KNOW THE WAY

JUNIOR CERTIFICATE RELIGIOUS EDUCATION

Orla Walsh
(Section D: Orla Philips)

First published 2007 by
Veritas Publications
7/8 Lower Abbey Street, Dublin 1, Ireland
Email publications@veritas.ie   Website www.veritas.ie

ISBN 978 1 84730 043 0

Copyright © Irish Episcopal Commission on Catechetics, 2007
Printed with Ecclesiastical Approval

The material in this publication is protected by copyright law. Except as may be permitted by law, no part of the material may be reproduced (including by storage in a retrieval system) or transmitted in any form or by any means, adapted, rented or lent without the written permission of the copyright owners. Applications for permissions should be addressed to the publisher.

A catalogue record for this book is available from the British Library.

Veritas books are printed on paper made from the wood pulp of managed forests. For every tree felled, at least one tree is planted, thereby renewing natural resources.

Veritas would like to thank:
The teachers, students, principals and post-primary diocesan advisers in Religious Education who assisted in the piloting of Section A of this programme, and those who willingly gave of their time for interviews and research in this text.

Consulters to the programme:
Robert Dunne and Grainne Wilson for advice on early drafts of the text; Caroline Renehan for advice on the text; Katherina Broderick for advice on Section D; and Eoin O'Mahony (Council for Research and Development, Maynooth) for advice on the statistics in Section D, Part 1.

Those who offered advice on particular lessons and sections of text:
Patrick Mullins OCarm STD

Veritas would like to acknowledge the influence of the *Community of Faith* and the *Fully Alive* series.

Theological Advisor: Brendan Leahy BL STD
Syllabus Adviser and Co-writer of Journal: Brendan O'Brien
Consultant to the Programme: Maura Hyland
Designer & Typesetter: Paula Ryan
Text Editor: Elaine Campion
Copyright Research: Caitriona Clarke
Picture Research: Paula Ryan and Ruth Kennedy
Origination: Digital Prepress Imaging
Printed in the Republic of Ireland by Microprint Ltd, Dublin

Family of 'Know' characters illustrated by Ronan Kennedy; © Ronan Kennedy/Orla Walsh, 2007; other illustrations by Ronan Kennedy (pp.89,90,105, 284,285) © 2007.

Scripture quotations are from the *New Revised Standard Version Bible* © 1993 and 1998 by the Division of Christian Education of the National Council of the Churches of Christ in the USA; used with permission; lyrics from 'I Will Follow' by U2, Columbia/Island Records, 1980 (p. 272); lyrics from 'I Still Haven't Found What I'm Looking For' by U2, Island Records, 1987 (p. 272);'Shackles (Praise You)' by Mary Mary, Columbia Records, 1999 (p.343,346); extract from 'Spraying the Potatoes' by Patrick Kavanagh, courtesy of the trustees of the estate of the late Catherine B. Kavanagh, through the Jonathan Williams Literary Agency, (p.355); lyrics from 'Baby Can I Hold You?' by Tracy Chapman, Elektra/Asylum Records, 1988 (p.461).

Stock photography supplied by www.sxc.hu; photographs supplied by Getty images (pp.14,27,29,39,50,59,69,174,176,177,180,222,239); photographs supplied by Free Stock Photos (pp.88,188,328); photograph of Dudley Farrell supplied by John Quirke Photography (p.25); photograph of domes courtesy of Anna Lauk (p.157); photograph of horse courtesy of Julia Borysewicz (p.278); photograph of teenage boy courtesy of Emanuel Lobeck (p.293); paintings by Bill Bolger (p.103,115,142,153,390).

Every effort has been made to contact the copyright holders of the material reproduced in *Know the Way*. If any infringement has occurred, the owners of such copyright are requested to contact the publishers.

Contents

Section A
Communities of Faith

Part 1 Community
1	We Belong to Many Communities	7
2	Characteristics of Community	12
3	Community Life and the Freedom of the Individual	16

Part 2 Communities at Work
4	The Role of Communities in Society	20
5	Local, National and International Communities	24

Part 3 Communities of Faith
6	World Religions – Founders and Followers	30
7	Christian Denominations	34
8	Religious Identity	36
9	Called to Serve	38
10	The Roman Catholic Church	40
11	Roles within the Catholic Church	43
12	Roles in a Parish	46
13	The Anglican Communion	48
14	A Church Organisation – Trócaire	51
15	Religious Orders and Organisations In Ireland	54

Part 4 Relationships between Communities of Faith
16	Words can Hurt; Words can Heal	56
17	Sectarianism	59
18	Respecting Our Differences	62
19	The Ecumenical Movement	64
20	Inter-Faith Dialogue	67

Part 5 (Higher Level Only) Organisation and Leadership in Communities of Faith
21	Styles of Leadership	71
22	Leadership as Service	74
23	Leadership and Authority in two Christian Churches	76

Section B
Foundations of Religion – Christianity

Part 1 The Context
24	The Land of Palestine	82
25	Palestine in the Time of Jesus	84
26	Political and Religious Structures in the Time of Jesus	86
27	Religious Groups in the Time of Jesus	89
28	Messianic Expectation	91

Part 2 Evidence about Jesus
29	Sources of Information about Jesus of Nazareth	93
30	From Oral Tradition to the Written Word	96
31	The Evangelists and the Gospels	98
32	The Synoptic Gospels	102

Part 3 The Person and Preaching of Jesus
33	Jesus and the Kingdom of God	104
34	The Kingdom of God in Parables	108
35	The Kingdom of God in Miracles	113
36	The Kingdom of God in Table-fellowship	117
37	The Kingdom of God in Discipleship	119
38	The Call to Discipleship Today	121
39	The Kingdom of God in the World Today	123

Part 4 The Death and Resurrection of Jesus
40	Conflict in the Life of Jesus	126
41	The Last Supper	130
42	The Passion of Jesus	133
43	The Resurrection of Jesus	137
44	The Appearances of Jesus after the Resurrection	140

Part 5 Faith in Christ
45	The First Christian Communities	145
46	The Characteristics of the First Christian Communities	149
47	Titles for Jesus (Higher Level)	152

Section C
Foundations of Religion
Major World Religions

Judaism

Part 1 The Context
48	The Historical and Geographical Background of Judaism	158

Part 2 Sources of Evidence
49	The Origins of Judaism	161
50	The Tanakh – The Sacred Text of Judaism	167
51	From Oral to Written Tradition	169
52	Other Records and Sources	171

Part 3 Rites of Passage and Other Rituals
53	Jewish Beliefs and Practices	173
54	Jewish Rites of Passage	178
55	Jewish Feasts and Festivals	183
56	Jewish Places of Worship	187

Part 4 Development of Tradition
57	The Development of Judaism	190
58	The Recent History of Judaism	193
59	The Jewish Community Worldwide	195

Part 5 (Higher Level Only) Tradition, Faith and Practice Today
60	Community Structure	198
61	Faith and Practice Today	201

Islam

Part 1 The Context
62	The Geographical, Historical and Cultural Background of Islam	204

Part 2 Sources of Evidence
63 The Story of Muhammad — 207
64 The Qu'ran – The Sacred Text of Islam — 210
65 Other Records and Sources — 213

Part 3 Rites of Passage and Other Rituals
66 The Core Beliefs of Islam — 215
67 The Practice of the Islamic Faith — 217
68 Signs and Symbols of Islam — 220
69 Islamic Rites of Passage — 222
70 Ritual Events and Sacred Times of Islam — 224
71 Islamic Prayer and Places of Worship — 227

Part 4 Development of Tradition
72 The Development of Islam — 229

Part 5 (Higher Level Only) Tradition, Faith and Practice Today
73 Islamic Faith and Practice Today — 233
74 Conflict and Dialogue Between the Major World Religions — 237
75 Islam, Judaism and Christianity: A Comparison — 241

Section D
The Question of Faith

Part 1 The Situation of Faith Today
76 Religious Belief and Practice Among Adolescents Today — 246
77 Religious Belief and Practice in Ireland — 252
78 Religious Belief and Practice in Europe — 258

Part 2 The Beginnings of Faith
79 Reflection – A Time of Discovery — 266
80 Questions of Meaning — 269
81 Awe and Wonder — 275
82 Finding Answers — 277

Part 3 The Growth of Faith
83 Images of God — 283
84 Christian Images of God — 288
85 Stages of Faith — 291

Part 4 The Expression of Faith
86 A Living Faith — 296
87 People of Faith — 301

Part 5 (Higher Level Only) Challenges to Faith
88 Religious and Scientific World Views — 307
89 World Views in Modern Culture — 315

Section E
The Celebration of Faith

Part 1 The World of Ritual
90 Places of Significance — 323
91 Pilgrimage Sites — 327
92 Times of Significance — 331
93 The Liturgical Year — 334
94 Actions of Significance — 339

Part 2 The Experience of Worship
95 The Language of Worship — 342
96 The Elements of Worship — 346

Part 3 (Higher Level Only) Worship as Response to Mystery
97 The Impact of Mystery — 349
98 Responses to the Encounter with Mystery — 353
99 Religious Responses to Mystery — 356

Part 4 Sign and Symbol
100 Signs and Symbols — 361
101 Symbolism in Religious Life — 364
102 Icons — 366
103 Encountering Religious Symbols — 369
104 Sacraments — 371
105 The Seven Sacraments of the Catholic Church — 375
106 The Celebration of the Eucharist in two Christian Traditions — 378

Part 5 Prayer
107 Communication with God — 382
108 The Nature and Function of Prayer — 386
109 Vocal Prayer — 389
110 Meditation and Contemplation — 392
111 Difficulties and Challenges of Prayer — 395
112 Important People in the Spiritual Traditions — 398

Section F
The Moral Challenge

Part 1 Introduction to Morality
113 What is Morality? — 402
114 Actions and Consequences — 404
115 Rights and Responsibilities — 409
116 Influences on our Morality — 412

Part 2 Sources of Morality
117 Sources of Morality — 415
118 Moral Vision — 418
119 Formal and Informal Codes of Behaviour — 420
120 Authority and Tradition — 423
121 Religious Moral Vision — 426

Part 3 Growing in Morality
122 Moral Growth — 429
123 Conscience and Morality — 433

Part 4 Religious Morality in Action
124 Moral Decision-making — 437
125 A Religious Moral Vision — 440
126 Morality in Action — 445
127 Social Justice — 448
128 Moral Failure — 452
129 Stewardship of the Earth — 456
130 Forgiveness and Reconciliation — 461

Part 5 (Higher Level Only) Law and Morality
131 The Relationship between Law and Morality — 466
132 State Law and Religious Morality — 470

Preparing the Journal — 473
Past Exam Questions — 487
Glossary of Key Concepts — 501

Community

LESSON 1 We Belong to Many Communities

GROUNDWORK
In this lesson we plan to:
- identify some of the forms and types of community to which we belong.

DIGGING DEEPER
How do the communities to which I belong help me to realise my full potential?

 **Key Concepts**
Co-operation/Lack of Co-operation

What do you think of when you hear the word 'community'?
List five words that come into your mind.

We can say that a community is a group of people who share something or have something in common, for example, a neighbourhood, a hobby or a set of religious beliefs. Usually, a community is made up of people who want to achieve a common goal.

There are many different types of community. How many can you think of?

Write down all the communities that you are part of.

What do the people who belong to these different communities share or have in common?

We Belong to Many Different Communities

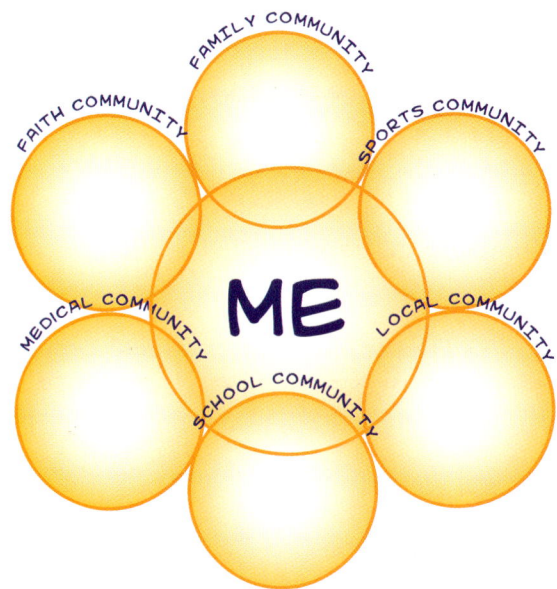

Draw a larger version of the above diagram in your Religion folder and write the name of a community you belong to around each circle, for example, family community, school community, faith community, parish community. Inside each circle, list the people who share this community with you, for example, sisters, brothers, friends, parents/guardians, teachers, priests, sports coaches and so on.

It is only when we take the time to think, that we realise we belong to a huge variety of communities! Can you explain why this may be so?

KNOW HOW

An acrostic is a poem or a puzzle in which particular letters spell another word. The word that is spelled out by the letters is the theme of the poem or puzzle. Usually, the particular/special letters come at the beginning of each line, but they can also appear elsewhere. Here are some examples:

WAVE**S**
BLU**E**
AQU**A**

FAITHFUL
RELIABLE
IMPORTANT
EARNEST
NOBLE
DEVOTED

In pairs, write an acrostic poem using the word B E L O N G.
Then read and comment on each other's work.
What were the most commonly used words?
What do these words tell us about belonging to a community?

Co-operation/Lack of Co-operation

Communities don't just happen! It takes a lot of effort on the part of each member and then on the part of the group as a whole to build a community. **Co-operation** is the word we use to describe working together in this way. **Lack of co-operation** can lead to the breakdown of a community.

Group Challenge: Steppping Stones

You have fifteen minutes to complete this task!

- Break up into groups of six.
- Each group will need seven A4 sheets of paper, to represent stones.
- Lay out the 'stones' for each group as follows: three on the left, three on the right, and one in the centre. Three students stand on the left-hand stones, facing the centre. The other three students stand on the right-hand stones, also facing the centre. The centre stone is not occupied.

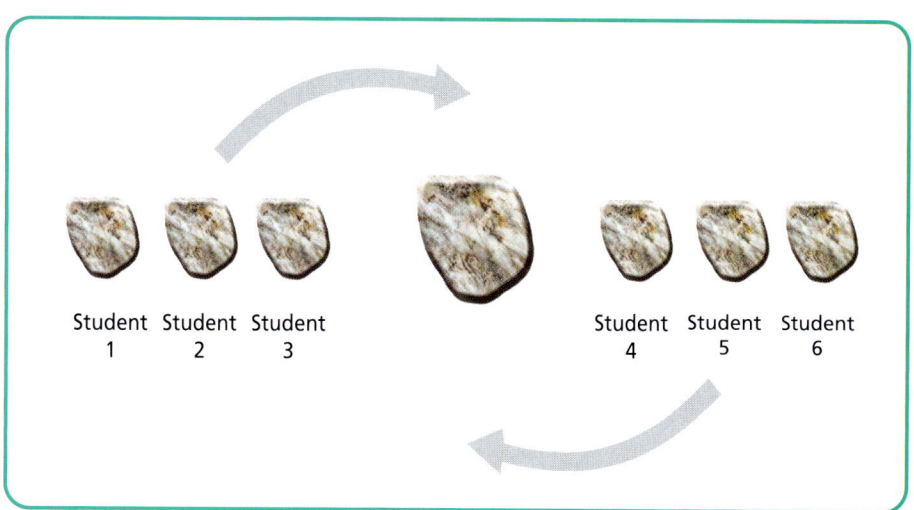

The challenge: exchanging places

Everyone must move so that the people originally standing on the right-hand stepping stones are on the left-hand stones, and those originally standing on the left-hand stepping stones are on the right-hand stones, with the centre stone remaining unoccupied.

How to play

After each move, each student must be standing on a stepping stone.

- If you start on the left, you may only move to the right. If you start on the right, you may only move to the left.
- You may 'jump' another student if there is an empty stone on the other side. You may not 'jump' more than one student.
- Only one student may move at a time.

TAKE FIVE

1. Did you enjoy your task? Why?/Why not?
2. How easy/difficult was the task?
3. Why did you have to work as a community?
4. What happened when a) you didn't work as a community, and b) you did work as a community?
5. Why is this game a good example of co-operation/lack of co-operation within a group?

The Human Need to Live in Community

Story: The Wild Boy of Aveyron

In 1798, three hunters spied a young boy, aged about twelve, walking through woods near Caine in France. He appeared to be moving like an animal, and when he caught sight of the hunters he leapt for cover among the leaves. Eventually, the hunters managed to capture the boy and they brought him back to their village.

The villagers named the boy Victor, and a local man called Jean Itard began to work with him. Everyone in the village was amazed that Victor had none of the abilities that people use all the time as they go about their normal daily lives. He moved like an animal, he was completely without the ability to relate to others and he tried to bite and scratch anyone who came near him. Poor Victor showed no signs of affection, even to those who were helping him. His eyes were without expression and he was unable to concentrate. He could not distinguish between flat and raised surfaces, between music and noise, or between perfume and bad smells.

After many years of work with Jean Itard, Victor showed some signs of progress. However, he did not develop some of the basic social, intellectual and physical skills that we take for granted in human beings.

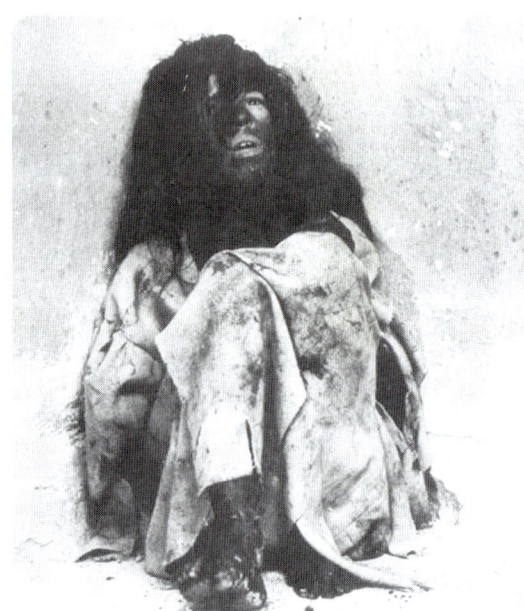

The Wild Boy of Aveyron

DIGGING DEEPER

This story helps us to understand that human beings, by our very nature, need other people in order to become fully human and fully alive. From the very beginning of our lives, we learn how to be human by imitating others and sharing our lives with them. This was impossible for Victor, as during his early years he had no one to imitate, no one with whom he could share his life. Human beings need to belong, to be in community with others, in order to realise their potential as human beings.

KNOW WHAT

1. Identify two things which show that Victor did not belong to any community.
2. Name three factors that caused Victor to develop as he did.
3. What does this tell us about the human need to be with others and to live in community?

DIGGING DEEPER

1. Do you know of any other examples where young people were left alone without love, attention or care and, therefore, did not achieve their full potential as human beings?
2. Identify some of the ways in which the people you live with have helped you to develop as a human being.

New Communities

Your new school is an example of a new community to which you now belong.

List five words that come to mind when you think of your new school community.

KNOW WHAT

1. In your opinion, what has to happen within your class group to enable your class to become a community?
2. In what ways do your classmates show co-operation/lack of co-operation in the class group?
3. What do you think are the difficult/not so difficult things about being a class community?

Co-operation: Working together to achieve a common goal.

Lack of co-operation: Not working together.

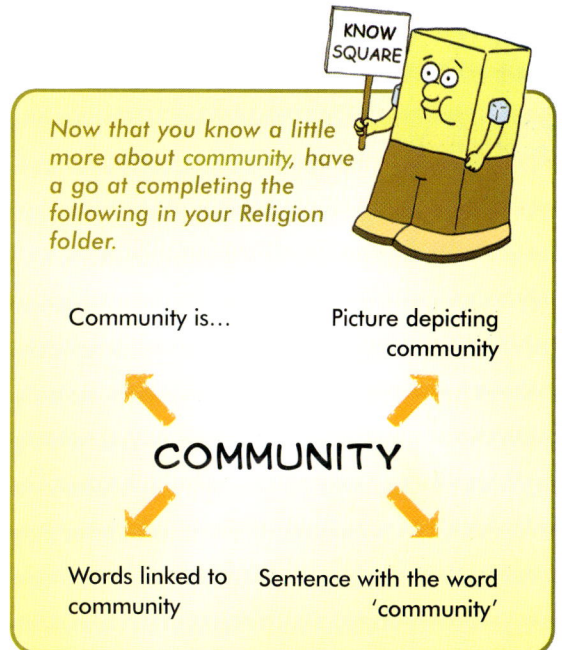

Now that you know a little more about community, have a go at completing the following in your Religion folder.

Community is...   Picture depicting community

COMMUNITY

Words linked to community   Sentence with the word 'community'

LESSON 2 Characteristics of Community

GROUNDWORK
In this lesson we plan to:
- identify the main characteristics of a community.

DIGGING DEEPER
What are the values that enable a community to work well?

 **Key Concepts**
Sharing/Co-operation/Communication

The word 'characteristic' means a feature or quality that makes somebody or something recognisable. When we talk about the characteristics of community, we are talking about the features or qualities that make people recognisable as a community. How do we recognise a community? We recognise a community by its characteristics or qualities of sharing, co-operation and communication.

When we demonstrate the characteristics of community, we are showing respect for ourselves and for others. To respect means to care for and to value others in our communities. It means that we give attention to others and avoid causing harm to them. 'Respect' may be seen as an umbrella term for the characteristics of community, because each characteristic involves respecting others in a particular way.

Sharing means more than dividing out the 'goodies' or the workload. The boy from Aveyron did not realise his full potential as a human being because he had no human contact in the early years of his life, no one with whom he could share his feelings and his experiences. Sharing involves caring for others, giving of yourself as well as giving of your goods. When we are born, we are immediately part of a family. We share with our families from the very beginning; we share our experiences, our time, our care. Sharing within a community involves making a genuine effort to see the needs of others and to respond to them.

Co-operation means working together as a team to achieve a common goal.

Communication is about giving and receiving information. We have often heard the phrase to 'keep the lines of communication open'. These 'lines' are the channels that flow from one source to another. There are many ways to communicate, from verbal communication to body language to written communication.

Group Challenge: Team Tower

You have ten minutes to complete this task!

- Divide into groups of four.
- Each group must have fifty drinking straws and a stapler.
- Your task is to build the tallest free-standing tower in the allocated time.
- Each team member must play a role in the task.

KNOW WHAT
1. How difficult/easy was the task?
2. Which characteristics of community were evident in your group?
3. Why was it important to work together?
4. Discuss this statement in relation to your task:
   'Communities are made up of people who work together by co-operating, by sharing and by communicating with one another.'

Body Talk – A Form of Communication

- Divide into pairs.
- Write the following phrases on small pieces of paper.

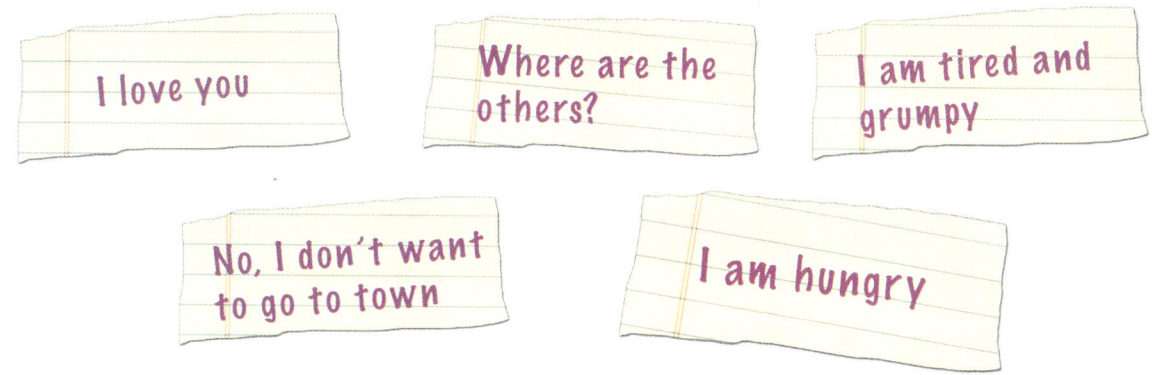

- Fold them up and choose one.
- Without making a sound, communicate the phrase to your partner.

DIGGING DEEPER
1. Have you ever had to give someone an important message? What did this involve and how did you communicate it?
2. Was there ever a time when someone you know did not receive a message due to a breakdown in communication? What happened and how was the situation resolved?
3. What are the consequences of not paying enough attention to the method of communication within a group? Has this ever happened to you?
4. How do we make sure that the 'lines of communication' within our communities are always kept open?
5. Did you ever get the wrong message? How did this happen?

Story: A Dream Come True…

It was 1976 and Paul was finding his teenage years a little difficult. His school-work was not going well and it seemed like everyone except him was heading for a bright future. Paul was clever, but he just couldn't concentrate enough to be keep his grades up.

He always had these melodies in his head, whether he was alone, at the local club or in a church hall. Whenever he found himself beside a piano, he would put his finger on a key and play a note. He reckoned that if he pressed a pedal under that note, that one little note, he could fill the whole hall with an incredible sound. He could hear a rhyme for the note in his head and he knew that he would be able to find another note, and another. He just had no way of letting these notes out, no way of making them heard.

Then one day in school, Paul received a note from Larry, who played the drums, saying he was interested in forming a band. Paul was excited about the idea and so he and his friend Robbie decided to visit Larry at home. They found him in his kitchen, with his drum kit set up. There were a few other lads with him. There was a brainy looking guy called Dave, who was fifteen, and he had an electric guitar. Paul felt excited now. He reckoned the musical notes in his head would soon find their voice.

U2 in concert

When young Larry began to play the drums, they made an amazing sound. The other guy, Dave, hit a chord on his guitar, and Paul felt a surge of excitement, as he had never heard an electric guitar before.

This was a day that Paul would never forget. The band formed and began to play together. Within a month, Paul had started going out with a girl called Ali. Now life was looking good and his dreams and ambitions were wrapped in wings, destined to soar.

TAKE FIVE

1. At the beginning of the story, we read that Paul knew he could fill a room with music. So why didn't he?
2. Why was Paul excited about the note he got from the young drummer?
3. What did the young people in the kitchen have in common?
4. What did they have to do together to achieve their dreams and ambitions?
5. Why could Paul not achieve his dreams on his own?

The above true story is based on an interview with Paul Hewson, whom we all know as Bono from the rock band U2. In the interview, Bono recalled the beginnings of the community of U2. Today, more than three decades later, U2 has an ever-increasing and devoted following. The band performed three homecoming concerts in Dublin's Croke Park in the summer of 2005, and many people singled out this event as their most precious memory of that year. Fans spanning over three decades, many accompanied by their children, shared in the community that is U2.

KNOW IT ALL

Write five sentences about U2. In each sentence, use one of the following words:

BELONG   COMMUNICATION   RESPECT
CO-OPERATION   SHARING

KNOWING ME KNOWING U2
Find out five interesting facts about the community that is one of the world's greatest rock bands – U2.

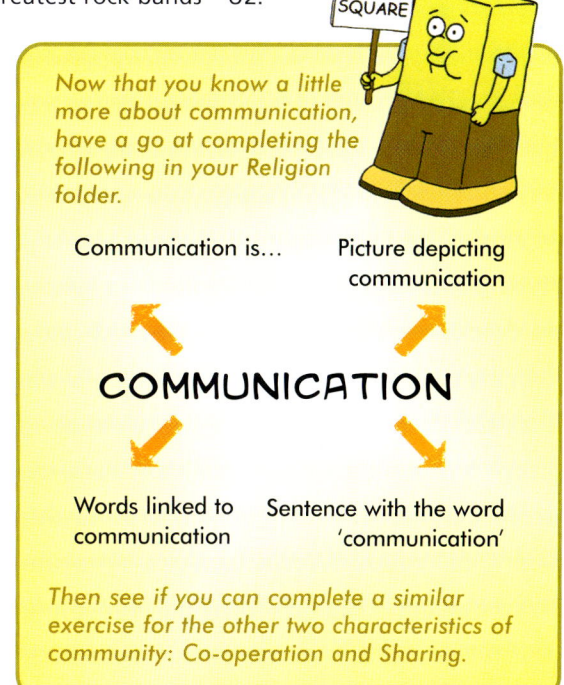

Now that you know a little more about communication, have a go at completing the following in your Religion folder.

Communication is…   Picture depicting communication

COMMUNICATION

Words linked to communication   Sentence with the word 'communication'

Then see if you can complete a similar exercise for the other two characteristics of community: Co-operation and Sharing.

DIGGING DEEPER

1. Name and describe two of the values that motivated the friends in the story.
2. Were you ever in a situation where you felt you needed support from others to achieve your goals? What happened? Write about your experience.
3. Did you ever encourage and support others in order to enable their dreams to come true? Tell your story.

Sharing: Willing and unselfish giving to others.

Communication: Sharing of experiences, thoughts or feelings.

SECTION A COMMUNITIES OF FAITH

LESSON 3 Community Life and the Freedom of the Individual

GROUNDWORK
In this lesson we plan to:
- explore the tension between individual and community responsibility.

DIGGING DEEPER
How do we ensure that the needs of each person are met within a community?

Key Concepts
Roles/Community breakdown

KNOW WHAT
1. Write one word to match each section of the illustration shown and then share your six words with the class.
2. What do the donkeys want to do?
3. What happens when they work together?

DIGGING DEEPER
1. Why might the donkeys want to go in different directions?
2. Have you ever wanted to take a different direction from the others in your group? What did that feel like?

Roles within Communities

There are many different communities in society, and each one has its own set of **roles**. For example, the roles within a committee would include treasurer, secretary and chairperson.

All of the people who make up a community have different gifts and talents, which can be used for the good of the whole community. Each person has a different role to play, and no one person has all the gifts and talents needed for the community to work. It is important that each person's gifts and talents are accepted and valued.

Story: What's My Role?

There once was a group of four people: Every Body, Some Body, Any Body and No Body. There was an important job to be done and Every Body was asked to do it. Every Body was sure Some Body would do it. Any Body could have done it, but No Body did it. Some Body got angry with that, because it was Every Body's job. Every Body thought Any Body could do it, but No Body realised that Every Body wouldn't do it. In the end, Every Body blamed Some Body when No Body did what Any Body could have done.

KNOW WHAT
1. Do you find this story confusing? Why?/Why not?
2. Why is it important for members of a community to take on different roles within the community?
3. Read the last line again: 'In the end, Every Body blamed Some Body when No Body did what Any Body could have done.' In your own words, explain what this line means.

DIGGING DEEPER
1. Name a community to which you belong. What is your role within that community? Why is this your role?
2. Why is it true that no one person can play all the roles within a community?

The Strengths of Community

When we live in community, we receive the support and help that we require to enable us to fulfil our needs. Our needs vary from physical needs (for food, water, shelter and so on) to personal growth and fulfilment needs (to feel good about ourselves, to succeed at something, to build our confidence). The help and support that we receive is one of the great strengths of a community.

KNOW WHAT
1. Name two groups who have shown you the strengths of community. In each case, explain how being part of the group provided you with support and enabled you to fulfil your needs.
2. Has there ever been a case where you, as part of a group, have helped another member to succeed? If so, how did this feel? Write about this time.

The Weaknesses of Community

In any community, there will always be some tension between the needs of the group and the needs of the individual. This means that a person can be made to feel 'left out', 'unaccepted' or even 'isolated' if they do not 'go along' with the group. There can be many reasons why people don't just 'go with the flow' within a community group. They may not agree with the decisions being made, or they may not feel able to take part in the activity for one reason or another. For those individuals, this may be experienced as a weakness of community.

Let's explore some situations that will help us to understand more clearly the weaknesses of community.

Situation 1

James has just finished his last two Christmas exams and he is totally wrecked! On his way home from school, he decides to buy a new CD to cheer himself up – sure why not? He will spend the first hour of his Christmas break chilling out to some new sounds. When he arrives home, he drops his jacket in the hall and races upstairs to his room. There is a snag, however! James shares his room with Andy, his brother. Andy has formed a study group with four friends and they have just got together to study for a really important college exam on Monday – they are hard at work in James' and Andy's bedroom!

KNOW WHAT

1. What is the source or cause of tension here?
2. How do you think James feels when he sees the room occupied?
3. If you were James, what would you do? Why?

Situation 2

The Junior Certificate exams are over and the gang have organised a party. Susie hears one of her pals saying that she is getting money together to buy alcohol for the celebrations and will be collecting from the gang the next day. Most of the group eagerly agree and say they can't wait, but Susie is not so sure. She has a bad feeling about sneaking alcohol into the party and a worse feeling about getting caught! Who can she talk to about this? Will she sound like a total nerd? How is she going to enjoy the night if she is the only one not drinking alcohol?

KNOW WHAT

1. In this situation, what is the source or cause of tension between the needs of the group and the needs of the individual?
2. Sometimes a person can feel isolated within a group. Explain how this has happened here.
3. What must happen if the needs of the individual are to be met within the group?

DIGGING DEEPER

1. Think of two ways in which Susie's needs could have been met.
2. Think of a time when there was a tension created by what you wanted to do and what the group you were part of wanted to do. What happened? What might have helped the situation? How was the situation resolved?
3. If you were asked to give advice in situations like the two above, what would your advice be?

Community Breakdown

When the tension between the needs of the group and the needs of the individual is not addressed, people can feel isolated and even unaccepted. How do you think Susie felt at the end of the story? Tension can lead to **community breakdown**. This occurs when the characteristics of community are not being practised by the members.

Community breakdown can often be resolved if the lines of communication are kept open and are accessible to all members within the group. For example, in the second situation above, Susie was unsure as to how she could communicate her thoughts about alcohol at the party. If Susie could have found a way to tell her friends how she felt, they may have been prepared to listen.

In order to avoid community breakdown, it is often necessary to reach a compromise. With a compromise, there are usually two sides, each of which has a different viewpoint. To reach a compromise, each party must agree to let go of their own preference and accept a way forward that is somewhere between the two. The following story is a good example of this.

Story: The Seattle Olympics

At the Seattle Olympics, nine athletes, all mentally or physically challenged, gathered on the start line for the 100 metre race. The gun fired and the race began. They ran in threes. Then suddenly, one of the male athletes tripped, spun on the track and fell. He began to sob with sheer disappointment. When the other eight athletes heard him crying, they slowed down and looked behind

Athletes at the Seattle Olympics

them. Then they stopped and went back – all of them. One of the girls sat next to him, hugged him and asked, 'Are you feeling better now?' Then, all nine walked shoulder to shoulder to the finish line. The whole crowd stood up and applauded.

KNOW WHAT

1. What do you think it would feel like to be at the start line in an Olympic race?
2. How do you think the young athlete felt when he fell?
3. People who watched this race still talk about it. Can you explain why?
4. Why is this story a good example of compromise within a group?

Strengths of community	Weaknesses that lead to community breakdown
Co-operation	Lack of co-operation
Sharing	Not sharing
Good communication	Poor communication
Fulfilling roles	Failure to carry out roles
Help and support	Failure to deal with tension between the members

KNOW IT ALL

Copy the following exercise into your Religion folder and fill in the blanks.

1. The characteristics of community are c_____ , c_____ and s_____ .
2. A strength of a community is _____ .
3. A weakness of a community is _____ .
4. There is often t_____ between the needs of the individual and the needs of the group.
5. Sometimes this tension can be resolved if the lines of c_____ are kept open.
6. A community may not always be able to look after everyone's individual n_____ .
7. Sometimes we have to let go of our own preferences in order to avoid c_____ b_____ .
8. A c_____ is often required.

Roles: Specific tasks or functions within a group, e.g. member, leader, secretary, etc.

Community breakdown: Occurs when a group stops working/sharing and breaks apart.

Communities at Work

LESSON 4   The Role of Communities in Society

GROUNDWORK
In this lesson we plan to:
- describe the role of communities in society.

DIGGING DEEPER
How do the communities in our society help us to fulfil our needs?

Key Concepts
Commitment/Service

Commitment
Commitment involves a promise or pledge to do something. It requires time and attention. If we are to be committed to something, we have to make time for it and devote attention to it.

Record-Breakers – Commitment in Action
On 10 September 2005, 7,664 dancers took to the streets of Cork to set a new record for the Largest Irish Dance. Also in September 2005, the Titans Basketball Club from Galway set a new Basketball Marathon record of forty hours and three minutes.

On 26 September 2003, Macmillan Cancer Relief held the largest coffee morning, with 576,157 people attending over 26,000 meetings across the United Kingdom at the same time.

On 1 December 2002, a group of thirty-eight surfers rode the same wave simultaneously at Manly Beach, Sydney.

On 7 September 2001, 559,493 people began jumping up and down for one minute to mark the launch of Science Year in the UK. There were actually 569,069 participants – the extra numbers represent people with disabilities who took part by dropping objects onto the ground.

KNOW HOW

1. In your opinion, what kind of commitment was required to achieve these results?
2. If you were asked to take the leadership role within one of these record-breaking communities, which one would you choose, and why?
3. Imagine that you have the opportunity to break a record with a group. Decide on the record and write four tasks that you need to carry out in order to achieve your common goal.

Communities Call for Commitment

Jamie's Story

The summer songs were belting out from the radio and Jamie was feeling g-r-e-a-t! He was working in the local café for July and August and was hoping to save enough money for his first electric guitar. He reckoned his dad might get him a good deal on a Squire Telecaster.

Jamie had a laugh with all the customers. He particularly enjoyed the banter with old Mrs Murphy, who came in for her tea and scone every Friday morning after collecting her pension. Jamie shared his plan with her, and she smiled as she told him that she loved to swing and dance at the carnivals when she was his age.

Jamie was part of a local band that played pop rock. All the gang were mad into them and at this stage they were kinda famous, well in Galway anyway. From the day Jamie joined the band, he felt part of something good. He was committed to the group and wanted to work hard to make them the best they could be. All the lads practised together and hung out together. They were all waiting for Jamie to get his new guitar. Jamie was doing fairly well on the tips front this week, so maybe Saturday would be the day.

Katie's Story

Katie loved being part of the sports club. All the members had a major laugh together and every weekend meant another team to play against and another place to travel to. As vice-captain of the basketball team, Katie helped Jenny, the captain, to get the team organised for each match. Sometimes this was hard work, especially getting the kits washed and ordered, but most of the time the team members were attentive and helpful and the preparatory work was easily done. Katie also helped out with the club's committee and acted as assistant treasurer. This meant she was a back-up for Josh, who was the club's full-time treasurer. She liked Josh and they worked well together.

Katie was also developing an interest in soccer. She reckoned it would be an exciting new skill to learn and would help her to maintain her fitness at a high level. She decided that she would take part in the upcoming trials and do her best to get a place on the team.

KNOW WHAT
1. List all the groups, teams and committees that Jamie and Katie are part of.
2. Describe the commitment they have towards these groups.
3. What difference does being part of something make to their lives?
4. What difference does a local group, a local band or a local sports club make to your area?

DIGGING DEEPER
Choose *three* of the following groups and answer the questions below:
GAA, Swimming Club, Soccer Club, Meals on Wheels, Karate Club, Gaeilge Group, Simon Community, Residents' Association, Equestrian Centre, Pottery Club, Gardening Ireland.
1. What is the role of these community groups in our society?
2. How do these groups help people to fulfil their different needs?

Service

The communities to which we belong provide us with a **service**, i.e. they fulfil some of our needs. (The table opposite explains the different levels of need.) Our local shops are communities that provide us with clothes, food and drinks; our school is a community that provides us with an education and a safe place in which to grow and reach our full potential. Communities enable us to grow and change and they work with us to help us achieve our goals in life. As we grow up and move on, we become part of new communities and we also leave particular communities. A specific community group that you belonged to when you were five may no longer fulfil your needs, so you move on and join other communities.

Think of some of the community groups you belonged to when you were younger, but have now outgrown. What new community groups have you joined in the recent past?

KNOWING ME KNOWING YOU
Community groups also provide services in the local area. Name one community at work in your area and describe the service it provides.

KNOW HOW

Think of a community to which you belong, for example, school, youth club, band, family, football team, etc. Copy the grid below into your Religion folder and list the ways in which this community helps you to fulfil each of the five levels of needs.

1st level – Physical needs, such as food, water, etc.	
2nd level – Safety needs, such as shelter and a safe environment	
3rd level – the need to belong, to feel as if you are part of something	
4th level – the need to be confident within yourself, to know that you are okay	
5th level – the need to realise your true potential	

Commitment: Pledge/promise to a group or community to carry out a task or role.

Service: Work done by a person or group for the good of another person or group.

LESSON 5 Local, National and International Communities

GROUNDWORK
In this lesson we plan to:
- explore the work done by a local community, a national community and an international community;
- examine the inspiration for this work;
- recognise the variety of roles within these communities, including leadership roles.

DIGGING DEEPER
What inspires people to work together for a common vision?

 **Key Concepts**
Vision/Commitment/Service/Leadership

What is your **vision** for the future? What inspires (motivates) you to do your best?

In groups of two, write down four words that come into your mind when you talk about a) your vision and b) your inspiration. Share your words with the rest of the class.

A Local Community – The Gaelic Athletic Association (GAA)

Have a go at answering the following questions in your Religion folder.

1. What does GAA stand for?
2. What is your favourite GAA sport?
3. What GAA team do you support?
4. What is the name of your local GAA club?
5. What are your local colours?
6. Who is your favourite GAA sportsperson?

The Inspiration for the Work of the GAA

The GAA is an example of a local community. It was founded in 1884 by Michael Cusack and Maurice Davin. Their inspiring vision was to create an organisation to encourage and promote the national games of hurling and football. Dr T. W. Croke (Archbishop of Cashel) was the first patron of the Association, and Croke Park in Dublin (the Association's headquarters) was named in his honour.

Vision

The GAA community is run by men and women who share the vision of their founders. They agree with the notion that the national games of hurling and football should be encouraged and promoted. They realise this vision (make it happen) through the work they do in a spirit of co-operation and commitment.

Commitment and Service

A tremendous amount of commitment is required to provide the year-round service of training and support for the members, which is provided free at both local and national levels. All

KNOW THE WAY

24

youngsters over the age of five, both male and female, are encouraged to play, and they are trained in the pursuit of excellence.

Hurling is the oldest of Irish sports, dating from pre-Christian times, and it is played by 100,000 people in Ireland. Women's hurling, called 'camogie', is played according to the same basic rules, but with a smaller pitch and smaller sticks. There are 50,000 camogie players in Ireland. Gaelic football is played by approximately 250,000 males and females, making it the most popular sport in Ireland.

The Variety of Roles

There is a variety of roles in the local GAA clubs. Whether these roles involve making sandwiches or making speeches, each one is necessary and important. The role of the players is to play together as a team. Trainers are required to train the teams, referees to referee ongoing matches, and club managers to organise meetings at county level and to plan matches, training sessions and celebratory events. The overall manager plays a leadership role, which involves co-ordinating the programme of events for the year.

As well as training and co-ordinating matches during the year, the GAA, sponsored by VHI Healthcare, runs intensive football and hurling summer camps, called Cúl Camps.

The following is an extract from an interview with Dudley Farrell, who plays a **leadership** role with the GAA in County Meath.

How long have you been involved in your local GAA community?
Since I was a child – about thirty-five years.

Why are you involved in the GAA?
I grew up playing football and my parents were GAA supporters. Now I want to give something back to the organisation that has been such a big part of my life.

What is your role in your local GAA club?
I am the supervisor of all the Meath 'Cúl camps' and I work as Coaching and Games Development Officer during the year. Over three thousand players have attended twenty-three camps this summer, and there are sixty-two clubs with between five and ten teams that play during the year. My role takes me to all of these clubs and camps.

Do you organise both football and hurling?
Yes, I work with and enjoy both.

What/Who is the inspiration for your work with the GAA?
My parents. They brought me to play at a young age and they always supported me and my involvement with the GAA. I am also inspired by the teams and by individual players who have developed into skilled sportspeople.

What motivates you to stay involved?
My love of football and hurling and the pleasure they give to me. The GAA has always been part of my life and it is wonderful to see young players get so much enjoyment out of it. It keeps them fit and healthy and develops their team spirit. Another motivation is the life-long friendships that have developed over the years; being part of something, to belong to something, is a great motivation to keep it up!

What kind of service does the local GAA provide for your area?
In Nobber, County Meath, our GAA club has wonderful facilities for the local youth. We have an all-weather floodlit pitch, which provides year-round facilities. There are many skilled sportspeople who provide training, refereeing, supervision and support for the players.

What do you think is the role of the GAA in society?
The GAA provides a service to society at local and national levels. It is a club for all ages and levels of players to go and enjoy football and hurling. In the GAA, there is what is known as the 'parish rule'. This means a player can only play with their parish. This builds relationships in the local community. Players work together at a local level and are proud to play for their parish. When a team is playing, they also have community support, family support and club support. To be a part of that is great encouragement for any young boy or girl as they start out in life.

TAKE FIVE

1. What kind of service does the GAA provide at local level?
2. How can the GAA be both a local community and a national community?
3. How would you describe the commitment and service of GAA club members?
4. Discuss the variety of roles in a local GAA club.
5. Write a page on the leadership role we have explored in the above interview.

DIGGING DEEPER
1. Are you or have you ever been part of a local GAA club or any other local group? Describe what the experience is/was like.
2. Have you ever attended a Cúl camp? Describe the experience.
3. What are the advantages of being part of a club or group? Why are any of the local clubs or groups important for our society?
4. What other leadership roles do people have in your community?

A National Community – Special Olympics Ireland

A national community is a community that is co-ordinated (organised) at national level, with local branches in other areas.

> *'Let me win. But if I cannot win, let me be brave in the attempt.'*

The above athletes' oath is from Special Olympics Ireland, a national community that was founded in 1978. It provides year-round training and competition in many Olympic-type sports for people with a learning disability. This gives the members of Special Olympics Ireland 'an ongoing opportunity to develop physical fitness, show courage, experience joy, and participate in a sharing of gifts, skills and friendships with their families, other Special Olympics athletes and the community'.

The Inspiration for the Work of Special Olympics Ireland
The initial inspiration for the work of Special Olympics came from Eunice Kennedy Shriver, who founded Special Olympics in the USA in 1968. Her vision was to improve the way

society deals with people who have learning disabilities. Eunice had grown up with her sister Rosemary, who had a learning disability. At that time in America, a person with special needs was seen as a cause of embarrassment to the entire family. Eunice and Rosemary were very close and, as a tribute to her sister, Eunice wanted to work for a change in attitude towards people with special needs. The organisation has since spread to over one hundred and sixty countries worldwide.

Vision

The members and the volunteers who work for this community share the vision that 'there is a place for everyone'. There are over thirty-four thousand people with a learning disability in Ireland. Over ten and a half thousand of those people take part in Special Olympics Ireland. Because of the vision of this national community, these athletes have benefited socially, emotionally and physically.

Commitment and Service

Special Olympics Ireland provides training and competition opportunities in eleven summer sports and one winter sport. The volunteers and the athletes are dedicated to their goals and show ongoing commitment to their roles. Over seven thousand volunteers provide a dedicated and committed service to the organisation. The athletes who participate in Special Olympics benefit greatly from this commitment and service. They become physically fit and develop greater self-confidence and a more positive self-image. Their participation in sport allows them to demonstrate amazing courage and enthusiasm, and to enjoy the rewards of friendship and teamwork.

The Variety of Roles

Special Olympics Ireland would not exist as a national community without the time, energy, dedication and commitment of its volunteers. Thousands of volunteers are required to co-ordinate local Special Olympics programmes. Anyone over the age of fifteen years can become involved. Students, senior citizens, business people, families and relatives of athletes, amateur and professional athletes, coaches and many others come together to fill a wide variety of roles in Special Olympics programmes.

Leadership

The headquarters of Special Olympics Ireland is located at North Circular Road in Dublin. The community is led by a director. Each province also has a regional director, who co-ordinates the activities and sports for that area.

TAKE FIVE

1. What is a national community?
2. What is the role of Special Olympics Ireland in society, at both local and national levels?
3. What kind of a service does Special Olympics Ireland provide?
4. What roles exist within this national community?
5. In your opinion, what kind of commitment is required to make this community as successful and effective as it is?

DIGGING DEEPER

1. Have you or has anybody you know ever been involved in Special Olympics Ireland? If so, describe the type of work it entailed.
2. Anyone over the age of fifteen can volunteer to help run local Special Olympics. Would you like to become involved when you reach that age? Why?/Why not?
3. Who is the director of Special Olympics Ireland? Research his or her role and explain why this role might be a good example of commitment and service.

KNOWING ME KNOWING YOU

Look up the following website and then write an account of the inspiration for the work of Special Olympics Ireland.
http://www.specialolympics.ie/en/?page=connaught_families

An International Community – Greenpeace

The Vision of Greenpeace

> 'Greenpeace exists because this fragile earth deserves a voice.
> It needs solutions.
> It needs change.
> It needs action.'

1. What strikes you about this vision?
2. To what is Greenpeace alerting the world?
3. What is Greenpeace calling for?

The Inspiration for the Work of Greenpeace

Greenpeace was founded by a small team of activists who, in 1971, motivated by their vision of a green and peaceful world, set sail from Vancouver, Canada, in an old fishing boat. Their aim was to focus worldwide attention on US underground nuclear testing at Amchitka, a tiny island off the west coast of Alaska. They believed that even a small group of people could make a difference. Though their boat was intercepted before it got to Amchitka, the journey sparked a lot of public interest. The United States still detonated the bomb, but the voice of reason had been heard. Nuclear testing on Amchitka ended that year and the island was later declared a bird sanctuary.

This tradition of 'bearing witness' in a peaceful and non-violent manner continues today, and Greenpeace ships are an important part of the organisation's campaign work. This non-profit international community has since spread to forty countries across Europe, America, Asia and the Pacific Ocean. The vision and courage of the founders continues to inspire the community today in its campaign to:

- STOP CLIMATE CHANGE
- PROTECT THE ANCIENT FORESTS
- SAVE THE OCEANS
- STOP WHALING
- SAY NO TO GENETIC ENGINEERING
- STOP THE NUCLEAR THREAT
- ELIMINATE TOXIC CHEMICALS
- ENCOURAGE SUSTAINABLE TRADE

Commitment and Service

Greenpeace is committed to maintaining its independence and, therefore, it does not accept donations from governments or corporations, but depends on contributions from individual supporters and foundation grants. Greenpeace shows its commitment to the international community by focusing on the most crucial worldwide threats to our environment.

Greenpeace believes that the struggle to preserve the future of our planet involves everybody. It has 2.8 million supporters worldwide, and it encourages many millions more than that to take action every day. One of the longest banners Greenpeace ever made summed up its mission:

> 'When the last tree is cut, the last river poisoned, and the last fish dead, we will discover that we can't eat money.'

The Variety of Roles

Greenpeace employs more than one hundred and fifty staff, from all over the world. The roles necessary to operate this international community include project managers, fundraising officers, video editors and marine officers, to name but a few.

Leadership

All of Greenpeace's global campaigns are led from the head office in Amsterdam. The headquarters also supports the national and regional offices, which are funded by millions of members worldwide. Greenpeace International's team of fundraising and development personnel provides all these offices with leadership, direction and support.

KNOW WHAT
1. What type of work is done by Greenpeace?
2. What is the role of Greenpeace in our society?
3. What is the inspiration for the work of Greenpeace?
4. Describe some of the roles within Greenpeace.

DIGGING DEEPER
1. How important do you think the work of Greenpeace is for the worldwide community?
2. Log on to the Greenpeace website at: *http://www.greenpeace.org/international/*
    - Report on two recent news items from this website.
    - Identify two ways in which your class can support the work of Greenpeace.

KNOWING ME KNOWING YOU
Log on to *http://www.greenpeace.org/international/fungames* to explore a fun and games page on the Greenpeace site.

Vision: A powerful image of what the world or a person or a group could be.

Leadership: Setting a goal or aim for a person or a community and guiding them towards it.

Communities of Faith

LESSON 6 World Religions – Founders and Followers

GROUNDWORK
In this lesson we plan to:
- recognise and be able to tell the stories of the founders and earliest followers of the five major world religions.

DIGGING DEEPER
What is the founding story of my faith?

 **Key Concepts**
Faith/Belief/Religions/Founder/Inspiring Vision/Preaching/Sacred text

The Major World Religions

We have learned that a community is a group of people who have something in common and we have looked at examples of communities at local, national and international levels.

A community of faith is a group of people who share a particular set of religious beliefs. This set of religious beliefs is at the heart of their religion/their **faith**.

There are many different religions in the world. Can you identify the religions to which each of these symbols belong?

Five of the most significant world **religions** are: Christianity, Islam, Judaism, Hinduism and Buddhism. These are referred to as the 'major' world religions. The map opposite shows the central locations of these religions.

There are people who belong to all of the major world religions living in Ireland today.

TAKE FIVE

1. Name four places where Christianity is practised.
2. Where do the majority of people who belong to the Islamic faith community live?
3. Name two communities of faith that are found in Africa.
4. What is the predominant religion in India?
5. What religion is mainly found in South-East Asia?

> ### DID YOU KNOW?
> In 1894, a man named Will Keith Kellogg was trying to improve the vegetarian diet of hospital patients. In the process of searching for a digestible bread substitute, he accidentally left a pot of boiled wheat to stand, and the wheat became very soft. When he rolled the softened wheat and let it dry, each grain of wheat changed into a large thin flake. The flakes turned out to be a tasty cereal. Kellogg had invented cornflakes!

An 'inventor' is another word for the creator of something, i.e. the person who brings the product into being. Inventors do for products what founders do for communities!

- The **founder** is the person whose vision leads to the formation of a community, which works to make that vision a reality.
- A founder of a religion is one whose beliefs, lifestyle and **inspiring vision** lead to the formation of that religion.

There are many similarities and differences between the major world religions. Not all of them have a founder, but each one did have a group of early followers.

Monotheism/Polytheism

The different religious faiths or traditions fall into two broad categories. The first category is *monotheism*, which means to believe in one God. This is the category into which the three major world religions of Judaism, Christianity and Islam belong. The other category is *polytheism*, which means to believe in more than one God. This is the category to which Hinduism and Buddhism belong.

MONOTHEISM = BELIEF IN ONE GOD

POLYTHEISM = BELIEF IN MORE THAN ONE GOD

We will now look at Christianity, Hinduism and Buddhism. (Judaism and Islam will be dealt with in Section C.)

Christianity

Founder/ Significant leader	Jesus Christ
When?	2000 years ago
Where?	Israel
Earliest followers	The Apostles and other converted people
Sacred text	The Bible – Old and New Testaments

Jesus founded the Christian faith. He travelled throughout the Holy Land **preaching** the Good News and telling the people about God and how God wanted them to live. The apostles and other early followers of Christianity travelled with Jesus, listened to him, were healed by him and witnessed his words and deeds.

It was in Jerusalem that the apostles witnessed the trial and death of Jesus. After his death and resurrection, Jesus appeared to them many times. They did not recognise him at first, but Jesus helped them to understand that he had overcome death. Before his ascension to heaven, Jesus told his apostles about their future role as leaders of his Church on earth.

At Pentecost, the apostles and the other followers received the gift of the Holy Spirit, which filled them with courage and confidence to go and 'teach all nations'.

Christians believe that Jesus is the Son of God and the Saviour of the world.

KNOW IT ALL

Copy the following exercise into your Religion folder and fill in the blanks using the wordbank given below.

The Christian faith community was _____ by Jesus. The _____ were the earliest followers of Jesus. The teaching of Jesus was called the _____ _____. All of Jesus' teachings are found in the _____, which is the sacred text of the Christian faith. Jesus died in _____ . It was at Pentecost that the apostles received the _____ of the Holy Spirit.

WORDBANK

Jerusalem • Apostles • Bible • Founded • Good News • Gift

(We will explore Christianity in greater detail in Section B.)

Hinduism

Founder/ Significant leader	None
When?	3000 years ago
Where?	India
Earliest followers	The people who lived beside the Indus river
Sacred text	The Vedas

Hinduism began in India about 3000 years ago. At that time, India was being invaded by the Aryan tribes, who brought with them hymns to the many different gods they believed in. As the tribes made their way through India, the cultures and beliefs that they encountered became very significant for them. This was how the religion known as Hinduism began.

The word 'Hindu' comes from an ancient Indian language called Sanskrit. It was the name given to the people of faith who lived beside the Indus river. Together with the Aryan tribes, these were the earliest followers of the Hindu religion.

KNOW IT ALL

Copy the following paragraph into your Religion folder and fill in the blanks using the wordbank given below.

Hinduism began about _____ years ago. India was being invaded by the _____ tribes, who brought with them _____ to the many different _____ they believed in. As the _____ made their way through India, the _____ and _____ that they encountered became very _____ for them. This was how the religion known as _____ began. The earliest followers of Hinduism were the _____ tribes and the people of faith who lived beside the _____ river.

WORDBANK

Aryan • Hymns • Tribes • 3000 • Hinduism • Aryan • Gods • Beliefs • Significant • Indus • Cultures

Buddhism

Founder/ Significant leader	Siddhartha Gautama (The Buddha)
When?	2500 years ago
Where?	North-east India
Earliest followers	A group of monks known as the Sangha
Sacred text	Tripitaka/Mahayana Sutras

Buddhism grew out of Hinduism. The founder of Buddhism, Siddhartha Gautama, had a wealthy upbringing and he experienced little of the pain and poverty of the world. At the age of twenty-nine, Siddhartha left his wife, child and home to begin his search for meaning in life. When he was thirty-five years old, he achieved enlightenment. From this time on, he was called the Buddha, which means the awakened or the enlightened one. After he became Buddha, Siddharta passed on his insights to a group of monks, known as the Sangha. This group became the earliest followers of Buddhism. The Buddha's main teachings are called the Three Universal Truths, the Four Noble Truths and the Eightfold Path.

KNOW IT ALL

Copy this chart into your Religion folder and fill in the details.

Name of religion	Buddhism
Founder/ Significant leader	
When?	
Where?	
Earliest followers	

DIGGING DEEPER

1. Write about the founding story of your faith.
2. How did the belief and inspiring vision of the founder lead to the formation of your religion?

Faith/belief: Something accepted as true by a person or group. Our faith or belief in God is at the heart of our religion.

Religions: Systems of practices and rules to express and respond to the search for and belief in God.

Founder: A person whose teaching and example leads to the formation of a group or community vision.

LESSON 7   Christian Denominations

GROUNDWORK
In this lesson we plan to:
- explore the meaning of a community of faith and learn what a denomination of a community of faith is.

DIGGING DEEPER
What did Jesus mean when he said, 'I am the vine, you are the branches?'

Key Concept
Denomination

Christianity is one of the five great world religions. Within Christianity, there are a number of different denominations. Each **denomination** is a community of faith with its own organisation and practices. The Church of Ireland and the Methodist Church are both denominations of Christianity.

Divisions within Christianity

Throughout history, there have been a number of splits and divisions within Christianity. The first occurred during the fourth and fifth centuries, when there were theological disputes about Jesus being truly God and truly human. Churches such as the Coptic Church, the Armenian Church and the Ethiopian Church came from that time and are called Oriental Orthodox Churches or Ancient Eastern Churches. These churches are small in number.

The second major split was between East and West. In 1054, most of the eastern part of the Christian community split from Rome, under the leadership of its most important bishop, the Patriarch of Constantinople. (Constantinople is now called Istanbul.) This split is referred to as the Great Schism.

The Great Schism happened because of divisions and difficulties that had come about after the fall of the Roman Empire. It happened also because the Eastern community did not accept the authority of the Pope in Rome. Eastern Christianity became known as Orthodox and Western Christianity became known as

Roman. So we have the Russian Orthodox Church in Russia and the Greek Orthodox Church in Greece.

There are strong links between the Roman Catholic Church and the Eastern Orthodox churches. Although they have different leaders, they share a common belief in the Trinity, the sacraments and sacred scripture.

The next division after the Great Schism came with the Reformation in Western Europe, when the Church further divided into many different churches or denominations. The first of these divisions took place in the sixteenth century and is known as the Protestant Reformation. (We will explore this division in greater detail in Lesson 13.)

Jesus wanted his followers to be united. Christians today realise that, despite their divisions, they are still united in many ways in Jesus. Christians today are making renewed efforts to overcome the divisions that still exist. This is why Christians of different denominations try to respect and learn about one another.

Jesus said: 'I am the vine, you are the branches. Those who abide in me and I in them bear much fruit, because apart from me you can do nothing' (John 15:5).

The Great Schism (1054)

Roman Catholic Church → Orthodox churches

Roman Catholic Church → Reformation (Sixteenth century) → Protestant churches / Roman Catholic Church

Protestant churches → Church of Ireland (in England known as the Church of England), Methodist Church, Presbyterian Church, Baptist Church, Salvation Army, Society of Friends, or Quakers

KNOW WHAT
1. What is a denomination?
2. What is a schism?
3. What was the Great Schism within Christianity?
4. Looking at the above chart, how many Christian denominations are there? Name four of them.

DIGGING DEEPER
Invite people from different Christian denominations to come and talk to your class.

 **Denomination:** Community of faith, with its own particular organisation and practices.

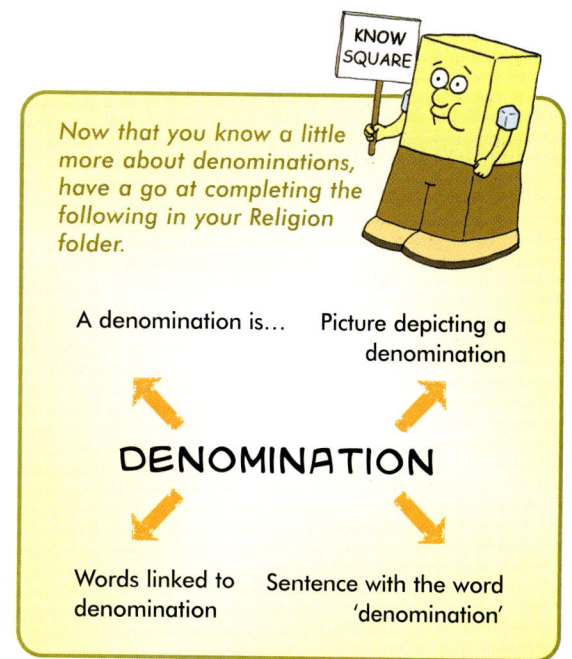

Now that you know a little more about denominations, have a go at completing the following in your Religion folder.

A denomination is... | Picture depicting a denomination

DENOMINATION

Words linked to denomination | Sentence with the word 'denomination'

LESSON 8 Religious Identity

GROUNDWORK
In this lesson we plan to:
- explore the term 'identity' and be aware of the significance of a religious identity.

DIGGING DEEPER
How do I express my religious identity?

Key Concept
Identity

Name Game Challenge
You will need five coloured 'post-its' for this game. Also, five 'volunteers' to take up the challenge!

- Five volunteers stand in front of the class.
- The other class members write down the names of well-known people on a sheet of paper. For example, pop stars, politicians, actors. This must be done in secret!
- A representative of the class then writes the five most popular names on the post-its and sticks one on each volunteer's forehead.
- In turn, the five volunteers then ask the rest of the class questions about their 'new' identity.
- Only 'Yes' and 'No' answers may be given.

From the questions asked and the answers given, the five volunteers must try to uncover their famous identity.

Identity
The Name Game Challenge helps us to realise that our **identity** is what makes us different from everybody else. Each one of us has our own unique identity.

KNOWING ME KNOWING YOU
What are the unique qualities that mark you out as different? Write a paragraph to explain how your unique qualities identify you from everyone else.

Religious Identity
The community of faith to which you belong (i.e. your religion) further identifies you as a person. For example, if you are from the Christian community of faith, you will have a Christian identity. This means that you take seriously the inspiring vision of Jesus, the founder of Christianity, and all that being a Christian involves. You will believe that Jesus is risen from the dead and is still present in the world through his Word, the Church and the sacraments. If you are from the Islamic community of faith, you will have an Islamic identity and take seriously the inspiring vision of Muhammad.

KNOW WHAT

1. What does the word 'identity' mean?
2. What is your religious identity?
3. What does the term 'Christian identity' mean?
4. If you were a Christian, how would you show your Christian identity?
5. What does the term 'Islamic identity' mean?
6. If you were a Muslim, how would you show your Islamic identity?

DIGGING DEEPER

1. When/how do you think that you show your religious identity to others?
2. Have you ever had an experience where your religious identity affected other people's opinions of you? Explain what happened.
2. Have you ever witnessed or heard about someone else's religious identity causing them to be treated in a different way? Explain what happened. What might have helped in this situation?

When do you receive your religious identity?

When babies are born, there is usually an initiation ceremony into their particular community of faith. When babies are born into the Christian community, they receive their identity as members of that community by celebrating the sacrament of Baptism. Baptism is one of the sacraments of initiation. For a Christian, initiation means becoming a member of the Christian community of faith and a follower of Jesus. It is through the sacrament of Baptism that all Christians are freed from sin, become members of God's family and are called to serve God and others and to live as followers of Jesus. It is also through the sacrament of Baptism that Christians become connected as sisters and brothers to every other member of the Christian community. Because of their Baptism, they now have a religious identity as Christians.

All of the Christian denominations celebrate Baptism. (You will learn more about the sacrament of Baptism in Section E.)

KNOW WHAT

1. What is a sacrament of initiation?
2. What does the celebration of the sacrament of Baptism mean for a person?
3. What is the relationship between Baptism and Christian identity?

Identity: That which makes it possible to know who a group or a person is.

SECTION A — COMMUNITIES OF FAITH

LESSON 9 Called to Serve

GROUNDWORK
In this lesson we plan to:
- find out what it means to have a vocation.

DIGGING DEEPER
How are we called to serve?

Key Concepts
Vocation as a calling to serve/Mission/Gospel

Story: A Life-changing Experience

Like most twelve-year-old boys, canadian Craig Kielburger enjoyed being with his friends and having a good time. One day, as Craig reached for the comic section of the newspaper, the *Toronto Star*, a picture on the front page of the paper caught his attention; it was a picture of a boy wearing a bright red vest with his fist held high. The headline read: 'Boy, twelve, murdered for speaking out against child labour.'

Craig Kielburger

Craig's curiosity was aroused. The article told the story of Iqbal Masih, a young boy from Pakistan who was sold into child labour at the age of four, as a carpet-weaver, to repay a loan that his parents had taken out. Iqbal worked twelve hours a day, six days a week, tying tiny knots to make carpets. He lost his freedom to laugh and to play. He lost his freedom to go to school. The article told how, when he was twelve years old, the same age as Craig, he was murdered.

Craig had never heard about child labour and wasn't even certain where Pakistan was, but the differences in their lives shocked him. When Craig read that there were 250 million child labourers in the world, half of them working full time, and many in very dangerous conditions, he knew he had to help.

Craig, along with a group of his twelve-year-old friends, formed an organisation called 'Free the Children', whose aim was not only to free children from abuse and exploitation, but to free children from the idea that they are not old enough or smart enough or capable enough to help change the world.

Within six months, Craig had many meetings and raised $150,000 to build a rehabilitation and education centre in India for children who were freed from slavery as carpet-weavers. He travelled to South Asia to see the situation for himself and he is now responsible for a world-wide movement that promotes justice issues concerning young people.

Craig felt called to respond, and he did so in a very worthwhile way. His experience was a life-changing one. As a result of this experience, and of reading that newspaper article when he was twelve years old, he made many new choices in his life.

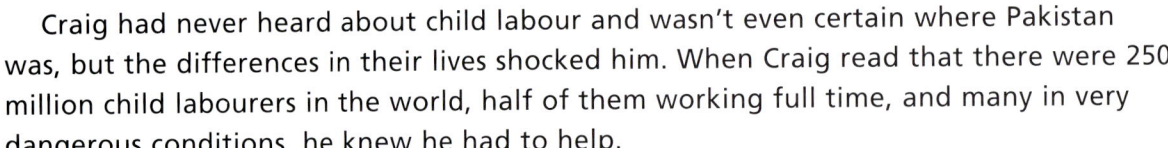

KNOW WHAT
1. In what way was Craig's life changed by his calling to serve?
2. Do you know of any other person who felt called to respond to any of the many crises in our world today?

DIGGING DEEPER

1. How do you respond if you are invited to take part in a charity fun run, a danceathon, a sponsored fast, a soccer marathon or any other event organised to raise money for a charity?
2. Have you ever initiated (started) a charity event to help others or do you know someone who organises such events?
3. What are the outcomes of charity events and what kind of response do they show to a calling to serve?

KNOWING ME KNOWING YOU

1. Go to your internet search engine and type in Craig's full name. Try to find out what he is working at today.
2. Gather some newspaper or magazine cuttings that tell the story of people who have had life-changing experiences and were called to serve others as a result.
   - What were the life-changing events?
   - How were they called to serve?
   - What happened to their lives as a result of these life-changing experiences?

Vocation as a Calling to Serve

Every Christian has a vocation. The word 'vocation' comes from the Latin *vocatio*, which means 'a calling'. Through Baptism, each Christian is called by God to become more like Jesus Christ – to live and love like him, to grow in knowledge and love of God, and to use their personal gifts and talents to help and serve others. This is their **mission** or role as Christians.

Some examples of famous Christians who responded in a very significant way to their baptismal call:

Mother Teresa, Michael Courtney, Eunice Kennedy Shriver, Sr Stanislaus Kennedy, Fr Peter Mc Verry, Adi Roche, Bono, Fr Maximilian Kolbe, Archbishop Oscar Romero, Mel Gibson.

Ali Hewson, Bono and Adi Roche

KNOW WHAT

1. What do you know about any of the people mentioned above?
2. How did/do they help to spread **Gospel** values?

KNOWING ME KNOWING YOU

Write a page on a person (or group) from your area who works to spread Gospel values.

Vocation as a calling to serve: God calls people to carry out their roles/tasks in their community of faith for the benefit of others.

Mission: A specific task given to a person or group.

Gospel: Means 'good news' and refers to the Good News of God's love that Jesus brought to all people. The first four books of the New Testament are called gospels because they tell of the new life that Jesus offers to all.

LESSON 10   The Roman Catholic Church

GROUNDWORK
In this lesson we plan to:
- name the leaders of churches in Ireland today;
- begin a study of the Roman Catholic Church.

DIGGING DEEPER
How can I show my religious commitment?

Key Concepts
Church/Inspiring vision/Founder/Religious Commitment

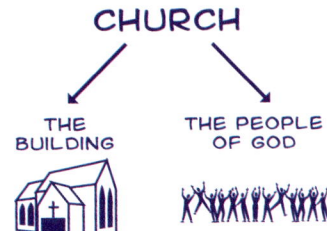

All the major world religions have communities of faith living and worshipping in Ireland. The Catholic Church and the Church of Ireland have the largest number of followers, while the other main Christian churches are the Presbyterian Church, the Methodist Church and the Baptist Church.

Each **church** has its own leader. The Catholic Church in Ireland is led by the Archbishop of Armagh, who is the *Primate of All Ireland*. Similarly, the Church of Ireland's Archbishop of Armagh is *Primate of All Ireland* for that community of faith. A *Moderator* is appointed each year to lead the Irish Presbyterian Church, while the Irish Jewish community is led by the *Chief Rabbi*. The Islamic community in Ireland looks to the local *imam* for direction and leadership.

The Roman Catholic Church

The Catholic Church is a community of followers of Jesus Christ who believe in God the Father, God the Son and God the Holy Spirit, and who gather to pray and to celebrate the sacraments, especially the Eucharist.

The Catholic Church is the largest Christian denomination in the world. There are approximately three million members of the Catholic Church living in Ireland. The word 'Catholic' has its origin in the Greek language, and means 'universal'. When other Christian denominations speak of Catholicism, they usually refer to it as Roman Catholicism. This is to underline the central role of the Pope in the organisation of the Catholic Church.

The inspiration or **inspiring vision** for the work done by the Catholic Church comes directly from the **founder** of Christianity, Jesus Christ. *The Catechism of the Catholic Church* states:

> *The one mediator, Christ, established and ever sustains here on earth his holy Church, the community of faith, hope and charity, as a visible organisation through which he communicates truth and grace to all people. (para. 771)*

St Paul called the Christian community of believers the 'Body of Christ'. They work together as all the parts of the body work together. The head of the body is Jesus Christ himself.

Jesus is always gathering people into one community through his word, through the sacraments and through community life. He does this through the Holy Spirit.

Religious Commitment

Belonging to any community calls for commitment, i.e. a promise to work on behalf of the group. Belonging to a church or other religious group calls for **religious commitment**. Every baptised Catholic is called to serve God and others. By doing this, they show their commitment to their baptismal identity.

All members of the Catholic Church show their religious commitment by striving to spread Gospel values in their homes, in their work, in their leisure activities and in their wider communities.

- **Lay people** show their religious commitment by working for God and others in their families and by helping to build up their faith community at local, national and international levels. They do this above all by the way they live and relate to others, and by giving witness to the Gospel through their work and through their involvement in economics, culture, sport, politics, etc. Teenagers can show their religious commitment by fundraising for organisations like Concern, Goal or Trócaire, by helping to distribute St Vincent de Paul hampers or by singing together at a school Mass or prayer service. They might also show their religious commitment by standing up for a classmate who is being bullied, by sharing their lunchtime treats or by encouraging a teammate at a match. Religious commitment, therefore, involves working for and with others at all times; it means action as well as words.

- Men and women who are members of **religious orders or communities** show their religious commitment through their daily work and their life choices. In Ireland, many of our hospitals and schools were founded (set up) by members of religious orders. For example, the Mercy Sisters established many hospitals and girls' schools and the Christian Brothers established many boys' schools. A particular focus of many religious orders is to work with people who are in need.

- **Priests, bishops and all other ordained ministers** show their religious commitment in the same ways as lay people, but they also show it by their choice to dedicate all of their life's work to spreading the Gospel, celebrating the sacraments, especially the Eucharist, and working as instruments of Christ in building up the Christian community.

Members of all faiths demonstrate religious commitment when they gather together as a community to worship. In the Catholic Church, people gather to celebrate the sacraments. Members of the clergy play a special leading role in these celebrations.

> *'For where two or three are gathered in my name, I am there among them.'*
> (Matthew 18:20)

KNOW WHAT

1. What is religious commitment?
2. How do the laity (lay people), the clergy and members of religious orders show their religious commitment in ways that are similar?
3. How do the laity, the clergy and members of religious orders show their religious commitment in ways that are dissimilar?
4. 'Worshipping together, for example attending Sunday Mass, nourishes us on our journey through life.' What do you think this statement means?

DIGGING DEEPER

> 'Paddy Murphy went to Mass, he never missed a Sunday.
> All the wrong that Paddy did, he did it on a Monday.'

1. What is this rhyme about?
2. How does Paddy show/not show his religious commitment?
3. How does this rhyme help us to understand that religious commitment involves how we live our lives, treat others and practise our faith every day of the week?
4. Why might it be difficult to show religious commitment in the modern world?

KNOW HOW

Copy the following chart into your Religion folder and then name two ways in which each person can show his/her religious commitment.

The religious leader of my faith	Me
1.	1.
2.	2.

DIGGING DEEPER

1. Give an example of a time when you witnessed or heard about a lay person showing their religious commitment by working to serve God in their community.
2. Give an example of a time when you witnessed or heard about a priest or religious sister or brother showing their religious commitment by working to serve God in their community.
3. Give an example of a time when you showed your religious commitment by working to serve God in your community.

Church: A community of faith. Also used to describe a building in which people worship.

Religious commitment: Pledge/promise to live as God asks; may involve taking on a new task or role.

LESSON 11 Roles within the Catholic Church

GROUNDWORK
In this lesson we plan to:
- learn about the variety of roles within the Catholic community of faith, including leadership roles.

DIGGING DEEPER
What are the different roles within my community of faith?

Key Concepts
Roles/Leadership/Vocation as a calling to serve/Service

Roles within the Catholic Church

In Lesson 10, we looked at the three broad groups of people within the Catholic Church and we examined how each group shows their religious commitment. We will now look more closely at the variety of **roles** within the Catholic Church, including **leadership** roles.

Leadership roles provide a service to all the members of the Church. This **service** is given by:

- the Pope, cardinals, bishops, priests;
- lay people within the Church;
- religious orders within the Church;
- groups such as Meals on Wheels, CYC (Catholic Youth Council), the Society of St Vincent de Paul, Trócaire, etc.
- movements such as Charismatic Renewal, L'Arche, Legion of Mary, etc.

Just as a wheel requires all the spokes to move forward, and each spoke on the wheel helps and supports the other spokes, as well as supporting the wheel, a community of faith works in the same way. See if you can add any other names to the great wheel that is the Church!

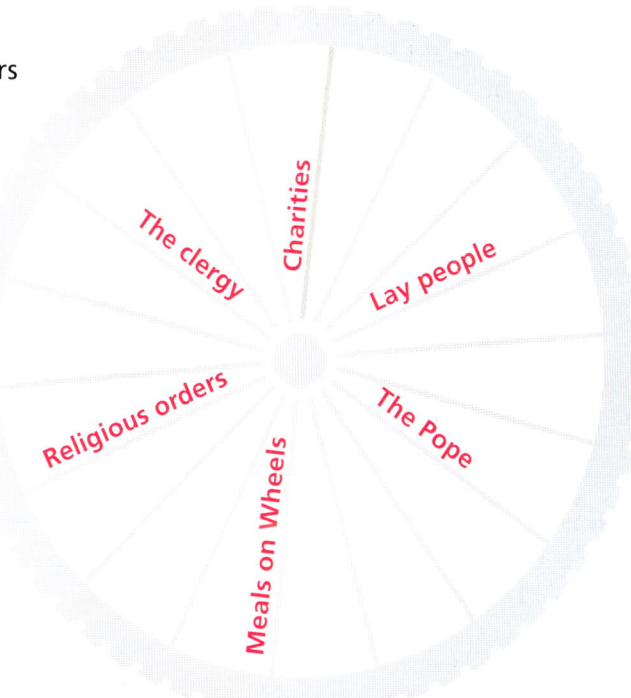

The Organisation of the Catholic Church

The Pope, also known as the Holy Father, is the leader of the Catholic Church. He is like the apostle Peter at the time of the early Church. The Pope lives in Vatican City in Rome, Italy. Rome was one of the earliest centres of Christianity and the city in which the apostles Peter and Paul lived and were martyred.

43

As head of the hierarchy of the Church, the Pope has supreme authority and universal power over the Catholic Church.

The Catholic Church holds that the Pope is infallible, i.e. he cannot err when he teaches officially on matters of faith and morals. The term used to describe this is *ex cathedra*.

The Pope is supported and assisted in his work by the cardinals, archbishops, bishops, men and women of religious orders and lay people.

Part of the Pope's ministry and mission in leading the Church is to write papal encyclicals (letters), which guide and inform the community of faith on the teachings of the Church.

Pope Benedict XVI

Cardinals are chosen by the Pope. They have authority in the Church, as they inform the Pope on important issues. One of the most important roles that cardinals have is to help elect a new Pope. This is a very honourable and responsible role.

Bishops look after their dioceses. The bishop is the leader of all the priests in his diocese, as well as the local spiritual leader of all the Catholics in the diocese. An archbishop leads an archdiocese. Bishops and archbishops also have authority in making decisions on how the Catholic faith is handed on and celebrated in their diocese/archdiocese.

Priests play a leading role in their parish. Each diocese is divided into a number of parishes. Until now, each parish had a parish priest, as well as one or more curates. Because of a reduction in the number of priests, many parishes must now share the priests of their dioceses. Priests support the community of faith, celebrate the sacraments and work for growth in the Church.

Religious orders serve the community in many of the caring and educational professions, as well as through their prayer and work within their own religious communities.

Lay people play a vital role in the Catholic Church, including a variety of leadership roles within community groups and committees, and in the area of religious education.

TAKE FIVE

1. Who is the leader of the Roman Catholic Church?
2. Which group plays a special leadership role in the election of a new Pope?
3. What role do lay people play in the Catholic Church?
4. What is the role of a priest?
5. What role does a bishop play in a diocese?

KNOWING ME KNOWING YOU

Copy the following sentences into your Religion folder and then draw lines to match the descriptions with the people listed.

I am a teenager who works with children in the First Holy Communion class	A mother
I am a religious leader with a large diocese	An archbishop
I am a woman who enjoys helping out with parish work	A married couple
I am a woman who lives and works in a religious order	Transition Year student
I am an ordinary person who works to build up the community of faith	The Pope
I am the leader of the Catholic Church	A religious sister
We are a couple who run a local youth group	Lay person

What is the impact or effect of the work of the Catholic Church?

The various organisations run by the Catholic Church, whether they be medical, educational or charitable organisations, all support and care for the local communities throughout Ireland.

The many aid agencies who carry out the work of the Catholic Church have been responsible for great progress in improving the lives of people at local, national and international levels, resulting in:

- communities escaping from the poverty trap;
- communities being consoled and supported in times of suffering;
- communities being able to enjoy a better standard of living.

KNOW WHAT

1. Where does the inspiration for the work of the Catholic Church come from?
2. Where does the help and guidance for the work of the Catholic Church come from?
3. Give three examples of work being carried out by the Catholic Church.
4. Name two examples of the impact of the work done by the Catholic Church.

LESSON 12 Roles in a Parish

GROUNDWORK
In this lesson we plan to:
- explore a specific example of the variety of roles within the Catholic Church at parish level.

DIGGING DEEPER
What role can I play in my parish?

Key Concepts

Roles/Service

The specific **roles** within a parish community provide an important **service** to the community. Let's meet some of the people from the Parish of St Peter and St Paul, as each describe their own role.

Fr Gerard, the parish priest
'I support my community of faith through preaching the word of God. I make the love of God available by celebrating the sacraments. I build unity by preaching the truth and by helping people to use their talents for the good of the community. The people in this parish are warm, friendly and always ready to work together. There is always a friendly face to talk to here!'

Miriam, the sacristan
'I prepare the church for Mass and any other liturgical events. I really enjoy my work and I make sure that everything is always in its right place. I have a very creative altar group to help me.'

Róisín, a minister of the Eucharist
'I trained with a group to become a minister of the Eucharist. Now I give out Holy Communion at Mass. I also bring Holy Communion to people who are not well enough to come to Mass. I enjoy helping out in the parish.'

Donal, a minister of the Word
'I read from the Bible at Mass on Sundays. I always practise to make sure I don't get nervous!'

Seamus, the caretaker
'I look after the maintenance of the church. I love gardening and I know the parishioners enjoy my flowerbeds, especially the rose garden.'

Dermot and Jim, who collect the baskets
'We co-ordinate the collections at Mass. There are five others who share the duties with us. Both of us are retired now and we enjoy giving a helping hand in the parish.'

Sr Jacqueline, who runs the parish shop
'I open the shop at the back of the church after Mass. You can buy Holy Communion medals, Mass cards and many other gifts there. It is a great way to meet and chat with people.'

Angela, who co-ordinates the Meals on Wheels group
'I work with a great group of people in the community. We ensure that the food is bought, cooked and delivered hot to all who avail of our service. There is a great sense of co-operation and sharing in our kitchen.'

Catherine and John, who are in the choir
'We meet up every Thursday evening to practise with the choir. We really enjoy taking part in the Sunday Mass and sharing our gifts and talents with the community. There are always extra practices for Christmas and Easter. It really lifts our spirits to be part of the choir.'

Teresa, who is an altar server
'I serve at Mass on a Sunday morning. I mostly serve at the Youth Mass in our parish. Most of the others in my class are altar servers too.'

Cathal and Cathy, who co-ordinate the Youth Mass
'We are a young couple who enjoy working with the youth group. We co-ordinate the Youth Mass in the parish and we get a tremendous response from all the young people. The Youth Mass is an amazing celebration for our community.'

Joy, who is secretary at the Parish Centre
'I am a full-time secretary at the Parish Centre. It's a very busy parish. There is always something going on in the Parish Centre during the evening or at the weekends. We also run a homework club after school each day. I really enjoy my work.'

David, a young person in the parish
'I really enjoy belonging to this parish and taking part in the various activities and celebrations.'

5-4-3-2-1
1. Name **five** roles played by lay people in your parish.
2. Name **four** ways in which you could become involved in your parish.
3. Suggest **three** ways in which young people are involved in your parish community.
4. Name and describe the service of **two** people who work full-time in your parish.
5. Write **one** newsletter to let people know what is going on in your parish.

DIGGING DEEPER
'All members of the Catholic community of faith play an important role.'

Write a page on this statement, giving sufficient reasons for your viewpoint.

KNOW IT ALL
Choose *five* of the following and explain each person's role and identity.

Pope • Mother • Bishop • Student • Priest • Father • Member of a religious order
Lay person • Leader • Cardinal • Reader • Altar server • Sister • Brother

KNOWING ME KNOWING YOU
Try to arange a visit to your local Catholic church.
- Draw a sketch of the inside of the church.
- Read what is on the parish noticeboard.
- Find out at what times the Masses are on.
- Find out about communities or groups that are working in your parish.

LESSON 13   The Anglican Communion

GROUNDWORK
In this lesson we plan to:
- understand the term 'Protestantism' and explore the Anglican Communion as a community of faith.

DIGGING DEEPER
What do you know about the Anglican communion?

Key Concepts
Church/Sacred text/Roles

The Protestant Reformation

In Lesson 7, we read about the Great Schism (split) that took place within Christianity in 1054. In the sixteenth century, another division occurred. A Catholic Augustinian monk named Martin Luther began to protest about specific practices in the Catholic Church. Luther believed that people were saved and brought to heaven by faith alone, while the Catholic Church taught that people had to do good works as well as have faith in order to get to heaven. Luther was particularly against the Church's practice of granting 'indulgences' as it was taught and explained by some priests at that time, i.e. people could give money to the Church in order to shorten their journey to heaven. On 31 October 1517, Luther pinned his '95 Theses' (arguments) on the door of the main church in Wittenberg, Germany.

Martin Luther

Luther was sincere in questioning some of the practices that were happening in the Catholic Church. However, he refused to obey the Pope at the time (Pope Leo X) and gradually, as often happens when people argue and there is disagreement, his position became more extreme. Eventually, Luther was excommunicated (expelled) from the Catholic Church and he formed his own **church** in Germany. This was called the Lutheran Church.

The churches that emerged from this division are called Protestant churches, because they were founded following a protest. The 'Protestant Reformation' is the term used to describe this time of change and division within Christianity.

TAKE FIVE
1. Who was Martin Luther?
2. What did he do on 31 October 1517?
3. What happened to him as a result of this?
4. What church did Luther establish in Germany?
5. What is meant by the term 'Protestant Reformation'?

The Anglican Communion

The Church of England was established after the Protestant Reformation, with King Henry VIII as its leader. Later, as the British Empire spread, Church of England missionaries set up similar communities of faith in other parts of the world, which they named after the countries concerned, for example, the Church of Ireland, the Church of India, the Church of Canada, and so on. Together, these communities of faith are now known as the Anglican Communion. They are all in communion (in community) with the Church of England and its leader, the Archbishop of Canterbury.

The Church of Ireland is an important part of the worldwide Anglican Communion. Today, there are over 370,000 Irish members of the Church of Ireland.

Some important aspects of the Anglican Communion today

Sacred text

Like all other Christians, members of the Anglican Communion have great respect for the Bible. They believe that it is the Word of God and that, when applied to daily life, it offers all that is needed to help a person to grow in their relationship with God. Like all other Christians, they believe that the Bible is a **sacred text**.

Sacraments

The churches of the Anglican Communion celebrate the sacrament of Baptism and the sacrament of the Eucharist (Holy Communion). The other five sacraments celebrated by the Catholic Church are recognised as celebrations of God's grace rather than sacraments. ('Grace' is the word for God's loving presence and action in people's lives.)

Roles within the Anglican Communion

Local parish – Ministers/Rectors

In the Church of Ireland, the local clergy are called *ministers* or *rectors*. In the Church of England, they are usually called *vicars*. Since 1990, both men and women can be ordained in the Anglican Communion and all clergy are free to marry. The ministers work within the local community at many levels. They invite every age-group to become involved in working for the good of the whole community. Ministers lead the *Sunday Worship*, of which there are two kinds: *Sunday Service* and *Holy Communion*. In Ireland, Holy Communion is celebrated on the first and third Sunday of every month.

Lay people

As with all the Christian churches, lay people play an important role in the Anglican Communion. They participate at Sunday Worship by reading the scriptures and other prayers and by joining in singing the hymns. Lay people work with the local minister to build community within their families and their parish. Some lay people are elected as members of the lay vestry. This means that they can play a leading role in the running of their parish.

The Organisation of the Church of Ireland

The Church of Ireland is divided into two provinces: Armagh and Dublin. Two Anglican archbishops lead the two provinces. The two provinces are subdivided into twelve dioceses, each with its own bishop. The archbishops and bishops work to build the faith community and play a guiding role in the leadership of the Church. Each year, the Church of Ireland holds an assembly called a Synod, where the bishops and representatives of the clergy and lay people come together to discuss and decide on important issues.

Rt Rev Alan Harper, Archbishop of Armagh and Most Rev Fr John Neill, Archbishop of Dublin

KNOW IT ALL

Copy the following paragraph into your Religion folder and fill in the blanks using the wordbank given below.

The Church of Ireland is part of the _____ _____ . This faith community has great respect for the _____ . There are two _____ celebrated in the Anglican Communion: they are _____ and _____ _____ . Both men and women can be _____ in the Anglican Communion. The clergy at parish level are called _____ or _____. They lead the Sunday _____, of which there are two kinds: Sunday Service and _____ _____ . There is a great variety of _____ within the Anglican Communion. The Archbishop of _____ is the spiritual leader of the worldwide Anglican Communion.

WORDBANK

Holy Communion • Ministers • Roles • Anglican Communion • Sacraments
Holy Communion • Baptism • Bible • Ordained • Worship • Rectors • Canterbury

DIGGING DEEPER

1. Outline two important aspects of the Anglican Communion.
2. What is the role of a lay person in the Anglican Communion?
3. What is the role of a lay person in your community of faith?

Sacred text: Writings relating to a community of faith, which are considered holy and inspired.

LESSON 14   A Church Organisation – Trócaire

GROUNDWORK
In this lesson we plan to:
- look at the type of work done by a religious organisation;
- recognise the variety of roles in the organisation, including leadership roles.

DIGGING DEEPER
How does a church organisation work to spread Gospel values?

Key Concepts
Inspiring vision/Roles/Service/Commitment

Trócaire – A Church Organisation at Work
- What do you know about Trócaire?
- Google the word 'Trócaire' and discuss your findings in class.

Trócaire is one of the many Catholic organisations that imitate the work and teachings of Jesus. The Trócaire community works for justice and peace in the world and promotes global awareness of the poverty that exists.

Who?
Trócaire is the official overseas development agency of the Catholic Church in Ireland. It was set up by the Irish Catholic Bishops in 1973 to express the concern of the Irish Church for the suffering of the world's poorest and most oppressed people.

What?
Trócaire was formed to carry out the following aims:

- To support long-term development projects overseas.
- To provide relief during emergencies.
- To inform the Irish public about the root causes of poverty and injustice.
- To work with the public to bring about global change.

Inspiring Vision
Trócaire, which means 'compassion' in the Irish language, draws its **inspiring vision** from Scripture and the social teaching of the Catholic Church. The Trócaire community strives to promote human development and social justice in line with Gospel values. It works for a just world, where people's dignity is protected, rights are respected and basic needs are met; where there is fairness in the sharing of resources, and people are free to control their own development. Its work of **service** and **commitment** is influenced by the experiences and the hopes of the poor and oppressed.

Where?
Trócaire offers its support in Africa, Asia, Latin America, the Middle East and in any emergency situations. Map available from website at:
http://trocaire.com/international/internationalintroduction.htm

When?
This support is offered on an ongoing basis and in times of emergency, regardless of race, gender, religion or politics.

The Variety of Roles Within Trócaire

There are many **roles** within Trócaire. There are the leadership roles held by the chairperson and the director, as well as by the managers and team co-ordinators in Ireland and in Trócaire's offices in Africa, Asia and Latin America. There are also the programme officers who work on different programmes involving themes like emergencies, gender, HIV/AIDs, human rights and the environment. Some of these people are based in Ireland and some in the overseas offices.

In Ireland, there are education and campaign teams who talk to young people in schools and parishes all over the country, telling them about the work of Trócaire and about how they can contribute to this work, for example by signing postcards, attending human rights workshops, taking part in solidarity events or fundraising activities, buying Fair Trade products, joining the Just World social networking site *(apps.trocaire.org/justworld)* or simply learning more about a particular issue, like Burma or The Wall in Palestine, and sharing this information with others.

KNOW WHAT
1. Why is there a variety of roles within Trocáire?
2. Where does Trócaire's vision come from?

DIGGING DEEPER
1. Have you ever been involved in a Trócaire campaign? How do you think your involvement helped the campaign?
2. Now that you know more about Trócaire, do you think you will become more involved in their campaign this year? Explain your answer.
3. Invite someone from Trócaire to talk to your class.

KNOW IT ALL
Copy the following paragraph into your Religion folder and fill in the blanks using the wordbank given below.

_____ is a religious organisation. It received its name from the _____ language. Trócaire means _____. The organisation draws its _____ from _____ and the social teaching of the _____ Church. Trócaire has several aims: to _____ long-term development projects overseas; to provide _____ during emergencies; to inform the Irish public about the root causes of poverty and injustice, and to work with the _____ to bring about global change.

WORDBANK

Relief • Compassion • Scripture • Trócaire • Public • Support • Vision • Catholic • Irish

KNOW THE WAY

The Impact of Trócaire's Work on Individuals and Communities

The Global Gift Plan

Trócaire's Global Gift Plan provides a wonderful opportunity for all of us to work together as a community that is co-operating, communicating and sharing with some of the world's poorest people. Since the start of the Global Gift Plan in the year 2000, gifts have transformed the lives of thousands of people in developing countries. By taking part in the Global Gift Plan, we can work together to ensure that these families have a promising future to look forward to. In 2006, almost 81,000 global gifts were purchased, amounting to €3.2 million /£2.25 million. Chicks for Central America were the most popular gift, with over 31,000 purchased. Can you imagine that? Here is a story about some of the people who have benefited from this positive action plan.

A Report from Honduras

Forty-seven families in the rural community of San Juan Pueblo in northern Honduras received the global gift of a consignment of chicks. San Juan Pueblo is a wonderful example of a community where people work together on projects that will benefit others. When they received news of the arrival of the global gift chicks, the community began to work together to prepare for receiving them. They built chicken hutches, using wood and corrugated metal for the roofs, and sticks and mud for the individual pens. The chicks are fed on maize and they drink rainwater collected in gutters lying on the ground. They have provided an extra source of food and income for the whole community.

KNOW WHAT

1. In your own words, explain what the Trócaire Global Gift Plan is.
2. What are the advantages of such a project?
3. In the light of the above report from Honduras, write a paragraph to explain how the Global Gift Plan does more than offer short-term benefits.
4. What is the impact of the work of Trócaire on individuals and on the wider community?
5. Log on to *www.trocaire.ie* and see if you can name two other gifts that have been added over the years. How have each of these gifts helped people?

DIGGING DEEPER

Can you suggest any other type of gift for the Trócaire Global Gift Plan? Explain your choice.

KNOWING ME KNOWING YOU

If your class would like to take part in the Global Gift Plan for Christmas, you can:

- Write to: Trócaire, Maynooth, FREEPOST, Co Kildare.
- Callsave: Trócaire at 1850 408 408.
- Order your gifts online at: *www.trocaire.org*
- Purchase your global gifts from: Trócaire, Maynooth, County Kildare; 12 Cathedral Street, Dublin 1; 9 Cook Street, Cork, or your nearest Veritas store in Dublin, Cork, Clare, Sligo, Derry, Donegal or Monaghan.

LESSON 15 Religious Orders and Organisations In Ireland

GROUNDWORK
In this lesson we plan to:
- research religious orders and organisations in Ireland.

DIGGING DEEPER
How do the religious orders and organisations in Ireland respond to their vocation?

Key Concepts
Vocation as a calling to serve/Mission

Serving God in a Religious Order

When a person joins a religious order, we say that they are answering their '**vocation**' or 'calling' to serve God in a special way. We can also refer to this as their '**mission**'. Before their final entry into the religious order, each person makes three vows (promises). These vows shape their life's work and their lifestyle: poverty (they will not personally own material things, e.g. house, car); chastity (they will not get married or have sexual relationships); obedience (they will always do what God wants).

KNOW WHAT
1. How might these vows affect/influence a person's work of serving God?
2. How might they shape a person's lifestyle?

Examples of religious orders in the Catholic Church:
The Loreto Sisters, The Presentation Brothers, The Presentation Sisters, The Poor Clares, The Christian Brothers, The Carmelite Sisters, The Daughters of Charity.

The Carmelite order of Sisters in New Ross, Co Wexford, is an enclosed contemplative order. An enclosed order is an order of sisters (nuns) or monks who live in a very quiet and prayerful environment. Such enclosures provide space and freedom for those within to enjoy their life of prayer and reflection. Here is an interview with Sister Brenda, one of the sisters of the Carmelite order in New Ross.

Who is the founder of your order?
The Carmelite tradition has no recognised founder but we originated when some hermits opted to stay on Mount Carmel and pray. Eventually they had to flee to Europe and they became known as the Brothers of Our Lady of Mount Carmel. This all happened in the twelfth century. In the fifteenth century, groups of women joined the order. From the monastery in Avila, Spain, St Teresa emerged to reform the order. We are all descended from this group, called the Discalced (barefoot) Carmelites.

What was St Teresa's inspiring vision?
St Teresa of Avila was a very special and holy person. She devoted her life to God and shared her experience of God with the world through her writings. For Teresa, God and things of God were central, and this was her vision, which has inspired us to live a life filled with prayerful reflection. She has helped us to develop a deep relationship with God, to be friends of God.

How do the Carmelite Sisters respond to their vocation as a calling to serve?

We devote much of our day to prayer and quiet contemplation. Our prayer life is at the service of the Church. When we pray the Divine Office, we are praying in the name of the People of God for the world's needs and intentions. At a different level, we serve the local community of faith by making altar bread for the sacrament of the Eucharist at Mass. The local children who are making their First Holy Communion actually come and cut their own hosts for the First Holy Communion Mass.

What kind of impact does your work have on the community?

We have a big impact on the local community and beyond. We know this from the number of people who contact us looking for our prayerful support in all their needs. People have great faith and they believe that our prayers help them. Many come back in gratitude, including exam students!

What is the variety of roles within your community of faith?

Roles within the community include:

- A portess, who meets those who call to the door or phone.
- A prioress, who is chosen by the group to be the leader for three years.
- A bursar, who looks after the financial matters.
- A sacristan, who looks after everything to do with the church, preparing for Mass and the Divine Office, and other liturgical celebrations.

Serving God in a Lay Organisation

People can also serve God in the Catholic Church by becoming involved in lay organisations that seek to carry out the Church's work and spread Gospel values.

Examples of lay organisations in the Catholic Church:
The Society of St Vincent de Paul, Trócaire, The Legion of Mary, Accord, Catholic Youth Care, Catholic Girl Guides, and so on.

KNOW IT ALL

We will now do some research on a religious order or a lay organisation in the Catholic Church. You may take one of the examples given on the opposite page or choose your own. You could use the internet or the library or a combination of both. You may also decide to add additional headings to those suggested below.

Suggested topics for your research

1. Name of order/organisation
2. Name of founder
3. When was it founded?
4. Where was it founded?
5. What is its inspiration?
6. What is the effect of its work on other individuals and on other communities?
7. What are the different roles in this community?

Share your answers with the class. You could develop this task further by displaying your work on poster sheets.

KNOWING ME KNOWING YOU

For more information on Catholic religious organisations, go to:
www.cori.ie/congregation.html

DIGGING DEEPER

What was the most interesting point that you learned from the religious order/organisation you chose to research?

See page 485 for past exam questions on this topic.

Relationships between Communities of Faith

LESSON 16 Words can Hurt; Words can Heal

GROUNDWORK
In this lesson we plan to:
- recognise the importance of respecting one's own religious beliefs and the beliefs of others.

DIGGING DEEPER
How can I show tolerance for people of different faiths?

Key Concept
Tolerance

'The highest result of education is tolerance.' (Helen Keller)

What is 'tolerance'?

Tolerance is respect, acceptance and appreciation of the rich diversity (differences) in our world. It is a way of thinking and acting that shows respect for those who are different from us.

The Greek term *agape* is used to describe the kind of love that Jesus brought on earth. The great American civil rights leader Reverend Martin Luther King described this as a universal love that 'discovers the friend in every person it meets'.

Class activity: Words to Hurt; Words to Heal

Cut out the outline of a person on a large sheet of coloured paper. This person may be given a fictitious name. This 'person' represents a new student who has just arrived into a close-knit group. Every other student has a best buddie or is in a group of three or four, so the new class member is not finding it easy to fit in. Some students automatically put up barriers to the new student, deciding that they dislike him/her without even trying to get to know them.

- Each student must use their imagination and say something that is not particularly kind to the new 'student'. For example, 'Hey, find your own pals' or 'Your hair is a m-e-s-s', and so on.
- Every time a nasty thing is said, a strip of the 'new student' is torn off and handed to the person who said it. (Each strip must be easily recognised as a body part.)
- When many students have had a chance to say something unkind, it is time to put the 'new student' back together again.
- Invite the students to say something good/apologise to the new student and tape back the body part.

When the 'new student' has been put back together again, she/he is no longer quite the same as at the start.

TAKE FIVE

1. In what way can words be destructive?
2. How did the group rebuild the 'new student'?
3. What does this exercise say about lack of tolerance of difference?
4. Why is it always important to think before you speak?
5. What have you learned from this task?

DIGGING DEEPER

1. Have you ever witnessed other people showing a lack of tolerance towards a person's beliefs? What happened? What would have helped the situation?
2. Name two things that we can do to ensure that we don't respond with a lack of tolerance to the beliefs of others.

KNOW HOW

How many different communities of faith are there in your class? Let's find out more about each of these communities!

Each student answers the questions given on the next page in their Religion folder. Afterwards, the class discuss the different answers.

The word 'Creed' comes from the Latin word 'Credo' and it means 'I believe'. This gave the name Creed to any statement of belief.

Name:

Community of faith:

1. What is the creed of your religion?

2. What is the moral code of your religion?

3. What is the sacred text of your religion?

4. Name two elements of your religion that make it different from others.

5. Name two elements that make it the same as others.

6. What would you miss most about your religion if you could not practise it?

7. What would your family miss the most if they could not practise it?

8. Have you ever had cause to defend your religious beliefs due to the intolerance of others?

9. What is it about your religion that causes you to respect and value it?

KNOW WHAT

1. Did you find the exercise difficult to complete? Why?/Why not?
2. What did you learn from this exercise?
3. What do you think leads to intolerance between people of different religious beliefs?
4. Can you come up with one idea for your school that would help the students to build respect and tolerance for their own beliefs and for the beliefs of others?

 **Tolerance:** Being willing to recognise and respect the beliefs and practices of others, while valuing and studying one's own beliefs and religious practices.

KNOW THE WAY

LESSON 17 Sectarianism

GROUNDWORK
In this lesson we plan to:
- explore the implications of sectarianism and religious conflict in Ireland.

DIGGING DEEPER
How does religious conflict affect my faith?

Key Concepts
Sectarianism/Religious Conflict/Tolerance

What is 'sectarianism'?

Sectarianism is a type of *prejudice*. Prejudice means to pre-judge someone and form an opinion of them based, for example, on their gender, their social status, their cultural background or their religious beliefs. You may have heard the saying 'Don't judge the book by the cover'. This saying is a warning against prejudice. It is wrong to pre-judge people.

Belfast murals

Sectarianism is a prejudiced opinion based on religion, which can result in conflict and the exclusion of those of a different faith community. Sectarianism occurs when people reject others because they do not share the same religious beliefs as themselves.

Sectarianism and Religious Conflict

In Northern Ireland, there has been a long history of conflict. Unfortunately, there is much evidence of a lack of **tolerance** between people from the Protestant community and people from the Catholic community. The 'Troubles', as the conflict in Northern Ireland has often been called, grew from the rise of the civil rights movement in 1969. Between 1969 and the signing of the Good Friday Agreement in 1998, over three and a half thousand people were killed. While the reasons for the conflict are complex, stemming from political as well as religious differences, intolerance has played a major role, and, out of this, sectarianism has raised its ugly head.

Today, there is much work being carried out to promote mutual acceptance of the differences between all of the denominations of Christianity. It is important to realise that respect for one's own religious beliefs must go hand in hand with respect for the religious beliefs of others. To show respect means to value and to care about someone or something.

When each denomination works for the good of the worldwide Christian community, they are being true to the inspiring vision of Jesus Christ, the founder of Christianity.

KNOW WHAT

1. What is sectarianism?
2. What is religious conflict?
3. Give an example of religious conflict in Ireland.
4. What can happen when the denominations of Christianity work together?

The Times

HUNDREDS HOLD VIGIL FOR MURDER VICTIM

Hundreds of people gathered last night for a candlelit vigil at the scene where eighteen-year-old Gavin Brett was murdered. Residents of Glengormley and elsewhere stood in silence as the teenager's father, Michael, thanked them for turning out. He said the vigil was the start of the family's healing process.

KNOW THE WAY

The cross-community vigil that followed the death of Gavin Brett in 2001 was remarkable when we consider the circumstances of his murder. Gavin was an eighteen-year-old Protestant who was chatting with a group of his Catholic friends outside St Enda's GAA club in Glengormley, on the outskirts of Belfast, when loyalist gunmen shot him. One of his friends, Michael Farrell, was shot in the ankle. Gavin was shot because the gunmen thought he was a Catholic. At his funeral, Reverend Baylor told the congregation, 'These men who murdered Gavin were Protestants, loyalists, and they killed one of their own, thinking he was a Roman Catholic. They bring shame on the name of Protestantism. They represent the evil, wasteful path which is dead and useless in us all. Gavin, in the way he lived his life, friends with Protestants and Roman Catholics, represents the only future, the only hope, the only purpose we have.' Gavin's father, Michael, was an experienced paramedic who had helped to treat victims of the Omagh bombing which killed twenty-nine people in 1998. He was quickly on the scene after his son was shot and he tried desperately to help him. At his son's

Gavin Brett

funeral, he helped Michael Farrell, who was using crutches to enter the church. In describing his son he said, 'There wasn't one bigoted bone in his body, and basically bigots took his life away.'

DIGGING DEEPER
1. In what way is this incident an example of sectarianism/intolerance?
2. Do you know of any similar attacks that have happened in the world news recently? Explain what happened and why it happened.
3. What do you think would help to resolve the type of conflict that occurs between people of different religious beliefs? Explain your suggestions.

Did you know?

Did you know that sectarian attitudes can form in children as young as three?

In 2006, it was announced that the children's TV programme *Sesame Street* and the Northern Ireland Pre-School Playgroup Association (NIPPA) were joining together to create a new series of the programme, which would be set in Northern Ireland, in an effort to deal with the problems of sectarianism faced by young children. According to Barney McNeany, Chief Executive of the Northern Ireland Commission for Children and Young People: 'We know from research that attitudes can be formed by children as young as three into very difficult areas such as sectarianism, and that they can be affected by issues such as discrimination, bullying and attitudes to disability.'

Sesame Street productions focus on positive messages and, therefore, this is a very creative way to intervene at an early stage to help change attitudes that stem from conflict and intolerance.

DIGGING DEEEPER
1. How do you react to learning that children as young as three may be affected by sectarianism?
2. Can you suggest one other way that sectarianism could be avoided?

Sectarianism: Excluding (even hating) others who do not belong to one's own community of faith.

Religious conflict: Occurs where two or more groups oppose one another because of their differing faiths or religious beliefs.

See page 486 for past exam questions on this topic.

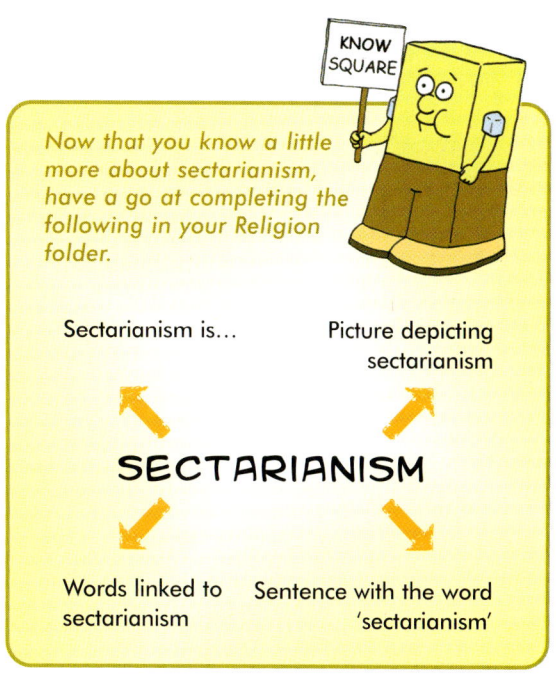

SECTION A COMMUNITIES OF FAITH

LESSON 18 Respecting Our Differences

GROUNDWORK
In this lesson we plan to:
- consider the implications of religious conflict and sectarianism in the world.

DIGGING DEEPER
What is my response to religious conflict?

Key Concepts
Religious conflict/Sectarianism

On 28 August 1963, the American civil rights leader Martin Luther King made a very famous speech, which is known as the 'I have a Dream' speech.

In 2006, a twelve-year-old student wrote her own 'I have a dream' poem. This is what she wrote:

I Have a Dream

I have a dream that all people will be treated equally.
I have a dream that people would lay down their differences and be friends.
I have a dream that people will respect themselves and others.
I have a dream that violence will end and that peace will begin.
I have a dream that my dreams will become your dreams too.

Reverend Martin Luther King

KNOW WHAT

1. What does the title tell you about the poem?
2. 'I have a dream that my dreams will become your dreams too.' What does this last line of the poem mean?
3. According to this twelve-year-old, what does respecting others involve?

KNOW HOW
Remember our earlier attempts at writing an acrostic poem. Let's write another one now using the word 'respect'. As explained earlier, the 'special letter' does not always have to be at the beginning of each line.

Moving Beyond Sectarianism

Today, there are many places in the world where members of different communities of faith are in conflict with one another, for example, Jews and Muslims in Israel, Christians and Muslims in the former Yugoslavia, Hindus, Sikhs and Muslims in India, to name but a few.

This kind of **religious conflict** goes against the teaching of the major world religions, which is summarised in the 'Golden Rule' of each faith community.

The Golden Rule of the Major World Religions

In everything, do to others as you would have them do to you.

Matthew 7:12
CHRISTIANITY

What is hateful to you, do not do to your fellow man.

The Talmud
JUDAISM

No one of you is a believer until he desires for his brother that which he desires for himself.

Hadith
ISLAM

Hurt not others with that which pains yourself.

Udama-Varqa
BUDDHISM

This is the sum of duty; do nothing to others which would cause you pain if done to you.

The Mahabharata
HINDUISM

DIGGING DEEPER

1. How could the characteristics of community, i.e. co-operation, sharing and communication, help to eradicate (do away with) **sectarianism**?
2. What does the Golden Rule of each religion have to say about respecting the beliefs of others?

KNOW HOW

'The aftermath of non-violence is the creation of the beloved community, while the aftermath of violence is tragic bitterness.' (Martin Luther King)

Consider this quote and write a short essay on the effects of violence resulting from religious conflict. Try to use as many of the following words and phrases as you can:

Conflict, religious conflict, tolerance, co-operation, communication, community, communities of faith, sectarianism, unity.

LESSON 19 The Ecumenical Movement

GROUNDWORK
In this lesson we plan to:
- explore two examples of the ecumenical movement in Ireland.

DIGGING DEEPER
What part can I play in the Irish ecumenical movement?

Key Concepts
Ecumenism/Religious conflict

Ecumenism in the Christian Community

In the past, relationships between the Roman Catholic Church and other Christian denominations have often been spoiled by disagreements and resentment. Today, many Christians are committed to developing a greater sense of understanding of one another. **Ecumenism** is the name given to this work for Christian unity. Restoration of Christian unity was one of the principal aims of the Second Vatican Council. The ecumenical movement has brought a greater degree of tolerance, encouraging active participation and discussion between the different Christian denominations. We can see evidence of this in Ireland.

The Glencree Centre for Reconciliation

The Glencree Centre for Reconciliation, at Glencree, Enniskerry, County Wicklow, offers a welcome and a 'safe space' to all those who share its goal of building world peace. It is open to people of all faith traditions.

The members of the Glencree community see peace-building as a process that helps people to understand the nature and meaning of conflict and to seek to resolve such conflict without violence.

Glencree Centre for Reconciliation

The members of the Glencree community recognise that peace-building is a task that requires ongoing dedicated and courageous effort, as well as time and patience.

DIGGING DEEPER
1. How does the Glencree community help to bring about peace and reconciliation?
2. How does the Glencree community promote tolerance and respect for the beliefs of different people?

KNOWING ME KNOWING YOU
Try to organise a class trip to the Glencree Centre for Reconciliation. You can find out more about the Glencree community by checking out their website at: *www.glencree.ie*

Sr Noreen Christian and the Currach Community

This small community is made up of men and women, both religious and lay, from a variety of backgrounds. They live on the Springfield Road in Belfast, in what used to be two run-down buildings. This area is called the 'peace line', as it lies between Catholic and Protestant communities. The people of the Currach Community live a simple lifestyle that involves both work and prayer. They reach out to the local community by working on a variety of projects aimed at promoting peace and reconciliation, such as group work with young people, projects that help to develop community awareness, and justice work. The Currach Community is one of the four partners responsible for 'Forthspring', a community centre for local people.

KNOWING ME KNOWING YOU
1. You can find out more about the Currach Community by checking out their website at: www.ccommunity.fsnet.co.uk
2. Invite someone from the Currach Community to talk to your class.

DIGGING DEEPER
1. Why do you think it is important to have groups like the Glencree Centre for Reconciliation and the Currach Community in our society?
2. How could you become involved in building ecumenism?

The Worldwide Ecumenical Movement

At his first Sunday Mass as Pope, Benedict XVI described the divided Church of Christ as a torn net no longer holding together all that it should contain. He prayed:

> 'Alas, beloved Lord, with sorrow we must now acknowledge that [the net] has been torn! But...let us do all we can to pursue the path towards the unity you have promised... Grant that we may be one flock and one shepherd! Do not allow your net to be torn; help us to be servants of unity!'

For centuries, Catholic, Orthodox and Protestant Christians were completely divided. This went against the vision of Jesus Christ. Then in 1910, a World Missionary Conference was held in Edinburgh, Scotland, attended by representatives of many Protestant denominations, who started to work together for the worldwide unity of Christians. This became known as the ecumenical movement.

The word 'ecumenical' comes from the Greek word *oikoumene*, meaning 'one world'.

This is the logo of the World Council of Churches, which works for ecumenism.

During the twentieth century, the Catholic Church made greater efforts towards healing the divisions that exist between Christians. In particular, Pope John XXIII (1958-63), Pope Paul VI (1963-78) and Pope John Paul II (1978-2005) all worked to help end such divisions. Pope Benedict XVI is continuing this work. Today, representatives of the Catholic Church and the World Council of Churches gather to work together for ecumenism.

KNOW WHAT
1. Where does the word 'ecumenical' come from and what does it mean?
2. Write down three words that describe the logo for the World Council of Churches. Explain your choice of words to the class.
3. What does this logo tell us about the WCC?

Church Unity Week
Every January, Christians all over the world have a Week of Prayer for Christian Unity. During this Church Unity Week, Christians from all over Ireland gather to pray together and dialogue with one another.

DIGGING DEEPER
1. Do you have a Church Unity Week in your school? If so, discuss what happens. If not, try to organise one in your school this year.
2. Have a go at designing your own logo for Church Unity Week.
3. Write a prayer for Church Unity Week based on the following Scripture quotation: *'No one can lay any foundation other than the one that has been laid; that foundation is Jesus Christ.'* (1 Corinthians 3:11)
4. Find out more about ecumenism on the following website: *http://www.oikoumene.org/en/home.html*

KNOWING ME KNOWING YOU
Class activity: Interview someone from another Christian denomination. The following are some suggested questions for your interview.

1. What is the name of your Christian denomination?
2. What role do you play in your church?
3. Can you describe a day in your life?
4. How does your church participate in the ecumenical movement?
5. What do you do to celebrate Church Unity Week?
6. Why is the ecumenical movement important for your Christian community of faith?
7. What plans have you for any future ecumenical services?

 **Ecumenism:** Name given to the movement that works to promote greater unity between the different Christian denominations.

KNOW THE WAY

LESSON 20 Inter-Faith Dialogue

GROUNDWORK
In this lesson we plan to:
- explore the meaning of inter-faith dialogue in our world today.

DIGGING DEEPER
What impact does inter-faith dialogue have on my faith?

Key Concepts
Inter-faith dialogue/Religious conflict

Class Activity: Different Leaves, Different Lives

On a large poster, the teacher or one of the students draws the trunk of a tree, with bare branches extending from it.

Then each student takes a sheet of A5 paper, with which to complete the following exercise.

- Copy the outline of one of your hands on to the sheet.
- On the outline:
    1. Write a sentence about yourself.
    2. Name your favourite band.
    3. Name your favourite sports star.
    4. Name your favourite colour.
    5. Name your favourite item of clothing.
    6. Name your favourite TV programme.
- Cut out and colour in the outline of your hand.
- Attach all the 'hands' as leaves to the tree.

Create a banner for your tree entitled: 'Different Leaves, Different Lives!'

KNOW WHAT
1. What does the title 'Different leaves, different lives' mean?
2. 'No two people are the same. To recognise difference is to get to know one another better.' Explain this statement.

DIGGING DEEPER
1. Have you or has anyone you know ever been treated badly because you/they were different from others? If so, describe what happened.
2. What do you think would have helped resolve the situation?

Inter-Faith Dialogue

We recognise that people belong to different kinds of families, have different coloured skin, different likes and dislikes, different political opinions and different experiences of life.

So too, each religion has its own history, set of beliefs, moral code and acts of worship. The following chart summarises the main differences between the five major world religions. Although there has been a lot of conflict between religions in the past, today all the major religions are working hard to understand one another better and to build a world where people can live together in peace.

Religion	Christianity	Islam	Hinduism	Buddhism	Judaism
Followers	1820 million	971 million	732 million	314 million	18 million
Sacred text	Bible	Qur'an	Vedas	Tripitaka/ Mahayana Sutras	Tanakh (Torah)
Moral code	Two Great Commandments Beatitudes	Five Pillars	Doing good and meditation	Four Noble Truths Eightfold Path	Ten Commandments
Place of worship	Church/Chapel Cathedral	Mosque	Mandira	Temple	Synagogue

Inter-faith dialogue is the term we use to describe different religions talking to one another. Inter-faith (or inter-religious) dialogue is different from ecumenism because it refers to dialogue between all of the world religions, not just the Christian churches.

KNOW IT ALL

Copy the following paragraph into your Religion folder and fill in the blanks using the wordbank given below.

Communication between people of different religions is based upon _____ . Each religion has its own _____ set of beliefs, _____ _____ and acts of worship. Ecumenism is the work being done by _____ churches to being about _____ amongst Christians. Inter-faith _____ is the term used to describe different religions _____ to one another.

WORDBANK
Dialogue • Respect • Christian • History • Talking • Moral code • Unity

Ecumenism involves the Christian churches. Inter-faith dialogue involves all the world religions.

The Search for World Peace

On 11 September 2001 (also referred to as 9/11), there was a series of terrorist attacks within the US. Two planes crashed into the World Trade Center in Manhattan, New York city, causing both towers to collapse. A third plane ploughed into the US Department of Defense headquarters, the Pentagon, in Arlington County, Virginia. A fourth plane crashed into a rural field in Somerset County, Pennsylvania, having been diverted from its intended target following passenger resistance. The official count records 2,986 deaths in the attacks.

At an Inter-faith Prayer Service for World Peace which took place in St Patrick's Cathedral, Dublin, one month after the terrorist attacks of 9/11, the Reverend Robert McCarthy, Dean, commented:

'The events of the last few weeks have exposed a Western world largely ignorant of Islam and Judaism. This ignorance must be confronted. Jews, Muslims and Christians are all children of Abraham. Now is the time for the great faiths to foster together a greater understanding of their common values and heritage.'

DIGGING DEEPER
1. How might the events of 9/11 encourage more concentrated inter-faith dialogue?
2. Have you ever taken part in an inter-faith service? If so, describe the experience.

World Day of Prayer

During the World Day of Prayer in 2002, Pope John Paul II led two hundred other religious leaders in prayers for world peace in Assisi, the birthplace of St Francis.

The members of each community of faith had travelled to Assisi from the Vatican's seldom-used rail station in a seven-car train supplied by Italy's State-run railway. Pope John Paul II said that he wanted to use the 'peace train' to make all participants of the World Day of Prayer feel equal.

The Pope wanted that year's day of prayer to reinforce his message that religion must not be a motive for conflict in the twenty-first century.

During the afternoon, the members of the various faith communities joined together for a final ceremony, each carrying a candle as a symbol of peace. The Pope told them: 'Never again violence. Never again war. Never again terrorism.'

> **Inter-faith dialogue:** When members of different communities of faith (different religions) talk together in order to come to a better understanding of their beliefs.

See page 486 for past exam questions on this topic.

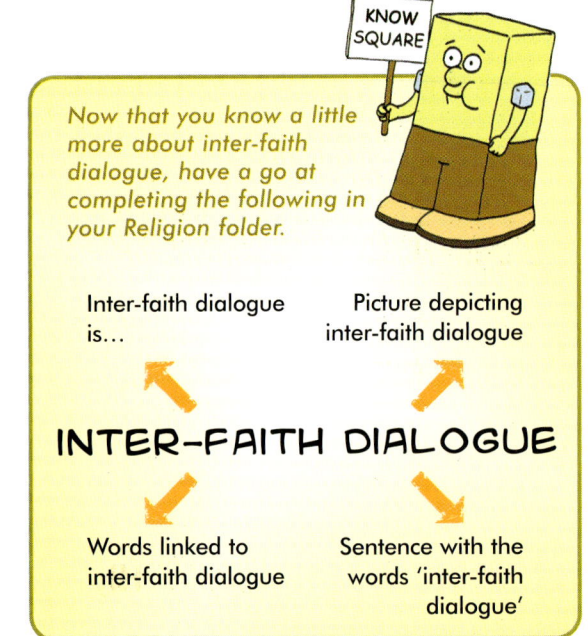

Now that you know a little more about inter-faith dialogue, have a go at completing the following in your Religion folder.

INTER-FAITH DIALOGUE

- Inter-faith dialogue is…
- Picture depicting inter-faith dialogue
- Words linked to inter-faith dialogue
- Sentence with the words 'inter-faith dialogue'

(Higher Level Only)

Organisation and Leadership in Communities of Faith

LESSON 21 Styles of Leadership

GROUNDWORK
In this lesson we plan to:
- identify and describe different styles of leadership and their impact on human communities.

DIGGING DEEPER
What qualities are required for good leadership?

 **Key Concept**
Leadership

Introductory Activity: Take me to your Leader!
Working in groups of three:
1. List four different types of leader.
2. Decide on two words that describe how each of these leaders lead.
3. Briefly explain your choice of words.
4. Now share your work with the other groups in your class.

Styles of Leadership

There are many styles of leadership. Different styles of leadership are required for different situations, and no style is the perfect one. The main styles of leadership are:

- Authoritarian leadership
- Enabling leadership
- Consultative leadership

Authoritarian leadership is often referred to as traditional leadership. An authoritarian leader does not allow anyone else to become involved in the decision-making process. An authoritarian leader always 'leads' and expects others to follow.

Enabling leadership is about motivating and helping the group to make their own decisions.

Consultative leadership is where the leader listens to everyone in the group and allows their suggestions to influence his/her final decision.

Which diagram fits which style of leadership? Give reasons for your choices.

KNOW WHAT
1. Describe two situations that call for different styles of leadership.
2. Write one paragraph about the kind of impact these styles of leadership have on communities.

KNOW HOW
1. Write three words to describe each of the three main styles of leadership.
2. In pairs, work out what styles of leadership would be required in the following situations:
   - Organising the school sports day.
   - Preparing a group to clear up the litter from around the neighbourhood.
   - The school bus breaks down and it begins to rain; all the students must get home.
   - The under fives are having a party!
   - A member of your class is moving to America, and you want to organise a farewell celebration.

Qualities for Good Leadership

To be a good leader requires good communication skills. This means that a leader must be able to communicate to the members of the community the task to be completed and how it should be carried out.

A good leader uses a combination of leadership styles, depending on each situation.

As well as recognising what is best for the community, a good leader also enables the members to be involved in making decisions.

A good leader must remind the community members of what has happened in the past, help them to work together in the present, and motivate them to plan for the future.

Everyone cannot be a leader, because not everyone has good leadership qualities.

KNOW IT ALL

Copy the following into your Religion folder and fill in the blanks using the wordbank given below.

Leaders are people who:
- Listen and hear the _____ of all the members of the group/community.
- Can make _____ for the good of the group.
- Can _____ on behalf of the group.
- A good leader must remind the community members of what has happened in the _____ , help them to work together in the _____ , and motivate them to plan for the _____ .

WORDBANK
Communicate • Opinions • Present • Past • Decisions • Future

DIGGING DEEPER
1. Write about a time when you played a leadership role. What style of leadership did you use?
2. Are there any other qualities required for effective leadership?

LESSON 22 Leadership as Service

GROUNDWORK
In this lesson we plan to:
learn about leadership as
- that which provides a service;
- a part of ministry.

DIGGING DEEPER
How do leaders serve?

Key Concepts
Service/Ministry

Class Challenge: Line Up!

You have fifteen minutes to perform this task!

The whole class must line up in order of age, from the youngest to the oldest, whilst keeping noise levels to a minimum. The line must be in order not only by month, but also by day.

You have no instructions on how to organise this task – just a time-limit!

Answer the following questions when the time is up.

1. How noisy did the group become?
2. Did anyone stand out as particularly bossy? What effect did this have?
3. Was it a frustrating exercise? Discuss your answer.
4. What did you do to help?
5. Who did the most work in order to complete the line?
6. 'The leaders gave a service to the group.' Discuss this statement.

DIGGING DEEPER

1. Have you ever been in a group with a good leader? What do you think it was that made him/her a good leader?
2. How do leaders provide a service?

Service Within the Christian Community

Jesus showed the world that leadership involves **service**. Jesus lived for others. He healed the sick. He forgave sinners. He gave comfort to those who were sad. He included those who were left out or ignored by others. He blessed children and listened to what they had to say. He did all this because of his love for God the Father and for us. The Holy Spirit was with Jesus as he lived his life by serving God and others. Every Christian is invited to a similar life of love and service. Christians live out this love and service of God by taking part in the various ministries (jobs) in their community of faith.

Ministry

Ordained ministry involves sharing in Christ's continuing ministry of building up the Church through the sacraments, especially at Mass, and spreading the Gospel. Ordained clergy do this by:

- ministering the sacraments;
- ministering to the sick;
- ministering to schools;
- ministering to the wider community.

Lay people support the ministry of the Church. They do this by:

- leading prayer groups;
- working at the parish office;
- being Ministers of the Word;
- being Ministers of the Eucharist;
- visiting the sick;
- using their talents for the good of the community.

KNOW WHAT
1. What is 'ministry'?
2. Name two examples of ministry for a) a lay person and b) a priest.

DIGGING DEEPER
Think of a ministry that you can become involved in within your community of faith.

 **Ministry:** Role of service given to a member by a community and/or its leader.

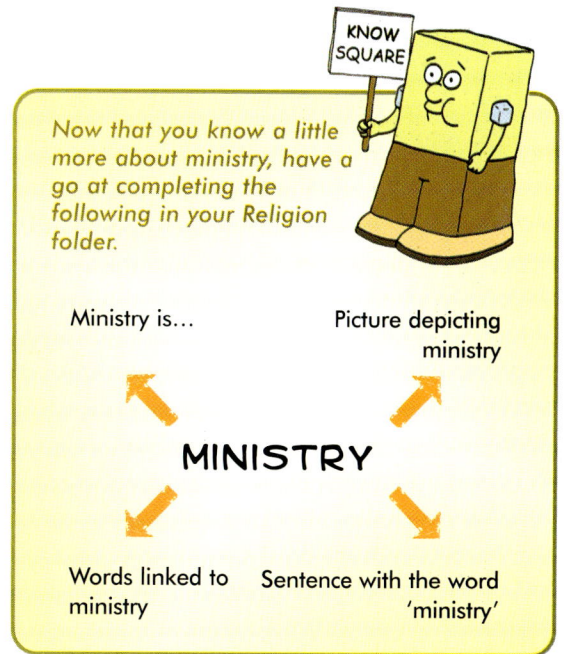

Now that you know a little more about ministry, have a go at completing the following in your Religion folder.

Ministry is…　　Picture depicting ministry

MINISTRY

Words linked to ministry　　Sentence with the word 'ministry'

LESSON 23   Leadership and Authority in two Christian Churches

GROUNDWORK
In this lesson we plan to:
- explore the connection between Christian leadership and authority in two Christian churches.

DIGGING DEEPER
What is the relationship between leadership and authority within these two churches?

Key Concepts
Leadership/Authority/Ministry/Service/Religious commitment

Leadership always involves some degree of 'authority'. **Authority** is the power that a person in a position of leadership has to make decisions for or about a group or community. Leadership and authority are, therefore, connected.

A story of leadership, authority and steadfast teamwork

In April 1970, America's third scheduled moon mission, Apollo 13, lifted off without a hitch. On board was a crew of three men – Commanders Jim Lovell, Jack Swigert and Fred Haise. They were supported on the ground by a Mission Control Center, under the command of flight director Gene Krantz.

On the second day after the launch, the crew aboard the spacecraft routinely switched on the fans in the oxygen tanks for a short while. Straight away, the quantity indicator showed that there was a problem with the oxygen levels, and a master alarm indicated low pressure in a hydrogen tank. The Mission Control Center swiftly reacted to this and commanded the crew to switch on all tank stirrers and heaters. Suddenly the crew heard a loud 'bang' and felt unusual vibrations in the spacecraft. It was at this point that Commander Jack Swigert issued the alert, 'Houston, we have a problem' – a catchphrase that was to be made famous by the film *Apollo 13*.

Led by Krantz on the ground and Lovell in space, the team devised a brilliant plan. They realised that they could use the lunar module as a 'lifeboat'. Now their survival depended on the lunar module's oxygen and water supplies, as well as the teamwork and leadership skills of Lovell and Krantz.

The first critical leadership decision was to get the crippled spacecraft back on course. While this was being accomplished, the team on the ground at Mission Control worked out a new flight plan that would minimise the consumption of oxygen, water and electricity, while keeping vital systems in operation.

While all this was taking place, the crew members were aware of the dangers: they could suffocate if the oxygen ran out; they could freeze to death if there was insufficient power, or they could be poisoned by carbon dioxide because of a faulty filtering system. If, by some miracle, they escaped these catastrophic events, there was always a chance that they would be incinerated upon re-entry into the earth's atmosphere.

After many heart-stopping moments of decision-making and the emergence of problem after problem, the Apollo 13 mission arrived home safely. Its safe return was the result of a combination of teamwork, leadership, authority and, above all, courage. From that day forward, the Apollo 13 mission was known as the 'successful failure'.

KNOW WHAT
1. How is this story a good example of leadership and teamwork?
2. How does it show the connection between leadership and authority?
3. How does it show the connection between leadership and service?
4. What styles of leadership were used by the different people? Explain your answer.
5. To what extent do you think Krantz and Lovell would have relied upon the support and expertise of others in getting through this situation?
6. How did the leaders in this situation provide a vital service?

DIGGING DEEPER
1. Unless you are an astronaut, you have not been in this kind of situation! However, you may have been in a similar situation, i.e. one that demanded strong and responsible leadership and authority. If so, describe this experience.
2. What do you think helps make a good leader in a difficult and pressurised situation? Name any leaders who have proved they can work well under severe pressure.

Leadership and Authority in the Catholic Church

The earliest followers of Jesus were the apostles. It was Jesus who invited them to preach and teach the Good News. This was the beginning of the Christian story. When Jesus rose from the dead, Christianity spread. Leaders and people in roles of authority were chosen to continue Jesus' ministry, to spread the Gospel and to celebrate the sacraments.

The role of all church leaders includes working to hand on the faith tradition; this is part of their **ministry** and **service** to the People of God. They carry out this role by sharing the central beliefs of the faith and abiding by the moral code.

Since the Second Vatican Council, the Catholic Church has stressed the importance of the leadership roles that lay people can play.

All work done in service of God and others is a sign of one's **religious commitment**.

Leadership Roles in the Catholic Church
We have looked at the leadership roles of the various members of the Catholic Church, which you might like to revise at this point. (See Lesson 11.)

1. Write four sentences to describe the leadership role of the Pope.
2. How do the bishops exercise their role of authority and leadership?
3. How do priests show leadership qualities in their parish?
4. How do the leaders of the Catholic Church show their religious commitment?

The Magisterium of the Catholic Church
All baptised people have a duty to teach the Catholic faith that was handed down by the apostles. The Magisterium is the teaching authority of the Catholic Church, i.e. those members of the Church who have a special gift of the Holy Spirit to teach and explain the truths of the faith. The Magisterium comprises the Pope, cardinals, archbishops and bishops. Together, they are referred to as the hierarchy of the Church. The Pope is the direct successor of St Peter and the head of the Catholic Church. The successors of the apostles are the bishops, and it is their special role to ensure that the teaching of the

Catholic Church is handed on in their own diocese. Thus, the leaders of the Church provide a very important service to the Catholic tradition.

'And I tell you, you are Peter, and on this rock I will build my church.' (Matthew 16:18)

The Irish Bishops' Conference

The Irish Bishops' Conference (IBC) meets four times a year in Maynooth College, County Kildare. The head of the IBC is the Archbishop of Armagh and the members are the bishops and archbishops from the other dioceses.

KNOW WHAT

1. What purpose does the Magisterium of the Catholic Church have?
2. Which people are part of the Magisterium? What other term is used to describe this group of people?
3. What do the letters IBC stand for?
4. Describe the connection between the various leadership roles in the Church and the authority (or power) given to those roles.

DIGGING DEEPER

1. How does the authority of the leadership in your church help you in your life?
2. How is the leadership of the Catholic Church modelled on the leadership of Jesus?

Leadership and Authority in the Church of Ireland

The General Synod is a meeting of representatives of all the dioceses in the Church of Ireland. It is used to direct the leadership and authority of the Church of Ireland. The General Synod meets annually in May.

The main function of the Synod is to pass laws for the whole Church of Ireland. By passing laws and approving acts, the members of the General Synod guide and teach the members of the Anglican community of faith in Ireland (the Church of Ireland).

There are three Orders present at the General Synod; they are made up of bishops, clergy and lay people. The three Orders work together as two Houses: the House of Bishops (comprising of archbishops and bishops) and the House of Representatives (comprising of other clergy and lay members).

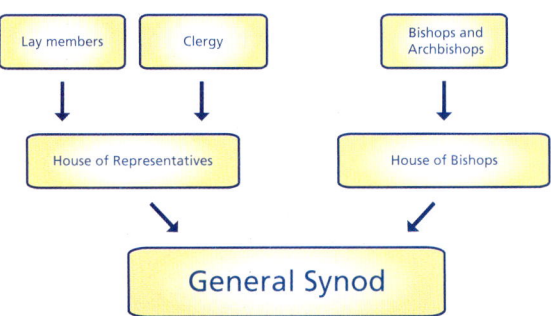

The Archbishop of Armagh leads the General Synod.

TAKE FIVE

1. What meeting is used to direct the leadership and authority of the Church of Ireland?
2. Who is represented at this meeting?
3. What is the main aim of the Synod?
4. How many Houses are there at the Synod?
5. Where does the archbishop who leads the Synod come from?

Authority: The power that a person in a position of leadership has to make decisions for or about a group or community.

See page 486 for past exam questions on this topic.

Before beginning Section B...

Note for teachers: *Many of the exercises in Section B require the use of a Bible. It is important, therefore, that students be familiar with the Bible and know how to look up a Bible reference.*

The Bible

The word Bible comes from the Greek word *biblia*, meaning 'books'. The Bible is like a library of books. It is divided into two parts: the Old Testament and the New Testament. Each of these parts contains many different books. The Old Testament and the New Testament are closely linked because, when put together, they tell a single story.

Old Testament
46 books:

Torah (5)

Historical books (16)

Wisdom books (7)

Prophetic books (18)

New Testament
27 books:

Gospels (4)

Acts (1)

Letters (21)

Revelation (1)

The Old Testament tells the story of God's relationship with the Jewish people before the coming of Jesus. Jewish people call the Old Testament the Hebrew Scriptures.

The New Testament tells the story of the founder of Christianity, Jesus Christ, and of the earliest followers of Christianity. The gospels belong to the New Testament.

The Bible was written over hundreds of years by different people from different backgrounds. They all had one thing in common: they were inspired by God to put words on what God wanted people to know. For Christians, the Bible is a sacred text because they believe that it is truly the Word of God.

Looking up a Bible Reference

Each of the books in the Bible is made up of chapters and verses. In order to find specific stories or quotations in the Bible, you need to know how to read a Bible reference.

A Bible reference has three parts:

1. The name of the book (which is often abbreviated or shortened).
2. The chapter.
3. The verse.

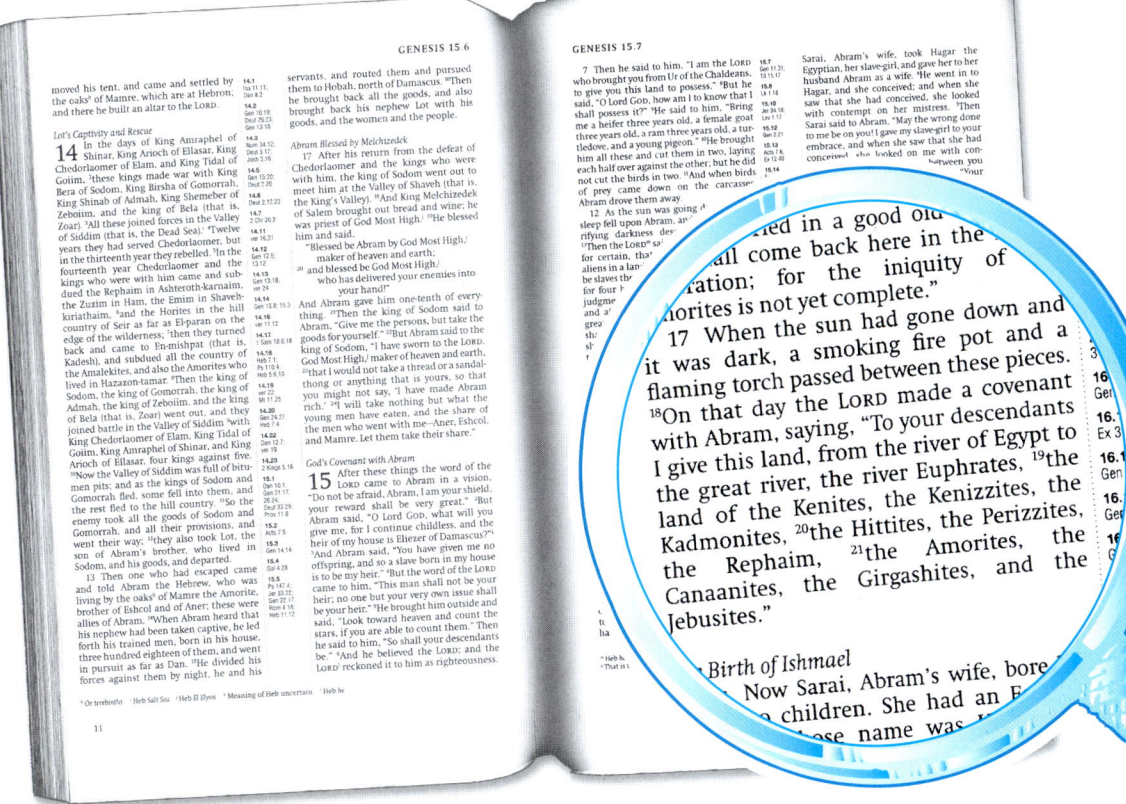

Let's take an example: Gen 15:18.

Spot the three components:
1. The first word 'Gen' (a shortened form of Genesis) is the name of the book.
2. The number '15' is the number of the chapter.
3. The number '18' is the number of the verse.

> *'To your descendants I give this land…'*
>
> **(Gen 15:18)**

Here are two other examples:

Old Testament
Gen 17:5

New Testament
Mk 1:4

Sometimes we are instructed to read more than one verse, for example Gen 12:1- 4. This means Genesis, chapter 12, verses 1 to 4.

The Context

LESSON 24 The Land of Palestine

GROUNDWORK
In this lesson we plan to:
- explore the geography of Palestine in the time of Jesus.

DIGGING DEEPER
As a boy, what did Jesus learn from the place where he lived?

Key Concept
The Holy Land

The Holy Land

The country where Jesus lived is known as the **Holy Land**. This is because the origins of Judaism, Christianity and Islam are found there. At the time of Jesus, the Holy Land was called Palestine. (Today, this country is known as Israel.)

Palestine was small, being about the size of Northern Ireland. It consisted of three main provinces (regions): Galilee, Samaria and Judaea. It had two lakes: the Sea of Galilee and the Dead Sea. The river Jordan connected these two lakes.

The capital city of Palestine was Jerusalem, in the province of Judaea. There were also several small villages and towns, for example, Nazareth and Capernaum in Galilee, and Bethlehem and Jericho in Judaea.

Ireland and Palestine

A Land of Contrasts

The north of Palestine was very different from the south. Galilee, in the north, with its lake called the Sea of Galilee, was a place of rich fertile plains and steep hills. Jesus grew up here, in the town of Nazareth, where Joseph was a carpenter. As a young boy, he probably watched the fishermen sorting their catches on the lake-shore and the traders selling their wares at the market-place. But he would also have experienced country life and would have seen shepherds minding their sheep and vineyard workers tending to their vines. Further south, the greenery gave way to desert. The town of Jericho is built in an oasis near the river Jordan, and from there the land moves steeply uphill to Jerusalem.

DIGGING DEEPER
How might the people whom Jesus met as a boy have influenced his later teaching?

TAKE FIVE
Study the map before answering these questions.
1. Name the three main provinces of Palestine.
2. What are the two lakes called?
3. What river connects these two lakes?
4. Name four towns or villages in Palestine.
5. What is this country known as today?

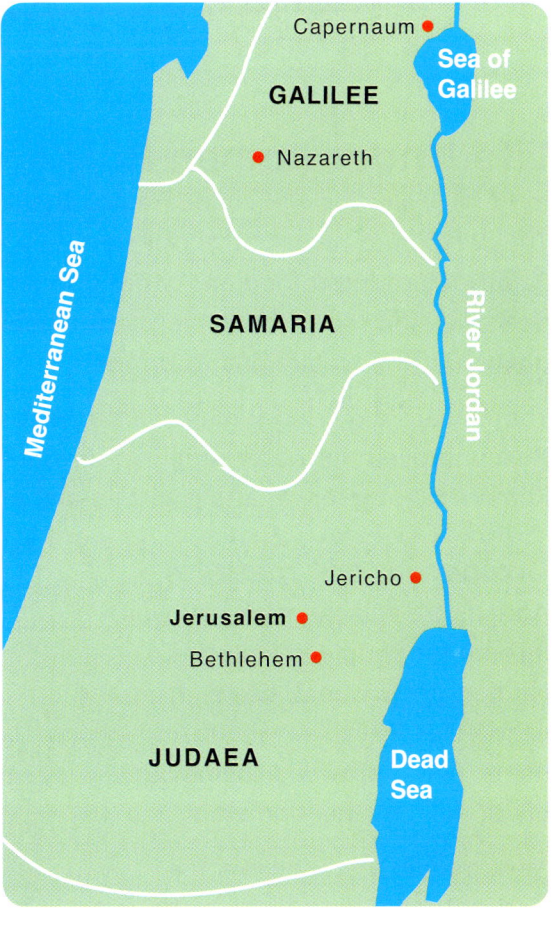

DIGGING DEEPER
You will need a Bible for this exercise.
Match the scripture references given below with the name of a city, town, river or sea.
1. The town in which Jesus was born (Matthew 2:1).
2. The town where Jesus lived with Mary and Joseph (Luke 2:39-40).
3. The place where John the Baptist often preached (Matthew 3:1).
4. The city in which Jesus fed the five thousand (Luke 9:10).
5. The town in which Jesus raised Lazarus from the dead (John 11:1).
6. The town where Jesus attended a wedding and performed a miracle (John 2:1).
7. Jesus travelled to this city to visit the Temple (Luke 2:22).
8. The river in which John baptised Jesus (Mark 1:9).
9. The province where Jesus spent most of his life (Luke 2:39).
10. The sea/lake where the apostles spent some time fishing (Mark 4:18).

 **The Holy Land:** The country where Jesus lived and taught. Called Palestine, prior to the creation of the modern state of Israel.

LESSON 25 Palestine in the Time of Jesus

GROUNDWORK
In this lesson we plan to:
- look at the impact of historical and geographical factors on the lives of the people at the time of Jesus.

DIGGING DEEPER
What kind of lifestyle did Jesus of Nazareth have?

Key Concept
The Roman Empire

Life Under Roman Rule

In 63 BC, Palestine was conquered by the Romans and became part of the **Roman Empire**. The decision to take control of Palestine was a very profitable one for the Romans, as Palestine produced food and other goods for export, including fruit, oil, wine, fish, perfumes and skins. The Romans also imposed heavy taxes on the people to pay for the upkeep of the empire and its armies.

The Romans did bring some advantages to Palestine, for example, they built new roads, they improved the water supply in Jerusalem and they constructed many buildings. Under Roman rule, there was also a certain amount of political stability.

Occupations and Lifestyles

Agriculture was the main source of income for people in Palestine. Farmers grew wheat, barley, fruit and vegetables. They kept sheep and goats, which provided them with meat, milk, leather and wool.

Most people used donkeys for transport and agricultural work, and camels for heavier work. Horses were a luxury that only rich people could enjoy.

Fishing was another valuable source of income. Fish could be dried and preserved in salt and there was a vibrant fishing economy around the Sea of Galilee.

Although there was money in circulation, a barter system also operated in Palestine, which meant that one type of produce could be exchanged for another.

There was great tension between the rich and the poor in society. Most farmers were in debt and found it difficult to make ends meet. Labourers, who often worked on a day-to-day basis, were among the poorest in society, along with the unemployed and the slaves. There was no social welfare or State benefit for those who were sick, but the Jewish community had a religious obligation to give alms (money, food or other kinds of assistance) to those who were ill.

Towns and Buildings

The marketplace was a common feature of all Palestinian towns. It was the centre of trade, a meeting-place for friends and a place where casual labourers could gather in search of work.

Houses were simple and functional. They usually consisted of one large room that was used for a variety of purposes, including eating, washing, praying and sleeping. At night-time, this room could become extremely hot, so the family climbed on to the flat roof and slept there. As the winter nights were usually very cold, farming families often brought their animals into their homes to keep them safe and warm. The animals were a valuable source of heat for the family.

The Languages of the Roman Empire

There were four different languages spoken. The official language of the Roman Empire was Latin, but the people of Palestine continued to speak their own language, called Aramaic. This was the language that Jesus, his family and his followers would have spoken. Jewish scriptures were written in the ancient language of Hebrew, and the Jewish people used Hebrew during religious services. All Jewish boys learned to read and speak Hebrew. In the eastern part of the Roman Empire, Greek was commonly spoken. This was the area where many of the first Christian communities were established. In fact, the New Testament was written in Greek.

Hebrew: the language of Sacred Scripture and religious services

Latin: the official language of the Roman Empire

Greek: spoken in the eastern part of the Roman Empire

Aramaic: the language spoken by Palestinians

Log on to *http://www.v-a.com/Bible/prayer.html* to hear the Lord's Prayer being read in Aramaic.

5-4-3-2-1

1. Identify **five** new pieces of information that you have learned about life in Palestine in the time of Jesus.
2. Name **four** ways in which people made a living at this time.
3. Write **three** sentences about the typical family home.
4. Name **two** types of people that you would have met if you lived in Palestine in the time of Jesus.
5. Have a go at drawing **one** picture of a family home in Palestine.

DIGGING DEEPER

1. Imagine you are a teenager living in Palestine in the time of Jesus. Write a short account describing your life.
2. From what you have learned so far, what might have influenced the type of person that Jesus became?

The Roman Empire: The name used to describe the regions of the world ruled by Rome. Palestine was part of the Roman Empire.

LESSON 26 Political and Religious Structures in the Time of Jesus

GROUNDWORK
In this lesson we plan to:
- learn about the political and religious structures in operation at the time of Jesus.

DIGGING DEEPER
How do the political and religious structures of my country impact on my faith?

Key Concept
Ancient Judaism

Ancient Judaism

Jesus was born into the Jewish faith. The Jewish faith has its origins in God's special relationship with Abraham and later with Moses. God called Abraham to lead the people from the city of Ur in Mesopotamia (modern-day Iraq) to the land of Canaan. God made a covenant with Abraham whereby Abraham and his followers would be God's chosen people. In return for this, the people would be asked to obey God's laws.

Abraham's descendants settled in Canaan, but eventually they moved down to Egypt, where, as time went by, they were persecuted and treated as slaves. Hundreds of years later, God sent them a leader, Moses, to free them from slavery. In the book of Exodus, we read of how Moses led the Israelites out of slavery in Egypt and on towards the Promised Land (modern-day Israel).

The story of **ancient Judaism**, of Abraham and Moses, would have been very familiar to Jesus.

Political Structures in the Time of Jesus

Over the centuries, the Israelites had many rulers: first they were ruled by prophets called judges, then by kings, beginning with Saul, then David, then David's son Solomon. After Solomon's death, the land was divided into two kingdoms: the Kingdom of Israel and the Kingdom of Judaea. In 63 BC, the Romans conquered the land and called it Palestine. In 40 BC, they appointed Herod as king. Because Herod was not a Jew, the Jewish people never accepted him.

At the time of Jesus, Palestine (the Holy Land) was still part of the Roman Empire, and Roman laws and customs were being imposed on the Jewish people. The Jews didn't like the Romans and there was always a great deal of tension between them.

The Roman emperor was called Caesar. He allowed Herod to continue as a token leader (i.e. without any real power), but he sent governors to Palestine to take care of his interests and, therefore, the real power was firmly held by Rome. Pontius Pilate was the Roman governor (procurator) from AD 26 to 36. His job was to keep law and order in Palestine and make sure the Jewish people paid their taxes.

Timeline of the main events around the time of Jesus

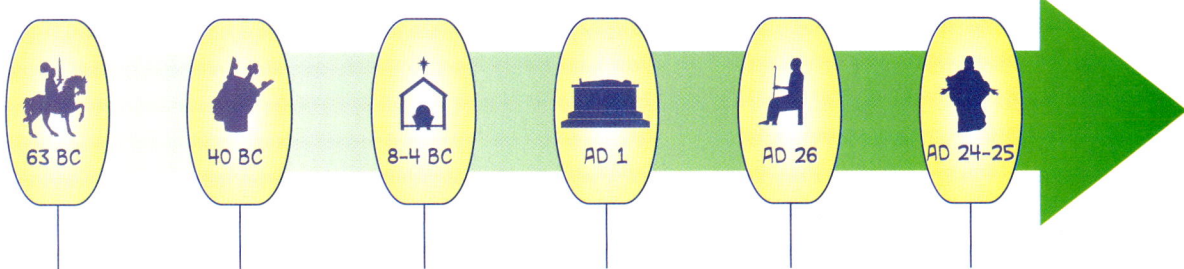

63 BC — Palestine was conquered by the Romans.

40 BC — The Romans appointed Herod as king. Because Herod was not a Jew, the Jewish people never accepted him.

8–4 BC — Birth of Jesus. (Herod was king at the time of the birth of Jesus.)

AD 1 — Death of Herod. (Herod died when Jesus was still a boy.)

AD 26 — Pontius Pilate was made governor of the province of Judaea.

AD 24–25 — Around this time, Jesus began his mission.

KNOW WHAT

1. What religion was Jesus born into?
2. What happened in 63 BC?
3. Who was appointed king in 40 BC?
4. Who was born in 8–4 BC?
5. What happened in AD 1?
6. Who was made governor in AD 26?
7. What was the role of the Roman governor?
8. When did Jesus begin his mission?

Religious Structures in the Time of Jesus

The Romans found the Jewish faith baffling. They were polytheists (i.e. they believed in many different gods) and the Jews were monotheists (i.e. they believed in one God). The Jews called their God 'Yahweh'. (The name 'Yahweh' is considered so sacred that it is never said out loud.) The Romans allowed the Jewish people to continue to practise their religion. They saw this as a way of keeping the people happy and so making it easier for them to govern Palestine.

The Sanhedrin

The Sanhedrin was the religious governing body located in Jerusalem. It also served as the highest court of Jewish law in Palestine. The High Priest was president of the Sanhedrin and its members were made up of Sadducees and Pharisees, two religious groups who disagreed on many issues. (You will learn more about these two groups in the next lesson.)

The Romans allowed the Sanhedrin to:

- act as a court of law;
- punish Jewish people who broke the Jewish law;
- keep its own guards, who maintained order.

This was quite a cunning plan on behalf of the Romans because now they had a situation where the two main Jewish groups were fighting and disagreeing amongst each other and inflicting punishment on their own people for not upholding the strict Jewish laws.

87

TAKE FIVE

1. What was the Sanhedrin?
2. Who was the president of the Sanhedrin?
3. Who were the two main Jewish groups that were involved in the Sanhedrin?
4. What powers did the Sanhedrin have?
5. Why were the Romans happy to have a court like the Sanhedrin?

The Temple

All Jewish people wanted to visit the Temple in Jerusalem at least once a year because it was considered the dwelling place of God and Judaism's most sacred building. The chief authority of the Temple was the High Priest.

The Western Wall of the Temple in Jerusalem

The Synagogue

By the time Jesus was born, all towns and cities in Palestine had synagogues. The synagogue was a meeting-place for prayer and the study of the Law, and it was run by the elders in the Jewish community. Services were held there on the Sabbath and on feast days. Jesus attended the synagogue regularly.

The Sabbath

The Jewish Sabbath begins on Friday evening and ends on Saturday evening. It is considered a holy day and a day of rest. Traditionally, it is traced back to the Ten Commandments given to Moses: 'Remember to keep holy the Sabbath day' (Exodus 20).

KNOW WHAT

1. Why did the Jewish people visit the Temple?
2. Who was the High Priest?

DIGGING DEEPER

1. How do you think the political and religious structures described above might have impacted upon (affected) Jesus as he was growing up?
2. Find out about the political and religious structures in Palestine/Israel today. How do they compare with those that existed at the time of Jesus?
3. How do the current political and religious structures of Ireland impact upon you/upon others?

 **Ancient Judaism:** The religion into which Jesus was born, based on the Five Books of Moses (also called the Torah), which are the first five books of the Bible.

LESSON 27 Religious Groups in the Time of Jesus

GROUNDWORK
In this lesson we plan to:
- explore further the religious groupings at the time of Jesus.

DIGGING DEEPER
How was Jesus' outlook different to the outlook of the religious groups at this time?

Key Concept
Ancient Judaism

The Religious Groups of Ancient Judaism

The Sadducees

Who were they?	Wealthy aristocracy (many of whom were priests).
What did they do?	Controlled the office of the High Priest.
What did they accept?	The Torah – the written Law of Judaism.
What did they reject?	The ancient traditions of the Pharisees.
Why were they unpopular with the poor?	They were too powerful and they co-operated with the with Romans.
What did they believe about a Messiah?	The Sadducees were not waiting for a Messiah. They did not believe in a resurrection or afterlife of any kind and they did not expect to be freed from the Romans.

The Pharisees

Who were they?	A group of learned laymen who rejected Roman rule.
What did they do?	Religious leaders/teachers in the local synagogues.
What did they accept?	The Torah – the written law of Judaism.
What did they reject?	Those who did not follow the strict law of the Torah.
Why were they unpopular with the poor?	They were too pious and their laws were too strict.
What did they believe about a Messiah?	The Pharisees believed in an afterlife, a final judgement day and freedom from Roman rule. They expected the Messiah that was promised in the Hebrew Scriptures.

SECTION B FOUNDATIONS OF RELIGION – CHRISTIANITY

The Zealots

Who were they?	A revolutionary group.
What did they do?	Fought to rid Palestine of the Roman authorities.
What did they accept?	A violent and military route to freedom.
What did they reject?	The Romans, peaceful protest and paying taxes.
Why were they unpopular with the poor?	They used violence to achieve their goals.
What did they believe about a Messiah?	The Zealots believed that a militant Messiah (i.e. a Messiah who favoured the use of violence) would come to their rescue and free them from Roman rule. Today, Zealots would be called terrorists.

The Essenes

Who were they?	A community of monks who led a quiet and prayerful life.
What did they do?	Left society to live and pray in the desert. It is likely that the Essenes established the monastic community at Qumran, where the Dead Sea Scrolls were found.
What did they accept?	A peaceful and prayerful religious life.
What did they reject?	Corruption and religious carelessness amongst the Jews.
Why were they unpopular with the poor?	They removed themselves from the rest of society.
What did they believe about a Messiah?	They believed that a Messiah of David would come and bring with him a new kingdom.

KNOW IT ALL

Imagine that you are a member of one of the groups described above and write a paragraph about yourself, e.g. 'I am a Pharisee and I live in Jericho. I have studied for many years and I think that the law of the Torah must be respected…'

DIGGING DEEPER

1. If you had the choice of belonging to one of the religious groups at the time of Jesus, which one would you choose and why?
2. Which group (if any) do you think Jesus was part of? Give reasons for your answer.

KNOW IT ALL

You have four minutes to unscramble the letters and find the words! The first letter of each word is a capital letter.

HEPAIRESS   OROP   NSSSEEE

ETLOAZS   DEESDSUCA

LESSON 28 Messianic Expectation

GROUNDWORK
In this lesson we plan to:
- explore and understand the concept of Messianic expectation.

DIGGING DEEPER
Who is the Messiah?

Key Concept
Messianic expectation

At one time or another, we've all used the words 'I can't wait' as we looked forward to something really special that was to happen in the future.

Think of a time when you really looked forward to something, for example, a holiday or a special trip. Write a paragraph in your Religion folder describing how you felt in the weeks/months leading up to the event and then as the actual day got closer.

It is always good to have a goal or a dream to work towards and focus on, because this gives us hope and promise in our lives.

Messianic Expectation – Waiting for the Messiah

The Jewish people had great hope and expectation. Their hope for the future centred on the arrival of the Messiah. 'Messiah' means 'someone who has been anointed'. In their sacred scriptures, especially in the writings of the prophets, the Jewish people read of 'the anointed one' who would be sent by God to bring everlasting peace. It is easy to understand their excitement at the thought of the coming of the Messiah.

Opinions were mixed as to who the Messiah would be. Many believed that he would be a descendant of the great King David, a mighty leader born into luxury and wealth, who would bring them prosperity and liberate them from the Romans. Others looked forward to a saviour who would use force if necessary in order to drive the Romans out of Palestine.

KNOW HOW
You will need a Bible for this exercise.
What do the following references say about the Messiah?
Isaiah 9:1-7, Jeremiah 23:5-6, Ezekiel 34:22-25, Zechariah 9:9-10, Matthew 1:18, 22-23, Luke 2:11, 26, Mark 8:27-30, John 4:25-26, Acts 18:5.

Jesus, the Christ
In the beginning, the apostles did not recognise Jesus as the Messiah, the Son of God. And because of the different Jewish interpretations of what the Messiah would be like, Jesus did not like to use the term. As they got to know Jesus better, the apostles began to think that he might be the Messiah, and so they called him 'Jesus, the Christ'. ('Christ' also means 'The anointed one'.)

He asked them, 'But who do you say that I am?' Peter answered him, 'You are the Messiah.' (Mark 8:29)

But it was only after Jesus' death and resurrection, and with the help of the Holy Spirit, that they fully recognised him as the Son of God. Then they looked back at the times they had travelled together and they had a better understanding of some of the things that Jesus had said to them and of some of the amazing incidents that they had witnessed.

KNOW IT ALL

Copy the following grid into your Religion folder and fill in the missing information based on what you learned about each group in the previous lesson.

Group	Messianic Expectation
Sadducees	Not waiting for a Messiah
Pharisees	
Zealots	
Essenes	
Poor	

DIGGING DEEPER

1. Imagine that you have just entered a local shop. Someone rushes past you, but you pay no attention to them. Then you find out that this was a very famous person. How would you feel? Would you regret not recognising him or her?
2. What do you think the disciples expected the Messiah to be? Was this similar or different to any of the expectations of the other groups mentioned in this lesson?

KNOW HOW

Write an acrostic poem based on the word 'Messiah'.

🗝️ **Messianic expectation:** The belief of the Jewish people that God would send a great political and religious leader to solve their problems.

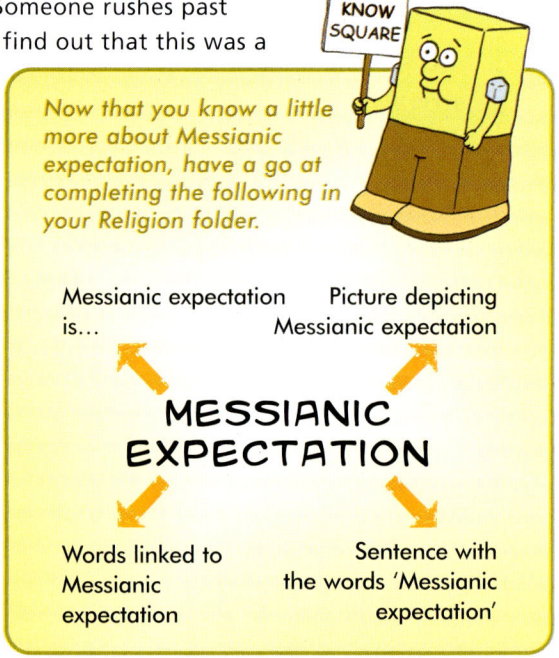

Now that you know a little more about Messianic expectation, have a go at completing the following in your Religion folder.

- Messianic expectation is…
- Picture depicting Messianic expectation
- Words linked to Messianic expectation
- Sentence with the words 'Messianic expectation'

MESSIANIC EXPECTATION

Evidence about Jesus

LESSON 29 Sources of Information about Jesus of Nazareth

GROUNDWORK
In this lesson we plan to:
- name some of the sources of information about Jesus of Nazareth.

DIGGING DEEPER
Where do we learn about Jesus of Nazareth?

Key Concepts
Evidence/Gospel/Witness

Sources of Evidence about Jesus

The *source* of any piece of information tells you where the information comes from; the **evidence** refers to the *information* itself. The New Testament is the main source of evidence about Jesus.

The gospels are part of the New Testament. The word **Gospel** means 'good news'. The New Testament presents the Gospel or Good News about Jesus according to Matthew, Mark, Luke and John. The other books in the New Testament are the Acts of the Apostles, the letters of Paul, Peter, John, James, Jude, the letter to the Hebrews and the book of Revelation.

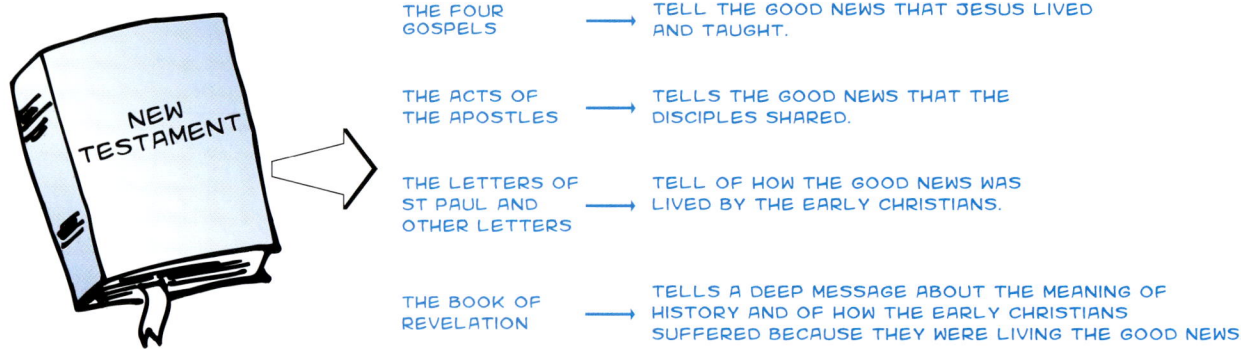

KNOW WHAT

1. What is the main source of evidence about Jesus?
2. Where do we find most of the evidence about Jesus in the New Testament?
3. What does the word 'gospel' mean?

Documents of Faith

The gospels are not biographies of Jesus in the normal sense of the word. They do not tell us, for example, about his appearance, his youth or his school days. Instead, they tell us about:

- **his teachings**
- **his miracles**
- **his healing work**
- **his death and resurrection**

as experienced by the earliest followers of Christianity.

The gospels are not concerned with precise details the way a document of history would be, but instead they deal with the meaning and importance of Jesus' words and actions.

The gospels are called 'documents of faith' because the authors believed that Jesus was more than just a good man; they believed that he was also the Messiah, the Son of God. Matthew, Mark, Luke and John wrote their gospels to help other people to believe the same.

Each of the gospels gives **witness** to the story of Jesus. This means that they give evidence (information) about the person and preaching of Jesus.

For example, Jesus was aware that the people needed him, but he also knew that his time on earth would be short and that his followers would require help to continue to preach his message. In Matthew's gospel, we can read about Jesus' concern for his people:

> *Then Jesus went about all the cities and villages, teaching in their synagogues, and proclaiming the good news of the kingdom, and curing every disease and every sickness. When he saw the crowds, he had compassion for them, because they were harassed and helpless, like sheep without a shepherd. Then he said to his disciples, 'The harvest is plentiful but the labourers are few, therefore ask the Lord of the harvest to send out labourers into his harvest'.* (Matthew 9:35-38)

KNOW WHAT

1. If the gospels were historical documents, what sort of evidence do you think you would find in them?
2. What is the difference between a document of history and a document of faith?
3. In reference to the above passage from Matthew's gospel, why do you think Jesus felt sorry for the crowd?
4. 'The harvest is plentiful but the labourers are few.' What do you think this means?

The gospels are documents of faith.
The gospels give witness to the story of Jesus.

DIGGING DEEPER
1. How do the gospels give witness to the story of Jesus?
2. What good news do the gospels contain for people of faith?
3. The Bible helps us to 'get to know' the story of Jesus. What other ways can we 'get to know' the person of Jesus?

Documents of History

Apart from documents of faith such as the gospels, there is also evidence about Jesus to be found in documents of history, such as the writings of the historians Josephus and Tacitus.

Josephus was a Jewish historian who died in Rome about AD 98. He was famous for writing several books for the Romans, in which he tried to explain Judaism to them. In one passage, Josephus mentions Jesus:

> *About this time arose Jesus, a wise man, who did good deeds and whose virtues were recognised. And many Jews and disciples of other nations became his disciples. Pilate condemned him to be crucified and to die. However, those who had become his disciples preached his doctrine. They related that he had appeared to them three days after his crucifixion and that he was alive. Perhaps he was the Messiah in connection with whom the prophets foretold wonders.*

Although this account of Jesus does not give dates and specific details, it does make historical reference to him.

Tacitus was a Roman historian who wrote about the people and their experiences in the Roman Empire. Like Josephus, he too wrote about Jesus. When he was writing about the persecution of Christians in Rome by the Emperor Nero in AD 64, Tacitus explained who the Christians were and where they got their name:

> *The name Christian comes from Christ, who was executed in the reign of Tiberius by the procurator Pontius Pilate.*

Josephus and Tacitus wrote documents of history.

KNOW HOW
Write a paragraph each on Josephus and Tacitus, explaining who they were and what they said about Jesus.

Evidence: Information that provides a reason for believing in something.

Gospel: Means 'good news' and is the name used for each of the first four texts of the New Testament because they tell of the new life that Jesus offers to us.

Witness: Something that serves as evidence or proof. The gospels give witness to the story of Jesus.

LESSON 30 From Oral Tradition to the Written Word

GROUNDWORK
In this lesson we plan to:
- trace the gospels from the oral tradition to the written word.

DIGGING DEEPER
Who wrote the Christian story?

Key Concepts
Evidence from Oral and Written Tradition/Gospel

Recording the Past

If you wanted to write a story about the schooldays your grandparents had, the story would have to go through three stages before it would appear in your copy.

- The first stage is **the life stage**. This means that your grandparents would actually have lived the story. This stage is the very beginning, the *actual experience*.
- The second stage is **the oral stage**. This is the stage where your grandparents tell you what their schooldays were like. It is the *talking about* stage.
- The third and final stage is **the written stage**. This is when you record the *information* that you gathered during the oral stage.

KNOWING ME KNOWING YOU
- Ask a grandparent or a local senior citizen what their schooldays were like (stage one).
- Together, chat about the experience (stage two).
- Write an account of what you have talked about (stage three).
- In class, share your accounts and discuss the three stages that you followed.

The Writing of the Gospels

The above example helps us to understand the three stages that were involved in the writing of the gospels. The life stage began with the birth of Jesus and ended with his ascension into heaven.

The second stage was when the followers of Jesus recognised who Jesus was, and brought news of him beyond Palestine to other countries, eventually reaching Rome. This oral stage is part of the Christian **oral tradition**.

The third stage was when the followers of Jesus began to write down the story of Jesus' ministry and the circumstances of his death and resurrection. These stories, together with letters written by the early Church leaders to the first Christian communities, were gathered together to form the New Testament and are part of the **written tradition** of Christianity.

KNOW WHAT

1. What three stages or processes were involved in the writing of the gospels?
2. What is the oral tradition relating to Jesus' life, death and resurrection?
3. What is the written tradition of Christianity?
4. How did the written tradition ensure the continuous spread of the Good News?

The writing of the gospels and the rest of the New Testament was inspired by the Risen Jesus Christ and the Holy Spirit.

DIGGING DEEPER
How do you think the Risen Jesus and the Holy Spirit inspired the writers of the New Testament?

KNOW IT ALL
Copy the following sentences into your Religion folder and fill in the blanks using the wordbank given below.

The _gospels_ tell the story of the b_irth_, d_eath_ and r_esurrection_ of Jesus Christ.

There were _three_ stages involved in the formation of the gospels.

The ~~actual life~~ stage began with the birth of Jesus and ended with his ascension into heaven.

The _oral_ stage is part of the Christian o_ral_ t_radition_. During this stage, the apostles shared what they had learned about Jesus.

The final stage, the _written_ stage, is part of the w_ritten_ t_radition_ of Christianity.

WORDBANK
Gospels • Birth • Three • Oral tradition • Death • Life • Oral • Written • Written tradition • Resurrection

🔑 **Evidence from oral tradition:** Information that is handed on by word of mouth from one group to another.

Evidence from written tradition: Information that is written down, e.g. in the gospels and the letters of the apostles.

See page 487 for a past exam question on this topic.

LESSON 31 The Evangelists and the Gospels

GROUNDWORK
In this lesson we plan to:
- explore further how the gospels came to be written.

DIGGING DEEPER
The four gospels tell the same story of the Good News in different ways.

Key Concepts
Gospel/Evangelist

The same, yet different!

You have six minutes to complete this task.

- Which picture interests you the most? Explain your answer.
- The four pictures are of the same geographical location. Where do you think it is? (Clue: The A _ p _)
- Explain why it is possible to see the same place, person or object from many different perspectives.

The Gospels Tell the Story of Jesus

The gospels were written by Matthew, Mark, Luke and John, who are called **evangelists**, from the Greek word *euangelistes*, meaning 'one who announces the Good News'. They were inspired by the Holy Spirit to write what God wanted people to know. They knew that it was important to write down the Good News about Jesus before all those who had lived with Jesus had died. Each evangelist was a person of great faith and each one told the same story about Jesus, but in different ways. Each of them wanted to emphasise different things. Through their writings, they were aiming to show people who Jesus really was and to explain the meaning of his life, death and resurrection. They also wanted to write about Jesus in a way that would be understood by the different groups for whom they were writing.

The Gospel of Mark

When you open the New Testament, the first gospel you see is Matthew's gospel. You might be surprised, therefore, that we are starting with Mark's gospel, but we are going to look at the gospels in the order in which they were written, and Mark's was written first.

Mark probably wrote his gospel in Rome around AD 65 and he wrote it for Gentile Christians (i.e. non-Jewish people who had become Christians). Because Mark's audience was not Jewish, there are very few references to the Old Testament in Mark's gospel. Mark knew some of those who had met Jesus and who continued to preach the Good News. He became a follower of Peter and he listened very carefully to all that Peter told him about Jesus. Peter would have had difficulty preaching to Gentile Christians because he spoke Aramaic, while they spoke Greek. Mark is sometimes described as the interpreter of Peter. This is because he heard Peter telling the stories of Jesus in Aramaic but he then wrote them down in Greek for a Greek-speaking audience. Mark presents Jesus as the *teaching* Messiah and also as the *suffering* Messiah.

The Gospel of Matthew

Matthew's gospel was written around AD 85, at least twenty years after Mark's gospel. It was also written in Greek and it seems that Matthew was familiar with Mark's gospel. It is thought that Matthew was a teacher and that he worked as a rabbi for a while, which would explain his great knowledge and understanding of the Scriptures.

Matthew's gospel is the most Jewish of the gospels and it contains plenty of references to the Old Testament. Matthew was writing for Jews who had converted to Christianity. Not everyone believed that Jesus was the Messiah and so it was often difficult for these new Christian converts. They were no longer allowed to pray in the synagogues and so they often felt despair. Matthew reminded them that they had hope; their hope was in Jesus Christ, the awaited Messiah.

When writing his gospel, Matthew worked hard to show the Jewish Christians how Jesus and his teaching, as portrayed in the New Testament, fulfilled (brought about) what was foretold in the Old Testament. Matthew's gospel presents Jesus as *the* Messiah.

The Gospel of Luke

Luke's gospel was also written around AD 85. Luke was a Gentile Christian writing for other Gentile Christians. As a young man, he was a companion and helper to the apostle Paul. Luke also wrote the Acts of the Apostles. He was a wonderful storyteller.

Luke's gospel tells us about Jesus' journey towards Jerusalem and the effect of his death and resurrection. Luke is thought to have been a doctor. He was very aware of the suffering and pain of the poor and the oppressed and he greatly respected the way Jesus healed people and cared for everyone, rich and poor, Gentile and Jew. Luke's gospel presents Jesus as a compassionate Messiah, one who *heals* people and *cares* for them.

The Gospel of John

John's gospel was written in AD 95 and it was the last gospel to be written. It is quite different from the other gospels. John was writing for people who had already been converted to Christianity and had been followers of Jesus for many years. His gospel is concerned with the meaning of Jesus' teaching and with exploring Jesus' message. John was trying to deepen the faith of the Christians for whom he was writing.

The opening lines of John's gospel identify Jesus as the Messiah, the word and wisdom of God, and introduce the themes to be developed (John 1:1-18). John sought to explain how Jesus had come to give eternal life: 'I came that they may have life and have it to the full' (John 10:10). John identifies Jesus with God's name 'I am' from the Old Testament (Exodus 3:14):

- 'I am the bread of life.' (John 6:35)
- 'I am the light of the world.' (John 8:12)
- 'I am the good shepherd.' (John 10:11)

John's gospel presents Jesus as a *life-giving* Messiah. This means that life will be richer and fuller for those who listen to Jesus and come to a greater understanding of his teachings.

KNOW WHAT

1. What does the term 'evangelist' mean?
2. How do we know that the evangelists were people of faith?
3. Which gospel was written for Christian converts from Judaism?
4. Name the evangelist who was most likely a doctor and the one who is thought to have been a teacher.
5. Which gospel is different from the others? How is it different?
6. What type of Messiah does each evangelist describe?

KNOW HOW

Copy the following chart into your Religion folder four times and fill it in for each gospel.

Name of Gospel:	
Two points about the author	1.
	2.
Two points about the gospel	1.
	2.

KNOW THE WAY

KNOW IT ALL

Match the references with the headings listed:

Matthew 8:14-15	Cure of Peter's mother-in-law
Mark 1:21-22	Cure of a leper
Luke 5:12-16	Death of Lazarus
John 11:1-44	Jesus teaches in Capernaum

Evangelist: The name given to each of the four writers of the gospels: Matthew, Mark, Luke and John.

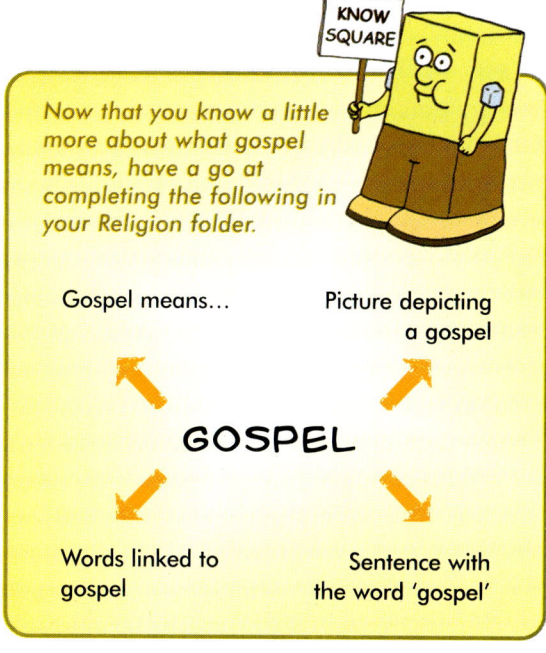

Now that you know a little more about what gospel means, have a go at completing the following in your Religion folder.

Gospel means…

Picture depicting a gospel

GOSPEL

Words linked to gospel

Sentence with the word 'gospel'

LESSON 32 The Synoptic Gospels

GROUNDWORK
In this lesson we plan to:
- explore the synoptic gospels.

DIGGING DEEPER
How do the synoptic gospels help to increase Christian faith?

Key Concept
Synoptic

The Three Synoptic Gospels

The gospels of Matthew, Mark and Luke have many similarities. Because of this, they are referred to as the **synoptic** gospels. The two syllables in the word 'synoptic' are: *syn*, which means 'together', and *optic*, which means 'seen'; when 'seen together', the three gospels are very similar. It is obvious from reading the first three gospels that they record many of the same events in the life of Jesus, but the context (circumstances) of each gospel is different. They were written by different individuals, with different points of view, for different groups of people. There are different perspectives (outlooks) on the life of Jesus of Nazareth in each gospel.

We will now look at one event from the life of Jesus – the Calling of the Disciples – and compare how it is presented in each of the three synoptic gospels.

Matthew 4:18-22
As he walked by the Sea of Galilee, he saw two brothers, Simon, who was called Peter, and Andrew his brother, casting a net into the sea – for they were fishermen. And he said to them, 'Follow me, and I will make you fishers for people.' Immediately they left their nets and followed him. As he went from there, he saw two other brothers, James son of Zebedee and his brother John, in the boat with their father Zebedee, mending their nets, and he called them. Immediately they left the boat and their father, and followed him

Mark 1:16-20
As Jesus passed along the Sea of Galilee, he saw Simon and his brother Andrew casting a net into the sea – for they were fishermen. And Jesus said to them, 'Follow me and I will make you fishers for people'. And immediately they left their nets and followed him. As he went a little farther, he saw James son of Zebedee and his brother John, who were in their boat mending the nets. Immediately he called them; and they left their father Zebedee in the boat with the hired men, and followed him.

Luke 5:1-11
Once while Jesus was standing beside the lake of Gennesaret, and the crowd was pressing in on him to hear the word of God, he saw two boats there at the shore of the lake; the fishermen had gone out of them and were washing their nets. He got into one

of the boats, the one belonging to Simon, and asked him to put out a little way from the shore. Then he sat down and taught the crowds from the boat. When he had finished speaking, he said to Simon, 'Put out into the deep water and let down your nets for a catch.' Simon answered, 'Master, we have worked all night long but have caught nothing. Yet if you say so, I will let down the nets.' When they had done this, they caught so many fish that their nets were beginning to break. So they signalled their partners in the other boat to come and help them. And they came and filled both boats, so that they began to sink. But when Simon Peter saw it, he fell down at Jesus' knees, saying, 'Go away from me, Lord, for I am a sinful man!' For he and all who were with him were amazed at the catch of fish they had taken; and so also were James and John, sons of Zebedee, who were partners with Simon. Then Jesus said to Simon, 'Do not be afraid; from now on you will be catching people.' When they had brought their boats to shore, they left everything and followed him.

KNOW WHAT

1. Compare the three accounts by listing all the words that they have in common.
2. Having examined the three accounts, decide what is the perspective (outlook) of each evangelist on the life of Jesus.
3. In your opinion, what are the most important things that the evangelists wanted people to know about the calling of the first four disciples?
4. Using your Bible, see if you can find two other stories that the synoptic gospels have in common.

DIGGING DEEPER

1. What do the similarities in the synoptic gospels teach us about Jesus?
2. How do stories from the synoptic gospels help to increase Christian faith?

Synoptic: Means sharing a point of view. The gospels of Matthew, Mark and Luke are called synoptic gospels because they share so many of the same stories about Jesus.

See page 487 for a past exam question on this topic.

The Person and Preaching of Jesus

LESSON 33 Jesus and the Kingdom of God

GROUNDWORK
In this lesson we plan to:
- explore what Jesus meant when he preached about the Kingdom of God.

DIGGING DEEPER
What does the Kingdom of God mean for me?

 **Key Concepts**
Kingdom of God/Kingdom of God in Parable/Miracle/Table-fellowship/Discipleship

DIGGING DEEPER
Read an account of John the Baptist from one of the gospels and describe the kind of person he was and the work that he was doing. Choose from one of the following references: Matthew 3:1-12; Mark 1:1-8; Luke 3:1-20; John 1:19-34.

of the boats, the one belonging to Simon, and asked him to put out a little way from the shore. Then he sat down and taught the crowds from the boat. When he had finished speaking, he said to Simon, 'Put out into the deep water and let down your nets for a catch.' Simon answered, 'Master, we have worked all night long but have caught nothing. Yet if you say so, I will let down the nets.' When they had done this, they caught so many fish that their nets were beginning to break. So they signalled their partners in the other boat to come and help them. And they came and filled both boats, so that they began to sink. But when Simon Peter saw it, he fell down at Jesus' knees, saying, 'Go away from me, Lord, for I am a sinful man!' For he and all who were with him were amazed at the catch of fish they had taken; and so also were James and John, sons of Zebedee, who were partners with Simon. Then Jesus said to Simon, 'Do not be afraid; from now on you will be catching people.' When they had brought their boats to shore, they left everything and followed him.

KNOW WHAT

1. Compare the three accounts by listing all the words that they have in common.
2. Having examined the three accounts, decide what is the perspective (outlook) of each evangelist on the life of Jesus.
3. In your opinion, what are the most important things that the evangelists wanted people to know about the calling of the first four disciples?
4. Using your Bible, see if you can find two other stories that the synoptic gospels have in common.

DIGGING DEEPER

1. What do the similarities in the synoptic gospels teach us about Jesus?
2. How do stories from the synoptic gospels help to increase Christian faith?

Synoptic: Means sharing a point of view. The gospels of Matthew, Mark and Luke are called synoptic gospels because they share so many of the same stories about Jesus.

See page 487 for a past exam question on this topic.

The Person and Preaching of Jesus

LESSON 33 Jesus and the Kingdom of God

GROUNDWORK
In this lesson we plan to:
- explore what Jesus meant when he preached about the Kingdom of God.

DIGGING DEEPER
What does the Kingdom of God mean for me?

 **Key Concepts**
Kingdom of God/Kingdom of God in Parable/Miracle/Table-fellowship/Discipleship

DIGGING DEEPER

Read an account of John the Baptist from one of the gospels and describe the kind of person he was and the work that he was doing. Choose from one of the following references: Matthew 3:1-12; Mark 1:1-8; Luke 3:1-20; John 1:19-34.

Jesus Announces the Kingdom of God

The Jewish people were waiting for a Messiah to come and establish a great and peaceful kingdom. They remembered better times in their history, when they were not occupied by a foreign power, but had their own kingdom led by King David. The prophets had encouraged them not to despair, promising that God would send the Messiah.

After being baptised by John the Baptist, Jesus called the apostles to follow him as he began his public ministry. The *ministry* of Jesus refers to the work of *serving* God and others that Jesus came on earth to do. The main aim of the ministry of Jesus was to proclaim and show people that 'the Kingdom of God is at hand'.

Jesus spoke about the **Kingdom of God** as a way of life rather than an actual physical place. In the Kingdom of God, people live together in love, peace, truth and justice. The Kingdom of God is based on love, not power. Jesus explained that the Kingdom of God is in people and among people. It is about the way people treat one another and live as God calls them to. The Kingdom of God is right here, right now, in the response that people make to the invitation given by Jesus to follow God and to rely on the saving power of God's love in their lives. Living in the Kingdom of God involves trusting in God and listening to the voice of the Spirit, which offers guidance.

KNOW WHAT
1. What is the Kingdom of God?
2. Where is the Kingdom of God?
3. When is the Kingdom of God going to begin?
4. Why did Jesus invite every person into the Kingdom of God?

DIGGING DEEPER
1. Do you think you are invited into the Kingdom of God? How does that make you feel? What is your response to that invitation?
2. Why do you think it might have been difficult for the people to understand the kind of kingdom that Jesus was preaching about?

What Jesus did…

Jesus revealed the Kingdom of God through his **parables**.

- Jesus told stories called parables to help his followers to understand what the Kingdom of God is like.

Jesus revealed the Kingdom of God through his **miracles**.

- Those who travelled with Jesus witnessed the miracles and experienced Jesus' kindness and compassion. As they journeyed with him, they began to understand that their lives would never be the same again.

Jesus revealed the Kingdom of God through his **table-fellowship**.

- The term 'table-fellowship' means 'sharing a meal with others'. To sit down and eat a meal with someone was an important part of life in Palestine. Jesus included everyone at his table.

Jesus revealed the Kingdom of God through his **discipleship**.

- The word 'disciple' comes from the Latin *discipulus*, meaning a follower, pupil or student. Jesus called people to be his disciples. The Greek word *metanoia* is used to describe the change that must occur if a person is to become a disciple of Jesus; it means 'a change of heart'. Jesus called his disciples to make a complete change of heart by responding to the immense love and mercy of God and following him in the ways of the Kingdom of God.

KNOW IT ALL

Copy the following exercise into your Religion folder and fill in the blanks using the wordbank given below.

1. The main message in the ministry of Jesus was the _____ of _____ .
2. Jesus showed the meaning of the Kingdom of God through his _____ and _____ .
3. He revealed the kingdom through p_____ , m_____ , t_____ _____ and d_____ .

WORDBANK

Discipleship • Miracles • Words • Kingdom • Actions • Parables • Table-fellowship • God

By witnessing Jesus' words and actions, many people came to know God and to develop a greater understanding of the kingdom. Jesus reached out to people who were looked down on by the rest of society, like tax-collectors and prostitutes. His message about the Kingdom of God was good news because it brought hope into the lives of all people. It taught them how to love everyone and it gave them examples of how to imitate Jesus' love in practical ways.

KNOW IT ALL

You will need a Bible for this exercise.

Look up the following gospel references and find out what each one says about the Kingdom of God. Each reference relates to parable, miracle, table-fellowship or discipleship.

- Matthew 8:23-27
- Mark 1:40-44
- Mark 4:30-32
- Luke 11:37-54
- Luke 9:10-17
- Luke 10:29-37
- John 1:43-48

 **Kingdom of God:** God is always present in the world. The Kingdom of God is brought about when people respond to God's presence in their words and actions and by treating others and the earth as God calls them to. The Kingdom of God, therefore, refers to a way of life rather than a physical place. It means trusting in God and listening to the voice of the Holy Spirit.

in parable: Jesus told short stories called parables to teach his followers what he meant by the Kingdom of God. These stories invited people to respond by changing their behaviour.

in miracle: Jesus performed wonderful actions called miracles to show people that the Kingdom of God is present and at work in the world. These miracles invited a response.

in table-fellowship (shared meals): Jesus loved to share meals, expecially with those who were looked down upon or excluded by others. By doing so, he showed that the Kingdom of God includes everyone.

in discipleship: Becoming a follower or disciple of Jesus means working to build the Kingdom of God in the world.

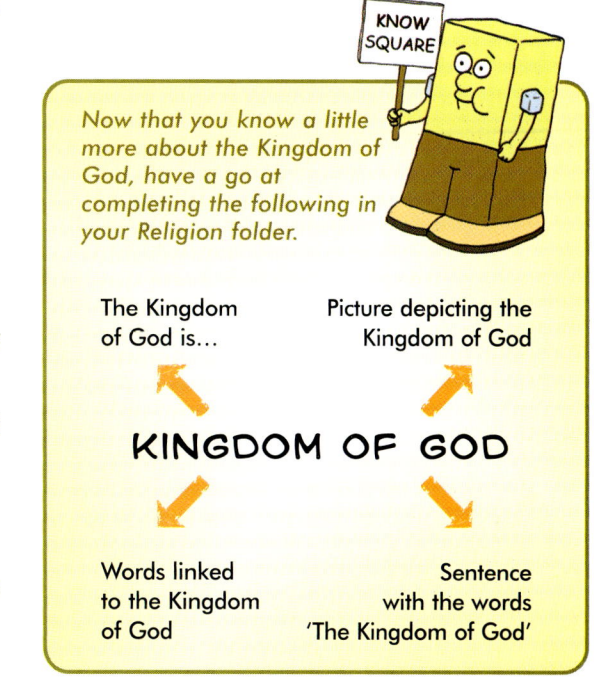

Now that you know a little more about the Kingdom of God, have a go at completing the following in your Religion folder.

The Kingdom of God is...

Picture depicting the Kingdom of God

KINGDOM OF GOD

Words linked to the Kingdom of God

Sentence with the words 'The Kingdom of God'

Lesson 34 The Kingdom of God in Parables

GROUNDWORK
In this lesson we plan to:
- identify the characteristics of the Kingdom of God as preached by Jesus in his parables.

DIGGING DEEPER
How do Jesus' parables speak to people today?

Key Concept
Kingdom of God in Parables

We listen to stories because they grab our attention and then they share some knowledge and information with us. Sometimes we tell stories when we want to explain something very important and we want to make sure that the listeners hear, understand and remember what we are saying.

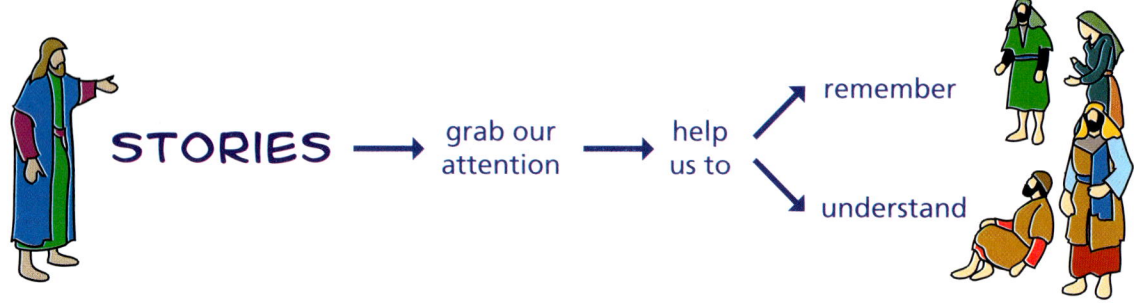

DIGGING DEEPER
1. Think of a story you have heard that has helped you in your understanding of something. What was the story and how did it help?
2. Think of a time when you told a story to explain something. What was the story and the message?

The Parables of Jesus

Jesus told short stories called parables to help his followers to understand what he meant by the Kingdom of God. Jesus' parables were based on the lifestyles that ordinary people were familiar with at that time; they told of farm workers, fishermen, shepherds, kings and so on. They dealt with very ordinary events, such as paying workers, minding sheep, sowing crops or catching fish. The parables were sometimes about life in the city. Often, there was a question asked in the parable, or a puzzle to be solved. Usually, the story did not give the answer, but left the listeners to figure out the answer from their own experience of life.

KNOW WHAT
1. Why did Jesus tell parables?
2. Why do you think most of Jesus' parables were about life in the countryside rather than in the city?

Two Levels of Meaning
The parables of Jesus work on two levels, i.e. they have two levels of meaning. There is the first and obvious meaning of the story, and then a deeper, challenging message about the Kingdom of God.

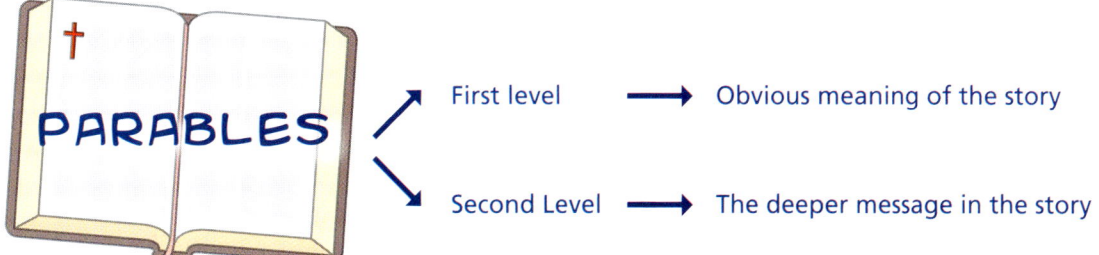

KNOW IT ALL
Copy the following exercise into your Religion folder and fill in the blanks using the wordbank given below.

A parable is a short .... about .... events.
A parable always has a ....
Jesus told many parables in order to teach people about the .... of ....
Parables work on .... levels.
The first level shows the .... meaning of the story and the second level shows the .... message in the story.

WORDBANK
Story • Kingdom • Obvious • Hidden meaning • God • Deeper • Ordinary • Two

Let's look at one of Jesus' parables and examine the two levels of meaning that it contains.

The Parable of the Sower
'Listen! Once there was a man who went out to sow corn. As he scattered the seed in the field, some of it fell along the path, and the birds came and ate it up. Other seed fell on rocky ground, where there was little soil. The seeds soon sprouted, because the soil wasn't deep, but then the sun came up and it burnt the young plants; and because the roots had not grown deep enough, the plants soon dried up and died. Some of the seed fell among thorn bushes, which grew up and choked the plants, and they didn't produce any corn. But some seeds fell in good soil, and the plants sprouted, grew and produced corn: some had thirty grains, others sixty and others a hundred. Listen, then, if you have ears!' (Adapted from Matthew 13:1-23)

The Meaning of the Parable

The first level of meaning in this parable is obvious: if someone is sowing seed, it's best to sow it in good soil, where it will thrive and grow and produce a good crop. But what is the second level of meaning? Let's explore it!

The different kinds of soil represent the people who hear the Word of God.

- Some seeds fell along the stony path. The stony path represents those who hear God's message but then they fall into temptation and ignore what they have heard.
- Other seeds fell on rocky ground. The rocky ground represents those who hear the message, receive it gladly, but if it requires any extra work or effort from them, they will eventually give up and reject the message.
- Some seeds fell in the bushes. The bushes represent the people who hear and understand the message, but then material wealth and worries about other things smother their enthusiasm, and so they reject it.
- The last seeds were sown in good soil. The good soil represents those people who hear and understand the message and respond by making changes in their lives in order to follow in the footsteps of Jesus.

The parables of Jesus are as relevant and challenging today as they were when he told them some two thousand years ago.

KNOW WHAT
Explain the two levels of meaning in the parable of the Sower.

DIGGING DEEPER
1. How is the parable of the Sower relevant today?
2. Have a go at drawing some pictures to explain this parable.

Parables and the Kingdom of God

Through his parables, Jesus helped people to understand the meaning of the Kingdom of God. He demonstrated the characteristics (signs or features) of the kingdom by showing:

- how sinners and outcasts (outsiders) are to be treated in the kingdom;
- how people living in the kingdom should love their neighbour;
- how there should be a special place for the poor;
- how women should be treated;
- how people must love and forgive their enemies.

The Parable of the Good Samaritan

A man once asked Jesus, 'Who is my neighbour?' Jesus answered, 'A man was going down from Jerusalem to Jericho, and he fell among robbers, who stripped him and beat him, then departed, leaving him half dead. By chance, a certain priest was going down that way. When he saw the man, he passed by on the other side. In the same way, a Levite came to the place and saw him, and he too passed by on the other side. But then a Samaritan came upon the injured man. When he saw him, he was moved with compassion and he bandaged up his wounds, pouring oil and wine on them. He put him on his own animal and brought him to an inn, and took care of him. The next day, before he left, he took out two denarii, and gave them to the innkeeper, and said to him, "Take care of him. Whatever you spend beyond that, I will repay you when I return."' Then Jesus asked, 'Now which of these three do you think was a neighbour to the man who fell among the robbers?' The man who had questioned Jesus said, 'He who showed mercy on him.' Then Jesus said to him, 'Go and do likewise'. (Adapted from Luke 10:30-37)

The parable of the Good Samaritan helps us to understand **how people should love one another in the Kingdom of God**.

KNOW WHAT

1. What does this parable tell us about the Kingdom of God?
2. Why do you think Jesus told this parable?
3. Which of the following characteristics of the kingdom do you recognise in this parable: Treatment of sinners and outsiders; Treatment of women; Special place of the poor; Love of neighbour; Love of enemy. Explain your choice.

DIGGING DEEPER

1. What does this parable mean for us today?
2. Think of a 'Good Samaritan' story that you have witnessed or heard about. Write about this story and the people who were involved.

The Parable of the Lost Sheep

'If any of you has a hundred sheep, and one of them gets lost, what will you do? Won't you leave the ninety-nine in the field and go and look for the lost sheep until you find it? And when you find it, you will be so glad that you will put it on your shoulder and carry it home. Then you will call in your friends and neighbours and say, "Let's celebrate! I've found my lost sheep. In the same way there is more happiness in heaven because of one sinner who turns to God than over ninety-nine good people who don't need to.'
(Luke 15:4-7)

The parable of the Lost Sheep helps us to understand **how the poor and outsiders of society are treated in the Kingdom of God**.

KNOW WHAT

1. What does this parable tell us about how sinners and outsiders should be treated?
2. What does it tell us about the Kingdom of God?
3. Why do you think Jesus told this parable?
4. Which of the following characteristics of the kingdom do you recognise in this parable: Treatment of sinners and outsiders; Treatment of women; Special place of the poor; Love of neighbour; Love of enemy. Explain your choice.

DIGGING DEEPER

1. What does this parable mean for us today?
2. Think of a 'Lost sheep' story you have witnessed or heard about . Write about this story and the people who were involved.

Welcoming the Kingdom into our Hearts

Through the parables, Jesus explained that if God's kingdom is welcomed into the hearts of people and is lived by people, the effects will be huge. Jesus challenged people to open up their hearts and to listen to God in their lives.

KNOW HOW

1. Divide your class into groups of three or four. Each group must look up *one* of the following parables and then answer the questions below. (All the parables must be read.)

   The parable of the Good Servant (Matthew 24:45-51)
   The parable of the Weeds (Matthew 13:45-46)
   The parable of the Yeast (Luke 13:20-21)
   The parable of the Hidden Treasure (Matthew 13:44)
   The parable of the Net (Matthew 13:47-50)
   The parable of the Prodigal Son (Luke 15:11-32)
   The parable of the Ten Bridesmaids (Matthew 25:1-13)

   1. In the parable you have read, to what is the Kingdom of God compared?
   2. What is the main message in this parable?
   3. Which characteristics of the kingdom do you recognise in this parable?

2. Look for some volunteers in your class to act out a modern-day version of one of the parables.

DIGGING DEEPER

1. What does the parable you chose say to you today?
2. How do parables help people to make sense of their lives and work for God's kingdom here on earth?

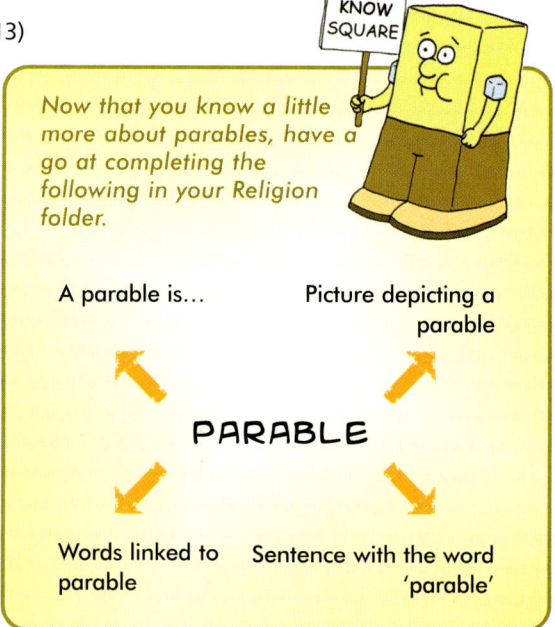

Now that you know a little more about parables, have a go at completing the following in your Religion folder.

A parable is…   Picture depicting a parable

PARABLE

Words linked to parable   Sentence with the word 'parable'

Lesson 35 The Kingdom of God in Miracles

GROUNDWORK

In this lesson we plan to:
- identify the characteristics of the Kingdom of God in the miracles performed by Jesus.

DIGGING DEEPER

How is the Kingdom of God reflected in the miracles of Jesus?

Key Concept
Kingdom of God in Miracles

Write down five words that come to mind when you hear the word 'miracle'.

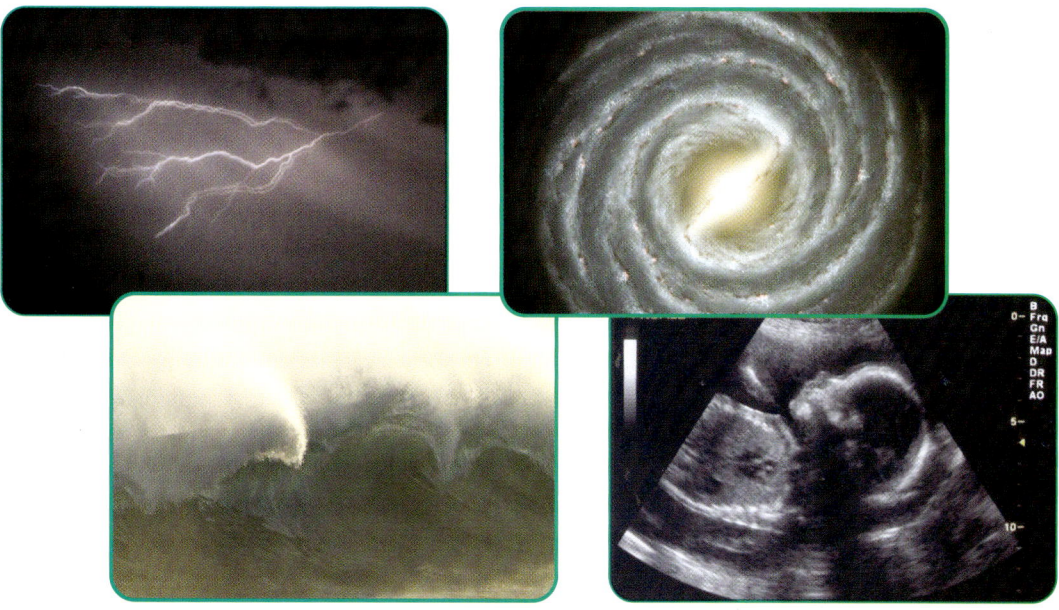

The Miracles of Jesus

Throughout the gospels, Jesus is shown reaching out to people and helping to ease their pain. The miracles of Jesus included healing the sick and curing lepers, the blind and the lame. Jesus even brought the dead back to life.

Jesus did not perform these miracles to show off some sort of special power. In many cases, he performed his miracles with only a few people present.

In John's gospel, the miracles are called 'signs'. John wanted people to understand that the miracles Jesus performed were signs of God's love, showing people that the Kingdom of God is present and at work in the world. God continues to act in an extraordinary way in people's lives today.

Like the parables, the miracles show us some of the characteristics of the Kingdom of God. They are examples of how Jesus treated sinners and outsiders, women and the poor. Jesus shows the meaning of love of neighbour and love of enemy by his words and deeds. 'The very works that I am doing testify that the Father has sent me' (John 5:36).

Two Levels of Meaning

Just as the parables work on two levels, the miracles of Jesus also work on two levels.

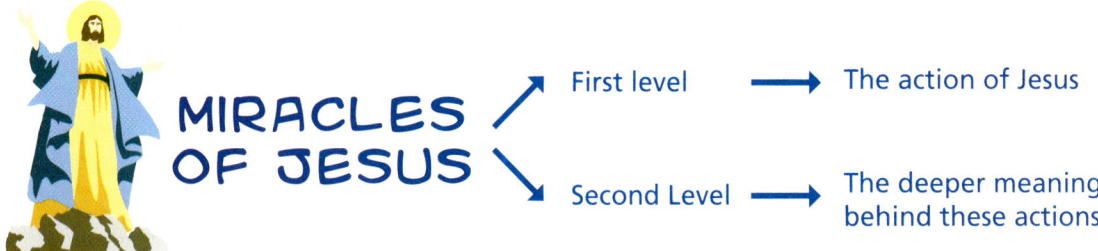

The miracles of Jesus were invitations to people to respond to God's love and to the message of the Kingdom of God. Jesus asked people to open their hearts to this message. Jesus performed many of the miracles in response to people's faith. 'Go; let it be done for you according to your faith' (Matthew 8:13).

DIGGING DEEPER
1. What do you think Jesus meant when he asked people to open their hearts?
2. What do you think Jesus meant when he told the people to 'repent and believe in the good news'?
3. Think of an example of someone who has opened his/her heart to the message of the Kingdom of God.

The Four Types of Miracle in the Gospels

Healing miracles – At the time of Jesus, an illness was seen as a punishment from God for one's own sins or the sins of the family. Therefore, people who were ill were treated as outcasts. Jesus mixed with those who were ill and he felt tremendous compassion for them. He healed them and showed them the power of God's love to overcome suffering and pain.

Nature miracles – Jesus performed wonderous acts in nature. He changed water into wine, calmed the storm and fed five thousand people with five loaves and two fishes. These miracles were not about Jesus showing off his power, but about showing the power of God's love for all people.

Miracles to cast out demons – Jesus performed exorcisms (the casting out of evil spirits) to enable people to see that by opening their hearts to God's love, they would get the courage to confront and overcome evil and the suffering and pain it brings.

Miracles to restore life – There are three accounts of these miracles in the gospels. Jesus raised people from the dead to show that God's love and power is stronger than death. When people think they have lost something for ever, having trust and faith in God can restore hope. Jesus performed such miracles to show that nothing is impossible with God. God can restore (give back) what had been considered lost for ever.

We will now look at two miracles: a healing miracle and a nature miracle. Very often, the healing miracles of Jesus showed his concern not only for people who were suffering from an illness but also for the outcast in society.

A Healing Miracle: Jesus Cures a Sick Woman

Now there was a woman who had been suffering from haemorrhages for twelve years. She had endured much under many physicians and had spent all that she had; and she was no better, but rather grew worse. She had heard about Jesus, and came up behind him in the crowd and touched his cloak, for she said, 'If I but touch his clothes, I will be made well.' Immediately her haemorrhage stopped; and she felt in her body that she was healed of her disease. Immediately aware that power had gone forth from him, Jesus turned about in the crowd and said, 'Who touched my clothes?' And his disciples said to him, 'You see the crowd pressing in on you; how can you say, "Who touched me?"' He looked all around him to see who had done it. But the woman, knowing what had happened to her, came in fear and trembling, fell down before him, and told him the whole truth. He said to her, 'Daughter, your faith has made you well; go in peace, and be healed of your disease.' (Mark 5:25-34)

KNOW WHAT
1. Why do you think the woman 'came in fear and trembling' to Jesus?
2. What does Jesus tell us about the treatment of women in the Kingdom of God by his words and actions on this occasion?

DIGGING DEEPER
1. Have you ever witnessed a time when a female was badly treated? What happened?
2. In our world today, why might a person of a particular gender (i.e. male or female) or a particular group of people be treated unfairly? How can we help to resolve situations like this?

Healing miracles help us to understand **how those who are weak or outsiders in society are treated in the Kingdom of God**.

A Nature Miracle: A Storm on Lake Galilee

One day, Jesus and his disciples got into a boat, and he said, 'Let's cross the lake.' They started out, and while they were sailing across, he went to sleep. Suddenly a storm struck the lake, and the boat started sinking. They were in danger. So they went to Jesus and woke him up, 'Master, Master! We are about to drown!' Jesus got up and ordered the wind and waves to stop. They obeyed, and everything was calm. Then Jesus asked the disciples, 'Don't you have any faith?' But they were frightened and amazed. They said to one another, 'Who is this? He can give orders to the wind and the waves, and they obey him!' (Luke 8:22-25)

KNOW HOW
1. Draw or paint a picture to represent the story 'A Storm on Lake Galilee'.
2. Imagine that you overhear a conversation between two disciples about Jesus on the day after the storm. Write it down.

DIGGING DEEPER
1. If people in our world today followed the example of Jesus, what would be different?
2. Do you know of anyone who follows the example of Jesus in their treatment of the weak and outsiders in today's society?

The miracles of Jesus explained the meaning of the Kingdom of God

- Jesus' miracles showed people that the Kingdom of God is present in the most difficult situations of people's lives.
- Everyone is welcome in the Kingdom of God, no matter what their ability or disability.
- Jesus performed miracles in response to people's faith.
- The miracles are a sign of God's love and of God's power over nature, sickness, evil and even death.

KNOW IT ALL
Choose *three* miracles from the lists below and:
- Report on the first one for the national News.
- Draw a picture to represent the second one.
- Write a paragraph on the third one to show how this miracle explains the meaning of the Kingdom of God.

Nature Miracles
Calming of the storm (Matthew 8:23)
Feeding the five thousand (Luke 9:10)
Walking on the water (Matthew 14:25)

Healing Miracles
Cleansing of a leper (Luke 5:12)
Healing a centurion's servant (Matthew 8:5)
Healing a paralysed man (Mark 2:15)

Restoring Life
Raising the ruler's daughter (Matthew 9:18, 23)
Raising of a widow's son at Nain (Luke 7:11)
Raising of Lazarus (John 11:1-32)

Casting out demons
Casting out an unclean spirit (Luke 4:33)
Healing a boy with a demon (Mark 19:17)

LESSON 36 The Kingdom of God in Table-fellowship

GROUNDWORK
In this lesson we plan to:
- explore the meaning of the Kingdom of God in the table-fellowship of Jesus.

DIGGING DEEPER
How does sharing a meal with others describe the Kingdom of God?

 **Key Concept**
Kingdom of God in Table-fellowship

At Yer Granny's

'Sit down at the table' she said,
'Sit down and eat your lunch.
There's lots of room in Granny's house
For you and the whole bunch.'

'I baked bread and scones today,
Flapjacks and muffins too.
I bet you'd love a glob of jam,
As does your auntie Lu.'

Granny has a special table,
Everyone feels at home.
She always has the kettle on
Whenever you will roam.

She makes you feel warm inside
With all her healthy nosh.
Granny has a place for you
Even though she's not that posh!

KNOW WHAT
1. What is so special about Granny's table?
2. How does Granny welcome people into her home?
3. Explain the last two lines of the poem.
4. What is the deeper message of this poem?

Table-fellowship

Table-fellowship is about sharing food around a table. Sharing a meal creates a special bond between the people gathered at the table. In the poem, it is Granny who helps to create that special bond for all those who eat at her table. People eat together at special times, like birthdays, religious festival days or any significant family days. Some people, especially some families, eat together every day.

KNOW WHAT
1. What is table-fellowship?
2. When was the last time you shared a meal with your family members and friends?

Jesus and Table-fellowship

In Jewish life, meals are very important times. So Jesus grew up to value mealtimes too.

In the Middle East during the time of Jesus, people would only eat and drink with members of their own class and with those of whom they approved. It would have been a scandal to eat with people of a lower class. But Jesus included everyone at his table. For Jesus, the happiness and unity of a shared meal gave a taste of what life is like in the Kingdom of God. Jesus was saying something very important by eating with particular types of people. It is difficult for us to imagine the scandal that he caused by mixing socially with the likes of 'tax-collectors and sinners' (see Matthew 11:9).

Jesus said:

'When you give a lunch or a dinner, do not invite your friends or your brothers or your relations or rich neighbours, in case they invite you back and so repay you. But when you have a party, invite the poor, the crippled, the lame, the blind; then you will be blessed, for they have no means to repay you and so you will be repaid when the upright rise again.' (Adapted from Luke 14:12-13)

KNOW WHAT
1. How did table-fellowship mean something different for Jesus than for Jewish people at the time of Jesus?
2. What did Jesus have to say about sharing meals with people?

DIGGING DEEPER
1. What does it mean to us when we share a meal with our family and friends?
2. Have you ever been invited to share a special meal with others? How did this feel? Write about this time.

KNOW IT ALL
The meals Jesus shared, as described in Luke's gospel
Meal at Levi's house (5:27-39)
Dinner with Simon the Pharisee (7:36-50)
Feeding of five thousand (9:10-17)
Welcomed into the house of Mary and Martha (10:38-42)
Dinner with a Pharisee (11:37-54)
Sabbath meal with a Pharisee (14:1-24)
Welcomed into the home of Zacchaeus (19:1-10)
The Last Supper (22:7-23)
Supper in Emmaus (24:13-35)
Eating with disciples in Jerusalem (24:36-53)

Choose *two* meals from the above list and answer the following questions.

1. What does each of these meals tell us about the Kingdom of God?
2. Why do you think Jesus explained the characteristics of the kingdom through table-fellowship?

DIGGING DEEPER
If you were present at any of these meals with Jesus, what do you think your reaction to Jesus would have been? Discuss your answers in class.

LESSON 37 The Kingdom of God in Discipleship

GROUNDWORK
In this lesson we plan to:
- explore the meaning of the Kingdom of God in the discipleship of Jesus.

DIGGING DEEPER
What does it mean to be a disciple of Jesus?

 **Key Concepts**
Kingdom of God in Discipleship/Mission

Sir Ernest Shackleton was famous for exploring the South Pole. He was born at the end of the nineteenth century in County Kildare and was forty-eight when he died in the Antarctic, where he is buried. Once, before an expedition, he put an advertisement in *The Times*. It read: 'Men wanted for hazardous journey. Small wages, bitter cold. Long months of complete darkness. Constant danger, safe return doubtful. Honour and recognition in case of success.' Five thousand people replied to this advertisement. Ernest Shackleton selected twenty-seven to join him on this great journey.

KNOW WHAT
Why do you think Sir Ernest received so many replies?

DIGGING DEEPER
1. Why are we excited by the call to adventure? How does it make us feel about life?
2. Have you ever had a call to adventure? What was it like? Describe what happened.

Jesus and Discipleship

This story may help us to understand the call of **discipleship**. Jesus singled his disciples out from the crowd and *called* them to follow him. He chose them; they did not choose him. The word 'disciple' actually refers to a student or one who learns from a teacher and then carries on the work of the teacher. Jesus had many disciples, and they carried on his work after his death and resurrection.

Being called to become a disciple of Jesus means being asked to have a complete change of lifestyle and, more importantly, a complete change of heart (a *metanoia*) in response to the immense love of God as experienced in Jesus' words and deeds.

To be a disciple of Jesus means:

- working for the Kingdom of God;
- treating everybody as equals;
- loving others as Jesus did;
- putting others first;
- welcoming all;
- spreading the Good News.

A New Mission

In Luke's gospel, the disciples of Jesus are numbered at around seventy (Luke 10:1-20). However, Jesus chose twelve disciples to be his constant companions. He called these twelve people the apostles. We know about the calling of the apostles because it is recorded for us in the New Testament.

The twelve apostles were a mixed bunch, with different backgrounds, ideas and abilities. Some were brothers and fishermen, some may have been shepherds, one was a tax-collector and one was a member of a Jewish group of freedom fighters. Some were married; others were not. They all had one thing in common: the new role or **mission** that Jesus had given them. Their mission was to follow Jesus and to share his work of spreading the Good News. The apostles went everywhere with Jesus: they shared meals together, laughed together and prayed together.

> In the Catholic Church, the Pope and the bishops are successors to the apostles and hold the apostolic office to preach the Gospel to the whole world, to protect and pass on the faith, to celebrate the sacraments and to nurture the Church.

5-4-3-2-1

In groups of two, complete the following exercise. You will need your Bible.

1. Name **five** of the apostles. (Luke 6:12-16)
2. Describe what talents the following **four** apostles brought to the group: Matthew, Peter, James and John.
3. Find the gospel references telling you how **three** of the apostles were chosen.
4. Name and describe the **two** sets of brothers among the twelve apostles. (Mark 1:16-20)
5. Name and describe the **one** apostle who betrayed Jesus. (Mark 14: 66-72 and Luke 22:47-53)

DIGGING DEEPER

Imagine that you are one of the chosen apostles of Jesus. Give your name and write an account of the day that you were singled out and chosen to follow Jesus.

KNOW IT ALL

Copy the following into your Religion folder and complete the sentences.

Discipleship is _____
Metanoia is _____
An apostle is the name given to _____
Discipleship means working for the kingdom by _____

> **Mission:** Task given to a member of a community of faith to continue the work of Jesus, i.e. making people aware of God's presence and action in the world and inviting a response.

See page 487 for past exam questions on this topic.

LESSON 38 The Call to Discipleship Today

GROUNDWORK
In this lesson we plan to:
- explore the response Jesus asked for when he issued his call to discipleship during his ministry.

DIGGING DEEPER
What is Jesus asking when he issues his call to discipleship today?

 **Key Concept**
Discipleship

'What's with the attitude?'

'What's with the attitude?' is a phrase we often hear. What is an attitude? An attitude is defined as our 'approach' to something or our 'way of thinking' about something. Our attitude can change depending on the task involved.

Think of an attitude to go with each of the following tasks:

- Getting out of bed on a Monday morning
- Going to a party
- Emptying the bins
- Going on holidays
- Studying on a hot day

Discuss the different attitudes listed by your class.

Love One Another

The great commandment of Jesus was to 'love one another'. This is what he called his disciples to do in order to build the Kingdom of God. In a speech called the Sermon on the Mount, Jesus taught people a set of attitudes that they should have in order to 'be' in the Kingdom of God. This set of attitudes is known as the Beatitudes (Be-attitudes). Jesus said that these attitudes are specially blessed by God.

To become a disciple of Jesus means having a complete change of heart, called a 'metanoia'. If one has a change of heart, one sees the world in a different way. The Beatitudes are a guide to be-ing the Kingdom of God here on earth. In other words, Be-attitudes show people the way of **discipleship**, i.e. how to 'be' disciples of Jesus.

KNOW HOW

Find and read the Beatitudes in Matthew 5:3-12 (also Luke 6:20-23).

The Be-attitudes and Discipleship

Jesus says that God blesses…	In other words God blesses…	This suggests that God blesses…
People who depend on God	People who know they don't have all the answers; people who are aware of God in their lives	People who have a loving relationship with God
People who are gentle	People who treat others with kindness; people who treat the earth with respect	Gentleness Being kind-hearted Compassion
People who mourn	People who are mourning the loss of someone they love	Friendship and relationships – and will restore them in heaven
People who hunger and thirst for what is right	People who strive to make life fair; people who won't settle for inequality	Justice Equality
People who are merciful	People who don't take revenge; people who forgive and give others a fair chance to change	Mercy Forgiveness
People whose hearts are pure	People who are honourable; people who don't take advantage of others	Right living Thinking properly about others
People who make peace	People who work to end war, conflict and division; people who aim to unite others	Unity Peace Peacemaking
People who are treated badly for doing right	People for whom others make trouble because they do the right thing	Truth Honesty Fair play
People who are abused for following Jesus	People who live like Jesus, who see life as Jesus did and who trust in God's promises	What Jesus taught People's love for Jesus People's respect for Jesus

DIGGING DEEPER

1. Choose one of the Beatitudes. How could this beatitude affect your life?
2. Choose two beatitudes and think of a modern-day example of each one in action. Share your examples with your classmates.

LESSON 39 The Kingdom of God in the World Today

GROUNDWORK
In this lesson we plan to:
- identify the characteristics of the Kingdom of God in the followers of Jesus, both past and present.

DIGGING DEEPER
How is God's kingdom made present in the world today?

Key Concepts
Vocation/Mission

Vocation and Mission
Disciples of Jesus are called to share the Good News with all people. We refer to their calling to serve others as their **vocation**. The task they are called to do is their **mission**.

The Disciples Lived the Gospel
Jesus asked his disciples to go out into the world and spread the Good News. He asked them to help people everywhere to get to know him, to learn from him, to copy his attitude and to live it. Jesus asked them to teach others to do everything that he had told them. This included loving God and one's neighbour (Matthew 22:34-40), looking after the poor, the weak, the outsiders in society, the sick (Matthew 25: 21-46), as well as caring for those in prison.

Jesus' disciples were like family to one another. They shared meals and prayed together. They often met in one another's homes. They would sell their property and possessions and give the money to whoever needed it. Day after day, they met together in the Temple to give praise to God. (See Acts 2:42, 44-47.)

KNOW WHAT
How do we recognise the characteristics of the kingdom in the words and actions of Jesus' early followers?

Living the Gospel Today
When people respond to the call of Jesus, God's kingdom is seen in their lives.

Pope John Paul II (1978-2005) expressed how people today can be followers of Jesus when he said:

> *Solidarity [being united with others and concerned for others]… is not a feeling of vague compassion or shallow distress at the misfortunes of so many people, both near and far. On the contrary, it is a firm and persevering determination to commit oneself to the common good;*

Pope John Paul II

that is to say, to the good of all and of each individual, because we are all really responsible for all. (Solicitudo Rei Socialis, 1987, para 38)

Let's look at some examples of people responding to Jesus' call to live the Gospel today.

The L'Arche Community

Jean Vanier, a Catholic layman, founded the L'Arche community in France. The members – many of whom have learning disabilities – are an example of how people can live the Gospel today. They work, pray and celebrate together. This is what Jean Vanier had to say about his calling (vocation) to work with people with learning disabilities:

'Over the past thirty years, I have had the joy of welcoming a number of men and women from psychiatric institutions to L'Arche. When these people with mental handicaps arrived in the community, they often had a lot of anger and depression inside them. I have seen them gradually change. I could even say that I have often been a witness to a kind of resurrection in them, which is a source of hope for me… I believe that, by understanding their brokenness, we can understand more of our own brokenness; and that by opening ourselves up and being willing to relate to others, we can be healed. In this way, we can enter into forgiveness and reconciliation between people in a small but fundamental way.'

Members of the L'Arche community

Jean Vanier lives his vocation to be a disciple of Jesus by working with those who are so often rejected or neglected by society. God's kingdom can be seen today in the way this disciple treats those with learning disabilities. To be a disciple of Jesus in the world today means to pay attention to those who are in need. Jesus calls everyone to be his disciples. Christians are called to be disciples of Jesus when they are baptised.

Trócaire

Trocaire is an example of an organisation in which people work to ease human suffering and to remove the causes of such suffering. Such work is an example for us of what it means to be a disciple today.

Mother Teresa and the Missionaries of Charity

Mother Teresa made a life-changing decision when she found a woman who had been left to die on the streets of Calcutta, India. She described what happened:

The woman had been half eaten by rats and ants. I took her to the hospital, but they could do nothing for her. They only took her because I refused to go home until something was done for her. After they cared for her, I went straight to the town hall and asked for a place where I could take people like this woman, because that day I found more people dying in the street. An employee of the health services brought me to the temple of Kali… the building was empty and he asked me if I wanted to use it. Within twenty-four hours we brought our sick and our suffering and started the Home for the Dying Destitutes.

Mother Teresa started an order of nuns called the Missionaries of Charity in Calcutta to help look after people who were destitute and dying. Today, the sisters live and work in over five hundred places around the world. They, like their founder, are an example of what it means to be true disciples of Jesus.

See *www.catholic.net/RCC/People/MotherTeresa/mother.html* for more information on Mother Teresa.

KNOW WHAT
1. What similarities are there between the words of Pope John Paul II, Jean Vanier and Mother Teresa?
2. How have the lives of people been changed by working as disciples of Jesus?

DIGGING DEEPER
1. How do Christians show the characteristics of the kingdom in their words and actions today?
2. What kind of life does a true follower of Christ live today?
3. Name and describe a national and an international example of a follower of Christ working for the Kingdom of God in their lives.

KNOWING ME KNOWING YOU
Find two newspaper cuttings that show that the Kingdom of God as taught by Jesus is a) alive and well in the world and b) being ignored by some people in the world.

Vocation: Calling to a particular kind of work or role. As a religious term, it is a calling from God to serve others as Jesus did, by taking on a role/task in the community of faith for the benefit of others.

The Death and Resurrection of Jesus

LESSON 40 Conflict in the Life of Jesus

GROUNDWORK
In this lesson we plan to:
- explore moments of conflict in the life of Jesus.

DIGGING DEEPER
Jesus had to cope with much conflict in his life. What can I learn from his response?

Key Concept
Conflict with authority

Many people experience conflict in their lives. In the following story, James and Jack learn how to deal with conflict and even use it to their advantage.

Story: SK8 4 EVER

Skating was what James and Jack did. Sure they got their homework done, sure they did their chores (well sorta) but their lives revolved around their boards. These guys were skilled when it came to their boards. They could 'ollie up' and 'flip' since they were eight years old.

As teenagers, they were finding it hard to avoid conflict with the local Garda. In their town, there was no proper place to skate. The Market Square was cool until it was cobbled, the Post Office was class before they planted around it, and now the town hall was being turned into a library and they would no longer be able to skate in front of it.

The only place where they could skate was in the car-park, but Garda Walsh said he was having no more of it, and that chasing them out on a Saturday evening was not his idea of fun. Garda Walsh had issued fines of fifty euro each to their parents. The parents had blown a fuse and grounded the boys and now there was a major conflict at home to deal with as well.

Jack and James decided to approach their school principal, who was really good at providing space for the pupils to practise their hobbies – so why not skateboarding? They decided that if they were to be taken seriously, they would have to make some proposals and offer some compromises. Jack offered to work on the school grounds to raise the money they owed to their parents, and James offered to clean the teachers' cars for two weeks! Their principal was impressed with their approach to the situation and she agreed to their proposals. Then she offered them a further suggestion: she proposed that they form a working committee and launch a fundraiser to build a small skate park at the back of the local scouts' hall.

The boys agreed. They worked hard to pay off their debts, and Garda Walsh was so impressed with them that he joined their working committee. They enlisted parents, scout leaders, Fr Andy and three teachers! Together they organised fun days and race nights, cake sales and sponsored walks and many other fundraising activities.

Two years, four months and three days later, Jack and James launched 'SK8 4 EVER', a new skate park for teens. They had demos, contests, tipsters and free boarding for all on the day.

Jack and James now own five major skateboarding parks in Ireland. They have kids of their own who skate as a hobby. What was a constant source of serious conflict for them as teenagers has turned into a most pleasurable and profitable lifestyle for them as adults!

KNOW WHAT
1. Why was it so difficult for Jack and James to find a place to skateboard?
2. How did they deal with conflict?
3. Is there always a solution to conflict? Why?/Why not?

DIGGING DEEPER
1. Think of a time when you had to deal with conflict. Describe what happened.
2. See if you can come up with one piece of advice that would help others to deal with conflict.

Conflict in the Life of Jesus

From the very beginning of Jesus' public ministry, the question on everyone's lips was 'Who is this man?' It was not uncommon at that time for preachers to travel around the Holy Land, but there was something different about Jesus. The message he preached was one of love, peace and reconciliation and he spoke with an authority and a compassion that was new – and different from that of other preachers. Yet this message led to conflict with both the political and the religious authorities.

People like the scribes, who were experts in the Law as given to Moses, were scandalised when they witnessed some of the words and actions of Jesus, especially when he dared to forgive sins. The religious authorities were particularly disturbed when Jesus broke the Sabbath, the penalty for which was stoning to death. In Mark's gospel we read:

> *One Sabbath Jesus was going through the grainfields; and as they made their way his disciples began to pluck heads of grain. The Pharisees said to him, 'Look, why are they doing what is not lawful on the Sabbath?' And he said to them, 'Have you never read what David did when he and his companions were hungry and in need of food? He entered the house of God, where Abiathar was high priest, and ate the bread of the Presence, which it is not lawful for any but the priests to eat, and he gave some to his companions.' Then he said to them, 'The Sabbath was made for humankind, and not humankind for the Sabbath; so the Son of Man is lord even of the Sabbath.'*
> (Mark 2:23-28)

By reminding them of a time when the great King David found it necessary to break the Law, Jesus showed his knowledge of the history of the Jewish people. More than that, he also claimed to be Lord of everything, even of the Sabbath. He made matters worse when, later on and still on the Sabbath, he healed a man with a paralysed hand. The scribes and Pharisees had been waiting to see what would happen and, before he healed the man, Jesus turned to look at them. Mark describes what happened:

> *He looked around at them with anger; he was grieved at their hardness of heart and said to the man, 'Stretch out your hand.' He stretched it out, and his hand was restored. The Pharisees went out and immediately conspired with the Herodians against him, how to destroy him.* (Mark 3:5-6)

KNOW WHAT
1. Why was there conflict in the life of Jesus?
2. What groups in authority entered into conflict with Jesus?
3. Would you say that Jesus met the conflict head on or ignored it? Why?/Why not?

Growing Opposition to Jesus

On Palm Sunday, Jesus entered Jerusalem riding on a donkey. He was greeted by happy crowds waving palm branches, obviously overjoyed to welcome him. Unfortunately, the great welcome the crowd gave Jesus worked against him. The religious authorities, who were already deeply suspicious of him, were dismayed at the number and enthusiasm of his followers. After all, he was only a wandering preacher, a humble carpenter. How dare he put himself forward like this!

On one occasion, Jesus challenged the practice of changing money and selling things at the Temple. The religious authorities, the chief priests and the Pharisees were deeply troubled by this and by the huge support Jesus received from his followers. (You can read about this in Mark 11:15-19, Matthew 21:12-17, Luke 19:45-48 and John 2:13-22.)

Jesus Challenges the Teachers of the Law

The religious leaders were particularly unhappy when they felt that Jesus was challenging their authority.

Jesus told a large crowd who had gathered to hear him, 'Watch out for the teachers of the Law, who like to walk around in their long robes and be greeted with respect in the market-place, who choose the reserved seats in the synagogues and the best places at feasts. They take advantage of widows and rob them of their homes, and then make a show of saying long prayers. Their punishment will be all the worse.'
(Adapted from Mark 12:38-40)

Religious leaders at the time of Jesus used their position to exert power over people. They did not always live religiously themselves.

KNOW WHAT
1. What kinds of conflict did Jesus experience?
2. What was Jesus doing that made the scribes and Pharisees question him?
3. Why do you think this kind of conflict kept arising?
4. In your Bible, find two other examples of Jesus experiencing conflict. In each example, describe what happened.

Conflict with authority: An open clash with the person/group that makes the community's or group's decisions. Jesus clashed with the Pharisees and, more particularly, with the Sadducees.

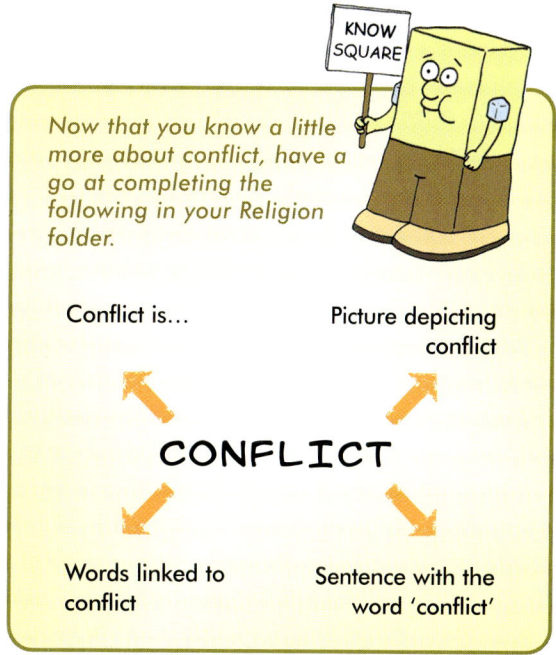

Now that you know a little more about conflict, have a go at completing the following in your Religion folder.

Conflict is…   Picture depicting conflict

CONFLICT

Words linked to conflict   Sentence with the word 'conflict'

See pages 487 and 488 for past exam questions on this topic.

129

LESSON 41 The Last Supper

GROUNDWORK
In this lesson we plan to:
- explore the Last Supper as a meal in the Passover tradition.

DIGGING DEEPER
What is the meaning of the Last Supper for Christians?

Key Concepts
Memorial/Passover/Eucharist

Memorial

The Irish poet Patrick Kavanagh celebrated the beauty in the ordinary, everyday things of life. He particularly appreciated the beauty of nature and this became the inspiration for much of his poetry. When Kavanagh died in 1967, his friends wanted to create a memorial of him. A memorial is something that remembers or pays tribute to a person or an action from the past. Kavanagh had found great peace and comfort sitting beside the Grand Canal in Dublin and he had written a poem about this. The following lines are from this poem.

> *O commemorate me where there is water,*
> *Canal water preferably, so stilly*
> *Greeny at the heart of summer. Brother*
> *Commemorate me thus beautifully.*

Kavanagh's friends were inspired by this poem and so they decided to place a seat by the canal as a memorial of his life and his work.

KNOW WHAT
Why do you think Patrick Kavanagh's friends chose this particular memorial?

The Last Supper as a Memorial Meal

Here is what St Paul wrote about the Last Supper in his first letter to the Christians in the city of Corinth:

> *…the Lord Jesus on the night when he was betrayed took a loaf of bread, and when he had given thanks, he broke it and said, 'This is my body that is for you. Do this in remembrance of me.' In the same way he took the cup also, after supper, saying, 'This cup is the new covenant in my blood. Do this, as often as you drink it, in remembrance of me.'* (1 Corinthians 11:23-25)

Just before he died, Jesus shared his last meal with his friends. This meal is now known as the Last Supper. Jesus was thinking of his own death, which was soon to happen. He died to bring forgiveness for the sins of all and he wanted to leave the apostles with a **memorial** of this event.

KNOW WHAT
Why is the Last Supper known as a memorial supper?

The Last Supper as a Passover Meal

Jesus linked his death and resurrection to the escape of the Israelites from slavery in Egypt. Moses told the Israelites, on the night of their escape from Egypt, to kill and roast a lamb so that they would have a good meal inside them for their long journey, during which they would 'pass over' from slavery to freedom. The blood of the lamb was painted on their door-frames to protect them from the great plague that was to strike Egypt. Moses then led them to freedom. Every year, Jews remember their escape from Egypt during their festival of **Passover**. They celebrate with a special Passover meal, at which they eat roast lamb, just as their ancestors did before leaving Egypt.

At the Passover meal, Jewish people remember how Moses led the Israelites from slavery to freedom. Jesus ate the Last Supper at the time of Passover, so it was a Passover meal. Jesus, by his life and death, showed the way to new freedom and new life for all his followers. The blood of the lamb reminded the Jewish people of the journey of their ancestors from slavery to freedom. Jesus is sometimes called the Lamb of God because, by his death, he too led the people to a new freedom.

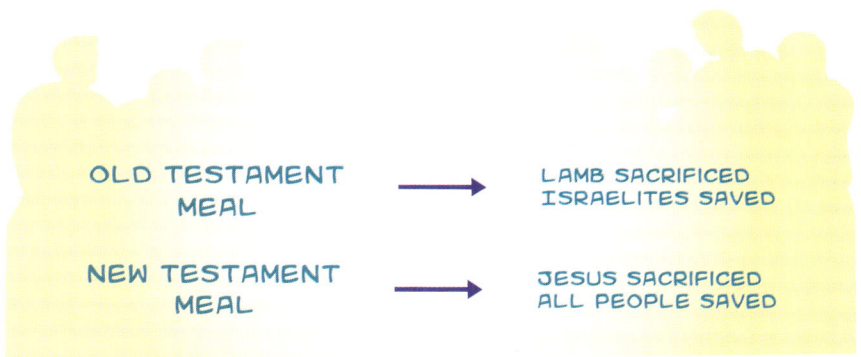

(You will learn more about the Passover festival in Section C.)

KNOW WHAT
1. Briefly explain the tradition behind the Passover meal.
2. What is the connection between the Passover meal and the Last Supper?
3. Why is Jesus sometimes called the Lamb of God?

The Last Supper as Eucharist

The Acts of the Apostles tells us that the first Christians gathered in one another's houses to celebrate the 'Breaking of the Bread', or **Eucharist**, as it has become known. 'Eucharist' literally means 'to give thanks'. It is the name that Christians have given to the sacrament based on the command of Jesus at the Last Supper: 'Do this in memory of me.' The apostles, the first Christians, did again what Jesus had done at the Last Supper.

They repeated the actions and words of Jesus by blessing and sharing the bread and wine among the group, just as Jesus had asked them to do. They knew, as they did this, that Jesus was really present with them. He was present under the appearances of bread and wine. When they shared the bread and wine, he was with each one of them, giving them the strength and the confidence they needed to live as his followers. Nourished by the Eucharist and filled with praise and thanks for the gift of God's Son, Jesus, they went out to live like him.

From Lanfranco's 'The Last Supper'

Every Eucharist is a memorial of this Last Supper because every Eucharist makes real for us again the life, death and resurrection of Jesus.

KNOW WHAT

1. What is the connection between the Last Supper and the Eucharist?
2. Why did the earliest followers of Jesus feel nourished and strengthened by the Eucharist?

DIGGING DEEPER

Read the story of the Last Supper in Mark 14:12-26 before answering the following questions.

1. How do you think Jesus felt during the Last Supper?
2. Tell the story of the Last Supper from the point of view of either Peter or Judas. Remember that both were faithful followers of Jesus, who would soon betray him in one way or another.

Memorial: An action that recalls the past. The Eucharist is a memorial because it recalls and makes present the actions of Jesus at the Last Supper and it reminds us that the Risen Jesus continues to be with us.

Passover: The name given to the meal and the festival that celebrates God's action in freeing the Hebrew people from slavery in Egypt.

Eucharist: Literally 'to give thanks'. It is the name that Christians give to the sacrament based on the command of Jesus: 'Do this in memory of me.' Also used to refer specifically to the body and blood of Christ, who is truly present in the Eucharist under the appearances of bread and wine.

LESSON 42 The Passion of Jesus

GROUNDWORK
In this lesson we plan to:
- read and become familiar with the gospel accounts of the death of Jesus.

DIGGING DEEPER
How does the passion of Christ impact on the lives of Christians today?

Key Concepts
Sacrifice/Martyrdom

The Passion of Jesus refers to his great suffering between the night of the Last Supper and his death on the cross. All over the world today, there are people who are suffering. The following story is a tale of great suffering and, unfortunately, it is a story that continues to unfold.

Story: Innocent Voices

Innocent Voices is a film based on the true story of screenwriter Oscar Torres' difficult childhood. It is a story about Chava, an eleven-year-old boy who suddenly becomes the 'man of the house' when his father leaves the family in the middle of a civil war. The story is based in El Salvador in Central America in the 1980s. At that time, the government's armed forces were recruiting twelve-year-olds to fight against the peasant rebels. Young boys were snatched from their classrooms or caught on the streets. In the film, Chava has just one year of childhood left. On his twelfth birthday, he will be recruited to fight in the government's war. Chava's life becomes a game of survival, not only from the bullets of the war, but also from the tension and conflict that wars always bring. By day, he tries to make money to pay the bills and by night he tries to keep alive the childish spirits of his brother and sister. All the while, he runs for his life and hides from the army sweeps. The tension of battle is all around.

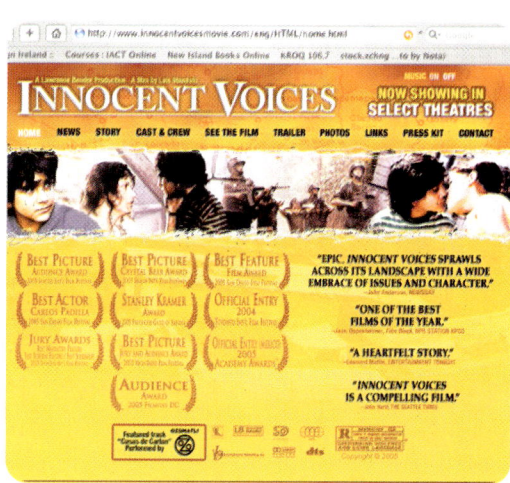

Unfortunately, Oscar Torres' story is not unique. Today, an estimated 300,000 child soldiers – boys and girls under the age of eighteen – are taking part in more than thirty conflicts worldwide. Many are as young as Chava. Wars kill and maim children, forcing them out of their childhood and disrupting their societies. For decades, organisations like UNICEF have worked to help children affected by armed conflict.

KNOW WHAT
1. What does the title tell us about the film?
2. Why was Chava's life full of tension and conflict?
3. What did he do to make the best of his situation?
4. What does this story tell us about the violence and terror that always accompanies armed conflict?

DIGGING DEEPER

What do you think could help in difficult situations such as the one outlined above?

Find out more about this award-winning film on *www.innocentvoicesmovie.com*.

Sacrifice

What does the word 'sacrifice' mean to you? Look at the following pictures and, in each case, outline what the sacrifice might be.

Jesus sacrificed himself for others by giving his time and energy to do what God wanted and to love others as himself. Jesus knew that he would be killed if he continued to preach his message, but he was prepared to suffer and even to die in order to do so. He made this huge sacrifice because of his love for God and for all God's people. He knew that, through his sacrifice, others would enter the new life of the Kingdom of God because his Spirit would pour into their hearts.

KNOW WHAT

1. Lent is a special time of sacrifice for Christians. Explain why this is so.
2. Have you ever made a sacrifice during Lent? Discuss your answer in class.

Martyrdom

The word 'martyr' comes from the Greek word for 'witness'. The word 'witness' in this sense describes someone who stands up for what they believe in, even if there is a heavy price to be paid for doing so. Jesus gave his whole life as a witness to God's love, particularly in his death on the cross. Ever since, people who have died for their faith have been called martyrs. St Stephen is the first martyr to be mentioned after the death of Jesus. (You can read about his death in Acts 6.) His feast day is on 26 December. This day was chosen to link Stephen directly with Jesus. Like Jesus, Stephen was a witness to belief in God's love, even in the face of death.

KNOW IT ALL

Copy the following into your Religion folder and complete the sentences.

1. A martyr is…
2. St Stephen was a martyr because …
3. 26 December is the feast of St Stephen because…

The Gospel Accounts of the Passion and Death of Jesus

The early Christians would have heard the story of Jesus' sacrifice in his passion (suffering) and death. This story was an important part of Christianity's first oral tradition – the first preaching of the apostles. (See Acts 2:32, 36; 5:30-31; 10:39-40.) While the accounts of the passion and death of Jesus are different in places, they all share a broadly similar order of events.

Class Task

Divide your class into four groups. Each group must read and summarise, in poster or role-play format, a gospel account of the death of Jesus. The gospel references are as follows:

The arrest of Jesus: Mark 14:26-52; Matthew 26:30-56; Luke 22:39-53; John 18:1-12.

Before the Temple authorities and Peter's denial: Mark 14:53-72; Matthew 26:57–27:10; Luke 22:54-71; John 18:13-27.

Roman trial: Mark:15:1-20; Matthew 27:11-31; Luke 23:1-25; John 18:28 – 19:16a.

Crucifixion, death and burial: Mark 15:21-47; Matthew 27:32-66; Luke 23:26-56; John 19:16b-42.

When each group is familiar with the gospel accounts of the death of Jesus, have a go at the following table quiz. The class should divide up into equal-sized teams.

Table Quiz on the Passion and Death of Jesus

There are eighty points in total to be awarded, two for each correct answer. Where there are two parts in an answer, the team is awarded two points for each correct part.

Round 1 (12 points)

1. At what place did Jesus arrive? — 2 points
2. Which three apostles were with him? — 2 points
3. What did the three apostles do? — 2 points
4. Who arrived with some armed men? — 2 points
5. Who sent them? — 2 points
6. What did Jesus say when he was arrested? — 2 points

Round 2 (22 points)

1. Who questioned Jesus? — 2 points
2. What were the two main questions the Sanhedrin asked of Jesus? — 2x2 points
3. When false witnesses gave conflicting evidence suggesting that Jesus said he would destroy the Temple, what did Jesus say? — 2 points
4. What was the name of the High Priest? — 2 points
5. What did he ask Jesus? — 2 points
6. What was Jesus' answer? — 2 points
7. How was Jesus treated by those who questioned him? — 2 points
8. What was happening at the same time, out in the courtyard? — 2 points
9. What did Peter say? — 2 points
10. When the truth of what he had done dawned on Peter, what did he do? — 2 points

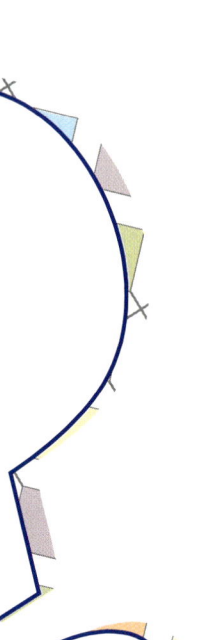

Round 3 (18 points)

1. What happened the following morning? — 2 points
2. Who was Pilate? — 2 points
3. What did he ask Jesus? — 2 points
4. How did Jesus react to this question? — 2 points
5. Pilate proposed to release Jesus. What did the chief priests want Pilate to do? — 2 points
6. What was Pilate's final decision? (Two parts) — 2x2 points
7. What did the soldiers do to Jesus? (Two parts) — 2x2 points

Round 4 (28 points)

1. To where did Jesus carry the cross? — 2 points
2. How many times did the weight of the cross cause Jesus to fall? — 2 points
3. Who intervened and helped Jesus to carry the cross? — 2 points
4. Who else did Jesus meet on this journey? — 2 points
5. Who wiped his face? — 2 points
6. Who gambled for Jesus' clothes? — 2 points
7. How long did Jesus suffer the torture of crucifixion? — 2 points
8. What psalm did Jesus cry out? — 2 points
9. What were the words of that psalm? — 2 points
10. What happened next? (Two parts) — 2x2 points
11. What well-known Jew asked Pilate for the body of Jesus? — 2 points
12. What was this man given permission to do? (Two parts) — 2x2 points

KNOW IT ALL

1. Which of the following characters feature in all four gospel accounts of the passion (suffering) and death of Jesus?
   Jesus/Peter/Judas/The Pharisees/The Jewish Temple authorities/Mary/The apostles/Pilate/Pilate's wife/Herod/A centurion/Barabbas/The young man who runs away when Jesus is arrested/Caiaphas, the High Priest/Simon of Cyrene
2. List the events that happened during the last week of Jesus' life. How did these events influence/affect the followers of Jesus?

DIGGING DEEPER

How do you think the passion (suffering) of Christ impacts on the lives of people today?

KNOW HOW

'The Stations of the Cross' are a Christian meditation on the passion of Jesus. They are a powerful way to contemplate the last journey of Jesus. Divide into groups and present the Stations of the Cross as a set of posters or role-play each scene. Each group must present their station and explain what is happening.

 **Sacrifice:** Giving of oneself out of love in order to achieve a goal or purpose.

Martyrdom: Suffering or being put to death because of your religious beliefs.

LESSON 43 The Resurrection of Jesus

GROUNDWORK
In this lesson we plan to:
- explore the resurrection of Jesus.

DIGGING DEEPER
When do I celebrate the Resurrection of Jesus?

Key Concept
Resurrection

The Resurrection

The story of Jesus did not end on the cross. An amazing thing happened on the third day after Jesus' death: God raised Jesus from the dead. This event is called the **Resurrection** and it is recorded in the gospels.

The death of Jesus must have been a very difficult experience for the disciples. They had developed a deep and loyal relationship with Jesus, whom they looked up to as their leader, but now he was dead and they were alone. Of course, they were frightened and fearful of what was coming next, and some of them lost all hope and ran away, while others huddled together and tried to come to terms with their grief. Jesus had told them that he would be with them always, and now their faith was being tested. It is important to look at the Resurrection with this setting or background in mind.

DIGGING DEEPER
Were you ever told that something amazing was going to happen and you didn't quite believe it. Then, it happened. Describe what happened and your reaction to it.

The Gospel Accounts of the Resurrection

There were no witnesses to the actual resurrection of Jesus. The gospels tell us about what happened after the Resurrection.

Before answering the questions given below, read the following gospel accounts of the Resurrection: Mark 16:1-8, Luke 24:1-12, John 20:1-10.

KNOW WHAT
1. How did Mary and Joanna feel when they found the empty tomb?
2. How do you think you would have felt?
3. Who told the women that Jesus had risen from the dead?
4. Why would the women have been afraid?
5. Which of the apostles arrived at the tomb?
6. Peter and the other apostles knew that Jesus had said he would rise again in three days, and this was the third day. Would you say they felt better or worse because of this knowledge?

DIGGING DEEPER
When do we celebrate the resurrection of Jesus?

Class Activity

Form into groups of five and act out the following drama based on Luke's account of the Resurrection.

Drama: The Mystery of the Empty Tomb

Joshua: (Broadcaster) Good morning, Jerusalem! You're listening to 2JM Radio and this is Joshua Johnson with *Sabbath Sequence*, the religious affairs programme. Later, we'll have a report from the Temple, where eighteen thousand Passover lambs were slaughtered without a hitch. But before that, let's turn to the report we received early this morning, about the disappearance of a body from a new tomb outside Jerusalem. We sent our reporter, Daniel, along. He's on the line now. Hello Daniel! What can you tell us?

Daniel: (Outside broadcast reporter) Good morning, Joshua. I am standing in the garden where the tomb of Jesus of Nazareth is located. Jesus was crucified last Friday, and his body was put in a tomb belonging to Joseph of Arimathea. Some time in the last thirty-six hours the tomb was opened, and the body of Jesus is no longer there. I have Mary of Magdala with me here. She is one of the women who found the tomb open and empty. Mary and Joanna, what brought you to the tomb this morning?

Mary: We came here at first light to finish the burial properly, with spices. We hadn't enough time on Friday — the sun was about to set and we had to get home for the start of Sabbath. When we got here this morning, the huge stone that covered the entrance to the tomb had been rolled away, the body was gone and the tomb was empty.

Daniel: What was your reaction, Mary?

Mary: We couldn't understand it. I dropped the spices in fright. I took a better look and found the linen cloth lying where Jesus' body had been.

Daniel: Could you have made a mistake and gone to the wrong tomb?

Mary: Absolutely not. You don't forget where someone is buried.

Daniel: Joanna, let me turn to you. You were with Mary when you discovered that the body was missing. What happened next?

Joanna: All of a sudden, the place seemed very bright and there were two people speaking to us. 'Why are you looking for the living among the dead?' they said. 'He is not here. He has risen.' Then they reminded us of what Jesus said when he was in Galilee: 'The Son of Man must be crucified and three days later rise to life.' We were terrified.

Daniel: What did you do then?

KNOW THE WAY

Joanna:	We ran back to the city to the room where the other friends of Jesus were hiding. Mary got there first.
Mary:	I was out of breath when I got there. I told them that the tomb was empty and that we had been told that Jesus had risen from the dead.
Daniel:	How did they react?
Joanna:	They told us that we were in shock after Friday and to go home and rest. We couldn't, so we came back here instead. They didn't believe us.
Daniel:	Hold on a moment. Someone has just rushed past us into the tomb. I think it is Peter. *(Goes after Peter)* Peter, why are you here?
Peter:	I wanted to see for myself. The tomb is empty, just as Mary said. I'm really puzzled and a bit frightened.
Daniel:	What do you think has happened?
Peter:	I don't know. Jesus told us that he would suffer and die and that in three days he would rise — and this is the third day.
Daniel:	Peter, what do you say about the rumours that one of your own people stole the body to make it look like Jesus had risen from the dead?
Peter:	That's mad! How would we remove that stone and carry a dead body without being seen? Why would we leave the linen cloth behind?
Daniel:	What do you and the other disciples intend to do now?
Peter:	I'll tell the other disciples what I've seen here. I don't know what conclusions to draw. We need more to go on. We'll have to lie low for a while and see if there are any further developments.
Daniel:	Well, that's all from here for the time being. We go back now to the studio to rejoin Joshua Johnson and the *Sabbath Sequence* team.

 Resurrection: The event in which Jesus was raised to new life after his death on the cross.

See page 488 for past exam questions on this topic.

LESSON 44 The Appearances of Jesus after the Resurrection

GROUNDWORK
In this lesson we plan to:
- explore the impact of the resurrection appearances on the followers of Jesus.

DIGGING DEEPER
How does the resurrection of Jesus impact on the lives of Christians?

 **Key Concepts**
Resurrection/Transformation/Presence

After Jesus' death, the disciples felt alone and afraid. They were unsure as to what would happen next. Jesus had promised them that his death would not be the end. But the events that had just occurred tested their faith. In the following story, young Oisín puts his faith in Brad… and his faith pays off.

Story: Going for Gold

Oisín had trained hard on Brad. Brad was a good horse and Oisín knew he would give a top performance on Saturday. His dream of being a champion show-jumper was on the verge of becoming a reality.

During the week, Oisín was nervous. 'Sure that's to be expected, young fella,' said Carmel, his trainer, 'but don't let Brad feel your nerves. You'll put him off his stroke, you know.'

Six a.m. on Saturday morning, Oisín and Brad rode out over the hills of Meath. Oisín felt a wonderful calmness as they cantered across the fields with only the dew and the birds for company.

His nerves were a little less calm later in the day when he prepared to enter the arena with Brad in Dublin's RDS stadium. After an endless number of show-jumping events, their turn had finally come. A huge cry from the loudspeaker filled the air: 'Oisín Breathnach, number six, to take arena number two, with Brad, for the final gold.'

'Go for gold, Brad, go for gold,' Oisín whispered, just before the off. 'Elegant', 'skilled' and 'accurate' were the words the commentator used as Oisín and Brad cleared every jump without touching a cross-pole.

The final double fence was waiting. Oisín glanced at the large arena clock and knew they were okay for time. He steadied Brad and prepared himself for the jump. Oisín could feel Brad's stride pattern and it was perfect. In one fluid motion, they soared into the air and effortlessly

landed safely on the other side. Everyone rose to their feet and gave a thunderous applause. 'Yes!' cried Oisín, as he threw his arms around Brad's neck, 'I knew we could do it. I knew we could win the gold!'

KNOW WHAT
1. How do you think Oisín felt at the end of the final round?
2. What do you think made him happier – winning, or the fact that he and Brad had gone for gold together? Explain your answer.
3. What do you think was the impact of the win for Oisín?

DIGGING DEEPER
1. Write about an event in your life that you had prepared for and were anxious about. How did things work out?
2. What do you think causes major events in our lives to have different impacts/effects on us and on the people around us?

Transformation and Presence

On Easter Sunday, the tomb in which Jesus was buried was found empty. The body of Jesus was no longer there. At first, those who visited the tomb thought that the body must have been stolen or hidden, and they were shocked. The followers of Jesus had to wait until the **resurrection** appearances to find out what had really happened.

When they met the Risen Jesus, they did not recognise him because he was different – he was **transformed**. But after he had spoken to them, they were convinced that it was truly Jesus.

The resurrection of Jesus was not the revival of a dead body. Although Jesus still had the marks of his crucifixion, his body was transformed into a new and glorious body. Death had no more power over him.

The friends of Jesus realised that from now on he would always be with them because he was alive in this new way. They would always feel his **presence** among them.

Jesus Appears to Two Friends on the Road to Emmaus

On the same day that Mary Magdalene and the other women discovered the empty tomb, two of Jesus' disciples, Cleopas and a friend, were walking with a heavy step to a small village outside Jerusalem, called Emmaus. The curious events of the day dominated their sad conversation. 'What are you talking about?' a stranger enquired. Taken aback, Cleopas replied, 'Surely you must be aware what has happened here in Jerusalem in these last few days?' 'What things?' the man asked. So they explained all about Jesus and all that he had done before being crucified by the Roman authorities. 'But the strangest thing of all is that his body is no longer in the tomb. It has disappeared off the face of the earth.' 'If only you had believed the holy prophets!' the man replied, and he began to explain all that the scriptures had said about these things. Later that evening, they invited the man to share a meal with them. As they were eating, he broke the bread and gave thanks. At that moment, they realised that it was Jesus, but he vanished before them. 'That explains our excitement as he was talking to us along the road,' they said. Without delay, the two friends hurried back to Jerusalem. Bursting in on the apostles, they told them all that happened on their journey. 'It's true, the Lord is alive again!' they said. (Adapted from Luke 24:13-35)

KNOW WHAT
1. Have a go at drawing five cartoons that explain the Emmaus story and write one caption under each cartoon.
2. When did the disciples realise that it was Jesus who was with them and why do you think they came to this realisation?

Jesus Appears to the Eleven Apostles

Peter returned to Jerusalem to tell the other eleven apostles about the empty tomb. He found them gathered in a room with some other companions. Then Cleopas and his friend joined them, and they all told of the events that had occurred. When the others heard their stories, they were filled with excitement and they began shouting, 'Jesus is alive! He has risen.'

Suddenly, the room went quiet. There, in the middle of them, stood Jesus. 'Peace be with you,' he said.

The apostles were afraid and unsure of how they should react. Jesus reassured them by saying, 'Why are you alarmed? Look at my hands and my feet, see the wound in my side from the nails and the spear.'

He then said to them, 'Come and eat.' Because he ate with them, they realised that Jesus was not a ghost. They ate together and then he began to talk to them and remind them of what he had taught them through his words and actions. He talked about the Law of Moses, the writings of the prophets and the psalms. He reminded them of how it was foretold in the Old Testament that the Messiah would suffer and then rise from the dead three days later. In this way, Jesus helped them to understand the true meaning of the Scriptures and of all that had happened to him.

After this, the apostles stopped being afraid and they grew in courage and confidence. Soon, they became excited and eager to spread the Good News. Jesus asked them to wait in Jerusalem until he had sent the Holy Spirit to help them.

KNOW WHAT
1. Why do you think the apostles were tense and unsure of how to react when Jesus first appeared among them?
2. What did Jesus do and say to reassure them?
3. What did Jesus ask the apostles to wait for in Jerusalem?
4. Why was this worth waiting for?

KNOW IT ALL
You will need a Bible to answer the following questions.

1. What happened in Luke 24:1-12?
2. What was the name of the village mentioned later in the story, in Luke 24:13-25?
3. Where did Jesus appear to the group in Luke 24:36-49?
4. What happened in Luke 24:50-53?

The Impact of the Resurrection

When the followers of Jesus realised that he had risen from the dead, they were confident once again. Jesus had not abandoned them, but had come back to them as he had promised, to be with them until the end of time. Now they fully understood who he was. The resurrection of Jesus from the dead and his subsequent appearances finally revealed to his followers that he was more than they could ever have imagined. Jesus had surely come from God: 'Whoever has seen me has seen the Father' (John 14:9).

Imagine the joy and the excitement that followed such a difficult time of grief and hopelessness. The followers of Jesus were no longer alone. After the Resurrection, the words and actions of Jesus took on a new meaning for them. They now knew that:

- Jesus had overcome death and would be with them always.
- Jesus truly was the awaited Messiah.
- Jesus was the Son of God.

All of this had a wonderful effect on the followers of Jesus. They celebrated Christ's victory over death and were ready to be his co-workers for the Kingdom of God and to go and spread the Good News. Now they would prepare to be strengthened by the Holy Spirit.

DIGGING DEEPER
1. How do you think the resurrection appearances affected the followers of Jesus?
2. How do you think the resurrection of Jesus affects the followers of Jesus today?
3. The disciples didn't fully understand that Jesus was God's Son until after his death and resurrection. After the death of Jesus, they learned more about who he really was. How do you think this helped them to understand more about the things he had said and done during the time they spent with him?

The Ascension of Jesus

For forty days after his resurrection from the dead, Jesus appeared to the apostles from time to time. Gradually he explained to them that it would soon be time for him to leave and return to his Father. He reminded them of the promise he made to them at the Last Supper, that he would send the Holy Spirit to help and guide them.

Then Jesus took them with him to the hillside near Bethany, where they had so often stayed. Jesus told them: 'Go therefore and make disciples of all nations, baptising them in the name of the Father and of the Son and of the Holy Spirit, and teaching them to obey everything that I have commanded you. And remember, I am with you always, to the end of the age' (Matthew 28:19-20).

Then he said goodbye. The last words of Luke's gospel read:

'While he was blessing them, he withdrew from them and was carried up into heaven.'

KNOW WHAT
1. What is the Ascension?
2. What three things did Jesus say to the apostles before he returned to the Father?
3. How do you think the apostles felt after the Ascension?

DIGGING DEEPER
Before Jesus ascended into heaven, he assured the apostles that he would be with them always, until the end of time. What is it like to be reassured and made feel confident at a time when you are worried or nervous? Write about a time when you felt reassured and filled with confidence.

Transformation: A core change in a person or thing, i.e. a change in essential qualities or character or way of life.

Presence: Opposite of absence. Something seen or felt or heard or available.

See pages 488–489 for past exam questions on this topic.

KNOW THE WAY

Faith in Christ

LESSON 45 The First Christian Communities

GROUNDWORK
In this lesson we plan to:
- explore of the emerging identity and development of the first Christian communities.

DIGGING DEEPER
What happened when the Good News was first preached?

Key Concepts
Pentecost/ Missionary

Pentecost – The Coming of the Holy Spirit

Pentecost is the name given to the day when the followers of Jesus experienced God's gift of the Holy Spirit, as promised by Jesus. The following 'interview' with the apostle Peter is based on the events of that day.

An interview with Peter the Apostle

The apostles of Jesus have come out of hiding. They are preaching openly in Jerusalem about Jesus and his message. Moshe, a reporter from the local radio station, has spoken with Peter, the leader of the group. Here is his report.

Moshe: How long were you hiding out and what did you expect to happen?

Peter: We waited for days. We were waiting for what Jesus promised before he left. He promised to send the Holy Spirit to help us and to give us courage.

145

Moshe: What was it like for you as you waited on the Holy Spirit to arrive?

Peter: At first I wondered if it would ever happen. How could we hope for better than Jesus, our Master?

Moshe: So, would you say you had sort of given up then?

Peter: No. We kept telling each other that Jesus would not forget us. Because Jesus had appeared to us, we wanted to tell the Good News of his resurrection. We wanted to carry on the work Jesus began. But we lacked confidence. How were we to do this by ourselves?

Moshe: Peter, can you describe for us exactly what happened that changed you?

Peter: Well, we had locked ourselves in this room. We were afraid. We prayed together. Then we heard a noise like a wind blowing through the whole house. We were frightened. No one moved. Suddenly the room began to feel very bright and warm. I looked up and saw over our heads what looked like tongues of fire. They spread out over us. I felt a surge of life run through me, as if my life had begun again.

Moshe: What difference has the Holy Spirit made to you and the other friends of Jesus?

Peter: Before this we were lost, lonely and afraid. In spite of our failings, we are now strong, full of hope and confidence. We are changed. Somehow, foreign visitors can understand us, even though we don't speak their language. Isn't that amazing?

Moshe: Yes, it really is. What reaction have you got so far?

Peter: We were so excited that some people thought we were drunk. We are driven by God's Spirit in our hearts. It must be working! People are amazed when they hear our story of Jesus. Many become believers and get baptised. Some three thousand people joined our group – and that was just on the first day!

Moshe: That's really incredible, Peter. I wish you and your fellow apostles every success in your mission. That's all for now from the Holy City.

KNOW WHAT
Why do you think the apostles felt as they did before and after the coming of the Holy Spirit?

KNOW THE WAY

DIGGING DEEPER
Imagine you are one of the people who listed to Peter and chose to become a believer and be baptised. Describe what it was about his message that impressed you and what changes being a Christian will bring about in your life.

KNOWING ME KNOWING YOU
Interview a friend who has been confirmed and ask them the following questions.

1. How did you feel on the morning of your Confirmation?
2. What preparation did you do in school and at home?
3. What did the bishop say to you at your Confirmation?
4. How did the bishop confirm you?
5. How were you strengthened by the Holy Spirit?
6. How was your Confirmation Day a day of celebration for your family?
7. Think of four words to describe the day.

KNOW HOW
Make a wall chart with the title 'Pentecost' using a collage of some of the words and quotes from your interviews.

Christian Missionaries
We have often watched movies about superheroes engaged in a mission (task), so we will have some understanding that a mission usually involves tough and tiring work. Christian **missionaries** are not superheroes, but they do engage in demanding and difficult work. Christian missionaries are involved in a mission for their faith. That mission involves telling others about the Good News of God's kingdom and inviting their response. The disciples were sent out as missionaries and they worked hard to spread the Good News and build the early Christian community.

KNOW WHAT
Why did the disciples become missionaries and what did their work involve?

The Early Christian Community
There were difficult times ahead for the early Christian community. The established Jewish community and the new 'Christian' movement didn't always get on, and the gap between them widened as the Christian community grew and Gentiles (non-Jewish people) were accepted into it. This led to official Judaism breaking formal links with Christianity, which made life very difficult for Christians; they were now unpopular both with the Roman Empire, who considered them a security threat, and with the Jewish authorities. As time passed and it became obvious that the Christian movement was growing rapidly, the opposition to Christianity turned violent and the Christian community had to become almost a secret organisation.

The Christian community in Jerusalem consisted mostly of Jewish Christians (Jews who had become Christians). Antioch, the capital of Syria, was where the first community of Gentile Christians lived. The Christian community in Antioch grew as Christians fled from Jerusalem, where Christianity was outlawed. It was at Antioch that the name Christian was first given to the followers of Jesus. One of the challenges that faced the early Christian community was the tension between the Jewish and Gentile Christians.

KNOW IT ALL

Copy the following exercise into your Religion folder and fill in the blanks.

The disciples worked as m _____ for their faith.
The early C _____ c _____ had to face difficult times.
Both J _____ and G _____ were accepted into the Christian community.
The Christian community became unpopular with both the R _____ authorities and the J _____ authorities.
Opposition became violent, so the Christian community had to become almost a s _____ o _____ .
Many of the Jewish Christians lived in J _____ .
The Gentile Christians lived in A _____ , the capital of S _____ .
It was in Antioch that the name C _____ was first given to the followers of Jesus.
A major challenge for the first Christians was the t _____ between the Jewish Christians and the Gentile Christians.

Pentecost: The day, described in Acts 2, when the followers of Jesus experienced God's gift of the Holy Spirit.

Missionary: The word used to describe a person or community that continues the work of Jesus, telling others about the Good News of God's kingdom and inviting their response.

LESSON 46 The Characteristics of the First Christian Communities

GROUNDWORK
In this lesson we plan to:
- compare and contrast the early faith communities with modern faith communities.

DIGGING DEEPER
What is the difference between the early followers of Jesus and the followers of Jesus today?

Key Concept
People of God

The Growth of the First Christian Communities

In the Acts of the Apostles, we learn that the apostles were inspired by the gift of the Holy Spirit at Pentecost and immediately went out on to the streets of Jerusalem and began preaching. The result was instant: 'So those who welcomed Peter's message were baptised, and that day about three thousand persons were added' (Acts 2:41). Soon Christianity spread from Jerusalem all over Palestine and then to the non-Jewish people in neighbouring countries.

The People of God

The Kingdom of God is made up of the **People of God**. Through his words and deeds, Jesus made it clear that everyone was welcome to join the People of God. Jesus summed up how the People of God were to live when he said:

> 'I give you a new commandment: love one another. As I have loved you, so you must love one another.' (John 13:34)

Faith

The early Christian communities put their faith and trust in the Risen Jesus. They believed that Jesus was the Son of God, the Messiah, and they knew that they were the People of God. They listened to the Good News, they believed it and, therefore, they lived it.

Because of their strong belief and faith in the Good News, they too began to work for the Kingdom of God. Their faith led them to live in a particular way – as the People of God working for the Kingdom of God.

Worship

The early Christian communities prayed and worshipped together. They were faithful to the teachings of the apostles and to their own mission as newly baptised Christians. They celebrated the Lord's Supper and spent time praying in their homes and in the Temple.

> Day by day, as they spent much time together in the temple, they broke bread at home and ate their food with glad and generous hearts, praising God and having the goodwill of all the people. And day by day the Lord added to their number those who were being saved. (Acts 2:46-47)

Way of Life

As the Good News about Jesus spread, more and more people recognised him as the Messiah. They tried to live their lives according to his commandment to love one another. There was evidence all around them of injustice in society. There were rich people who had plenty, while many people were in need. The followers of Jesus took seriously their responsibility as Christians to love one another; they shared what they had and cared for the weak and the outsiders of society, the poor and the sick.

They would sell their possessions and goods and distribute the proceeds to all, as any had need. (Acts 2:45)

Community

People lived in community and were led by ministers called bishops and elders. These people were gifted in leadership, teaching and preaching. Every community had people with different gifts but they all worked together for the good of the community.

For just as the body is one and has many members, and all the members of the body, though many, are one body, so it is with Christ. (1 Corinthians 12:12)

KNOW IT ALL

Write about the characteristics of the first Christian communities under the following headings:

- A people of faith
- A worshipping people
- A people of action
- A people in community

Modern Faith Communities

There are many wonderful examples of Christians working as communities of faith in the world today. One such community is 'Restoration Ministries'.

The word 'restoration' means repairing or restoring. Restoration Ministries is a faith-driven organisation that aims to restore and strengthen the faith and confidence of people who have been hurt by others and by life.

In Restoration Ministries, people find:

- someone to talk to;
- someone to pray with;
- someone to listen.

Restoration Ministries is a multi-denominational organisation, i.e. it is made up of people from different religious backgrounds.

From its base at Restoration House in Dunmurry, County Antrim, this community engages in a ministry of reconciliation (forgiveness), healing, listening, hospitality and prayer. It provides:

- a place of safety, where people can tell their story and be heard;
- a place where people are helped to develop a vision;
- a place where people can feel welcomed and loved.

'Jesus' prayer was that we might be one so that the world would believe.'

Through networking around the world, but particularly in Ireland, under the guidance of the Holy Spirit, Restoration Ministries seeks:

- to be an image of unity in a world with so many divisions and differences;
- to be an effective inspiration in this world;
- to see others develop a ministry of restoration (healing).

KNOW WHAT
1. What is the faith community of Restoration Ministries about?
2. How does this faith community live according to the teachings of Jesus?
3. How do those involved in Restoration Ministries show their faith in God?
4. How do those involved in Restoration Ministries worship God?

DIGGING DEEPER
1. 'Restoration Ministries is a faith-driven organisation.' Explain what this statement means.
2. Describe two things about Restoration Ministries that are the same as the early Christian communities and two that are different. Discuss your answers in class.
3. Name two other modern faith communities and describe the work they do.
(If you look back on Section A, you will find more examples of modern Christian faith communities at work.)

You can find out more about Restoration Ministries at www.restorationministries.co.uk

 **People of God:** The term used to describe the Hebrew people whom God freed from slavery in Egypt. In Christian use, it is the name given to the community of those who believe in Jesus. (See Acts 2:44-46 for the first written description.)

151

LESSON 47 Titles for Jesus (Higher Level)

GROUNDWORK
In this lesson we plan to:
- deepen our understanding of the meanings attached to the various titles for Jesus.

DIGGING DEEPER
What do the titles of Jesus tell us about him?

Key Concepts
Son of Man/Son of God/New Creation/Christ/Messiah

What's in a Name?

Write an acrostic poem based on your name. Then share what you have written with your classmates.

After viewing all the acrostics, discuss the following questions.

1. What is the significance of a name?
2. Why do you think it is important to remember someone's name?

In this lesson, we will deepen our understanding of the meanings attached to the different titles/names for Jesus.

Jesus is Branded

When the religious authorities captured and questioned Jesus, they branded him as a false prophet. They also accused him of having political ambitions against the Romans. Jesus' disciples – particularly Peter, who was supposed to be the leader – totally abandoned him. On Easter Sunday, they were to get their first surprise – Jesus was risen, alive in a new way! Perhaps their second surprise was even greater: Jesus forgave them for abandoning him in his hour of need. In the space of a few days, they went from being people of deep despair to being people with a new and strong identity. With the help of the Holy Spirit, they went even further, to being people with a message – a message they wanted to pass on to others.

This was the background to their struggle to find titles that would help them to explain their experience of Jesus. If the religious authorities had tried to 'brand' Jesus as one thing, the friends and disciples of Jesus went on to 'brand' him as something else. They had to find new ways of talking about Jesus to the Jewish people of Palestine and to the Greek-speaking people who lived in neighbouring countries.

Son of Man

In Mark's gospel, Jesus uses the title **Son of Man** fourteen times when he describes himself. This was a term that would have been familiar to the disciples of Jesus, as it is found in two of the books of the Old Testament: Daniel and Ezekiel. In chapter 7 of the book of Daniel, the Son of Man is portrayed as:

- a heavenly representative of great power and dignity, who would show the true meaning of people's difficulties and sufferings;
- remaining faithful to God in the face of suffering;
- acting for God and for the people in the event of a final time of trial or crisis.

Jesus probably used the title because of his faithfulness to God, despite his suffering, and because he called others to be faithful too. However, this is not a title that lived on after the death of Jesus.

KNOW WHAT

1. How many times did Jesus describe himself as the Son of Man in Mark's gospel? Why did he use this term?
2. Give an example of how the Son of Man was described in the Old Testament.
3. Look up the following Bible references and summarise what Jesus said about his identity as the Son of Man: Mark 2:1-12 and Mark 10:32-34.

The Messiah/Christ

Because the friends and disciples of Jesus and the first Christian community were Jewish, they were brought up in expectation of the **Messiah**. They had learned that the Messiah was the one whom God would send to save the people. Because the country was occupied by the Romans, it was believed that the Messiah would be a political figure. People remembered the time when Israel was a great kingdom, free from occupation and ruled by King David. It seemed only right to them that the Messiah would be in some way related to David. The word 'Messiah' means 'one who has been anointed'. Kings are

The Tower of David

anointed to show their God-given authority. By using the word 'Messiah', they showed that they believed that this Messiah would be some kind of king. (The terms 'Messiah' and 'Christ' have the same meaning – Messiah is the Hebrew word and Christ is Greek.)

Jesus was not a political figure but one who made the ultimate sacrifice – facing suffering and death on the cross. This sacrifice united him with God. After Jesus' resurrection, his followers could clearly see that he had been sent by God and that he was the Messiah for whom they had been waiting. They re-read the Old Testament in the light of this and concluded that:

- the death of Jesus on the cross was predicted (foretold) in the Old Testament;
- Jesus had suffered just as the prophets before him had done;
- Jesus was the 'Suffering Servant' of whom the prophet Isaiah had spoken.

The use of the term Messiah showed the early followers of Christianity that the saviour who had been foretold by the scriptures had come to them. He had offered his body and blood for them and made himself a sacrifice for the whole world. Jesus truly was the Messiah.

KNOW WHAT
1. Find another place in the gospels where the title Messiah/Christ is used and write about the context (background) in which it was written.
2. How did the title Messiah/Christ influence the faith and practice of the early Christians?

KNOW HOW
Have a go at designing a poster that describes Jesus as the Messiah.

Son of God

It was not long before Jesus was heard of in the Greek-speaking world that surrounded Palestine. Some of the people there were aware of the Jewish traditions/prophecies about the Messiah, but some were not – particularly the Gentiles (those who were not Jews). Telling these people about the Risen Jesus in a meaningful way would need a different kind of language. The followers of Jesus turned to another term from the Old Testament, where God's power or word was spoken of as God's 'Son'.

> *Those in the boat worshipped him, saying, 'Truly you are the Son of God.'*
> (Matthew 14:33)

This new title, **Son of God**, was then used to describe the Risen Jesus. It referred to someone who was very close to God and committed to living as God wanted. This term helped the early Christians to understand the one-ness between God and God's Son, Jesus Christ. It emphasised the fact that Jesus was not just a very powerful human, but that he shared in the very nature of God. Jesus was the 'Son of God'.

> *For God so loved the world that he gave his only Son, so that everyone who believes in him may have eternal life.* (John 3:16)

This term is used many times in the gospel of St John. As this was the last gospel to be written, we can see that at this stage the early Christians were very aware of the relationship between God and Jesus Christ. They appreciated that Jesus was all that he said he was. They appreciated that to use the title 'Son of God' would help the people of God to understand and appreciate the bond between God and Jesus. Jesus' death was proof of his unique unity with God. This led to a deeper understanding of the mystery of God, which we call the Trinity.

KNOW WHAT
1. Where did the followers of Jesus find the title 'Son of God' for Jesus?
2. What did the title 'Son of God' refer to?
3. Why did they use this title?
4. When was this title used and fully understood?

New Creation

St Paul was a significant figure in the early Christian community. After his conversion on the road to Damascus, his life was totally transformed. He found a new purpose in life: sharing the Good News of the Risen Jesus with people, especially Gentiles. Paul used several images when describing Jesus to them, including **New Creation**. Although this term had been used in the Old Testament (for example, Isaiah 65 talks about God's promise to make all things new), Paul used it in a new way. He gave Jesus the title 'New Creation' because, in Jesus, God had done something very new that affected every human being. There was now a living link between the Risen Jesus and the People of God that would never be broken. Christians share in this new relationship by faith and by Baptism. Paul also says that the people of God express this unity in the Eucharist.

Some examples of Paul's use of the term 'New Creation' can be found in Colossians 1:15 and following verses, in 2 Corinthians 5:17 and in Ephesians 2:10.

TAKE FIVE

1. Who used the title 'New Creation' to describe Jesus?
2. Where was this term originally used?
3. How did Paul use it in a new way?
4. How do Christians share in this new relationship between the Risen Jesus and the People of God?
5. Look up one of the above Bible references for an example of a time when St Paul used this title for Jesus.

KNOW HOW

1. Design and create a backdrop for your school's Easter celebration, using the words: 'Jesus Christ, today, yesterday and forever.'

Or

2. Design four symbols, one for each of the four titles of Jesus.

DIGGING DEEPER

1. What do the varioius titles of Jesus tell us about him?
2. How could the titles of Jesus help to increase Christian faith?
3. Why is it possible to use all these titles to describe Jesus?

Son of Man: A title that Jesus gave himself, especially in the gospel according to Mark.

Christ/Messiah: 'Christ' and 'Messiah' are English versions of the same word in Greek and Hebrew, meaning 'anointed'. For the first Christians, Jesus was the Messiah promised by God, for whom the Jewish people had waited.

Son of God: A name for Jesus that helped Greek-speaking Gentiles to understand the unity of Jesus and God.

New Creation: St Paul described Jesus as God's 'New Creation' to underline how the presence of Jesus was God's new start in the world.

Judaism

The Context

LESSON 48 The Historical and Geographical Background of Judaism

GROUNDWORK
In this lesson we plan to:
- explore the historical and geographical background to life at the time of the foundation of Judaism.

DIGGING DEEPER
How did the historical and geographical background at the time of the foundation of Judaism affect the people?

Key Concepts
Location/Cultural context

MY BIRTH DAY!

I can feel it coming,
I know I'm on my way.
I think it's gonna happen,
My birthday'll be today.

Whoosh! I think I've landed,
I'm here, I'm here, it's me.
This place is full of colours.
There's lots and lots to see.

I'm born today, I'm shouting,
I can't believe it's true.
This is the first day
Of my whole life with you!

Location and Cultural Context

Imagine that you want to tell everyone about the place where you were born. Draw a map of your county, with the main towns marked and named. Include any rivers or mountains in your map. Then indicate the town in which you were born. You have now shown the **location** or place of your birth!

Now go a step further and give some details of what life is like in the country of your birth. You might like to include the following information in your account:

- The name of the political party that leads the government.
- The number one hit single.
- The most fashionable item of clothing for your age-group today.
- The cost of a newspaper or magazine.
- Two popular television programmes.
- The typical climate.
- The world religion(s) practised in your area.
- The kinds of jobs people have.
- The way people spend their free time.

Such information gives us a picture of the society and culture in which you live. We call this the **cultural context**.

The Origins of Judaism

Location

Judaism began almost four thousand years ago in a large area of land in the Middle East known as the Fertile Crescent. It stretches from the ancient city of Ur in Mesopotamia (modern-day Iraq), where Abraham was born, up and around an arc to Haran (where he began his journey to the Promised Land) and down to the land of Canaan (later to be known as Palestine). Three very important rivers water the Fertile Crescent: the Nile in Egypt and the Tigris and Euphrates in Mesopotamia.

KNOW HOW

Study the map opposite to find the location of the following places:

- The city of Ur
- Haran and the land of Canaan
- Mesopotamia
- The three large rivers
- The position of Canaan as a crossroads between Egypt and Mesopotamia

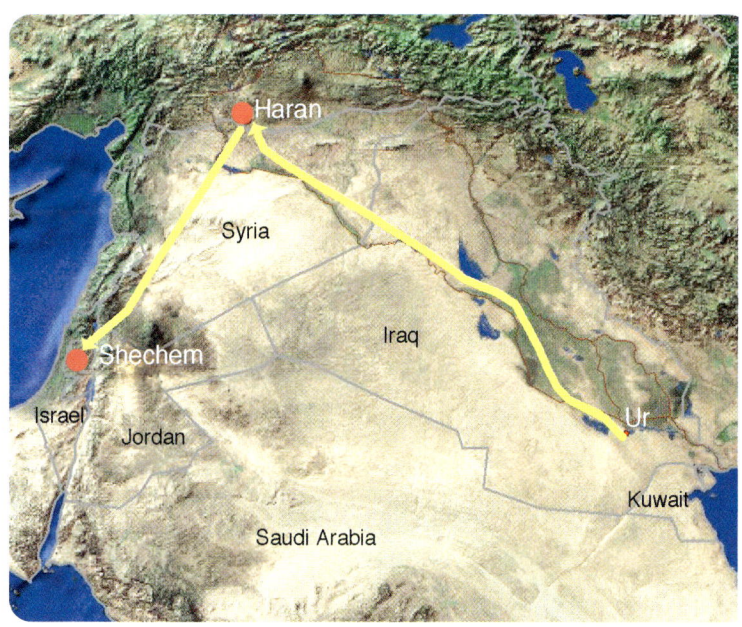

The Fertile Crescent

Cultural Context

At that time, many people lived a nomadic lifestyle as hunters and herders. As the land was fertile, wild wheat and barley grew in abundance. Gradually, these nomadic people settled down along the banks of the rivers, becoming the world's first farmers. This was a very different way of life for them, as these settlements were the first urban (city) dwellings in the land.

Although the climate was hot and dry, with seasonal flooding, the new farmers learned to control the flooding rivers and they were able to produce crops such as barley, wheat, flax, sesame and different kinds of fruit and vegetables. On the one hand, their lives were now less difficult, but on the other hand, they lost their simple way of life, as their tribal clans were replaced by a centralised political system and they had to adapt to the anonymity of a city lifestyle.

Important cities sprung up in the land of Mesopotamia. These walled cities were surrounded by smaller villages. The people lived in well-built houses and trading took place with passing merchants from distant lands. At the time of the origins of Judaism, Assyria and Babylonia were important states in Mesopotamia.

KNOW HOW

1. Draw a map of the journey travelled by Abraham and Sarah from Haran to the land of Canaan. Mark in the placenames of the surrounding area, e.g. Egypt and the Red Sea.
2. Try to imagine what the people's clothing would have been like at that time and give a brief description.
3. Describe the lifestyle of the nomadic people.
4. Briefly explain the kind of impact the location and climate would have had on the lives of the people at that time.

DIGGING DEEPER

1. Look at the map of the birthplace of Judaism. Would you like to have lived there at this time in history? Why?/Why not?
2. How do you think the historical and geographical background to life at the time of the foundation of Judaism affected the lives of the people?

> **Location:** A particular place, e.g. a town, city or country.
>
> **Cultural context:** The events, facts, stories and customs of a particular culture or society that connect with and influence other events, e.g. the founding of a major world religion.

Sources of Evidence

LESSON 49 The Origins of Judaism

GROUNDWORK
In this lesson we plan to:
- study the biography of the founders of Judaism – Abraham and Moses.

DIGGING DEEPER
Why did God call Abraham and Moses?

Key Concepts
Founder/Inspiration/Vision/Dream/Prophet

Abraham – The First Founder of Judaism

Abraham's First Vision – God calls Abraham

Almost four thousand years ago, God called Abraham to leave his home in the city of Haran and journey with his family to Canaan (later known as Palestine). For Abraham, this was a journey of faith.

> 'Leave your country, your family and your father's house, for the land that I will show you. I will make you a great nation; I will bless you and make your name so famous that it will be used as a blessing.' (Genesis 12:1-2)

This was how the Covenant between God and the Hebrew people (the Israelites) was first established. A covenant is an agreement. The Hebrew people promised to obey God's law and, in return, they would be God's chosen race.

Abraham's Second Vision

While on the journey to the land of Canaan, Abraham built an altar to God. God spoke to Abraham and asked him to have faith and to continue to worship the one true God (at that time, the people worshipped many gods). In return for Abraham's faith and the faith of his people, God would lead Abraham and his descendants to the Promised Land. This was the covenant that God made with Abraham.

> *'To your descendants I give this land…'* (Genesis 15:18)

Abraham's Third Vision – God gives Abraham his new name
Once again, God spoke to Abraham. Up to this, Abraham had been known as Abram. God changed Abraham's name from Abram to Abraham, which means 'father of many'.

> *'You shall no longer be called Abram; your name shall be Abraham, for I make you father of a multitude of nations.'* (Genesis 17:5).

Abraham is one of the **founders** of Judaism because he was the first person to be called by God to set up the Covenant between God and the chosen people. God inspired or motivated Abraham to keep this agreement. It was God's **inspiration** that gave Abraham the **vision** to make the journey with his wife Sarah to the land of Canaan.

As a physical sign of this covenant, all Jewish males are circumcised (the foreskin of the penis is removed) when they are eight days old.

KNOW WHAT

God spoke to Abraham three times. In your own words, describe what happened.

DIGGING DEEPER

1. Why is Abraham known as a founder of Judaism?
2. What were the key moments in the life of Abraham? Your class group might like to make a storyboard of these key moments.
3. What do you think it was like for Abraham to be called by God to establish the Covenant?
4. Have you ever felt called by God? Have you ever been asked to do something by a parent or guardian that you knew was going to be difficult, e.g. keep agreements? How did you react and what did you do?
5. What have been key moments in your life?

Factfile

Name:	Abraham, originally called Abram.
Born:	Ur, in Mesopotamia (modern-day Iraq). Later moved to Haran.
Family:	Wife, Sarah, and sons Ishmael and Isaac.
Called by God:	At the age of seventy-five to move with his wife from Haran. In response to God, he set out on a journey from Haran to the land of Canaan (later called Palestine).
Response:	Abraham said 'Yes' to God and began a dangerous and difficult journey to a land far from his friends and his home.
Amazing facts:	For many years, Sarah and Abraham had no children. God promised them a son after they had settled in Canaan. God kept that promise.
Famous for:	His trust in God. God chose Abraham to be the father of a great nation.

Moses – The Second Founder of Judaism

The descendants of Abraham eventually had to flee from Canaan and were forced into slavery by the Egyptians. God called Moses to lead the people to freedom again.

When Moses was a baby, his mother hid him in a basket among reeds by the river Nile to save him from an order from the Pharaoh of Egypt that all Jewish male babies should be killed (Exodus 1:22). He was found by the Pharaoh's daughter and taken to the royal palace, where he was reared as an Egyptian prince. Moses knew, however, that he was of Hebrew background.

On one occasion, Moses witnessed an Egyptian soldier beating a Hebrew slave. Angered by the situation, Moses killed the soldier. He was then forced to flee to the Sinai desert. There he worked as a shepherd and lived a contented life (Exodus 2:11).

Moses' Vision – The Burning Bush

One day, God appeared to Moses in the form of a burning bush. God told Moses that he must return to Egypt and lead the Hebrews out of slavery. God said to Moses 'I shall be with you' (Exodus 3:12).

Moses returned to Egypt and asked the Pharaoh to let the people go, but he refused. Through Moses, God sent ten plagues on the Egyptian people: they suffered rivers of blood, plagues of frogs, gnats, flies, animal diseases, boils, hail, locusts and darkness (Exodus 7:14–11:9).

The final plague sent on the Egyptians was the death of all their firstborn infants. The Hebrew people were spared this plague. Through Moses, God asked the Hebrews to paint the blood of a lamb on their doors so that the angel of death would 'pass over' their homes (Exodus 12:12). That night, the Hebrews ate a meal of unleavened bread (flat bread), as there was no time for the bread to rise before they made their escape. Led by Moses, the people had great faith in God, who protected them by day and by night (Exodus 13:21-22).

After the plague, Pharaoh agreed to let the people go. But soon afterwards, he regretted his decision and ordered his army to set after them and bring them back. The Red Sea parted for the Hebrews, allowing them to escape, whilst the Egyptian army was drowned by the tide (Exodus 14:31).

This release of the Hebrew people from slavery, led by Moses, is known as the Exodus. Each year, the Jewish people remember this event and celebrate it at their Passover meal, where the story of the Exodus is retold.

The Oral Torah and The Ten Commandments – God's Covenant with Moses

While the Israelites were on their journey through the desert, God appeared to Moses on Mount Sinai and gave him the oral Torah (the Law), as well as the Ten Commandments, which were written on two tablets of stone.

Then Moses turned and went down the mountain, carrying the two tablets of the covenant. The tablets were the word of God, and the writing was the writing of God, engraved on the tablets. (Exodus 32:15-16)

The Ten Commandments and the Torah or Law are the moral code of the Jewish people. (A moral code tells people what is right and what is wrong.)

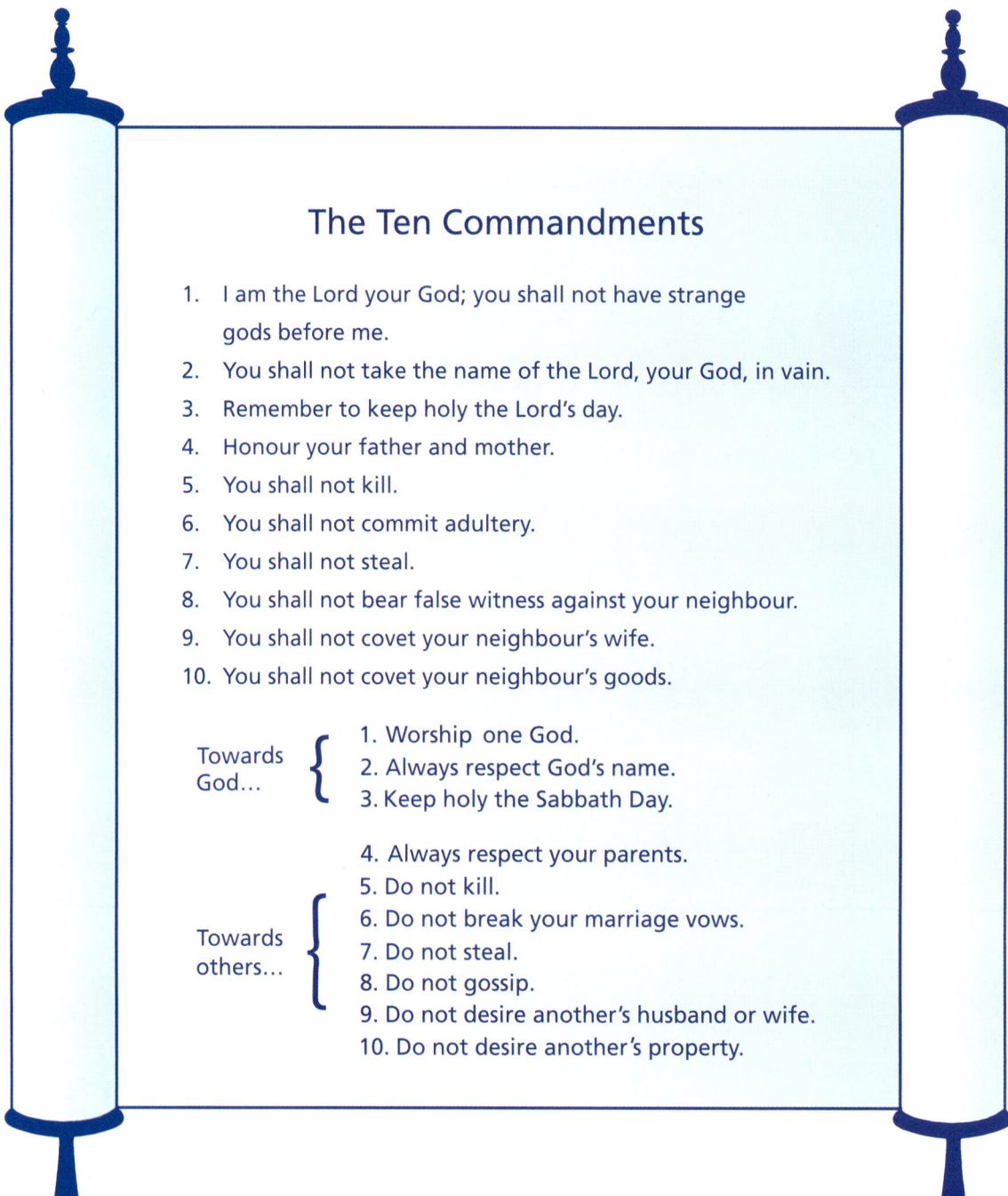

The Ten Commandments

1. I am the Lord your God; you shall not have strange gods before me.
2. You shall not take the name of the Lord, your God, in vain.
3. Remember to keep holy the Lord's day.
4. Honour your father and mother.
5. You shall not kill.
6. You shall not commit adultery.
7. You shall not steal.
8. You shall not bear false witness against your neighbour.
9. You shall not covet your neighbour's wife.
10. You shall not covet your neighbour's goods.

Towards God…
1. Worship one God.
2. Always respect God's name.
3. Keep holy the Sabbath Day.

Towards others…
4. Always respect your parents.
5. Do not kill.
6. Do not break your marriage vows.
7. Do not steal.
8. Do not gossip.
9. Do not desire another's husband or wife.
10. Do not desire another's property.

DIGGING DEEPER
Why did God call Moses and Abraham?

The Impact of the Ten Commandments on the Jewish People

The Ten Commandments were a renewal of the Covenant that had already been established between God and the Hebrew people. They gave the Hebrew people a blueprint or guide to help them remain faithful to God. Therefore, the Hebrew people were called 'People of the Covenant'. By obeying the Ten Commandments, the people kept their side of the covenant with God. They said: 'All the words that the Lord has spoken we will do' (Exodus 24:3). Whenever the people failed to live by the Ten Commandments, the prophets reminded them of their covenant and of their special relationship with God. Because of their reverence, the Hebrew people used the term 'YHWH' to refer to God.

DIGGING DEEPER
How do the Ten Commandments influence the lives of Jews and Christians today?

KNOW WHAT
You will need a Bible for this exercise.
Read Exodus 3:1-6, 11-15 and Exodus 4:1-5, 10-12 before answering the following questions.

1. Describe how the call of Moses was different to the call of Abraham.
2. Why do you think that Moses was at first reluctant (unwilling) to answer God's call?
3. What helped Moses to answer the call of God?
4. Why is Moses known as a founder of Judaism?

Factfile

Name:	Moses
Born:	Son of a Hebrew slave in Egypt. Hidden in a basket by the river Nile and discovered by the daughter of the Pharaoh. Raised as an Egyptian prince.
Family:	Wife called Zipporah and a son called Gershom.
Called by God:	As a young adult at the burning bush.
Response:	Reluctant at first. Finally, he did as God asked and led the Hebrew people out of slavery in Egypt to the land of Canaan.
Amazing facts:	Through Moses, God performed amazing miracles to persuade the Pharaoh to let the Hebrew people go free. These included a variety of plagues, hailstorms and the parting of the Red Sea.
Famous for:	The Exodus. Moses led the Hebrew people from slavery to freedom. God gave Moses the Ten Commandments and the oral Torah on Mount Sinai.

KNOW IT ALL
You will need a Bible for this exercise.

1. Where did Abraham and his family settle after they left Ur? (Genesis 11:31-32)
2. Where did Abraham go to after he left Egypt? (Genesis 13:1)
3. What age was Abraham when the Lord appeared to him? (Genesis 17:1)
4. How did Moses show that he was afraid? (Exodus 3:6)
5. What physical change had happened to Moses when he came down from the mountain with the tablets of stone? (Exodus 34:28)
6. What did Moses say about the Sabbath day? (Exodus 35:2)

Covenant with Abraham
- God's covenant with Abraham was God's gift to Abraham and his descendants.
- The Hebrew people would believe in one God and obey God's laws.
- Abraham would be the father of a great nation.
- Abraham's descendants would be God's chosen people.
- All Jewish boys would be circumcised as a sign of the Covenant.

Covenant with Moses
- When God had led the Hebrew people out of slavery, he made a covenant with Moses on Mount Sinai.
- The people would live according to the Torah (Law) and the Ten Commandments.
- Name of God – YHWH (Lord).
- People of the Covenant.

In summary…
- Abraham and Moses were the founders and great **prophets** of the Jewish community of faith.
- They were both called by God in a series of visions/dreams.
- They both answered the call from God and carried out their mission as requested by God.
- The story of Abraham (as told in the book of Genesis) and of Moses (as told in the book of Exodus) paved the way for the beginning of the Jewish culture.

Founder: One who sets up or inspires a new organisation, e.g. a religious community.

Inspiration: Something that stirs our imagination and that influences us to new thinking or action.

Vision/dream: A powerful image of what the world or a person or a group could be.

Prophet: A person who speaks on behalf of God.

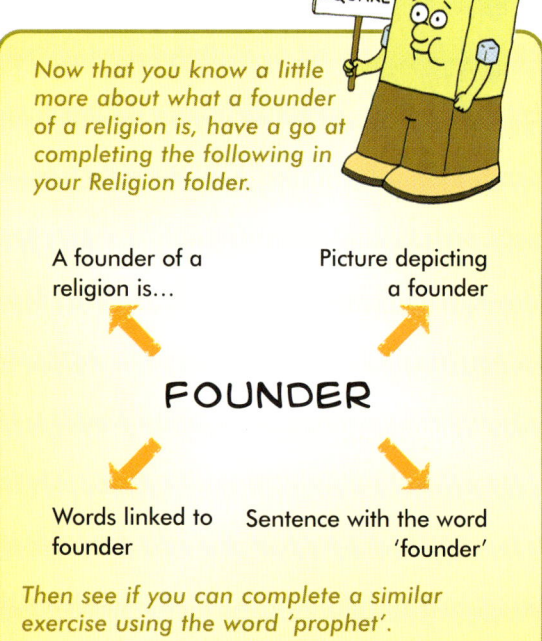

Now that you know a little more about what a founder of a religion is, have a go at completing the following in your Religion folder.

A founder of a religion is…

Picture depicting a founder

FOUNDER

Words linked to founder

Sentence with the word 'founder'

Then see if you can complete a similar exercise using the word 'prophet'.

KNOW THE WAY

166

LESSON 50 The Tanakh – The Sacred Text of Judaism

GROUNDWORK
In this lesson we plan to:
- explore the primary source of information about Judaism.

DIGGING DEEPER
What is the sacred text of Judaism?

Key Concepts
Sacred text/Evidence/Prophet

The Tanakh is the Hebrew name for the **sacred text** or Bible of Judaism. It is a document of faith and the primary source of **evidence** (information) about the foundations or origins of Judaism. It is known as the Hebrew Bible or the Hebrew Scriptures.

The Tanakh was written in Hebrew and has three main sections:

- The Torah
- The Prophets
- The Writings

The name Tanakh comes from the first letters of the Hebrew names for these three sections, i.e.

T for Torah
N for Nevi'im (Prophets)
K for Ketuvim (Writings)

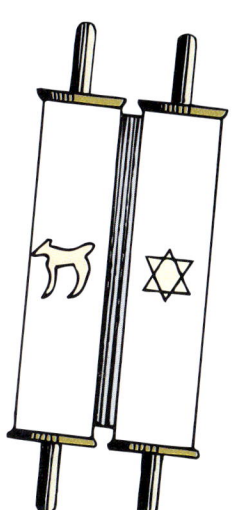

The Torah

The written Torah is also called the Pentateuch, a Greek word meaning 'five books', because it is made up of the first five books of the Hebrew Bible, which Christians call the Old Testament. All the books in the Torah – Genesis, Exodus, Leviticus, Numbers and Deuteronomy – instruct the Jewish community of faith on what God is asking of them.

T	Genesis	The Garden of Eden to the land of Egypt
O	Exodus	Flight from Egypt to Mount Sinai
R	Leviticus	The Lord speaks to Moses on Mount Sinai
A	Numbers	From Mount Sinai to the plains of Moab
H	Deuteronomy	The plains of Moab, where Moses dies

167

The Prophets (the Nevi'im)

The **prophets** were people chosen by God to speak for God and to explain to each generation the meaning of the Word of God in their lives. There were many great prophets, such as Isaiah, Jeremiah and Ezekiel. Their teachings are found in this section of the Tanakh.

The Writings (the Ketuvim)

This final part of the Tanakh is a collection of writings about the history of the Jewish people. It contains poetry, songs, proverbs and many stories of people and the events they experienced.

KNOW IT ALL

Copy the following exercise into your Religion folder and fill in the blanks using the wordbank given below.

1. The T_____ is the sacred text of Judaism.
2. The Tanakh is a document of f_____.
3. The Tanakh was written in H_____.
4. The written T_____ is also called the P_____, a Greek word meaning 'f_____ b_____'.
5. All the books in the Torah – G_____, E_____, L_____, N_____ and D_____ – instruct the Jewish community of faith on what God is asking of them.
6. The p_____ were people chosen by God to speak for God.
7. The prophets were sent by God to explain to each generation the meaning of the W_____ of G_____ in their lives.
8. There were many great prophets, including I_____, J_____ and E_____.
9. The W_____ is the final part of the Tanakh.
10. This section contains poetry, _____, proverbs and many stories of people and the events they experienced.

WORDBANK

Isaiah • Jeremiah • Ezekiel • Faith • Exodus • Pentateuch • Word of God • Torah • Leviticus • Tanakh
Songs • Genesis • Numbers • Writings • Deuteronomy • Hebrew • Prophets • Five books

DIGGING DEEPER

1. Why is a sacred text of a religion the primary source of information about that religion?
2. What is the sacred text of your faith? Why is it the primary source of information about your faith?

🔑 **Sacred text:** Writings relating to a community of faith, which are considered holy and inspired.

Evidence: Information that provides a reason or basis for believing something.

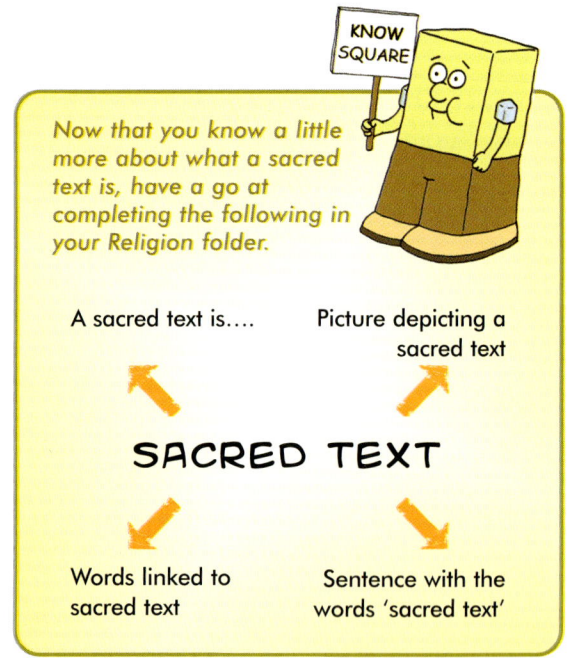

Now that you know a little more about what a sacred text is, have a go at completing the following in your Religion folder.

A sacred text is….   Picture depicting a sacred text

SACRED TEXT

Words linked to sacred text   Sentence with the words 'sacred text'

LESSON 51 From Oral to Written Tradition

GROUNDWORK
In this lesson we plan to:
- trace the development of the sacred text of Judaism from its origins to its present form.

DIGGING DEEPER
How did the Jewish people preserve the story of their faith?

Key Concepts
Sacred text/Inspiration/Revelation/Oral tradition

Introductory Exercise

1. What kind of information would you expect to find in a history book?
2. The following words are sometimes used in relation to a history book: Evidence • Facts • Source • Information • People. Choose one of these words and use it to complete the following sentence: A history book is…
3. The following words are sometimes used in relation to a sacred text: Document of faith • Witness • Story • Followers • Revelation. Choose one of these words and use it to complete the following sentence: A sacred text is…

The Hebrew Scriptures as Sacred Text

When the Jewish people read the Tanakh, the Hebrew Scriptures, they are reading a document of faith. While there is always some information of a historical nature contained in documents of faith, the Tanakh primarily teaches the story of the faith journey of their ancestors, the ancient Hebrew people, also known as the Israelites.

The Hebrew Scriptures reveal (show) God to the Jewish people. The writers were **inspired** by the Holy Spirit to tell the people about what God is like and about how God wants people to live. The Hebrew Scriptures are, therefore, part of God's **revelation**.

KNOW WHAT

You will need a Bible for this exercise.
Read *two* of the following texts before answering the questions below:

- Genesis 12:1
- Genesis 17:12
- Exodus 3:10
- Exodus 31:18

1. Do your chosen passages state facts and statistics?
2. How would you know that these passages are from a document of faith?
3. How is the information contained in these passages different from the kind of information you might find in a history book?
4. What information do these passages give you about the founding story of the Jewish faith?

169

The Oral Tradition of Judaism

The Jewish people wanted to remember the story of their faith and of how God had made them a 'chosen people', so they passed on the story by word of mouth to their children and to their children's children. We refer to this method of handing on a faith story as an **oral tradition**. The purpose was not to provide a specific historical record but rather to teach the people about their relationship with God and about God's covenant or agreement with them.

KNOW WHAT
1. What story was handed on through the oral tradition of the Jewish faith?
2. Why was it so important for the Jewish people to hand on their faith story by the oral tradition?

DIGGING DEEPER
1. Was it difficult for the Jewish people to remember their faith story? Why?/Why not?
2. Describe how the earliest followers of your faith tradition preserved their faith story?

From Oral to Written Tradition

Eventually the Jewish people began to write down the stories from their oral tradition. The Hebrew Bible took over a thousand years to be recorded in its present form. There were hundreds of writers involved in this great task.

The very first books were written on *papyrus*, a paper-like material made from a plant that grows wild all over the Nile river valley. Long stalks were cut and then soaked in water until they began to rot. Then they were laid down next to each other, crushed tightly together and left to dry until they formed what looked like a sheet of paper.

Another material, called *parchment,* was used for the copies of the Torah that were read in the synagogue. Parchment was a hardwearing 'paper' made from animal skins, chiefly from goats or sheep. The skins were scraped and rubbed smooth, ready to write on.

As papyrus and parchment wore out, the scriptures had to be transcribed (copied) to preserve the truths of the faith. The people who carried out this work were called *scribes*.

KNOW WHAT
1. What documents form the written tradition of the Jewish faith?
2. Explain one of the following words: papyrus/parchment.
3. Briefly outline the development of the Jewish faith tradition from the time it was spoken about (oral tradition) to the time it was written down (written tradition).

 **Revelation:** The act of revealing or showing something. Used to describe how God and God's message were revealed to the founders of Judaism, Christianity and Islam.

Oral tradition: Information that is handed on by word of mouth from one person or group to another.

LESSON 52   Other Records and Sources

GROUNDWORK
In this lesson we plan to:
- explore other records and sources for the foundation of Judaism.

DIGGING DEEPER
How do Jewish documents of faith affect the faith of the Jewish people?

Key Concepts
Oral tradition/Evidence/Sacred Text

The Oral Torah

The ancient rabbis (Jewish teachers) believed that God gave Moses a set of written laws – the Ten Commandments – and an oral Torah. The oral Torah is a commentary on the laws in the written Torah and it explains how to apply the laws to different life situations. Like the written Torah, the oral Torah provides further **evidence** of the history and key beliefs of the Jewish faith. The oral Torah is part of the **oral tradition** of Judaism.

While the written Torah remained the most significant reference for the Jewish community of faith, the oral Torah helped the people in their understanding of what God was asking of them. As the Jewish people faced new hardships and trials, their rabbis frequently re-read the written Torah and applied it to new situations. Eventually, two new documents were written: the *Mishnah* and the *Talmud*.

The Mishnah

The Mishnah was written and developed by about two thousand rabbis. It is based on the oral law that was given to Moses. Jewish students use the Mishnah as a textbook on Jewish Law. It helps the Jewish people to focus on what God has asked of them through the Covenant.

The Talmud

The Talmud is a detailed commentary on the Mishnah. It contains large collections of rules and interpretations, collected over the centuries. It is a difficult text to read but it is still studied by Jewish children up to the present day.

KNOW WHAT
1. What is the principal sacred text in Judaism?
2. What is the oral Torah and how did it develop?
3. Who wrote the Mishnah and what does it teach the Jewish people?
4. What is the Talmud?

The Dead Sea Scrolls

In 1947, an Arab shepherd boy called Mazra was minding his sheep and goats near the shore of the Dead Sea. One of his goats had gone missing, so he wandered up to the nearby caves to search for it. When Mazra began to throw stones into one of the caves, he heard a jar break and this frightened him. He raced home, but he decided to return with his cousin the following day. Together they climbed up the cliff to investigate. What they discovered changed the study of the Bible for ever. There, in that cave, rolled up in jars, were many handwritten papyrus scrolls of almost every book of the Old Testament, the Hebrew Scriptures.

Over the following nine years, eight hundred more scrolls were found around the same area, but the scrolls found by the young boy are the only writings of Hebrew Scripture known to exist. They are at least as old as Jesus and John the Baptist. The scrolls had been placed there around AD 68 by the Qumran religious community, probably in order to protect them from destruction by the Romans.

When the most recent copy of the Hebrew text of the book of Isaiah was compared with the Dead Sea scrolls, it was found to be virtually identical. This is clear evidence of the excellent work carried out by the scribes as they handed on the truths of the Jewish faith over two thousand years. It also indicates the accuracy of the Scriptures and the faith story they tell.

KNOW HOW

1. Imagine you are a sister or brother of Mazra, the shepherd boy. Write a diary account of what happened the day your brother came home with the Dead Sea scrolls.
    or
2. Have a go at drawing the scene where Mazra found the Dead Sea scrolls and write a brief description of what happened.

DIGGING DEEPER

1. In what ways do Jewish documents of faith, such as the Tanakh, the Mishnah and the Talmud, affect the faith of the Jewish people?
2. How do the documents of your faith affect your belief?

KNOW THE WAY

Rites of Passage and Other Rituals

LESSON 53 Jewish Beliefs and Practices

GROUNDWORK
In this lesson we plan to:
- identify essential elements of the beliefs and practices of Judaism.

DIGGING DEEPER
What are the beliefs and practices at the heart of Judaism?

What are the beliefs and practices at the heart of my faith?

Key Concepts
Creed/Practice/Prayer/Meditation

The Central Beliefs of Judaism

The Jewish people believe that there is only one God and that they have a special relationship with God because of the Covenant. Let's take a closer look at each of these beliefs.

One God

Judaism is the oldest of the three monotheistic faiths (alongside Christianity and Islam). 'Monotheistic' is the term used to describe belief in one God, who created everything.

The Covenant

Jewish people believe that God made a very special covenant or agreement with Abraham that they would inherit the Promised Land and be God's chosen race. They believe that this covenant was renewed when God rescued the Jewish people from slavery in Egypt and gave Moses the Ten Commandments. The Covenant is central to Judaism. It places a deep obligation on the Jewish people to live good and faithful lives according to God's will. They believe that although it is sometimes hard to live up to the demands of the Covenant, God's love for them remains constant. (Revise the covenant diagrams on page 166 of Part 1).

KNOW WHAT
In your own words, describe the central beliefs of Judaism.

DIGGING DEEPER
1. What are the beliefs and practices at the heart of your faith?
2. In what ways are the central beliefs of Judaism different/the same as the central beliefs of your faith?

The Creed of Judaism

The **creed** of a religion is the statement of that religion's beliefs. The Shema is the major Jewish prayer and is the closest thing to a creed in Judaism. The Jewish people pray the Shema daily. It affirms the belief in one God and asks the Jewish people to remember God each day of their lives. For Jews, God is the creator of everything and God sustains all of creation. God is the beginning and end of all things.

GOD IS ALL POWERFUL	GOD IS EVERYWHERE	GOD KNOWS ALL AND SEES ALL
OMNIPOTENT	OMNIPRESENT	OMNISCIENT

The following is part of the Shema: *'Hear, O Israel: the Lord is our God, the Lord alone. You shall love the Lord your God with all your heart, with all your soul and with all your might. Keep these words that I am commanding you today in your heart. Recite them to your children and talk about them when you are at home and when you are away, when you lie down and when you rise. Bind them as a sign on your hand, fix them as an emblem on your forehead, and write them on the doorposts of your house and upon your gates.'* (Deuteronomy 6:4-9)

Tefillin

The words of the Shema are written on tiny scrolls and placed in small leather pouches, called *tefillin*, which are strapped to the forehead and left arm of Jewish men and boys, and worn during prayer. Similar scrolls are also placed in small boxes, called *mezuzah*, which are tied to the doorposts of Jewish homes.

The name most often used for God in the Hebrew Scriptures is 'Yahweh'. However, the Jewish people have such reverence for God that, although this name can be written down (as YHWH), they do not say it out loud; they generally say 'the Lord' instead.

KNOW WHAT
1. What is the Shema?
2. Explain the following words: creed, tefillin, mezuzah.
3. Why would Jewish people write YHWH instead of Yahweh?

DIGGING DEEPER
1. What is the creed of your faith?
2. Where and how often would you pray the creed of your faith?
3. Why do you think it is important to pray the creed of one's faith with others as well as in private?

The Practice of the Jewish Faith

When people live according to the central beliefs and teachings of their religion, we say that they are *living* or *practising* their faith. The following are the key elements in the **practice** of the Jewish faith.

The Ten Commandments

The Ten Commandments are the moral code or laws accepted by the Jewish people. In living according to the Ten Commandments, the Jewish people are living their faith.

(The Ten Commandments are dealt with in greater detail in Section B and in Section F.)

DIGGING DEEPER
1. Choose three of the commandments and give an example of how each one could help someone to show respect for God and for others.
2. Briefly describe the moral code of your faith and mention how it helps you in your life choices.

The Sabbath

Each week, the members of the Jewish community gather at the synagogue on the Sabbath day (known to Jews as *Shabbat*). The Sabbath begins at sunset on Friday and continues until after sunset on Saturday. The traditional Sabbath candles are lit, usually by the mother of the family, and special prayers are said. The men and the boys attend the synagogue to welcome in the Sabbath. At the end of the day, there is a special celebratory meal, with prayers and singing.

The Sabbath is welcomed as a great blessing and is a reminder of people's dependence on God the Creator. As a mark of their religious commitment to the Sabbath, Jewish families prepare their meals the previous day and no work of any kind is done on the Sabbath, which is treated as a day of rest, prayer and meditation.

On the Saturday morning, many Jewish people attend a service in the synagogue. The high point of the Sabbath is the solemn opening of the Ark of the Covenant and the carrying of the Torah scroll around the synagogue. This is a clear sign of the respect and commitment of the Jewish people for the law of the Torah, which asks them to 'remember to keep holy the Sabbath day'.

Prayer and Meditation

Jewish people show their religious commitment through the practice of daily **prayer**. They pray and meditate to increase their awareness of God with them. **Meditation** is a type of silent prayer, during which the person focuses all their attention on God. The formal language for Jewish prayer is Hebrew, though of course Jewish people can pray in any language they choose. Devout Jewish people pray five times a day: before going to bed, after rising in the morning and at the three meal times. In the evening and in the morning, the Shema is recited. (The Jewish day begins in the evening.)

KNOW WHAT
1. What is the Sabbath and when is it observed?
2. How do the Jewish practices on the Sabbath help us to recognise the beliefs of their faith?
3. Describe the daily ritual of prayer in the life of Jewish people and explain how this daily prayer shows their religious commitment.

Prayer shawl or *tallit*

Special Clothing for Prayer

While in the synagogue, Jewish men tie leather pouches called *tefillin* to their arms and their foreheads to show their commitment to the Shema.

Jewish men wear a *tallit*, a special prayer shawl with tassels on the corners, at morning synagogue services. The tassels are a reminder of God's commandments. Some devout Jewish men wear the shawl under their shirts at all times, so as to keep God's word close to them.

In Eastern cultures, covering the head is a sign of respect. This is probably why Jewish people cover their heads during prayer; it shows respect to God. The *kippah* is a skull-cap worn by Jewish men during prayer. It is similar in shape to the small white head-covering worn by the Pope and it may be of any colour.

KNOW HOW
Draw and label a diagram of *two* of the following items of clothing worn by Jewish men during prayer: a tefillin, a tallit or a kippah.

Boy wearing the *kippah*

The Kosher Rule

Jewish food laws, called *kashrut*, relate to what may be eaten and to how animals are slaughtered (killed) and cooked. These rules, which come from the Torah, divide foods into two categories: *kosher* (allowed) and *terefah* (forbidden). The basic law of kosher is found in Leviticus 11:3, which states that an animal can be used for food if it has '…divided hoofs and is cleft-footed and chews the cud'.

Traditional kosher butcher

Food that is allowed – kosher

Oxen, goats, cows, sheep, chickens, ducks and geese. Fish that have both fins and scales, such as salmon and cod. Milk and eggs from kosher animals.

Food that is forbidden – terefah

Any animal that does not have split hooves and does not chew its cud, especially the pig. Also shellfish.

Meat and dairy products may not be eaten together or at the same meal.

KNOW IT ALL

Imagine that you are a member of the Jewish community. You have been asked to speak at a local youth club about your faith. Write your speech and explain how people from other faith traditions would be able to recognise the central beliefs of Judaism by the words and actions of a Jewish person.

DIGGING DEEPER

1. How does the creed and the practice of the Jewish faith show the religious commitment of the Jewish people?
2. What are the outward signs of your religious commitment?
3. Why do you think each religion has a specific creed and code of practice for its members?

Creed: A statement of religious beliefs.

Practice: The practice of a faith tradition means the living of that faith according to its central beliefs and teachings.

Prayer: Communication between people and God.

Meditation: A form of silent prayer during which the person empties the mind of all other thoughts and focuses on the divine.

LESSON 54 Jewish Rites of Passage

GROUNDWORK
In this lesson we plan to:
- explore the rites of passage in Judaism.

DIGGING DEEPER
How do Jewish people celebrate the key stages in their lives?

How do people from my faith tradition celebrate the key stages in their lives?

Key Concepts
Rite/Ritual/Sign/Symbol/Ceremony

Introductory Exercise: Life-map
In your Religion journal, draw a 'map' of your life so far. You could use boxes (as shown below) to help you to display your journey.

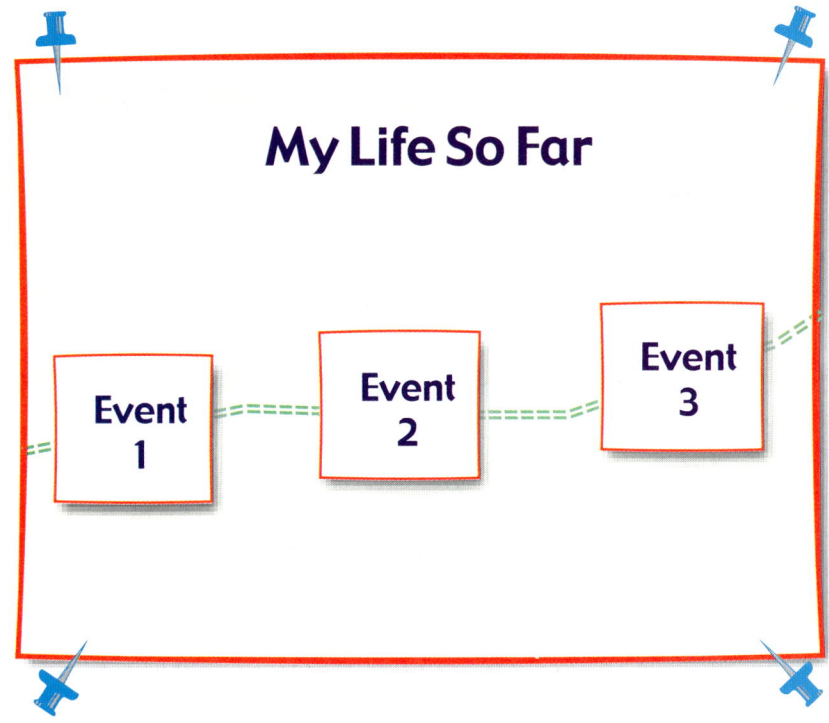

Mark in significant events, dates and celebrations that you have experienced so far. For example, the date of your first birthday.

Write four sentences about your 'life-map', using one of the following words in each sentence: Happy; Sad; Fun; Difficult.

For example: My family told me I was very *happy* playing with balloons the day of my first birthday.

KNOW THE WAY

Rites and Rituals

As you grow and mature, you move through different stages in life. These stages may be marked by 'rites of passage'. A **rite** is a set of words or actions used to celebrate or mark a particular event. In the case of rites of passage, they mark the 'passage' from one stage of life to another. Jewish rites of passage are celebrated through **ritual** in the synagogue, the sacred place of worship for the Jewish community.

Symbols

A **symbol** is a type of **sign** but with a deeper meaning. For example, a white flag can symbolise peace. Symbols are more powerful than signs because they affect the way we feel. Religious symbols can put us in touch with what is sacred or gives meaning to life. Symbols are used in the rites and rituals of every religion. As we explore the following Jewish rites of passage, we will note some of the symbols of Judaism.

The menorah, a seven-branched candlestick, is a very old symbol of Judaism. The central branch represents the Sabbath, the day God rested after creating the world.

Jewish Rites of Passage

Brit Milah – The naming of a Jewish infant

Any child born to a Jewish mother is considered a member of the Jewish community. The Brit Milah is the name of the **ceremony** at which Jewish baby boys are circumcised. This 'initiation' ceremony recalls the covenant that God made with Abraham, whereby all Jewish baby boys are circumcised as a physical sign of the covenant. Usually, this takes place when the child is eight days old. The circumcision is performed by a highly trained surgeon. Baby boys are also given their Hebrew names at this ceremony.

Jewish baby girls have an initiation ceremony that is more simple. They are named and given a blessing during a public reading of the Torah in the synagogue.

Bar Mitzvah – Male coming of age

As soon as they can speak, Jewish boys are taught to read and speak Hebrew, the formal language of Jewish worship. They learn the commandments and memorise many prayers and texts, for example, the Shema. They also learn the Psalms.

At the age of thirteen, a Jewish boy is considered old enough to take responsibility for himself and for keeping the Jewish Law or Torah. At a special ceremony called the Bar Mitzvah, the Jewish community welcomes the boy as an adult member. This is a rite of passage and is a symbol of the boy's 'coming of age'.

Before his Bar Mitzvah, a Jewish boy attends special classes with the rabbi (Jewish teacher). The day that is usually chosen for the ceremony is the first Sabbath day after the boy's twelfth birthday. During the service, the boy is usually called up to the *bimah* (reading platform) to read the day's passage from the Torah. He reads the passage in Hebrew. He is presented with the *kippah* (skull-cap) and allowed to wear the *tallit* (prayer shawl). He is also given the *tefillin* (leather box/pouch containing the text of the Shema) and a *siddur* (prayer book). The kippah, tallit, tefillin and siddur are all symbols of the Jewish faith and are presented to the boy as a sign of his maturity and his faith.

Bat Mitzvah – Female coming of age

In the Reform tradition of Judaism (which you will learn about in Lesson 61), a girl who reaches the age of twelve becomes a *bat mitzvah* or 'daughter of the law'. Until recently, there were no special ceremonies associated with this. Now, many synagogues of the Reform tradition have introduced special prayers during the Sabbath synagogue service, with a party to follow.

In some Irish synagogues, a girl may read a portion of the Torah during the Bat Mitzvah ceremony, just as the boy does at his Bar Mitzvah. In the Orthodox tradition (which you will also learn about in Lesson 61), girls have the opportunity of becoming *bath chayil*, meaning 'daughter of valour', at a special service on a day other than the Sabbath.

Bat Mitzvah celebration

As with the Bar Mitzvah, this ceremony is a symbol of the girl's coming of age.

KNOW HOW
Have a go at designing a leaflet that outlines the religious ceremonies celebrated by a Jewish young person up until the age of fourteen.

DIGGING DEEPER
1. How do people from your faith tradition celebrate the key stages in their lives?
2. What rites will you have celebrated in your faith tradition by the time you are a teenager? Describe these celebrations. (You will learn more about these rites and rituals in Section E.)

Jewish Marriage Ceremony

Jewish people are expected to marry others of the same faith. This is in order to pass on the faith through the generations.

The Jewish wedding ceremony is a very symbolic ceremony. The bride is veiled as a reminder (symbol) of how Rebekah veiled her face when she was first brought to Isaac (Genesis 24:65). The bride goes to the groom and walks around him. Wine is blessed twice, the second time with a special marriage blessing. The groom places a ring on the bride's finger and says: 'Be sanctified to me with this ring in accordance with the law of Moses

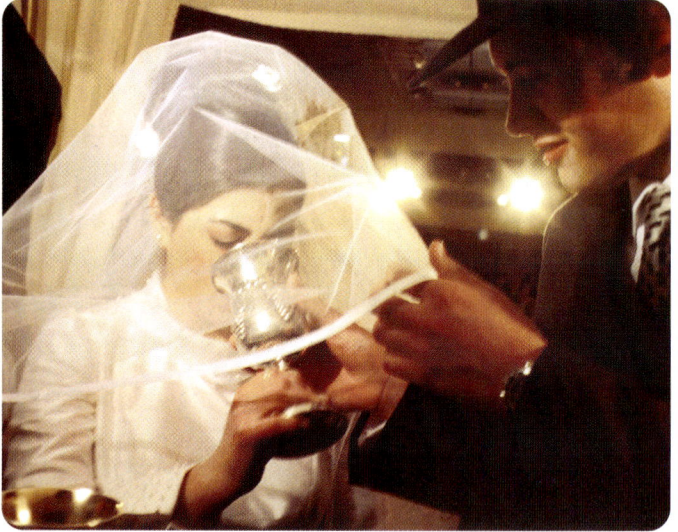

Jewish wedding celebration

and Israel.' The ring is a symbol of their love for each other and of the life they will spend together. The marriage contract is read aloud. It outlines the groom's obligations to the bride. The bride and groom then stand under a canopy (or cover) held up by four posts. This is a symbol of the home they will share together. Before those present, they say seven special blessings and drink the blessed wine. The man smashes the wine glass as a symbol of the destruction of the Temple in Jerusalem. The wedding ceremony is followed by a special celebratory meal.

KNOW HOW
Draw two representations of the first two photographs that would be likely to appear in the wedding album of a Jewish couple.

DIGGING DEEPER
1. Why is the Jewish wedding ceremony a very symbolic ceremony?
2. How is marriage celebrated in your faith tradition? Could the ceremony also be described as a 'very symbolic ceremony'? Explain.
3. Have you ever been to a wedding within the Christian tradition? If so, can you remember any of the symbols that were used? Describe what took place.

Death and Mourning

Jewish people believe in life after death. Every Jewish person hopes that their last words will be the Shema.

Jewish people show respect for the dead person by:

- cleaning the body and wrapping it in a plain linen cloth;
- placing lighted candles nearby;
- never leaving the body alone;
- never displaying the body for others to see;
- not eating or drinking in the presence of the body;
- burying the body in such a way that it touches the earth;
- burying the body without delay.

Even if they do not touch the body, Jewish people believe that being in the presence of a dead body makes them unclean in some spiritual way. Afterwards, they will wash their hands as a sign of becoming spiritually clean again. On hearing the news of the death of a close family member, Jewish people may tear their clothing and say a prayer.

The body must be buried as soon as possible after death, usually within twenty-four hours. After the burial, the family has a special meal of eggs (symbols of life) and bread. Only after this time do people call to offer their sympathy. When they call, they allow the mourners to start the conversation. Only after the first year do mourners resume a fully normal life again.

KNOW WHAT
1. How do Jewish people view death?
2. Name three ways in which Jewish people show respect for their dead.

DIGGING DEEPER

1. What symbols are used in the Jewish practice associated with death and mourning? What do they symbolise for the Jewish people?
2. How are the Jewish and Christian practices that are connected with death: a) the same, b) different?

5-4-3-2-1

1. Name **five** Jewish rites of passage that are celebrated through ritual.
2. Describe **four** items used during a Bar Mitzvah/Bat Mitzvah celebration.
3. Identify and explain **three** symbols used during a Jewish marriage ceremony.
4. What **two** sentiments are expressed in the Jewish practice associated with death and mourning?
5. Write **one** paragraph explaining the following words in relation to Judaism: rite, ritual, sign, symbol and ceremony.

KNOWING ME KNOWING YOU

Find out more about Jewish traditions connected with death and mourning at: *www.jewfaq.org/death.htm*

Rite: A set of words or actions used to celebrate or mark an important event. 'Rites of passage' celebrate different stages in a person's life.

Ritual: A series of actions carried out in a set way. Religious rituals are usually repeated regularly by the faith community to express the relationship between God and the community.

Sign: A word, drawing or action that gives information.

Symbol: A type of sign, but with a deeper meaning. A symbol is a visible sign of something invisible.

Ceremony: A formal event to celebrate and to show respect for something, for example, a baptism or a wedding.

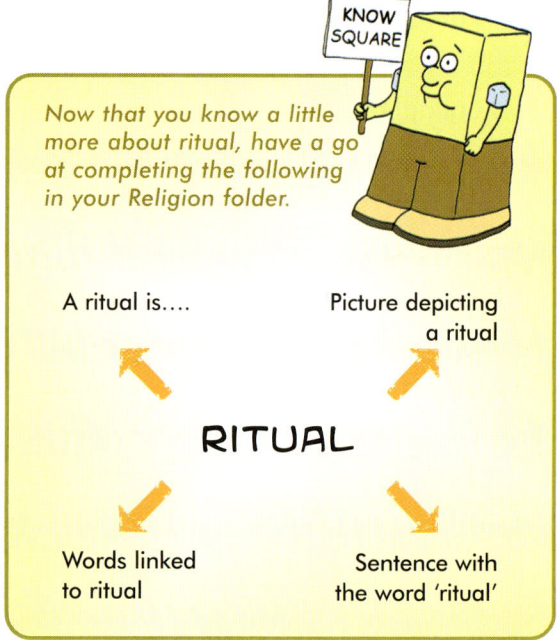

Now that you know a little more about ritual, have a go at completing the following in your Religion folder.

A ritual is....   Picture depicting a ritual

RITUAL

Words linked to ritual   Sentence with the word 'ritual'

See pages 489 and 490 for past exam questions on this topic.

KNOW THE WAY

LESSON 55 Jewish Feasts and Festivals

GROUNDWORK
In this lesson we plan to:
- explore the feasts and festivals of Judaism.

DIGGING DEEPER
How do Jewish people celebrate their sacred times?

How are sacred times celebrated by people in your faith tradition?

Key Concepts
Sacred time/Calendar/Festivals/Ritual

Introductory Activity: Feasts and Festivals
Copy these three circles, including the headings, into your Religion folder:

In the circles, write the date and name of a festival or feast that is celebrated each year by your family, your country and your religion.

The discuss the answers to the following questions:

1. What occasions did you choose?
2. How do you celebrate these occasions?
3. Why do you celebrate them?

Sacred Times in the Jewish Calendar

In every religion, there are **sacred times** that are marked by celebrations. Each year, Christians celebrate special events in the life of Jesus, and these dates are recorded by a liturgical calendar. The Jewish **calendar** is based on an ancient lunar calendar; this means that the months of the year were originally calculated according to the time between two full moons – about twenty-nine-and-a-half days. As a result, the Jewish year is normally 354 days long.

The twelve months of the Jewish year are:

Tishrei
Cheshvan
Kislev
Tevet
Shevat
Adar
Nisan
Iyar
Sivan
Tamuz
Av
Ellul

Jewish **festivals** are either linked to the season in which they are celebrated or are related to Jewish history. These festivals are **ritual** events because they are celebrated in the same way every year.

The use of a lunar calendar means that the dates on which the festivals are celebrated change from year to year. In a leap year, the Jewish people add an extra month to make sure that the festivals are kept in line with the seasons of nature. Also, the use of a lunar calendar means that a new day does not begin at nighttime or at sunrise but at dusk, when the first stars appear in the sky. We will now look at one festival in each season.

Autumn
Rosh Hashanah: The Jewish New Year. Ten days of reflection, ending with Yom Kippur – the Day of Atonement.
Sukkoth: Feast of Tabernacles.
Simchat Torah: Rejoicing of the law.

Summer
Shavuot: Festival of Weeks.
Tishah b'Av: Solemn day of mourning or fasting.

Winter
Hanukah: Festival of Lights.
Purim: Festival of Lots.

Spring
Passover or Pesach: Feast of Unleavened Bread.

Autumn Festivals

There are four autumn festivals in the Jewish calendar: Rosh Hashanah, Yom Kippur, Sukkoth and Simchat Torah.

The Jewish New Year is marked by a ten-day period of repentance, leading up to a special day known as **Yom Kippur**, the **Day of Atonement** (at-one-ment with God). This is the most holy day of the Jewish year. On this day, Jewish people fast, pray and confess their sins. Some devout people wear a white robe as a symbol of purity. In the evening, Jewish families have a special meal at home and then go to an evening service at their place of worship, the synagogue.

Winter Festivals

There are two winter festivals in the Jewish calendar: Hanukah and Purim.

Purim, also known as the **Festival of Lots**, is usually celebrated in March. It is a joyful occasion. It remembers how the villain Haman of Persia cast lots to decide when to destroy the Jewish people. They were saved by the bravery of Queen Esther, who was herself a Jew. Families gather at the synagogue to hear the story being read from the book of Esther, and whenever Haman's name is mentioned, everyone in the synagogue makes a noise to express their dislike; some stamp their feet and others make a noise with a rattle. Jewish families mark the festival by holding parties, and the children are encouraged to dress up as the characters in the story.

KNOW IT ALL
1. Yom Kippur is also known as the Day of _____ .
2. The Festival of Lots is also known as _____ .
3. Jewish families celebrate this festival by holding _____ .
4. The children _____ _____ as characters from the story of Queen Esther and Haman of Persia.

Spring Festival

There is one spring festival in the Jewish calendar: Pesach.

Pesach, the Festival of Passover, celebrates God's freeing of the Jewish people from slavery in Egypt. People eat *matzah* (flat bread baked without yeast, also called unleavened bread) during the festival to recall how the Jewish people ate unleavened bread before leaving Egypt, as they had no time to bake ordinary bread. No 'leavening' or yeast is used in any foods during the whole Passover season. This is why the feast is also known as the Feast of Unleavened Bread.

On the first night of the festival, the *seder meal* is eaten in the homes of Jewish people. This is a wonderful celebration for the whole Jewish community. Traditional foods are served and songs are sung. At the centre of the table there is a seder dish, which contains five foods that are associated with the Passover:

Bitter herbs	A reminder of the bitterness of slavery.
Shankbone of roast lamb	To recall the lamb sacrificed by their ancestors.
A roasted egg	A symbol of new life.
Haroset	A mixture of chopped apples, wine, cinnamon and nuts, symbolising the brick building material used by the slaves in Egypt.
Greens	Usually parsley and celery tops, to symbolise hope.

The youngest member of the family has an important role in the celebration. He/she always asks the same question: 'Why is this night different from other nights?' The father of the family answers by retelling the events of the Exodus or escape from Egypt. It is traditional to leave a vacant place and an extra cup of wine at the table during the seder meal; this is for the prophet Elijah, who is expected to arrive before the Messiah.

KNOW WHAT
1. What is the name of the festival that celebrates the escape to freedom of the Jewish people from Egypt? How did this festival get its name?
2. What is a seder meal? What are the ingredients required for a seder meal?
3. Name two other traditions associated with this meal.

Summer Festivals

There are two summer festivals in the Jewish calendar: Shavuot and Tishah b'Av.

Fifty days after Passover, Shavuot, or the Festival of Weeks, is celebrated. It remembers the giving of the Law to Moses on Mount Sinai. The Ten Commandments are read out loud in the synagogue. Some people stay in the synagogue all night to meditate on them. Shavuot is also called the Feast of the First Fruits because it marks the beginning of the wheat harvest. During this festival, the synagogues are decorated with fruit and food.

KNOW IT ALL

1. Name and describe four Jewish festivals.
2. Match the festivals listed below with the correct time of year and description.

Purim	Autumn	Festival of Weeks
Yom Kippur	Summer	Festival of Lots
Pesach	Winter	Day of Atonement
Shavuot	Spring	Festival of Passover

KNOW HOW

You own a beautiful Jewish restaurant! Plan and write the menu for a festive dinner at the festival of Pesach.

DIGGING DEEPER

1. How do we know that the sacred times of Judaism are very important for Jewish people?
2. What sacred times are celebrated in your faith tradition? How are they celebrated?

Calendar/Sacred time: A calendar is a system for dividing the year into definite periods. Sacred time refers to times of special religious importance, e.g. religious festivals.

Festivals: Special celebrations that recall the events, facts, stories and customs of a particular group, nation or religion.

See page 490 for a past exam question on this topic.

KNOW THE WAY

LESSON 56 Jewish Places of Worship

GROUNDWORK
In this lesson we plan to:
- explore the places of worship in Judaism.

DIGGING DEEPER
Where do Jewish people gather for worship?

Where do people from my faith tradition gather for worship?

Key Concepts
Places of Worship/Pilgrimage/Symbol

The Synagogue

The synagogue is the sacred **place of worship** in the Jewish faith. The word 'synagogue' comes from the Greek word for assembly or collection. Members of the Jewish community gather there for prayer and religious ceremonies. It is also used for education and socialising.

A synagogue must have windows and be facing in the direction of Jerusalem. Inside the main entrance, there is usually a small porch with two doors: one leading up to the balcony and the other into the main body of the building. The building is rectangular,

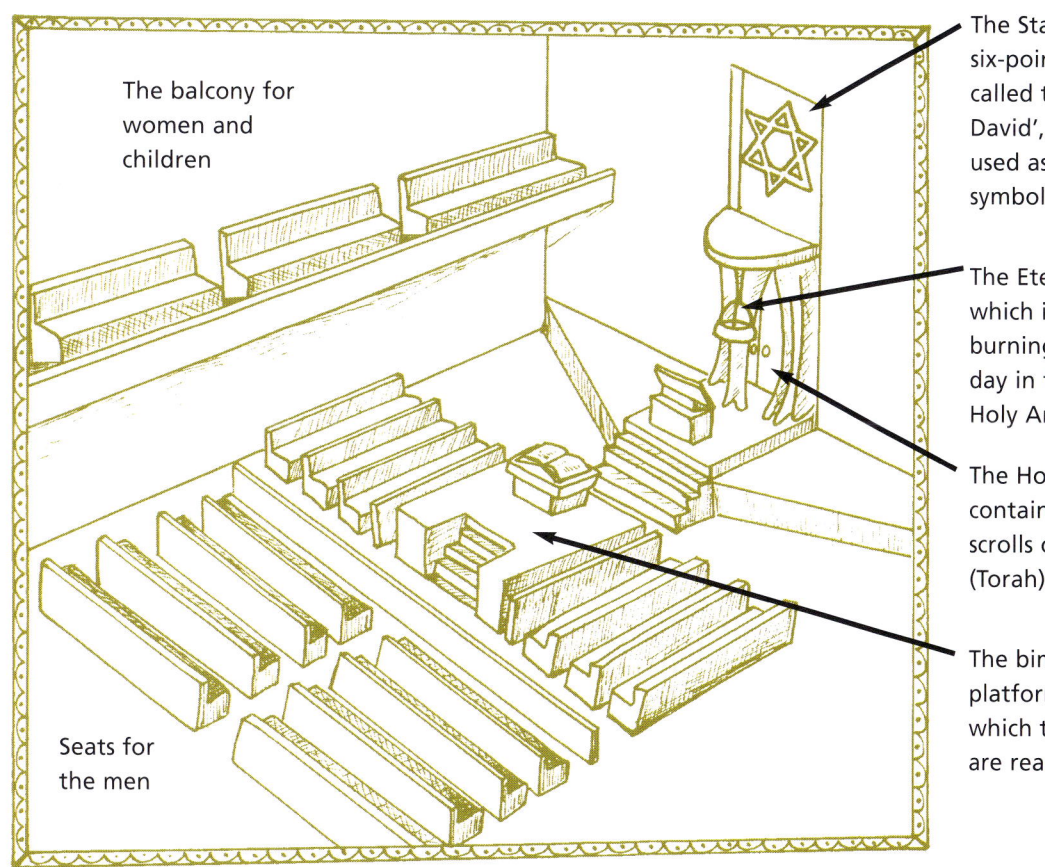

with seats arranged on three sides. The fourth side is most important, as it is where the Holy Ark is placed.

On Saturday mornings, Jewish families go the synagogue for worship (Sabbath service). The service is led by the local *rabbi*. It usually begins with a psalm, inviting the people to praise God. The leader says prayers and the people answer 'Amen'. A lesson from the Torah is read in Hebrew. The preacher reads a lesson from the Prophets and explains it. The service usually lasts for one hour and ends with a blessing.

Every synagogue has a set of handwritten scrolls of the Torah. The scrolls are made from parchment and have wooden rollers on each end. They are looked after very carefully and are never touched with the hand. When they are read, a special pointer is used. Before being placed in the Ark, the scrolls are covered with a cloth made from silk or velvet, which is decorated or embroidered to show its importance.

A copy of the Ten Commandments hangs over the Holy Ark.

KNOW HOW
Organise a visit to a synagogue. Alternatively, you can make a virtual visit to an Orthodox synagogue at: *http://scheinerman.net/judaism/synagogue/*

3-2-1
1. Name and describe **one** place of worship in the Jewish faith tradition.
2. Give **two** reasons for gathering at the synagogue.
3. Name and describe **three** items you would find in a synagogue.

The Temple

The Temple in Jerusalem contained the original Ark of the Covenant. The Ark of the Covenant held the tablets of stone engraved with the Ten Commandments that were given to Moses on Mount Sinai. The Temple was destroyed and rebuilt many times, but was finally destroyed by the Romans in AD 70. The only remaining part of this sacred place is the Western Wall, also known as the 'Wailing Wall', which is now a place of **pilgrimage** for Jewish people.

Men praying at the Western Wall

Large crowds pray at the Western Wall on Friday evenings and it is also a common gathering place on all Jewish festivals, particularly on the feast of Tishah b'Av, which commemorates the destruction of the Temples. Today, the Wall is a national **symbol**, and the opening or closing ceremonies of many Jewish events, including secular (non-religious) ones, are conducted there.

KNOW WHAT
1. Why is the Western Wall a significant place for Judaism?
2. At what specific time of year do people make a journey to this place?

DIGGING DEEPER
1. Why do people gather in a sacred place for worship and ritual?
2. What is the name of the place of worship in your faith tradition?
3. Name and describe a place of pilgrimage in your faith tradition.

Places of Worship: Places set apart for religious rituals.

Pilgrimage: A journey to a sacred place.

See page 491 for past exam questions on this topic.

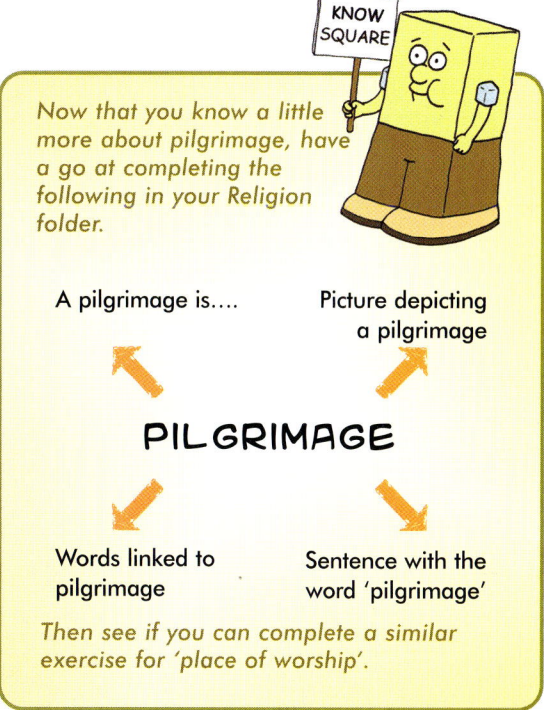

Development of Tradition

LESSON 57 The Development of Judaism

GROUNDWORK
In this lesson we plan to:
- study the development of Judaism.

DIGGING DEEPER
What events led to the Jewish faith as we know it today?

 **Key Concept**
Development

The Development of Judaism

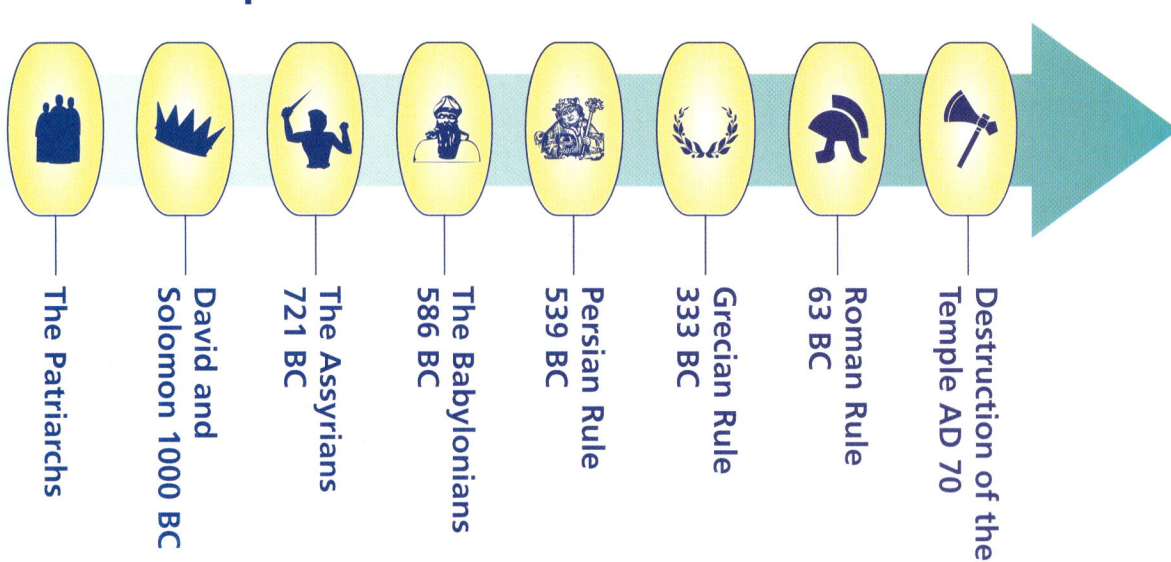

- The Patriarchs
- David and Solomon 1000 BC
- The Assyrians 721 BC
- The Babylonians 586 BC
- Persian Rule 539 BC
- Grecian Rule 333 BC
- Roman Rule 63 BC
- Destruction of the Temple AD 70

The Patriarchs
Judaism begins with the story of Abraham, the earliest patriarch, as told in the book of Genesis. The book of Exodus tells the story of Moses and how he freed the Hebrew people from slavery in Egypt. The Jewish faith is founded on God's covenant with Abraham and later with Moses.

David and Solomon 1000 BC
Israel's greatest king, David, captured Jerusalem. He brought together the tribes of the north and the south. His son, Solomon, continued his work, so that the people had a king, a land and a Temple. Around this time, stories about the Patriarchs and about other great events of the past, e.g. the Exodus, were written down.

After Solomon's death in 933 BC, the kingdom split in two; the Northern Kingdom was called Israel and it broke with the dynasty of David. The place of the kings in religious matters declined and the influence of the prophets increased. People turned to prophets like Elijah, Amos and Hosea to learn more about God.

The Temple in Jerusalem continued to be the centre of Jewish faith. It was considered to be the place where God lived among the chosen people.

The Assyrians 721 BC
In 721 BC, the Assyrians destroyed the Kingdom of Israel.

The Babylonians 586 BC
Jerusalem was conquered by the Babylonians and the Jews were taken away to Babylon. Half a century of exile followed. The people had lost everything: their homes, their land and their king. They were even in danger of losing their faith in God. They turned to prophets like Ezekiel to give them encouragement and hope for the future. They turned to the traditions of their faith to find meaning in the suffering they were going through.

Persian Rule 539 BC
Babylon was captured by the army of Cyrus II of Persia. Cyrus allowed the Jewish people to practise their faith and to rebuild their Temple in Jerusalem.

Grecian Rule 333 BC
The Greek Alexander the Great conquered the Middle East, and Hellenism (the influence of the Greeks) spread rapidly. The Jewish people remained true to their faith and resisted the Greeks. Every year when the Jewish people celebrate Hanukah (the Festival of Lights), they celebrate the return to use of the Temple at this time.

Roman Rule 63 BC
In 63 BC, Rome took over the Middle East and King Herod reigned from 40 to 4 BC. Under Herod's rule, a huge amount of building took place, with palaces, theatres and amphitheatres being constructed (all influenced by Greece and Rome) and, of course, the Temple in Jerusalem.

It was during this time of Roman occupation that the Jewish hope for a Messiah became prominent. The Messiah was expected to free them from the Romans and to restore the Judaean state.

Destruction of the Temple AD 70

There was much conflict between the Greek and Jewish communities and between the Roman governors and the local population. It all came to a violent conclusion in AD 70 when the Jews revolted against Rome and were badly defeated. The Temple was destroyed and all that remained was the Western Wall, which to this day is a place of pilgrimage. This had a devastating effect on the Jewish community.

As a result of these conflicts, Jewish people became scattered around the world, and those who did not live in Israel were now known as the *Diaspora*.

KNOW WHAT

1. Who were the Patriarchs and what did they do?
2. What part did Moses play in the history of the Jewish people?
3. Who were David and Solomon?
4. Name three other groups that ruled the Jewish people before the arrival of the Romans in 63 BC.
5. What Roman king reigned from 40 BC to 4 BC?
6. What is meant by the term 'Diaspora'?

DIGGING DEEPER

1. The Jewish faith suffered many trials and tribulations as it developed through the ages. Discuss this statement with reference to the above information.
2. What do you think helps a faith tradition to remain steadfast and strong when it is in the process of development?

Development: *Growth or change, e.g. the way in which a community of faith grows or matures over time.*

LESSON 58 The Recent History of Judaism

GROUNDWORK
In this lesson we plan to:
- identify important moments in the recent history of Judaism.

DIGGING DEEPER
What price did the Jews pay for their commitment to their faith?

Key Concepts
Commitment/Persecution

Introductory Activity

1. Divide up into approximately six groups according to specific qualities, e.g. hair colour, eye colour, hair type, height, sporting ability, musical ability.
2. Within your group, discuss your reactions to the 'new school rules' listed opposite.
3. Take a few minutes to role-play some students' reactions if the new 'rules' were going to be enforced in your school.

New School Rules

- Only students with brown hair can have time off for lunch.
- Music students must sing their answers in class.
- Only tall students are allowed to sit down in the classroom.
- Sporty students must come to school on Saturday mornings.
- Students with long hair can have every second class free.
- Students who wear glasses or contact lenses must sit at the front of the class.

Sometimes people are forced into very difficult situations because they are different or they don't 'fit in' with someone else's idea of what is acceptable. This is what happened to the Jewish people as they tried to practise their faith.

The Price of Commitment to Judaism

There is a long history – throughout Europe and beyond – of discrimination against the Jewish people because of their faith. The Jewish people have had to pay a huge price for their **commitment** to Judaism.

The greatest example of **persecution** or bad treatment of the Jewish people is also the most recent: the Jewish people call it the *Holocaust* or *Shoah*. When the Nazi party, led by Adolf Hitler, came to power in Germany in 1933, the country faced serious problems. The Nazis blamed these problems on the Jewish people. They told people to stay away from Jewish-owned shops and businesses. They did not allow Jewish people to own land or to work as doctors, dentists, teachers, lawyers, accountants, etc., even though these people were German citizens like everyone else.

Before the Second World War (1939-1945), the Nazis set up 'concentration camps' or prisons. During the war, they filled them mainly with Jewish people, gathered from all the lands they occupied. In 1942, the Nazis began to kill the Jewish prisoners at the Auschwitz concentration camp. They put them into sealed rooms or 'chambers' and pretended to offer them showers, but instead of water, gas came out of the showers and killed them. They burned the bodies or had other Jewish people bury their dead in mass graves.

By the summer of 1944, the Nazis were killing nine thousand people each day. There were other concentration camps, and approximately 870,000 people died in the one at Treblinka. Between 1940 and 1945, six million Jewish people, one third of the Jewish people in the world at that time, were killed.

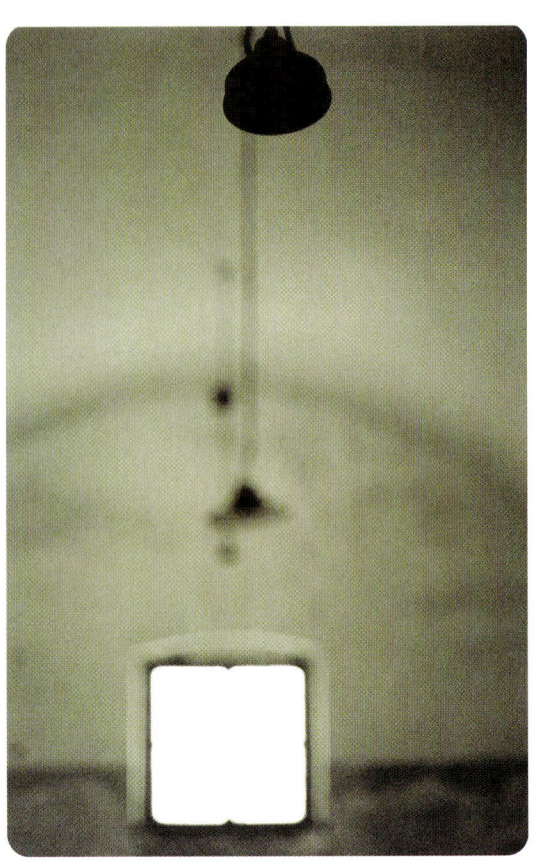

The persecution of Jewish people is called anti-Semitism. The effects of anti-Semitism have been far-reaching; it has had a deep impact on the relationship between Judaism and other communities, both political and religious.

KNOW WHAT
1. What is anti-Semitism?
2. What price did the Jewish community have to pay for their commitment to their faith?
3. From what you have learned about the development of the Jewish religion, can you give some other examples of how Jewish people were persecuted over the centuries?
4. Explain why the Holocaust has had a deep effect on the relationship between Judaism and other faith communities.

DIGGING DEEPER
1. What do you feel when you read about the price the Jewish people had to pay for their commitment to their faith?
2. Have you ever witnessed or heard about a person who suffered because of their faith? What happened?
3. What could help in a situation where a person is being discriminated against because of their faith?
4. Were the members of your own faith community ever persecuted for their beliefs? If so, describe what happened.

Commitment: Pledge/promise to a group or community to carry out a task or role.

Persecution: Deliberately causing loss, pain or death to a person or a group because of race, religion or way of life.

LESSON 59   The Jewish Community Worldwide

GROUNDWORK
In this lesson we plan to:
- learn about the global distribution of the Jewish community, with particular reference to Ireland.

DIGGING DEEPER
Who are my Jewish neighbours?

Key Concept
Expansion

The Jewish Community Worldwide

There are approximately thirteen million Jews worldwide: six million in the USA, three million in Israel and the rest divided throughout the world, including communities in Russia and Eastern Europe.

United States of America	6,000,000
Israel	3,000,000
Russia, Eastern Europe and rest of world	4,000,000

Members of the Jewish community who live outside of Israel are known as the Diaspora. However, many of the Jewish people are moving 'back' to Israel, so the population of Israel is rising and the Diaspora is in decline.

The Zionist Movement

Zionism refers to the movement to secure the homeland of Palestine for the Jewish people. The movement was founded by Theodor Herzl in the nineteenth century. Herzl had a vision that the Jewish homeland could be established in Palestine. Early Zionism was not fully supported by the Jewish people, but after the death of Herzl in 1904, the Zionists (supporters) were totally committed to the vision of their founder and they began to push for the support of major world powers.

In 1917, Britain (which had just conquered Palestine) issued the Balfour Declaration. This Declaration approved of Jewish emigration to Israel and declared that a homeland could later be established. The idea of the return of the Jewish people to the land of Israel is rooted in the Bible, where each prophet assures the exiles in Babylon that they will be brought back to the Promised Land.

In 1948, the modern state of Israel was created. The Jewish people, devastated by centuries of anti-Semitism and by the events of the Holocaust, turned towards Jerusalem as their spiritual homeland.

3-2-1
- Write **one** sentence to explain the term 'Diaspora'.
- Name **two** countries where there are over a million Jewish people.
- Write **three** sentences about the Zionist movement.

Jewish Communities in Ireland

Evidence of Jewish people arriving in Ireland can be traced back to the Annals (records) of Inisfallen (dated AD 1079). This document records the arrival of five Jewish people into Ireland, probably from Rouen in France. The expulsion of Jewish people from other parts of the world resulted in some Jewish people escaping to Ireland, but the numbers were very small.

It was not until the 1880s that larger numbers began to arrive in Ireland. Between 1880 and 1910, approximately two thousand Jewish people came to Ireland from Eastern Europe and settled in Belfast, Cork, Derry, Drogheda, Dublin, Limerick, Lurgan and Waterford. The following years saw some **expansion** of the Jewish population in Ireland, which peaked at approximately 5,500 in the late 1940s, but today it has declined to approximately 1,200.

Members of the Jewish community make an important contribution to all walks of life in Ireland, including professional, business, educational and political.

At the moment, there are six synagogues in Ireland: four in Dublin, one in Belfast and one in Cork. Five of these belong to the Orthodox Jewish community, while one of the synagogues in Dublin is a Progressive synagogue. The Progressive Jewish community is part of the Reform tradition. (You will learn about the Orthodox and Reform traditions of Judaism in Lesson 61.)

Members of the Jewish community can buy kosher food in Dublin and Belfast. This is extremely important in order to maintain the Jewish lifestyle.

Stratford College, based in Rathgar, Dublin, is the only Jewish school in Ireland and it educates both primary and post-primary students. Stratford College caters for all denominations of Judaism.

Stratford College, Rathgar

KNOW IT ALL

Copy the following exercise into your Religion folder and fill in the blanks using the wordbank given below.

1. The earliest evidence of Jewish people coming to Ireland can be found in the Annals of _____ .
2. The first Jewish people in Ireland were probably from _____ in France.
3. It was not until the _____ that more Jewish people began to arrive in Ireland.
4. The Jewish people settled in Belfast, C _____ , D _____ , D _____ , D _____ , L _____ , L _____ and W _____ .
5. Today there are approximately _____ members of the Jewish community in Ireland.
6. There are six _____ in Ireland.
7. In Ireland, kosher food can be purchased in _____ and _____ .
8. There is only one Jewish school in Ireland. It is called S _____ C _____ and it is in Dublin.

WORDBANK

Drogheda • Dublin • Synagogues • 1880s • Rouen • 1200 • Dublin
Belfast • Cork • Derry • Stratford College • Limerick • Lurgan • Waterford • Inisfallen

DIGGING DEEPER

Invite a young Jewish person to talk to your class about the Jewish community of faith in Ireland today.

 **Expansion:** Increase in size, area or number. A religious community expands when more people join it and when it spreads to other places.

See page 491 for past exam questions on this topic.

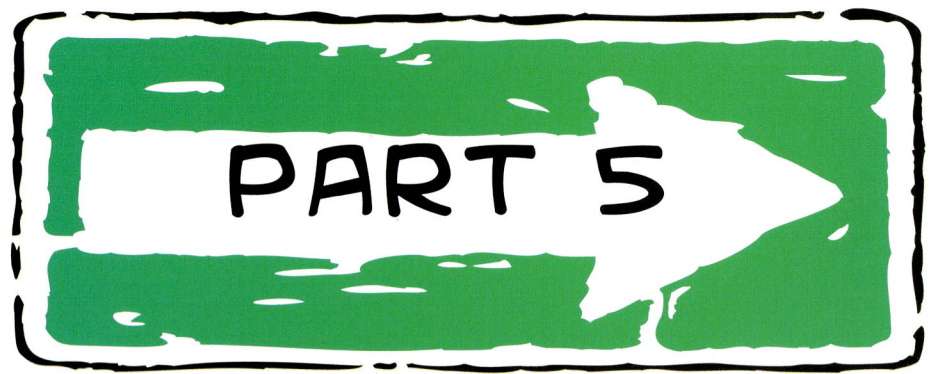

(Higher Level Only)

Tradition, Faith and Practice Today

LESSON 60 Community Structure

GROUNDWORK
In this lesson we plan to:
- learn about the roles within the Jewish community.

DIGGING DEEPER
What is the structure of the Jewish community?

 **Key Concepts**
Community Structure/Leadership/Education/Follower/Discipleship

The Structure of the Jewish Community

As in any community, there are various roles within the Jewish community of faith. These roles all contribute to building up the **community structure**.

Rabbi

The rabbi is the leader and teacher in the local Jewish community. In the Reform tradition of Judaism, a rabbi may be a man or a woman. Rabbis are very well educated in Jewish law and tradition and so have the authority to make decisions. They provide the Jewish community with **leadership** and **education**, and they answer questions and resolve disputes in matters relating to Jewish law. The rabbi also acts as a spiritual leader within the Jewish community, leading religious services and dealing with the day-to-day running of the synagogue.

Several rabbis may join together to form a *beth din* – a type of court. The beth din organises the divorce documents if a Jewish marriage has broken down. It also grants licences to kosher butchers.

The chief rabbi represents and leads the Jewish community in a country.

Chief Rabbi of Ireland, Dr Yaakov Pearlman

Chazan

The chazan (cantor) is the person who leads the Jewish congregation in prayer. Any person who lives in accordance with the Torah and has an in-depth knowledge of the prayers and music can lead the prayer services. In smaller faith communities, the rabbi often serves as both rabbi and chazan. However, because music plays such a major role in Jewish religious services, larger congregations usually hire a professional chazan, a person with both musical skills and training as a religious leader and educator. The playing of instruments is not allowed on the Sabbath, so a chazan must be able to sing the melodies for the congregation. This is a very important role in the Jewish community.

Gabbai

A gabbai is a lay person who volunteers to perform various duties in connection with Torah readings at religious services. This is like a Minister of the Word (a reader) in the Christian churches. To serve the community of faith as a gabbai is a great honour, and it is only given to a person who has a thorough knowledge of the Hebrew Scriptures.

Shochet

Jews are allowed to eat certain animals and birds, provided that they are slaughtered and cooked in accordance with Jewish law. The person who performs the slaughter is called a *shochet*. In the Jewish faith tradition, the shochet is not simply a butcher; he must be a pious man, well-trained in Jewish law and particularly in that which relates to *kashrut* (see page 177).

Followers

All communities of faith are made up of followers who work together in a spirit of co-operation, sharing and communication. To be a **follower** of a religion requires taking on a **discipleship** role. A disciple is someone who wants to learn about and practise their religion.

TAKE FIVE
1. What is the name of a religious leader in the Jewish faith?
2. Outline three things a rabbi would do during his/her day.
3. What is the role of the chazan? What kind of talents might a chazan have?
4. What is the name of the person who prepares the meat for the Jewish community?
5. What does the term *kashrut* refer to?

DIGGING DEEPER

1. How do the various roles that form the community structure of the Jewish people support them in the practice of their faith?
2. How does the community structure of your religion support the practice of your faith?

KNOW IT ALL

Copy the following into your Religion folder and match the roles with the definitions.

Chazan	Slaughters animals and prepares meat according to Jewish food laws
Rabbi	Leads prayer and singing
Gabbai	Represents the Jewish community in a country
Shochet	Local spiritual leader and teacher
Chief rabbi	Performs duties at services

Community Structure: Way in which a group of people with a common interest is organised, especially in its roles (leadership, membership, etc).

Leadership: Setting a goal or aim for a person or a community and guiding them towards it. Always involves some degree of authority.

Education: The teaching or passing on of knowledge.

Follower/Discipleship: A person becomes a follower when they take on discipleship. This means that they begin to live by the traditions of a community of faith.

LESSON 61 Faith and Practice Today

GROUNDWORK
In this lesson we plan to:
- compare and contrast the faith and practice of early Jewish communities with that of modern Jewish communities.

DIGGING DEEPER
How has the faith and practice of the Jewish community changed over the years?

Key Concepts
Tradition/Follower/Discipleship

The Jewish Faith Tradition

There are two branches of Judaism today, the Orthodox **tradition** and the Reform tradition. The Orthodox tradition upholds the beliefs and practices of the early Jewish communities, while the Reform tradition is a more modern branch of Judaism. There are **followers** of both traditions in Ireland today.

Orthodox Judaism

Followers of the Orthodox tradition are strongly committed to expressing and living the Jewish faith in the way that it has been handed down to them by their ancestors. God's gift of the Torah (the Law) at Mount Sinai is considered to be more important than anything else. So, while Orthodox Jews are involved in many aspects of life – art, music, literature, fashion, science and business – they never forget that the teachings of the Torah come first when making decisions about how to live. In Orthodox synagogues, men and women are seated separately and the service is conducted in Hebrew. Of all the branches of Judaism, Orthodox Judaism makes the greatest demands on its followers.

Reform Judaism

Reform Judaism came about in response to the new ways of thinking of the eighteenth century (often called the 'Enlightenment'). This was a time of scientific discoveries and progressive thinking. Until then, people turned to their faith, sacred scripture and figures of authority (like the rabbi) for an understanding of their world. During the Enlightenment, people found new sources of knowledge. Science was able to answer some of their questions about the world around them. They began to look at the world, and their relationship with it, in a new way. For some Jewish people, this meant a softening of the laws, the teachings and the worship of Judaism, as it adapted to a changing world. Many of the strict dietary laws were discarded. Prayers were translated from the original Hebrew into the spoken language of the local Jewish community. In the Reform tradition, the men and women sit together. Reform Judaism emphasises the *spirit* rather than the *letter* of the Jewish Law. This does not mean that the Reform tradition abandons the Law, but rather it incorporates and adapts it into modern Jewish living. This form of Judaism continues today to change and adapt with each new generation of followers.

Orthodox Jews...
- Follow the laws of the Torah and the Jewish tradition strictly.
- Accept male rabbis only.
- Use only Hebrew in their synagogues.
- Men and women sit apart in the synagogue.
- Keep strict dietary laws.

Reform Jews...
- Adapt the laws of the Torah and the Jewish traditions to modern life.
- Allow synagogue services to be led by rabbis and by others.
- Accept both male and female rabbis.
- Celebrate services in the local language.
- Men and women sit together in the synagogue.
- Do not keep strict dietary laws.

KNOW IT ALL
1. List two similarities and two differences between the Orthodox and Reform traditions.
2. Write a paragraph about the difference in lifestyle between a follower of the Orthodox tradition and a follower of the Reform tradition in Judaism.

A Modern Jewish Community

An example of a modern Jewish community is the American Jewish World Service (AJWS). This group (based in America, but with worldwide support from the Jewish community) was set up in April 2004 to provide humanitarian aid for Africa. It is supporting many of the displaced and traumatised people who have been violently forced from their homes and are now living in camps in Sudan and Chad. Like Trócaire, this group is working to educate all people about such atrocities and to put pressure on world leaders to help end the suffering.

The funds raised by AJWS are being used to develop water sources, build sanitation facilities, improve basic health care, and support feeding centres to care for the thousands of malnourished children. They are also used to pay for educational and recreational activities for children, to support centres that provide care and counselling for orphans, and to provide family-friendly spaces for social and recreational activities. (We will refer to this group again in Section F when we talk about the Jewish moral vision.)

KNOWING ME KNOWING YOU
You can find out more about the American Jewish World Service and its work for a just world at: *http://www.ajws.org/index.cfm*

DIGGING DEEPER

1. How has the faith and practice of the Jewish community changed over the years?
2. Why is it important for a religion to change and evolve through the ages?
3. How do you think a modern Jewish community, e.g. the American Jewish World Service group, compares with the early followers of Judaism?
4. What kind of changes have occurred down through the years in your religion? Identify two major differences between the practice of your faith and the practice of your grandparents' faith.

5-4-3-2-1

1. Name and describe **five** new things you have learned about the beliefs and practices of Judaism.
2. Describe **four** Jewish festivals.
3. Write **three** paragraphs describing the sacred text of Judaism.
4. Name and describe the **two** rites of passage a Jewish teenager would have celebrated.
5. Write **one** A4 page describing Judaism to a group from sixth class in primary school.

> **Tradition:** The handing down of information, beliefs and customs from one generation to the next. Religious tradition involves the handing on of religious practices, beliefs, etc.

See page 492 for past exam questions on this topic.

Islam

The Context

LESSON 62   The Geographical, Historical and Cultural Background of Islam

GROUNDWORK
In this lesson we plan to:
- explore the geographical, historical and cultural background of Islam.

DIGGING DEEPER
Where was Islam founded? What religion was practised in Saudi Arabia before the foundation of Islam?

Key Concepts
Location/Cultural Context

Story: Moving to Melbourne

Jack looked out the airplane window. The buildings were the tallest he had ever seen and their glass windows sparkled like diamonds in the morning sun. There were swimming pools in back gardens, red brick roofs, and a few green patches of grass here and there. Jack was so excited. His dad had been transferred to a new job in Australia.

In the taxi *en route* to their new home, they noticed that Melbourne was a hive of multicultural activity. There were street traders and performers busy at their work in the summer sun. Bruce, the taxi driver, explained that they were now crossing the Yarra river. Jack remarked that the land was very flat except for the mountain range in the distance, and Bruce explained that this was the great dividing mountain range that runs along the southeast coast of Australia. 'This is so cool', thought Jack, 'I love moving to Melbourne!'

KNOW WHAT
What are the biggest changes that Jack will have to get used to in his new home?

The Location of Islam

Islam was founded in the seventh century AD in Saudi Arabia in the Middle East. Saudi Arabia is located between the Persian Gulf and the Red Sea. It is called 'the land of the two holy mosques' – a reference to Mecca and Medina, Islam's two holiest places.

Saudi Arabia is a land of enormous deserts and little rainfall. It is a huge, tilted block of rock, highest in the west and sloping gradually down to the east. Much of this rock is covered by large deserts. The landscape also contains mountain ranges and flat coastal plains.

DIGGING DEEPER
1. Where was the Islamic faith founded?
2. How does this **location** compare with the place where your religion was founded? How are they the same/different?

The Cultural Context

Life at the time of the foundation of Islam was very tough because of the landscape and the climate. The climate was hot and dry and there were no permanent rivers or lakes. The Arabs were a fiercely independent tribal people who led a nomadic lifestyle. The tribes were made up of several clans, led by a chief. They travelled from place to place in search of food and water for their flocks of sheep and camels.

To survive in these hot and dry lands, they had to be tough and ready to fight for their families and their tribes. Inter-tribal warfare was common, but it was limited by guidelines and rules.

A sense of community was important to the tribes, and strict rules were put in place to ensure that everyone worked as a cohesive unit. They were severely punished if they put the individual ahead of the group.

Mecca and Medina were oasis cities of great importance, as they were centres of trade and agriculture and they linked the Mediterranean world with South Arabia, East Africa and South Asia.

Because of the commercial success of the trading towns, people began to settle, and this affected the tribal communities and their way of life. The tribes began to break down because the individual members no longer needed the security of the tribe to survive. People were now beginning to look after themselves, as opposed to working within the tribal communities.

Religious Structures

The Arab tribes were polytheists, i.e. they worshipped many gods. They had a particular devotion to gods of nature, whom they believed protected them. The Ka'ba in the city of Mecca was the most important place of worship of the gods. It is a cube-shaped building, which at that time housed 360 idols of tribal gods. As well as believing in many nature gods, the Arab people believed in Allah, a supreme god and the creator of all life. They knew of the Jewish and Christian religions because many of the traders who travelled throughout the Middle East were Jews and Christians. However, this had little or no influence on the polytheism of the Arabs.

KNOW WHAT

1. What was life like at the time of the foundation of Islam (i.e. what was the cultural context)?
2. In your opinion, was this a difficult way of life? Why?/Why not?
3. How did the type of landscape affect the people and their way of life?
4. Who was in charge of the tribes?
5. What measures were put in place to make sure that each tribe worked as a community?
6. How did the people practise their religion at the time? What religious structures did they have?

DIGGING DEEPER

1. What do you know about polytheism?
2. What religion was practised in Saudi Arabia before the foundation of Islam?

KNOW IT ALL

Copy this exercise into your Religion folder and fill in the blanks using the wordbank given below.

> The _____ were a nomadic people who moved from one area to another in search of _____ and _____ . The tribes were led by a _____ . There was a great sense of _____ within the tribes. The towns of _____ and _____ were hives of commercial activity at the time. The tribes worshipped many _____, especially gods of _____. The _____ in Mecca was the main shrine. However, the people also believed in _____, the creator of all life. The commercial success of the trading towns led to the breakdown of the tribal communities, as people began to _____ down in order to avoid the harsh _____ life.

WORDBANK
Water • Arabs • Chief • Medina • Community • Food • Mecca • Nature • Gods • Settle Nomadic • Ka'ba • Allah

Location: A particular place or position, e.g. a town, city or country.

Cultural context: The events, facts, stories and customs of a particular culture or society that connect with and influence other events, e.g. the founding of a major world religion.

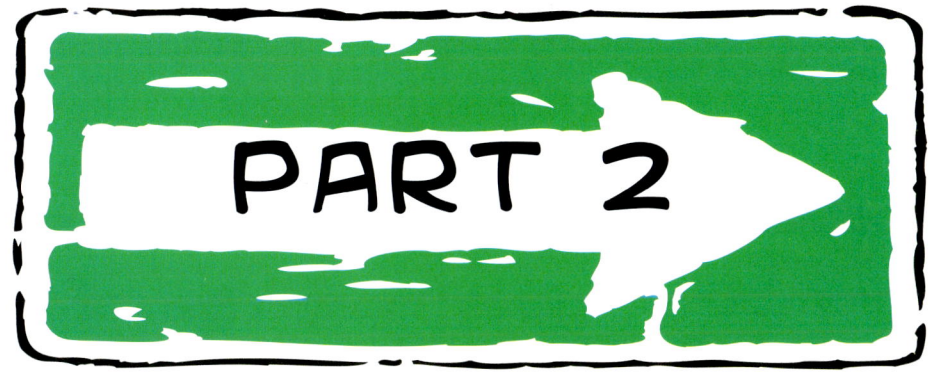

Sources of Evidence

LESSON 63 The Story of Muhammad

GROUNDWORK
In this lesson we plan to:
- explore the biography of Muhammad, the founder of Islam.

DIGGING DEEPER
How is the life of Muhammad a source of evidence (information) about the Islamic faith?

 **Key Concepts**
Founder/Vision/Dream/Revelation/Prophet

Muhammad – Founder of Islam

Muhammad was the **founder** of Islam. The word 'Islam' is an Arabic word that means 'submission'. Those who are members of the Islamic faith community are known as Muslims and they are called to have total submission to God, whom they call Allah. ('Allah' is the Arabic translation of the word 'God'. Christians in the Middle East also use the word 'Allah' for God.)

Muhammad was born in AD 570. He was orphaned at a very young age and was raised by his uncle. As he grew up, he developed into a responsible and kind young man, who worked hard, first as a shepherd and later as a trader.

When he was twenty-five, Muhammad went to work for a widow named Khadija, and despite the fact that she was almost forty years old, they married, had a family of six children and enjoyed a long and happy life together.

Muhammad was used to the familiar site of many different shrines to the gods. He was a deeply spiritual man, and he would often go to a cave on Mount Hira outside the city of Mecca to pray and meditate. It was while he was praying at Hira, at the age of forty, that something amazing happened, which would change his life for ever.

Muhammad's Vision/Dream

One day, in AD 610, while meditating in a cave at Mount Hira, Muhammad believed the archangel Gabriel appeared to him in a **dream** or **vision**. The angel told him to repeat the words he would tell him and to learn them by heart. This was Muhammad's first **revelation** from God, and it was the first of many such encounters. The words that were given to Muhammad declared that:

Mount Hira

- God is one.
- God is all powerful.
- God alone should be worshipped.

Like most people of that time, Muhammad could not read or write, so he learned everything he was told by heart. This revelation from God through the angel Gabriel became the beginnings of the Qur'an, the sacred text of Islam. The night of this first encounter is very special for the Islamic faith and is celebrated by Muslims as the Night of Power and Excellence.

After this first experience, Muhammad returned home. He told Khadija what had happened and she became the first convert to Islam. The seeds of Islam had begun to take root.

Muhammad the Prophet

Muhammad continued to receive messages from God and he began to teach about the oneness of God in the city of Mecca. His message made him very unpopular, as the people of Mecca were intolerant of anyone who tried to denounce or criticise their gods. Muhammad condemned their polytheism and proclaimed himself the **prophet** of a new monotheistic religion. He encouraged people to surrender their lives to the will of God and to take care of their fellow citizens. Some of the people found the idea of one God, Allah, who wanted the people to live good and honest lives, both strange and uncomfortable.

Muhammad endured the persecution of the Meccans for thirteen years. Eventually, he was driven out of Mecca, as were his followers, and they fled to the city of Yathrib in AD 622. This flight is called the *Hijra* and it remains a highly significant event in the Islamic calendar. Muslim dates are all calculated from this journey. Therefore, AD 622 is the year 1 AH (After Hijra), and AD 2000 is 1421 AH. The town of Yathrib later changed its name to Madinat al-Nabi (the town of the Prophet), which is now shortened to Medina.

Return to Mecca

Eight years after he had fled, Muhammad returned to Mecca. After his return, he went into the Ka'ba shrine and destroyed all of the idols and dedicated it to one God, Allah. Mecca has since been regarded as the holiest of all Islamic cities. During the last year of his life, Muhammad led a pilgrimage, or *hajj*, around all the significant places of worship to Allah. He preached to his followers on the Plain of Arafat as they made their pilgrim journey. By the time of the prophet Muhammad's death in 632, most of Arabia had converted to Islam.

Muslims revere Muhammad as the greatest and final prophet.

The Ka'ba in Mecca

KNOW WHAT
1. What message was revealed in a vision to Muhammad?
2. Why was Muhammad persecuted?
3. Why is the Hijra a very significant event for Muslims?

DIGGING DEEPER
1. How is the life of Muhammad a source of evidence (information) about the Islamic faith?
2. What do you think are the important things about the founder of any faith for its members?
3. Who is the founder of your faith? How did the life of the founder of your faith influence the followers?
4. Islamic followers show great respect for the founder of their faith. How do members of your faith show respect for their founder?

KNOW HOW
Compile a list of the key moments in Muhammad's life and explain why Muhammad is such a central figure in Islam.

Founder: One who sets up or inspires a new organisation, e.g. a religious community.

Vision/dream: A powerful image of what the world or a person or a group could be.

Revelation: The act of revealing or showing something. Used to describe how God and God's message were revealed to the founders and followers of Judaism, Christianity and Islam.

Prophet: A holy person sent by God to reveal (show) something of what God is like to others.

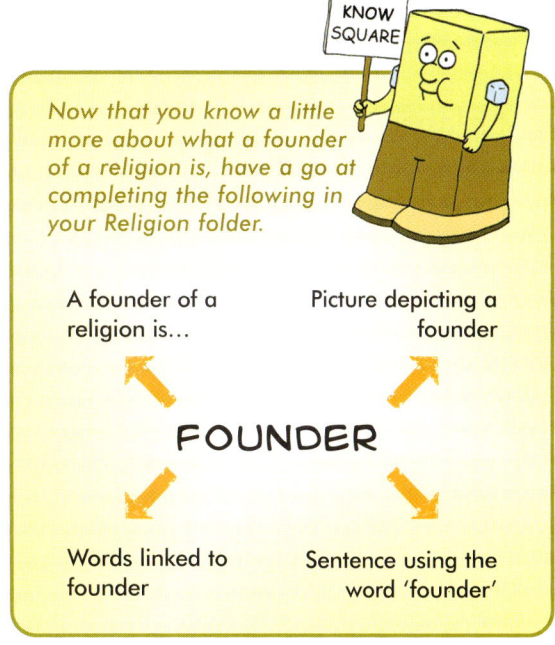

Now that you know a little more about what a founder of a religion is, have a go at completing the following in your Religion folder.

A founder of a religion is… Picture depicting a founder

FOUNDER

Words linked to founder Sentence using the word 'founder'

LESSON 64 The Qu'ran – The Sacred Text of Islam

GROUNDWORK
In this lesson we plan to:
- explore the primary source of information about Islam and trace the development of the Islamic faith from oral to written tradition;
- differentiate between faith documents and historical documents.

DIGGING DEEPER
How does a document of faith influence a person's faith?

Key Concepts
Evidence/Sacred text/Revelation/Inspiration/Oral tradition

The Qur'an – The Sacred Text of Islam

The primary source of information or **evidence** about Islam is the Qur'an (sometimes written as Koran). This **sacred text** was revealed in stages to the Prophet Muhammad over a period of twenty-three years.

The Qur'an is written in Arabic. It is slightly smaller than the New Testament and is divided into 114 chapters, called *suras*. Muslims today continue in the tradition of the earliest followers of Islam and memorise the text. Young Muslims attend lessons to help them learn Arabic if it is not their native language.

For Muslims, the Qur'an is Islam's earthly centre; this means that, as the literal Word of God (Allah), the Qur'an is respected and looked up to as a miracle of God. Before reading the Qu'ran, Muslims must wash their hands. While the Qur'an is being recited aloud, Muslims behave with great reverence and refrain from speaking, eating or drinking, or making any distracting noise.

As with the other world religions, the sacred text of Islam began with an **oral tradition**. Muhammad learned by heart all the **revelations** that he received from Allah. Under Allah's **inspiration**, he taught these to other Muslims, who in turn learned them off and recited them also. The word Qur'an means 'to recite'. Muhammad knew that these were messages from God and so he handed them on. This is why Muhammad is also known as the Messenger.

After the death of Muhammad, all that was revealed by Allah was brought together and written down to form the written text known as the Qur'an.

The Development of the Qur'an from Oral to Written Tradition

Oral Tradition:
- God revealed messages to Muhammad through the Angel Gabriel, and Muhammad learned all of the messages off by heart.
- Muhammad recited them to his companions, who in turn learned them off by heart.

Written Tradition:
- After the death of Muhammad, the revelations or messages from God were written down.
- The Qur'an, the sacred text of Islam, was compiled.

KNOW WHAT
1. What is the primary source of information about Islam?
2. How is the Qur'an laid out and what language is it written in?
3. Why is this sacred text still memorised by Muslims?

DIGGING DEEPER
1. Why do the Islamic people show such respect for the Qu'ran?
2. What is the sacred text of your faith? How do the members of your faith show respect for their sacred text?

KNOW IT ALL
Copy the following exercise into your Religion folder and fill in the blanks using the wordbank given below.

1. The _____ is the sacred text of Islam.
2. It is the primary _____ of information about Islam.
3. The Qur'an is the word of God as _____ through the angel _____ to _____ .
4. The Qur'an was not written down straight away, but was kept alive through the _____ _____ .
5. As Muhammad experienced each _____, he learned all the messages off by heart and _____ them to his followers.
6. After the death of Muhammad, all the information was written down and the _____ was formed.

WORDBANK
Vision • Qur'an • Muhammad • Source • Revealed • Gabriel • Taught • Oral Tradition • Qur'an

Documents of History; Documents of Faith

A historical document gives facts about when, where and how certain things happened. Your school History book is an example of such a document.

A faith document on the other hand explores the relationship between the members of a particular faith tradition and God. It includes information about what God wants to say to them and how God communicates with them.

(At this point, you might like to revise the opening exercise in Lesson 51 of 'Judaism', to examine the differences between documents of history and documents of faith.)

The Qur'an – A Document of Faith
When Muslims are reading and reciting the Qur'an, they are reading a document of faith. The Qur'an teaches the people of Islam about their faith and instructs them in their way of life. It is a document of faith because Muslims believe that it was written by God and revealed to Muhammad at different times in his life through the angel Gabriel.

The Qur'an instructs the Islamic community on:

- their behaviour towards God;
- the need to be honest and just in society;
- the need to balance the economic system;
- the need to show respect for the environment.

The imagery and language of the Qur'an is as beautiful as the handwriting used in its production. Here is one example:

> *'God is the light of the heavens and the earth. The parable of his light is as a niche and within it is a lamp, and the lamp is within a glass. And the glass as if it were a brilliant star lit from a sacred olive tree neither of the East nor of the West, whose oil almost glows forth, though no fire touched it. Light upon light, and God guides to his light whom he wills.'* (Qur'an 24:35)

KNOW WHAT

From what you have learned about the historical and religious sources of information for Christianity and Judaism and Islam, write four sentences that explain the difference between a document of history and a document of faith. (You might like to return to previous lessons on Christianity and Judaism to help you with this.)

KNOW IT ALL

Copy the following exercise into your Religion folder and match each word to its definition.

- Sacred text of Islam
- Monotheism
- Hijra
- Historical document
- Chapter from the Qur'an
- Revelation
- The great prophet of Islam
- Arabic
- Mecca
- Document of faith

- Belief in one God.
- The flight of Muhammad from Mecca
- Sura
- A religious document inspired by God
- Language of the Qur'an
- The Qur'an
- Holy city of Islam
- History book
- Muhammad
- Reveals or shows something of God

DIGGING DEEPER

1. In what ways do the Islamic documents of faith affect/influence the faith of Muslims?
2. How does the sacred text of your religion help you in your life?

Evidence: Information that provides a reason or basis for believing something.

Sacred text: Writings relating to a community of faith, which are considered holy and inspired.

Inspiration: Something that stirs our imagination and that influences us to new thinking or action.

Oral Tradition: Information that is handed on by word of mouth from one person or group to another.

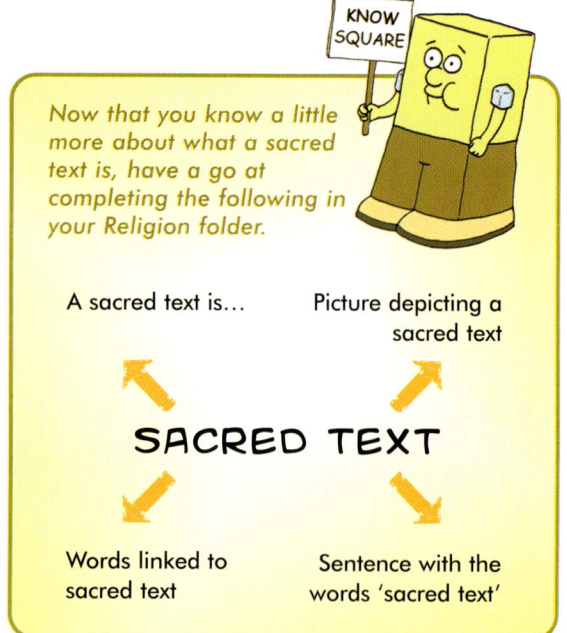

Now that you know a little more about what a sacred text is, have a go at completing the following in your Religion folder.

A sacred text is… — Picture depicting a sacred text

SACRED TEXT

Words linked to sacred text — Sentence with the words 'sacred text'

KNOW THE WAY

LESSON 65 Other Records and Sources

GROUNDWORK
In this lesson we plan to:
- examine the other sources of information about the foundation of Islam.

DIGGING DEEPER
What other sources give us information about the Islamic faith?

Key Concepts
Sacred text/Evidence

Introductory Exercise: Family and Friends

If you were to describe yourself through the eyes of a family member in one sentence, what would you say?

If you were to describe yourself through the eyes of a friend in one sentence, what would you say?

1. Is there a difference between both descriptions? Why?/Why not?
2. Does each sentence tell us something different about you? Explain.
3. Is it helpful to have more than one source of evidence or information about something? Why?/Why not?

The Sunna and the Hadith

Muhammad's followers kept a record of what he said and taught. This collection of stories and sayings of Muhammad is known as the Hadith and it covers almost every aspect of life: from table manners to the nature of the world about us.

Muhammad is believed to have interpreted the word of God by his actions, known as the Sunna or 'Way' of the Prophet. The Sunna sums up the way that the Prophet Muhammad lived his life. It serves as an example for all Muslims on how they too should act. The Sunna is embodied or included in the Hadith, which, after the Qur'an, is a further source of **evidence** about the Islamic faith.

Muslims today continue to use the Sunna and the Hadith to help them to gain a better understanding of life and of the Qur'an. While these are important elements of Islamic tradition, Muslims give clear priority to the Qur'an, because they believe that it is the direct word of God.

KNOW WHAT
1. What is the Hadith?
2. What is the Sunna?

DIGGING DEEPER
1. 'We can work out what's right on our own; we don't need a holy book to tell us what to do.' Do you agree with this statement? Discuss your answer.
2. Do you think a faithful Muslim would agree with that statement? Discuss your answer.
3. How do the documents of your faith affect your belief/your actions?

Sharia Law: The Way of Allah Expressed in Rules for Living

Followers of Islam look for guidance first to the Qu'ran and then to the life and sayings of Muhammad, as recorded in the Hadith. Through a process of argument and agreement, a huge range of laws and recommendations has emerged. This body of laws is called the Sharia or 'Allah's Law'. It includes rules for every area of life, including how to dress, how to pray, how a country should be governed, etc. Sharia is the ultimate authority in Islam. Teachers (or scholars) continue to play a most important role in Islam today because they work out how to apply Sharia law in new situations. But these teachers are not as important as the Sharia itself. Sincere Muslims strive (or go all-out) to follow Allah's Law in absolutely every area of their lives; they use the word *jihad* to describe this.

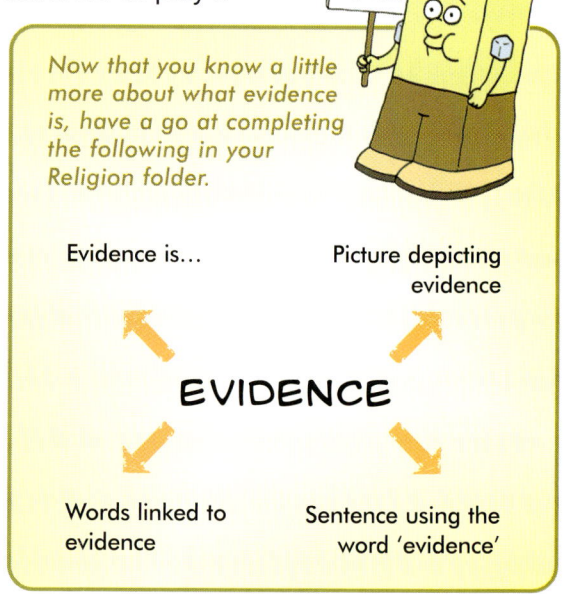

Now that you know a little more about what evidence is, have a go at completing the following in your Religion folder.

Evidence is…   Picture depicting evidence

EVIDENCE

Words linked to evidence   Sentence using the word 'evidence'

KNOW WHAT
1. What is Sharia law?
2. How did Sharia law come about?

DIGGING DEEPER
How is Sharia law a source of evidence about Islam?

Rites of Passage and Other Rituals

LESSON 66 The Core Beliefs of Islam

GROUNDWORK
In this lesson we plan to:
- identify the core beliefs of Islam.

DIGGING DEEPER
What is the belief system at the heart of Islam?

The Islamic Articles of Faith

1. Belief in Allah
Muslims believe in one God (*Allah* in Arabic), who controls everything. To be a Muslim means to live one's life according to God's will. The word 'Islam' means 'submission to God'. Muslims try to be obedient to the will of Allah rather than putting their own wishes first.

2. Belief in the Qur'an
The Qur'an is the sacred text of Islam. Muslims believe that the words of the Qur'an came directly from God (Allah) and were passed on through the prophet Muhammad. Every word of the Qur'an is sacred and is spoken in the original Arabic. Muslims show their respect for the Qur'an by:

- wrapping it in a clean cloth;
- keeping it on a high shelf so that no other book is placed before it;
- washing before touching it;
- placing it on a stand to read it, so that it does not touch the floor;
- not turning their backs on it;
- sometimes kissing it after reading it.

3. Belief in Angels

The angel Gabriel revealed the Word of God as it is written in the Qur'an to Muhammad.

4. Belief in the Prophet Muhammad and in the other prophets of the Hebrew Scriptures and the Bible

Muslims believe that Adam, Moses, Abraham, David and Jesus were prophets who also received revelations from God, and they call Jews and Christians 'People of the Book' out of respect for their belief in the Hebrew Scriptures and the Bible. Jesus is considered a particularly important prophet, but he is not recognised as the Son of God.

5. Belief in Judgement Day and life after death

Muslims believe in a Day of Judgement, when people will be either rewarded or punished by Allah, depending on the kind of life they have lived.

KNOW WHAT

1. What are the first three beliefs of Islam?
2. What does the fourth belief tell us about the Islamic faith?
3. How is the fifth belief similar to the Christian belief about life after death?
4. Do you think the Islamic faith asks a lot of its followers? Why?/Why not?

DIGGING DEEPER

1. What are the main beliefs of your faith?
2. How do these beliefs affect your daily life?
3. Choose *one* of the above beliefs and explain why you think a follower of Islam believes this?

LESSON 67 The Practice of the Islamic Faith

GROUNDWORK
In this lesson we plan to:
- explore how Muslims practise their faith through the Five Pillars of Islam.

DIGGING DEEPER
How is a person's lifestyle influenced by their faith?

Key Concepts
Practice/Creed/Prayer/Meditation/Ritual/Places of Worship

How do I show you?
I show you I like you by being your mate.
I show you I care by looking out when you're late.
I show you I believe when I act on your advice.
I show you I'm sorry when I say something nice.
I show you how much you mean by the things that I do.
I think you're a pal, the best through and through.

3-2-1
1. Think of **three** words that describe this poem.
2. List **two** ways in which the poet describes her relationship with her friend.
3. Write **one** paragraph or have a go at drawing one picture to describe the theme of the poem.

This simple poem is based on the theme of the classic poem 'How do I love thee? Let me count the ways...' by Elizabeth Barrett Browning. The poem above is hardly a love poem, but perhaps it's a 'buddie' poem! The poem demonstrates how the poet is committed to her friend. Commitment requires action; this means you must 'do' things to show you are committed to someone or something as well as 'say' you are committed.

- Name two things to which you are committed.
- Name two ways in which you show your commitment.

The Five Pillars of Islam

The Five Pillars of Islam are the five ways that Muslims express and live their faith. In the last lesson, we looked at the five core beliefs of Islam. The Five Pillars of Islam stem from these beliefs. By their **practice** of the Five Pillars, Muslims put their beliefs into action and show their religious commitment.

1. Shahada (Creed)
The Shahada is a **creed** or profession of faith that declares: 'There is no God but Allah, and Muhammad is his messenger.' These words are repeated in prayer several times a day. Muslims do not worship Muhammad; they worship Allah (God). Muhammad preached that

God can only be known through his messengers, therefore belief in God requires belief in the words of the Qur'an and the Messengers of God. The words of the Shahada are the first words whispered into a newborn baby's ear and, if possible, they are the last words prayed with a dying person.

2. Salat (Prayer)

Salat is the **ritual** of praying five times every day: at dawn, just after midday, in mid-afternoon, just after sunset and after dark. These **prayers** are mainly verses from the Qur'an, praising Allah and asking for his guidance. The prayers are said in Arabic. Muslims often wash and take off their shoes before praying. On Fridays, Muslim men are expected to perform the afternoon prayer in the mosque, one of the main **places of worship** for Muslims.

3. Sawm (Fasting)

Sawm is the fasting that takes place during the ninth month of the Islamic year, which is called Ramadan. During the hours of daylight in this month, adult Muslims don't eat or drink anything. This time of fasting reminds Muslims not to take the good things in life for granted and not to overindulge in them. It also helps them to identify with the poor. It is a time for prayer, **meditation** and reflection, when Muslims take stock of their lives.

4. Zakat (Almsgiving)

Zakat is the responsibility Muslims have to give, if they can afford it, at least two and a half per cent of their savings every year to the poor. Zakat is often described as the pillar of social action. Because the Islamic people see everything as belonging to God, they see this simply as a way of distributing the wealth more fairly and of purifying one's soul. In Islamic countries, this religious tax is collected by the government and then shared among the poor. In non-Islamic countries, the Islamic community organises this collection and distribution.

5. Hajj (Pilgrimage)

Hajj is the pilgrimage that every Muslim is expected to make (unless they are ill or cannot afford it) to Mecca to visit the Ka'ba, a place of worship to Allah. The Hajj takes place during the twelfth Muslim month, when many millions of pilgrims travel to Mecca.

Pilgrims at the Hajj

Shahada	A creed or profession of faith: One God, Allah.	Creed
Salat	The ritual of praying five times every day.	Prayer
Sawm	The fasting that takes place during the month of Ramadan.	Fasting
Zakat	The giving of money and care to the poor.	Almsgiving
Hajj	The pilgrimage that every Muslim hopes to make to Mecca.	Pilgrimage

TAKE FIVE

1. What is the creed of Islam?
2. What ritual happens five times a day?
3. How do Muslims try to distribute their wealth more fairly in society?
4. What takes place during the holy month of Ramadan?
5. What is the Hajj and when does it occur?

DIGGING DEEPER

1. How is the lifestyle of a Muslim influenced by his/her faith?
2. How is your lifestyle influenced by your faith?
3. Muslims fast during Ramadan. Is there a time when people of your faith are encouraged to fast? Describe this time.
4. Have you ever gone without certain foods or fasted as part of your religious commitment? What was it like? Why did you choose to do this?

KNOW IT ALL

Copy the following exercise into your Religion folder and match the words to their correct meaning.

- Sawm
- Zakat
- Ramadan
- Mosque
- Qur'an
- Shahada
- Salat
- Hajj

- Pilgrimage to Mecca
- Place of worship for Muslims
- Sacred text
- Holy month of fasting
- Prayer
- Creed or profession of faith
- Fasting
- To give alms to the poor

KNOWING ME KNOWING YOU

Find out more about the beliefs and practices of Islam at the BBC website: *www.bbc.co.uk/religion/religions/islam/index.shtml*

This website includes a very clear illustration of how Muslims pray.

 **Practice:** The practice of a faith tradition means the living of that faith according to its central beliefs and teachings.

Creed: A statement of religious beliefs.

Prayer: Communication between people and God.

Meditation: A form of silent prayer during which the person empties the mind of all other thoughts and focuses on the divine.

Ritual: A series of actions carried out in a set way. Religious rituals are usually repeated regularly by the faith community to express the relationship between God and the community.

Places of Worship: Places set apart for religious rituals.

See pages 489 and 490 for past exam questions on this topic.

LESSON 68   Signs and Symbols of Islam

GROUNDWORK
In this lesson we plan to:
- explore some of the signs and symbols of Islam.

DIGGING DEEPER
By what practices would you be able to identify a person of the Islamic faith?

Key Concepts
Sign and Symbol

Symbols of Islam

The crescent moon and star are a symbol of Islam. The Muslim calendar is based on the cycles of the moon and the five points of the star are said to remind Muslims of the Five Pillars of Islam. Muslims believe that Islam guides a person's life just as the moon and stars guide a traveller in the desert. This symbol on a country's flag usually indicates that it is a Muslim state.

The flag of Pakistan

The colour green is commonly used when representing Islam. It is often used in decorating mosques, tombs and various religious objects. Some say that this is because green was the favourite colour of Muhammad and that he wore a green cloak and turban, while others say that it symbolises vegetation. In the Qu'ran, it is said that the people in heaven will wear green clothes.

KNOW WHAT
Describe some of the symbols that are important for the Islamic faith community.

KNOW HOW
Draw the crescent moon symbol of Islam and explain what it symbolises.

Signs of Islam

Dress Code

Muslims believe in dressing modestly, without drawing attention to their bodies. This is an outward **sign** of their respect for their bodies and it also shows that they are part of the Islamic community. Muslim men are encouraged to cover themselves from the waist to the knee. Women are encouraged not to show bare skin in public; for this reason, many Muslim women wear a scarf (called a *hijab*) and cover their arms and legs when they go out. Some Muslim women choose to wear a *burka*, which is a long loose-flowing garment that covers the body from head to toe, with only a small opening for the eyes.

Muslim women wearing the burka

Food and Drink

There are strict dietary laws in Islam. Muslims eat what is called *halal* meat; that is, meat that has been slaughtered in the traditional Muslim way. The word *halal* means 'allowed', and while the animal is being slaughtered the name of Allah is said; the animal is also killed in such a way that the blood, which Muslims consider unclean, is drained away.

Muslims are not allowed to eat pork, and this includes any type of sausage that contains even small traces of pork. Because many food products contain animal fats, including the fat from pigs, Muslims have to be very careful about the type of foods they eat, especially processed foods, so they don't eat anything that has 'animal fat', 'lard', 'shortening' or 'fat' in the list of ingredients.

Muslims are also very strict about not drinking alcohol; they see this as part of the Prophet Muhammad's teachings concerning living a healthy lifestyle.

This strict dietary observance is an outward sign that the Muslim community is deeply committed to the Islamic faith.

KNOW WHAT
1. Look through the food press at home. See if you can find four foods that have animal fat listed in the ingredients. Why would a Muslim avoid these foods?
2. If you were having people from the Islamic faith community to lunch, what kind of foods would you serve? Name three foods or drinks that you would definitely not serve.

DIGGING DEEPER
1. Do you think it would be difficult to observe strict dietary laws? Why?/Why not?
2. By what practices would you be able to identify a person of the Islamic faith?
3. By what practices would you be able to identify a person of your faith?

Sign: A word, drawing or action that gives information.

Symbol: A type of sign, but with a deeper meaning. A symbol is a visible sign of something invisible.

LESSON 69 Islamic Rites of Passage

GROUNDWORK
In this lesson we plan to:
- explore the rites of passage of Islam.

DIGGING DEEPER
How do the Islamic people celebrate the key stages in their lives?

Key Concepts
Rite/Places of Worship/Ceremony/Ritual/Sign/Symbol

Islamic Rites of Passage

The Islamic faith has many special celebrations that mark the major stages of life. These celebrations are called **rites** of passage and they take place in the mosque, the sacred **place of worship** for Muslims.

Birth

At birth, words from the Qur'an are whispered into the ear of the newborn baby.

About seven days after the birth, the baby's family celebrates by having a naming **ceremony**. The choice of a name is very important to the Muslim people. If a boy has the name Abdul (a name recommended by Allah), it is usually followed by one of the ninety-nine beautiful names of God. Many of the baby girls are given the names of women from the Prophet Muhammad's family.

A popular custom is to cut the baby's hair and weigh it, and then give the weight of the hair in gold or silver to the poor.

If the baby is male, circumcision is usually performed at this time. This serves as a physical **sign** that the baby boy has become a member of the Muslim faith community.

Marriage

Marriage and family life are very important in the Islamic community. Marriage is, however, more of a legal contract than a religious one. There is often just a simple **ritual** of readings from the Qur'an and an exchange of vows in the presence of family and friends.

Some Muslim marriages are arranged (the couple are chosen for each other by family members), but this varies from country to country. Divorce is allowed but is greatly discouraged.

Islamic wedding ceremony

When a Muslim woman marries, her groom gives her a dowry for her own use. (A dowry is a sum of money or goods of value.) The bride keeps her own family name.

Death

Muslims are buried within a day of their death. First the body is washed and then it is wrapped in a white cloth. Muslims do not use coffins. The person who has died is laid to rest on their right side, to face Mecca. At the graveside, prayers from the Qur'an are recited. Cremation is not allowed.

Men and women are buried separately. As a **symbol** of respect for their dead, the graves of Muslims are sometimes raised above ground level. Large tombstones or decorations are not traditional.

KNOW WHAT

From your earlier exploration of the Jewish faith, can you describe the differences between the Muslim and the Jewish naming ceremonies, marriage ceremonies and funeral rituals?

DIGGING DEEPER

1. How do the Islamic people celebrate the key stages in their lives?
2. If you were a Muslim, how many key stages in your life would you have celebrated by now? Describe one.
3. If possible, arrange a meeting with Islamic teenagers from your community.

KNOWING ME KNOWING YOU

- Find out more about Islamic customs connected with birth at:
  www.bbc.co.uk/religion/religions/islam/features/rites/birth/
- Find out more about Islamic marriage celebrations at:
  www.bbc.co.uk/religion/religions/islam/features/rites/weddings.shtml
- Find out more about Islamic customs connected with death and burial at:
  islam.about.com/cs/elderly/a/funerals.htm

Rite: A set of words or actions used to celebrate or mark an important event. 'Rites of passage' celebrate different stages in a person's life.

Ceremony: A formal event to celebrate and to show respect for something, for example, a baptism or a wedding.

LESSON 70 Ritual Events and Sacred Times of Islam

GROUNDWORK
In this lesson we plan to:
- explore the feasts and festivals of Islam;
- explore pilgrimage as a key element of Islam.

DIGGING DEEPER
How do the Islamic people celebrate their sacred times?

Key Concepts
Calendar/Sacred Time/Festivals/Pilgrimage/Ritual

Story: A Special Day
It was 21 June, the longest day of the year, but it was also Chelsea's thirteenth birthday. She was really excited about being a teenager and was looking forward to the day's celebrations.

Her grandparents arrived in high spirits. 'Wait until you see what we have for you, young lady,' said Grandad John. 'We have planned this day since you were born,' said Granny Cecelia. Grandad John reached into the boot of their car and eased out an elegant birch tree.

'The Lady of the Forest is what she's often called,' Grandad John said with a smile. 'The day you were born, we bought this tree, planted it at home and watched it grow. Just like you, it has become strong and confident. Now it will be a sign of how much you're loved.'

Chelsea was thrilled with the thought that this beautiful tree was hers, and not only was it hers, but they shared the same birthday.

KNOW WHAT
1. How was the birch tree a sign of their love?
2. Why is it important to mark special occasions?
3. Do you know anyone who had an important occasion made really special by family or friends? Describe what happened.

In every religion, there are **sacred times** that are marked by celebrations. Let's learn about such times in the Islamic faith tradition.

Ritual Events and Sacred Times of Islam
The Islamic faith has its own **calendar**, calculated from AD 622, the year of the Hijra, when Muhammad fled from Mecca to Medina. It is a lunar calender, i.e. it is based on the cycles of the moon. There are twelve lunar months in the Islamic year, rotating in a thirty-year cycle, where the years are 354 days long, except for eleven leap years of 355 days. Muslim **festivals** happen at various times during the year and are not linked to the seasons like some of the festivals in the Christian and Jewish religious calendar.

Ramadan
Ramadan is the ninth month of the Islamic calender and it is regarded as the holiest month of the year. It was during this month that Muhammad received the first of the revelations of the Qur'an, so the focus of Ramadan is on the Qur'an, and many Muslims read it

through from beginning to end. During this month, Muslims fast from all food and drink during the hours of daylight.

Eid ul-Fitr

The festival of Eid ul-Fitr takes place at the end of Ramadan. There is great rejoicing and thanksgiving to God for the successful completion of the fast. After a ceremony in the mosque (which includes an address given by the spiritual leader), everyone gets together for a communal lunch. Throughout the day, Muslims give one another a traditional greeting, 'Eid Mubarak', which means 'Blessing and joys of Eid'. During the first three days of the new month, there is a lot of visiting between families and friends, with the giving and receiving of presents – very like the way Christians celebrate at Christmas.

Eid ul-Adha

This festival takes place during the twelfth month of the Islamic calendar, just over two months after Eid ul-Fitr. It coincides with the Hajj, the great **pilgrimage** to Mecca. This festival celebrates Abraham's willingness to sacrifice his son Ishmael to God. God commanded Abraham (known to Muslims as Ibrahim) to sacrifice a lamb instead, so the sacrifice of a lamb or a goat is an important part of this festival. Prayers are said in the mosque for those Muslims who have journeyed to Mecca. The festival lasts for four days.

The Hajj

Mecca is viewed as an extremely holy place and no non-Muslim is allowed to enter it. The Hajj involves three specific journeys within Mecca. Each journey includes prayers and **rituals** that recall events in the life of Abraham, his son Ishmael and the Prophet Muhammad.

Stage 1
When Muslims make their pilgrimage to Mecca, they dress in a special white gown that ensures modesty and symbolises purity. When they arrive at the Ka'ba, they pray and circle it seven times in an anti-clockwise direction. When they are finished the circles of prayer, if they are close enough, they kiss or touch the shrine. Then they journey seven times between two small hills near the Ka'ba.

Stage 2
The second part of the Hajj involves making a journey of over twenty kilometres to the Plain of Arafat, where the Prophet Muhammad preached his last sermon. Here the pilgrims ask God's forgiveness for their wrongdoings. They camp overnight in a place between Arafat and the village of Mina, and they collect stones for their next ritual, which will take place in Mina.

Stage 3
At Mina, the pilgrims throw their stones at pillars that represent Satan and his temptations. This ritual recalls a time when Abraham was tempted by Satan three times and he rejected him three times.

The Ka'ba in Mecca, where over a million Islamic pilgrims visit every year.

When stage three is complete, the pilgrims celebrate the festival of Eid ul-Adha, and a sheep or goat is sacrificed in thanksgiving.

KNOW WHAT

1. What happens during Ramadan?
2. What happens during Eid ul-Fitr?
3. What is the Hajj?
4. Which festival coincides with the Hajj?
5. What does this festival celebrate?
6. Where does the Hajj take place?
7. Outline the stages of the Hajj and what takes place at each stage.

KNOWING ME KNOWING YOU

With the guidance of your teacher, try to watch National Geographic channel's *Inside Mecca*. It will help you to identify each stage of the Hajj and to understand the significance of the pilgrimage for the followers of Islam.

DIGGING DEEPER

1. Why is pilgrimage an important part of the Islamic faith?
2. Why is pilgrimage an important part of any faith?
3. Name two sites of pilgrimage from your faith and briefly explain why they are pilgrimage sites.

KNOW IT ALL

Copy the following exercise into your Religion folder and fill in the blanks using the wordbank given below.

There are two main Islamic festivals: _____ and _____. Eid ul-Fitr takes place at the end of _____. Ramadan is the _____ month of the Islamic calendar and is celebrated because the Prophet _____ received his first _____ at this time. During Ramadan, many Muslims read the _____ from beginning to end. The end of Ramadam is a time of great _____ and _____.

Eid ul-Adha takes place during the _____ month. It recalls the willingness of _____ to offer his son _____ as a sacrifice to God. God told Abraham to sacrifice a _____ instead, and so Muslims repeat this ritual during this festival. The great pilgrimage called the _____ also takes place during this festival.

WORDBANK

Eid ul-Adha • Ninth • Revelation • Muhammad • Qur'an • Eid ul-Fitr • Thanksgiving
Rejoicing • Twelfth • Ishmael • Ramadan • Abraham • Hajj • Lamb

KNOW THE WAY

Festivals: Special celebrations that recall the events, facts, stories and customs of a particular group, nation or religion.

Calendar/Sacred time: A calender is a system for dividing the year into definite periods. Sacred time refers to times of special religious importance, e.g. religious festivals.

Pilgrimage: A journey to a sacred place.

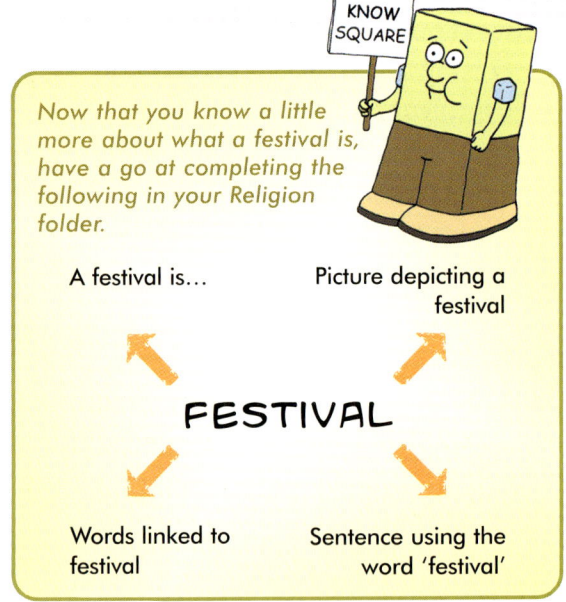

LESSON 71 Islamic Prayer and Places of Worship

GROUNDWORK
In this lesson we plan to:
- explore the practice of prayer within the Islamic faith.

DIGGING DEEPER
When do I pray?

Key Concepts
Practice/Ritual/Places of Worship

The Practice of Prayer

The second pillar of Islam is Salat: this is the call to prayer five times a day. For a Muslim, life revolves around this **practice**.

Before Salat, each Muslim prepares to pray by:

1. Having the right intention to pray.
2. Performing *wudu* (a cleansing of the body and the mind).
3. Laying out a prayer mat on clean ground.
4. Facing in the direction of Mecca.
5. Standing erect, with head down, hands at sides, and feet evenly spaced.

Muslims often pray at a mosque, but they may pray anywhere by simply using a prayer mat. Muslims remove their shoes before prayer and the women wear a scarf. Many Muslim men wear a prayer cap.

A prayer mat

Prayer Rituals

The prayers are accompanied by **ritual** actions, each of which has a specific meaning:

Standing	Listening to God
Bowing	Showing respect for God
Touching forehead to ground	Showing obedience to God

Prayer Beads

Some Muslims use prayer beads, similar to Catholic rosary beads. Each bead is passed and held through the thumb and forefinger, to keep count of the prayers. Each string has thirty-three or ninety-nine beads and is used to recite the ninety-nine 'Beautiful Names' of Allah that are given in the Qur'an.

TAKE FIVE

1. What is the second pillar of Islam?
2. How does a Muslim prepare to pray?
3. In what direction does a Muslim face during prayer?
4. What ritual actions are part of Muslim prayer?
5. What do Muslims wear during prayers?

Place of Worship – The Mosque

The mosque is an Islamic **place of worship**. Many mosques have dome-shaped roofs and a crescent-moon symbol on the top. They often have a tower called a *minaret*, from where the call to prayer is made, generally through a loudspeaker.

All male Muslims are expected to attend the mosque at midday on Fridays for prayers. An arched alcove or a decorated panel in the wall of the mosque shows them the direction of Mecca. Men and women sit in different parts of the mosque. A leader, called the *imam*, leads the prayers.

Islam forbids any image of Allah because Allah is considered too great to be limited to an interpretation by human hands. Therefore, there are no pictures or statues in a mosque. Instead, the walls are often decorated with beautifully written passages from the Qur'an; this is called calligraphy.

KNOWING ME KNOWING YOU

- With your teacher, try to organise a class visit to a mosque.
- You can also look up either of the following websites for a virtual tour of a mosque:
  http://www.lancashiremosques.com/discovery_mosque_tour.asp
  http://www.hitchams.suffolk.sch.uk/mosque/entrance.htm

DIGGING DEEPER

1. Name and describe three of the prayer times in your faith community.
2. Write about any particular times during your day that you set aside for prayer.

See pages 490 and 491 for past exam questions on this topic.

Development of Tradition

LESSON 72 The Development of Islam

GROUNDWORK
In this lesson we plan to:
- identify important people and key moments in the development of Islam;
- explore the division or split (schism) that occurred within Islam;
- learn about the global distribution of the Muslim people.

DIGGING DEEPER
What events led to the Islamic faith as we know it today?

 **Key Concepts**
Development/Expansion/Schism/Persecution/Commitment

The Development and Expansion of Islam

As with all of the major world religions, Islam began to **develop** and **expand**. As Islam grew throughout Arabia, it expanded to the borders of Afghanistan and India in the east and as far west as Spain and France.

Key Moments in the Development and Expansion of Islam

AD 570 — Birth of Muhammad.

AD 595 — Muhammad met and married Khadija, who became the first convert to Islam.

AD 610 — Muhammad had his first revelation from God through the Angel Gabriel. That event is celebrated by Muslims today as the Night of Power and Excellence.

AD 620 — Muhammad preached to people from Yathrib, a city north of Mecca.

AD 622 — The Hijra – the flight of Muhammad and his followers from Mecca to Yathrib, now called Medina. In Medina, Muhammad was embraced as a great religious and political leader.

AD 630 — Muhammad returned to Mecca. He initiated a *jihad* (a holy war) and after three major battles he conquered the city of Mecca. He then entered the Ka'ba shrine and destroyed all the idols and dedicated the Ka'ba to one God, Allah.

AD 632 — Muhammad made his final pilgrimage to the Ka'ba shrine. It was at Mount Arafat that Muhammad delivered his final sermon. Later that same year, he became ill and died in Medina.

AD 650 — After the death of Muhammad, there was a rapid expansion of Islam. Islamic armies from Arabia swept through parts of the east and by AD 650 many provinces of the eastern Roman Empire and also the Persian Empire were converted to Islam.

AD 700 — The conquest of the North African coast began. Roman Africa was taken, and in AD 711 the Islamic armies crossed over into Spain and the south of France.

Eighth to twelfth century — From the eighth to the twelfth century, Islam enjoyed what is called the Golden Age of Islam. This is because art, literature, architecture, science and mathematics flourished in the Islamic cities, such as Baghdad in Iraq, Cairo in Egypt and Damascus in Syria. A mathematical system, known as *al-jabar* in Arabic, was invented; in English we know this as algebra.

Middle Ages — During the Middle Ages, there was much conflict between Islam and the Christian states of Europe, although there were also episodes of peaceful co-existence and friendly contact.

Fifteenth century — The Islamic Turks overran what was left of the old eastern Roman Empire, took Constantinople (now Istanbul), and gained control of Greece and specific neighbouring territories in eastern Europe. This is why even today in some parts of eastern Europe, like Albania, there are still large Islamic communities.

KNOW THE WAY

KNOW WHAT
From what you have learned in the previous lessons, can you add in any extra information to these dates?

KNOW HOW
Divide the class into groups. Each group chooses one key moment in the development of Islam and represents it in words and pictures. When each group has finished, place the key moments in their correct order on the classroom wall. The leader of each group may then tell the class about the key moment they chose.

DIGGING DEEPER
What do you think helps a faith to remain steadfast and strong when it is in the process of development?

Islam after the Death of Muhammad

After Muhammad's death, the leadership of the Muslim community passed to a succession of 'caliphs' (deputies). The fourth Caliph was Ali, Muhammad's son-in-law. A dispute arose about Ali's right to be Caliph, and before it could be settled, Ali was killed. As a result, there occurred a **schism** or split within the Islamic faith tradition, and the Muslim community separated into two distinct groups. These two groups still exist today. While both groups are Muslim, they have developed somewhat different traditions over the years.

Sunni Muslims

The first group, the Sunni Muslims, make up about ninety per cent of Muslims worldwide. Sunni Muslims believe that no one could succeed Muhammad. They take their authority from the Sunna, the words and actions of Muhammad. They declare Muhammad to be 'the Seal of the Prophets' (i.e. the final prophet) and the Qur'an as the perfect revelation of Allah. They follow the Caliphs, who can only be seen as 'guardians' of this truth. The Sunni group have 'imams' – holy men whose main function is to lead the prayers in the mosque.

Shia Muslims

The second group, called Shia (or Shiite) Muslims, make up about ten per cent of the Muslim population. They are supporters of Ali, who refused to accept the authority of the Caliphs. The Shias believe that Ali was Muhammad's true successor because of his relationship with the prophet. The Shias suffered **persecution** for their faith, but this only added to their sense of **commitment** and of being the true preservers of Islam. Their main figure of religious authority is the Imam. This group has a different understanding of the term 'Imam'. The Shia believe that the Imam is someone who is able to lead them in all aspects of life. According to the Shia, the Imam is a leader who *must* be followed, since he is appointed by Allah and is a descendant of Allah.

In Iran, the homeland of the Shia group, there was a revolution in 1979. The people were taken over by the Ayatollahs (Shia religious leaders), who declared Iran to be an Islamic state, and strict Islamic laws were introduced.

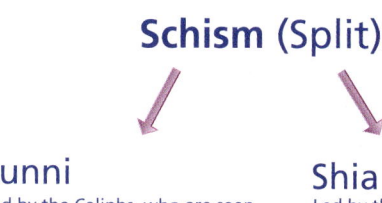

Schism (Split)

Sunni
Led by the Caliphs, who are seen as guardians of the truth that was revealed by Muhammad.

Shia
Led by the Iman, who must be a direct descendant of Muhammad.

KNOW WHAT
1. What happened after the death of the Prophet Muhammad?
2. Why did a schism occur in the Islamic faith tradition?
3. What is the main difference between the Sunni and Shia Islamic groups?
4. Where in the world today is the split between Sunni and Shia Muslims most obvious?

DIGGING DEEPER
1. What effect do you think a schism would have on a faith community?
2. Has there ever been a schism in your faith community? Describe what happened?
   Or
   Write about a schism that happened in any world religion. Describe the effects it had on the religion.

The Worldwide Community of Muslims

The majority of Muslims today live in countries of North Africa (e.g. Algeria, Libya and Egypt) and in the Middle East (e.g. Saudi Arabia, Iran and Iraq). Muslims are also present in significant numbers in countries as varied as Russia, China, India, England and the United States of America. These communities include many people who were born into the Muslim faith tradition in the country to which they had moved. There are approximately twenty thousand Muslims living in Ireland. The worldwide community of Muslims is known as the *Umma*.

KNOW IT ALL
In your own words, explain each of the following terms: Expansion; Development; Schism; Imam; Sunni; Shia; Caliph; Muhammad; Guardian; Umma; Prophet.

Development: Growth or change, e.g. the way in which a community of faith grows or matures over time.

Expansion: Increase in size, area or number. A religious community expands when more people join it and when it spreads to other places.

Schism: A split, especially in relation to a religious tradition.

Persecution: Deliberately causing loss, pain or death to a person or a group because of race, religion or way of life.

Commitment: Pledge/promise to a group or community to carry out a task or role.

See page 491 for past exam questions on this topic.

(Higher Level Only)

Tradition, Faith and Practice Today

LESSON 73 Islamic Faith and Practice Today

GROUNDWORK
In this lesson we plan to:
- explore the faith and practice of Islamic communities today with reference to Ireland.

DIGGING DEEPER
Who are the Irish Islamic faith community?

 **Key Concepts**
Community structure/Education/Leadership/Tradition

The Islamic Community in Ireland

In 1959, the first Islamic Society was established in Ireland. It was initiated by the Muslim students who were studying medicine in Ireland. At that time, there was no place where they could meet and worship together as a community. So they founded the Dublin Islamic Society (later called the Islamic Foundation of Ireland). They used their homes and rented rooms in order to pray and worship together. In 1976, the first mosque and Islamic centre in Ireland was opened on Harrington Street, Dublin 8. In the early eighties, there was a full-time *imam* (leader) for the mosque.

During the last twenty years, there has been a steady increase in the numbers of Muslims in Ireland. The Islamic Cultural Centre of Ireland in Clonskeagh, Dublin, is one of the centres of Islamic worship. It is also a place of **education** and socialisation for the Sunni Muslim community. There are both Sunni and Shia communities in Ireland.

> The imam usually acts as a **leader** of the local Muslim community, giving advice about Islamic law and customs. Imams are elected because they have a good knowledge of the Qur'an and lead by example. In the Islamic faith community, it is vital that the leaders show that they themselves are totally obedient to the will of Allah.

KNOW WHAT
Who are the religious leaders in the Islamic faith?

The Islamic Cultural Centre, Clonskeagh
In September 1996, the Islamic Cultural Centre of Ireland opened at Clonskeagh in Dublin. (There is also a centre on South Circular Road in Dublin.)

In the centre at Clonskeagh, there are five different areas: a mosque; a Muslim primary school; a library; a halal shop; a halal restaurant.

Approximately three hundred students attend the Muslim National School. The students represent a wide variety of nationalities and ethnic origins. They follow the Irish curriculum (including the Irish language). The only difference is in the area of Religious Education, where they concentrate on Islam.

Islamic Cultural Centre of Ireland, Clonskeagh

On Friday evenings and during the weekend, another school, called the Nur Al Huda Qur'anic School, is open in the centre. This school teaches two subjects: the memorisation of the Qur'an and Arabic.

KNOW WHAT
1. Why was an Islamic centre founded in Ireland?
2. How has the faith and practice of the Islamic community in Ireland changed as a result of such a centre being available?

DIGGING DEEPER
Describe the faith and practice of the modern Islamic faith community in Ireland.

A Young Person's Guide to Islam
Sayyed is fifteen years old and was born in Ireland. His father, who is Egyptian, met Sayyed's mother when he was studying to become a doctor in a large Cork hospital. Here Sayyed answers some questions from Paul, a student in his class who comes from a Catholic background and is trying to write an article on Islam for a project in Religion class.

Interview

Paul: Hi there Sayyed! How do you become a member of the Islamic faith? I was baptised into the Christian community as a baby. Do you have anything like that?

Sayyed: Well, both my parents are Muslim, so, naturally enough, faith is an important part of our life together. We believe that we are all born Muslim because as babies we naturally submit to God's will. We do have a ceremony when we are born, although I don't remember it. I have been told that when I was born my father whispered special words into my ear. It was a call to prayer. When I was seven days old, other rituals were performed.

Paul: What do you mean by rituals?

Sayyed: Well for a start, my hair was shaved off and weighed. In the past, the weight of a baby's hair was given in gold or silver to the poor. It is still expected that a donation be given to charity when a child is born. Being charitable to the poor is one way of celebrating the precious gift of a child. The next ritual was to give me a name. My name is Muhammad Sayyed, but I am called Sayyed to avoid confusion because lots of Muslim boys are named Muhammad.

Paul: Is it true that Muslim boys are circumcised?

Sayyed: Yes they are, but I was only a tiny baby when the doctor performed the circumcision, so I don't remember it.

Paul: Do you go to church on Sundays?

Sayyed: We don't go to church, we worship in a mosque, and our special day for worship is Friday, not Sunday. Prayer is a very important part of my life. Like all Muslims, I pray five times a day.

Paul: I heard that you go to special classes at the weekend. What kind of things do you learn?

Sayyed: I am learning Arabic to help me memorise the Qur'an, our holy book. The Qur'an can only be said in Arabic.

Paul: What about food? I've noticed some unusual things in your lunch-box.

Sayyed: You should try my food. It's really tasty. We eat halal food, which means food that is allowed. Meat is killed in a special way that is painless to the animal. My mum is a great cook and she makes lovely Egyptian dishes for us at home.

Paul: Thanks Sayyed. That has given me lots of information for my article!

KNOW WHAT
1. What happened when Sayyed was born?
2. What does Sayyed mean by the term ritual?
3. Where does Sayyed go to worship with other Muslim people?
4. Why is Sayyed learning Arabic?
5. What kind of food does he eat?

KNOW HOW
Write a page on the kind of lifestyle a Muslim boy like Sayyed has.

DIGGING DEEPER
Write a page that details the differences between your lifestyle and that of Sayyed.

KNOW IT ALL
Copy the following into your Religion folder and fill in the blanks using the wordbank given below.

1. There has been an _____ in the number of Muslims in Ireland in the past twenty years.
2. The Islamic Cultural Centre of Ireland is in _____ , Dublin.
3. It is a place of _____ , _____ and _____ for the Sunni Muslim community.
4. Approximately three hundred students attend the Muslim _____ _____ which is located in the centre.
5. The children follow the _____ curriculum.

WORDBANK
Education • Clonskeagh • National School • Increase • Irish • Worship • Socialisation

KNOWING YOU KNOWING ME
Find out more about Islam at the BBC website:
www.bbc.co.uk/religion/religions/islam/index.shtml

Community Structure: Way in which a group of people with a common interest is organised, especially in its roles (leadership, membership, etc).

Education: The teaching or passing on of knowledge.

Leadership: Setting a goal or aim for a person or a community and guiding them towards it. Always involves some degree of authority.

Tradition: The handing down of information, beliefs and customs from one generation to the next. Religious tradition involves the handing on of religious practices, beliefs, etc.

See page 492 for past exam questions on this topic.

LESSON 74   Conflict and Dialogue Between the Major World Religions

GROUNDWORK
In this lesson we plan to:
- explore conflict and dialogue between different communities of faith.

DIGGING DEEPER
How can inter-faith dialogue help to ease conflict within communities of faith?

 **Key Concepts**
Dialogue/Followers

KNOW WHAT
1. Think of two examples of situations of conflict that have been in the news headlines recently. What happened and why?
2. Why do you think that conflict sometimes arises between the different world religions?
3. What do you think might help to resolve the conflict that arises between religions?
4. Think of an example from the recent world news where there were some strategies put in place to resolve religious conflict?

Conflict and Religious Belief

Religious belief is one of the factors in many of the conflicts that are happening around the world today. However, it is also true to say that the core beliefs of the major world religions promote peace and reconciliation.

The five major world religions – Judaism, Christianity, Islam, Hinduism and Buddhism – agree on the Golden Rule: 'Treat others as you would like to be treated yourself.'

Judaism
The Talmud teaches: *'What is hateful to you, do not to your fellow men.'*

This respect for others comes from the Jewish people's experience of God's respect and love for them throughout their history. The Exodus (the escape from slavery in Egypt to freedom) is the main example of God's care for them. The Golden Rule is an expression of their belief that all life is precious to God because it is created and loved by God. The Jewish faith – including the Golden Rule – is honoured when Jewish families celebrate Shabbat.

Islam
'No one of you is a believer until he desires for his brother that which he desires for himself' (Hadith). The Qur'an clearly states the responsibility Muslims have to support and care for others. For example, the fourth pillar of Islam, Zakat, emphasises the need to share with those less fortunate. Islam is a religion, with ideals that are distinct from the political struggles and ideals of some of its followers. From the Qur'an, we can see that respect for all life is an important part of the Islamic faith.

KNOW WHAT

1. What are the 'Golden rules' of Judaism and Islam?
2. How do you think the 'Golden Rule' of a religion helps to resolve conflict?
3. Why do you think relationships between religions often break down?

Dialogue

Dialogue is about communicating and listening in order to understand someone else's point of view. In section A, we learned about inter-faith dialogue, which is based on respect for one's own beliefs and for the beliefs and convictions of others. The leadership of the major world religions can support inter-faith dialogue by encouraging education about other faiths among the members.

In the West, communities from some of the major world religions are in a minority. Their **followers** sometimes face prejudice when they try to practise their faith. For example, finding an appropriate place in which to kneel and pray, or eating kosher food, can be difficult if these things are not common practice.

In 1964, Pope Paul VI set up a special office at the Vatican to promote inter-faith dialogue, in line with the document of the Second Vatican Council called *Nostra Aetate*, which states:

> The Catholic Church rejects nothing which is true and holy in these [non-Christian] religions. She has a sincere respect for those ways of acting and living, those moral and doctrinal teachings, which may differ in many respects from what she holds and teaches, but which none the less often reflect the brightness of that Truth which is the light of all [people].
>
> (Website: *http://www.vatican.va/roman_curia/ pontifical _councils/interelg/documents/rc_pc_interelg _pro_ 20051996_en.html*)

Other groups have also been set up, for example, the Council of Christians and Jews (*see http://www. iccj.org/*). Through the Three Faiths Forum for members of the Jewish, Islamic and Christian communities (*see http://www.threefaithsforum.org.uk/*), closer ties have developed between members of the three monotheistic religions. Dialogue has also been established with both the Hindu and Buddhist communities.

KNOW WHAT

1. What is dialogue?
2. What is inter-faith dialogue?
3. Why is it important for followers of different religions to make an effort to engage in inter-faith dialogue?

DIGGING DEEPER

1. How do you think Irish society is responding to members of other religions who have made Ireland their home?
2. What can you do to show respect and understanding for other religions?
3. Think of an example where you have witnessed a person of another faith being treated with respect/not being treated with respect.

4. With reference to question 3, what may have helped in the second scenario?

Conflict and Dialogue between Islam and Christianity

In September 2006, Pope Benedict XVI, the leader of the Roman Catholic Church, gave a speech to an academic audience in Regensburg in his native Germany. He quoted a Byzantine emperor who had described Islam as a violent religion. Many Muslims around the world were angered by the speech and reacted strongly to it. The Pope immediately offered his regrets that the speech had caused offence and he stressed that the offending remarks did not reflect his personal views.

THE INTERNATIONAL TIMES
Pope Benedict visits Turkey and opens new dialogue with Islam.

THE WEEKLY INDEPENDENT
Pope visits mosque during Turkish trip.

THE PEOPLE'S POST
Pope and Muslim cleric pray at Blue Mosque.

THE DAILY NEWS
Pope Benedict defuses controversy with Islam through dialogue and diplomacy.

It is no surprise, therefore, that when Pope Benedict visited Turkey in November 2006, many newspapers and television stations around the world reported on the event. The visit was seen as a test of the Vatican's ability to mend ties with the Islamic world. Many newspapers described the Pope's actions in Turkey as gestures of reconciliation to the followers of Islam.

Pope Benedict referred to his trip as 'an unforgettable spiritual and pastoral experience, which I hope will produce the fruits for an increasingly sincere co-operation between all of Christ's disciples, and a useful dialogue with Muslims'.

Pope Benedict XVI and Muslim leaders at the Blue Mosque

The Pope visited the Blue Mosque, where he removed his shoes and, standing side by side with the Mufti of Istanbul and the Imam of the Blue Mosque, he faced towards Mecca and closed his eyes in prayer. This marked only the second papal visit in history to a Muslim place of worship. (Pope Benedict's predecessor, the late Pope John Paul II, visited a mosque during a trip to the Syrian capital of Damascus in 2001.)

KNOW WHAT
1. What, according to the newspapers, was the underlying cause of the strong reaction to Pope Benedict's speech?
2. How did Pope Benedict respond to the negative reaction?

3. Can you think of some practical ways in which Christians and Muslims could work together to achieve peace?

KNOW HOW

For more information on Pope Benedict's visit to Turkey, you might like to look up the following websites:

http://newsvote.bbc.co.uk/mpapps/pagetools/print/news.bbc.co.uk/2/hi/europe/61588...
http://www.beliefnet.com/story/205/story_20568.html
http://www.christianpost.com/pages/print.htm?aid=23795
http://www.time.com/time/personoftheyear/2006/people/3html
http://www.foxnews.com/printer_friendly_story/0,3566,233180,00.html

DIGGING DEEPER

Following the 9/11 attacks in New York in 2001, there were many inter-faith services throughout Ireland to commemorate the people of many faiths who died in these attacks. How might such services be seen as an example of people working together to achieve peace for the good of all humanity?

Dialogue: Talking and listening in order to develop greater understanding. Inter-faith dialogue leads to greater understanding between different religions.

Follower/Discipleship: A person becomes a follower when they take on discipleship. This means that they begin to live by the traditions of a community of faith.

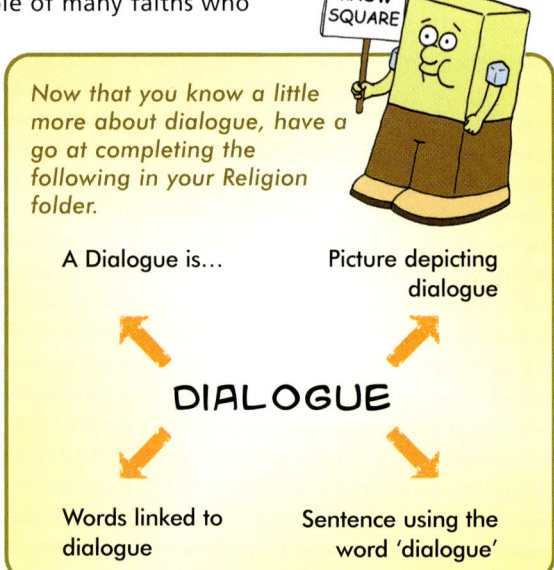

Now that you know a little more about dialogue, have a go at completing the following in your Religion folder.

A Dialogue is…

Picture depicting dialogue

DIALOGUE

Words linked to dialogue

Sentence using the word 'dialogue'

See page 492 for past exam questions on this topic.

KNOW THE WAY

240

LESSON 75 Islam, Judaism and Christianity: A Comparison

GROUNDWORK
In this lesson we plan to:
- revise the two major world religions studied and compare each of them to the Christian community of faith.

DIGGING DEEPER
What is the same and what is different about the Islamic and Jewish faith communities?

Name: Judaism

Founders: Abraham and Moses

Date: 4000 years ago

Earliest Followers: The descendants of Abraham and the Israelite or Hebrew people.

A follower of this major world religion is called: A Jew.

Beliefs: The Jewish people believe in one God who is the creator of everything. God has a unique relationship with the Jewish people because God established a covenant with them through Abraham and Moses. The Jewish people await the arrival of the Messiah.

Sacred Text: The Hebrew Scriptures

Location/Place of Origin: Israel

Holy Day: Saturday. The Sabbath begins at sunset on Friday and continues until after sunset on Saturday. The traditional Sabbath candles are lit and special prayers are said, usually by the mother of the family. The men and the boys attend the synagogue to welcome in the Sabbath. At the end of the day, there is a special celebratory meal, with prayers and singing.

Name: Islam

Founder: Muhammad

Date: 1500 years ago

Earliest Followers: The family of Muhammad and the people of Mecca.

A follower of this major world religion is called: A Muslim.

Beliefs: The Islamic people believe in one God, Allah, and in the Prophet Muhammad. The key beliefs are summed up by the Shahada: 'There is no God but Allah, and Muhammad is his messenger.' Muslims submit their lives to Allah and everything in their life is under the control of Allah.

Sacred Text: The Qu'ran

Location/Place of Origin: Saudi Arabia

Holy Day: Friday. All male Muslims are expected to attend the mosque at midday on Fridays for prayers. They turn to an arched alcove or a decorated panel in the wall to show them the direction of Mecca. Men and women sit in different parts of the mosque. A leader, called the imam, leads the prayers.

Prayer: The Jewish people pray daily. The formal language for prayer is Hebrew, though of course Jewish people can pray in any language. Devout Jewish people pray five times a day: before going to bed, after rising in the morning and at the three meal times. (The Jewish day begins in the evening.) In the evening and in the morning, the Shema is recited.

Place of Worship: The synagogue

Sacred Times /Festivals:

Autumn festivals – Rosh Hashanah/Yom Kippur/Sukkoth/Simchat Torah

Winter festivals – Hanukah/Purim

Spring festival – Pesach

Summer festivals – Shavuot/Tishah b'Av

Place of Pilgrimage: The Western Wall in Jerusalem is a sacred place of pilgrimage for the Jewish people.

Leadership: Chief Rabbi/Rabbi.

Rites of Passage: The Jewish people celebrate all the important events of life, from birth to death. The Bar Mitzvah (Coming of Age) for a boy, and the Bat Mitzvah for a girl are major celebrations within the Jewish family community.

Way of life: Jews live their lives in accordance with the Ten Commandments. They observe the Hebrew Scriptures quite literally and take instruction on many daily events, including dietary laws. Jewish people observe their Sabbath day strictly and take that time to rest and pray. When in the synagogue at prayer, Jewish men wear the kippah, the tallit and tefillin.

Symbol of this religion: The symbol of Judaism is called the Magen of David, also known as the Star of David. It is often worn as an ornament around the neck by young Jews.

Prayer: Muslims are called to pray five times a day. This is the second pillar of Islam, Salat. When Muslims pray, they turn towards Mecca. For a Muslim, life revolves around these prayer times. They have specific ritual actions that are carried out before prayer. Each action has a specific meaning.

Place of Worship: The mosque

Sacred Times /Festivals:

Eid ul-Fitr takes place at the end of Ramadan in the ninth month of the Islamic calendar.

Eid ul-Adha takes place during the twelfth month of the Islamic calendar.

Place of Pilgrimage: The holy city of Mecca, home of the Ka'ba, is the sacred place of pilgrimage for the Islamic people. Every Muslim tries to make the Hajj pilgrimage to Mecca once in their lifetime.

Leadership: The imam leads the prayer in the mosque on Fridays.

Rites of Passage: As with Judaism, the Islamic faith tradition celebrates all the major events of life, from birth to death. At birth, words from the Qur'an are whispered into the ear of the newborn baby. There is also a Naming Ceremony.

Way of life: The people of the Islamic faith observe their religion as their way of life. Muslims live their lives in accordance with the Five Pillars of Islam. They too have strict dietary laws and a sense of ritual around their prayer times. Pilgrimage is one of the Five Pillars of Islam and is to be observed at least once in the life of a Muslim.

Symbol of this religion: The crescent moon and star is a symbol of Islam. The five points of the star symbolise the Five Pillars of Islam. The moon and the stars remind Muslims of God, the creator of everything.

KNOW HOW
Write an essay describing the lifestyle of a follower of one of the above traditions in Ireland today.

You might like to include the following in your essay:
Faith and practice / Sacred times and places / Community structure / Leadership and education.

Christianity and Judaism: Similarities and Differences
Here is a brief summary of the main similarities and differences between Judaism and Christianity:

Christians and Jews believe in
- One God
- Life after death
- God's final judgement of us
- Prayer, fasting and almsgiving
- Mary, the mother of Jesus
- The books of the Old Testament
- The existence of evil

Christians and Jews disagree on
- God as Father, Son and Holy Spirit
- Jesus as the Son of God
- Jesus' death and resurrection
- Jesus as saviour (The Jewish people are still waiting for the Messiah)
- The New Testament and the Old Testament being God's final word

Christianity and Islam: Similarities and Differences
Here is a brief summary of the main similarities and differences between Islam and Christianity:

Christians and Muslims believe in
- One God
- Life after death
- God's final judgement of us
- Prayer, fasting and almsgiving
- Mary, the mother of Jesus
- Angels
- The existence of evil

Christians and Muslims disagree on
- God as Father, Son and Holy Spirit
- Jesus as the Son of God
- Jesus' death and resurrection
- Jesus as saviour
- The Bible as God's final word

DIGGING DEEPER
What is the same and what is different about the Islamic and Jewish faith communities?

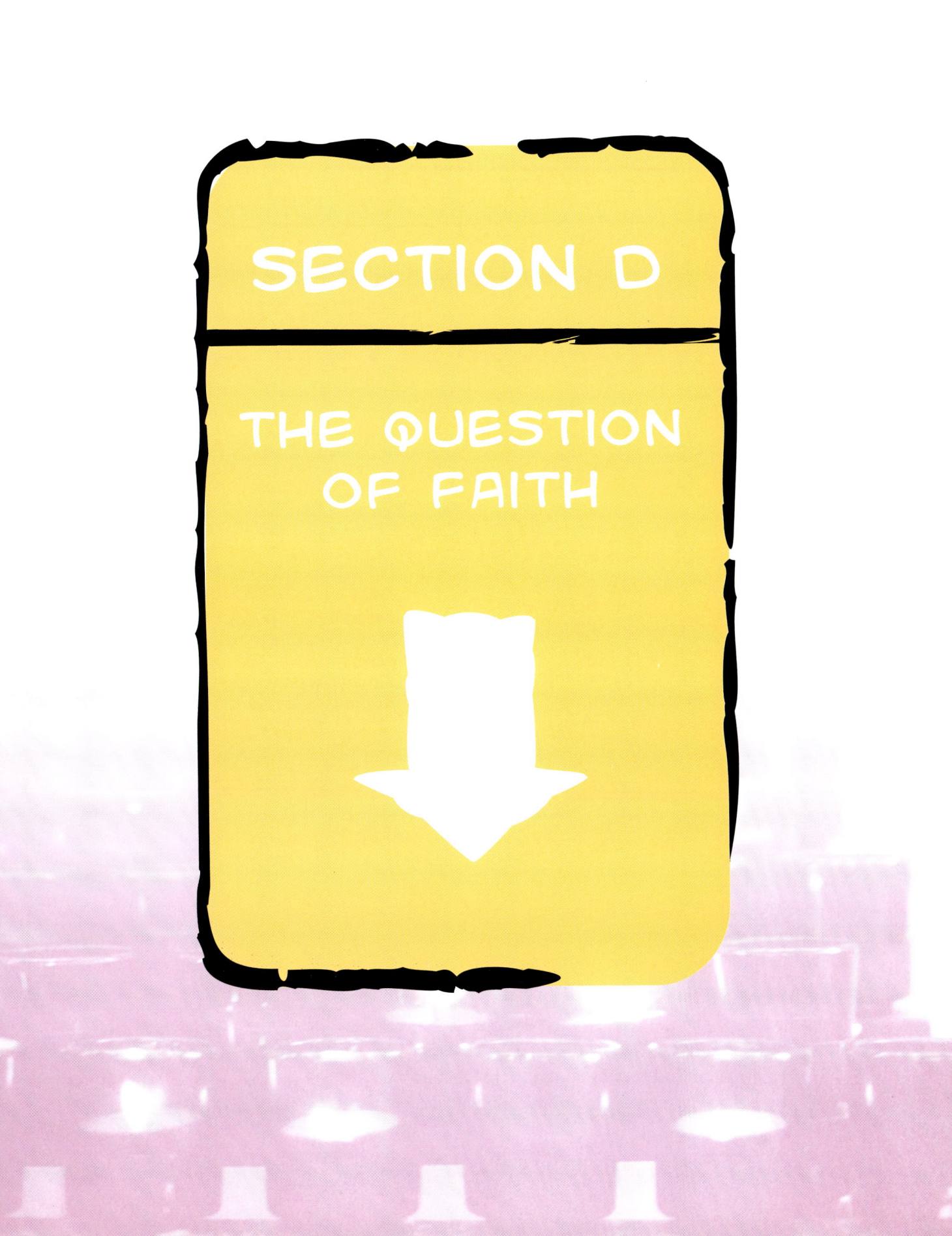

The Situation of Faith Today

LESSON 76 Religious Belief and Practice Among Adolescents Today

GROUNDWORK
In this lesson we plan to:
- explore religious beliefs and practices among adolescents in the locality;
- identify factors that influence the religious beliefs and practices of adolescents.

DIGGING DEEPER
What are my main religious beliefs?
How do I express my religious beliefs?
Who/what has influenced my religious beliefs and practices?

Key Concepts
Religious belief/Religious practice

Religious Belief

Religious belief is what people believe to be true about God and about their relationship with God. Some examples of Christian beliefs are:

- There is only one God.
- Jesus is the Son of God and the Saviour of the world.
- There is life after death.
- The Word of God is to be found in the Bible.
- Those who have loved God in this life will live in eternal friendship with God.

KNOW WHAT

1. List one other Christian belief.
2. Name another world religion you have studied. What are its main religious beliefs?
3. Imagine that a person from another country visited your local area. What signs of religious belief would they see?

Religious Practice

People express their religious beliefs through their actions. **Religious practice** is the system of behaviour and set of activities that people use to express their belief in God. Christians express their religious belief through a variety of religious practices, including:

- Prayer
- Worship, e.g. celebrating the Eucharist
- Celebrating sacred times, e.g. Christmas and Easter
- Going on pilgrimage to sacred places
- Following Jesus' commandment to love God and to love your neighbour as yourself

KNOW WHAT

1. List one other Christian practice.
2. Name another world religion you have studied. How do the followers of that religion express their religious belief?
3. What similarities and differences do you notice between the religious practices of members of that world religion and those of Christians?

KNOWING ME KNOWING YOU
Survey on Young People and Religion

As a class group, organise a survey of all the classes in your year to examine young people's attitudes to religious belief and practice. You could use the following questions or add some more of your own.

		Yes	No
1.	Do you believe in God?	✓	
2.	Do you pray at least once a week?	✓	
3.	Do you attend religious services at least once a week?	✓	
4.	Do you believe in heaven?	✓	
5.	Do you believe in hell?		✓
6.	Do you try to keep the moral code of your religion, e.g. Jesus' commandment to love God and neighbour?	✓	
7.	Do you believe in an afterlife?	✓	

This activity will require some careful planning, including the allocation of different tasks to individual students. For example:

- Once the questions have been finalised, they will need to be typed up on a single sheet of paper and then photocopied.
- The questionnaires will need to be distributed to the students in the various classes, and then collected later when they have been completed.
- Most importantly, the results will have to be compiled and presented so as to give a concise picture of the information collected. This could be done using a bar chart or by simply listing in descending order the number of students who gave positive answers to the questions, e.g.

    Of the _____ (total number) students questioned:
    _____ said that they believe in God.
    _____ said that they attend religious services at least once a week, etc.

Note: Students who complete the questionnaire should not be asked to write their name on the sheet. The survey is not concerned with the views of individual students, but rather with adolescent religious belief and practice in general.

Influences on the Religious Beliefs and Practices of Adolescents

Adolescents live in a world of relationships – relationships with family, friends, the local community and the wider world. These relationships, as well as other events in life, influence adolescents' religious beliefs and practices. Read the following statements from young people:

'When I was little, my mum said our bedtime prayers with us each night. Religion is important to my mum and dad. They brought us to Mass each Sunday. Now I have a choice about going to Mass, but I still go.' *(Mike, 17)*

'At school I learn about religion, but I do not go to church a lot because my parents don't go.' *(Jane, 16)*

'My mum and dad think I go to church, but I don't. It's boring!' *(Stephen, 14)*

'In Transition Year, I joined a folk group. It's made up of young people from around the town and we have a great time. I have learnt to play the guitar. For me, religious services are about friendship and music, but also something more …' *(Sarah, 17)*

'My friends don't go to church. And when they don't go, I don't go. I want to be with them, doing whatever they're doing.' *(Tom, 15)*

'I like the meditations that we sometimes do in Religion class. It's good to have a bit of quiet time to talk to God about what's going on in my life. God has become more of a friend to me.' *(Melissa, 16)*

KNOW WHAT
What has influenced each of the above young people's religious beliefs and practices?

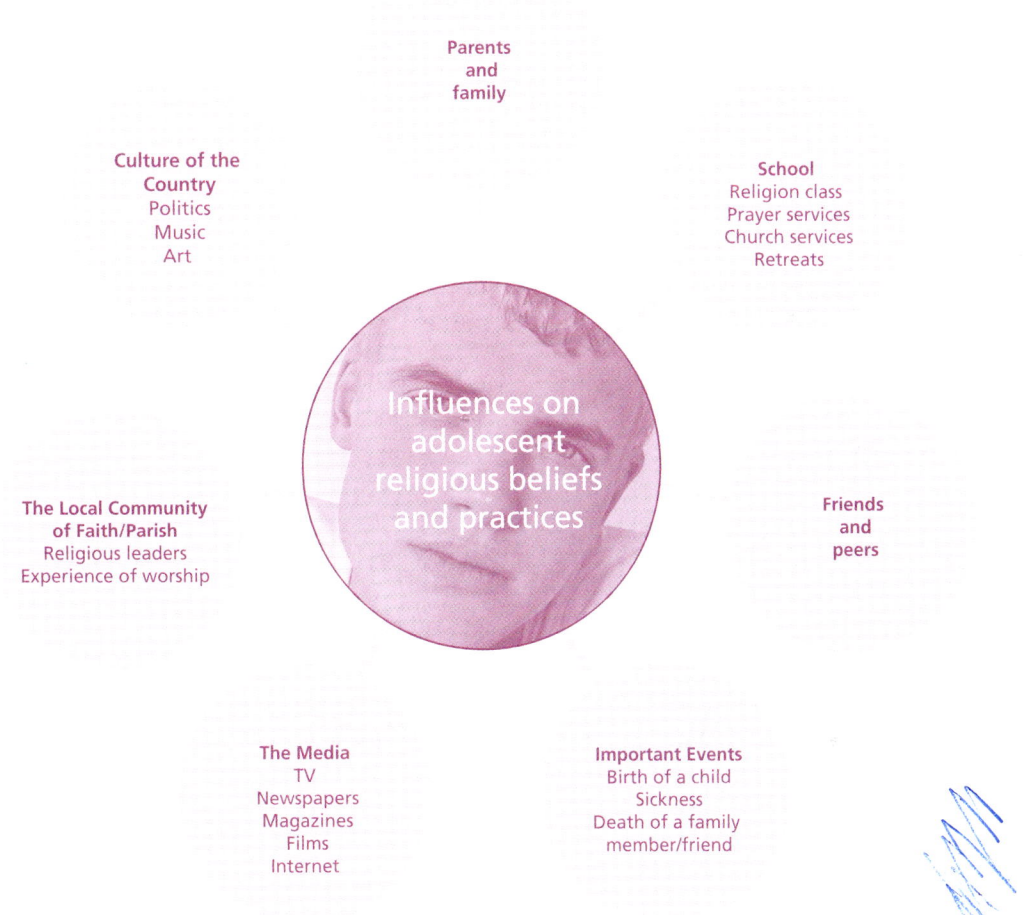

Family:	The family has a big influence on the religious beliefs and practices of teenagers. Many parents/guardians encourage the religious belief and practice of their children from a young age by praying with them and by taking them to religious services. However, in some homes, God or religion are never mentioned. As a result, children pick up the attitude that religion is not important.
	The religious influence of the family continues during adolescence. Research suggests that when teenagers see that their parents value religion, they are more likely to value it themselves. If parents do not pray or attend religious services, teenagers are less likely to pray or attend religious services themselves.
Friends and Peers:	The influence of the peer group and friends is very strong during adolescence. Teenagers want to be accepted by their peers. They find it easier to go to religious services or to take part in a folk group or choir when their friends also take part.
School:	In Ireland, most students attend Religion class in school. There, they learn about their own religion and about other communities of faith and they join in class discussions on religious matters. This may help to strengthen their

religious beliefs. Sometimes, students are given the opportunity to take part in a meditation during class. Many students like this type of prayer and some even use it at home.

In many schools, students also take part in religious services, such as class Masses and carol services. Many teenagers like being involved as readers, musicians, members of the choir, etc. Sometimes this experience can lead them to become more involved in religious services in their parish or local community.

Parish/Local Community of Faith: The experience of worship in the local community has a big influence on religious practice. Research suggests that many Irish teenagers find Mass boring and see no point in going to Mass. Other teenagers make a big effort to go to Youth Masses, where young people take part as readers, collectors, members of the folk group or choir, etc. They enjoy the sense of being together with other young people and feel God's presence at the Youth Mass.

KNOW WHAT
1. What do you think is the greatest influence on the religious beliefs and practices of adolescents? Explain your choice.
2. List the factors that might strengthen and have a positive effect on the religious beliefs and practices of adolescents.
3. List the factors that might weaken and have a negative effect on the religious beliefs and practices of adolescents.
4. Choose *two* factors that influence the religious beliefs and practices of adolescents. Explain their influence.

DIGGING DEEPER
1. What are your main religious beliefs?
2. How do you express your religious beliefs through your actions?
3. Who/what has shaped your religious beliefs and practices? Explain.

Signs of Hope Among Young People

A recent sign of religious faith among young people was the 2005 World Youth Day in Cologne. Some 400,000 young people from Europe and other parts of the world travelled to Cologne to take part in a week-long event of prayer and discussion. Over one million young people attended the Mass celebrated by Pope Benedict XVI on the last day of this festival of faith.

Young people at World Youth Day in Cologne

KNOW HOW

Now that you know a little bit more about religious belief and practice, copy the following statements into your Religion folder and indicate whether they are true or false.

True or False

		True	False
1.	Religious belief is what people believe to be true about God and their relationship with God.	☐	☐
2.	Christians do not believe that Jesus is the Son of God.	☐	☐
3.	Religious practice is the system of behaviour and set of activities people use to express their belief in God.	☐	☐
4.	Worship and prayer are not examples of religious practice.	☐	☐
5.	Family and friends are important influences on adolescent religious belief and practice.	☐	☐
6.	People who believe in God do not try to keep the moral code of their religion.	☐	☐

Religious belief: What we believe to be true about God and our relationship with God.

Religious practice: The system of behaviour and set of activities people use to express their belief in God.

See page 493 for past exam questions on this topic.

LESSON 77 Religious Belief and Practice in Ireland

GROUNDWORK
In this lesson we plan to:
- identify the characteristics of religious belief and practice in Ireland at present and over the last century;
- identify factors that have influenced religious belief in Ireland.

DIGGING DEEPER
What similarities and differences are there between my religious beliefs and practices, and those of older people in my locality? Does the situation of faith in my country affect my religious beliefs and practices?

Key Concepts
Religious belief/Religious practice

Religious Belief and Practice in the Past

An interesting way to find out about religious belief and practice in your locality or country in the past is to talk to an older person. In the following interview, Claire, a Roman Catholic who grew up in rural Ireland in the 1930s and 1940s, tells us about religious belief and practice in her area when she was young.

When you were growing up, what were your religious beliefs?
I believed in God, in Jesus and in his mother Mary. I also believed in heaven and hell.

How often did you pray?
I prayed in the morning and in the evening. After tea, I used to kneel down with my family and say the Family Rosary.

Were there any religious objects in your home?
We had the Sacred Heart picture in our kitchen. There was a lovely Sacred Heart lamp in front of it that was lit day and night. Nearly every house had a Sacred Heart picture and lamp.

The Rosary
The Rosary is a prayer of devotion to Mary, the mother of Jesus. This prayer is divided into five decades. Each decade consists of the Our Father, ten Hail Marys and the Glory Be to the Father. In the past, there were three sets of five decades, called the Joyful, Sorrowful and Glorious Mysteries. In 2002, Pope John Paul II introduced another set of mysteries of the Rosary, called the Luminous Mysteries or Mysteries of Light. In the past, people went to the church for Rosary and Benediction each evening in October and May. The Family Rosary was a very popular religious practice in Ireland.

There was a holy picture in every room in our house. We also had a holy water font inside the front door. People had great faith in the power of holy water, especially if there was a storm.

How often did you go to church?
We always went to Mass on Sunday. Every Sunday, we put on our best clothes and cycled four miles to the church. The Mass was in Latin. The priest celebrated Mass with his back to us. We did not have any breakfast until we came home from Mass because you had to fast from midnight in order to receive Holy Communion.

In your parish, what other religious practices did you take part in?
When I went to secondary school, I went to Rosary and Benediction each evening during the months of May and October. We got a half an hour off from Study each evening to go. I also went to confession once a month.

Did any other religious practices take place in your parish?
Each year there was a Procession of the Blessed Sacrament in our village. Before the procession, houses were repainted, windows cleaned and bunting was put up. A small altar with a holy picture and flowers was erected outside each house. In the procession, the priest carried a monstrance containing the Blessed Sacrament through the village. Everyone followed, singing hymns and praying the Rosary. This happened in all the towns and villages around us.

Every few years, there was also a Parish Mission. A group of priests visited our parish for a week or a fortnight. They celebrated Mass each morning. Each evening there was Rosary, Benediction and a long sermon.

Were there any places of pilgrimage near where you lived?
Each summer there was a Pattern at the holy well in my parish. People set up stalls and you could buy sweets and minerals. The grown-ups prayed at the holy well.

Benediction

In the past, people went to Benediction each evening during October and May. They also went to Benediction on a Sunday evening. At Benediction, the priest places the Blessed Sacrament (Body of Christ) in a monstrance on the altar. The people kneel in front of the Blessed Sacrament and sing hymns of praise. Then the priest blesses the people with the Blessed Sacrament. After the blessing, the people say prayers of adoration.

Procession of the Blessed Sacrament

In the past, most parishes celebrated the feast of Corpus Christi (Body of Christ) with a Procession of the Blessed Sacrament. The priest carried a monstrance containing the Blessed Sacrament through the town or village. He blessed the people with the Blessed Sacrament at various points along the way. Most people took part in the procession. They honoured the Blessed Sacrament by singing hymns and saying the Rosary.

We also went to Knock every year. My father hired a hackney car and the whole family went to Knock for the afternoon. We said the Rosary around the church and did the Stations of the Cross inside.

What religious practices did you take part in at secondary school?

Each morning there was Mass. At the beginning of the first class, the nun said a prayer. Then at noon, we stopped our lessons to say the Angelus together.

How did you celebrate sacred times such as Christmas, Lent and Easter?

Lent was much stricter in the past than it is now. You could only have one main meal, like in the middle of the day, and two smaller meals. There were no dances or weddings during Lent. Easter and Christmas were lovely times. Before Christmas, we decorated the house with holly and paper decorations and hung up our stockings at the fireplace. On Christmas morning, we opened our presents and went to Mass. Afterwards, we had a big Christmas dinner.

How important was religion in people's lives back then?

Religion was very important. People prayed for fine weather, they prayed for a good harvest or if someone was sick. Back then, times were not easy. People prayed that everything would be all right.

What do you think is the biggest change in religious practice that has happened since you were young?

Many people don't go to confession any more. Also, the Mass is not as important as it was. Many young people don't go to Mass now.

Note: It is important to remember that many of the religious practices mentioned above, such as the Rosary, Benediction, Procession of the Blessed Sacrament, Parish Mission and pilgrimages, are still part of the religious beliefs and practices of the Catholic community in Ireland today.

Parish Missions

In the past, a Parish Mission was held in nearly every parish in Ireland. Visiting priests celebrated Mass and the sacrament of Reconciliation. They also celebrated the Rosary and Benediction. During the mission, the priests gave long sermons encouraging devotional practices such as the Family Rosary, Benediction and the Stations of the Cross. The Parish Mission was usually well attended.

Places of Pilgrimage

In the past, pilgrimages (journeys to sacred places) were a popular religious practice. People went on pilgrimage to Croagh Patrick, Knock and to many other places, including holy wells.

The Stations of the Cross

In the past, many people prayed the Stations of the Cross. During the Stations of the Cross, a person reflects on fourteen points along Jesus' final journey to Calvary. Images of these fourteen points are displayed on the walls of Roman Catholic churches. Usually, a person prays the Stations of the Cross on their own. However, on Good Friday, Roman Catholics gather together to pray the Stations of the Cross.

KNOW WHAT

1. What religious beliefs did Claire have as a young girl?
2. Name some of the religious objects that were in her home.
3. What differences are there between how Mass was celebrated in the past and how it is celebrated today?
4. What religious practices did Claire take part in at school?
5. What religious practices did the people of her parish take part in?
6. 'Lent was much stricter in the past than it is now.' Do you agree? Give reasons for your answer.
7. According to Claire, what are the biggest changes that have taken place in religious practice?

KNOW HOW

Write a paragraph about *two* of the following religious practices: Rosary; Benediction; Procession of the Blessed Sacrament; Parish Mission; Stations of the Cross.

KNOWING ME KNOWING YOU

Using the questions in the above interview, conduct your own interview with an older person in your locality. You could do this activity in groups or on your own.

Afterwards, share your answers with other students in your class. In your classroom, display the main points learned under the heading 'Religion in My Locality in the Past'.

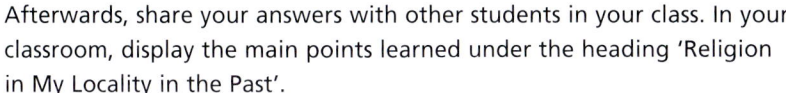

DIGGING DEEPER

What similarities and differences are there between your religious beliefs and practices and those of the person you interviewed?

KNOW WHAT

In the interview, Claire mentioned the religious beliefs and practices that were popular in her local area in the 1930s and 1940s:

Belief in God	Belief in Jesus as the Son of God	Devotion to Mary
Belief in heaven	Belief in hell	Family Rosary
Latin Mass	Sacred Heart picture in the house	Holy water font
Monthly confession	Eucharistic fast from midnight	Angelus
Strict observance of Lent	Blessed Sacrament procession	Pilgrimages
Sunday Mass	Rosary/Benediction in May and October	Parish Mission

1. Which of these religious beliefs and practices were popular in your local area in the past?
2. Which of these are popular in your local area today?
3. Which of these are not popular in your local area today?
4. List the main changes that have taken place in religious belief and practice in your local area.

Changes in Religious Belief and Practice in Ireland

Look at the following charts, which relate to religious beliefs and practices in Ireland, and then answer the questions below.

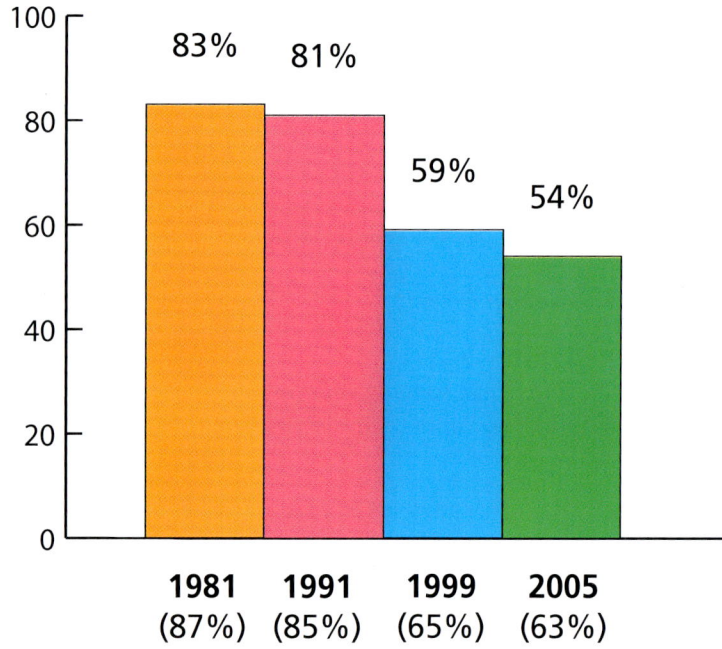

Attendance at Religious Services At Least Once a Week

1981	1991	1999	2005
83%	81%	59%	54%
(87%)	(85%)	(65%)	(63%)

(European Values Study, 1981, 1990, 1999 and the European Social Survey, 2005)

Note: Mass attendance for Roman Catholics is in brackets under each year.

1. Between 1981 and 2005, what was the percentage change in attendance at religious services in Ireland?
2. In what decade did the biggest decline in attendance at religious services in Ireland take place?

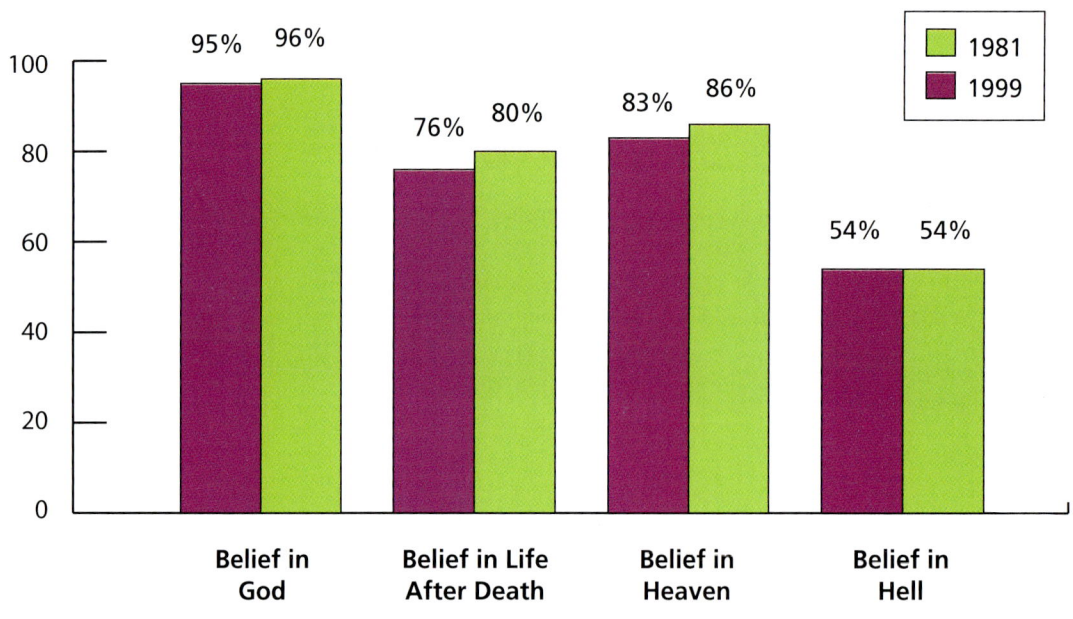

Religious Beliefs

Legend: 1981, 1999

	Belief in God	Belief in Life After Death	Belief in Heaven	Belief in Hell
1999	95%	76%	83%	54%
1981	96%	80%	86%	54%

(European Values Study, 1981 and 1999)

KNOW THE WAY

1. What religious beliefs increased between 1981 and 1999?
2. What religious belief remained the same?
3. What does this chart show about Irish people's religious beliefs?

Since the 1930s and 1940s, there have been many changes in religious belief and practice in Ireland:

- Some religious practices have died out, e.g. the strict Lenten fast, monthly confession and the Eucharistic fast from midnight. Others have become less popular, e.g. fewer people say the Family Rosary or take part in the Procession of the Blessed Sacrament. Many homes no longer contain religious pictures or statues, e.g. Sacred Heart picture.
- As a result of the decisions taken by the Second Vatican Council (1962–1965), there have been important changes in the way the Mass is celebrated. Since Vatican II, the Eucharist is usually celebrated in the language of the people rather than in Latin. The priest faces the people and they may choose to receive Communion in the hand. In the past, people received Communion only on the tongue.
- Between 1981 and 2005, there was a big decline in the number of people attending religious services – from 83 per cent to 54 per cent.
- In recent years, there has been a big increase in the size of some communities of faith in Ireland. For example, between 2002 and 2006 the Orthodox community in Ireland doubled in size and the Muslim community increased by 70 per cent (to over 32,000).

Is there a crisis of faith in Ireland?

Some people say that there is a crisis of faith in Ireland. They look at the fall in some religious practices and say that religion is in decline in Ireland. What do you think?

Before you make up your mind, consider the following points:

- Surveys show that most Irish people continue to believe in God, life after death, and heaven and hell. Irish people's commitment to these four Christian beliefs remained constant between 1981 and 1999.
- Surveys also show that most Irish people pray at least once a week. Between 1999 and 2005, the number of people who pray at least once a week increased from 70 per cent to 73 per cent.
- In the 2006 Census, only 4.4 per cent of Irish people said that they had no religion. In contrast, 87 per cent of Irish people said that they were Roman Catholic, and another 3 per cent said that they were members of the Church of Ireland.

Figures like these suggest that religion is still a strong force in Ireland.

KNOW HOW

Imagine that you have been asked to give a talk on radio about the differences and similarities between the religious beliefs and practices of Irish people today and in past generations. Outline your talk.

KNOWING ME KNOWING YOU

Research and debate the following motion in class: 'Religious belief and practice is in crisis among young people in Ireland.'

LESSON 78 Religious Belief and Practice in Europe

GROUNDWORK
In this lesson we plan to:
- identify the characteristics of religious belief and practice throughout Europe;
- identify factors that have influenced religious belief and practice throughout Europe;
- examine the distribution of religions around the world;
- explore the differences between religion in Europe and religion elsewhere.

DIGGING DEEPER
How does the situation of faith in a country affect a person's religious beliefs and practices?

Key Concepts
Religious belief/Religious practice

Changes in Religious Belief and Practice in Europe

As in Ireland, there have been many changes in the religious beliefs and practices of Europeans in the last century. The following story highlights the changes in religious practice and belief in Germany following World War II. After the war, Germany was divided into two parts: East Germany and West Germany. A communist government ruled East Germany between 1945 and 1989. Communism is a system of government in which the welfare of the State takes priority over the rights of individuals, and people are encouraged to believe in the State rather than in a religion or God.

Hans' story...

My name is Hans. I was born in the south-eastern part of Germany, near Leipzig, in 1944. My parents were Roman Catholics and I was baptised. After the war, Germany was divided into two parts and a communist government was set up in East Germany. Like other communist governments, it tried to reduce the influence of the churches by banning the teaching of religion in schools. But my mother taught me to pray and she brought me to Mass. She also saw to it that I made my First Communion and Confirmation. However, shortly after I got an apprenticeship, I stopped going to church. By then, taking part in religious services was considered bad for your career – it could stop you getting a job or promotion. When I had children, I did not have them baptised, nor did I teach them about God. Today, like most East Germans, my children and grandchildren do not believe in God. My grandchildren think that religion is old-fashioned. They are more interested in having a good time and in buying all the things they see advertised on television than they are in religious matters. Since I am free again to take part in religious services, I have gone back to the church of my childhood. But it is a changed church – the seats are emptier and the Mass is no longer in Latin. The priest now faces us and we can receive Communion in the hand. I suppose it is just another change for me to get used to.

KNOW THE WAY

KNOW WHAT

1. How did Hans' parents influence his faith as a child?
2. How did the communist government in East Germany try to reduce the influence of the churches?
3. Why did Hans stop going to church?
4. Give two reasons for the changes in religious belief and practice in Eastern Germany in the last century.

As Hans' story suggests, there have been many changes in religious belief and practice in continental Europe over the last century. Consider the following:

- Traditionally, Southern Europe was Roman Catholic and Northern Europe was Protestant. From 1900, there was a steady decline in the number of people taking part in Catholic and Protestant religious practices in some European countries. In 1998, a survey showed that regular attendance at religious services in Europe ranged from a high of 73 per cent in Ireland to a low of 5 per cent in Russia. Attendance at religious services was less than 10 per cent in five European countries: Norway, Cyprus, Denmark, Sweden and Russia.
- While religious belief has remained strong in some European countries, e.g. Cyprus, Poland and Ireland, it has fallen significantly in other countries, e.g. Former East Germany, Czech Republic and Sweden. In 1998, belief in God ranged from a high of 96 per cent in Cyprus to a low of 26 per cent in the Former East Germany.
- There has been an increase in the size of some world religions in Europe, e.g. Islam, Buddhism and Hinduism.

(Figures taken from International Social Survey Programme, 1998)

KNOW WHAT

What do you think has been the most important change in religious belief and practice that has taken place in Europe? Explain.

KNOWING ME KNOWING YOU

Using the library and/or the internet, research the religious beliefs and practices of people in one European country. Present your findings to the class.

Influences on Religious Belief and Practice in the Last Century

There are many reasons for the changes that have taken place in religious belief and practice in Ireland and Europe over the last century. These include:

The Rise and Fall of Communism

In 1917, a communist government was set up in Russia. After World War II, Russia set up communist governments in many countries in Eastern Europe, e.g. East Germany, Poland, Czechoslovakia and Hungary. In these countries, communist governments tried to discourage people from practising their religion. As a result, religious belief and practice declined in many communist countries, particularly Russia, East Germany and Czechoslovakia.

In 1989, communism came to an end in most of Eastern Europe and people were free to practise religion again. Recent surveys suggest that there has been a slight rise in religious belief and practice in some Eastern European countries. (International Social Survey Programme, 1991, 1998.)

The Growth of the Mass Media

Since 1960, there has been a huge increase in the number of television channels in Europe. In 1961, RTÉ opened the first Irish television station. Today, many people can tune in to a large number of TV channels in their homes. They can also surf the internet. Many TV programmes and websites promote non-religious values, such as casual sexual relationships or putting worldly matters before spiritual ones. The influence of the media has been very powerful.

The Second Vatican Council

The Second Vatican Council was a meeting of Roman Catholic bishops from all over the world. It took place in Rome and lasted from 1962 to 1965. One of its aims was to update the structures and practices of the Church, so that it could better proclaim the teachings of Jesus. Another aim was to work for greater unity among all Christians and for greater understanding among followers of all religions. As we have seen, the Second Vatican Council made changes to the way the Mass was celebrated. It also encouraged people to read the Bible and to work for peace and justice. The documents produced by the Council cover many different topics and are an important source of reference and guidance for Catholics.

Migration

Since the 1950s, many immigrants have come to continental Europe from Africa and Asia, bringing with them the influence of non-Christian religions such as Islam, Hinduism and Buddhism. In recent years, Ireland has also received immigrants from Africa, Asia and Eastern Europe, many of whom are members of the Muslim or Orthodox communities.

The Holocaust

During World War II, six million Jews, or two-thirds of all the Jews in Europe, were murdered in extermination camps by the Nazis. This event is known as the Holocaust. As well as reducing the number of Jews living in Europe, the Holocaust caused people to question how God could allow something like this to happen. Some people stopped believing in God.

KNOW WHAT

1. Identify *two* factors that might have weakened religious faith and practice in Ireland in the last century.
2. Identify *two* factors that might have weakened religious faith and practice in Europe in the last century.
3. Identify *one* factor that might have strengthened religious belief and practice in Ireland or Europe.

KNOW IT ALL

Copy the following exercise into your Religion folder and fill in the blanks using the wordbank given below.

In the second half of the twentieth century, many _____ took place in the way Irish people practised their religion. Monthly _____ and the _____ fast from midnight disappeared. The _____ Mass was replaced by Mass in the language of the people. _____ people now attend religious services or say the _____ _____. However, most Irish people continue to believe in God, life after death and heaven and _____.

In continental Europe, changes also took place in religious belief and practice. In some European countries, fewer people believe in _____ today than in the past. There has been a big decline in religious _____ in many countries. A survey taken in 1998 showed that regular attendance at religious services in Europe ranged from a high of _____ per cent in Ireland to a low of _____ per cent in Russia. Attendance at religious services was less than 10 per cent in five _____ countries. In Europe, there has also been an increase in the size of some _____ religions.

Many factors have caused these changes in religious belief and practice, including the Second _____ Council, the growth of the _____ and _____.

WORDBANK

European • Fewer • Latin • 5 • Media • Changes • Vatican • Eucharistic • Migration • Confession • World • Family Rosary • Practice • 73 • Hell • God

The Global Distribution of Religions

The following chart shows the distribution of religions in the world at present.

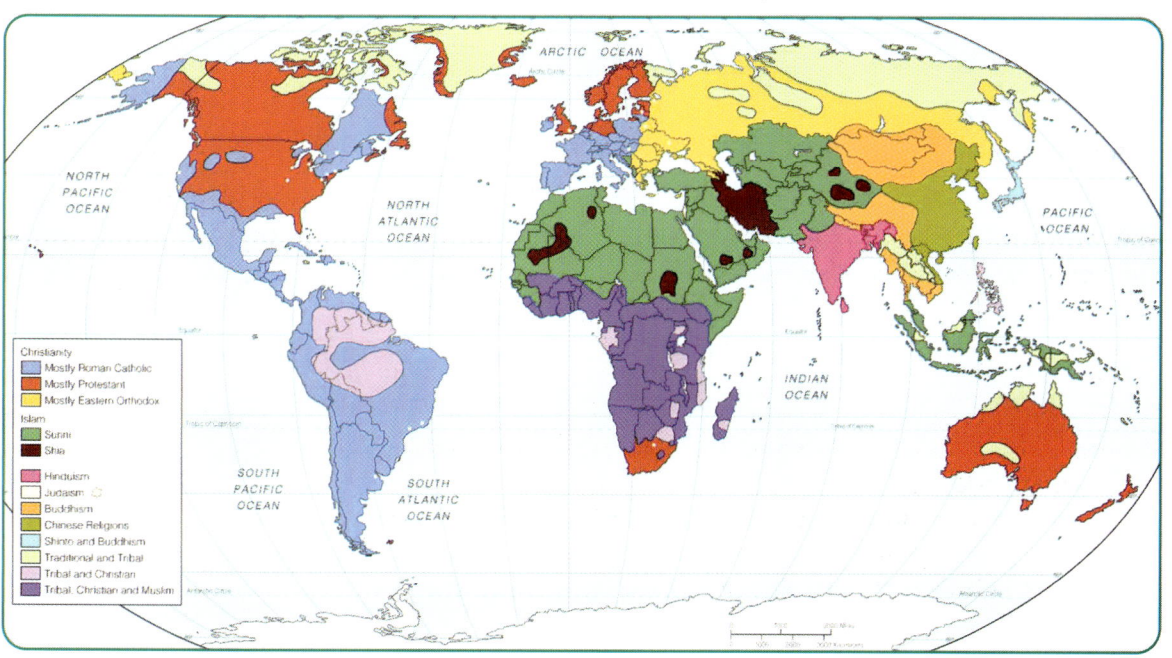

KNOW WHAT

Answer the following questions with reference to the above map:
1. Which countries have you or members of your family visited?
2. What is the main religion in each of these countries?
3. What are the main religions in Europe?
4. What are the main religions in North and South America?
5. What are the main religions in Africa?
6. What are the main religions in Asia?

The Main Religions in Europe and Elsewhere

- Christianity is the main religion in Europe (77 per cent). The next largest is Islam (4 per cent). A significant percentage of Europeans (18 per cent) do not believe in God or have no religion.
- Christianity is also the main religion in North America (79 per cent) and South America (95 per cent).
- In Asia, Islam is the main religion (23 per cent), followed closely by Hinduism (21 per cent). A significant percentage of people in Asia (20 per cent) do not believe in God or have no religion. Only 9 per cent are Christian.
- In Africa, Christianity is the main religion (46 per cent), followed closely by Islam (41 per cent).

KNOW WHAT

1. Name the continents on which Christianity is the main religion.
2. Name two continents where a significant percentage of people do not believe in God or have no religion.
3. Name two continents where a significant percentage of people are Muslim.

A Survey of Religious Belief and Practice

In 1998, a survey on religious belief and practice was carried out in over thirty-two countries, including Ireland. Most of the countries surveyed are in Europe. Obviously, religious beliefs and practices in Ireland and elsewhere are continually changing, and the figures produced by this survey would almost certainly have changed if the same survey was carried out today. What we are studying here is the underlying patterns or trends in religious belief and practice in Europe and elsewhere, rather than the specific figures.

The following chart shows the percentage of people in each country who stated that they believe in God.

Belief in God – Ireland, Europe and Elsewhere

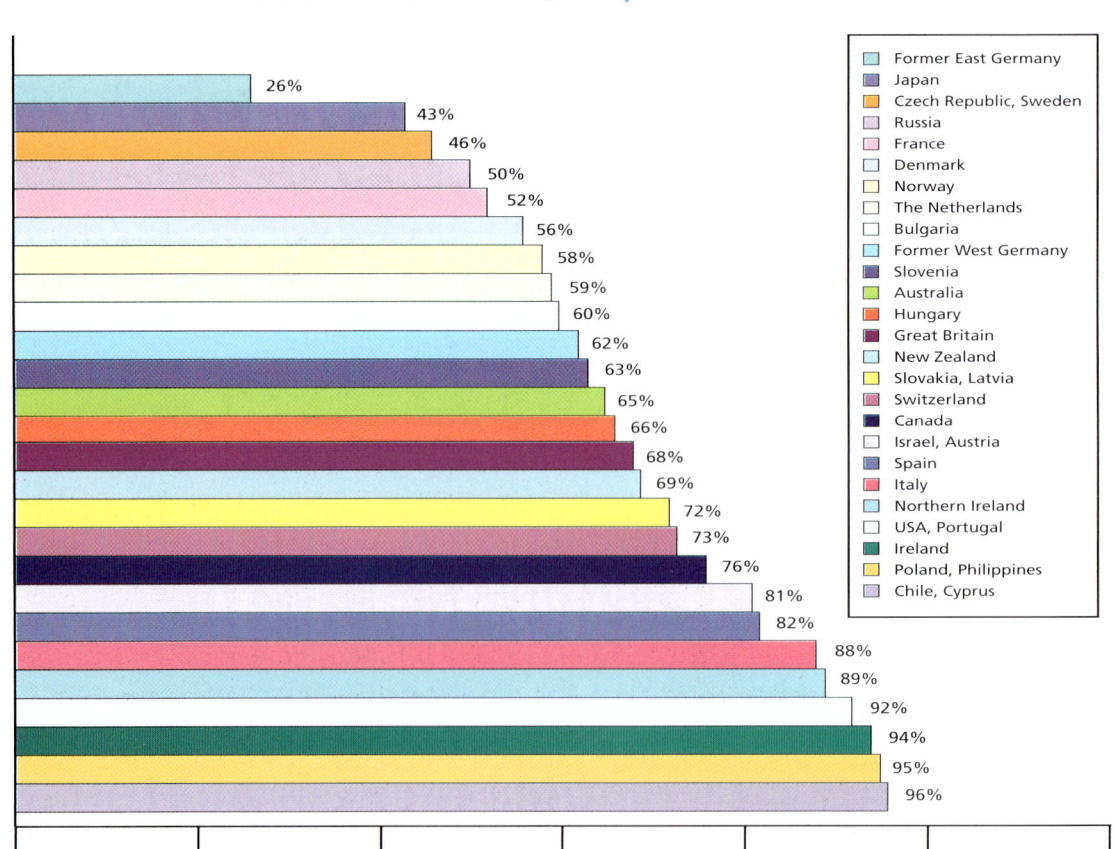

(International Social Survey Programme, 1998)

From this survey, we see that belief in God in the non-European countries compares well to belief in God in many European countries. Nine of the ten countries that were found to have the lowest levels of belief in God were in Europe, e.g. Former East Germany, Czech Republic and Sweden. Ireland had the fifth highest level of belief in God (94 per cent).

KNOW WHAT

1. According to this survey, what country had the lowest level of belief in God?
2. What four countries had the highest level of belief in God?
3. Where did Ireland rank in terms of belief in God?
4. What European countries ranked higher than Ireland in terms of belief in God?
5. What non-European countries ranked higher than Ireland in terms of belief in God?
6. How does belief in God in the non-European countries compare with belief in God in the European countries according to this survey?

The 1998 survey also asked people how often they attended religious services.

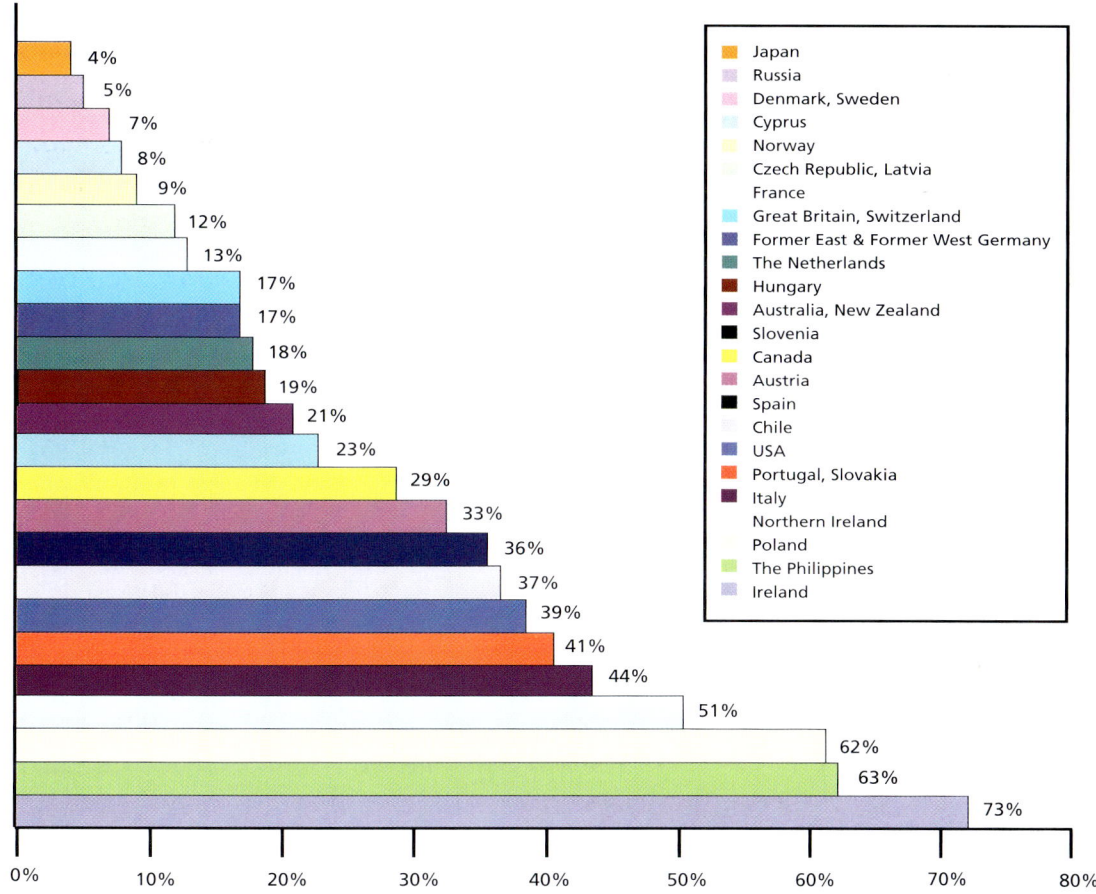

(International Social Survey Programme, 1998)

According to this survey, attendance rates in the non-European countries compare well to attendance in the European countries. Nine of the ten countries with the lowest levels of attendance at religious services are in Europe, e.g. Denmark, Sweden and Russia. In Ireland, more people were found to attend religious services regularly than in any other European or non-European country.

KNOW WHAT

1. What countries had attendance levels under 10 per cent?
2. Which country had the highest attendance at religious services?
3. Which non-European country had the highest level of attendance at religious services?
4. How does attendance at religious services in the non-European countries compare with attendance levels in the European countries?

DIGGING DEEPER

1. If you were born in Former East Germany, would you be more or less likely to believe in God than if you were born in Ireland? Give a reason for your answer.
2. If you were born in Russia, would you be more or less likely to attend religious services than if you were born in Ireland? Give a reason for your answer.
3. Does the situation of faith in Ireland affect your religious belief and practice? Explain.

KNOW WHAT

Now that you know a little bit more about religious belief and practice in Europe and the rest of the world, copy the following statements into your Religion folder and indicate whether they are true or false.

True or False

		True	False
1.	Christianity is the largest religion in Europe, North America and South America.	☐	☐
2.	Europe and Asia have a large number of people who do not believe in God or have no religion.	☐	☐
3.	Islam is the largest religion in Africa and Asia.	☐	☐
4.	Belief in God varies a lot from country to country.	☐	☐
5.	According to the 1998 ISSP survey, nine out of ten countries with the lowest levels of belief in God are in Africa.	☐	☐
6.	According to the 1998 ISSP survey, the Philippines has the second highest level of attendance at religious services.	☐	☐

KNOW IT ALL

Copy the following exercise into your Religion folder and fill in the blanks using the wordbank given below.

Christianity is the largest religion in Europe, _____, and North and South America. Islam is the largest religion in _____ . A sizable percentage of people in _____ and Asia do not believe in God or have no religion. Religious belief and practice in non-European countries compares _____ to religious belief and practice in European countries. According to a survey taken in 1998, _____ of the ten countries with the lowest levels of belief in God are in Europe. Nine of the ten countries with the _____ levels of attendance at religious services are also in Europe.

WORDBANK
Africa • Europe • lowest • Asia • nine • well

KNOW HOW

Write an account of the similarities and differences between religion in Europe and religion elsewhere.

KNOWING ME KNOWING YOU

Research the religious beliefs and practices of people in one non-European country and compare them to religious beliefs and practices in one European country. Present your findings to the class.

PART 2

The Beginnings of Faith

LESSON 79 Reflection – A Time of Discovery

GROUNDWORK
In this lesson we plan to:
- explore the importance of reflection.

DIGGING DEEPER
Why is it important to take time to reflect?

Key Concepts
Reflection/Question/Meaning

Guided Meditation

Sometimes life gets very busy. It is good to take time to reflect on life. Your teacher will lead you in this guided meditation:

- Sit quietly and forget about the other students around you. This time is for you!
- Make yourself comfortable. You might find it helpful to sit with your back straight and your two feet flat on the floor. Let your hands rest comfortably on your lap. (If you are sitting at your desk, you might prefer to rest your head and arms on the desk.)
- Allow your body to relax and close your eyes.
- Listen for any sounds from outside the room. Pay attention to each sound, the softest … the loudest … listen to them all.
- Turn your attention to the sounds you can hear inside the room. Listen to each of these sounds.

- Now become aware of your own breathing. Don't change the way in which you breathe, just pay attention to it. Listen to your breathing as you breathe in and as you breathe out. Do this for several minutes.
- Now, in your imagination, take yourself back to a time in the past when you were very happy. Picture that scene in your mind … the different features of the place … the objects … colours … sounds … everything that is part of the place. If there are any other people there, pay attention to them … Who are they? …What are they doing? … How do you feel about them? Now, focus on yourself … What are you doing? …How are you relating to any other people that are there? Become aware of any activities or conversations that are going on. Take a few minutes to relive the scene … What do you enjoy about being in this place? What is making you happy? … Savour this feeling of happiness.
- When you are ready, come back into the present. Become aware of where you are … notice the sounds around you. Now, open your eyes.

DIGGING DEEPER
1. From this exercise, what did you learn about the kind of things that make you happy?
2. Why is it important to be aware of what makes you happy?
3. Why is it important to take time to reflect on life?

Reflection

Reflection is an important human characteristic. Only human beings are able to reflect. When people reflect, they think deeply about life and they become more aware of their own feelings and actions. Sometimes when people reflect on their experiences, they ask **questions** about the **meaning** of life, for example: 'Who am I? What do I want to do with my life?' In taking time to reflect, they learn more about themselves and about life. As a result, they are better equipped to make important decisions.

The Monastery

A few years ago, BBC 2 broadcast a reality TV show called *The Monastery*. The programme followed five men who had volunteered to spend forty days and nights living with Catholic monks in a remote monastery. The cameras recorded these men as they tried to meet the challenge of leading a monk's life of study, prayer and work.

The five men came from very different backgrounds. One of them, Gary McCormick, was thirty-six years old. As a teenager in Belfast, he had joined a paramilitary organisation and served time in prison. For him, the time in the monastery was very worthwhile: 'It freed my demons. I

The Monastery of Christ

had a very bad image of myself up to six months ago and going to the monastery helped me to ask myself important questions and getting away from it all brought me closer to God. Modern life is so fast-paced and there are so many pressures. This gives you an opportunity to take stock of your life and make decisions about the things that are really important.'

KNOW WHAT

1. What challenge did the five men face?
2. What kind of questions do you think Gary asked himself during his time at the monastery?
3. How did Gary benefit from his experience?
4. What does this story teach you about the importance of reflection?

DIGGING DEEPER

1. Think of a place that you find relaxing. What kind of things do you think about when you are there?
2. Read Mark 6:45-46. Mark tells us that Jesus went up on the mountain to pray. What do you think Jesus reflected on when he prayed to God the Father?
3. Why is it important to take time out for reflection?

Reflection: Inner personal thought. Focusing on or searching for something meaningful in a sacred text, in the events of life or in the world of nature.

Question: To ask or argue about things that are uncertain or debatable.

Meaning: When people search for meaning in life, they look for relationships or things that make life feel worthwhile, that bring satisfaction and that make sense of life.

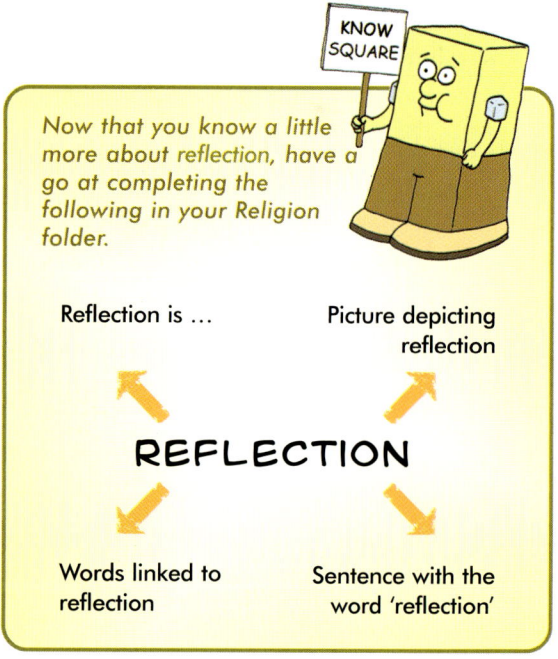

Now that you know a little more about reflection, have a go at completing the following in your Religion folder.

- Reflection is ...
- Picture depicting reflection
- Words linked to reflection
- Sentence with the word 'reflection'

REFLECTION

LESSON 80 Questions of Meaning

GROUNDWORK
In this lesson we plan to:
- be aware that the facility for questioning is an essential human characteristic;
- look at the questions that human beings ask at different stages of their development;
- explore examples of questions of meaning in youth culture.

DIGGING DEEPER
What questions of meaning do I ask?

Key Concepts
Question/Questioner/Search/Meaning

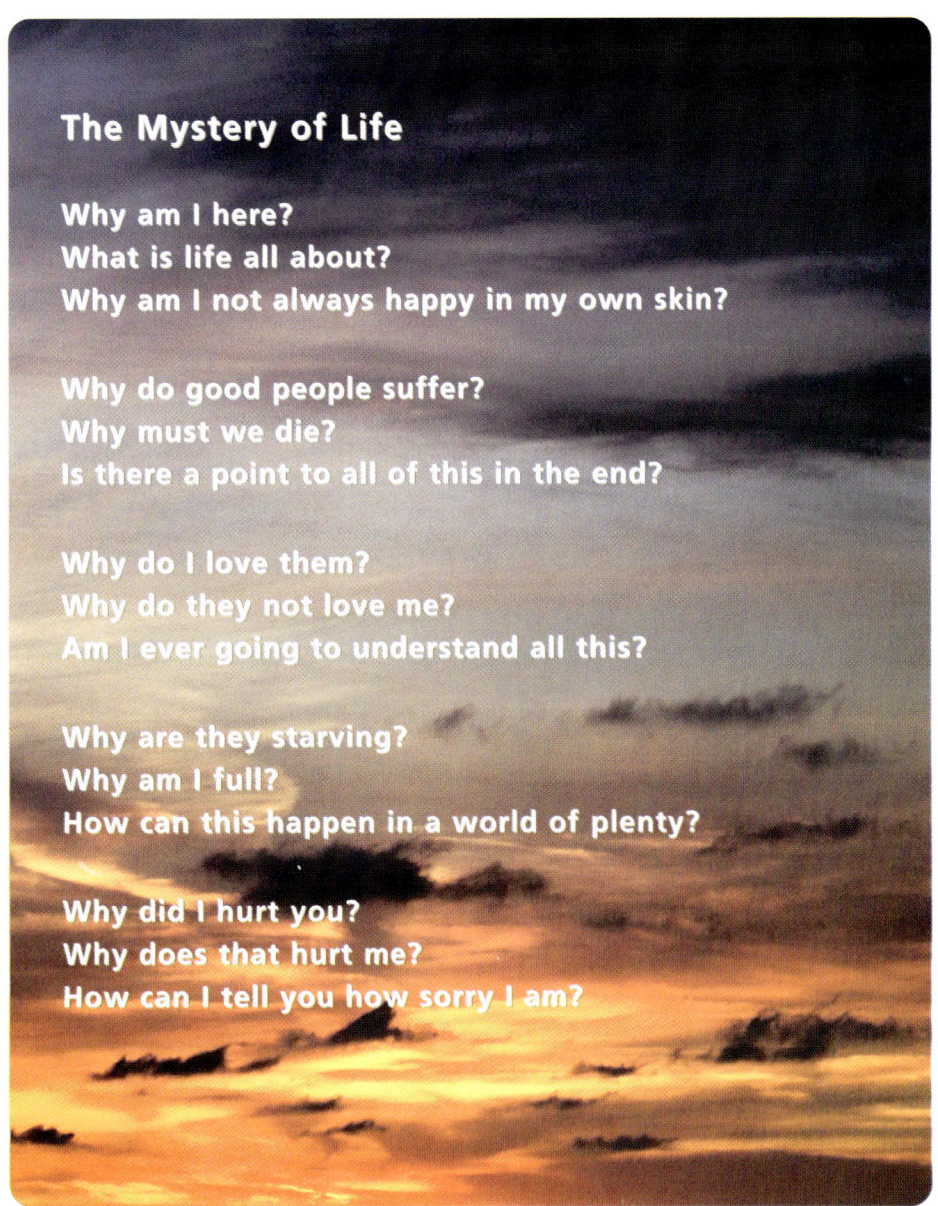

The Mystery of Life

Why am I here?
What is life all about?
Why am I not always happy in my own skin?

Why do good people suffer?
Why must we die?
Is there a point to all of this in the end?

Why do I love them?
Why do they not love me?
Am I ever going to understand all this?

Why are they starving?
Why am I full?
How can this happen in a world of plenty?

Why did I hurt you?
Why does that hurt me?
How can I tell you how sorry I am?

KNOW WHAT

1. Which of the questions in the poem have you asked?
2. List any questions in the poem that you find difficult to answer.
3. Do you think 'The Mystery of Life' is a good title for the poem? Why?/Why not?

DIGGING DEEPER

1. Which of the questions listed below do you often ask?
2. Which of these questions do you never ask?
3. From the list, choose *two* questions that you think are difficult to answer. Explain your choice.

What time is it?
What is my goal/purpose in life?
Can I have some money?
What will make me happy?
What films are on in the cinema?
Why do people suffer and die?
What time do I have to be home?
Who am I?
What homework do we have?
What happens to people when they die?
What marks did I get in my test?
What is life all about?
What time will we meet in town?
Why is there evil in the world?
Why should I be good?

The Search for Meaning

One important difference between human beings and other creatures is that human beings ask **questions**. Children, teenagers and adults are all **questioners**. We ask questions in order to learn about other people, about life and about the world around us. Some of the questions that we ask are difficult to answer. For example:

Who am I?
What is the goal/purpose of life?
How can we find happiness?
What happens to people when they die?
Why do people suffer?
Why is there evil in the world?
Why be good?

Such questions are part of the **search** for the **meaning** of life. When people search for meaning, they are looking for a sense of purpose in life. They are looking for something that makes sense of life and that makes life feel worthwhile.

KNOW WHAT

1. List the questions of meaning in the poem 'The Mystery of Life'.
2. What questions of meaning do you ask?
3. How are the questions of meaning that you ask similar to the questions asked by the child in the poem?
4. How are the questions of meaning that you ask different from the questions asked by the child in the poem?

DIGGING DEEPER

1. Keep a diary/log of all the questions that you ask in the next twenty-four hours.
2. Review the questions and put a tick beside all the questions of meaning that you ask.
3. Do you agree or disagree with the statement: 'Asking questions is an essential human characteristic'? Give reasons for your answer.

Questions of Meaning from Childhood to Adulthood

While children, teenagers and adults all ask questions of meaning, there are differences as well as similarities in the kind of questions that they ask.

Young children ask questions in order to make sense of what they see or experience. For example, the death of a pet or a relative may lead to questions such as:

'Will Fluffy go to heaven?'
'Why did Grandad get sick and die?'

Similarly, the birth of a baby brother or sister may lead a child to ask questions about the beginning of life:

'Where do babies come from?'
'Does God make babies?'

Children's questions are concrete questions about people and events that they have experienced.

During adolescence, teenagers develop the ability to reflect and to think about their lives. In trying to make sense of the world around them, they begin to ask questions that they never asked before. For example, when they see or experience birth, sickness, goodness or death, they often ask abstract questions about the meaning or purpose of these experiences:

Why do people suffer and die?
What is life all about?
Why be good?

Teenagers also begin to ask questions about what will make them happy. All human beings want to be happy. The search for happiness is part of the search for the meaning or purpose of life.

How can I find happiness?
What do I want to do with my life?
What is my goal/purpose in life?

Like teenagers, adults also ask questions about what will make them happy. They, too, try to make sense of human experiences like death, birth, suffering, goodness, evil, etc. Just like teenagers, they continue to ask abstract questions about the meaning of life:

What happens to people when they die?
Where can human beings find true happiness?
Can good come out of suffering?

KNOW HOW
In your Religion folder, give three examples of questions of meaning asked by (a) children, (b) teenagers and (c) adults.

DIGGING DEEPER
What question of meaning would you most like to be able to answer? Why?

Questions of Meaning in Youth Culture

Modern music, film and literature explore issues that are relevant to people today. In these media, young people recognise questions and themes that are relevant to their own lives. Music is a particularly important part of youth culture, as many song lyrics reflect the issues and the questions of meaning that young people face.

Read and/or listen to the following excerpt from the U2 song 'I Will Follow', which Bono wrote after his mother's death.

I was on the outside when you said
You needed me
I was looking at myself
I was blind, I could not see

A boy tries hard to be a man
His mother takes him by the hand
If he stops to think, he starts to cry
Oh why?

If you walk away, walk away
I walk away, walk away … I will follow (x2)

I was on the inside
When they pulled the four walls down
I was looking through the window
I was lost, I am found

DIGGING DEEPER
1. What issue(s) is explored in the song?
2. What question is expressed in the second verse?
3. Do you know any other songs that deal with similar issues? Explain.

Finding ways to make sense of and to cope with loss is part of the search for meaning in life. Another part of the search for meaning is trying to make sense of who we are and what our purpose is in life. U2 explore this aspect of the search for meaning in their song 'I Still Haven't Found What I'm Looking For':

I have climbed the highest mountains
I have run through the fields
Only to be with you
Only to be with you

I have run, I have crawled
I have scaled these city walls
These city walls
Only to be with you

But I still haven't found what I'm looking for
But I still haven't found what I'm looking for

DIGGING DEEPER
1. Where has the singer searched for a sense of purpose in life?
2. Do you know any other songs about the search for a sense of purpose or identity in life? Explain.

Group Exercise
- Break into four groups.
- Choose a leader and a reporter for each group. The job of the leader is to make sure that the group completes the task. The job of the reporter is to write down the group's answers to the questions and to report these to the rest of the class.
- Each group chooses a song, film, book/magazine or TV programme that is popular with young people and that deals with issues relevant to young people.
- In your group, discuss the following in relation to the example you have chosen:
    What questions of meaning are expressed in it?
    How are these questions expressed?
    How are these questions relevant to the lives of young people today?
- When all the groups have finished, the reporters outline their groups' answers to the class.

DIGGING DEEPER
Describe how people express questions about the meaning of life in *two* of the following:

Music   TV programmes   Books/Magazines   Films

KNOW IT ALL

Copy the following into your Religion folder and fill in the blanks using the wordbank given below.

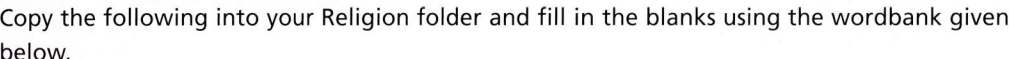

An important difference between humans and other creatures is that humans ask _____. Asking questions is a characteristic of being _____. Questions about the meaning of _____ can be difficult to answer. Children ask questions to make sense of what they see or _____. For example, the death of a pet or a relative can cause a child to ask many questions about what happens after_____. During adolescence, teenagers develop the ability to _____ on their lives. They begin to ask questions about what will make them _____. This desire for happiness is part of the search for the ———— of life. Teenagers also search for the meaning of experiences like birth, death, ————, etc. Like teenagers, _____ search for happiness and ask questions about the meaning of life.

WORDBANK

Adults • Death • Experience • Goodness • Happy • Meaning • Life • Questions • Reflect • Human

Questioner: Person who asks questions.

Search: To look for, to seek out, to enquire, to ask – in order to find meaning or answers.

See page 493 for past exam questions on this topic.

LESSON 81 Awe and Wonder

GROUNDWORK
In this lesson we plan to:
- look at experiences of awe and wonder;
- explain how such experiences cause people to reflect on the meaning of life.

DIGGING DEEPER
When do I reflect and ask questions about the meaning of life?

Key Concepts
Awe and Wonder/Reflection/Meaning

Experiences of Awe and Wonder

From time to time, we have experiences that fill us with **awe and wonder**. We feel amazed, surprised and moved by something wonderful. Sometimes these feelings are awakened by our relationships. At other times, the beauty of nature can stop us in our tracks. Often, as we **reflect** on our experiences of awe and wonder, we begin to ask questions about the **meaning** of life. Consider the following:

John was truly on a high! Jane had just agreed to go the cinema with him on Friday night. A part of him still couldn't believe it. She was so cool, he was amazed that she could be interested in him. As John slowly came down to earth, he remembered the question that Mr Donoghue had asked them earlier in Religion class: 'What makes you happy?' Well, John had found the answer to that question … JANE. However, he wouldn't be sharing that piece of information with Mr Donoghue or with the class.

Elaine looked in awe at her newborn baby boy. She could feel her heart swell with love and happiness. From this moment, she knew that her life would never be the same again. She now had a new purpose in life: to love and cherish this tiny infant. As she continued to gaze at her newborn son, she realised that she had found an answer to her question about the meaning of life.

Lunar eclipse

'Thousands of people gazed in awe as the skies remained clear on Saturday night for the most spectacular lunar eclipse in more than a decade. … The phenomenon occurred because the Earth passed directly between the Moon and the Sun.' (*Irish Independent*, 5 March 2007)

TAKE FIVE

1. To what question of meaning had John found an answer?
2. Why do you think Elaine was filled with awe as she looked at her baby?
3. What question of meaning had she found an answer to?
4. What have the two stories in common?
5. What questions of meaning do you think a person watching a lunar eclipse might ask themselves?

KNOW HOW

1. From the following list, choose *one* experience that caused you to reflect and ask questions about the meaning of life. Describe the experience and write about how it caused you to reflect.

A newborn baby	A beautiful sunset	A star-filled sky
A kind act	A storm at sea	The feeling of being loved
An accident	A film	Fun
A relationship	A holiday	Illness
A death	Music	A beautiful painting
The perfection of small things in nature, e.g. a ladybird, a spider's web, etc.	A rainbow	The sense that the world couldn't be here by chance

2. Collect photographs/pictures of scenes/events that awaken awe and wonder. Make a collage of these and display them in the classroom.

 **Awe and Wonder: Emotion (combining amazement and reverence) inspired by deep (significant) experience.**

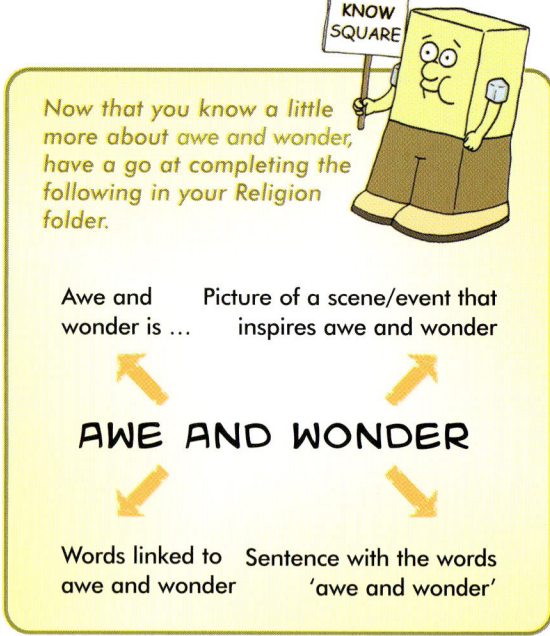

KNOW THE WAY

276

LESSON 82   Finding Answers

GROUNDWORK

In this lesson we plan to:
- identify some of the sources of meaning in human life;
- look at the position of the secular humanist.

DIGGING DEEPER

What are my sources of meaning? How do they influence my choices and behaviour? How important to me is my friendship with God?

Key Concepts
Meaning/Meaninglessness/Humanism

Introductory Activity

Imagine that you are offered a sports or music scholarship to a school in America for a year. As part of the package, you can choose three of the following:

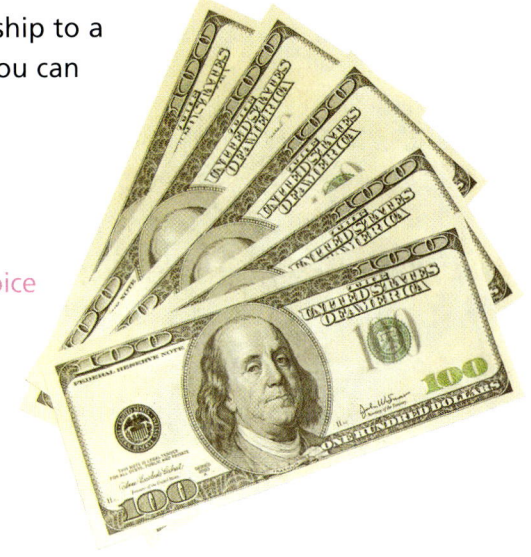

An air ticket for your best friend to visit
Air tickets for your family to visit
A car for the year
Two tickets to any concert or sports event of your choice
A music system for your room
A holiday in any other American city
Help from an expert tutor
One thousand dollars of spending money
Any other item of your own choosing

1. List your three choices.
2. Do your three choices have anything in common? Explain.
3. Why did you choose these three items?
4. What do your choices say about what makes you happy or gives your life meaning?

Sources of Meaning

Everyone has a built-in longing to be happy. All human beings search for things that will bring satisfaction and a sense of **meaning** to their lives. The search for happiness is part of the search for meaning. People find meaning in many different places:

- For some people, the key to happiness is having a loving relationship with their *family*. They enjoy spending time with their family. They keep in touch with family members and are there for them when they need help.
- Others feel that *friendship* gives most meaning to their lives. They spend a lot of time with their friends. They are loyal to their friends in good times and bad.
- Some regard *music* as the key to happiness. They enjoy listening to and playing music or they may compose their own music.
- Some people find the meaning of life in *work*. They like to do their job or school work well. Often, they work long hours to get the job done properly.

SECTION D   THE QUESTION OF FAITH

277

- Some people feel that *money* makes them happy. They feel secure when they have money. They spend time thinking up ways to make money.
- For others, the meaning of life is to achieve *success*. They feel alive when they are successful.

KNOW HOW

Read the following list and choose *five* items that give your life meaning.

My family	Being successful	Wearing cool clothes
Being popular	My friends	Getting good results
Having money	Sport	Work
Music	Being independent	Travel
My hobbies	Looking good	A friendship with God
Having a boy/girlfriend	Getting on with people	Cars
Art	Making the world a better place	Helping people

1. Compare your five choices with the choices of the other students in your class. What were the most popular choices?
2. List the three most popular choices for your class.

DIGGING DEEPER

1. Choose *two* of the five items that you picked out in the previous exercise. Write a paragraph explaining how they influenced how you spent your time in the last week (i.e. your choices and behaviour).
2. Look back at the *three* most popular choices for members of your class. Outline how each of these can help people to find answers in their search for meaning in life.

Meaninglessness

As we have seen, many people find answers to their search for happiness and meaning in their relationships with family and friends, in sport, music, work, money, success, etc. They feel content when they are involved with these things.

However, there are some people who say that these things do not give meaning to life. Some people do not find any happiness in life. According to them, 'life is **meaningless**!'

Story: Starting Over

Mark loved horses. He spent all his free time after school and at weekends riding the horses at his father's training yard. He dreamt of becoming a top jockey and of winning all the big races. Mark worked hard to make his dream come true. He left school at sixteen and went to work for Pat O'Brien, one of the best trainers in the country. He worked hard and never complained about the long hours or the travelling. Soon his efforts began to pay off. At eighteen, he won his first major race at Listowel and at nineteen he won three races at the Cheltenham Festival. Racing became his life. Frequently, he raced six days a week.

But when Mark was twenty-three, disaster struck. At Aintree, his horse unseated him and Mark was left paralysed from the waist down. Suddenly, there was nothing to look forward to. Mark could no longer do what he enjoyed. He felt that his life was meaningless.

When Mark was eventually released from hospital, he was filled with self-pity. But slowly, he began to watch his father out in the training yard with the horses. At meal-times, he started to make suggestions about their training. One evening, his father handed him an envelope. Inside, Mark found a licence to train horses. Suddenly, life looked better. Mark knew that although he was no longer able to ride, he could still work with horses and train them to win all the big races. Once again, his life had meaning.

KNOW WHAT
1. Before his accident, what gave meaning to Mark's life?
2. After the accident, why did Mark feel that his life was meaningless?
3. How did Mark find meaning in his life once again?

God and the Search for Meaning

People who believe in God say that a person can only be fully happy when they have faith in God. Religious people say that the secret of real happiness is having a friendship with God.

Ann's Search for Meaning

Ann Lee is a young woman who works at Knock Shrine, Co. Mayo. As part of her work, she gives retreats to primary and secondary school students. Here she talks about her search for happiness as a teenager:

> … like everyone, I searched for the ultimate happiness. I searched everywhere: in my appearance, in drink and drugs, in popularity and fashion, in success, and men, and I was doing very well in those areas. All of those things gave me a 'high on life' feeling but the only thing was that happiness didn't last very long. I always ended up flat and … searching for something else to make me happy. When I was twenty years of age, my dad died suddenly, my heart was broken and none of those anaesthetics could fix it. I was left very empty and disillusioned with life; I could find no meaning in it. One day I went back to Mass and I really asked Jesus to help me; that was thirteen years ago.
>
> I always say to my First Year classes about their Confirmation: 'Remember how you were really looking forward to the big day; how you couldn't wait'. They all nod. Then I ask them what they were most excited about. No one ever said 'The Holy Spirit'. They say the clothes, the money and, above all, what they were going to buy. Then I ask them if those things they bought are still making them happy. The answer is always 'No'! Now they're looking forward to Christmas or the next birthday or whatever. 'I'll be happy if or I'll be happy when…'
>
> … No person or created thing can make you fully happy. God made us like little egg cups with a dip in the centre; an emptiness inside that only God can fill. … We will always be restless, we will always be searching until we find God.

KNOW WHAT
1. As a teenager, what gave Ann a 'high on life' feeling?
2. Why do you think Ann went back to Mass?
3. Why did the things the students bought with their Confirmation money not make them fully happy?
4. 'God has made us like little egg cups with a dip in the centre.' What does Ann mean by this?
7. According to Ann, what is the source of true happiness?

St Augustine's Search for Meaning

Augustine was born in North Africa in AD 354. Like Ann, he searched for happiness as a teenager by having a hectic social life. But no matter what he tried, he still felt restless and unhappy. Eventually, he turned to God and became a Christian. Later, he became a bishop. When Augustine was reflecting back over his life, he wrote these lines: 'You have made us for yourself, O Lord, and our hearts are restless until they rest in Thee.' Augustine believed that true happiness could only be found by having a loving friendship with God.

KNOW WHAT

1. Why did Augustine feel restless and dissatisfied?
2. How did Augustine find real happiness?
3. What did Augustine mean by the words: 'Our hearts are restless until they rest in Thee'?
4. How is Ann's story similar to that of St Augustine?

DIGGING DEEPER

1. According to Ann and St Augustine, true happiness can only be found by having a loving friendship with God. What do you think?
2. How important is having a friendship with God to you?

Copy this diagram into your Religion folder:

Religious Answers to the Search for Meaning – Major World Religions

The world religions help people to answer questions about the meaning of life. Let us look at the answers that Christianity, Judaism and Islam give to some of the questions that people ask about life today.

	Judaism	Christianity	Islam
What is the goal/purpose of life?	Jewish people believe that God has invited them into a special relationship called the Covenant. The purpose of life is to love God and to live according to the moral law, as given in the Ten Commandments and in the Torah.	Christians believe that life is a gift from God. The purpose of life is to develop a loving relationship with God. Christians try to keep Jesus' commandment to love God and love one's neighbour.	For Muslims, the purpose of life is to serve Allah and to live according to the moral code given in the Qur'an and the Hadith.
What happens when we die?	Some Jews believe that the dead will be raised to life when the Messiah comes. However, there is no mention of an afterlife in the Torah.	Christians believe in life after death. They believe that if a person has loved God in this life, their soul will go to heaven after they die.	Muslims believe that Allah will raise all people to life on the Day of Judgement. Depending on how they have lived their lives, Allah will send them to heaven or hell.
Why is there evil in the world?	The Hebrew Scriptures teach that God gave human beings free will. Evil occurs when human beings disobey God.	The Bible teaches that God created people with free will. Evil occurs when people misuse their freedom.	Muslims believe that human beings have free will. Evil occurs when people sin.

KNOW WHAT

Choose *one* of these three religions: Judaism, Christianity or Islam. In your own words, outline its answers to the following questions:
1. What is the goal/purpose of life?
2. What happens when we die?
3. Why is there evil in the world?

Non-Religious Answers to the Search for Meaning – Humanism

Some people do not believe in God or in any religion. Instead, they believe in human beings. These people are called humanists. Humanists value human beings, not God. They put their trust in human goodness and in human intelligence.

Humanists believe that this life and this world is all there is. Therefore, it is important to try to be happy. Humanists do not turn to God or to religion to find answers to the search for happiness. Instead, they work out the answers by using human reason. Humanists give non-religious answers to questions about the meaning of life. This way of looking at life is called **humanism**.

Let us look at the answers that humanism gives to some of the questions that people ask about the meaning of life.

What is the goal/purpose of life?	Humanists do not believe that God created human beings. They believe that human beings developed through evolution. For humanists, this world is all there is. Therefore, human beings should enjoy life and develop their potential in ways that respect other people.

| What happens when we die? | Humanists do not believe in life after death. For them, this life and this world is all there is. |
| Why is there evil in the world? | Humanists say that we should treat people as we would like to be treated. Evil occurs when people do not do this. |

Copy this diagram into your Religion folder:

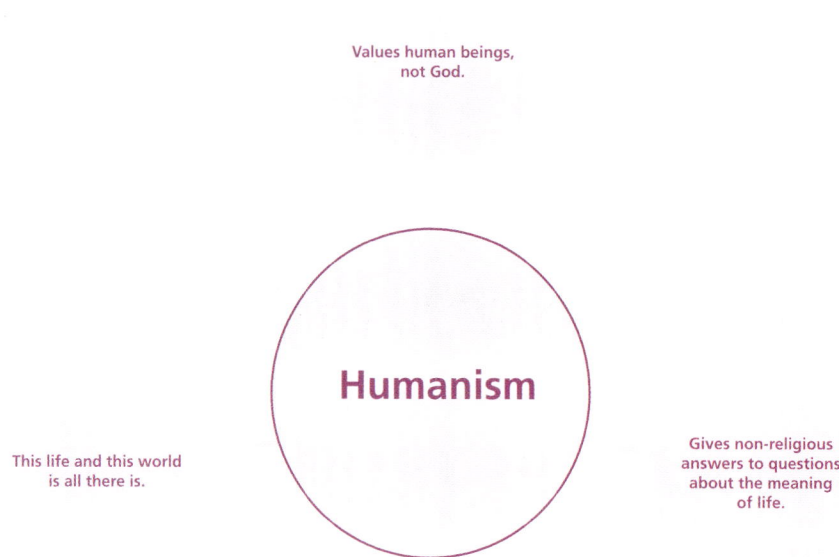

KNOW WHAT

In your own words, outline the answers humanism gives to the following questions:
1. What is the goal/purpose of life?
2. What happens when we die?
3. Why is there evil in the world?

 **Meaninglessness:** People experience meaninglessness when they feel life is not worthwhile, when they can find no reason to suffer their present difficulties.

Humanism: Looks to life (not religion) as a source of meaning; to base one's plans or beliefs on factual evidence and scientific ways of enquiry only.

See pages 493 and 494 for past exam questions on this topic.

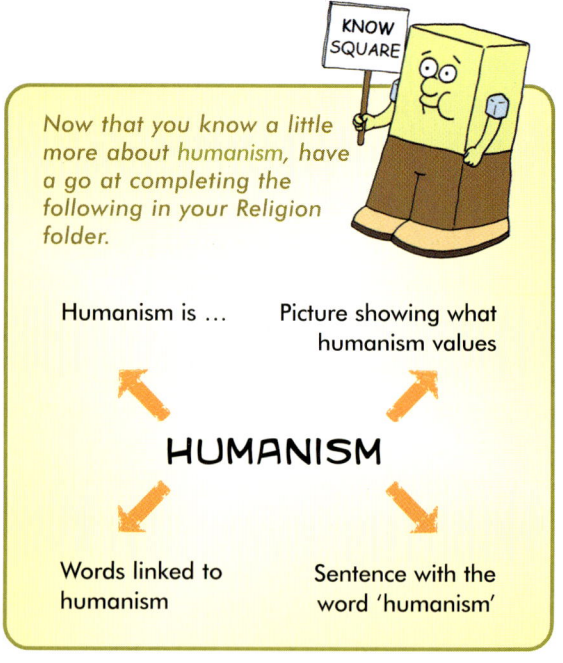

The Growth of Faith

LESSON 83 Images of God

GROUNDWORK
In this lesson we plan to:
- look at images of God from a variety of sources, including the students' own experiences.

DIGGING DEEPER
What are my images of God?
Who/What shaped my images of God?

Introductory Activity: Guided Meditation

Your teacher may play some relaxing music to help you to enter into this meditation.

- Sit quietly and forget about the other students around you. This time is for you!
- Make yourself comfortable. You might find it helpful to sit with your back straight and your two feet flat on the floor. Let your hands rest comfortably on your lap. (If you are sitting at your desk, you might prefer to rest your head and arms on the desk.)
- Allow your body to relax and close your eyes.
- Listen for any sounds from outside the room. Pay attention to each sound, the softest … the loudest … listen to them all.
- Then turn your attention to the sounds you can hear inside the room.
- Now become aware of your own breathing. Don't change the way in which you breathe, just pay attention to it. Listen to your breathing as you breathe in and as you breathe out. Do this for several minutes.
- Now, in your imagination, travel to one of your favourite places … perhaps the seaside, or beside a stream, or a hilltop or a garden. Choose a place where you feel happy and comfortable on your own.
- In your mind's eye, picture the scene around you. Notice the features of the place … the colours … the smells … the sounds … Relax and enjoy being there.

- Now become aware of God's presence in this place. … Where do you notice God? … What is God doing? … How do you feel toward God?
- Take this opportunity to speak to God … What does God say in reply? … Continue your conversation with God for as long as you wish …
- It's almost time for you to leave … Show God with a gesture or words what God means to you. … What does God do in response?
- When you are ready, come back into the present. … Become aware of where you are … Open your eyes and take a gentle stretch.

DIGGING DEEPER

1. Draw a picture or a symbol that represents what you think God is like. Complete this sentence and use it as a title for your drawing: 'God is like…'

Or

2. On a sheet of paper, list all the words you can think of to describe God. Using these words, write three or four sentences describing what you think God is like.

KNOWING ME KNOWING YOU

In pairs, share your drawings and/or written descriptions of God. What were the most common pictures/symbols/words used to describe God?

Images of God

Even though we cannot physically see God, each of us has an image or mental picture of God. Our image of God is the way we view God. It is the set of ideas that we have about what God is like.

Research into popular images of God among Irish children and young people found the following images to be the most common:

God as a kind old man
God is a kind old man with a beard and white hair. He is dressed in white robes and sits on a cloud, from where he guides the world.

God as controller
God is a ruler who controls everything that happens to us.

God as a stern judge
God watches us from heaven. He sees and judges everything we do.

God as forgiver
God forgives us when we are truly sorry.

God as a loving father
God is a loving father who is always there to listen to us, to comfort us and to guide us.

God as friend
God is a friend who is always there to listen, to comfort and to help.

God as a power for good
God is not a person. God is the goodness we see in nature and in people.

TAKE FIVE
1. Which of these images is closest to your own image of God?
2. Which of these images do you like (a) best and (b) least? Why?
3. In your opinion, are any of these images of God unhelpful? Explain.

Sources of Our Images of God
Our images of God come from a variety of sources – our parents/guardians, our teachers, our community of faith, experiences of life, film, music, books, etc. Let's look at three of these sources.

Parents
Parents have a big influence on children's images of God. Usually, children first hear about God from their parents. The messages they hear are varied, for example: 'God loves you and will always take care of you' or 'God is watching you, so you better be good'. These messages influence children's images of God.

Parents also influence their children's images of God by the way they relate to their children. Research suggests that young children who are strictly disciplined by their parents tend to see God as a punisher. On the other hand, children who see their parents as loving and powerful tend to imagine God as loving and powerful.

Community of Faith

The stories, beliefs and religious practices of a community of faith help to shape a person's image of God. Research suggests that there are some differences in the way that people of different religions think about God.

Film

In many films, for example *Bruce Almighty*, God is shown as a man dressed in white. This image of God encourages people to imagine God as a human being, usually male. In contrast, the three monotheistic religions – Judaism, Christianity and Islam – teach that God is Spirit and does not have a body.

KNOW WHAT
1. Give one example of how parents influence children's images of God.
2. Give one example of how film influences people's images of God.

The Development of Our Images of God

As we saw earlier in this lesson, young children often think of God as a kind old man living in the sky or as a stern judge. As they mature and get to know God better, their images of God tend to change. Many older children see God as a loving parent or as a spirit, while some teenagers also think of God as a guide or friend. Such images of God can be helpful in encouraging a child or adolescent to pray and to trust in God.

Sometimes our images of God are not helpful images. Some images can give us a wrong impression of God or damage our relationship with God. Examples of unhelpful images of God are God as a controller and God as a stern judge. For Christians, the image of God as controller is not a true image of God because the Bible tells us that God respects human freedom. Similarly, the image of God as a stern judge is an unhelpful image because it can make people afraid of God. For Christians, the best way to develop a truthful and helpful image of God is to look at the images of God in the Bible, especially at Jesus' understanding of God.

While people of all religions try to develop a truthful and helpful understanding of God by studying the images of God in their sacred texts, they also realise that no matter how wise they become, they will never understand God fully. Our human minds are not able to understand fully the mystery of God. We are human and God is God.

TAKE FIVE
1. What images of God are commonly found among young children?
2. What images of God are often found among older children?
3. Identify a helpful image of God and explain why it is helpful.
4. What do people of faith believe is the best way to develop a truthful and helpful image of God?
5. Why can people not understand God fully?

Kevin's Image of God

Here, nineteen-year-old Kevin talks about how his image of God has changed since he was a child:

My idea of God has changed a lot since I was young. When I was small, my dad used to say 'God is watching you. You'd better be good'. I had this idea that God was like a judge, looking down on me and ready to punish me when I did wrong. But now it's different. For me, God is like a really good friend. When I was in Fourth Year I joined a folk group. The guy in charge was really into it. He used to take us to these workshops on music and there I'd meet young people who would talk about God and religion and stuff! Then, we had a brilliant retreat in Leaving Cert. After that, I started to pray a bit more. Now I trust God fully and talk to him about lots of things. God always listens. He's like a great friend.

KNOW WHAT

1. What image of God did Kevin have when he was young?
2. Who or what influenced this image?
3. As he grew older, what caused his image of God to change?
4. What image of God does Kevin have now?

DIGGING DEEPER

1. Think back to when you were a child. What are your first memories about God or religion?
2. How has your image of God changed since you were a child?
3. Below is a list of some of the people and things that can influence a person's image of God. Choose *one* of these items and explain how it has influenced your image of God.

Parents	Grandparents	Other people
School	Friends	Community of faith
TV	Films	Art
Music	A sacred text	Events in life
Books	Magazines	

KNOW IT ALL

Copy the following into your Religion folder and fill in the blanks using the wordbank given below.

Young Irish people have a range of images of God, including: God as a kind old _____, God as _____, God as forgiver and God as _____. People's images of God come from a variety of sources. The messages that _____ give their children about God influences children's images of God. The stories, beliefs and religious practices of a _____ of _____ also influence a person's image of God. As children grow older and learn more about God, their images of God frequently _____. Sometimes the images of God that children and teenagers have are not _____ images. For Christians, the best way to develop a truthful and helpful image of God is to look at the images of God in the _____, especially at _____ understanding of God.

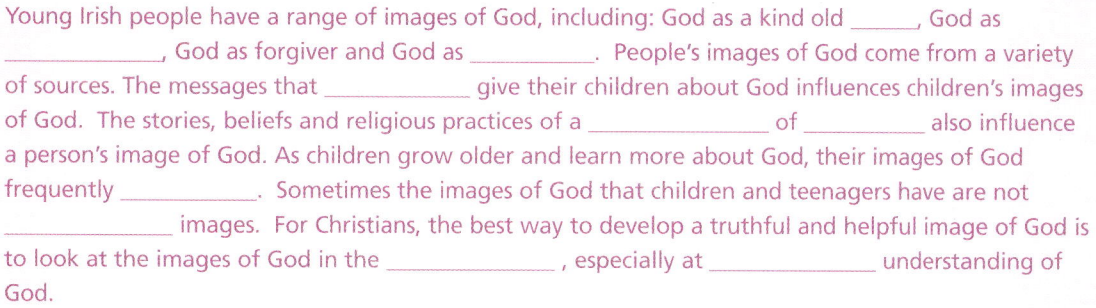

WORDBANK

Jesus' • Change • Controller • Parents • Faith • Helpful • Community • Man • Friend • Bible

See page 494 for past exam questions on this topic.

LESSON 84 Christian Images of God

GROUNDWORK
In this lesson we plan to:
- explore some Christian images of God.

DIGGING DEEPER
How do Christian images of God compare with my image of God?

For Christians, the Bible is the inspired Word of God. Christians believe that the best way to develop a truthful and helpful image of God is to look at the images of God in the Bible, especially at Jesus' understanding of God.

Images of God in the Old Testament

The images of God in the Old Testament are important to both Christians and Jews. The ancient Hebrew people used many images to describe God and God's relationship with them. In the following story from the book of Exodus, the Hebrew writers describe how God guided the people on their journey from slavery in Egypt:

The Lord went in front of them in a pillar of cloud by day, to lead them along the way, and in a pillar of fire by night, to give them light, so that they might travel by day and night. Neither the pillar of cloud by day nor the pillar of fire by night left its place in front of the people.

(Exodus 13:21-22)

KNOW WHAT
1. In the passage, what did God do to help the people of Israel?
2. What images are used to describe God's guiding presence?
3. Choose one of the images and say why it is a suitable image for God.
4. Using your Bible, match the following images of God with the correct Bible reference:

King	Isaiah 66:13
Eagle	Malachi 2:10
Creator	Psalm 47:7-8
Father	Psalm 78:52-53
Mother	Exodus 19:4
Shepherd	Jeremiah 1:4-5

5. Which one of these images do you like best? Why?
6. What does the image you have chosen say about God?

Images of God in the New Testament

Christians believe that we can most clearly see what God is like when we look at Jesus. Jesus said, 'Whoever has seen me, has seen the Father' (John 14:9). Christians believe that God became a human being in Jesus. This event is called the Incarnation.

The story of Jesus' baptism is the first story in the New Testament that reveals God as the Trinity, i.e. as Father, Son and Holy Spirit, three distinct persons. Each person of the Trinity is revealed in this story.

> *And when Jesus had been baptised, just as he came up from the water, suddenly the heavens were opened to him and he saw the Spirit of God descending like a dove and alighting on him. And a voice from heaven said, 'This is my Son, the Beloved, with whom I am well pleased.'* (Matthew 3:16-17)

KNOW WHAT
1. Identify the three images of God in this story.
2. What do Christians call the three persons in one God?

KNOW HOW
In your Religion folder, summarise the story of Jesus' baptism by drawing a picture for each of the following scenes:

- Jesus coming up from the water;
- the Spirit of God descending on Jesus;
- a voice from heaven saying, 'This is my Son, the Beloved.'

Images of God in Jesus' Parables
Jesus used a variety of images of God in his parables and in his teaching. For example, Jesus compared God to:

- a forgiving father
- a shepherd who searches for a lost sheep
- a housekeeper who searches for a lost coin
- a generous employer

The images that Jesus used portray God as loving, caring, generous and merciful. Frequently, Jesus used the image of God as 'Father'. He taught his followers to call God 'Our Father' and he encouraged them to pray to God. Jesus wanted his followers to understand that God loves, forgives and receives everyone with open arms.

KNOW HOW
1. Using your Bible, match each of the following images of God with the correct Bible reference:

The shepherd who searches for the lost sheep	Luke 15:11-24
The woman who searches for a lost coin	Matthew 20:1-16
The forgiving father	Luke 15:8-10
The generous employer	Luke 15:3-7

2. Choose *one* of these parables and, in your Religion folder, tell the story using either words or pictures. Then explain what the parable tells us about God.
3. From what you learned in Sections A and C, write a paragraph about the understanding of God in *one* of the following world religions: Judaism, Islam, Hinduism or Buddhism.

KNOW IT ALL

Copy the following into your Religion folder and fill in the blanks using the wordbank given below.

Christians believe that the best way to see what God is like is to look at _____. They believe that God the Son became a _____ being in Jesus. This event is called the _____. Two images of God that Jesus used are: God as the forgiving father and God as the _____ who searches for his lost sheep. Christians believe that there are _____ persons in the one God. This belief is called the doctrine of the _____ .

WORDBANK

Trinity • Incarnation • Three • Shepherd • Jesus • Human

LESSON 85   Stages of Faith

GROUNDWORK
In this lesson we plan to:
- explore the search for God from childhood to adulthood: from simple human trust to religious commitment.

DIGGING DEEPER
What do I believe about God?
What questions do I have about God and religion?
Do I have trust in God?

Key Concepts
Trust/Faith/Personal faith/Stages of faith/Childhood faith/Mature faith

Story: A Leap of Faith

One night, Peter woke up to find his bedroom full of smoke. Feeling very afraid, he grabbed his teddy and ran to the door of his room. When he opened it, he saw fire on the landing. His father and mother were standing on the far side of the flames but they were not able to reach him. Peter started to cry. Then he heard his father call out, 'Peter, go to the window and open it.' But Peter was too frightened to move. His father shouted louder, 'Peter, go to the window and open it!' Hugging his teddy, Peter went to the window and opened it. By this stage, Peter's parents had made their way out of the blazing house. The neighbours had gathered but the fire brigade had not yet arrived. Standing beneath the window, Peters' father called out, 'Jump, Peter, and I'll catch you.' But Peter could not see his father. All he could see were flames and smoke. 'No, Daddy, I can't see you,' he cried. Then his mother reassured him: 'Peter, we can see you and that's all that matters. Jump!' Peter hugged his teddy tightly and jumped. Within seconds, he found himself safe and sound in his father's arms.

TAKE FIVE
1. How did Peter feel when he woke up and found that his room was full of smoke?
2. Why were his parents not able to reach him?
3. Why was Peter afraid to jump?
4. In the end, why did Peter jump?
5. Do you think that Peter trusted his parents? Explain.

Trust and Faith

When we trust people like our parents or our friends, we believe in them. We know that we can rely on them. The word **trust** means to believe in, to rely on. Peter trusted his parents because he had certain beliefs about them. He believed that:

- his parents loved him;
- his parents would always help him;
- his parents wanted what was best for him.

As a result of what he believed about his parents, he trusted them to catch him when he fell. Belief and trust are closely connected. Our beliefs about people influence our trust in them.

291

Faith is similar to trust. When someone says that they have faith in you, it means that they believe in you, they have trust in you. When someone says that they have faith in God, what they mean is that they have trust in God. A person with religious faith says 'yes' to a friendship with God. They know that they can trust God because of what they have learnt and believe about God. People of faith put their trust in God because they believe that:

- God loves each person very much.
- God is always ready to help.
- God wants what is best for each person.

Personal faith is a person's own relationship with God. It refers to the way a person trusts in God and their beliefs about God. Each person is free to put their trust in God or not. Religious faith is a free act.

KNOW WHAT
1. How is trust connected with belief?
2. What do people mean when they say that they have faith in God?
3. What is personal faith?

DIGGING DEEPER
1. Think of someone you trust a great deal. Explain why you trust this person.
2. What do you believe about God?
3. Do you have trust in God? Why?/Why not?

Stages of Faith

As we saw earlier, our images of God change as we grow from childhood to adolescence and on to adulthood. Just as our relationship with our parents changes as we get older, so also does our relationship with God. Usually, as people grow older, they pass through different **stages of faith**: **childhood faith**; adolescent faith; **mature faith**.

Childhood Faith

'My name is Sandra. I am eight years old. This year I am making my First Communion. I will wear a beautiful dress and receive Jesus for the first time. My teacher says that receiving Jesus in Holy Communion is very special. My mam and dad have told me a lot about Jesus. Every Christmas we go to see the baby Jesus in the crib and light a candle. My mam taught me a prayer that Jesus said – it is called the "Our Father". I think God is like Jesus, but sometimes I think that God is probably an old man who lives in the sky.'

Usually, young children learn about God and religion from their parents or guardians, and sometimes from their grandparents. From their example, many young children learn how to take part in religious rituals, e.g. to bless themselves or to light a candle in front of a crib or holy picture. Once they are able to talk, they start to learn simple prayers and religious stories, e.g. stories about Jesus. As they grow older, they develop a better understanding of the stories, beliefs and practices that are part of their religion. They may also participate in some important rituals in their community of faith, e.g. Catholic students participate in the sacraments of Reconciliation, Eucharist and Confirmation. Like Sandra, many children have images of God as a judge or as an old man who lives in the sky.

Childhood faith is an *imitative faith* – children imitate the faith and religious practices of their parents and other important adults.

KNOW WHAT

1. Name two people who have influenced Sandra's faith and explain how they have influenced her faith.
2. What are Sandra's images of God?
3. How is Sandra's faith typical of a child's faith?
4. 'Childhood faith is an imitative faith.' Do you agree with this statement? Give reasons for your answer.

Adolescent Faith

'My name is Neil. I am fifteen years old. I no longer think that God is like an old man. Instead, I think that God is a loving friend who knows me and loves me as I am. But I still can't understand how God lets bad things happen. Like last year, my best friend's mother died and he has been going through a difficult time. Why are some people's lives so hard? I have asked my Religion teacher about this and he says that God gives people the strength to cope. But why does God allow bad things to happen in the first place? I'd love to be able to make sense of it all.'

Usually, teenage faith is a *searching* or *questioning* faith. Many teenagers are searching for happiness and meaning. They frequently ask questions about suffering and death, e.g. 'Why does God allow bad things to happen?' They also ask questions about their religious tradition, e.g. 'Why can't there be women priests?' Some teenagers may 'experiment' with their religion, e.g. by showing interest in other religious traditions. These teenagers are not losing their faith. Rather, they are searching for answers that make sense to them. Unfortunately, some teenagers never enter this questioning stage of adolescent faith; they fail to question the religious beliefs and practices that they had as children. They either stay at the stage of childhood faith or lose interest in religion altogether.

Teenagers want to be accepted by their friends and peers (i.e. by people of their own age). As a result, friends and peers have a big influence on what teenagers think about God and religion. Teenagers often find it easier to believe in God and take part in religious practices when their friends also do so.

Many teenagers have an image of God as the Friend who knows them and loves them as they are.

KNOW WHAT

1. What is Neil's image of God?
2. How is Neil's faith an adolescent faith?
3. Identify one influence on adolescent faith.
4. What image of God do many teenagers have?
5. 'Teenage faith is a searching or questioning faith.' Do you agree with this statement? Give reasons for your answer.

Mature Faith

'My name is Joanne. Even though I am twenty-eight years old, I still have a lot of questions about life and about God, but I think that's OK. Although I know that God is a mystery, I have a deep sense that God is with me, loving and guiding me. I pray every day and try to be patient and kind towards other people. In my spare time, I train the local Special Olympics swimming team.'

Many adults search for the meaning of life and ask questions about their religion. They also make choices about their religious beliefs and practices. They decide for themselves what religious beliefs and practices they want to keep and what community of faith they want to be part of. Some adults may give up on their religious faith. However, a lot of adults choose to have a close relationship with God and this relationship influences the way they live their lives. These adults pray to and worship God and try to live as they believe God wants them to live. For example, Christian adults try to keep Jesus' commandment to love God and to love their neighbour as themselves.

Some adults who reach the stage of mature faith see God as a mysterious and loving presence. Others never reach the stage of mature faith; they never move beyond the stage of childhood or adolescent faith.

KNOW WHAT

1. What is Joanne's image of God?
2. How does her faith influence the way she lives her life?
3. How is Joanne's faith a mature faith?
4. What image of God do many adults have at the stage of mature faith?
5. Write a paragraph describing the stage of mature faith.

DIGGING DEEPER

1. As a teenager, what questions do you ask about God and religion?
2. Is your faith an adolescent faith? Give reasons for your answer.
3. Read Luke 2:41-51 and answer the following questions:
   a) What was Jesus doing when his parents found him in the Temple?
   b) Would you describe the boy Jesus' faith as being similar to childhood or adolescent faith? Give reasons for your answer.

KNOW THE WAY

KNOW HOW

1. Make a wall display of the questions that the students in your class ask about God and religion. Choose an appropriate title for the display.
2. Imagine that you have been asked to write a newspaper article describing how faith develops from childhood to adulthood. In your article outline:
   a) The characteristics of childhood, adolescent and mature faith.
   b) The main influences on faith at each stage.
   c) The changes in one's image of God from childhood to adulthood.

KNOW IT ALL

Copy the following into your Religion folder and fill in the blanks using the wordbank given below.

The word _____ means to believe in or to rely on.

A person with religious faith says _____ to a relationship with God.

_____ _____ is a person's own relationship with God.

Many people pass through three _____ of faith.

Childhood faith is an _____ faith.

Adolescent faith is a _____ faith.

Many teenagers ask _____ about God.

Many adults see God as a mysterious and loving _____.

Christian adults with mature faith try to keep Jesus' commandment to love God and to love their _____ as themselves.

WORDBANK

Stages • Imitative • Searching • 'Yes' • Personal Faith • Questions • Presence • Neighbour • Trust

---

Trust: To rely on or to put one's confidence in someone or something.

Faith: The response of a person or a group to God's revelation.

Personal Faith: One's personal response to God and what is known about God. Grows and develops as a person grows.

Stages of Faith: Different ways of expressing the same faith/belief that go with different stages of life (e.g. childhood, adolescence, adulthood).

Childhood Faith: A child's first stage or expression or personal response to God and what is known about God.

Mature Faith: A fully developed (worked out) expression of a personal response to God and what is known about God.

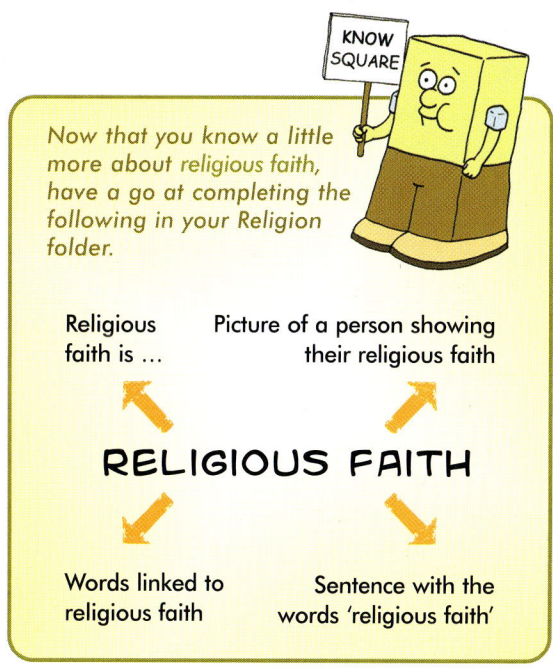

295

PART 4

The Expression of Faith

LESSON 86   A Living Faith

GROUNDWORK
In this lesson we plan to:
- explore prayer, worship and way of life as expressions of religious faith and of the search for God.

DIGGING DEEPER
How do I express my religious faith?

Key Concepts
Prayer/Worship

We Express Our Feelings

It is natural for people to express their feelings through words, facial expressions, gestures or actions. For example, when a person feels angry, they may frown, shout or slam a door. Similarly, when someone has feelings of trust in another person, they may express that trust by confiding in them or by depending on them.

Study each of the following photographs.

  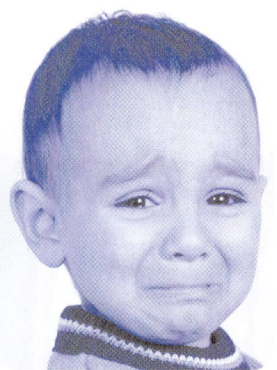 

KNOW WHAT
What feelings are being expressed in each photograph and how are they being expressed or communicated?

We Express Our Faith
People with religious faith put their trust in God and they express their faith through prayer, worship and way of life.

Prayer
Good friendships take time and energy. In order for our friendships to grow, we need to pay attention to our friends and to talk and listen to them. Communication is an important part of human friendship. Similarly, communication is an important part of a relationship with God. If our friendship with God is to grow and develop, we need to pay attention to God and to talk and listen to God. **Prayer** is communication with God. Prayer is part of the search for God. (We will look at prayer in greater detail in Section E.)

Worship
Another element of the human search for God is **worship**. People take part in worship in order to honour and praise God and to grow closer to God. Some examples of worship are private prayer, meditation, pilgrimage and religious services. (We will look at worship in greater detail in Section E.)

Way of Life

Derval O'Rourke, Seán Óg Ó hAilpín and Ronan O'Gara are three examples of modern, committed and successful Irish sportspeople. Their commitment to sport has a major effect on their way of life. It influences their diet, fitness routine, the amount of travel they do, etc.

In a similar way, when people have a deep faith in God, their faith influences the way they live. Each of the world religions has a moral code – a set of guidelines about how people should live. These moral codes influence the choices that people of faith make.

At the heart of the Christian moral code is Jesus' commandment to love God and to love your neighbour as yourself. Sincere Christians try to live by Jesus' commandment. They try to grow in friendship with God through prayer and worship and to behave in a loving way to everyone they meet. (We will look in greater detail at religious moral codes in Section F.)

KNOW WHAT

Copy the following statements into your Religion folder and indicate whether they are true or false.

True or False

	True	False
1. Religious faith can be expressed in a variety of ways.	☐	☐
2. Prayer is communication with God.	☐	☐
3. To pray is to show a lack of religious belief.	☐	☐
4. Worship involves giving honour and praise to God.	☐	☐
5. People who take part in worship do not believe in God.	☐	☐
6. A moral code is a set of guidelines about how to live.	☐	☐
7. Christians try to live by Jesus' commandment to love God and to love your neighbour as yourself.	☐	☐

Jack's Story

My name is Jack. I am fourteen years old. My parents are Catholics and they brought me up to believe in God. When I was small, they taught me how to bless myself and how to pray the 'Our Father'. They also brought me to church with my brothers and sisters.

Right now, there is a lot I don't understand about God. Last year, my baby cousin, Michael, was born blind. I can't understand why God allows bad things like that to happen.

It's just not fair! Even though I don't understand this about God, I still believe in God. I believe that God loves me and wants me to be happy. My image of God is of a good friend.

My religion is important to me. I go to church on Sunday and I also try to pray to God every day, even if it is just for a few minutes before I go to bed. I do my best to live as Jesus asked by helping other people. I try to be a good friend and I listen to my mates when they have a problem. When I am older, I would like to take a year off to work in the developing world. I want to help to make life better for other people.

KNOW WHAT
1. Who has influenced Jack's faith and how have they done so?
2. What does Jack believe about God?

KNOW HOW
Copy the following diagram into your Religion folder and give examples of how Jack expresses his faith in God through his prayer, worship and way of life.

How Jack expresses his faith in God

Prayer	
Worship	
Way of Life	

KNOWING ME KNOWING YOU
Interview someone who has faith in God. Ask them the following questions:
1. How important to you is your religious faith?
2. What are your main religious beliefs?
3. How often do you pray?
4. How often do you take part in religious services at your local church or place of worship?
5. How does your faith affect the way you live your life?

DIGGING DEEPER
1. How important is your faith to you?
2. How do you express your faith?
3. How does your faith influence your way of life?

KNOW IT ALL

Copy the following into your Religon folder and fill in the blanks using the wordbank given below.

People express their religious faith through prayer, _____ and way of life. Prayer is _____ with God. Through prayer, people talk to God and _____ to God. Prayer is part of the _____ for God. Worship is another _____ of the human search for God. Worship involves giving _____ and _____ to God. Some examples of worship are _____ and religious _____. Each religion has a _____ code. A moral code is a set of _____ about how people should live. Moral codes influence the _____ made by people of faith. Sincere Christians try to live by Jesus' _____ to love God and their _____.

WORDBANK

Search • Choices • Honour • Listen • Services • Commandment • Worship • Guidelines
Communication • Element • Meditation • Moral • Neighbour • Praise

Prayer: Communication between people and God.

Worship: Response of a group or individual to the sacred, often expressed through ritual.

LESSON 87 People of Faith

GROUNDWORK
In this lesson we plan to:
- explore stories of faithful people from two religious traditions.

DIGGING DEEPER
How do the lives of faithful people affect or challenge me?

Key Concepts
Monotheism/Polytheism/Prayer/Worship

Faithful People

In all of the world's religions, whether they are **monotheistic** (believing in one God) or **polytheistic** (believing in many gods), there are many examples of people who express their religious belief through their **prayer**, **worship** and way of life. In this lesson, we will look at the stories of two such faithful people – Sr Stanislaus Kennedy and Mahatma Gandhi.

KNOW WHAT
1. What is monotheism?
2. What is polytheism?
3. Name three monotheistic world religions.
4. Name a polytheistic world religion.

Sr Stanislaus Kennedy – An Example of a Christian Person of Faith

Sr Stanislaus Kennedy, or Sr Stan as she is known, is a Religious Sister of Charity. She lives in Dublin. Sr Stan was born in Kerry during the Second World War. At the age of eighteen, she joined the Religious Sisters of Charity. For the past fifty years, she has worked with poor and disadvantaged people.

Her main achievements include:

- Developing *Kilkenny Social Services* in the 1960s with Bishop Peter Birch.
- Setting up *Focus Ireland* in 1985. Focus Ireland is one of the most important organisations working with homeless people in Ireland today.
- Opening a spirituality centre called the *Sanctuary* in 2000. Located in Dublin's inner city, the Sanctuary runs courses and provides a quiet space to help people develop their spirituality.

Sr Stanislaus Kennedy

- Setting up the *Immigrant Council of Ireland* in 2001. This Council promotes the rights of immigrants by providing information, advice and legal aid.
- Developing the *Young Social Innovators Programme* (YSI). It provides an opportunity for young people to become actively involved in social issues.

KNOW WHAT

Have you heard of any of these organisations? If so, what do you know about them?

An Interview with Sr Stan

Q. What inspired you to become a Religious Sister of Charity?

A. When I was in my late teens, I decided I wanted to work with the poor and disadvantaged people of the world. I particularly wanted to help the poor children that I had read about. I discovered that the Religious Sisters of Charity had a vow of service to the poor and that they served the poor in many ways in Ireland and elsewhere. So I decided to enter with the Sisters of Charity. I discovered that they had a spiritual way of life, a religious way of life of prayer and service. That really appealed to me and, through them, I was able to dedicate my life to Christ and to the service of the poor.

Q. Tell us about a typical day in your life.

A. Usually, I rise at around six a.m. and after breakfast I pray for about an hour and fifteen minutes. Then I walk to Mass, after which I go to work. This might mean going to work at the Immigrant Council of Ireland, where we provide information, advice and legal aid for immigrants; it might mean working with the homeless people in Focus Ireland's coffee shop or attending a meeting on issues such as housing, immigration, poverty or justice; it might include spending time with staff who want to discuss issues with me or ask my advice; or it may involve answering letters or preparing lectures. So my days are varied and very full; sometimes they are in Dublin, sometimes they are outside of Dublin, depending on what the need is. In the middle of each day, I spend some time in prayer. Each evening, I spend about thirty minutes in prayer. I try to spend time each day with nature and some time reading and writing. I pray each night before I go to bed.

Q. What motivates your life and work?

A. I am motivated by people, especially people who are in need – those who are poor or homeless – and I feel the need to assist them. I am motivated by the great generosity of people who come to work with me and who give generously to the services. I am also motivated by the injustice and inequality I see around me in society and I want to do something to bring about greater equality and justice. I am motivated by the resilience of the poor and their ability to bounce back when they are given support and help. I am motivated by the light and spirit of God within me, which was given to me, not for myself but to light up the lives of other people and to lighten their burden and to light up society and the world. I am motivated by the words of Jesus Christ who said, 'whatever you do to the least of these, my little ones, you do it onto me'.

Q. Looking back on your work to date, what do you see as your greatest achievement?

A. I think my greatest achievement is being able to get many people to assist me in serving the poor and in developing services to respond to the needs of disadvantaged people in society. This includes people who came and helped me to develop Kilkenny Social Services, Focus Ireland, the Immigrant Council and the Young Social Innovators, and the many young people who have developed projects as young social innovators. It also includes the people who worked in the development of the Sanctuary, which is a spirituality centre in Dublin.

Q. How important is prayer and worship in your life?

A. Prayer and worship are at the very core of my day and of my life. My prayer and my communion with God give me the strength to move out and serve him in the persons of the poor.

Q. What gives you hope for the future?

A. Humanity gives me hope. People give me hope – with their extraordinary strength, their extraordinary courage, often in the face of many difficulties and problems. I get hope, too, when I experience the generosity of people. I get hope when I see nature all the time changing, all the time being renewed. I get great hope from the words of Christ who tells us, 'I will be with you always, even until the end of time.'

KNOW WHAT

1. From the interview, what is your impression of Sr Stan?
2. What words of Jesus motivate her life and work?
3. What gives her strength to serve the poor?
4. Imagine you were going to interview Sr Stan for a radio programme. Write down five questions you would like to ask her.

KNOW HOW

1. Copy the following diagram into your Religion folder and give examples of how Sr Stan expresses her faith in God through her prayer, worship and way of life.

How Sr Stan expresses her faith in God

Prayer	
Worship	
Way of Life	

2. Write a paragraph describing how Sr Stan's religious beliefs influence her life.

Mohandas Gandhi (1869–1948): An Example of a Hindu Person of Faith

Mohandas Gandhi was born in India into a Hindu family in 1869. At that time, the British ruled India. In 1888, Gandhi went to London to study law. There he read the Hindu sacred text, the *Bhagavad Gita*, for the first time. He also studied Christianity and admired Jesus' teachings, especially the Sermon on the Mount. While he remained a committed Hindu, Gandhi had great respect for the other world religions. He believed that they were like different roads leading to the same point.

In 1891, Gandhi qualified as a barrister and returned to India. However, he found it difficult to find work there and so he took a job as a legal adviser in South Africa. When Gandhi arrived in South Africa, he quickly discovered that Indians were treated as inferiors. One evening when he was travelling by train, a white man entered his carriage. When he saw that Gandhi – a 'coloured' man – was sitting in a first-class carriage, he complained to the conductor. Gandhi was ordered to move to a third-class carriage. On refusing to move, he was forced to leave the train. This experience was a turning point for Gandhi. He decided to work to get better rights for Indians living in South Africa.

Shortly afterwards, Gandhi began to teach Indians a method of non-violent disobedience called *satyagraha* (which means 'truth-force' or 'love-force'). He encouraged Indians not to co-operate with unjust laws. In 1907, the South African government brought in the Black Act. All Indians had to have their fingerprints taken and to carry a permit. Gandhi organised meetings and demonstrations against this law. He told Indians not to obey this law. Gandhi and his supporters were often sent to jail.

Mohandas Gandhi

In 1914, the government granted better rights to Indians. Gandhi's method of peaceful disobedience had been successful. Significantly, Gandhi got the inspiration for this method of peaceful disobedience from Jesus' teachings and from the Hindu teaching of *ahimsa* (which advocated non-violence towards living things). During his stay in South Africa, Gandhi was also inspired by the teachings of the *Bhagavad Gita* to take a vow of non-possession. On achieving his goal of better rights for Indians, Gandhi left South Africa with just a few material possessions and returned to India.

Back in India, Gandhi began to dress like the lowest Indian, wearing a loincloth and shawl. He also set up an *ashram* or religious community, where he lived with his family and other people. Each morning and evening, he held a prayer service at the ashram. Worship and prayer were important to Gandhi. He believed that prayer brought him inner peace. At each prayer meeting, a hymn was sung and part of the *Bhagavad Gita* was recited. In keeping with Gandhi's respect for other world religions, passages from other sacred texts such as the Bible and the Qur'an were often read. The ashram hymnbook also contained hymns from a variety of religions, including Christianity. Gandhi's favourite hymn was the Christian hymn, 'Lead Kindly Light'.

Shortly after World War I ended, Gandhi started to work for India's freedom from Great Britain. Once again, he taught Indians to use the method of non-violent disobedience called *satyagraha*. He organised peaceful meetings, demonstrations and marches against British rule. He also told Indians to boycott British goods and to use Indian-made goods instead. Gandhi became known as Mahatma (Great Soul). As a result of his work, he was put in prison many times.

Finally, in 1948, India received its independence from Great Britain. India was partitioned into two separate, independent states: Pakistan, which would have a Muslim majority, and a smaller India, which would have a Hindu majority. As a firm believer in Hindu–Muslim unity, Gandhi was upset by the decision to partition India into two separate states. When fighting broke out between Hindus and Muslims in Calcutta and New Delhi, Gandhi visited each city and fasted until the fighting stopped. Shortly after he ended his fast in New Delhi, Gandhi was shot on his way to his evening prayer meeting by a Hindu fanatic. His last words were, 'He Ram! He Ram!' ('Oh God! Oh God!').

KNOW IT ALL

Copy the following exercise into your Religion folder and fill in the blanks using the wordbank given below.

Gandhi's religion was _____.
While he was in London, Gandhi read the _____ _____, a sacred Hindu text.
He admired Jesus' teachings, especially the _____ __ ____ _____ .
Gandhi's method of peaceful disobedience was called _____.
_____ is the Hindu teaching that advocates non-violence towards all living things.
On returning to India, Gandhi lived in a religious community called an _____.
The title given to Gandhi in India was _____. It means Great Soul.
When fighting broke out between Hindus and Muslims, Gandhi _____ until the fighting stopped.

WORDBANK

Ashram • Satyagraha • Mahatma • Bhagavad Gita • Ahisma • Hinduism
• Fasted • Sermon on the Mount

KNOW HOW

1. Copy the following diagram into your Religion folder and give examples of how Gandhi expressed his faith in God through his prayer, worship and way of life.

How Gandhi expressed his faith in God

Prayer	
Worship	
Way of Life	

2. Write a paragraph describing how Gandhi's religious beliefs influenced his life.

DIGGING DEEPER

1. Reflect on what you have learned about Sr Stan or Gandhi.
   a) Explain what you admire about her/him.
   b) How are you affected or challenged by what you have learned about her/him?
2. Considering all the people of faith that you have studied, who do you admire the most? Explain your choice.
3. Would you describe yourself as a faithful person? Explain.

Additional Research Activities

1. In groups, research the official website of *one* of the following organisations:

   Focus Ireland – *http://www.focusireland.ie*
   The Immigrant Council of Ireland – *http://www.immigrantcouncil.ie*
   Religious Sisters of Charity – *http://www.rsccaritas.ie*
   The Sanctuary – *http://www.sanctuary.ie*
   Young Social Innovators of the Year – *http://www.youngsocialinnovators.ie*

   Prepare a report for your class on the work of the organisation, under the headings:

   - Role of Sr Stan in the organisation.
   - Inspiring vision/aim(s) of the organisation.
   - Work of the organisation.
   - Impact of the work on individuals and communities.

   Or

2. Watch the film *Gandhi* at home or research Gandhi on the internet.

   Prepare a report on Gandhi for your class, making reference to the following:

   - Main events in his life
   - Religious beliefs
   - Prayer and worship
   - Way of life

   Useful websites:

   http://www.gandhiinstitute.org/AboutGandhi/index.cfm
   http://www.bbc.co.uk – type Gandhi into the explore bbc.co.uk search engine

   Monotheism: The belief in only one God.
   Polytheism: The belief in many gods.

See page 494 for a past exam question on this topic.

(Higher Level Only)

Challenges to Faith

LESSON 88 Religious and Scientific World Views

GROUNDWORK
In this lesson we plan to:
- explore the religious and the scientific world views of creation.

DIGGING DEEPER
What is my world view?
What is my relationship with God like?
Where do I stand regarding the question of creation?

 **Key Concepts**
Reflection/World view/Creation/Fundamentalism

Our World View

Have you ever looked in wonder at the world around you and asked questions such as:

- How did the world begin?
- Why is there life on earth?
- Where did all the different species of life come from?
- What is the future of the world?

For centuries, people have looked at the amazing world in which we live and **reflected** on questions like these. The answers that people give to these kinds of questions are influenced by their **world view**. Whether we know it or not, each of us has a set of ideas about what the world is like. This set of ideas about the basic make-up of the world is called a world view. Our world view is like a pair of spectacles or contact lenses through which we look at the world. It shapes the way we see the world and influences our behaviour and attitudes.

Story: Seeing Things Differently

One Sunday morning, Steve was travelling on a New York subway. People were sitting quietly. Some were reading newspapers, some were dozing, others were simply contemplating with their eyes closed. It was a rather peaceful, calm scene.

At one stop, a man and his children entered the car. The children were soon yelling back and forth, throwing things, even grabbing people's newspapers. It was all very disturbing, and yet the father just sat there next to them and did nothing. It was not difficult to feel irritated. Steve could not believe the man could be so insensitive as to let his children run wild and do nothing about it. It was easy to see that everyone else in the car was annoyed as well.

So finally, with what he thought was admirable restraint and patience, Steve said to the man, 'Sir, your children are really disturbing a lot of people. I wonder if you couldn't control them a little bit more?' The man lifted his gaze as if coming into consciousness for the first time and said, 'Oh, you're right. I guess I should do something about it. We just came from the hospital where their mother died about an hour ago. I don't know what to think, and I guess they don't know how to handle it either.'

Steve says, 'Can you imagine what I felt at that moment? Suddenly I saw things differently. Because I saw differently, I felt differently. I behaved differently. My irritation vanished. I didn't have to worry about controlling my attitude or my behaviour. My heart was filled with this man's pain. Feelings of compassion and sympathy flowed freely. "Your wife just died? Oh, I'm so sorry! Can you tell me about it? What can I do to help?"'

Nothing changed in that subway car. All was the same: the same people, the same irritation, the same kids. What did change was a way of seeing it all and, with the seeing, a change of behaviour.

KNOW WHAT
1. At the beginning of the story, what was Steve's opinion of the man and his children?
2. By the end of the story, how had his way of seeing the man and his family changed?
3. How did the change in Steve's way of seeing the man and his family affect his behaviour towards them?

Just as Steve's way of seeing the man and his chidren influenced his behaviour towards them, our way of seeing the world influences the way we live.

DIGGING DEEPER – What is your world view?

Our world view shapes the answers we give to questions of meaning. Explore your own world view by answering the following questions in your Religion folder:

- Where does the world come from?
- Where do people come from?
- Why is the world the way it is?
- Where is the world heading?
- Who am I?
- What is good? What is evil?
- How should people behave?
- What is true?
- What is false?

KNOWING ME KNOWING YOU

As a class, share your answers to the above questions.
1. What were the most common answers to each question?
2. What do you think has influenced the world views of students in your class?

The Christian World View

The Christian world view is rooted in the Bible. For Christians, the Bible is the inspired Word of God. Christians believe that:

- God is the creator of the world.
- God created human beings in God's image and likeness.
- The world that God has created is good.
- God invites us to develop a loving friendship with him. Evil comes about when we refuse to co-operate with God.
- God sent Jesus to teach people how they should live.
- The Word of God is to be found in the Bible.
- Those who have loved God in this life will live in eternal friendship with God.

KNOW WHAT

1. What parts of this Christian world view were you familiar with already?
2. Does anything about this Christian world view surprise you? Explain.
3. Do you have any questions about this world view? Explain.

DIGGING DEEPER

Do you have a loving friendship with God?

KNOWING ME KNOWING YOU

Choose *one* of the following world religions: Judaism, Islam, Buddhism or Hinduism. Research the world views of this religion.

Creation in the Christian World View

Up to five centuries ago, most Christians and Jews believed the story of **creation** as it was told in the book of Genesis in the Bible – that God created the world in six days. No one saw any reason for not believing the story. However, as we will see, science began to make new discoveries about the world, which challenged the version of the creation story as told in Genesis.

KNOW HOW

Read the story of creation in Genesis 1:1-31. Then, in your Religion folder, match each of the following Days of Creation with what God created on that day:

Day 1	God created all kinds of sea creatures and the birds in the sky

Day 2	God created the sun, the moon and the stars

Day 3	God created animals and human beings

Day 4	God created light. He named the light 'day' and the darkness 'night'

Day 5	God created the sky

Day 6	God created dry land ('earth') and all kinds of plants

Finally, summarise the story of creation by drawing a picture for each of the six days of creation as it is described in Genesis.

KNOW WHAT

1. What is the image of God that is presented in the Genesis story of creation?
2. According to the Genesis account, in whose image and likeness did God create human beings?
3. What responsibility did God give to human beings?
4. What message does this story contain about a) God, b) human beings and c) creation?

KNOWING ME KNOWING YOU

In pairs, choose *one* of the following world religions: Islam, Buddhism or Hinduism. Research its view of creation and prepare a report for your class.

The Scientific World View

Science helps us to understand the world. Scientists study the world of matter and energy. They learn about the world by observing what happens and by carrying out experiments.

They suggest theories to explain how things happen, e.g. how the universe started, and then they carry out experiments and look for evidence to show that these theories are true. The following are some of the key people whose discoveries have shaped our understanding of the world.

Galileo Galilei (1564-1642)

Galileo was an Italian scientist who studied the planets and stars. He was fascinated by a new invention, the telescope, and he built one that was more powerful than any other at the time. Later, he wrote a book

Galileo Galilei

agreeing with the view of an earlier scientist called Copernicus that the earth revolved around the sun. This was at odds with the teaching of the Roman Catholic Church at that time. Reflecting the biblical story in which God created the earth before the sun, the Church taught that the earth was at the centre of the universe and that the sun and the other planets travelled around the earth. Because of his views, Galileo was tried by the Court of Inquisition. Under pressure from the Court, he stated that his ideas were wrong. He was kept under house arrest until he died in 1642.

KNOW WHAT
How did Galileo's ideas conflict with the story of creation in Genesis?

KNOW HOW
Copy the following fact file into your Religion folder and fill in the details.

Fact file: Galileo Galilei	
Born	
Interested in	
Worked as	
In his book he wrote that	
How his ideas conflicted with the story of creation in Genesis	

Charles Darwin (1809–1882)

Charles Darwin was a British scientist who wrote a famous book called *On the Origin of the Species*. In this book, he said that all life on earth had developed from much simpler forms of life over millions of years. Darwin maintained that plants and animals gradually changed or adapted to their environment in order to increase their chances of survival. In this way, new species or forms of life developed. Darwin called this process 'natural selection'. Later, Darwin wrote that human beings had developed in this way from lower animals. This theory of how life developed is known as the 'theory of evolution'.

Charles Darwin

In the past in particular, religious leaders had different opinions about Darwin's ideas. Some religious leaders supported Darwin while others opposed him. Scientists were also divided in their support for Darwin.

Some religious leaders opposed Darwin because they believed that the story of creation in Genesis described exactly how the world was created.

- They pointed out that Darwin's theory of evolution went against what Genesis tells us about how God created each form of life separately.
- They also said that it went against what Genesis tells us about how God created human beings in his own image and likeness, and that it seemed to put human beings on the same level as animals.

The Catholic Church holds that the Bible is not a scientific textbook. Its authors were inspired by God and it tells us what God wants us to know about ourselves, about God and about the world we live in. It contains different types of writing: poetry, story, metaphor, song, history, prayer. God makes himself known to us through the Bible and also through the teachings of the Church throughout the ages. To take a literal interpretation of scripture as the whole truth is called **fundamentalism**.

Today, the differences of opinion regarding Darwin's theory still remain and his ideas are not yet universally accepted.

KNOW WHAT
1. How did Darwin's ideas conflict with the story of creation in Genesis?
2. What is fundamentalism?

KNOW HOW
Copy the following fact file into your Religion folder and fill in the details.

Fact file: Charles Darwin	
Born	
Interested in	
Worked as	
In his book he wrote that	
How his ideas conflicted with the story of creation in Genesis	

Edwin Hubble and Other Scientists

In 1929, a scientist called Edwin Hubble found signs that the universe is expanding in all directions. As a result, many scientists began to accept a theory which became known as the Theory of the Big Bang. This theory says that the universe began with a huge explosion of energy and heat some ten to fifteen billion years ago. This explosion sent tiny pieces of matter hurling outwards. Gradually, some of these pieces of matter came together to form the stars and the galaxies. This theory of how the universe began is accepted by most scientists today.

Edwin Hubble

KNOW WHAT
How is the theory of the Big Bang different from the story of creation in Genesis?

DIGGING DEEPER
'The Big Bang theory does not tell us why the Big Bang happened?' Do you agree or disagree with this statement? Explain.

Can Science and Religion Work Together?

In the past, there was a lot of disagreement between the worlds of science and religion concerning creation. In recent history, however, there have been moments of harmony between them:

- In 1951, Pope Pius XII welcomed the theory of the Big Bang, saying that it should lead scientists to the Creator.
- In 1992, Pope John Paul II said that the Church had made a mistake in the way it treated Galileo. He also suggested that there are 'points of contact' between religion and science – each helps us to understand 'different aspects of reality'.

Today, many people believe that science and religion can work together to help us to understand the beginnings of the world. They point out that science and religion are similar in that they both search for answers to questions of meaning. Science sets out to answer the 'How?' questions – *How* did the universe and life begin? Religion, on the other hand, tends to ask the 'Why?' questions – *Why* do the universe and life exist? Since religion and science search for truth by asking different questions, we need both in order to make sense of life and the world.

While fundamentalist Christians disagree with the idea that we need both science and religion in order to understand the world, many other Christians think differently. They point out that since the authors of Genesis were not scientists, they could not give us a scientific description of how the world was created. Instead, these writers wanted to give us some important messages about God and the world:

- God made the world and everything in it.
- The world that God created is good.
- People are made in God's image and likeness.

So, while science seeks to tell us about *how* the universe and life developed, Genesis gives us an insight into *why* they were created.

Today, many Christians believe that the Big Bang was the way that God chose to create the world. They also accept that life and the human body evolved over time. They believe, however, that each human soul was created by God. In this way, human beings are different to the rest of creation.

KNOW WHAT

1. What are the main differences between the scientific and religious views of creation?
2. What are the main similarities between the scientific and religious views of creation?
3. Why do many Christians believe that both science and religion are needed in order to understand creation?
4. Why do some Christians disagree with the idea that we need both science and religion in order to understand the world?

KNOW IT ALL

Copy the following exercise into your Religion folder and fill in the blanks using the wordbank given below.

In the past, most Christians and Jews believed that the story of _____ as told in the book of _____ described how the world was created. This belief is an example of _____. Fundamentalists believe that what is written in a _____ _____, such as the Bible, is literally true. When Galileo wrote a book saying that the _____ was at the centre of the universe and that the _____ revolved around it, the _____ forced him to take back his ideas. Later, when Darwin wrote his theory of _____, many religious leaders disagreed with it.

Today, many people think that we need both _____ and religion in order to understand the origins of the world. Science seeks to tell us _____ the universe began. Religion seeks to tell us _____ it began. The story of creation in Genesis tells us that God is a _____ creator who made human beings in his own _____ and appointed them as caretakers of the world.

WORDBANK

Genesis • How • Fundamentalism • Loving • Earth • Church • Image • Sun • Why
Evolution • Sacred text • Creation • Science

DIGGING DEEPER

1. Outline what you believe about how the universe was created.
2. Outline what you believe about how life was created.
3. In your opinion, why do the universe and people exist?

World view: Way of thinking about the world (its origin, the way it works, etc.) that guides the way we live.

Fundamentalism: A literal, rigid style of belief. Relies solely on a literal interpretation of the community's sacred text and teachings. Rejects attempts to update or modernise the way in which community belief is expressed.

Creation: The coming into existence of the world. In religious terms, God's unique act of causing the whole world to exist.

See page 495 for a past exam question on this topic.

LESSON 89 World Views in Modern Culture

GROUNDWORK
In this lesson we plan to:
- explore the variety of world views in modern culture, including their origin;
- examine challenges to religious experience (such as materialism, individualism, etc.).

DIGGING DEEPER
What are the challenges to my religious belief in today's culture? When do I experience God's presence?

Key Concepts
World view/Experiencing God/Atheism/Agnosticism/Materialism/Secularism

Religious Experience

People with a religious **world view** believe in the existence of God. They believe in God even though they cannot see God. The three monotheistic world religions – Judaism, Christianity and Islam – teach that God is present everywhere. At different times in our lives, we become more aware of the presence of God. This **experience of God** can happen at times of great sadness or happiness or in moments of great beauty. In the following passage, astronaut Jim Irwin describes his sense of God on his first flight to the moon:

> *The first time we could see the whole earth, we saw it as a ball in the sky. It was about the size of a basketball, and the most beautiful thing you could ever want to see in all your life. Then, as we got farther and farther away, it diminished in size. We saw it shrink to the size of a baseball, and then to the size of a golf ball, and finally to the size of a marble, the most beautiful marble you can imagine. The earth is uncommonly lovely. It is the only warm object that we saw on our flight to the moon …*
>
> *During this sort of flight, you are too busy to reflect on the splendour of space … You have to try to register these experiences and examine them later … The ultimate effect has been to deepen and strengthen all the religious insight I ever had. It has remade my faith. I had become a sceptic about getting guidance from God, and I know I had lost the feeling of His nearness. On the moon, the total picture of the power of God and His Son, Jesus Christ became abundantly clear to me.*
>
> *I felt an overwhelming sense of the presence of God on the moon. I felt His spirit more closely than I had ever felt it on the earth, right there beside me – it was amazing.*

DIGGING DEEPER
Write about a time when you felt the presence of God in your life.

SECTION D THE QUESTION OF FAITH

315

KNOW HOW
Bring in a photograph or picture from a magazine, a newspaper or the internet that you think expresses God's presence in our world today. Make a collage of all the photographs/pictures for your class noticeboard.

Non-religious World Views

As modern science advanced from the sixteenth century onwards, people began look for scientific or logical explanations for everything. New ways of looking at the world developed, in which God had little or no part.

Atheism

The word **atheism** means 'without God'. Atheism is the view that God does not exist. Atheists are people who believe that there is no such thing as God.

Agnosticism

Agnosticism means 'not knowing'. Agnosticism is the view that people cannot know for sure whether or not God exists because there is not enough evidence to decide one way or the other. Agnostics are people who are unsure if God exists.

Materialism

Materialism is the theory that only material things are real. If something is real, then it must have a definite physical size or weight. If we cannot see it or touch it or measure it, then it does not exist. Since we cannot measure God or observe God with our senses, materialists say that God does not exist. Similarly, they say that the human soul does not exist. For materialists, human life ends when the body dies.

Since they believe that this life is all there is, many materialists say that the meaning of life is to have a lot of material possessions – because they help to make life more enjoyable.

Secularism

Secularism is the view that religion should have no part in civil matters. Secularists believe that religion should not have any influence on the laws of a country or on what happens in its schools or in the media, etc. They want religion and the State to be completely separate. Let's take some examples:

- A few years ago, there was a discussion in the media about whether RTE should continue to broadcast the Angelus on radio and TV. Some people felt that RTE should stop this practice – they felt that a religious practice like the Angelus did not belong on national radio and TV. This view is an example of secularism. Other people disagreed – they pointed out that the Angelus was a reminder to religious and non-religious people alike to spend a few minutes in reflection each day. In the end, RTE decided to continue broadcasting the Angelus.
- In 2004, the French government passed a law forbidding children from wearing obvious religious symbols at school, e.g. the Muslim headscarf or large crosses. They passed this law because they wanted religion and the State to be completely separate in France.

Individualism

Individualism is the view that each person should pursue their own goals and interests rather than the goals and interests of the group, e.g. a family or class group. This view is very different from the religious world view. Each of the monotheistic world religions calls us to serve God and to show concern for other people. For example, Jesus told his followers, 'Love God and love your neighbour as you love yourself.'

KNOW HOW

Read the following statements and match each one with the world view that it represents, i.e. atheism, agnosticism, materialism, secularism, individualism.

'I don't care if God exists or not. I think that religion has too much influence over what happens in this country and I want it to stop. Religion should not be able to influence the laws of a country or what happens in its schools. It should have no place in public life – it should be a private matter for each person.' **(Kate)**

'I don't believe that God exists. I think people in the past invented God to explain how the world began. Now, science tells us that the world began with the Big Bang. We no longer need God to explain things. Anyway, there is no evidence that God exists.' **(Tom)**

'Live life for yourself! That's my motto. It's difficult enough to take care of your own interests without having to worry about others as well. I look after Number One – that's ME! – and I expect others to do the same.' **(John)**

'I don't know if God exists or not. There is not enough evidence to show that God exists. On the other hand, there is not enough evidence to show that God does not exist. I'm keeping an open mind until some real proof is found.' **(Sarah)**

'Since I cannot see God with my own eyes, I don't believe in God. For me, only material things are real.' **(Richie)**

The Technological World View

Technology is the application of science to trade and industry in order to improve performance and methods of production. It is reflected in the development of tools and machinery and in the techniques for making goods. Since the 1700s, technology has grown rapidly and many important devices have been invented that have improved people's lives. However, technology and its production has caused a lot of damage to the environment. It is a major source of air, water and land pollution.

The technological world view sees the earth as a resource that can be used in any way in order to bring about progress. Nature is often seen as existing solely for the purpose of technological advancement and human consumption. In this world view, people are often seen in the same way: as resources or tools to be used to produce goods as quickly and cheaply as possible. People with this world view tend to put profit before people.

KNOW WHAT
1. Describe the technological view of the world and the person.
2. What are the main benefits of technology?
3. How does the environment suffer as a result of technological progress?

Challenges to Religious Experience
Each of the above world views challenges religious belief. For example:

- *Materialism* is a challenge to the experience of God. When someone believes that God does not exist, it is harder for them to recognise God in the everyday experiences of life.

- *Secularism* challenges religious belief by reducing the influence of religion in society.

- *Individualism* can limit a person's ability to sense the presence of God. Individualists may get so caught up in pursuing their own interests that they fail to become aware of the presence of God in the world around them.

- The *technological world view* conflicts with the religious view of the world and of the human being. The story of creation in Genesis tells us that human beings are created in the image and likeness of God and that our role is to imitate God the Creator by looking after all parts of creation. We are called to be stewards of creation. This means that we must use technology sensibly for the benefit of all people and all forms of life on this planet.

KNOW WHAT
1. Explain how materialism can challenge religious experience.
2. Explain how secularism can challenge religious experience.
3. Explain how individualism can challenge religious experience.
4. Explain how the technological world view can challenge religious experience.

Apathy and Religious Indifference

Shane's Story
Shane is sixteen. He plays bass guitar and is a member of a band. When he talks about music and his hopes for the future, you can hear the passion and enthusiasm in his voice. You know that music is important to him.

It's different if you ask Shane about religion. Then, he will just give you a dismissive look and change the subject. Even though he was baptised and received his First Communion and Confirmation, Shane does not go to church. He finds it too boring. Religion class also holds no interest for him – he passes the time by thinking up song lyrics in his head.

When a person shows a lack of enthusiasm or emotion, it is a sign of apathy. When people react to religion with apathy, it is a sign of religious indifference. In Ireland today, some young people have lost interest in religion. Even though they were born into a community of faith, religion now plays a very small role in their lives. They may say that they believe in God but they make very little time for God. Rather than deliberately rejecting God, they have drifted away from their religion. Apathy and religious indifference are challenges to religious belief.

KNOW WHAT

1. What does apathy mean?
2. Why do you think some young people have become indifferent to their faith?
3. What can be done to encourage them to return to their faith?
4. How do apathy and religious indifference challenge religious belief?

DIGGING DEEPER

1. Below is a list of statements that reflect the different world views discussed in this lesson. Read each statement carefully. Show your level of agreement or disagreement with each statement by circling the appropriate number on a scale of 1 to 5.

    1. Totally disagree; 2. Disagree; 3. Unsure; 4. Agree; 5. Agree totally.

I believe that God exists.	1	2	3	4	5
Religious faith gives meaning to my life.	1	2	3	4	5
Having a relationship with God is important to me.	1	2	3	4	5
Religion influences how I treat other people.	1	2	3	4	5
I pray regularly to God.	1	2	3	4	5
Religion plays a very small role in my life.	1	2	3	4	5
Religion is more important to me as I get older.	1	2	3	4	5
I believe that God created the world.	1	2	3	4	5
Both science and religion are needed to help us to understand the origins of the world.	1	2	3	4	5
Religion should not influence the laws of a country.	1	2	3	4	5
Only material things are real. If we cannot measure it or observe it with our senses, then it does not exist.	1	2	3	4	5
The world is a machine that people are free to use in any way they like in order to bring about progress.	1	2	3	4	5
People should concentrate solely on working towards their own goals.	1	2	3	4	5

2. Based on your responses to Question 1, do you think you have a religious world view? Explain.
3. Do any of the non-religious world views discussed in this lesson challenge your religious belief? Explain.

KNOW IT ALL

Copy the following into your Religion folder and fill in the blanks using the wordbank given below.

1. In the Bible, the book of _____ contains an account of creation.
2. _____ is the belief that there is no God.
3. A person who believes that life is about having lots of possessions is called a _____.
4. According to the Bible, humans are made in the _____ and likeness of God.
5. An _____ is a person who questions the existence of God.
6. _____ is defined as a lack of emotion or enthusiasm.
7. _____ was an Italian scientist who got into trouble with the Church for saying that the earth revolved around the sun.
8. _____ is the author of *On the Origin of the Species*.
9. The view that religion should not influence civil matters is called _____.
10. _____ reflects the view that people should put their own goals and interests before those of others.
11. A literal interpretation of a sacred text reflects a _____ world view.

WORDBANK

• Darwin • Materialist • Apathy • Secularism • Genesis • Atheism • Agnostic
• Galileo • Image • Fundamentalist • Individualism

Experiencing God: Being aware of God's presence in an immediate and personal way.

Atheism: World view that does not include God and in which the term 'God' does not refer to anything real.

Agnosticism: World view that neither includes nor excludes God. Belief that there is not enough proof to decide one way or another whether God exists.

Materialism: World view that includes only physical and measurable things. Since we cannot see or measure God, materialists say that God does not exist.

Secularism: World view which states that religion should have no part in the running of a country.

See page 495 for a past exam question on this topic.

The World of Ritual

LESSON 90   Places of Significance

GROUNDWORK
In this lesson we plan to:
- explore how particular places come to be significant.

DIGGING DEEPER
Why are there places of religious significance?

Key Concepts
Places of Significance/Sacredness

Introductory Exercise: Favourite Places

You have just won five thousand euros to spend on a family holiday! Everyone is really excited. Your eight-year-old brother Ben wants to go to Disneyworld in Florida, eighteen-year-old Ava would like to go to Greece, and Mum wants to relax on Valentia Island in Kerry. Dad has suggested visiting Old Trafford in Manchester, but you want to go to Universal Studios in Los Angeles!

1. Why do you think each of the suggested destinations are favourite places?
2. Which destination will you definitely *not* choose, and why?
3. Where do you decide to go on holiday? Explain your choice.

A favourite place is a very special place. We decide that somewhere is a favourite place because it holds a special meaning for us: for example, it may remind us of good times spent there as a young child, a family member/a loved one lives there, or simply because we always have a really good time there.

A favourite place is, therefore, a very significant or meaningful place.

Places of Significance

Take a moment to examine the photographs.

1. In pairs, match the names of the following Irish places of significance with the photos: Newgrange/Aillwee Caves/Croke Park/Wall outside Windmill Lane recording studios/Phoenix Park/Mansion House.
2. Choose *three* of these places and explain why they are places of significance.

A **place of significance** is one where something important or meaningful has occurred. Something happened in that place to *set it apart* from other places and to mark it as having special significance. For example, Trim Castle is a place of special significance because it is the largest and one of the most important Norman military constructions in Ireland. Over eight hundred years ago, King Henry II of England granted Hugh de Lacy the liberty (freedom) of Meath and de Lacy took possession of the castle. There is a huge history surrounding the events that happened at the castle from its takeover by de Lacy in 1172 to its appearance in the film *Braveheart* in 1995.

5-4-3-2-1

1. Write **five** words that describe a place of special significance.
2. Name a place of significance in Ireland and write **four** sentences about it.
3. Name **three** places of significance outside of Ireland and explain their significance.
4. Name and describe **two** places of significance that you have visited.
5. Write **one** paragraph to explain why a place can become a place of significance.

DIGGING DEEPER
1. Name two places of special significance in your life.
2. Why have these places become significant for you?

Common Characteristics of Places of Significance

Places of significance have at least three common characteristics:

- They stand for or represent something.
- Certain meaningful events happened there or are associated with them.
- Because of what they represent, people continue to visit these places today.

For example, in the case of Trim Castle:

- It is one of the most important Norman constructions in Ireland.
- Many historical events happened there.
- People continue to visit the site because of what it represents.

KNOW THE WAY

KNOW HOW
Choose *two* places of significance and state how each of the common characteristics of places of significance applies to them.

Places of Religious Significance

A place has religious significance when it is a sacred place. The word 'sacred' comes from the Latin word *sacra*, meaning holy.

Sacred places are associated with holy people, with founders and leaders of religions, with prophets, with saints or with the location of significant religious events or happenings. For example, Christians visit Lourdes in France, Muslims travel to Mecca in Saudi Arabia and Jews pray at the Western Wall in Jerusalem. People visit places of religious significance because they can be inspired there and can encounter God in a deep and meaningful way.

Places of worship, such as churches, mosques and synagogues, are also sacred places because they have a special religious significance. They are places in which people can encounter God through prayer and ritual.

The Sanctuary of the Catholic Church
The picture below shows the sanctuary (which means 'holy place') of a Catholic church. The sanctuary is the place where the Eucharist is celebrated. It is a raised area within the church. There are ornate statues and candles in the sanctuary. These help people to focus on their prayers to the saints, Our Lady and God.

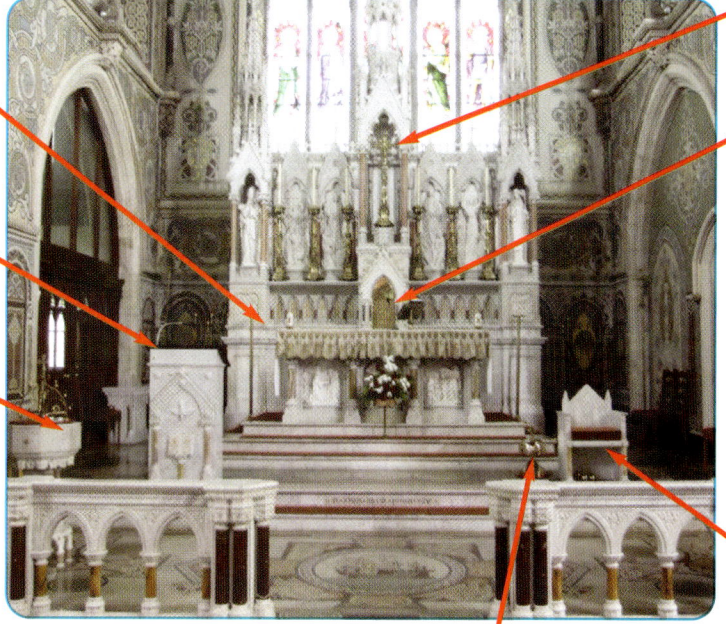

Altar: The altar is like a table. It reminds us of the table where Jesus gathered with the apostles for the Last Supper. It is here that the celebrant recalls the sacrifice that Jesus made for all.

Lectern: This is a tall stand from where the Bible – the Word of God – is read.

Baptismal font: This is the place where babies are baptised into the Catholic community of faith.

Paschal candle: This is a large candle located near the baptismal font. It is lit for the first time at the Easter vigil and is used throughout the year to remind people that Jesus is 'the light of the world'.

Gong: The gong or bell is sounded during the celebration of Mass to alert people to the real presence of Jesus Christ.

Crucifix: The crucifix is behind the altar and is the universal symbol of Christianity.

Tabernacle: The tabernacle is a small safe that holds the Blessed Sacrament, the body and blood of Jesus Christ. When people enter the church, they genuflect (kneel) to show their respect towards the Blessed Sacrament. The Sanctuary Light is lit to signify the presence of the Blessed Sacrament in the tabernacle.

Celebrant's chair: The priest sits here during Mass.

KNOW HOW
Draw a diagram of the inside of your local Catholic church. Locate and label all of the components shown above and, in your own words, describe their functions.

KNOW IT ALL
Complete the following sentences in your Religion folder.

1. The difference between a place of significance and a place of religious significance is…
2. A place of religious significance is a sacred place because…
3. A place of worship is a place of religious significance because…

Common Characteristics of Places of Religious Significance

Places of religious significance are *set apart* because they are places of **sacredness**. As well as having the characteristics associated with places of significance, they are also places where people can encounter God and have a religious experience. For example:

- They may be the birthplace or the burial place of a religious founder or leader.
- Apparitions or visions or other events of religious significance may have taken place there.
- People gather there to pray, to meditate and to celebrate, either alone or through ritual.
- They are places where people encounter God in a meaningful way, through prayer and quiet reflection.

KNOW WHAT
1. What are the common characteristics of places of significance?
2. What are the common characteristics of places of religious significance?
3. What are the main differences between the two?

DIGGING DEEPER
1. Name and describe two places of religious significance for your community of faith.
2. How did these places come to be places of religious significance?
3. What kind of prayer and celebrations take place there?
4. What kind of sacred encounters take place there?

KNOW HOW
Look up the following website and explore the module on Sacred Places and Sacred Spaces:

http://www.teachnet.ie/fwilliams/2005/index.htm

🗝️ **Places of significance:** Places that have a special meaning for people.
Sacredness: Regarded as holy, set apart, reserved, connected with God.

See page 495 for past exam questions on this topic.

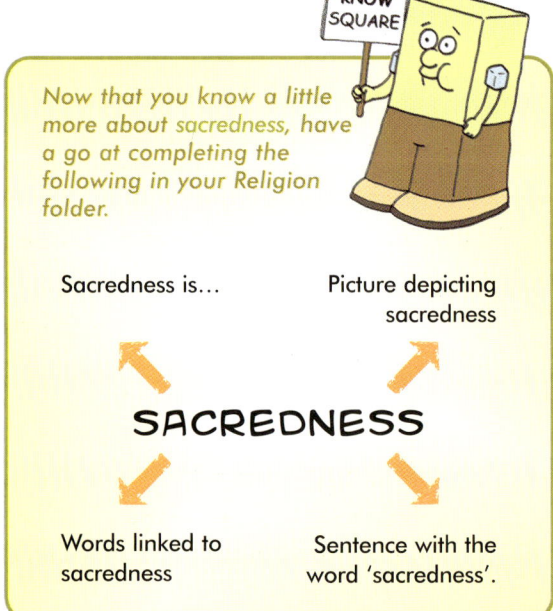

KNOW THE WAY

LESSON 91 Pilgrimage Sites

GROUNDWORK
In this lesson we plan to:
- take a closer look at some places of religious significance.

DIGGING DEEPER
Why is a place of pilgrimage regarded as a place of religious significance to a community of faith?

Key Concepts
Places of Significance/Sacredness

A Pilgrimage Site is a Place of Significance

A pilgrimage is a journey to a place that is regarded as sacred because it is associated with a person or event of religious significance. It is a spiritual journey because it involves an encounter with God, usually through prayer.

A pilgrimage is also a physical journey because it requires the pilgrims to give of themselves in order to enter into and focus on:

- the religious significance of the place;
- the religious significance of the time;
- the religious significance of the actions involved.

A pilgrimage is often physically demanding, as people of all age-groups and all levels of abilities and disabilities journey together. The physical journey of faith is as important as the spiritual journey of faith. In the past especially, pilgrimages were often long and difficult. People would try to walk faster or even go barefoot, so as to make the journey harder on themselves.

People make pilgrimages in order to:

- journey closer to God;
- ask for God's forgiveness and guidance;
- increase their faith;
- travel to the place where their religious founder or leaders lived;
- seek physical or spiritual healing.

Lourdes

KNOW WHAT
1. Explain why places of pilgrimage are considered to be sacred.
2. Explain how a pilgrimage is both a spiritual and a physical journey.
3. Why do people make pilgrimages?

DIGGING DEEPER

1. Places of pilgrimage have become very popular with young people. Why do you think this might be so?
2. Do you know of any places of pilgrimage in your community of faith? If so, tell the class what you know about them.
3. Name and describe a Christian place of pilgrimage.

A person who makes a pilgrimage is called a pilgrim.

Christian Pilgrimage Sites

There is a very strong tradition in the history of Christianity of people going on pilgrimage. Christian pilgrims spend time in the presence of God as they journey to a place of **sacredness**.

The Holy Land – Israel/Palestine

Christians often go on pilgrimage to the places where Jesus lived, for example, to Bethlehem at Christmas time or to Jerusalem at Easter.

On Good Friday, many pilgrims visit Jerusalem to walk the road to Calvary, known as the Via Dolorosa, and to pray the Stations of the Cross, as they recall and reflect on the final journey of Christ. At the end of this journey, they arrive at the Church of the Holy Sepulchre. This church was built on what is believed to be the site of Jesus' crucifixion and burial.

Jerusalem at night

St Peter's Basilica, Rome

Detail from the ceiling of St Peter's Basilica

St Peter's Basilica is in the centre of Vatican City in Rome, where the Pope lives. St Peter was martyred and thought to be buried at this sacred place. Every day, all year round, thousands of people from around the world make the pilgrimage to the basilica.

Pilgrims at St Peter's Basilica:

- Pray daily in the grounds of the basilica;
- Go to confession;
- Attend Mass;
- Light candles for their own intentions and the intentions of others;
- May attend an audience with the Pope.

Knock, County Mayo

The pilgrimage site of Knock in County Mayo was established on a dark and wet night in 1879, when fifteen people witnessed the appearance, or vision, of Mary, the Mother of God, along with St Joseph and St John, at the south gable of Knock Parish Church. They described Our Lady as clothed in white robes, with a beautiful crown on her head and a golden rose in full bloom on her forehead, with her eyes and hands raised in prayer. They saw St Joseph standing to the right of Our Lady and St John on her left, both of them dressed in white. St John appeared to be holding an open book in his left hand, as though he were preaching. Behind the three figures was a plain altar, upon which stood a lamb and a cross, with angels circling all around. Since then, Knock has grown to the status of an internationally recognised Marian shrine. Over one million pilgrims make their way to Knock each year. The personal pilgrimage of Pope John Paul II in 1979, the centenary of the apparition, gave rise to an even greater devotion to the shrine, as it emphasised the Vatican's approval of it. Mother Teresa of Calcutta made a visit to the shrine in June of 1993.

Pilgrims at Knock:

- Visit the Blessed Sacrament chapel;
- Go to confession;
- Attend Mass;
- Pray the Stations of the Cross;
- Pray the Mysteries of the Rosary;
- Walk in procession around the church;
- Pray the Litany of the Blessed Virgin, followed by the Prayer to Our Lady of Knock.

Statue of Our Lady, Knock

Walsingham, England

Walsingham is a small village in East Anglia. Since 1061, it has been the most famous shrine in England to Our Lady. It is believed that a woman named Richeldis de Faverches experienced a vision of Our Lady there. She was asked by Our Lady to build a house on the site similar to the one in Nazareth where Mary was told she would become the Mother of God. The original house that she built was made of wood and it had a wooden statue of Mary with the baby Jesus on her knee. The shrine, known as 'England's Nazareth', became a sacred pilgrimage site for Christians of all denominations.

Unfortunately, the shrine at Walsingham was destroyed during the Reformation in England. However, in 1894 it was restored and a new statue of Our Lady and the baby Jesus was installed. Since then, it has become a centre of ecumenism as well as a popular place of pilgrimage, with Catholics, Anglicans and Orthodox all having their own sacred spaces and shrines at the site.

Catholic pilgrims at Walsingham:

- Stop to pray at a small chapel known as the Slipper Chapel;
- Take off their shoes and walk the last mile to the shrine barefoot;
- Go to confession;
- Attend Mass;
- Pray the Stations of the Cross;
- Join other pilgrims in prayerful procession;
- Pray the Rosary;
- Spend time in prayerful reflection with God.

KNOW WHAT

1. In your own words, describe how a pilgrim might make a pilgrimage in any of the above sacred places.
2. Name and describe one sacred place of pilgrimage associated with Mary, the Mother of God.
   - Why is this place associated with Mary?
   - Why do you think pilgrims go there today?
3. Why is Rome a sacred place of pilgrimage for Christians?
4. What are the common characteristics of the places of pilgrimage mentioned above?

DIGGING DEEPER

1. Did you (or someone close to you) ever journey to a pilgrimage site? Describe what happened.
2. Why do people of faith from all over the world make pilgrimages?
3. Why would a pilgrimage strengthen a person's faith?
4. Why might a person try to make a pilgrimage harder for themselves?
5. If you were asked to make a pilgrimage, where would you go and what would you hope to encounter there?

KNOW HOW

Research the following websites:

http://www.request.org.uk/main/dowhat/pilgrimage/places/places01.htm
http://www.teachnet.ie/fwilliams/2005/
http://www.loughderg.org/AboutUs/
http://www.ltcconline.net/barclay/courses/Study_in_Spain/camino.htm
http://www.lourdesfrance.com/index.php?page=menu&texte=1&old=&langage=en

From your research, design a brochure that:

- tells the story of a pilgrimage site (how it became a sacred place);
- describes a pilgrim's schedule during a pilgrimage;
- provides a prayer to be prayed at the pilgrimage site.

LESSON 92 Times of Significance

GROUNDWORK
In this lesson we plan to:
- explore how particular times come to be significant.

DIGGING DEEPER
What makes my time significant? What makes my time sacred?

Key Concepts
Times of significance/Actions of Significance

1. What is being celebrated in each of these pictures?
2. How do you know that the people are celebrating?
3. Why do we celebrate events in our lives?

Times and Actions of Significance

We all enjoy celebrating important events and times in our lives. We mark our birthdays or our significant family or school events by celebrating together. Our year is divided up not only by days, weeks and months, but also by special times to be marked and remembered. These are all **times of significance**.

Think about your school year: what are the special times? Think about a year in the life of your family: what are the special times you remember? Our lives are punctuated with such special times of significance.

Youth clubs, sports clubs and community groups all celebrate significant times in their history: a victory in a game, an award for their achievements. They do this through a variety of **actions of significance**. For example, the youth club might hold a celebration for the more senior members of the community at Christmas time; the school might hold a graduation ceremony for the senior class and present them with certificates to mark their time in school. Through significant actions, we grow in our understanding of significant times in our lives.

Every community of faith has special times of significance. In section C, we saw how the followers of Islam and Judaism celebrate the significant times of their religion through significant actions, such as rites of passage and other rituals. We examined how such times are *set apart* as significant religious times.

DIGGING DEEPER

1. What are the times of significance in your life? How do you mark/celebrate these times?
2. What actions do you undertake to mark/celebrate these times?
3. What are the times of religious significance in your life? How do you mark/celebrate these times?
4. What actions do you undertake to mark/celebrate these times?
5. Do the non-religious times of significance and the times of religious significance in your life ever overlap? Explain your answer.

Times of Significance for Christians

Christians have developed their own way of dividing time – it is called the Church Year or the Liturgical Year. It begins with Advent, four Sundays before Christmas. Advent means 'coming' or 'arrival' and is the name of the Church season or time when people prepare for Christmas.

In the following diagram of the Christian Liturgical Year, we see that Advent, Christmas, Lent and Easter are all times of special significance for Christians. They are called seasons, because (like the seasons of nature) they last for a specific length of time and have their own particular character. In the diagram, the liturgical seasons form the inner circle. Within these seasons, there are special days of significance, which are named in the outer circle of the diagram.

KNOW WHAT

1. How is the Christian Liturgical Year divided?
2. What season marks the beginning of the Liturgical Year?
3. List the main times of significance in the Liturgical Year.

DIGGING DEEPER

1. Christians have many ways of celebrating the Liturgical Year. Describe how they celebrate one of the times of significance during the year.
2. Choose one of these times of significance and explain how it came to be significant.

Times of Significance for Jewish People

In Section C, we learned that the Jewish year is normally 354 days long. Jewish religious festivals are based on the Bible and are linked either to the time of year or to Jewish history. The dates of festivals change from year to year because Jews, like Muslims, use a lunar calendar.

Let's recap on the times of significance for Jewish people:

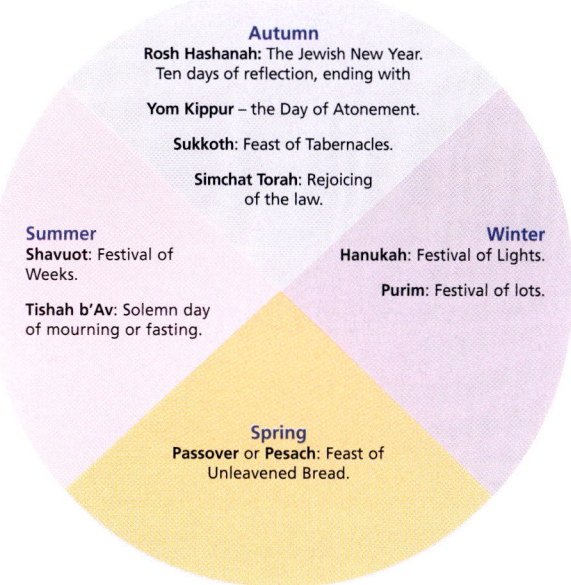

KNOW WHAT

1. Looking at the above diagrams, have a go at describing the main difference between the Christian and Jewish times of significance?
2. What is the main similarity? Explain your choice.

 **Times of significance:** Times when people respond to what is meaningful in their lives.

LESSON 93   The Liturgical Year

GROUNDWORK
In this lesson we plan to:
- take a closer look at the Liturgical Year in the Roman Catholic Church.

DIGGING DEEPER
How do Roman Catholics celebrate their Liturgical Year?

Key Concept
Times of significance

The Liturgical Year

Advent

Advent begins four Sundays before Christmas and ends early on Christmas Eve. It is a time of preparation for the Christmas celebration of the birth of Jesus. The First Sunday of Advent is the first day of the Liturgical Year. The liturgical colour for Advent is violet – the colour of preparation and desire to change life for the better.

During Advent, there is a special **time of significance** called 'The Immaculate Conception', on 8 December. This feast of Mary emphasises Mary's special place in God's work and how she was born free from Original Sin.

KNOW WHAT
1. What is Advent?
2. Why is it a time of significance?
3. What colour is worn by the priest during Advent liturgies?
4. What special time of significance, dedicated to Our Lady, is celebrated during Advent?

Christmas

The season of Christmas begins on Christmas Eve night and continues until the feast of the Baptism of the Lord, when Christians remember the day Jesus was baptised by John the Baptist.

The main celebrations within the Christmas season are:

- Christmas Day – recalling the birth of Jesus.
- Holy Family – remembering Jesus, Mary and Joseph as a family (Sunday after Christmas).
- Mary, Mother of God – celebrated on New Year's Day (also World Day of Prayer for Peace).
- Epiphany – Jesus came to save all people, represented by the Magi (6 January).
- Baptism of the Lord – Jesus was baptised by John in the river Jordan (Sunday after the Epiphany).

The celebratory colours of the Christmas season are white and gold.

Ordinary Time (Part 1)

During the Liturgical Year, when it is not Advent, Christmas, Lent or Easter, it is Ordinary Time. Ordinary Time occurs twice during the Church Year. Green is the colour used during this time. Green symbolises growth.

Some of the main days of this time are:

- Feast of the Presentation of the Lord – forty days after Christmas. It recalls how Mary and Joseph brought Jesus to the Temple forty days after he was born.
- St Brigid's Day.

KNOW IT ALL

Copy the following sentences into your Religion folder and fill in the blanks using the wordbank given below.

1. Ordinary Time occurs _____ during the Liturgical Year.
2. It occurs when it is not _____, Christmas, Lent or _____.
3. _____ is the colour for Ordinary Time. It symbolises growth.
4. The feast of the _____ of the Lord occurs during this time.
5. St _____ Day also falls within Ordinary Time.

WORDBANK
Presentation • Green • Advent • Brigid's • Twice • Easter

Lent

Lent recalls the forty days that Jesus spent in the desert before he began his public ministry. It is a season of preparation for Easter and of trying to change for the better. Lent is a time for prayer, fasting and almsgiving. The liturgical colour for Lent is violet. For adults who wish to become Christians, Lent is the final time of preparation before their Baptism.

The important days of Lent are:

- Ash Wednesday – first day of Lent. Ashes are put on the forehead.
- Sundays of Lent – very important for adults who are becoming Christians.
- Palm (Passion) Sunday – the last Sunday of Lent, when blessed palm is used to recall the triumphant entry of Jesus into Jerusalem before his suffering and death.
- Holy Thursday morning – when Lent ends.

KNOW WHAT

1. Why is Lent a time of significance?
2. What extra significance has Lent for adults who are in the process of becoming Christians?
3. Why is Palm Sunday a time of significance?
4. What is the colour for Lent?

The Easter Triduum (The Three Days of Easter)

Triduum (pronounced Trid-oo-um) is the Latin word for 'three days'.

Day 1: Holy Thursday evening to Good Friday evening

The time of the Triduum begins with the evening Mass of the Last Supper. You will remember that we looked at the Last Supper as a meal in the Passover tradition in Section B, when we were studying Christianity. The Last Supper also recalls the commandment of Jesus to love one another, the gift of the Eucharist and the start of the ministry of priesthood. Colour: white or gold.

This twenty-four hours includes the celebration of Good Friday, which recalls the passion and death of Jesus. People reverence (and kiss) the cross. This celebration does not include Mass. Colour: red – recalling bloodshed and martyrdom.

Day 2: From Good Friday evening to Holy Saturday evening

A quiet day, recalling the burial of Jesus. Colour: violet – the colour of mourning. No Mass is celebrated during this time.

Day 3: From Holy Saturday night to Easter Sunday evening

The third day of the Triduum begins with the Easter Vigil, which is celebrated after dark, recalling Jesus' resurrection from the dead. The paschal fire is blessed and from it is lit the paschal candle. Christians renew their baptismal promises at this special time. Adults who are to become Christians are baptised that night. Mass is celebrated with special music and joy. Colour: white or gold.

Easter

The Easter season begins on Easter Sunday and continues for fifty days. Colour: white or gold.

The important days of the season are:

- Easter Sunday – recalling the finding of the empty tomb and celebrating the resurrection of Jesus. At Mass, people renew their baptismal promises.
- Ascension Day – To ascend means to rise up. This day recalls Jesus returning to his Father in heaven.
- Pentecost Sunday – The last day of the Easter season marks the events in which the friends of Jesus received the power of the Holy Spirit. The colour red may also be used.

When we were studying Section B, we looked at the impact of Jesus' resurrection on his followers and on the work of the disciples afterwards. We continue to grow in our understanding of how this special time came to be significant in the lives of the first Christian communities and how it remains significant for modern Christian communities.

KNOW HOW

Write a short essay entitled 'Easter is a time of special religious significance'.
You might like to include the following:

- How Easter came to be significant
- Times of significance during the Easter season
- Places/buildings of significance associated with Easter
- Why Christians consider Easter a sacred time
- Actions of significance during Easter

Ordinary Time (Part 2)

The second stretch of Ordinary Time in the Liturgical Year begins on the Monday after Pentecost (the last day of the Easter season) and ends on the Saturday afternoon before the First Sunday of Advent. Once again, its colour is green, the colour of growth.

The important feasts of this time are:

- Trinity Sunday (the Sunday after Pentecost Sunday) – Christians recall the mystery of God the Father, God the Son and God the Holy Spirit, the divine community of love.
- The Body and Blood of the Lord (the Sunday after Trinity Sunday) – The focus is on the gift of Jesus in the Eucharist, the sacrament of love.
- The Assumption of the Blessed Virgin Mary (15 August) – Christians honour Mary, who has been taken completely by God into the life of heaven.
- All Saints' Day (1 November) – Christians honour all those who are in heaven.
- All Souls' Day (2 November) – Christians pray for all who have died.
- Feast of Christ the King – Last Sunday in Ordinary Time before Advent.

A Note on Holy Week

Traditionally, Holy Week begins on Palm Sunday and ends on Easter Sunday. It includes three particular parts of the Liturgical Year: the end of Lent, the Easter Triduum and Easter Sunday (when the Easter season starts).

A Note on Holy Days of Obligation

The resurrection of Jesus is recalled every Saturday night and Sunday morning. This is why Catholics gather for the Eucharist on Sundays.

Catholics also celebrate certain other days during the Liturgical Year that are considered special times of significance, and these are called Holy Days of Obligation: The Immaculate Conception (8 December), Christmas Day (25 December), The Epiphany (6 January), St Patrick's Day (17 March), The Assumption (15 August) and All Saints' Day (1 November).

Times of Significance in Three of the Major World Religions

Month	Christian	Jewish	Islamic
January	Epiphany		
February	* Ash Wednesday		Eid ul-Adha
March	* Ash Wednesday		Islamic New Year
April	*Palm Sunday, Holy Thursday Good Friday, Easter Sunday	First day of Passover (Pesach)	
May	Ascension Sunday	Feast of Weeks (Shavuot)	
June	Pentecost, Corpus Christi		
July			
August			
September		Jewish New Year (Rosh Hashanah), Day of Atonement (Yom Kippur)	
October		First Day of Tabernacles (Sukkoth)	
November			First day of Ramadan
December	First Sunday in Advent, Christmas Day		Eid ul-Fitr

Easter Sunday is always on the first Sunday after the first full moon after 21 March. Therefore, the month in which Ash Wednesday, Holy Thursday, Good Friday and Easter Sunday fall can change accordingly.

5-4-3-2-1

1. Name **five** months when there is 'Ordinary Time' in the Christian liturgical calendar.
2. Name **four** times of significance for two of the world religions.
3. Name the **three** times of significance noted in April for the Christian liturgical year.
4. Name **two** Jewish festivals.
5. Choose **one** of the times of significance listed in the above table and describe how it is celebrated.

See pages 495–496 for past exam questions on this topic.

KNOW THE WAY

LESSON 94   Actions of Significance

GROUNDWORK
In this lesson we plan to:
- explore how particular actions come to be significant.

DIGGING DEEPER
How do actions of significance strengthen my faith?

Key Concept
Actions of significance

Story: Healing Hugs

Diarmuid O'Connell is a twenty-nine-year-old man who has Down's syndrome. He lives on Valentia Island, County Kerry, in an independent living facility called Tig an Oileáin, which was built for people with special needs.

Diarmuid's medical condition at birth meant that he had to spend the first three months of his life in an incubator and a further month in a 'hot cot'. He had to receive twenty-four-hour care, which meant that much of this time was spent in people's arms!

As a young boy, Diarmuid had many illnesses that required hospital treatment, including undergoing heart surgery at the age of sixteen.

Because he had grown up with his parents, siblings and other family members holding him close, Diarmuid associated being held with being healed. He always felt better when he was being held close. So much so, that after his last operation, when his surgeon asked him if the pain was very severe, he raised his eyes and quietly asked for a hug.

For Diarmuid, a hug would lessen the pain. For him, a hug is an **action of significance**.

Times and Actions of Significance

Actions of significance often indicate the importance we attach to specific times. We clap to show our appreciation as an audience; we kneel to show our respect at times of prayer.

Times of significance often call for **actions of significance**.

TAKE FIVE

1. 'Significant' means special and important. What do you think is significant about the examples given above?
2. Which of the above actions has religious significance and which has non-religious significance?
3. Why do we have actions of significance in our day-to-day life?
4. Why do we have actions of religious significance?
5. Name and describe two actions of religious significance and two actions of non-religious significance.

Actions Speak Louder than Words

In any religion, there are many things that can be 'seen', for example, the sacred text, the statements of belief, the places of worship, and so on. In order to encounter the 'unseen', a community of faith has places of significance, times of significance and also actions of significance. Actions of significance embrace or capture what language cannot. We have all heard the old phrase 'actions speak louder than words'. In the story above, Diarmuid knew that words could not soothe his physical pain, but a hug would help him to cope with it.

Actions of Religious Significance

In the world of the sacred, actions of significance become symbolic, i.e. they have a deeper meaning. For example, kneeling for prayer becomes an action of respect and adoration; a handshake becomes a symbol of peace and reconciliation, and so on. When these actions are performed during communal acts of worship, they serve to strengthen and unify the community of faith.

The Sign of the Cross

When Christians pray, they usually begin with the sign of the cross. This is an action of significance because it directs the prayer to the three persons of the Trinity – God the Father, God the Son and God the Holy Spirit. It is also a statement of the person's belief in the Trinity and of the importance of the Trinity for Christians.

'Love' is at the heart of the Trinity. God loved people so much that he sent Jesus; Jesus loved so much that he died for all, and the Holy Spirit was sent to people out of love. Jesus always prayed to God the Father and identified himself as one with the Father. He also fulfilled his promise to send the disciples the gift of the Holy Spirit after his ascension into heaven. When people make the sign of the cross, they too are showing their love and reverence for the Trinity.

St Patrick, the patron saint of Ireland, tried to explain the Trinity by using a shamrock.

KNOW WHAT

Define an action of significance within the world of the sacred.

DIGGING DEEPER

1. Name and describe *two* actions of significance from your community of faith.
2. Which action of significance do you perform most often within your community of faith? Why do you think you perform this action of significance most often?
3. How does taking part in the actions of significance of your faith community strengthen your faith?
4. How can actions of religious significance 'speak louder than words'?
5. When Christians pray, they begin with an action of significance. What is this action and what does it mean?
6. If you were asked to explain the Trinity to your classmates, how would you do it?

KNOW IT ALL

The religions we have studied have many actions of significance. Copy the following chart into your Religion folder and have a go at filling it in. An example is already given for Christianity. You might like to choose another example of your own.

Name of Religion	Action of significance	Meaning
Christianity	Sign of the Cross	Indicates with reverence that a prayer time has begun and directs the prayer to the three persons of the Trinity. People also use this action as a sign of reverence when entering a sacred place.

Actions of significance: Actions through which people respond to what is meaningful in their lives.

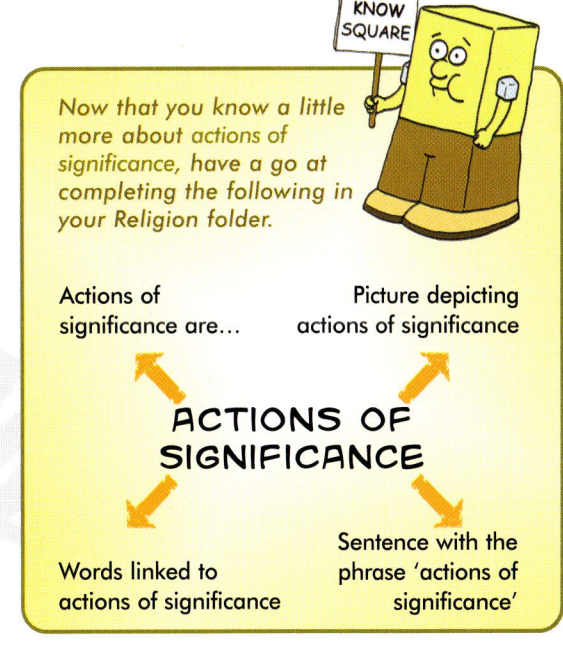

The Experience of Worship

LESSON 95 The Language of Worship

GROUNDWORK
In this lesson we plan to:
- explore the language of worship.

DIGGING DEEPER
What does it mean to worship?

 **Key Concepts**
Worship/Ritual/Participation

Worship

To **worship** means to give praise, to give worth, to show love, to honour, and to communicate one's faith. People worship privately through prayer and personal devotion and publicly through participation in rites, rituals and pilgrimage.

Gospel Music – An Example of Worship

In the Christian community of faith, people often offer praise and thanks to God in a physical and spiritual way through singing, which is sometimes accompanied by dancing and clapping. Gospel choirs are to be found all over the world, bringing great joy to the experience of praise and worship.

The gospel singer-songwriter sisters Erica and Tina Atkins chose 'Mary Mary' as their performing name. For Christians, this name sounds in itself like a prayer to Mary, the Mother of God. Mary Mary's music is a contemporary blend of funky, faithful, soulful and deeply spiritual prayer.

You may be familiar with the 'Shackles' song written and performed by Mary Mary. The sisters say that they wrote this song in order to share their Christian faith.

Let's look at a verse and a chorus from the song. (If someone has the music, you could listen to it together and even join in!)

> Been through the fire and the rain
> Bound in every kind of way
> But God has broken every chain
> So let me go right now
>
> Take the shackles off my feet so I can dance
> I just wanna praise you
> I just wanna praise you
> You broke the chains now I can lift my hands
> And I'm gonna praise you
> I'm gonna praise you

KNOW WHAT
1. What does the word 'worship' mean?
2. Why is gospel music an example of worship?
3. Explain what the verse and chorus of the above song are about.

DIGGING DEEPER
1. Have you ever worshipped God through song? Write about this experience.
2. 'They who sing, pray twice.' What does this statement suggest?

Ritual as Worship

We know that people often use the word **ritual** when they are describing a daily or weekly routine. For example, the breakfast ritual, the Sunday lunch ritual or even the homework ritual! When we describe ritual in this way, we are describing something that happens on a regular basis. In the world of the sacred, ritual has a slightly different meaning. Religious ritual invites people to communicate with God and others in a meaningful way. It is where people gather together and follow a specific pattern of behaviour that includes prayer and actions of religious significance. Religious ritual calls for **participation**. Although rituals may be repeated many times, they continue to offer new possibilities each time they are celebrated. For example, if you attend a regular prayer service in your school, each occasion will be a different experience for you. This is because you participate internally (through the mind, the heart and the soul) and externally (through the body) in different ways each time you take part.

What do religious rituals have in common?

- Physical movements, actions and gestures are used to express the relationship with God and with one another.
- Religious rituals connect with special events and times of significance.
- The words and actions are familiar to those present.
- Everyone participates in the majority of the actions.
- Religious rituals are part of every believer's past, present and future.

Participation in ritual is at the heart of worship.

As with all the major world religions, when Christians gather together as a community to express their relationship with God, they take part in ritual. As Christians grow and develop in faith, they experience something new about God and themselves each time they take part in ritual.

Participation in religious ritual helps people to be open to a meaningful encounter with God and others. One can then experience change and return to the daily routine renewed and regenerated. At the end of the Catholic Mass, the priest says 'Go in peace to love and serve the Lord', and the people reply 'Thanks be to God'.

KNOW WHAT

1. How is a religious ritual different to an everyday ritual?
2. When a person participates fully in religious ritual, what kind of change can come about?
3. What do you think the priest's words at the end of Mass convey?
4. Why do all the major world religions participate in sacred ritual?

3-2-1

1. Name **three** things that religious rituals have in common.
2. Describe **two** types of ritual in the Christian faith tradition.
3. Write **one** paragraph on the meaning of religious ritual.

DIGGING DEEPER

1. Give three examples of sacred ritual from your community of faith.
2. What was the last sacred ritual that you took part in? Explain what happened and the role you played.

Rites of Passage

Rites of passage are the most common of all rituals and are found both in ordinary life and in religious traditions. A rite of passage celebrates a person moving on from one stage of life to another. An example from ordinary life would be a birthday party or a graduation celebration. Religious rituals also mark the stages in a person's life. In Judaism, the bar mitzvah for boys or the bat mitzvah for girls is a celebration of the young person's 'coming of age'. In Christianity, there are many rites of passage celebrated through the ritual of the sacraments.

KNOW IT ALL

Copy the following grid into your Religion folder and place the entries in columns two and three in the correct order. (You may need to revise the relevant lessons from Section C to complete this exercise.)

Ritual	Religion	Explanation
Baptism	Judaism	Beginning of adulthood
Bar mitzvah	Christianity	Christian journey to a sacred place
Eucharist	Judaism	Jewish initiation ceremony
Confirmation	Christianity	Receiving the Holy Spirit
Pilgrimage to the Western Wall	Judaism	Christian initiation ceremony
Salat	Christianity	Prayer five times a day
Pilgrimage to Knock	Islam	Islamic journey to a sacred place
Brit Milah	Christianity	Confession
Penitential service	Christianity	Jewish journey to a sacred place
Pilgrimage to Mecca	Christianity	Receiving the Body and Blood of Jesus Christ

KNOW HOW

'Participation in ritual is at the heart of worship.'

Write half a page on the above statement.
Or
Create a poster to depict this statement.

 **Worship:** Response of a group or individual to the sacred, often expressed through ritual.

Ritual: A series of actions carried out in a set way. Religious rituals are usually repeated regularly by the faith community to express the relationship between God and the community.

Participation: Taking an active part in an action or activity.

Note for teachers: *Alongside 'participation', the syllabus includes 'observing' as a means of allowing students of a different faith or of no faith to identify the elements of worship, i.e. ritual and participation.*

LESSON 96 The Elements of Worship

GROUNDWORK
In this lesson we plan to:
- identify the elements of worship.

DIGGING DEEPER
What takes place during my worship?

Key Concepts
Worship/Ritual/Participation

'Take the shackles off my feet so I can dance. I just wanna praise you.'

We have explored the language that is used when we speak about **worship**. Let's now explore what happens during worship, i.e. the elements of worship.

The Elements of Worship

Taking the first letter of each element of worship, here is an easy way to remember them:

- **P** People gather to celebrate.
- **R** Rites and rituals take place.
- **A** Actions of significance take place.
- **I** In a holy (sacred) place.
- **S** Special events and times of significance.
- **E** Experiencing God and others in a meaningful way.

DIGGING DEEPER
With your teacher, organise a prayer service to mark a special time of significance. After the prayer service, answer the following questions.

1. Who gathered?
2. What rite/ritual was involved?
3. What actions of significance took place?
4. Where did the worship take place?
5. What was the special time of significance that you were celebrating?
6. How did you experience God and others in a meaningful way?
7. How did you participate in or observe the experience of worship?
8. What actions, gestures, movements, words, hymns or music were used during this experience of worship?

In Section C we studied Judaism and Islam, two major world religions, and we learned about the acts of worship that are characteristic of each religion. Every religion has its own times and actions of significance. During a pilgrimage, for example, a special type of worship takes place. Look back at Section C and, with the help of your teacher, see if you can identify any of the elements of worship in Jewish and Islamic times and actions of significance.

KNOW WHAT
1. What actions of significance do Muslims undertake during the Hajj?
2. What actions of significance do Jews undertake during the Passover?
3. What actions of significance do Christians undertake during the Easter Triduum?

The Elements of Worship in the Sacrament of Baptism
Through the sacrament of Baptism, all Christians are called to serve God and others and to live as followers of Jesus. Let's take a look at the elements of worship in the sacrament of Baptism as it is celebrated in the Catholic tradition.

People gather to celebrate:
The members of the community of faith gather together to participate in the celebration of the sacrament of Baptism.

Rites and rituals:
The priest leads the people through the rite of Baptism, which involves several different **rituals**. The main ritual is the actual baptism of the baby with holy water.

Actions of significance:
During the sacrament of Baptism, there are many actions of significance. For example, after the priest has baptised the baby with holy water, he anoints the baby's head with the oil of chrism. The anointing with chrism signifies the gift of the Holy Spirit to the newly baptised baby. The child is anointed with a new relationship with God and with others, and is now part of the Christian community, part of the Body of Christ.

Baptismal font

In a holy place:
The celebration of Baptism takes place in a church. This is a sacred place within the Christian community of faith.

Special events and times of significance:
Baptism is celebrated to welcome a new member into the Christian community. This is a very special time for the family and the entire community.

Experiencing God and others in a meaningful way:
Participation in an act of worship such as the sacrament of Baptism gives people the chance to take time out from their ordinary routine to spend some special time in a special place doing something very worthwhile and meaningful, i.e. welcoming new members into the community of faith. During the celebration of Baptism, people communicate with God and with others through rite and ritual. Afterwards, they go back to their ordinary routine, renewed and regenerated as followers of Christ.

DIGGING DEEPER
1. Why is the sacrament of Baptism an act of worship?
2. Identify the elements of worship in this sacrament.
3. Write about a time when you participated in or observed the sacrament of Baptism. In what ways do you think the sacrament of Baptism can strengthen the faith of Christians?
   Or
   Write about a time when you participated in or observed an act of worship within a community of faith. In what ways can such an act of worship strengthen a person's faith?

KNOWING ME KNOWING YOU
Create a sacred space in your school. Choose a time of special significance and build your sacred space with symbols that encourage prayer and reflection around this time. Try to include symbols from both the religious and the natural season.

Or

Organise and participate in or observe a prayer service to celebrate a special time of significance for a local hospital, a school for people with special needs or any other group in your local area. Create a centrepiece for the prayer service that encourages people to pray and reflect.

See page 496 for past exam questions on this topic.

(Higher Level Only)

Worship as Response to Mystery

LESSON 97 The Impact of Mystery

GROUNDWORK
In this lesson we plan to:
- explore the effect that the experience of mystery has in human life.

DIGGING DEEPER
How does the experience of mystery affect my life?

 **Key Concepts**
Encountering mystery/Wonder

Introductory Activity: Puzzles

1. A number has sixteen digits. It contains two 8s separated by eight digits; two 7s separated by seven digits; two 6s separated by six digits; two 5s separated by five digits, and so on. The last three digits of the number are 526. What is the number?

2. Where does 'Z' go: above or below the line? Give your reason.

   A EF HI KLMN   T VWXY
   BCD G   J   OPQRS U

3. What do you see?

Answers on page 352

349

Mysteries and Puzzles

When talking about religion and spirituality, we often use the term 'mystery' or we hear the phrase **'encountering mystery'** (i.e. coming face to face with mystery). Our relationship with the Divine involves mystery. People, too, are full of mystery. But what does this really mean?

To help us to understand what a mystery is, we need first to look at something that it is not. A mystery is not the same as a puzzle. The puzzles given above have definite answers. Mystery is different. In trying to figure out a mystery, we need to have more than one answer. Often, the more we know of a mystery, the harder it can be to understand it. We begin to realise that while every answer may be helpful, no single answer is enough. Every answer brings with it another 'angle' to explore.

The word 'mystery' has many meanings. The Oxford Dictionary defines mystery as 'a matter that remains unexplained'. A common meaning is that a mystery involves something hidden that needs to be revealed. Religion has a very important part to play in helping us to understand the existence of God and the mysteries of life and death. Science is very limited when it comes to the mystery of life and death, because often the more facts we gather about life and death, the harder it is to understand the mystery within them.

Mysteries of Life

Listed below are some of the most common mysteries that people wonder about.
Look at these mysteries carefully and then complete the exercise that follows.

1. Where does life come from? Why does it exist at all? Why are there so many different forms of life?
2. How is it that, of all the millions of people in the world, two particular people meet and fall in love? Do they choose whom they will love? Can we fall in love with just anyone? What makes two people fall in love with each other?
3. Why are some children born into wealth and other children born into poverty? How is it decided where and how we are born? Where are we before we are born?
4. What about death? Why do people have to die, especially young people who should have so much life in front of them? What happens to people when they die?
5. Why do bad things happen to good people? Why does suffering exist? Can it have any purpose?
6. Why do people follow evil leaders? Why is there war? Why are there weapons of destruction?
7. How is it that the world we live in – this amazingly complex planet we inhabit – is populated with plants and animals that can sustain life for all of us?

KNOW WHAT
1. Name two mysteries that you think will be solved one day.
2. Name two mysteries that you think will never be solved.
3. Where might you find the answers to these mysteries?

Questions like these arise from our experience of the mystery of life. None of them has a simple answer. For some, there is no answer available to us. As soon as we begin to discuss them, other questions arise.

People look for the answers to such mysteries in a number of different areas. For example, our previous experience might inform us about them. Sometimes people will look to religion or science to help solve these mysteries. The followers of a religion often seek the help of their religion to grow in their understanding of the mystery of God or of evil or of life after death. One of the ways they express their response to these mysteries is through worship.

Awe and Wonder

In the film *Shrek*, the ogre describes himself as resembling an onion! He suggests that he is not just the scary ogre everybody sees, but a creature with many layers hidden underneath. We can describe mystery in a similar way: the more layers we peel away, the more layers we find. Layers of mystery cause us to **wonder**. Wonder is an emotion that is stirred within us when we are faced with something that is amazing, astonishing or spectacular. We are often filled with wonder when we encounter something that we don't understand.

Let's read about one person's experience of awe and wonder.

Story: A Journey in Space

On 18 September 2006, Anousheh Ansari captured headlines all over the world when she became the first female space tourist as well as the first astronaut of Iranian descent. Anousheh blasted off for an eight-day expedition into space, along with two other NASA astronauts.

For Anousheh, this journey was the realisation of a lifelong dream. She decided to share her experience and wrote a daily blog for anyone who might be interested. To her complete surprise, the blog created worldwide interest and received more than fifty million hits.

The following is an extract from one such entry and it describes Anousheh's first sight of the earth from space:

Anousheh Ansari

> 'The launch was very smooth. The trip to the station felt long but it was worth it. I cannot keep my eyes off the windows. Earth is magnificent and peaceful from up here. You don't see any of those awful things you hear on the news from up here. The earth is so beautiful and if we could all see it this way I'm sure we would do everything in our power to preserve it. I truly hope that more and more people get to experience this trip first hand.'

In another blog, Anousheh spoke about the highlights of her trip:

> 'But that is not the best part. The best part and by far my favourite view up here is the view of the universe at night. The stars up here are unbelievable… It looks like someone has spread diamond dust over a black velvet blanket. The Milky Way is easily visible… like a rainbow of stars over the entire earth… I cannot keep my eyes off of them. I put my head to the window and stay there until the coldness of the glass gives me a headache… then I pull my head back a little and continue gazing out.'

Anousheh put words on her experience of the wonder of the planet. From her writings, we can see that she is a person of faith:

> 'As I gaze out I thank God once again for helping me be here and experience this. I have been thanking him for letting my inner voice carry out to you all and ask him to give me the vision to see my path in life and the strength to pursue it. These are the most peaceful moments I have had in my life and I feel a great source of positive energy. I have a hard time sleeping too long because I keep forcing my eyes open to just see this beauty and take it all in… only a second longer…'

5-4-3-2-1

1. Identify **five** words that Anousheh used to describe what she saw out of the spacecraft's window.
2. List **four** sights that she saw.
3. What **three** things does Anousheh thank God for?
4. Name **two** ways the experience of this wonder has made Anousheh feel.

351

5. Imagine you are inside a spacecraft, looking down upon the earth. Write **one** blog describing the wondrous sights you can see.

DIGGING DEEPER
Anousheh's experience of being in space led her to wonder about the universe. Are there things in your life that cause you to wonder? Write about them.

KNOWING ME KNOWING YOU
Log on to *http://spaceblog.xprize.org/2006/09/12/the-road-to-baikonur/* to find out more about Anousheh's experience.

The Wonder of Creation

5 billion years ago (approximately):	The sun formed
4.6 billion years ago:	The earth formed
2 billion years ago:	Oxygen produced by plants
1.3 billion years ago:	Multi-cellular species appeared
670 million years ago:	Worms appeared
500 million years ago:	Fish appeared
425 million years ago:	The first life on land
370 million years ago:	Amphibians appeared
360 million years ago:	Insects appeared
313 million years ago:	Reptiles, dinosaurs and birds appeared
216 million years ago:	Mammals appeared
114 million years ago:	Flowers appeared
300,000 years ago:	The earliest known modern human beings
2000 – 4000 years ago:	The rise of the great civilisations

DIGGING DEEPER
1. Does anything in this timeline of our planet surprise, amaze or especially interest you? Explain your answer.
2. Working in small groups, see if you can add three more recent entries to this timeline to bring it nearer to the present day.
3. What is your reaction to the wonder of creation?
4. Have you ever encountered or come face to face with a mystery in your own life? If so, how did you react to it? If not, how do you think you might react to it?

🔑 **Encountering mystery:** Being strongly affected by a meaningful experience that we do not fully understand.

Wonder: Feeling of respect and awe resulting from encountering or coming face to face with something amazing or spectacular.

Solutions to puzzles on page 349
1. The sixteen-digit number is 8131743568427526
2. Z goes above the line because it has only straight lines and no curves.
3. Two faces and a vase.

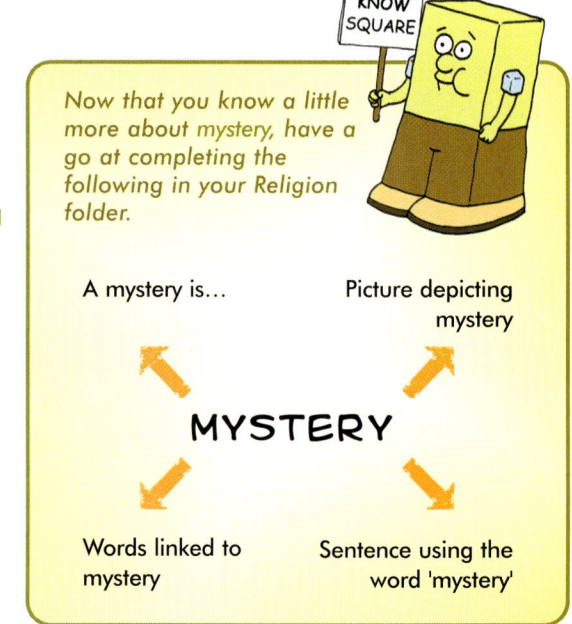

Now that you know a little more about *mystery*, have a go at completing the following in your Religion folder.

MYSTERY
- A mystery is…
- Picture depicting mystery
- Words linked to mystery
- Sentence using the word 'mystery'

LESSON 98 Responses to the Encounter with Mystery

GROUNDWORK
In this lesson we plan to:
- explore some responses to the encounter with mystery.

DIGGING DEEPER
How do I respond to mystery?

Key Concepts
Encountering mystery/Reflection

Newgrange – A Response to the Encounter with Mystery

This megalithic (i.e. great stone) passage tomb at Newgrange, County Meath, was built around 3200 BC, so it is even older than the great pyramids of Giza in Egypt. Newgrange is considered one of the most important ancient sacred sites in Ireland and is amazing for many reasons other than its age. Its construction was extremely precise for such an ancient building. It was built as a response to an encounter with the mystery of the sun. On 21 December, the shortest day of the year, the winter solstice sun lights up the whole passage and chamber. It would have been considered a place of significance because it was also a burial chamber.

It is interesting to reflect on what might have motivated those who built it. Why was it constructed so that sunlight passed all the way through to the central inner chamber at dawn on the shortest day of the year, when the sun begins to recover its cycle again? What were the builders hoping for? Perhaps they hoped that the recovering sun would in some way share its power with those who had died.

The very act of constructing the tomb was an action of significance, and it was followed by other rituals, like putting the bodies of those who had died into the chamber. Being in the presence of death is a sacred experience, as birth and death are the two most significant events of our lives. Visiting places like Newgrange reminds us that people of every place and time search for meaning and truth. The people who constructed this passage tomb knew what they believed in and they celebrated it.

KNOW IT ALL

Copy the following into your Religion folder and fill in the blanks using the wordbank given below.

The _____ tomb in Newgrange, County Meath, was built around _____ BC. It was used as a _____ chamber. It was built as a response to an encounter with the _____ of the _____. On 21 _____, the sun lights up the entire passage and chamber. Perhaps it was hoped that the recovering sun would share its power with those who had _____. By building this tomb, the people of Newgrange were celebrating one of the most _____ events of human life.

WORDBANK
Significant • Mystery • Burial • Passage • Died • Encounter • 3200 • Sun • December

Reflection as a Response to the Encounter with Mystery

We hear many people talking about life in the 'fast lane' and how they are stuck in the 'rat race'. These phrases refer to how full people's lives have become. With the introduction of electronic games, even recreation has become fast, furious and ultra competitive. It's only when life takes a slower pace that we can actually have the time to reflect.

Reflection involves taking time out to think about and try to make sense of our experiences and actions. It is often only through reflection that we can find our direction in life.

Even the very ordinary things in life can fill us with wonder and awe. For example, this picture is of something as ordinary as raindrops on a blade of grass, but when we take the time to look at it and reflect on its beauty and form, we can be 'stopped in our tracks'. This is what is called a moment of reflection, when time seems to stand still.

Other experiences in life that can cause us to reflect might be:

- the birth of a baby;
- the death of someone we love;
- getting to know people, including ourselves;
- making new relationships, especially falling in love;
- learning about the world of science.

DIGGING DEEPER

1. What does it mean when we reflect on something?
2. Sometimes we do not bother to take the time to reflect. Why do you think this is so?
3. Why might it be good for us to spend time reflecting on our lives?
4. Do you spend any time reflecting on your life? What causes you to reflect most often?

When the Ordinary becomes the Extra-ordinary

Sometimes we can have powerful moments when we sense the divine. This can happen when ordinary things or actions or events take on an extra-ordinary significance. Patrick Kavanagh was a famous Irish poet who came from County Monaghan. He had a wonderful ability through his use of language to transform the ordinary and the banal into something of significance. Kavanagh saw the extra-ordinary in the ordinary 'stuff of life'. Let's read the first three verses of one of Kavanagh's poems, 'Spraying the Potatoes'.

*The barrels of blue potato-spray
Stood on a headland of July
Beside an orchard wall where roses
Were young girls hanging from the sky.*

*The flocks of green potato stalks
Were blossoms spread for sudden flight,
The Kerr's Pinks in a frivelled blue,
The Arran Banners wearing white.*

*And over that potato-field
A lazy veil of woven sun.
Dandelions growing on headlands, showing
Their unloved hearts to everyone.*

KNOW WHAT
1. Would you regard spraying potatoes as an exciting way to spend your Saturday afternoons? Why?/Why not?
2. How does the poet make this 'ordinary' job sound extra-ordinary?

Kavanagh paints a glorious and vibrant picture for us. He describes a routine job such as spraying the potatoes as an extra-ordinary moment of beauty. In another poem, Kavanagh said that 'God is in the bits and pieces of Everyday…'. We experience extra-ordinary moments of beauty when we see the divine in our 'everyday'. Suddenly the ordinary becomes filled with newness and wonder. This experience comes through friends, family, the beauty of the world, music and the arts. God can be present to all in many and different ways.

DIGGING DEEPER
1. Kavanagh's poetry is famous for 'giving wings to ordinary things'. What does this phrase mean and why do you think it applies to Kavanagh's poetry?
2. How does Kavanagh's poetry help us to reflect on some of the 'everyday' mysteries of life?
3. Think of a time when you reflected on the everyday mysteries of life. It might be helpful for you to think of the place and the actions that were involved in this experience. Then briefly describe the experience.

KNOW HOW
Have a go at drawing a picture entitled 'The world is full of beauty waiting to be seen'.

 **Reflection:** Inner personal thought. Focusing on or searching for something meaningful in a sacred text, in the events of life or in the world of nature.

See page 496 for past exam questions on this topic.

LESSON 99 Religious Responses to Mystery

GROUNDWORK
In this lesson we plan to:
- explore some religious responses to the encounter with mystery.

DIGGING DEEPER
How do I respond to mystery through a religious experience?

Key Concepts
Worship as a response to mystery or an expression of ultimate concern/Celebration/Encounter with God/Communication

We all react to and reflect on mystery in different ways. Artists try to express in their works the mystery they sense in the world around them. Musicians use sounds to share their sense of mystery. How do you respond to the mysteries in your life? For example, have you ever wanted to be alone to listen to some piece of music that particularly appealed to you? Perhaps you have written something in a diary or journal in response to an experience or maybe you took the time to share a positive experience that you had with your friends. In a previous lesson, we learned that the followers of religions often seek the help of their religion to grow in their understanding of the mystery of God or of evil or of life after death. One of the ways they express this is through worship.

Let's take a closer look at worship, the sacraments, the psalms and pilgrimage as religious responses to the encounter with mystery.

Worship as a Response to Mystery

For people of faith, moments of mystery build up their sense of God. They react with awe and wonder, and they reflect on their experience. This is also what happens during worship. **Worship is a response to mystery** – in this case, the mystery of God. Through their worship, people give thanks and praise for the gifts of God, and so their worship becomes an **expression of ultimate concern** or love.

Acts of worship are a **celebration** of people's **encounter with God**. When people participate *fully* in rites and rituals (acts of worship), they are entering into a religious experience with the whole heart and mind. By so doing, they can encounter God or come face to face with God in a meaningful way.

KNOW THE WAY

The three major world religions that we have studied – Christianity, Judaism and Islam – all have their own special day of worship, or Sabbath. Through this special day of worship, Christians, Jews and Muslims respond to the encounter with mystery. Muslims keep Fridays as their special day, Jewish people keep Saturdays and Christians keep Sundays.

Catholics celebrate the Sabbath by attending Mass and taking part in various rituals and actions of significance: gathering, praying aloud as well as in silence, receiving the body and blood of Jesus Christ, etc.

Acts of worship that are celebrated within a community of faith result in **communication** with God and with others in a meaningful way. When the celebration is over, each person who has participated fully in the celebration will return to their ordinary life nourished and strengthened by what has taken place.

The Sacraments as a Response to Mystery

During his life on earth, Jesus showed people what God is like, through his actions and through his relationships with others. He invited people into a relationship with God. In the sacraments, through the use of ritual and symbol, Christians are helped to experience God's presence in their lives. For example, in the sacrament of Reconciliation, Catholics experience God's forgiving presence.

TAKE FIVE
1. Why is it necessary to reflect on and respond to mystery?
2. Explain how worship is a response to mystery.
3. What is celebrated on the Sabbath day?
4. How does worship enable people to communicate with God and with others in a meaningful way?
5. Explain the words 'celebration' and 'communication' as they are understood in the world of the sacred.

DIGGING DEEPER
1. Name and describe two acts of worship/celebrations that you have participated in? How did those acts of worship celebrate your encounter with God?
2. Catholics celebrate the seven sacraments as a response to their encounter with God. List the seven sacraments and describe what each one celebrates.
   Or
   Your community of faith celebrates important times and moments in your life. List these events and identify what each one celebrates.

The Psalms as a Response to Mystery

The vastness of the world around us reminds us that we are part of something greater than ourselves. The beauty of nature can lead us to be more aware of the mystery of God and of God's presence in the world.

But describing this mystery or encounter with God can be very difficult. In the book of Psalms in the Old Testament, we see many examples of efforts to capture the wonder and mystery of God and God's love in words. The book of Psalms contains prayers and hymns in which people expressed their feelings about God, often inspired by the world around them. These prayers and hymns were written in response to each writer's encounter with mystery.

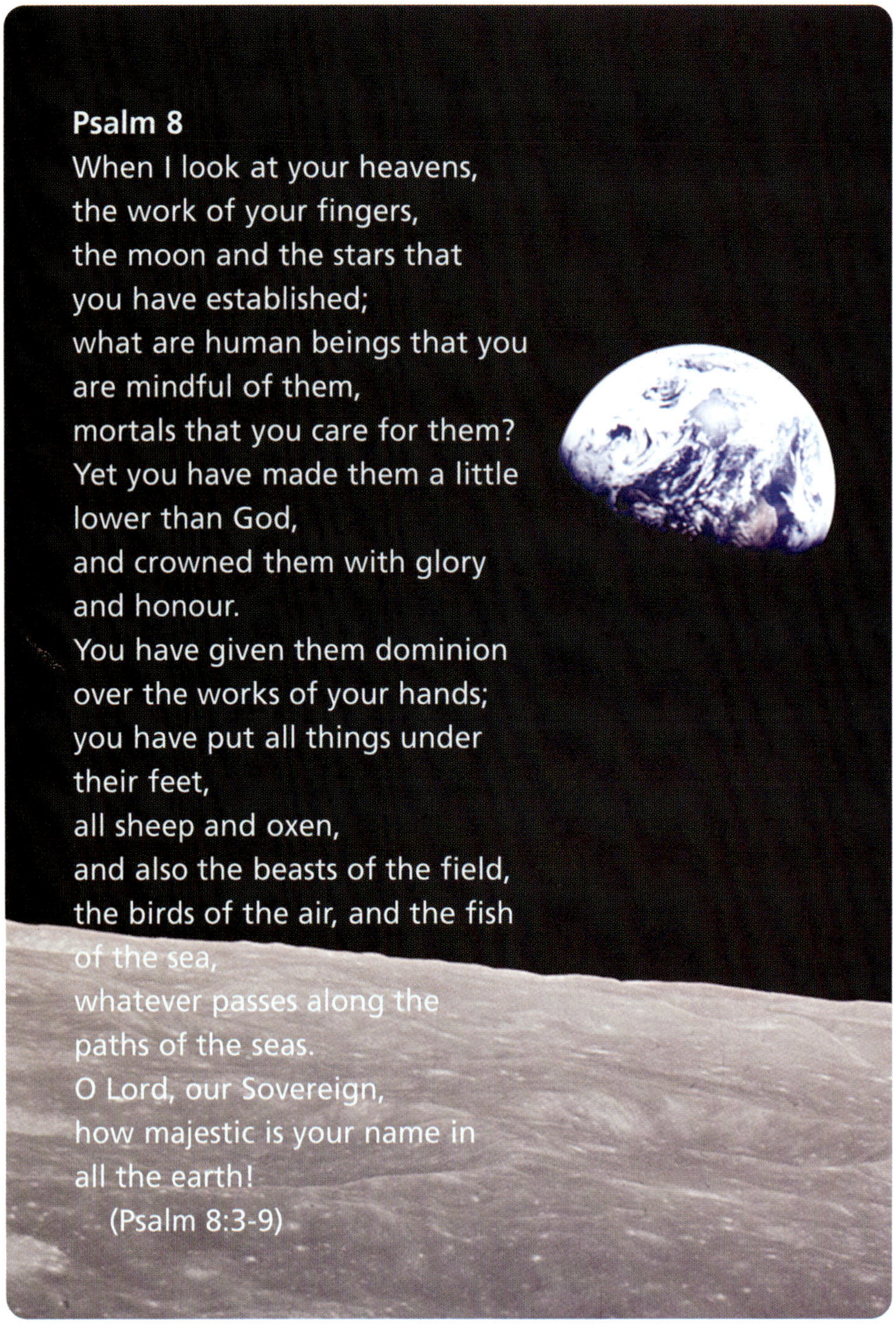

Psalm 8

When I look at your heavens,
the work of your fingers,
the moon and the stars that
you have established;
what are human beings that you
are mindful of them,
mortals that you care for them?
Yet you have made them a little
lower than God,
and crowned them with glory
and honour.
You have given them dominion
over the works of your hands;
you have put all things under
their feet,
all sheep and oxen,
and also the beasts of the field,
the birds of the air, and the fish
of the sea,
whatever passes along the
paths of the seas.
O Lord, our Sovereign,
how majestic is your name in
all the earth!
   (Psalm 8:3-9)

KNOW WHAT

1. What is this psalm saying about human beings and about creation?
2. Read the psalm again. How would you describe the writer's response to the encounter with mystery?

DIGGING DEEPER

You will need a Bible for this exercise.
1. Where would you most likely hear a psalm being read?
2. Look through the book of Psalms in your Bible. Choose one that you think illustrates a response to an encounter with mystery. Give reasons for your choice. Share your choice of psalm with the class.

KNOW THE WAY

Pilgrimage as a Response to Mystery

Pilgrimages are very popular, especially amongst young people. For centuries, people from all over the world have travelled great distances to sacred places of pilgrimage. They do this to show their personal devotion to a saint, a holy person or to embark on a journey of personal discovery. This journey of faith is a religious response to their encounter with mystery.

KNOW HOW

Working in pairs, choose *two* of the following pilgrimage sites and research them. (See the list of websites below.) When you have gathered enough information, answer the questions below in relation to each place.

The Knock Shrine (Ireland)   The Western Wall (Jerusalem)
Lourdes (France)   Santiago de Compostela (Spain)
Fatima (Portugal)   Mecca (Saudi Arabia)
Lough Derg (Ireland)   Taizé (France)

1. Where is this place of pilgrimage?
2. What holy person or event is associated with this area?
3. What is believed to have happened (or continues to happen) there?
4. Is there a particular time of year when people go there? Why?
5. How do the people who go there respond to the mystery of God at this place?
6. What actions do people carry out during the pilgrimage? What do these actions mean?
7. Would you like to visit this place of pilgrimage? Explain your answer.
8. Why do you think pilgrimages have become increasingly popular among young people?

Useful websites for your research:

www.taize.fr
www.loughderg.ie
http://www.lourdes-france.com/bonjour.htm
http://www.fatima.org/tour.html
http://www.knock-shrine.ie/
http://www.csj.org.uk/menu.htm – Camino de Santiago
http://instruct1.cit.cornell.edu/courses/nes266/page6.htm http://wordbytes.org/holyland/pilgrim063.htm

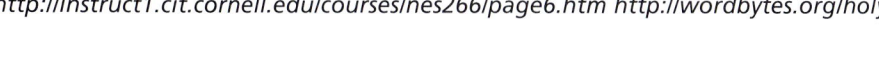

Here is a second-year student's reflection on her pilgrimage to Knock:

'Before I went to Knock I thought it would be a quaint little village. When I got there I was amazed at how vast and modern the grounds were. "Silence Please" signs were hung in many places, adding to the atmosphere of quiet contemplation.

The museum was a really exciting place to be. We encountered fascinating displays of Knock as it would have been in the ninteenth century.

When we had free time, my friend and I wandered around the religious shops. I bought a Saint Brigid's cross and a mini Bible. Then we both went to the basilica. It was massive and felt like a really holy place. I felt calm and relaxed there, even though it was probably the biggest building I have ever been in.

At 2.45pm we met at St John's rest-and-care centre, and then walked to Mass in the basilica. It was really nice to be there with my class. We smiled a lot during Mass. During the sign of peace we all shook hands and I really tried to mean it. Our teacher, Miss Finlay, had explained about pilgrimage to us so we felt a real kind of bond together, that we were making our pilgrimage together as a class. I can't quite explain it, but I know it felt really good to be there with my friends.'

TAKE FIVE

1. How would you describe this student's experience of Knock?
2. Why do you think the signs asking for silence were there?
3. Why do you think the student felt so calm and relaxed in the basilica?
4. Why do you think she really tried to make the sign of peace into a meaningful action?
5. Would you say that the pilgrimage to Knock caused this student to spend time in reflection? Why?

DIGGING DEEPER

Did you ever visit Knock Shrine or another place of pilgrimage? If so, write about your experience or describe it for the class.

Worship as a response to mystery or an expression of ultimate concern: When we find something or someone to be deeply meaningful, but normal words and thoughts are not enough to express our relationship or response, we turn to worship.

Encounter with God: Being strongly aware of the presence of God in a particular moment or place.

Celebration: Special gathering to honour one or more people or to mark a particular event.

Communication: Sharing of experiences, thoughts or feelings.

Sign and Symbol

LESSON 100 Signs and Symbols

GROUNDWORK
In this lesson we plan to:
- explore the place of sign and symbol in everyday life.

DIGGING DEEPER
What role do signs and symbols play in my life?

Key Concepts
Sign/Symbol/Communicating experience

Signs

A **sign** can be a word, a drawing or an action that provides information, for example, a road sign may tell us the direction we are travelling in and that the next town or our destination is a certain number of kilometres/miles away. Signs should be easy to recognise and their meaning should be obvious.

KNOW HOW
Draw signs to indicate:
- a narrow bridge ahead
- a one-way street
- a 'no smoking' zone

Now look again at your drawings.

Are they easy to recognise? Would a person be able to understand their message? Would you like to change or add anything to your signs to make them more understandable? Why are signs important?

361

Symbols

Symbols are more powerful than signs because they affect the way we feel. They touch us on many different levels and give us ways of expressing ourselves in more than just words. Symbols **communicate experience** where words are often not adequate. Unlike signs, which are easy to create, we don't usually just decide that something will be a symbol; it has to work for many people and draw a response from them because of the meaning it holds. Also, for a symbol to have any effect, its meaning must be understood. There would be little point in giving a red rose to someone you loved if they did not understand what it stood for.

When faced with strong symbols, we discover new meanings in life. They give us fresh energy and make us more sensitive to what matters in life. Through them, we are able to express deep experiences like love, joy, peace, faith and trust. For example, the dictionary defines a flower as 'the coloured (not green) part of a plant'. But that definition is far from the mind of someone buying flowers as a gift. When used as a symbol, a flower has a deeper meaning.

Signs or Symbols?

Identify whether each of the following pictures is a sign or a symbol. In your Religion folder, write out what it is that they signify or symbolise.

This spiral pattern is one of the oldest symbols in Irish history. It symbolises eternity because, if there was enough space to keep drawing, it could go on for ever.

KNOW THE WAY

KNOW WHAT

1. Divide up into pairs and write down what you think a Christmas tree could symbolise for each of the following people:
   - a three-year-old child;
   - a person in hospital;
   - a couple spending their first Christmas together;
   - a young person working abroad who is missing her family but is unable to return home for Christmas;
   - an old man.
2. Why is it that a Christmas tree can symbolise different things for different people?

DIGGING DEEPER

1. Have a go at drawing a symbol for a) love and b) friendship.
2. How do your drawings communicate the experiences of love and friendship?
3. The crest for each family name is made up of symbols. See if you can draw your family's crest and explain the family history (the experience) that it communicates. (If you don't know what your family crest looks like, you could create one!)

Actions as Symbols

Our actions can also act as symbols. For example, at the end of a good performance, the people in the audience clap their hands, symbolising their approval. See if you can think of any other actions that act as symbols.

KNOW IT ALL

Copy the following exercise into your Religion folder and match the actions with their meaning. (Note: A symbol can have more than one meaning.)

A frown	Impatience
Slamming a door	Welcome
A kiss	Annoyance
Patting someone's back	Love
Shaking hands	Comfort
Tapping fingers	Anger

Sign: A word, drawing or action that makes us aware of something.

Symbol: A type of sign, but with a deeper meaning. A symbol is a visible sign of something invisible.

Communicating experience: Being put in touch with a source of meaning – often through symbols.

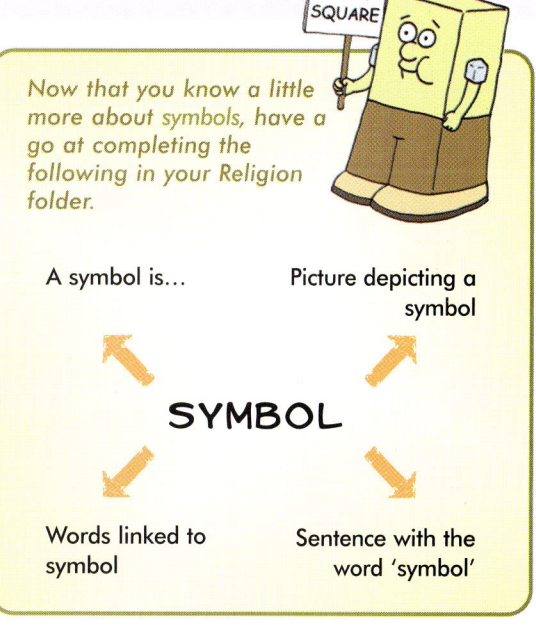

Now that you know a little more about *symbols*, have a go at completing the following in your Religion folder.

- A symbol is…
- Picture depicting a symbol
- Words linked to symbol
- Sentence with the word 'symbol'

SYMBOL

LESSON 101 Symbolism in Religious Life

GROUNDWORK
In this lesson we plan to:
- explore the purpose of symbols in religious life.

DIGGING DEEPER
What purpose do symbols have in my religion?

Key Concept
Symbol

The Use of Symbols in Religious Traditions

In the previous lesson, we explored what signs, symbols and symbolic acts mean in everyday life. **Symbols** and symbolic acts are also used within religious traditions. They help people to appreciate and recognise the depth of their faith because:

- they remind each religious tradition of their story (their religious history);
- they help each person to encounter the divine in a more meaningful way, e.g. they can act as aids to prayer or communication with the divine;
- they enable each person to overcome the limits of language;
- they bring about a change in the person who responds to them.

Let's look at some examples to illustrate these points.

Symbols and symbolic acts remind each religious tradition of their story.

Through the use of symbol, major events in the history and development of a religious tradition are recalled and celebrated.

Example A
At the Jewish Seder meal, a flat bread called *matzah* is eaten to recall how the Jewish people ate unleavened bread before leaving Egypt. It is also called the 'bread of freedom' because it symbolises their escape to freedom. Bitter herbs are served at the Seder meal, as a symbol of the bitterness of Egyptian slavery.

Example B
When a person is being welcomed into the Christian community through the sacrament of Baptism, they are anointed with oil of catechumens *before* they have been baptised, and with oil of chrism *after* they have been baptised. The oil of catechumens is a symbol of strength, while the oil of chrism is a symbol of the fact that the person has been specially chosen by God.

Symbols and symbolic acts help each person to encounter the divine in a more meaningful way.

Performing symbolic acts at the beginning of and during prayer enables the believer to leave the 'ordinary' space and move into the 'extra-ordinary' space, where there will be a more meaningful experience of the divine.

Example A
Every Muslim is expected to spray five times daily. Before prayer, they wash themselves in a procedure called *wudu*. This symbolic act is performed in order to cleanse the person from any wrongdoings and to help them concentrate on the prayers.

Example B
Before they begin to pray, Christians perform the symbolic act of blessing themselves. The sign of the cross calls upon the Trinity and brings the believer into a place where they are ready to encounter God through the words and actions of their prayers.

Symbols and symbolic acts enable each person to overcome the limits of language.
A gesture can say much more than words ever could. Symbols and symbolic acts can express what we cannot find words for. Symbolism allows the whole person to be involved in worship.

Example A
A newly baptised member of the Christian community of faith is presented with a lighted candle, symbolising the Risen Christ as the light and hope of the world. This symbol speaks more powerfully than any words ever could.

Example B
When the Jewish people partake in the Seder meal, it symbolises in a very powerful way their connection with their Jewish ancestors who escaped from slavery. It also helps the believers to enter completely into the Exodus experience, much more than just retelling the story could ever do.

Symbols and symbolic acts can bring about a change in the person who responds to them.
By responding to the symbols and symbolic acts used in the celebration of a special event or time of significance, the believers can leave the ordinary worries of daily life and experience the divine in a more powerful way.

Example A
When Christians gather to take part in the Good Friday services, they enter into the sorrow of the passion (suffering) and death of Jesus Christ. Through the use of symbol and symbolic action, Christians are transported to a different time and place, where they can encounter God in a meaningful way.

Example B
The final stage of *Hajj*, the Islamic pilgrimage to Mecca, takes place at Mina. There, the pilgrims throw stones at three stone pillars that represent Satan. This symbolic action recalls an occasion when Abraham was tempted by Satan three times and he rejected him three times. By entering into this symbolism, Muslims can encounter Allah in a more meaningful way.

KNOW HOW
Write a short essay on the use of symbols and symbolic acts in religious traditions.

3-2-1
1. Name and describe **three** symbols/symbolic acts from Judaism or Islam. What is their meaning?
2. Name and describe **two** symbols/symbolic acts from the Christian tradition. What is their meaning?
3. Name and describe **one** symbol/symbolic act that holds a deep meaning for you in your faith. Why does it hold a deep meaning for you?

LESSON 102 Icons

GROUNDWORK
In this Lesson we plan to:
- explore the 'icon' as a religious symbol.

DIGGING DEEPER
How does sacred art increase my faith?

Key Concepts
Icon/Symbol

What is an icon?

The word 'icon' is widely used in the world of computers. We are often directed to open a computer programme by clicking on its icon – a small image that appears on the screen. 'Icon' is the Greek word for 'image'. In the world of the sacred, an **icon** is a very precious religious image or painting.

Icons in the Eastern Orthodox Tradition

Orthodox Christians use icons of Jesus, Mary and the saints to help them to pray and become closer to God. These icons are painted on wood or created in mosaic with gold leaf.

The figures on an icon are deliberately painted out of perspective, and although they have a certain lifelike quality, they also have an 'other-worldly' look about them.

One important element of icons is the sense of non-movement that they portray. Every icon represents stillness and peace, and the suggestion that the figures painted are beyond change or decay.

'The Icon of the Trinity' by André Rublev

In pairs, look carefully at this icon and then answer the following questions on a sheet of paper.

1. Describe what you see in three sentences only.
2. Who do you think the people represent?
3. What colours are used in the icon?
4. Comment on the presence or absence of movement in the icon, and on the effect that this has on the viewer.
5. What do you think is the message in this icon?
6. Do you like this icon? Why?/Why not?

'The Icon of the Trinity' by André Rublev

It is said that an icon becomes a door that unites the visible with the invisible, the earthly with the heavenly. André Rublev, an artist monk from Russia, was inspired to paint this icon when he read Genesis 18:1-10.

The three figures in the painting represent the Father, the Son and the Holy Spirit. The colours are a little faded because this icon is approximately six hundred years old. Originally, it would have been very bright and vivid.

KNOW THE WAY

When we look at this, and indeed any icon, it is important to note that every single detail has a meaning and a purpose. The colours are deliberately chosen for their **symbolic** nature. For example, the colour blue symbolises heaven. The three figures in Rublev's icon are wearing blue to indicate that they are from heaven. Red is a symbol of royalty and it is also the colour of blood. The figure in the centre is wearing red and there is a chalice of blood on the table. This figure is associated with blood and royalty. Who do you think the central figure represents?

Gold is a symbol of holiness and of the power of God. All three figures are wearing some gold, suggesting that they each share in the power of God. The figure on the left is wearing the most gold and the other two figures are bowing towards him; this suggests that the figure on the left is God the Father. Who do you think the figure on the right represents?

As with all religious icons, there is a feeling of stillness and peace reflected in this icon of the Trinity. The empty space at the centre of the icon invites us in.

KNOWING ME KNOWING YOU
Visit your local library or use the internet to find out more about Rublev's icon of the Trinity. Try to find out what the following details in the icon represent: the building, the tree, the haloes, the mountain, the chalice of blood.

The Work of the Iconographer

Artists who paint icons are called iconographers. They live as monks, just like the Irish artists who designed the Book of Kells, and they look upon their task as a sacred one.

In the following interview, a young artist called Mimi talks to an iconographer.

Mimi: Good morning Petros, can you tell me why you decided to become an iconographer?

Petros: Good morning. Well, I was introduced to icon painting many years ago. It is very skilled work and it requires a lot of patience. People don't really decide to be iconographers – you are recognised as an icon painter only after prayer and meditation or if it is felt that you have a special gift. I myself am now teaching other monks in the icon tradition.

Mimi: What kind of preparations do you need to make before you begin your work?

Petros: Before I begin to create an icon, it is important that my attitude is right, so I pray and meditate in silence. I also prepare myself by fasting, by going to confession and by receiving communion. I choose the wood and the paint carefully and make sure that they are both blessed.

Mimi: Can you decide to paint any image you want?

Petros: No, an icon painter is not free to paint anything he likes. He must follow certain rules and traditions, unless it is revealed through prayer and meditation that the traditional pattern is to be changed.

Mimi: Could you briefly describe the methods you use when creating an icon?

Petros: There is a very special technique used in creating an icon. The icons are usually painted on wood in tempera. Tempera means colours that have been mixed with a natural emulsion, for example, egg yolk, or they can also be mixed with an artificial emulsion, such as oil. When I have finished painting an icon, it is blessed with holy water, and in this way the icon becomes more than just a painting.

Mimi: Why are icons used in Orthodox worship?

Petros: Icons are used in Orthodox worship to stimulate the imagination and to help people to move beyond the humdrum of everyday life and focus their minds on God. This is why icons are often referred to as 'doors to heaven'.

TAKE FIVE

1. What is a religious icon?
2. What do you call the artists who create icons?
3. What preparations are done before an icon is painted?
4. What makes an icon different to another piece of art?
5. Why are icons used during worship in Eastern Orthodox churches?

DIGGING DEEPER

1. Icons are described as 'doors that unite the visible with the invisible, the earthly with the heavenly'. What do you think this means for the members of the Orthodox churches?
2. What kind of sacred art is used in your religion?
3. How does sacred art help believers to become closer to a) the divine and b) their religious story?
4. Christians use statues and stained-glass windows to help them to become united with the story of their faith. How do you think they do this?
5. What does the sacred art and the stained-glass windows in your local church symbolise?

KNOWING ME KNOWING YOU

Visit this website to find out lots more about icons:
http://aggreen.net/iconography/icons.html

Icon: Picture with a religious content and meaning, used in the worship of the Orthodox Church.

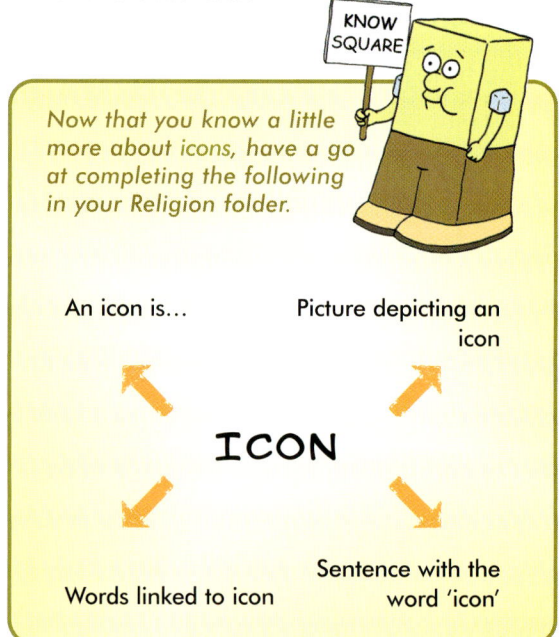

Now that you know a little more about icons, have a go at completing the following in your Religion folder.

KNOW THE WAY

LESSON 103 Encountering Religious Symbols

GROUNDWORK
In this lesson we plan to:
- encounter some religious symbols and their meanings.

DIGGING DEEPER
Where do we encounter religious symbols and what do they mean?

Key Concepts
Identity/Symbol

Introductory Activity: Symbols to Identify!
- Divide into groups of four.
- Each group must decide on a secret **identity**, e.g. detectives, goths, nurses, sports team, etc.
- Create two symbols (not signs) that will point to the identity of your group.
- Each group must present their symbols while the other groups quietly work out their identity. The winner is the group that works out the most identities!

When a **symbol** is used to represent a person, a group or a thing, it can help us to identify and recognise that person, group or thing. The symbols that are used to represent the different religions help us to identify and recognise those religions.

Let's take a look at the symbols that help us to build up the identity of each of the five major world religions.

Christianity – The Crucifix
The crucifix is an important symbol of faith, hope and love for all followers of Jesus Christ. It symbolises their faith in the Trinity: God the Father, God the Son and God the Holy Spirit. It symbolises the hope that life can be lived as Jesus taught, and it symbolises the love that Jesus showed for all by giving up his life.

Judaism – The Menorah
The Menorah is a very old symbol of Judaism, which was originally used in the Temple in Jerusalem. There is one in every synagogue throughout the world today. It is a seven-branched candlestick. The central branch represents the Sabbath, the day God rested after creating the world.

369

Islam – The Star and Crescent Moon
The five points of the star symbolise the five pillars of Islam. The moon and the stars remind Muslims of God, the creator of everything. Muslims use the moon to calculate the months of the year. This symbol on a country's flag usually indicates that it is a Muslim state.

Hinduism – The Symbol of 'Om'
This symbol is the written form of the sacred sound 'Om'. Om is a Hindu word used at the beginning of prayer and meditation. For followers of Hinduism, Om is a sacred syllable and it represents Brahma, an important Hindu God.

Buddhism – The Wheel
The wheel is the oldest of Buddhist symbols. The eight spokes represent the Eightfold Path to enlightenment. The circular shape represents the continuous circle of life and death.

5-4-3-2-1
1. Name **five** symbols associated with the five major world religions.
2. Name **four** religions that are identified by a specific symbol.
3. What are the symbols of the **three** monotheistic religions?
4. Have a go at drawing **two** symbols from the religious traditions.
5. Write **one** page entitled 'The symbols that identify each of the major world religions'.

DIGGING DEEPER
1. Why do you think each world religion has its own symbol to identify it?
2. What symbol did St Patrick use to explain the Trinity to the early Christian communities in Ireland?
3. What other Christian symbols do you know of? Draw one of them and explain what it symbolises.
4. Name and describe a symbol from two other faiths. Have a go at drawing them and explain what they symbolise.

 Identity: The individual characteristics that define a person or thing, or by which a person or thing can be recognised.

See page 497 for past exam questions on this topic.

LESSON 104 Sacraments

GROUNDWORK
In this lesson we plan to:
- explore the Christian understanding of sacrament.

DIGGING DEEPER
What does the celebration of the sacraments mean for Christians?

Key Concepts
Sacrament/Symbol/Identity

Introductory Activity
In pairs, draw a spider diagram with the word 'sacrament' in the centre. At the bottom of each 'leg', write a word that you associate with 'sacrament'. Share your words in class.

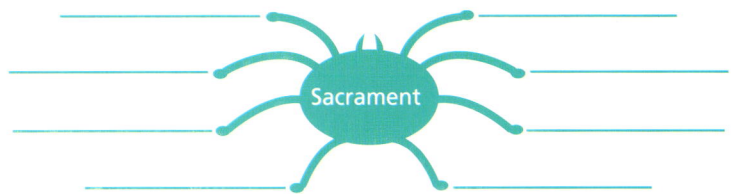

The Christian Understanding of Sacrament
Christians use the word 'grace' to describe God's loving presence in the world. A **sacrament** is a visible and effective sign of God's grace. Sacraments bring about what they signify. The celebration of the sacraments helps Christians to be open to the grace, or presence, of God in their lives. The sacraments remind them of the invitation from Jesus to enter into the Kingdom of God, because each of the sacraments is directly linked to the words and deeds of Jesus during his public ministry.

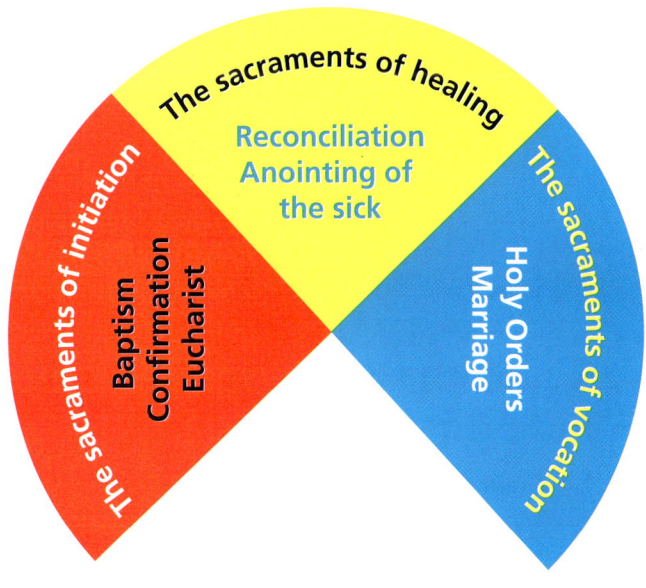

The Sacraments are Linked to Jesus

Each sacrament is linked to Jesus in a very special way. Christians believe that the sacraments were established or started by Jesus Christ, who still acts through the sacraments to pour out the Holy Spirit on the Church today.

Jesus called his disciples to follow him. The sacraments of initiation enable people to follow that same call. Through these sacraments, Christ draws all people to become members of the Church, he pours the Holy Spirit into their hearts and he comes to each person in the Eucharist.

Jesus healed and forgave people. In the sacrament of Reconciliation, he reconciles people with himself and with one another, and in the sacrament of the Anointing of the Sick he gives healing of body and soul.

Just as Jesus chose certain people for special tasks and ministries when he was on earth, he continues to call people. Some people are called to priestly ministry in the sacrament of Holy Orders, while others celebrate marriage in the sacrament of Marriage, and through living as Jesus asked us to they build up the Church.

KNOW WHAT
1. Why are the sacraments known as 'a visible sign of an invisible gift from God'?
2. How are the sacraments linked to Jesus?
3. Why are the sacraments grouped into three different categories?

DIGGING DEEPER
1. Have you celebrated any Christian sacraments? Name and describe the sacraments you have celebrated.
2. 'The sacraments are linked to Jesus.' What does this mean for Christian faith?

The Sacraments and the Christian Communities

Christianity is divided into three main groups:

- the Catholic Church
- the Orthodox churches
- the Protestant churches

The Catholic Church and the Orthodox churches teach that there are seven sacraments, while the Protestant churches believe that there are only two – Baptism and Eucharist (The Lord's Supper).

The Sacrament of Baptism – A Shared Identity

Christians have a shared **identity** because of their Baptism. All of the Christian churches and denominations celebrate the sacrament of Baptism. When babies are born into the Christian community, they receive their identity as members of that community through their Baptism. Baptism is one of the sacraments of initiation. At Baptism, Christians become followers of Jesus and, therefore, join the Body of Christ on earth. It is through the sacrament of Baptism that all Christians are called to serve God and others. It is also through the sacrament of Baptism that Christians become connected as sisters and brothers to every other member of the Christian community.

The churches of the Orthodox tradition celebrate the sacraments of initiation in one ceremony, where Baptism is followed directly by Confirmation and then Eucharist. These sacraments are celebrated with babies when they are still only days old – they are given communion from the chalice on a spoon.

KNOW IT ALL

Using this chart, find two similarities and two differences in the celebration of the sacraments in the different Christian churches. Discuss your answers in class.

Catholic Church	Orthodox Churches	Protestant Churches
Baptism	Baptism ⎫	Baptism
Holy Communion	Confirmation ⎬	The Lord's Supper
Confirmation	Eucharist ⎭	
Reconciliation	Reconciliation	
Anointing of the Sick	Anointing of the Sick	
Marriage	Marriage	
Holy Orders	Holy Orders	

3-2-1

1. Name the **three** sacraments of initiation.
2. Name **two** Christian churches that celebrate the sacrament of Baptism.
3. Christians have a shared identity because of their Baptism. Write **one** paragraph to explain this.

The Sacrament of the Eucharist/The Lord's Supper

The Catholic Church teaches that the bread and wine become wholly and completely the body and blood of Christ. This happens at Mass during the Eucharistic Prayer. The priest calls on the Holy Spirit to come upon the gifts of bread and wine at the Consecration. So when Catholics receive communion, they believe that they are receiving the actual body and blood of Christ under the appearances of bread and wine. Since there is no longer bread and wine but the body and blood of Christ, anything that is not consumed during the celebration is consumed afterwards, or else placed in the tabernacle.

The Protestant churches differ from the Catholic Church in their understanding of Eucharist. They call this celebration the 'Lord's Supper'. Generally, they do not celebrate it every Sunday, although this differs from church to church. Martin Luther taught that Christ is present in, with and under the signs of bread and wine. Therefore, when most Protestants receive communion, they believe that they are receiving the body and blood of Christ as well as bread and wine.

TAKE FIVE

1. Why is Jesus present in a special way during the sacraments?
2. How many sacraments are celebrated by the Catholic Church?
3. How many sacraments are celebrated by the Protestant churches?
4. Describe a major difference between the teaching on the sacrament of the Eucharist in the Catholic Church and in the Protestant churches.
5. Which church celebrates the sacraments of initiation during the same ceremony? At what age does this ceremony take place?

DIGGING DEEPER

The sacrament of the Eucharist nourishes and strengthens Christian faith. How does it do this?

Sacrament: A symbol of God's grace or presence, through which believers can communicate with God.

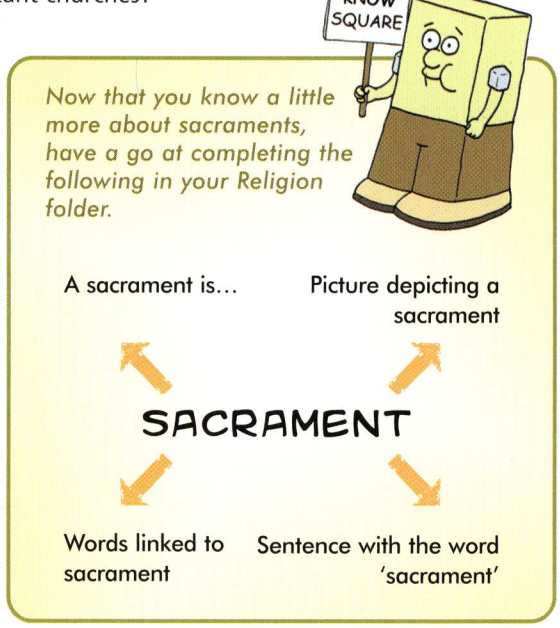

Now that you know a little more about sacraments, have a go at completing the following in your Religion folder.

A sacrament is…   Picture depicting a sacrament

SACRAMENT

Words linked to sacrament   Sentence with the word 'sacrament'

KNOW THE WAY

374

LESSON 105 The Seven Sacraments of the Catholic Church

GROUNDWORK
In this lesson we plan to:
- explore the understandings of sacrament specific to the Catholic Church.

DIGGING DEEPER
How is the faith of Catholics strengthened by the different understandings of sacrament?

Key Concept
Sacrament

Catholics use the word **sacrament** in three ways: they celebrate the seven sacraments during special times of significance and they also understand Jesus as sacrament and the Church as sacrament.

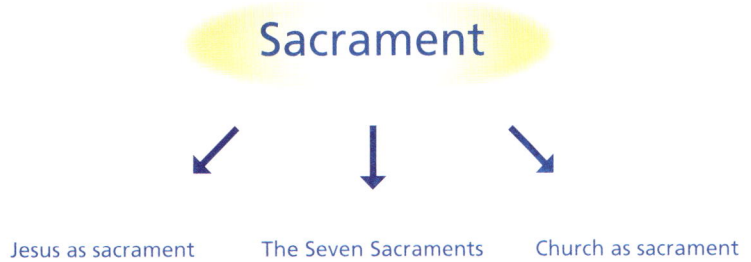

Jesus as Sacrament
Catholics believe that Jesus is the main 'sacrament' because, through the person of Jesus, God came among us. It is through Jesus that Christians come to know the One whom Jesus called 'Abba' or 'Father'. Jesus said: 'I am the way, and the truth, and the life. No one comes to the Father except through me. If you know me, you will know my Father also' (John 14:6).

The Catholic Church as Sacrament
Catholics believe that the Church that comes from Christ is also like a sacrament because it brings about unity between God and humanity. They believe that the Risen Jesus continues to be present with the Church – through the power of the Holy Spirit – particularly when the Church celebrates the seven sacraments.

The Seven Sacraments
The seven sacraments connect Catholics with the ministry of Jesus, with his words and deeds, whilst also connecting them with God today.

The Seven Sacraments

	Connect Christians with the Ministry of Jesus	Connect Christians with God today
Baptism	The gospels tell us that when Jesus was baptised, God said, 'This is my beloved Son.'	God has given life to all. At Baptism, Christians celebrate the forgiveness of sin and the wonderful gift of new life in Christ.
Reconciliation	Jesus preached and spoke powerfully of God's unconditional love and forgiveness. He himself forgave sins.	In the sacrament of Reconciliation, Catholics continue to share in God's loving forgiveness and receive God's mercy.
Eucharist	When Jesus celebrated the Last Supper with his disciples, he said: 'Do this in memory of me.'	At Mass today, the Risen Jesus is present to help those who celebrate the sacrament of the Eucharist to love God and others. He is present in the Eucharist, the sacrament of unity.
Confirmation	On Pentecost Day, the Holy Spirit was given to the apostles and disciples in the Upper Room in Jerusalem.	This same Holy Spirit is given to all Christians at Baptism and again at Confirmation to enable them to be the Body of Christ in our world and to proclaim Christ to the world in word and deed.
Marriage	Jesus supported the couple getting married at Cana as they took on their new commitment.	Through the sacrament of Marriage, couples celebrate the presence of the Risen Jesus with them as they pledge their love and commitment towards each other.
Holy Orders	Jesus chose apostles from among his disciples. They became the first leaders of the Church.	In the sacrament of Holy Orders today, members of the Church are ordained to continue Christ's ministry and leadership.
Anointing of the Sick	The gospels tell us of how Jesus brought healing and hope to the most difficult of human situations. At that time, those who were ill were often treated badly by others. Jesus showed the unconditional love and compassion of God through his healing.	When the sacrament of Anointing of the Sick is celebrated today, Catholics are reminded of the healing love and endless compassion of God.

KNOW WHAT

1. In your own words, explain how three of the sacraments connect Catholics with the ministry of Jesus.
2. In your own words, explain how three of the sacraments connect Catholics with God today.

DIGGING DEEPER

1. What is unique about the Catholic understanding of the word 'sacrament'?
2. How do you think the different understandings of the word sacrament strengthen the faith of Catholics?
3. Did you celebrate your first Holy Communion? What can you remember about the day? What did you learn about the sacrament of the Eucharist in preparation for the day?

KNOWING ME KNOWING YOU

Your teacher may bring your class to participate in or observe Mass in a local Catholic church.

Perhaps you could attend this Mass in a special way by making every effort to participate in it or observe it fully. What would help you to do this? Share your ideas with the class.

KNOW IT ALL

Quiz on the Sacraments

Ask for a volunteer to be Quizmaster and then divide into groups of three for this quiz! The marks to be allocated are given in brackets.

1. Name the seven sacraments in the Catholic tradition. (7)
2. How many sacraments are celebrated in the Orthodox churches? (4)
3. This sacrament involves a lifetime commitment between a man and a woman. (2)
4. What are the two sacraments celebrated in the Protestant churches? (4)
5. Which sacrament did Jesus receive? (2)
6. Which sacrament in the Catholic Church calls men and women to make a commitment to a lifetime of ministry? (2)
7. Which sacrament is celebrated on an ongoing basis by Christians? (2)
8. Name one sacrament that calls on the Holy Spirit for strength and guidance. (2)
9. Which sacraments are linked to the public ministry of Jesus? (7)

(Total marks: 32)

LESSON 106 The Celebration of the Eucharist in two Christian Traditions

GROUNDWORK
In this lesson we plan to:
- explore the sacrament of the Eucharist as it is celebrated in two Christian traditions.

DIGGING DEEPER
Why is the celebration of the Eucharist at the heart of Christian faith?

Key Concepts
Sacrament/Symbol

The Celebration of the Eucharist

The celebration of the Eucharist is at the heart of Christian faith. This means that it is *the* most special way in which Christians celebrate God's presence in their lives.

The word 'eucharist' comes from the Greek word *eucharistia*, meaning 'thanksgiving'. Sharing a meal is a wonderful way of showing thanks for something; for example, we have celebratory meals in thanksgiving for the gift of our life and the passing of the years on our birthday. (We have explored Eucharist and table-fellowship in Section B.)

All members of the Christian community are united with Christians in every other country in the world when they share the Eucharist.

The Celebration of the Eucharist in the Catholic Tradition

Catholics use the term 'Mass' to describe the celebration of the Eucharist. This name comes from the Latin word *missio*, meaning 'the sending'. In the past, the Mass was said in Latin and the final words spoken by the priest were 'Ite missa est', meaning 'Go, you are sent'.

Introductory Rite
The Mass begins with the introductory rite. The most important aspect of the introductory rite is that those present *gather* together as a community. Jesus said: 'Where two or three are gathered in my name, there I will be in the midst of them.'

Liturgy of the Word
This is the part of the Mass during which passages are read from the Bible and the priest gives a talk, or homily. Catholics believe that God speaks through the scriptures, so the

Liturgy of the Word is a very important part of the Mass. When listening to the scriptures, Catholics are listening to the stories that have brought them together and have shaped their community of faith. This follows the tradition in the Jewish synagogues, where passages from the Law and the Prophets are read each Sabbath.

During the homily, the priest explains important points raised by the scriptures and helps those present to connect the scriptures to their own lives.

By saying together the 'Creed' (or the 'Profession of Faith'), Catholics remember that they are one people who share one faith.

Liturgy of the Eucharist

At the beginning of the Liturgy of the Eucharist, the gifts of bread and wine are brought to the altar. These are key **symbols** in the Catholic tradition. This part of the celebration is called the Presentation of the Gifts.

When Jesus celebrated the Passover with his disciples at the Last Supper, he brought a new meaning to this very special meal. Through the Eucharist, Catholics take part in the paschal mystery (i.e. the death and resurrection of Jesus) and offer their thanks for all that God does for them in their lives.

A central part of the Liturgy of the Eucharist is the Eucharistic Prayer. It offers praise and thanks for God's mighty deeds. It also offers praise and thanks to God for Jesus Christ. This prayer is said by the priest on behalf of the whole Church. He calls the Holy Spirit to come upon the gifts of bread and wine so that they may become the body and blood of Jesus Christ. The Lord Jesus is present in a special way after the *Consecration*, when the bread is changed into the body of Christ and the wine is changed into the blood of Christ.

The priest also calls the Holy Spirit to come upon the people so that their lives, too, may be changed. Towards the end of the Eucharistic Prayer, Catholics remember all members of the Church, both living and dead. The Prayer concludes with the Great Amen, which is proclaimed by all the people.

Rite of Communion

The Rite of Communion begins after the Eucharistic Prayer. The 'Our Father' is said and the sign of peace is exchanged. The sign of peace is a symbolic action, whereby each person shakes hands or exchanges a blessing with the people around them, as a symbol of unity within the faith community. After the sign of peace, Holy Communion is distributed. The rite concludes with the 'Prayer after Communion'.

When Catholics receive the communion host, they believe that Jesus truly comes to them – really and substantially – under the appearances of bread and wine. Catholics believe that, through the Eucharist, they receive the gift of the living Jesus, who nourishes and strengthens their faith. The Eucharist is considered so important that Catholics have an obligation to receive it at least once a year and to live out this gift in their daily lives.

Concluding Rite

As they receive their final blessing and leave the church, Catholics bring with them, in their hearts, the peace and justice of Jesus Christ, the strength of the Holy Spirit and the love of God the Father.

KNOW IT ALL

Copy these sentences into your Religion folder and complete them.

1. The celebration of the Eucharist is at the heart of…
2. During the celebration of the Eucharist, all Christians across the world are…
3. The word 'Mass' comes from a Latin word meaning…
4. During the Introductory Rite…
5. During the Liturgy of the Word…
6. During the homily…
7. During the Liturgy of the Eucharist…
8. During the Rite of Communion…
9. During the Concluding Rite…

Important Aspects of the Eucharist

The *Catechism of the Catholic Church* helps Catholics to understand important parts of their faith. It reminds them of three important aspects of the Eucharist: thanksgiving, memorial and presence.

Thanksgiving

Catholics join with Jesus in giving thanks and praise to God for the wonder of creation and the great things that have been done for them. By celebrating the Eucharist, Catholics worship God; this means that they communicate with God in a deep and respectful way, giving thanks for the hope and forgiveness that have been shown to them through Jesus.

Memorial

Jesus' death on the Cross was a sacrifice because he gave his life for all. The Eucharist (Mass) is a sacrifice because it makes present the sacrifice of Jesus on the Cross. Christ's sacrifice present on the altar makes it possible for all generations of Christians to be united with his offering. (See *Catechism of the Catholic Church*, 1368.)

Presence

At Mass, Jesus is present in many ways:
- He is present where people are gathered in his name. Jesus told his disciples that whenever two or three are gathered in his name, he is with them.
- He is present when sacred scripture, the Word of God, is read. When people hear the gospels being read, they are experiencing Jesus with them today.
- He is present through the priest. Jesus acts through the priest at Mass. The priest reads the words of Jesus from the gospels and he repeats the words of Jesus during the Consecration.
- After the Consecration, the Risen Jesus is present under the appearances of bread and wine. This is why the Eucharist is also called the 'Blessed Sacrament'. Jesus invites everyone to his table. The Eucharist nourishes (feeds and strengthens) the people at Mass to live as disciples of Jesus.

DIGGING DEEPER

1. Why do you think the Eucharist is at the heart of Christian faith?
2. How can the celebration of the Eucharist be explained under the three headings of thanksgiving, memorial and presence?
3. What are the four ways in which Jesus Christ is present at Mass?
4. What does the Catholic understanding of the 'real presence' of Jesus Christ under the appearances of bread and wine say about the Catholic faith?
5. If you have received Holy Communion, explain how it nourishes and strengthens your faith.

The Celebration of the Eucharist in the Orthodox Tradition

The Orthodox churches call their Sunday Mass the Divine Liturgy. As with the Catholic Church, it is the main act of worship of the Orthodox churches.

The Divine Liturgy contains two parts. The first part is the Liturgy of the Catechumens (sometimes called the Liturgy of the Word). It is during this part of the liturgy that the Scriptures are read.

The second part of the Divine Liturgy is called the Liturgy of the Faithful (sometimes called the Liturgy of the Eucharist). It is at this stage of the service that the gifts of bread and wine are offered and consecrated. Like the Catholic Church, the Orthodox churches teach that the gifts truly become the body and blood of Jesus Christ.

```
An E-mail from Cyprus

Hi there,
    I'm on holiday with the folks in Cyprus! Just waiting for them to get ready for dinner,
    so I have time to email you about last Sunday's visit to an Orthodox church. They call
    their Sunday service the Divine Liturgy. It really was a fascinating experience.
    The first part focused mainly around the Bible. The centre doors of the icon screen
    opened and there was a big procession with candles and lots of incense. The priest
    carried the book of readings, held up high. After a first reading and a gospel reading,
    the priest spoke for a bit. Then he went back in behind the screen and the doors were
    closed.
    After a short while, the doors opened again and there was another procession. That was
    the start of the second part of the Divine Liturgy, which focuses on the Eucharist. The
    priest carried the bread and wine around the church. The people bowed so low, I thought
    they'd touch the ground. That's reverence! Then the priest went back through the doors
    to the holy table (the altar) and everyone said the Creed. My friend Irene told me that
    the priest then said a special prayer of thanks to God. During it, he used the words
    that Jesus used at the Last Supper. He took the bread and wine and offered them to God.
    He prayed that the Holy Spirit would change them into the body and blood of Christ. Then
    there was a short silence. The choir sang and the bells rang. I felt all tingly.
    After the Lord's Prayer, the people go to receive Communion from the priest. They
    receive Communion in both forms; the priest uses a special spoon to give them Communion
    from the chalice.
    After the blessing at the end, I was going to leave. But then I noticed that everyone
    lined up to kiss the cross that the priest was holding. We also got some cake bread. It
    wasn't Holy Communion; it was just a way of showing hospitality for all.
    Anyway, I'll show you the photographs I took when I get back. I hope the dog is
    behaving. Talk to you soon.
    Mary Kate
```

5-4-3-2-1

1. Name **five** parts of the sacrament of the Eucharist as it is celebrated in the Catholic Church.
2. Name **four** parts of the celebration of the sacrament of the Eucharist in the Orthodox Church.
3. Name **three** similarities between the celebration of the Eucharist in the Catholic tradition and in the Orthodox tradition.
4. Name **two** differences between the celebration of the Eucharist in the Catholic tradition and in the Orthodox tradition.
5. Write **one** page describing the understanding of sacrament in two Christian traditions.

Prayer

LESSON 107 Communication with God

GROUNDWORK
In this lesson we plan to:
- explore the idea of prayer as a need to communicate with God.

DIGGING DEEPER
How important is prayer in my life?

Key Concept
Communication with God

'For prayer is nothing else than being on terms of friendship with God.'

(Saint Teresa of Avila)

Introductory Activity: Friendship

To begin our lessons on prayer, let's first focus on friendships/relationships.

Take ten minutes to complete this task:
- Think of the names of two friends.
- Copy this chart into your Religion folder and fill it in.

Name of Friend	How long have we been friends?	How often do we meet?	How do we communicate with each other?	One word to describe this friend is...	A symbol of our friendship is...

Together, discuss your answers to the questions on the chart.

Communication

Showing an interest in people and communicating with them is a good way of opening up new relationships. Friendships are about making time for the 'other' in your life. Communication is a key ingredient in any relationship. It is a two-way process, involving the giving and receiving of messages in order to communicate experiences, thoughts and feelings. If for any reason the communication breaks down, so does the relationship.

DIGGING DEEPER
Try to think of an example where communication had broken down but was then restored.

1. What happened?
2. Why did it happen?
3. How was communication restored?

Prayer – Communication with God

Prayer is a two-way process of communication between the pray-er and God. God is no longer in the third person, but is now addressed directly. This is a key characteristic of prayer. Prayer is not talking *about* God, prayer is talking *to* God. In other words, prayer is **communication with God**.

'Say a Little Prayer'

Have a look at the prayers below and see if you can describe the context of each prayer, i.e. why it is being prayed. Discuss your suggestions in class.

- 'Please God, let me win!'
- 'I'll pray for you.'
- 'God bless!'
- 'Remember me in your prayers.'

- 'Thank God for that!'
- 'God help them.'
- 'I'll light a candle for you.'

Whether it is on the radio or at the dentist, in the exam hall or at the races, we hear prayers like these being prayed every day. People the world over feel the need to communicate with God, either to express their thanks or to look for guidance, strength and protection.

Two Christian examples of this:

- The *Glenstal Book of Prayer*, published in 2001, was a phenomenal success. This prayer book, described as a 'rich resource for the dark, mysterious but exciting journey that is prayer', was inspired by the Benedictine and Celtic traditions, and compiled by the monks of Glenstal Abbey in Limerick.
- The website www.*sacredspace.ie* was created by the Irish Jesuits in 1999. It guides people through a five- to ten-minute prayer session that focuses on a short scripture passage chosen for the day. Since its launch, it has had over twenty million hits.

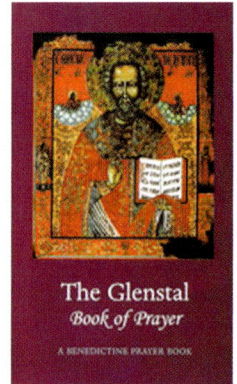

In his book *When Bad Things Happen to Good People,* Harold Kushner writes:

> *Prayer, when it is offered in the right way, redeems people from isolation. It assures them that they need not feel alone and abandoned. It lets them know that they are part of a greater reality, with more depth, more hope, more courage, and more of a future than any individual could have by himself.*

This is a good interpretation of the meaning of prayer, because the word 'prayer' literally means 'to request' or 'to ask for something'.

KNOW WHAT
1. What does 'communication with God' mean?
2. How do people communicate with God?

DIGGING DEEPER
1. Why and how often do you think people feel the need to communicate with God?
2. Do you know someone who prays regularly? Why do you think they do this?
3. How important is prayer in your life? Describe your experience of prayer.

The Importance of Prayer in Religious Traditions

Prayer strengthens people's awareness of God in their lives. We know that all the major world religions communicate with the divine through prayer. In Section B, we learned of how Jesus taught people to pray. In Section C, we explored the Shema prayer and the prayer life of the Jewish people. We also explored the practice of prayer in the Islamic faith.

Let's look at some of the prayers in the five major world religions:

The first line of the Jewish Shema prayer
Hear, O Israel: the Lord our God, the Lord is one.
Blessed be the name of the glory of His kingdom for ever and ever.

You shall love the Lord your God with all your heart, with all your soul and with all your might.

The Lord's prayer from the Christian tradition
Our Father who art in heaven,
Hallowed be thy name.
Thy kingdom come,
Thy will be done
On earth as it is in heaven.
Give us this day our daily bread
And forgive us our trespasses
As we forgive those who trespass against us.
And lead us not into temptation
But deliver us from evil. Amen.

An Islamic prayer
Praise be to Allah, The Cherisher and Sustainer of the World; Most Gracious, Most Merciful; Master of the Day of Judgement. Thee do we worship, and Thine aid we seek. Show us the straight way, the way of those on whom Thou hast bestowed Thy Grace, Those whose (portion) is not wrath, And who go not astray.

A Hindu meditation
The syllable Om is the call to knowledge.
We sing the praises of this syllable,
which is the key to every kind of knowledge.

A traditional Buddhist blessing and healing chant
Just as the soft rains fill the streams,
pour into the rivers and join together in the oceans,
so may the power of every moment of your goodness
flow forth to awaken and heal all beings,
those here now, those gone before, those yet to come.

KNOW WHAT
1. What do these prayers tell us about the place of prayer in these religious traditions?
2. Name one thing that strikes you about these prayers. Discuss your answer with your classmates.

KNOWING ME KNOWING YOU
Divide your class into five groups. Each group chooses a different religious tradition.

Research the place of prayer in your chosen religious tradition using your local library or the internet. Present your findings to the class.

 **Communication with God:** Sharing one's thoughts and feelings with God.

LESSON 108 The Nature and Function of Prayer

GROUNDWORK
In this lesson we plan to:
- differentiate between the different types of prayer.

DIGGING DEEPER
Why do people pray?

 **Key Concepts**
Praise and thanksgiving/Petition/Penitence

'The greatest thing anyone can do for God and others is pray. It is not the only thing; but it is the chief thing. The great people of earth today are the people who pray. I do not mean those who talk about prayer, nor those who say they believe in prayer; nor yet those who can explain about prayer; but I mean those people who take time to pray.' (S.D. Gordon)

Why do people pray?

When six teenagers were asked why they pray, they gave the following answers:

'I might just ask God for help or say thanks for something. I often tell God I am sorry for doing something wrong, like when I feel really bad and I know it's my own fault.' (Paula, 14)

'I don't really pray that much. Well, I do talk to God, asking for help and stuff, and I did thank God when my Nan got better, so I suppose I use my own words when I talk to God – is that prayer?' (Jamie, 15)

'I pray a good bit. I like to talk to God 'cos I think it makes me feel calm and kind of peaceful. I know that if I'm worried about something or before an exam I always pray. At home they pray a lot and I suppose I'm just used to it.' (Rob, 14)

'I pray when I'm skating or on a really sunny day. I pray because I feel happy and I thank God for all the good things in my life. I'm not talking about material wealth. I just have a happy life and I reckon it's worth saying thanks for that.' (Holly, 13)

'I feel a bit guilty because I only pray when things go wrong. This is a bit two-faced of me I suppose, but when things get tough I know I can always turn to God.' (John, 13)

'I pray when I am happy and I pray when I am sad. I try to remember to say a prayer in the good times as well as the bad.' (Steve, 14)

KNOW WHAT
1. What is the difference between Holly's attitude to prayer and John's attitude to it?
2. How does Steve view prayer?
3. What do you think of Paula's approach to prayer?
4. There are four different types of prayer mentioned above. Can you identify them?

DIGGING DEEPER
1. If you were to answer the same question, what would your answer be?
2. Which of the above answers would be most like your answer?
3. How does prayer strengthen your faith?

The Nature and Function of Prayer in the Christian Tradition

Christians divide prayer into four separate types: prayers of **praise**, **thanksgiving**, **petition** and **penitence**.

Praise
Christians praise God through prayer. Catholics praise God especially at the Sunday Mass.

> Jesus prayed prayers of praise and thanksgiving: 'At the same hour Jesus rejoiced in the Holy Spirit and said, "I thank you, Father, Lord of heaven and earth"' (Luke 10:21).

Thanksgiving
To thank God for the blessings received and for the happiness life can bring is another form of Christian prayer.

> Jesus prayed: 'I thank you, Father, Lord of heaven and earth, because you have hidden these things from the wise and the intelligent and have revealed them to infants' (Matthew 11:25).

Petition
'Petition' means to ask for something, literally to *request* help. Christians ask God to help them with problems; for example, to give them the confidence for an exam or a job interview, to give them strength to recover from an illness, and so on. Prayers of petition are also said during the celebration of the Eucharist, for people in need all over the world.

> Jesus prayed prayers of petition. When he was in the garden of Gethsemane, he asked God to help him: 'And going a little farther, he threw himself on the ground and prayed, "My Father, if it is possible, let this cup pass from me; yet not what I want but what you want"' (Matthew 26:39).

Penitence
Penitence is about saying sorry. Christians say sorry for the times they have hurt others or made the wrong choices. Before asking for forgiveness they must realise the wrongdoing and be prepared to make amends.

Jesus told this parable about penitence: 'Two men went up to the temple to pray, one a Pharisee and the other a tax collector. The Pharisee, standing by himself, was praying thus, "God, I thank you that I am not like the other people: thieves, rogues, adulterers, or even like this tax collector. I fast twice a week; I give a tenth of all my income." But the tax collector, standing far off, would not even look up to heaven, but was beating his breast and saying, "God, be merciful to me, a sinner!" I tell you, this man went down to his home justified rather than the other; for all who exalt themselves will be humbled, but all who humble themselves will be exalted.' (Luke 18:10-14)

KNOW WHAT

How would you describe the four types of prayer to children in a Confirmation class?

DIGGING DEEPER

1. The four types of prayer outlined above are present in the Lord's Prayer, which is also known as the 'Our Father'. See if you can work out where there is an example of each in this prayer.
2. Which of the four prayer types do you think people pray the most often/the least often? Give reasons for your answers.
3. Which of the four prayer types do you think Christians should say more often? Give reasons for your choice.

> **Praise and Thanksgiving:** To express approval of a person or thing; to express gratitude for a favour, kindness or mercy.
>
> **Petition:** A request/prayer that asks for a particular help or result.
>
> **Penitence:** Being sorry for past sins or failures.

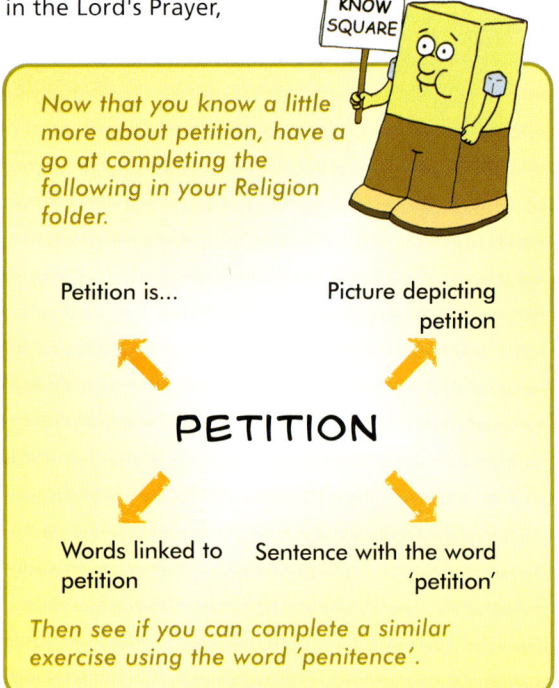

Now that you know a little more about petition, have a go at completing the following in your Religion folder.

Petition is...   Picture depicting petition

PETITION

Words linked to petition   Sentence with the word 'petition'

Then see if you can complete a similar exercise using the word 'penitence'.

KNOW THE WAY

LESSON 109 Vocal Prayer

GROUNDWORK
In this lesson we plan to:
- explore some of the different ways in which people pray.

DIGGING DEEPER
How do people pray?

 **Key Concepts**
Personal Prayer/Communal prayer

Prayer is a form of communication with God. In the Christian tradition, there are three main expressions of prayer: vocal, meditative and contemplative. Let's take a look now at vocal prayer.

Vocal Prayer

Praying vocally means using words to pray. We can pray vocally alone or with others. When Christians pray, they are following in the footsteps of their founder, Jesus Christ. The gospels tell us that prayer had a central role in the life of Jesus.

People sometimes pray when they are alone; this is called **personal prayer.** Vocal personal prayer can be very powerful, especially if the pray-er uses their own words to express their feelings. Personal prayer can take place anywhere; people can pray alone when they are walking to school, driving to work, before an exam, before or after a meal, etc. Personal prayer can often be a spontaneous prayer from the heart; for example, to give thanks.

Jesus regularly withdrew to deserted places to pray:

> 'In the morning, while it was still very dark, he got up and went out to a deserted place, and there he prayed.' (Mark 1:35)

> 'After saying farewell to them, he went up on the mountain to pray.' (Mark 6:46)

Another type of vocal prayer is **communal prayer**. This type of prayer takes place when members of any religious tradition gather as a faith community. Communal prayer happens most often when people gather for acts of worship in their place of worship; for example, Muslims in a mosque, Jews in a synagogue, Christians in a church.

Jesus celebrated the Sabbath day with his community of faith: 'When he came to Nazareth, where he had been brought up, he went to the synagogue on the Sabbath day, as was his custom.' (Luke 4:16)

Muslims at prayer

Many of the prayers of the Christian community have been passed down through several generations. Prayers like the 'Our Father', the 'Hail Mary', the 'Glory be to the Father' and the 'Angelus' give Christians a common language with which to talk to God.

TAKE FIVE
Complete these sentences in your Religion folder.

1. Vocal prayer means...
2. Personal vocal prayer is...
3. An example of personal prayer is...
4. Communal prayer is...
5. An example of communal prayer is...

DIGGING DEEPER
You will need a Bible for this exercise.
There are many references to the prayer life of Jesus in the gospels. Look up the following references and write down what they tell us about Jesus at prayer.

- Mark 6:41
- Luke 6:12
- Mark 14:32
- Luke 22:32
- Luke 3:21
- Luke 11:1
- John 17:20

1. How do we know that prayer played a central role in the life of Jesus?
2. How did Jesus pray?
3. How do you pray?

The Lord's Prayer

Jesus showed all Christians how to pray by teaching them the Lord's Prayer, which is also known as the 'Our Father'. The Lord's Prayer is a model of Christian prayer. Jesus began this prayer by calling God 'Abba'. Abba is an Aramaic word for 'Father', which was used within families; for us, Abba would be like Daddy or Dad. Jesus wanted all people to have a close relationship with God the Father and so he invited them to call God 'Our' Father.

This prayer can be an example of personal or communal prayer, as it can be said in private or with others. When the Lord's Prayer is recited at Mass, it is a communal prayer.

The Lord's Prayer teaches Christians:

- to recognise where God is and who God is (Matthew 6:9);
- to offer praise and thanksgiving to God (Matthew 6:9);
- to allow God's will to be done in their hearts and in their lives (Matthew 6:10);
- to find their daily needs in God (Matthew 6:11);
- to forgive others and ask for God's forgiveness (Matthew 6:12);
- to keep their hearts and minds free from wrong thoughts and actions (Matthew 6:13).

5-4-3-2-1

1. Identify **five** Bible references for times when Jesus prayed.
2. Explain **four** lines from the 'Our Father'.
3. What **three** requests does Jesus make to God in the 'Our Father'?
4. Write **two** paragraphs on the personal and communal prayer in the life of Jesus.
5. With what **one** name did Jesus begin the Lord's Prayer?

KNOW HOW

You will need a Bible for this exercise.
Look up the Bible references given below to find an example of each of the following:

1. Jesus praying a prayer of thanksgiving.
2. Jesus asking his followers to have courage.
3. A prayer of penitence.
4. Jesus asking people to continue to pray and not to lose heart.
5. Jesus praying a prayer of petition.
6. Jesus asking his followers to spend time in prayer.

Matthew 26:39	Mark 9:29	Luke 10:21	John 17:9
Matthew 6:9	Mark 11:25	Luke 18:1-2	John 17:15
Matthew 11:25	Mark 13:18	Luke 19:46	John 17:20
Matthew 14:23	Mark 14:32	Luke 22:32	

DIGGING DEEPER

1. The *Catechism of the Catholic Church* states:
   'The Lord's Prayer is truly the summary of the whole gospel.'
   Write one paragraph on this statement and discuss what you have written with the other members of your class.
2. What does the Lord's Prayer say to you about God?
3. How does praying the Lord's Prayer nourish your faith?
   Or
   Identify and describe a very important prayer that you pray as part of your religious tradition.

> **Personal Prayer: Taking time alone to be aware of God and to communicate with God.**
>
> **Communal Prayer: Taking time with the other members of your community of faith to be with God and to communicate with God.**

LESSON 110 Meditation and Contemplation

GROUNDWORK
In this lesson we plan to:
- examine meditation and contemplation as two expressions of prayer.

DIGGING DEEPER
Why do people use meditation and contemplation as ways of praying?

Key Concepts
Meditation/Contemplation

Meditation

Meditation is an expression of prayer that is used in many of the world religions. The goal of Christian meditation is to focus on God and on the mystery of God's love as given in the life, death and resurrection of Jesus Christ.

People who wish to meditate will find a comfortable position in a quiet place. They will close their eyes and relax. Many people begin by focusing on their breathing as a way of helping them to relax. Others will focus, for example, on feeling the heat in the palms of their hands. When they are quiet, calm and at ease, they are ready for prayer.

One form of meditation is guided meditation. You may have experienced this type of meditation as part of your Religion class. Guided meditation is where you are helped to meditate. The leader (teacher, chaplain or other spiritual guide) leads you through a process of becoming quiet and still. Then the leader slowly reads a gospel story or a prayer, giving you time to focus on its meaning. You can also pray like this on your own – and this would be an example of personal prayer.

Meditation has become a very popular way for people to pray because it gives them a chance to be quiet and still in a place where their minds and hearts are ready for prayer.

KNOW WHAT
1. What is meditation and why is it used as a form of prayer?
2. Why do you think it helps to be in a comfortable position before one begins to pray?
3. How can meditative prayer be a form of personal prayer?

DIGGING DEEPER

Have you ever prayed using meditation? If so, write about your experience.
Or
If you have never used meditation, do you think you would like to? Why?/Why not?

Contemplation

Contemplation is when we connect with God in a way that goes beyond words, gestures or images. Contemplation is not about thinking and reflecting, although these can lead a person into a state of contemplation, where words and thoughts become unnecessary.

Contemplative prayer allows a person to relax into the awareness that God is just there. Contemplation is about being aware of God, being with God and resting in God. St Teresa of Avila, a Carmelite sister, described contemplative prayer in this way: 'Contemplation is nothing more than a closer sharing between friends. It means taking time to be alone with Him who loves us.'

Contemplative orders of religious, such as the Carmelites, give time frequently to this form of communication with God, through which they become aware of God in the silence of their own hearts. One Carmelite sister described the identity of the Carmelite order in these words: 'Prayer is our real identity. The physical work we do is always simple so as to leave the mind free to be continually in the presence of God.'

The Rosary

The Rosary began in the Middle Ages, probably as a means of copying the way monks prayed in monasteries. The word 'bead' in 'rosary beads' comes from the old English word *bede*, meaning prayer or request.

The Rosary is an example of contemplative, meditative and vocal prayer. Saying the Rosary is a way of sharing in the memories of Mary, the Mother of God, and in the memories of the friends of Jesus. It gives Christians a chance to be with God, with Jesus and with Mary in a quiet, contemplative way. Repeating the 'Hail Mary' ten times (with the 'Glory be to the Father' and the 'Our Father' in between) helps those praying to find a quiet space inside themselves. It gives them an opportunity to learn from Jesus, to become like Jesus, to pray to Jesus and to celebrate Jesus.

Different themes or 'mysteries' are used to pray the Rosary on different days. The Rosary can also be a form of meditation, as the person praying can use their imagination to picture and reflect on the events connected with each mystery.

KNOW IT ALL

Copy the following sentences into your Religion folder and fill in the blanks using the wordbank given below.

1. Contemplation is a form of _____.
2. Contemplative prayer is a way of _____ with God.
3. Contemplative prayer involves being aware of and with _____.
4. Contemplative prayer is the form of prayer used in enclosed _____ orders.
5. The Rosary is a form of contemplative, meditative and _____ prayer.
6. The Rosary is a prayer to _____.
7. The Rosary is prayed using _____
8. The person saying the Rosary can use their _____ to picture the events connected with each 'mystery'.

WORDBANK

• Beads • Religious • Prayer • Communicating • Imagination • God • Presence • Our Lady • Vocal

KNOWING ME KNOWING YOU

Look up the following websites to find out more about prayer and the Rosary:

http://www.vatican.va/holy_father/john_paul_ii/apost_letters/documents/hf_jp-ii_apl_20021016_rosarium-virginis-mariae_en.html

http://www.ewtn.com/expert/answers/rosary_history.htm

http://www.catholic-truth.org/Essays/rosary.htm

DIGGING DEEPER

1. When you have found out more about the Rosary, perhaps your class could set aside a special time of significance to pray a decade of the Rosary together.
2. Ask a parent, guardian or grandparent about praying the Rosary. Write a paragraph based on the information you find out.

Meditation: Focusing attention/thoughts on a story, object or person in order to be more aware of them. Christian meditation focuses on God and the love of God as shown in Jesus Christ.

Contemplation: Focusing one's heart/feelings and being at rest with a particular subject or story. Christian contemplation brings Christians closer to God and to Jesus Christ.

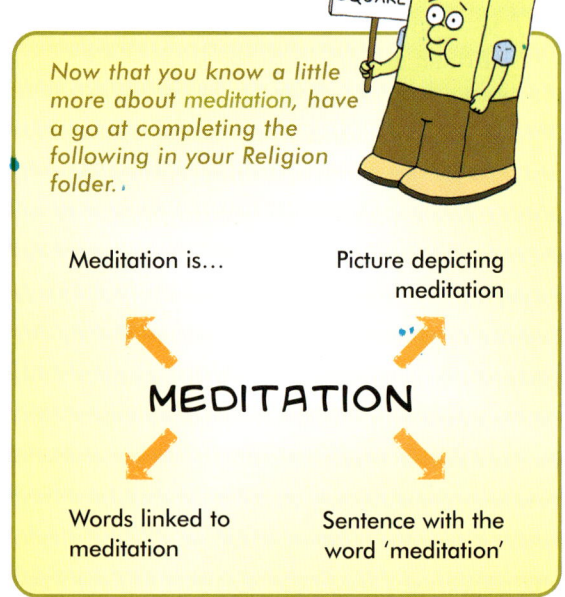

LESSON 111 Difficulties and Challenges of Prayer

GROUNDWORK
In this lesson we plan to:
- explore some of the difficulties and the challenges of prayer.

DIGGING DEEPER
Why do people often find prayer difficult?

Key Concepts
Communication with God

Trekker: I thought I was lost in the jungle, so I prayed to God to bring me out of it.
Friend: And did God answer your prayer?
Trekker: Before God could answer my prayer, an explorer turned up and showed me the way.

Was the trekker's prayer answered? Explain your answer.

A Time to Pray

Sometimes people find it hard to pray. They find it difficult to make the time and the space to pray. Prayer needs practice, patience and persistence.

Jesus urged his followers to pray and not to give up: 'Then Jesus told them a parable about their need to pray always and not to lose heart' (Luke 18:1).

THE THREE 'P'S OF PRAYER → PRACTICE, PATIENCE, PERSISTENCE

Prayer can be difficult because it seems like there is no immediate answer. However, Jesus said, 'If you believe, you will receive whatever you ask for in prayer' (Matthew 21:22).

The Four Stages of Prayer

St Teresa of Avila loved to garden. She described the pray-er in terms of a gardener watering their garden. She described four stages in the gardener's work, and then compared these to the way in which people advance in the art of prayer.

Stage One: The gardener goes to the well for buckets of water to water the whole garden.
A person decides to make prayer part of their lifestyle. Being still and quiet and leaving the world and its worries behind can be a very difficult task.

Stage Two: The gardener turns the crank of a water hose and gets more water with less labour and can rest without having to work constantly.
Having put their initial decision to pray more regularly into practice, the pray-er can now pray with more ease and is less distracted by the hustle and bustle of life.
Just as the gardener now has more time to spend actually watering the garden, the pray-er has more time to spend communicating with God through prayer.

Stage Three: The gardener waters the garden with running water from a river or a stream. There is just a small amount of work involved in directing the water into the garden. The river or stream now does the hard work.

> Just like this method of watering the garden, spending time in prayer becomes progressively more about what God does, and less about what the pray-er does.

Stage Four: The gardener sits quietly and allows the rain to fall and saturate the garden.

> The pray-er has now arrived at a stage whereby their communication with God is powerful and does not involve any work. This is contemplative prayer, which is about relaxing and resting in God.

By describing the four stages of prayer in this way, St Teresa helps us to understand that developing a prayer life takes time. Think of the three P's listed earlier: practice, patience and persistence.

KNOW WHAT
1. Why do people sometimes find it difficult to pray?
2. What did Jesus say about prayer?
3. Briefly describe St Teresa of Avila's four stages of prayer.

DIGGING DEEPER
1. In your opinion, what is the most difficult thing about prayer?
2. When do you find it easiest to pray?
3. Jesus asked his followers to pray always and not to lose heart. What do people 'lose heart' with in the practice of prayer?
4. Is there a particular prayer or prayer time that you share with your family or friends? If so, write a paragraph about it.

Challenges to Prayer

When people ask God for something, they might expect to get it. However, life's not like that. We often make petitions (ask for things) that we don't get. But before those who pray to God start thinking that God is not there or that God doesn't really care, it might be helpful to remember:

- Not everything that people want is right or good for them. God cannot be expected to give a person something that is bad.
- God gives people the freedom to make their own choices. People cannot expect God to undo the damage they do to themselves by making wrong choices.
- Other people can use their free will to hurt or offend you. If God were to stop people from hurting others, then God would be interfering with their free will.
- Even though what God made is good, there is still evil in the world. This is a mystery. Bad things may happen to us, even though they are not our fault. Bad things happened to Jesus: he was betrayed by his friends; he was killed on the cross. Jesus prayed not to have to go through his passion and death. Through the resurrection of Jesus, God showed that evil will not triumph. Good will win over evil in the end.

KNOW IT ALL
Copy the following sentences into your Religion folder and fill in the blanks using the wordbank given below.
1. People can often find it _____ to pray.
2. A prayer 'habit' takes time as well as the three P's: _____, _____, and _____.
3. We often make _____ for things that we don't get.
4. Not all the things that people want are _____ or _____ for them. God cannot be expected to give a person something that is bad.
5. God gives people _____ to make their own choices.
6. Other people can use their _____ _____ to hurt or offend you.
7. Through the _____ of Jesus, God showed that evil will not _____.

WORDBANK
Resurrection • Difficult • Patience • Right • Free will • Petitions • Good • Persistence • Freedom • Practice • Triumph

KNOWING ME KNOWING YOU

1. Look at the above pictures and explain how you know these people are praying.
2. Do you think all of these people are from the same community of faith? Explain your answer.
3. Which picture best represents you at prayer? Explain your answer.

Your Body Helps You to Pray
People often choose a posture that helps them to pray: some people sit upright during their prayer, while others kneel or stand. People also use gestures to help them to pray: Christians join their hands; they make the sign of the cross; they raise their hands in a gesture of praise; they bow their heads during the Consecration at Mass; they walk in procession. Muslims also use many gestures during their daily prayer (see page 227).

3-2-1
1. Identify **three** gestures that people use in prayer.
2. Identify **two** postures that people use in prayer.
3. Write **one** paragraph entitled 'My body can help me to pray'.

See page 497 for past exam questions on this topic.

LESSON 112 Important People in the Spiritual Traditions

GROUNDWORK
In this lesson we plan to:
- explore the importance of prayer in the lives of individuals from the Christian tradition.

DIGGING DEEPER
What is the spirituality of St Ignatius of Loyola and St Teresa of Avila?

Key Concepts
Communication with God/Personal prayer/Contemplation

We use the word 'spiritual' to describe things that relate to the world of religion as distinct from the material world in which we live. Our 'spirituality' refers to our attachment to religious values. We will now examine the spirituality of two figures from the Christian tradition.

St Ignatius of Loyola

Personal details: Ignatius was born in Spain in 1491, the youngest of eleven children. His mother died when he was very young and he spent his early childhood with foster parents. As he grew up, he enjoyed a wild social life, which included gambling. He was arrogant, vain and selfish.

Important moments in his life: That all changed after he joined the army and received a severe wound to his leg, which put him out of action for a long time. In desperation, he read any books that came to hand. Books were scarce and all he could find were biographies of the saints. He started to think about the lives of these people and about their relationship with God. Gradually, he began to develop his own relationship with God and to figure out what was really important in his life.

What happened next? He decided that he would live his life in the service of God. He began his journey of faith at the monastery of Montserrat. It look him a long time before he felt that he had really done penance for his earlier life. He then spent time in a Dominican monastery at Manresa, where he fasted, prayed and did penance. During this time, he developed a set of 'spiritual exercises', which Christians still use today. After he was ordained a priest, he founded a new religious order, the Society of Jesus, also known as the Jesuits.

His spirituality: Ignatius believed that God is present in people's lives at all times. His spiritual exercises are used today in retreats to help people to communicate with God in their lives, so that they can live as God wants them to. Ignatius stressed the importance of sharing the love of God with others, particularly the poor and oppressed. He also stressed the importance of daily personal prayer.

Prayer of St Ignatius of Loyola

Lord,
Teach me to be generous.
Teach me to serve you as you deserve:
To give and not to count the cost;
To fight and not to heed the wounds;
To toil and not to seek for rest;
To labour and not to seek reward,
Save that of knowing
I do your most holy will.

St Teresa of Avila

Personal details: Teresa was born in Spain in 1515. As a young child, she read the Lives of the saints with one of her brothers. They were particularly taken with the stories of the martyrs and they wanted to be martyrs too. As this wasn't possible, they decided to become hermits. Even at a young age, Teresa showed signs of the remarkable woman she would become. She had a heightened awareness of the poor, and her childhood games revolved around pretending to be a nun living in a community.

Important moment in her life: Teresa wanted to become a Carmelite nun, but her father was not happy about that. Eventually, she ran away from home and then secretly entered a Carmelite monastery. She was just twenty years old.

What happened next? There were 150 nuns in the Carmelite Monastery of the Incarnation, which Teresa joined. Their lives were rigidly set out: they fasted, they kept silence, they prayed the Divine Office together, and they saw to the spiritual and physical needs of the sick and needy.

St Teresa of Avila

Because of serious illness, Teresa had to return home for four years, but she went back to the monastery as soon as she was well again. She had strong opinions about prayer. She felt that prayer should be at the very centre of her life and that God was calling her to found a different type of Carmelite monastery, where the emphasis would be on a simpler and quieter lifestyle. After initial opposition from her superiors, St Teresa founded a new monastery, the Monastery of St Joseph. The sisters spent their time praying, gardening and caring for the poor. They owned nothing and lived on donations in return for simple services like sewing and spinning wool. Teresa died in 1582, leaving behind seventeen new monasteries where men and women could follow this simple lifestyle.

Her spirituality: At different stages of her life, Teresa preferred different types of prayer. As a girl she loved the Rosary; as a young adult she found that vocal prayer helped her to grow closer to God; later in life, she found that reading scripture and the Lives of the saints and focusing on the wonders of nature helped her to be aware of God's total and absolute love. Teresa realised that this practice of contemplative prayer was a very powerful way of communicating with God. She passed on this method of prayer to the other nuns in her order, making contemplative prayer into a way of life for the enclosed Carmelite orders.

(At this point, you might like to reread Lesson 15, Section A, where you will find some more information on the enclosed Carmelite orders.)

St Teresa's Bookmark

One of the most popular prayers of St Teresa is a brief prayer known as her 'bookmark'. It was found in her prayer book after her death. The following is an English translation of this prayer.

> Let nothing disturb you,
> Let nothing frighten you,
> All things are passing away:
> God never changes.
> Patience obtains all things.
> Whoever has God lacks nothing;
> God alone suffices.

KNOW WHAT
1. Describe St Ignatius of Loyola and the order he founded.
2. How do we know that prayer was very important to him?
3. Describe St Teresa of Avila and the order she founded.
4. How do we know that prayer had a great importance in her life?

KNOWING ME KNOWING YOU
Research these saints at your local library or on the internet and see if you can come up with any further information about them.

DIGGING DEEPER
1. How would you describe your spirituality? Give reasons for your answer.
2. If you had to suggest one way that your prayer life could be enhanced, what would your suggestion be?
3. What do you think might help ordinary people to reach a deeper level of spirituality in their lives?
4. Suggest a good time of year to begin developing one's prayer life in order to deepen one's spirituality. Give reasons for choosing this particular time.

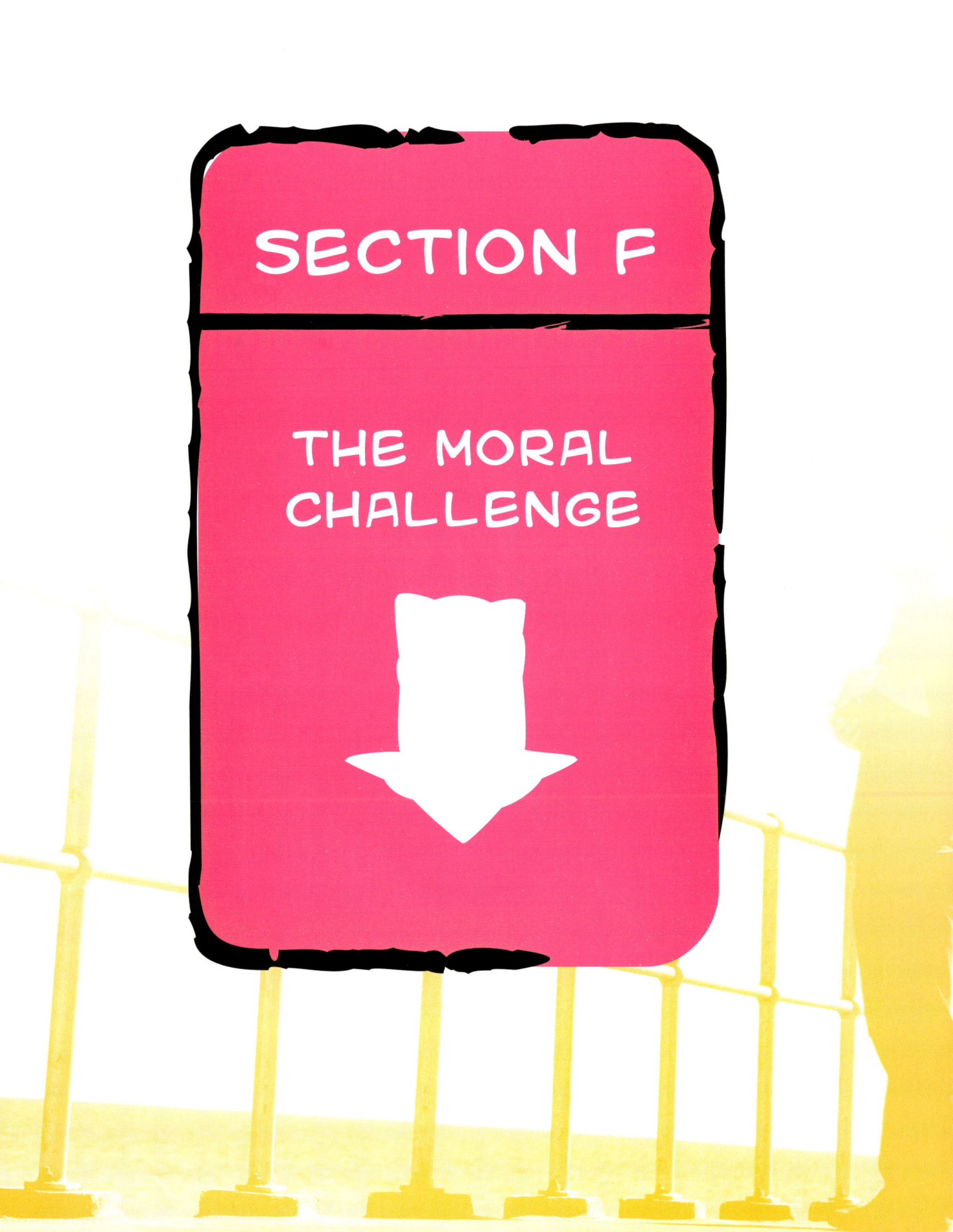

Introduction to Morality

LESSON 113 What is Morality?

GROUNDWORK
In this lesson we plan to:
- explore what it means to be moral.

DIGGING DEEPER
How moral am I?

 **Key Concepts**
Choice/Morality

Introductory Exercise

Read the following statements and decide which ones are about moral choices and which are not. How do you know which is which?

- It's not a good idea to tell lies.
- This fruit is rotten.
- It's right to help those in need.
- Susie got all the geography questions right.
- It's wrong to steal.
- This cake tastes good.
- Bullying is bad.
- Nelson Mandela is a good man.
- Speeding is not right.

Discuss the differences between the statements that involve moral choices and those that do not.

Morality and Choices

All of us have to make **choices**. Every day we decide about all sorts of things: blue jeans or black jeans? Lies or truth? Trainers or shoes? Help someone in need or ignore them? Choices that involve right or wrong and doing good or bad are called moral choices. The basis for making moral choices is called **morality**.

This section of our Religious Education programme is called 'The Moral Challenge'. The word 'challenge' is used because making moral decisions and leading a moral life can be difficult.

DIGGING DEEPER

1. Being a moral person means choosing right over wrong, good over bad. Why is it often difficult to be a moral person?
2. Have you ever had to make a difficult decision that involved right and wrong? What happened? How did you reach your decision? What helped you? Write about your choice.

Story: A Moral Choice

In February 2002, a retired County Monaghan farmer heard that Ireland was changing over to the new euro currency. He wondered what he should do. He had always kept his money at home and never used a bank. However, now, with the change to euro, all his old Irish money was going to be useless. Listening to the News on the radio one day, he heard how there was only a short time left for changing the old money into the new. He had to act. So, he gathered up all his old notes, stuffed them into a bag and slung it over the back of his bicycle.

Off he went. But something made him fall off his bicycle – probably a pothole! He gathered himself up quickly and pressed on, unaware of the commotion that he was about to leave behind him. For the bag at the back was torn in the fall and the notes had started to fall out. Cars were stopping everywhere along the road. People were rushing to pick up the money from the hedges and trees. But one motorist figured out what was happening. He caught up with the farmer and told him what had occurred. Together, they went back and gathered up what was left. When they added it up, it seemed that £10,000 was missing. Perhaps it was still up in the trees, but it seems more likely that it was in someone else's pocket.

DIGGING DEEPER

1. What is your reaction to this story? Do you feel sorry for the farmer? Why?/Why not?
2. How do you think you would have reacted if you had found the money? Would you have looked for the owner? Why?/Why not?
3. This story was reported on the national News. Would you have returned the money to the local police when you heard the News report? Why?/Why not?
4. What would be the only good moral choice a person could make in such a situation?

Choice: Opting for one thing rather than another.

Morality: The basis on which a person makes moral choices, i.e. between good and bad.

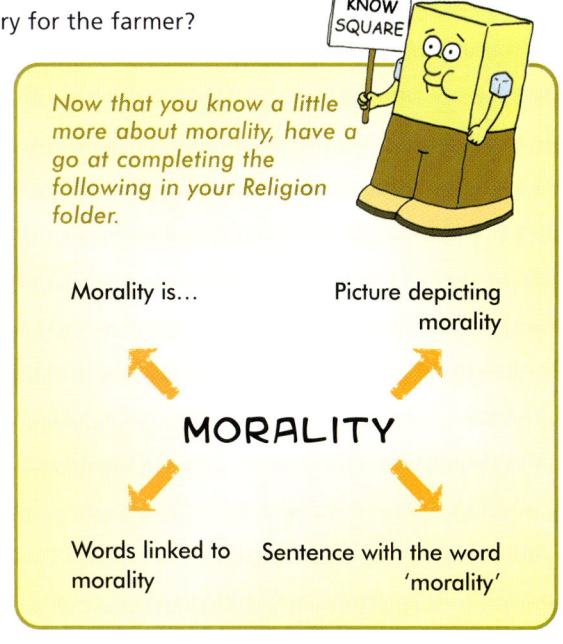

Now that you know a little more about morality, have a go at completing the following in your Religion folder.

Morality is…

Picture depicting morality

MORALITY

Words linked to morality

Sentence with the word 'morality'

LESSON 114 Actions and Consequences

GROUNDWORK
In this lesson we plan to:
- explore the consequences of actions and decisions on human relationships at personal, communal and global levels.

DIGGING DEEPER
What are the consequences of my actions?

 **Key Concepts**
Relationships/Freedom/Action and consequence

Human Relationships

The word **relationship** describes the way we connect with other people, either individually or in groups. We connect with people on three different levels: interpersonal, communal and global.

We have *interpersonal relationships* with people on a one-to-one basis; for example, with our family and our friends.

We have *communal relationships* with groups of people; for example, with the members of the different groups, clubs and communities to which we belong.

We have *global relationships* with people from all over the world; for example, much of what we eat comes from other countries, so we have a relationship with the people who produce that food.

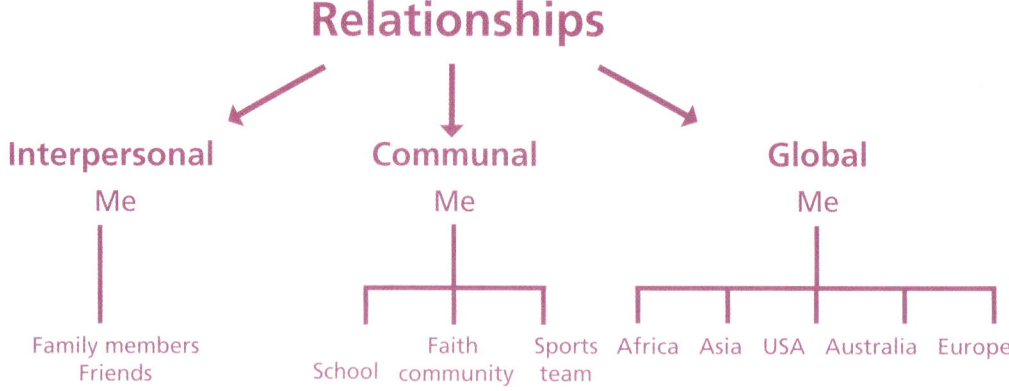

Freedom

We all value our **freedom**, but sometimes we have to accept that there are limits to our freedom; for example, the rules at home and in school or the laws of the land. It is important to respect the freedom of others while exercising our own freedom. Our freedom to choose right over wrong and good over bad is determined by our respect for the freedom of others. It is this respect for the freedom of others that builds up our relationships with others.

Actions and Consequences

As we grow up, we learn about the positive and negative **consequences** (results) of our **actions**. For example, we learn that if we don't get up early enough we will miss the bus, or if we don't work hard at school we will not do well in our exams. All of our actions have consequences; some positive, others negative. As we become more mature, we realise that sometimes making the right moral choice will result in hardship for ourselves. What is important in these situations is making sure our choice is true to who we are and to our relationship with God. Positive consequences are not always a measure of the morality of a decision.

- Stephen's friends have been stealing from the local shop. He knows that stealing is wrong and that he should tell someone about what is going on. However, Stephen also knows that if he tells on them, they will guess it was him and they will isolate him from their group.
- Pam would love to go to a hip-hop night in her local town. All her friends are going, but she doesn't have enough money to go. Then she spots the Trócaire box on the mantelpiece.
- Emma has been invited to a party in the house of one of the most popular girls in her class. She would love to go, but when she tells her younger sister, Laura, about it, Laura says that this girl has been bullying her for the past year.

Choices → Action → Consequences → Positive / Negative

KNOW WHAT

1. The next step in each of the situations described above is an action of some sort. For example, Stephen could tell his parents what has been happening, or he could ignore it and pretend he hasn't noticed anything, or he could join in the stealing in order to be 'one of the lads', and so on. Outline two possible actions in each of the other two scenarios.
2. What are the consequences of your proposed actions? Which of the consequences are positive and which are negative?

DIGGING DEEPER

1. What factors can help us to make good moral choices, i.e. choices that lead to actions with positive consequences?
2. Why is it a good idea to ask advice from others when we are faced with difficult moral decisions?

KNOWING ME KNOWING YOU

Interview a classmate about a time when they made a moral choice that led to an action with a) a positive consequence and b) a negative consequence.

Consequences and Relationships

Like ripples in a pool, the consequences of our actions extend out from our interpersonal relationships to our communal relationships and even to our global relationships.

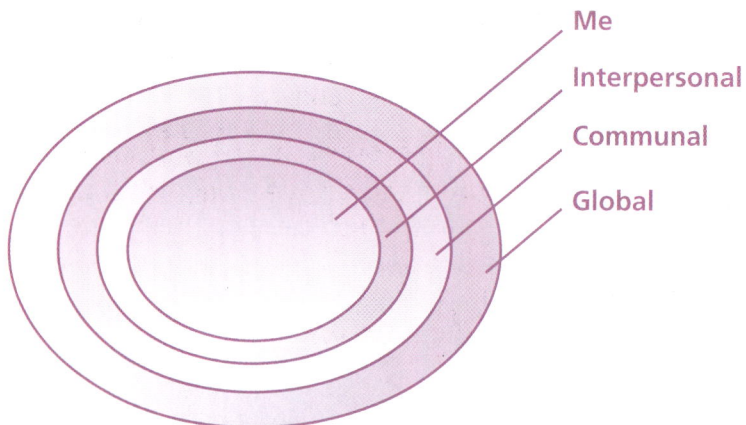

Example 1: The Niall Mellon Story

When Irish businessman Niall Mellon visited the township of Imizamo Yethu in Cape Town, South Africa, in 2002, he was so moved by the poor condition in which the residents were living that he set up the Niall Mellon Township Trust, a volunteer organisation with the aim of improving the lives of the people living in such townships.

Niall met with the township's community leaders and undertook to build 450 block houses to replace the cardboard, corrugated iron and hardboard shacks that the people were living in. Following this, he organised for 153 Irish volunteers to raise €3,000 each and to give up nine days in December and travel six thousand miles to Imizamo Yethu to build twenty-five houses in six and a half working days. So successful was this 'blitz' that in 2004 he gathered even more volunteers, raised even more money and built fifty houses in the same time-scale. The following year they built 106 houses in a two-week period. Work continued until the Trust met their target and completed 450 block houses in Imizamo Yethu. Since then, hundreds of houses have been built in Africa by volunteers working with the Niall Mellon Township Trust. You can read all about this work and see pictures of what has been achieved by logging on to *http://www.irishtownship.com/index.html*.

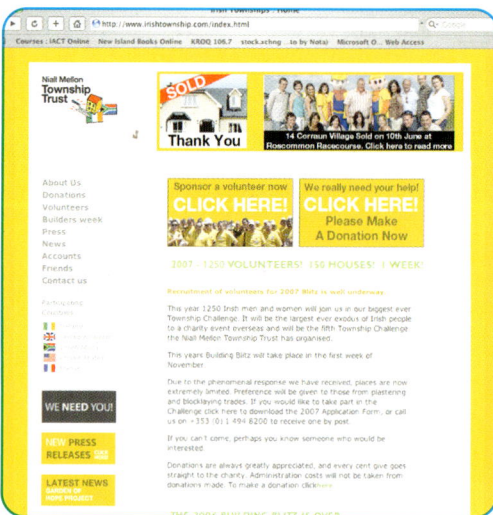

The Niall Mellon Township Trust is an example of how one person's actions can have amazing consequences of a positive nature on relationships at an interpersonal, communal and global level.

Interpersonal: Working on this project has had a very positive and lasting effect on every volunteer's relationship with family and friends. Linda McDonnell, a volunteer who has undertaken the challenge on several occasions, feels that such an experience changes one's life for ever. Bringing such hope to so many people has made her feel stronger and more confident. Niall Mellon himself suggests that 'your sore muscles, burnt faces and weary bodies will heal, but the pride you take home with you will never leave you'. In other words, the newfound gratitude and strength that such an experience brings, extends into one's relationships for a long time after the trip is over.

Communal: The work of Niall and the volunteers has a big impact on their relationships within both their local communities at home and at a national level. The local communities take an active role in the fundraising activities, and their pride in the achievement of the volunteers is shared by people throughout the country.

Global: The Niall Mellon Township Trust improves the quality of life for hundreds of people in Africa. The Irish people can be proud of this unique work, which strengthens their global relationship with these people.

Example 2: Drinking and Driving

A study on alcohol and fatal road deaths in Ireland, revealed at the launch of the Road Safety Authority's 2006 Christmas anti-drink-driving campaign, found that:

- Alcohol was a factor in 36.5% of all fatal crashes in 2003.
- Driver/rider alcohol was a factor in 28% of fatal crashes.
- Almost a quarter of drivers killed were over the legal limit when they died.
- Alcohol was a factor in 62% of single-vehicle, single-occupant fatal crashes.
- 90% of the drivers whose alcohol was a contributory factor in a fatal crash were male.
- Pedestrian alcohol was a factor in 38% of fatal pedestrian road crashes.
- Weekends through to Monday morning (the morning-after effect) is the zone for alcohol-related fatal crashes.

It is clear that combining alcohol and driving can have very negative consequences, which can be experienced in relationships at interpersonal, communal and global levels.

Interpersonal: The families and friends of people involved in serious car crashes have their lives changed for ever. They may have lost a loved one, or they may have to live with a loved one who now requires ongoing care.

Communal: Communal relationships can be changed for ever when people are severely injured or killed because of driving while under the influence of alcohol. There can be extreme sadness and a sense of hopelessness in the community, as people grieve with the families directly involved. Furthermore, there can be anger or resentment in the community towards the driver who caused the accident and towards their family.

Global: Driving over the alcohol limit is an action that affects global relationships. It drives up the statistics of drink-related fatalities and sends out a message worldwide.

For further information on the effects that drinking alcohol has on driving, visit: *www.rsa.ie*

KNOW WHAT

1. In your own words, outline the consequences of the volunteers' actions in the Niall Mellon story.
2. What are the consequences of drinking and driving?

DIGGING DEEPER

1. How do you think the positive consequences of the volunteers' actions affect their relationships with others?
2. How do you think the negative consequences of driving under the influence of alcohol affect the drivers' relationship with others?
3. How do the consequences of drinking and driving change people's lives?
4. How can paying attention to the consequences of our actions affect the type of people we become?
5. Think of two examples from your own life experience that show how relationships can be affected by a) the positive and b) the negative consequences of people's actions.

KNOWING ME KNOWING YOU

Log on to *http://www.irishtownship.com/index.html* and *www.rsa.ie* and then consider the following:

1. What could you do to support the Niall Mellon Township Trust?
2. What could you do to educate drivers about the consequences of drinking and driving?

What does Christianity teach about relationships?

Christianity teaches about right relationships. When relationships are right, justice is the result. Our moral behaviour affects our relationship with God and with others. Jesus' teaching on right relationships is centred around the commandment of love – the love of God and of neighbour: *'I give you a new commandment, that you love one another. Just as I have loved you, you also should love one another'.* (John 13:34)

Read the Good Samaritan story from Luke 10:25-37 and answer the following questions.

DIGGING DEEPER

1. What does Jesus say about right relationships in the story of the Good Samaritan?
2. In our world today, who do you think might take the place of a) the man who was attacked by thieves and b) the Samaritan who helped him?
3. What does Jesus show us about making good choices in this story? Is it easy to do this?
4. What is the Christian teaching on interpersonal, communal and global relationships?

 **Relationships:** Connections between people, through family, community, country, group or choice.

Freedom: The capacity to do what we want, i.e. to choose to do good or to do bad.

Action and consequence: A consequence is something that happens as a result of an action/choice.

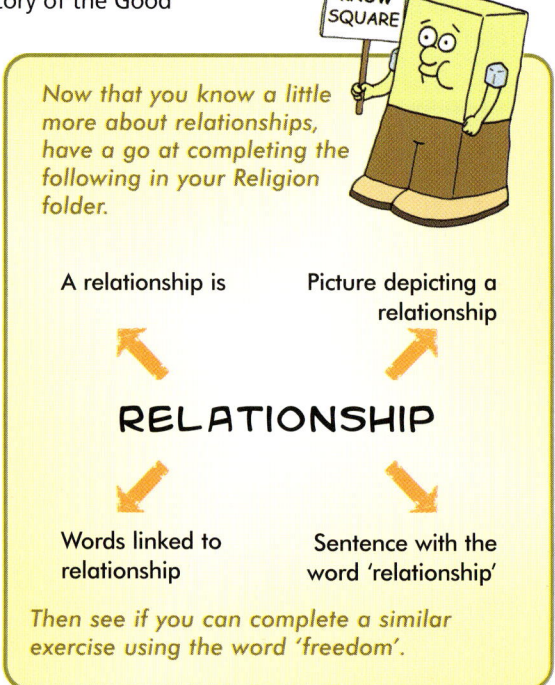

Now that you know a little more about relationships, have a go at completing the following in your Religion folder.

A relationship is / Picture depicting a relationship

RELATIONSHIP

Words linked to relationship / Sentence with the word 'relationship'

Then see if you can complete a similar exercise using the word 'freedom'.

KNOW THE WAY

408

LESSON 115 Rights and Responsibilities

GROUNDWORK
In this lesson we plan to:
- explore the connection between rights and responsibilities.

DIGGING DEEPER
What are my responsibilities in relation to my rights?

Key Concept
Morality

Rights

In our society, we hear much debate about rights – civil rights, students' rights, the rights of the working person and so on. *Rights* are things that people are entitled to in order to live a dignified and meaningful life. There is a difference between rights and privileges; for example, all people have the right to food and clothing, whereas owning a car is a *privilege*.

In order to become moral people, we must try to respect and protect the rights of others.

Universal Declaration of Human Rights

On 10 December 1942, the United Nations organisation published its *Declaration of Human Rights*. This declaration is universal, i.e. it applies to everyone throughout the world. It recognises the equality of all men and women and their right to live with dignity and freedom. It also establishes the responsibilities of all human beings. It was signed by the representatives of people from very different cultures, religions and political systems, from the developed and under-developed world. All of these people agreed on thirty basic rights that are a common standard of achievement for all peoples and nations.

You can find the full list of these human rights at: *http://www.un.org/Overview/rights.html*

All people have the right:
- to life;
- to liberty and security of person;
- not to be a slave;
- not to be tortured;
- to the protection of the law;
- to a fair and public hearing in the courts;
- to be presumed innocent until proven guilty;
- to freedom of movement and residence;
- to a nationality;
- to marry and have a family;
- to own property;
- to freedom of thought, conscience and religion;
- to freedom of peaceful assembly and of association;
- to freedom of opinion and expression;
- to seek and receive information and ideas;
- to take part in politics;
- to social security;
- to work;
- to fair wages and equal pay for equal work;
- to join a trade union;
- to rest and leisure;
- to adequate health care;
- to education.

5-4-3-2-1

1. Choose **five** rights that you think are the most important for your life at the present time. Give reasons for your choices.
2. Identify **four** rights that are not relevant to you right now.
3. Name **three** rights that you exercise every day.
4. Name **two** rights that you may never exercise.
5. Name **one** right that you are exercising as you read this textbook.

DIGGING DEEPER

Imagine yourself in a situation where you are deprived of a human right. Describe the situation and how you feel about it. How would you go about changing the situation?

Responsibilities

Rights and responsibilities go hand in hand. When we exercise our rights, we are called to take up the responsibility that goes with them. Once again, this involves making moral choices. For example, I have the right to education, therefore I have the responsibility to work hard at school.

Our rights and responsibilities also extend to our treatment of those around us. While I have the responsibility to work hard at school, I also have the responsibility to respect the other students in my class and their right to an education. I have the right to work, and with that right I have the responsibility to carry out my job to the best of my abilities, but I also have the responsibility to ensure that my work does not infringe on the rights of others to work.

See if you can come up with another example of the connection between rights and responsibilities.

KNOW HOW

Copy the following diagram into your Religion folder. In each circle, identify one way that you carry out the responsibility of showing respect for the rights of the group listed.

Responsibility for the Earth

As well as our responsibility to ourselves and to one another, we have a responsibility to the earth that we inhabit. Christians, Jews and Muslims all share the belief that the earth is a sacred gift from God, which has been given to us to take care of and pass on to each new generation. A lot of damage is being done to the earth, even while you are reading these words.

KNOW WHAT

1. What is the connection between rights and responsibilities? Explain your answer.
2. Is it fair that each right carries with it some responsibilities? Why?/Why not?
3. Why and how have we responsibilities in relation to others? What have these responsibilities got to do with being a moral person?
4. Why are we responsible for the earth? What has responsibility for the earth got to do with being a moral person?

DIGGING DEEPER

1. What do you think are the three most important responsibilities that you have as a moral person?
2. Was there ever a time when you did not take the proper responsibility for your actions? What happened?
3. Have you ever witnessed damage being done to the environment? What happened? What might have helped in this situation?

KNOWING ME KNOWING YOU

In groups of two, discuss the following question and then answer it in one sentence:

Who is responsible for ensuring that each person's human rights are respected and protected?

LESSON 116 Influences on our Morality

GROUNDWORK
In this lesson we plan to:
- explore the variety of influences on human behaviour and human choices at different stages of life.

DIGGING DEEPER
What influences my moral choices?

Key Concepts
Influence/Morality/Society

Introductory Activity: The Power of Influence

You will need: two sheets of paper and one volunteer to read out the statements.

- Using large lettering, write the words 'I agree' on one of the sheets of paper, and the words 'I disagree' on the other.
- Stick the sheets of paper at opposite ends of the classroom. The middle of the classroom is the 'I'm not sure' area.
- All students begin by standing in the middle of the room.
- The volunteer then reads out the following statements, one at a time. If you agree with a statement, you go to the 'I agree' position; if you disagree, you go to the 'I disagree' position. You may find yourself changing position as the questions change.

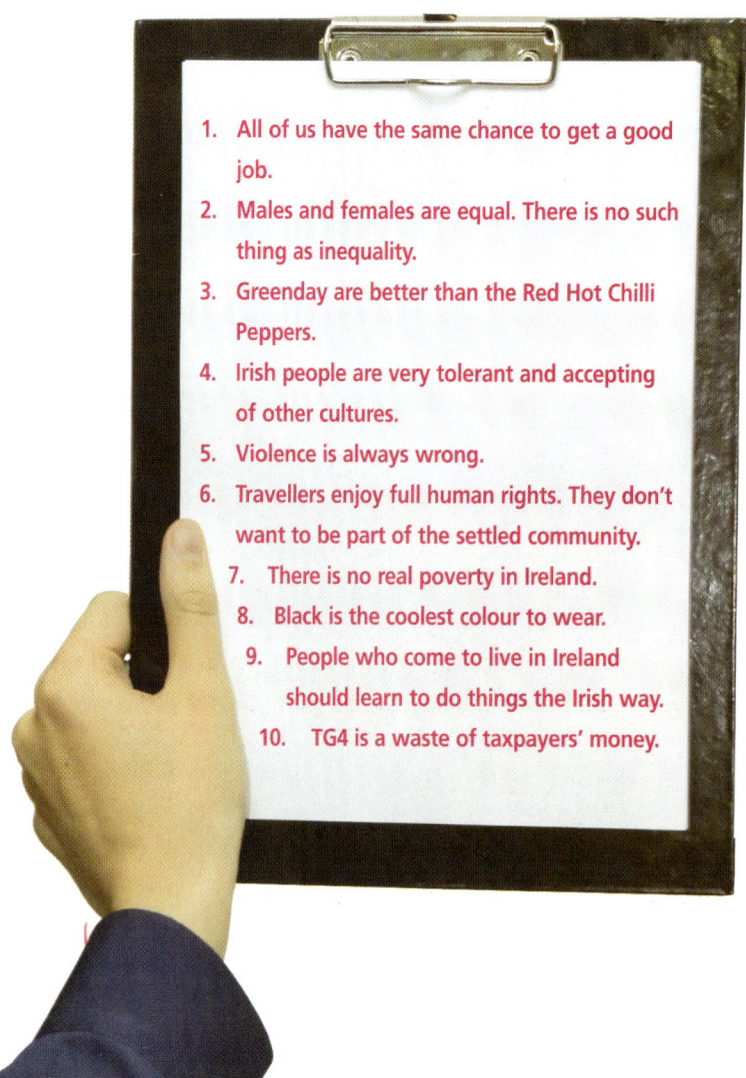

1. All of us have the same chance to get a good job.
2. Males and females are equal. There is no such thing as inequality.
3. Greenday are better than the Red Hot Chilli Peppers.
4. Irish people are very tolerant and accepting of other cultures.
5. Violence is always wrong.
6. Travellers enjoy full human rights. They don't want to be part of the settled community.
7. There is no real poverty in Ireland.
8. Black is the coolest colour to wear.
9. People who come to live in Ireland should learn to do things the Irish way.
10. TG4 is a waste of taxpayers' money.

- People at either end of the room should try to influence the group in the middle to join them.
- A quick discussion should follow each statement, i.e. people give brief reasons for their position in the classroom.

This exercise demonstrates how we can allow our opinions to be influenced by the opinions of others.

What influences our moral choices?

An **influence** is something that has an effect on the way we might think about a person, a place or a thing. Our opinions and choices are all influenced by many different factors. For example, our **morality**, what we believe to be good or bad, right or wrong, is influenced by our upbringing, the opinions of our family and friends, the place where we live, our religion and so on.

KNOW WHAT
Take a look at the chart below and note the groups of people that can influence Mike's behaviour. How do you think each group could influence his decision?

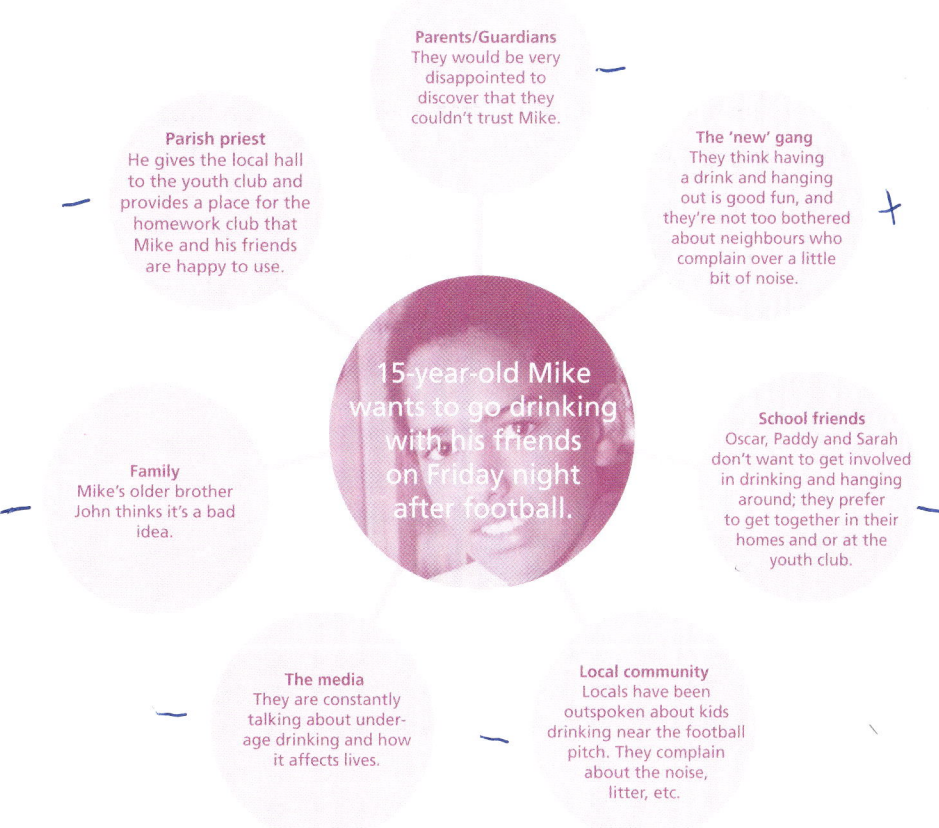

Think of another moral situation and draw a similar chart with all the groups of people that you think would have the potential to influence the person making the decision. Discuss your chart in class.

DIGGING DEEPER 3-2-1
1. List the last **three** decisions you made that were influenced by someone or something.
2. Name **two** people who are influenced by you.
3. What has been the **one** biggest influence on your behaviour this year?

Morality and Society

Our morality influences the kind of person we become: kind or harsh, honest or dishonest, trustworthy or untrustworthy. The kind of person we are influences the way we relate to others, not just to our family and close friends, but to all those in the wider community – our classmates, our work colleagues, the other members of our youth club/sports club, etc. It also affects the way we relate to people in our **society** whom we may not know personally, but with whom we are connected in various ways. Take a look at the following situations:

- Clare has just come out of a shop and she realises that the sales assistant has given her too much change. This happened before and she said nothing but felt a bit guilty. What should she do now?
- Paul takes the bus to school every day. His friends told him not to bother buying a ticket because they are very seldom checked. Paul has now stopped buying bus tickets, but he knows it's dishonest.
- There have been 375 deaths on the road this year. Over one hundred of them were drink-driving related. As usual for a Friday night, John has had a few too many drinks, but he only lives down the road, so he reckons he will be well able to drive.
- Simon is invited to a cider party at the weekend. He's not bothered about the cider but he knows the party will be a great laugh. His parents don't approve of the guy holding the party so even asking permission is going to cause major hassle. He could pretend he was going somewhere else, but then if something happened he would get caught. Should he risk it?

KNOW WHAT

1. What are the influences in each of these situations?
2. What do you think is the moral solution (the right/good thing to do) in each case?
3. What possible consequences can there be in each case?

DIGGING DEEPER

1. The above statements all refer to different moral issues. While all of them are of a personal nature (i.e. they relate to a single person), all of them could also be said to have the potential to affect more than one person. Discuss.
2. We know that our family and friends have an influence on our behaviour and on our choices. How can the people in the wider community have an influence on our behaviour and choices?

KNOW HOW

Find an example of a moral issue in this week's newspapers. In your own words, describe:

- the issue;
- the factors that have had an influence on the issue;
- the consequences – both personal and social;
- your proposed solution.

Influence: Something that affects a person's behaviour/decisions.

Society: The connection that exists between people when they share an outlook and way of life.

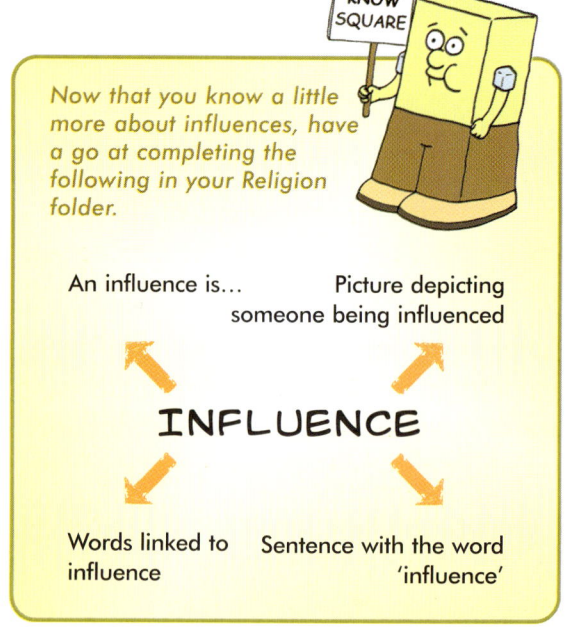

KNOW SQUARE

Now that you know a little more about influences, have a go at completing the following in your Religion folder.

An influence is…   Picture depicting someone being influenced

INFLUENCE

Words linked to influence   Sentence with the word 'influence'

KNOW THE WAY

Sources of Morality

LESSON 117 Sources of Morality

GROUNDWORK
In this lesson we plan to:
- identify the main sources of morality in people's lives.

DIGGING DEEPER
Who teaches me how to be a moral person?

Key Concept
Morality

'The strong must protect the sweet.' (Homer Simpson)

Dr Kris Jozajtis from Stirling University in Scotland suggests that in the American sitcom cartoon *The Simpsons*, many of the characters tend to end up doing the right thing; in other words, they take the moral option.

Perhaps Ned Flanders is the most consistently moral character in *The Simpsons*. He tries to do the right thing at every available opportunity. No matter how badly Homer treats him, Ned always turns the other cheek.

When Bart cuts off the head of Springfield's founder, Jebediah Springfield, in order to be popular with the bad boys at his school, he learns how important it is not only to respect such figures, but also to remember why we show respect in the first place. He learns this by witnessing the grief of the whole town (including the bad boys) when they discover the vandalism. He hears stories about Jebediah and how great he really was.

When Marge takes up bowling after Homer gives her a bowling ball as a birthday gift (which is really for himself), she almost falls in love with the dashing bowling instructor. However, after much deliberation, Marge chooses to visit Homer at his work as a special surprise for the man she truly loves!

This much-loved TV programme can teach us an important lesson about how our choices affect our relationships; regardless of how angry Homer, Marge, Bart, Lisa or even Maggie become with one another, they always end up doing the right thing for one another, and although the choices they make on the road to the right decision can often take a few detours, the destination of their decisions – choosing good over bad – is always the same.

KNOW WHAT
1. Why do you think Ned Flanders is suggested as perhaps the most moral person in the sitcom?
2. How are the members of the Simpson family a source of morality for one another?

Values

Our 'values' are those things we hold in high regard, such as freedom, friendship and honesty. Throughout history, people have fought and even died to defend such values. A person's values will always influence their choices. When you believe in a particular value, you try to live it and to apply it in every part of your life. As a result, you become a particular kind of person, with qualities that come from the values you hold. For example, if you believe in truth and live by that value, you will become an honest person.

David's Story

When David Huddie, a young college student, was diagnosed with terminal cancer, he dictated a letter, which his mother wrote down for him. He asked that the letter be sent to his friends after his death and he swore his mother to secrecy as to what was in it. David died on 4 July 2004, at the age of twenty-three. The letter was sent to eleven of his college and sporting friends. It read: 'I want to pay you back for your support and friendship by sending you all off on holiday.' He used half of his life-savings to pay for it. He did make one stipulation: there must be 'absolutely no misery or complaints' during the trip. The friends planned the holiday for that winter.

KNOW WHAT
1. What value did David cherish?
2. How did this value influence his actions?
3. David asked his mother to keep the letter a secret until after his death. What does this say about David's motivation (i.e. the reasons behind his action)?

DIGGING DEEPER
Name and describe two of the values you hold. Explain how those values help you to be a moral person.

Our values Our morality Our moral choices

Sources of Morality

Our morality (i.e. our sense of what is right and what is wrong) comes from our set of values. We get our values from the people and the traditions that surround us from the very beginning of our lives – our family, our friends, our school, our community, our religion and our State.

Family
Our family is the first source of our morality, as it is here that we first learn to differentiate between good and bad, right and wrong. For example, as small children, our family teaches us the value of sharing.

Friends
Our friends and peers are another source of morality for us. Our friends can have a positive or a negative influence on our moral values. They can encourage us to make choices that show respect and care for others or to make choices that do not show respect for others.

School
Our school community is a very important source of morality. The ethos and mission statement of our school describes the kind of place it tries to be. This influences how people within the school behave and how they treat others. Our school has a set of rules to help us to understand how we should act. During our school years, we meet with many different types of people and situations, and we are introduced to many new and exciting experiences. We learn important lessons about the consequences of our actions during our time in school.

Religion
The followers of a religion are greatly influenced in their moral choices by the teachings of their faith. For example, Christians believe in Gospel values. The Bible and the ministry of Jesus Christ encourage all Christians to 'love one another' and to 'treat others as you would like to be treated'. This influences the moral choices that Christians make in their relationships with others. We call the values that come from religion *religious values*.

The State
State representatives make decisions based on the 'common good', i.e. what they consider to be for the overall benefit of those who live in the country. This concern for the common good is a core belief or value of the State. Laws and rules emerge: we are not allowed to kill another human being; we are not allowed to steal from one another; we are not allowed to damage other people's property. Some people argue that some of the laws restrict freedom; for example, it is illegal to sell alcohol to people under the age of eighteen. The State takes the view that the overall good of society is best served by limiting the freedom of under-eighteens to buy alcohol. The State may be a source of morality for someone because they agree with its laws and rules; it may be a source of morality for another person because they do not want to end up in court.

It is from all of these groups that we learn a set of values. Our values influence us as we grow and mature, and they are the building blocks of our morality.

KNOW WHAT
List two ways in which each of the sources of morality mentioned above can influence your moral choices.

DIGGING DEEPER
1. Describe the main sources of your morality.
2. Do you think you could be a source of morality for anyone? Why?/Why not?
3. How does a person or a group of people become a source of morality?
4. How does your community of faith affect your morality?

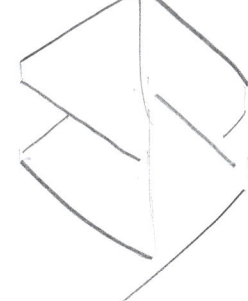

LESSON 118 Moral Vision

GROUNDWORK
In this lesson we plan to:
- explore the term 'moral vision'.

DIGGING DEEPER
What shapes my moral vision?

Key Concept
Moral vision

Moral Vision

Our **moral vision** describes the way we see the world from a moral point of view. It is most clearly seen in our moral choices, which reflect what we value in life, i.e. the ideals that we believe in and look upon as being important. Our moral vision is the overall expression of these values.

In the previous lesson, we learned that we are influenced by the moral values of our family, our friends, our school, our society and our faith community. In other words, we are influenced by the moral vision of others.

Our Morality

Our Moral Vision → Our Values → Our Moral Choices

Values learned from all the communities to which we belong

KNOW IT ALL

Complete the following sentences in your Religion folder.

1. A moral vision is…
2. My moral vision is influenced by…

Story: A Bad Moral Choice

Within a year of going to the Singapore branch of Barings Bank, young Nick Leeson sorted out a one-hundred-million-pound problem. Not only that, he also made another ten million pounds – ten per cent of the bank's entire profit that year. No wonder he became their superstar! Bank officials and bosses gave him complete freedom in his work. Nick and his wife Lisa had everything: money, weekends in exotic places, a smart apartment and frequent parties.

At work, Nick was never one for caution: he went with his gut feeling rather than taking carefully-worked-out choices. In 1994, his luck began to run out when the market finances did not go the way he expected. He began to lose the bank's money: hundreds of millions of pounds. Nick used a secret internal bank account to hide the losses and he continued to trade with money borrowed elsewhere. He kept trying for a miracle deal. But he had not counted on what happened next. On 17 January 1995, a huge earthquake devastated the Japanese city of Kobe. The stock market index plummeted. Nick used even more borrowed money to make deals for the bank, hoping to make profits and hide his previous losses. Finally, the losses were too huge to hide any more. So Nick Leeson and his wife went on the run. They were arrested in Germany. The final extent of the money he had squandered was revealed: £830 million. Nick was jailed and Barings Bank closed. He was released from prison in December 1999, homeless and penniless. He had serious health problems and he had separated from his wife.

Consequences

In Nick Leeson's case, the consequences in terms of his relationships were enormous:

Interpersonal relationships: He lost his employment, his earnings, his home and, most importantly, he lost his marriage.

Communal relationships: Not only did he and his wife suffer, but so did all the people who were connected with Barings Bank, e.g. the employees and their families, who lost jobs and incomes, and also all the account holders.

Global relationships: The worldwide businesses that were connected with the bank and those who invested money in the bank lost everything. In this case, many people suffered as a result of one person's bad moral choices. Some of those people will suffer the consequences of Nick Leeson's choices for the rest of their lives.

Bad consequences can often alert us that something is wrong, but consequences are not the only measure of how wrong a choice might be. You've probably heard the phrase 'The end justifies the means'. Suppose, by some miracle, Nick Leeson had been able to fix his problems without being caught. Would that mean that he had done nothing wrong? Would that make what he did all right? The answer is 'no'. Even if he had never been caught, Nick Leeson was really dishonest: he took enormous risks without telling his employers. He went to great lengths to conceal his dishonesty.

Nick Leeson's moral vision was flawed: if he could get away with doing wrong in pursuit of a particular goal, then it was all right as far as he was concerned. He put wealth, earnings and profit before other values, such as truth, his good name, marriage and friendship.

TAKE FIVE
1. What moral choices did Nick Leeson make?
2. What were the consequences of his choices?
3. How did the consequences of his choices affect his relationships at an interpersonal, communal and global level?
4. What kind of moral vision (outlook) did Nick Leeson have?
5. Why is it not true to say that 'the end justifies the means'?

DIGGING DEEPER
1. What kind of moral vision do you have? How do you think your moral vision developed?
2. How can your moral vision help you to become the person you really want to be?

Moral vision: Awareness of what is right and wrong, which guides a person's choices.

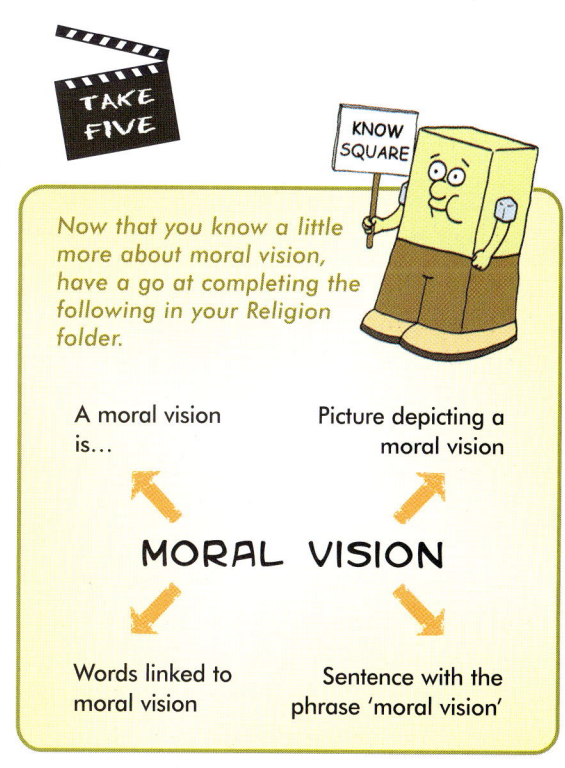

Now that you know a little more about moral vision, have a go at completing the following in your Religion folder.

A moral vision is…

Picture depicting a moral vision

MORAL VISION

Words linked to moral vision

Sentence with the phrase 'moral vision'

LESSON 119 Formal and Informal Codes of Behaviour

GROUNDWORK
In this lesson we plan to:
- **examine the evolution of formal and informal codes and principles of behaviour.**

DIGGING DEEPER
How do formal and informal codes of behaviour support my morality?

Key Concepts
Laws

Story: John's Dilemma

John enjoyed his job in the supermarket. Ok, so it was a bit boring at first, when all he could do was stack boxes on shelves, but ever since he had been put on the checkout it was much more fun. He was glad to see his friends, Declan and Ruth... someone to talk to, because it was a slow day. But his face fell when they brought packets of cigarettes to the checkout. He knew what that meant: they expected him to sell the cigarettes to them, even though they were under age...

KNOW WHAT
1. Describe two different endings to the story and identify the consequences for John in each case.
2. Who could be affected by John's actions? How would they be affected?
3. What steps do you think John should take if he wants to make a mature moral decision about what to do next?

When faced with the decision of whether or not to allow his friends to buy cigarettes, John's moral vision will give him a number of things to think about: Is it right to break the law and sell cigarettes to his friends? Is it right to allow his friends to break the law? Is it right for him to help them? Is it right to support his friends in a behaviour that could cost them their lives, or that could cost the lives of others through passive smoking? Does he have the right to make that decision for them? Is it right to lose the approval and companionship of his friends by not giving them what they want? Is it right that he could lose friends because of this? As you can see, the value John places on friendship can clash with other values.

DIGGING DEEPER
1. Think of one other situation where this could happen.
2. Have you ever experienced such a clash of values?

Formal and Informal Codes of Behaviour

Because values come into conflict from time to time, rules or codes have emerged to protect the higher values. In John's case, the value of protecting the lives of his friends and others is higher than the value of their friendship. In this example, we can see two different types of moral code at work: the informal code and the formal code.

Informal codes are the unwritten rules by which we learn to live in our community. They do not have the force of law behind them. They do, however, tell us what our community expects of us. They contain a moral vision of how people should live in community. Informal codes might deal with 'how to be a good neighbour' or 'how to respect the environment'.

Formal codes are written official rules or **laws** that state what is required of us. Formal codes may have begun as informal guidelines, but over time they have evolved into formal codes. In other words, they have been made formal or official by the leadership of a particular State, religious group or community. The Constitution and State legislation are examples of formal State codes; to break such laws usually incurs some degree of penalty. The Ten Commandments and the Beatitudes are examples of formal religious codes; they reflect the moral vision of a community of faith.

KNOW WHAT
1. Why do we have rules?
2. What is an informal code of behaviour? Give an example of an informal code of behaviour.
3. What in a formal code of behaviour? Give an example of a formal code of behaviour.

DIGGING DEEPER
1. How do formal and informal codes of behaviour support our morality?
2. Has there ever been a time when you have found it difficult to uphold formal/informal codes of behaviour? Why?/Why not?

The Law – Rooted in the Past

Ever since the first communities of people gathered together, they saw the need to formalise laws in the interest of the common good. The purpose of these laws or codes was to help people to live in community with one another. The laws upheld the values that the community lived by, such as respect, freedom, peace and so on. Each new generation interpreted the codes of the past in line with their own moral vision, instead of starting the process from scratch.

The Code of Hammurabi

Hammurabi (1795-50 BC) was a powerful Mesopotamian king. He is the first recorded example of a ruler making laws and publicising them for his people. His laws, known as the Code of Hammurabi, were carved in stone and put on public display so that everyone in the kingdom was aware of them and of their duty to keep them. An eight-foot-high black stone example still exists. Here is one of the laws inscribed on it:

'If any one buy(s) from the son or the slave of another man, without witness or a contract, silver or gold, a male or female slave, an ox or a sheep, an ass or anything, or if he take it in charge, he is considered a thief and shall be put to death.'

KNOW WHAT
1. Why do societies have laws?
2. What would happen if there were no laws?
3. What do you think was the moral vision behind the above example from the code of Hammurabi?

The Ten Commandments

The Ten Commandments were the basis of the moral code that Jesus grew up with. They give guidance on how people should live in right relationship with one another and with God.

1. I am the Lord your God: you shall not have strange gods before me.
2. You shall not take the name of the Lord your God in vain.
3. Remember to keep holy the Lord's day.
4. Honour your father and mother.
5. You shall not kill.
6. You shall not commit adultery.
7. You shall not steal.
8. You shall not bear false witness against your neighbour.
9. You shall not covet your neighbour's wife.
10. You shall not covet your neighbour's goods.

TAKE FIVE
1. What moral vision is contained within the Ten Commandments?
2. Write out a brief explanation of each of the Ten Commandments.
3. How do these commandments help people to live good lives?
4. Which of the Ten Commandments are similar to our State laws?
5. Which is the older code: our State law or the Ten Commandments?

🔑 **Laws:** Rules concerning behaviour.

KNOW THE WAY

LESSON 120 Authority and Tradition

GROUNDWORK
In this lesson we plan to:
- explore how authority and tradition influence a person's morality.

DIGGING DEEPER
How do authority and tradition influence my morality?

Key Concepts
Authority/Tradition

Introductory Exercise: What do you do?

In pairs, decide on a plan of action for each of the following situations.

1. You are handed a new baby to take care of for a week. You realise you have absolutely no experience with babies. What do you do?
2. You are on a Boeing 747 airplane flying to New York. A ferocious virus has begun to make the pilot and all the passengers extremely ill. Suddenly you realise you must land the plane! What do you do?
3. You have been asked to organise the funeral of a relative. What do you do?
4. While holidaying in the south of France, the French police arrest you for a crime you did not commit. You are not entitled to a lawyer and must defend yourself. What do you do?

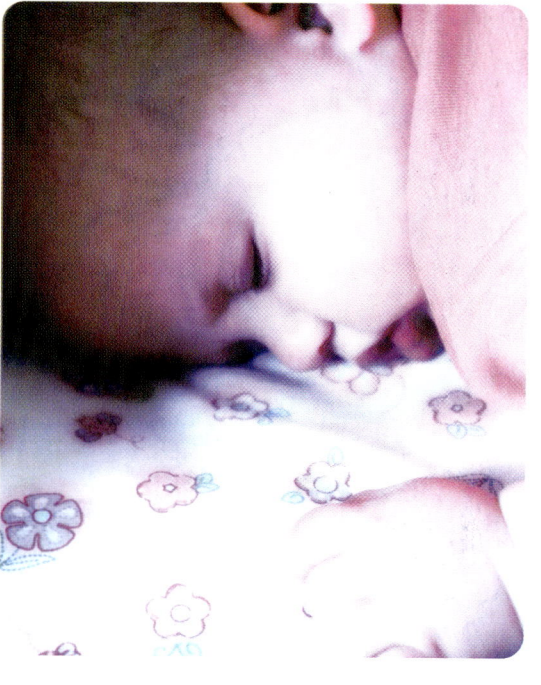

- Outline your decision in each case.
- What helped you to decide what to do in each situation?
- In relation to each of the above scenarios, briefly outline how the following might influence your decision: family, friends or peers, the State, religion.
- How might your moral vision influence your decision in the above cases?

Religious Authority and Tradition

When faced with a moral issue, we look for guidance to those in **authority**. By this we mean those people in positions of leadership who make and carry out decisions on behalf of others. We also turn to **tradition**, i.e. the body of knowledge that has built up on a particular subject over time and that has been handed on from one generation to another. For Christians, the source of tradition is the life of Christ and of the apostles and others who led holy lives down through the centuries. Authority and tradition are sources of morality for us. We look to the voice of authority for education and clarity; we look to the voice of tradition for tried and tested experience and wisdom. For people of faith, morality is largely guided by the authority and tradition of their religion. Members of every faith community look to their leaders for moral guidance throughout their lives. They also look to the tradition of that faith community for guidance.

Religious authority and tradition can be found within the sacred texts and in the teaching of religious leaders.

For example, Christians believe that the Bible was written under the inspiration of the Holy Spirit. They believe that the Holy Spirit continues to guide the Church today. Christian leaders have the authority to interpret this living tradition for the Church community. The religious leaders are not just giving their own opinion; they have the authority to interpret the sacred text and are guided by prayer and tradition. This means that they look to the set of beliefs and the body of religious teaching that has been handed down through tradition from the foundation of the faith, and they pass this on to others.

The Magisterium is the teaching authority of the Catholic Church. It is made up of the Pope and the bishops and it has the authority and the responsibility to offer direction and guidance to Catholics on all moral issues. The Magisterium presents its teaching in the form of:

- encyclical letters from the Pope;
- the *Catechism of the Catholic Church*;
- the documents of the Second Vatican Council (Vatican II);
- pastoral letters from a conference of bishops to the whole country or from a bishop to his diocese.

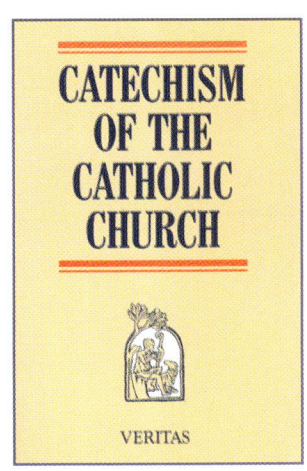

The teachings of the Catholic Church reflect the religious moral vision of Jesus Christ. The documents listed above enable Catholics to find out what the Church's teaching is on every moral issue. For example, Pope John Paul II's encyclical letter *Evangelium Vitae* (1995) explores the whole area of respect for human life. It outlines the Church's teaching on abortion and euthanasia.

Jesus promised to be with his Church always (Matthew 28:20). Christians continue to learn from scripture and tradition what it means to live good lives in imitation of Jesus and to work for justice, peace and truth in the world.

KNOW IT ALL

Copy this exercise into your Religion folder and fill in the blanks using the wordbank given below.

Authority and tradition can be found within the _____ _____ of a religion and in the teaching of _____ _____. For _____, the sacred scriptures are both an authority and a living _____. Religious _____ have a special responsibility and authority to give _____ on moral issues. The religious leaders are not just giving their own opinion, they have the _____ to interpret the sacred text and are guided by _____ and _____.

WORDBANK
Guidance • Tradition • Authority • Sacred text • Religious leaders • Tradition • Christians • Prayer • Leaders

KNOW THE WAY

Sources of Authority in the Five Major World Religions

Followers of the major world religions look to the authority of their sacred texts and religious leaders to guide them in living their moral lives. The teaching that is passed on through their religious tradition is also an important source of moral authority for them. Each of the major world religions has general principles such as a Golden Rule to encourage their followers to lead moral lives. You might like to revise the charts on pages 63 and 68 before completing the following exercise.

5-4-3-2-1

1. Name **five** sacred texts.
2. Name **four** religious leaders.
3. Identify the moral code of **three** world religions.
4. Choose **two** world religions that have a similar moral code.
5. Explain how the Golden Rule of **one** major world religion offers moral guidance to the followers of that religion.

KNOW WHAT

1. How do religious authority and tradition offer guidance to a person's morality?
2. Give an example of how authority and tradition work to inform and support the morality (good living) of Catholics.

DIGGING DEEPER

1. How does the authority and the tradition of your religion support your morality?
2. Identify and describe an area where you think you would need the authority and tradition of your religion to help you make a moral choice.

 Authority: Person or group that makes or carries out decisions for a community or State.

Tradition: Guidance or knowledge that is handed on, e.g. a law or custom.

LESSON 121 Religious Moral Vision

GROUNDWORK
In this lesson we plan to:
- explore the characteristics of a religious moral vision.

DIGGING DEEPER
What is my religious moral vision?

 **Key Concept**
Religious moral vision

Rules Rule!

- What rules do the above signs refer to?
- Some people say that rules can set you free. What do they mean when they say this?

The State puts rules and laws in place in order to help each person to respect themselves and others by keeping the moral code of society. The moral code of a society reflects its moral vision.

Moral code
(Set of rules or laws to guide behaviour)

Moral vision
(Moral view of the world, which reflects one's own set of moral values)

Religious Moral Vision

A **religious moral vision** is based on the set of beliefs, the sacred text and the life and teachings of the founder of each faith tradition. The moral choices of a believer give expression to that believer's religious moral vision.

The Christian moral vision is based on the example of Jesus' life. In section B, we learned that Jesus expressed his moral vision through his words and his actions. He expressed that moral vision in the Sermon on the Mount (Matthew 5:1–7:28), particularly in the Beatitudes (Matthew 5:1-12). The Beatitudes help Christians to live as followers of Jesus and, therefore, to embrace a Christian moral vision.

Religious moral code
E.g. The Beatitudes

Religious moral vision
E.g. To live according to the values outlined in the Beatitudes

The Christian religious moral vision has its origins in God's covenant with the people of Israel. We learned about this in Section C: the story of Abraham and Moses. The Hebrew people were invited into a special relationship with God. They responded to God in prayer and worship, in the way they lived and in the choices they made. God's special relationship with them was the foundation of their religious moral vision, which was expressed in the Ten Commandments.

By the time Jesus began his public ministry, the Jewish Law, including the Ten Commandments, had become complex and detailed in an effort to cover every aspect of daily life. Jesus reminded his listeners of the original spirit of the commandments – the invitation to all people to partake in a loving relationship with God. Jesus expressed this in two new commandments. He said:

> *'You shall love the Lord your God with all your heart, and with all your soul, and with all your mind. This is the greatest and first commandment. And a second is like it: You shall love your neighbour as yourself.'*

These two commandments sum up the Christian moral vision.

DIGGING DEEPER
(You might like to revise the Beatitudes on page 122 of Section B to help with this exercise.)

1. How do the Beatitudes express the Christian moral vision?
2. If all Christians lived according to this religious moral vision, what impact would it have on the world?
3. What do you think happens when the living out of a religious moral vision begins to break down? Think of an example of how this could happen.
4. Give one example of how the religious moral vision expressed in the Golden Rule of the five major world religions (see page 63) could make a difference to a member of one of these religions.

KNOW HOW
You will need a Bible for this exercise.

Read Luke 6:12.

- How do you think Jesus nourished his moral vision?
- What do you think can help to nourish the Christian religious moral vision?

What is different about a religious moral vision?

A person can have a moral vision without necessarily being a person of faith. Many good people throughout history have been motivated or driven to act justly out of concern for other human beings, rather than out of a religious moral vision. A religious moral vision has an 'extra' dimension or element. For example, a Christian is motivated to do good and to live a moral life out of the belief that:

- human life is a God-given gift;
- God is Creator and Father of all people;
- every person is created in the image and likeness of God and, therefore, has unique value, worth and dignity;
- each person must take full responsibility for their actions in order to maintain a right relationship with God and with others;
- the world is God's creation and we have been given responsibility to respect, protect and develop it. (We will explore this responsibility further in Lesson 129.)

Being true to a religious moral vision can be difficult, as the following story illustrates:

> Then someone came to Jesus and said, 'Teacher, what good deed must I do to have eternal life?' And he said to him, 'If you wish to enter into life, keep the commandments.' He said to him, 'Which ones?' And Jesus said, 'You shall not murder; You shall not commit adultery; You shall not steal; You shall not bear false witness; Honour your father and mother; also, You shall love your neighbour as yourself.' The young man said to him, 'I have kept all these; what do I still lack?' Jesus said to him, 'If you wish to be perfect, go, sell your possessions, and give the money to the poor, and you will have treasure in heaven; then come, follow me.' When the young man heard this word, he went away grieving, for he had many possessions. (Matthew 19:16-22)

The rich young man was sad because, although he observed the Ten Commandments, something more was asked of him. He was challenged to think about what it really means to live for God, to give oneself completely to God and to be prepared to follow God's ways, no matter what the personal cost.

Living out of a religious moral vision brings challenge into our lives. Jesus lived out of a religious moral vision and he certainly faced many challenges. Love was at the core of his life and in the end he sacrificed his life for this value.

A religious moral vision is an informed vision. It is arrived at through prayer and the guidance of religious leaders. Prayer can change a person's way of seeing what is right and what is wrong. So also can the guidance of religious texts and the teachings of religious leaders.

> The *Catechism of the Catholic Church* states: 'The Word of God is a light for our path. We must assimilate [absorb] it in faith and prayer, and put it into practice.'

KNOW WHAT
1. What is the difference between a moral vision and a religious moral vision?
2. Which vision is the more difficult one to live by? Explain your answer.

DIGGING DEEPER
1. How does the story of the rich young man help us to realise that living out of a religious moral vision takes a lot of time, effort and dedication?
2. How does having a prayer life support a person's religious moral vision?

KNOWING ME KNOWING YOU
Think of someone whose life choices clearly display their religious moral vision. Write about that person.

Religious moral vision: Awareness of what is right and wrong, as revealed by the sacred texts or founder of a community of faith.

KNOW THE WAY

Growing in Morality

LESSON 122 Moral Growth

GROUNDWORK
In this lesson we plan to:
- explore the development of personal morality;
- explore the human and religious need to move beyond selfishness to maturity.

DIGGING DEEPER
What stage of moral development have I reached?

Key Concepts
Moral growth/Moral maturity

Story: Changing the World

When I was young, I wanted to change the world. I found it was difficult to change the world, so I tried to change my country. When I found I couldn't change the country, I began to focus on my town. I couldn't change the town, so I tried to change my family. Now I am old and I realise the only thing I can change is myself. Suddenly I realise that if, long ago, I had changed myself, I could have made an impact on my family. My family and I could have made an impact on our town. That impact could have changed the nation and I could indeed have changed the world.

KNOW WHAT

1. What did the person in the story want to change? How did they go about it? Did they succeed?
2. How did the person's motivation (i.e. reasons for acting in a particular way) change over their lifetime?
3. What was the biggest realisation for this person?

DIGGING DEEPER

1. It is always easier to look back on a decision you have made and say that you could have made a better one. How can we try to make the best decision the first time round?
2. How much has the motivation for your thoughts and actions changed over the years? Give examples to illustrate your answer.

Stages of Moral Growth

In the story above, the person's thinking and the motivation for their actions changed as they grew older. The same process happens to our morality: it changes, grows and matures over time: this is called **moral growth**.

Moral growth is a gradual process, occurring in stages. While each stage is not always linked to a particular age-group, the movement of an individual from one stage to the next does represent a higher level of moral growth.

Stage 1 – Moral Immaturity

When we are very young, we do the right thing only if it benefits us in some way. Our motivation to do good is selfishness! We know that if we don't do the right thing, we will not be rewarded. For example, a toddler may share a toy simply because they know they will be given a treat. At this stage, the person is not making a choice based on the fact that something is right or wrong.

Stage 2 – Moral Steps

The second stage of moral growth relates to fear of punishment. Someone behaves well and makes 'good' moral choices but the motivation is to avoid punishment and gain reward, not because of what is right or wrong. For example, a child may behave well in the school yard in order to avoid detention from the supervising teacher, or a college student may visit their parents at the weekend just to avoid being given out to on the phone during the week. It is a step higher than moral immaturity, but the motivation is still immature.

Stage 3 – Moral Sheep

The third stage is motivated by approval from peers. We want to be the same, hence the name 'moral sheep'. We make decisions in order to be liked by others. At this stage of moral growth, the person becomes more aware of the positive and negative consequences that result from their actions and there is an increasing awareness of right and wrong. Groups of teenagers may agree to fundraise for a charity or make Christmas hampers for the local St Vincent de Paul group. This type of action encourages moral growth because those involved become more aware of the consequences of their actions.

Stage 4 – Moral Society

The fourth stage is about being influenced by society and promoting behaviour for the common good of all. For example, a person will pay their TV license because it is the right thing to do, as opposed to paying it just to avoid getting caught. At this stage of moral growth, the person is motivated by a concern for the common good, so they will abide by the laws of society which protect this value.

Stage 5 – Moral Maturity

A person reaches the stage of **moral maturity** when they behave in a way that upholds the values of justice, peace, respect, truth, love and forgiveness. The person at this stage of moral growth has an informed moral vision that serves to guide their morality. With moral maturity, the motivation for the behaviour comes from *inside* the person. This is different from moral immaturity, where behaviour in influenced from *outside* the person, i.e. peer pressure, fear of disapproval, fear of getting caught and so on.

The Five Stages of Moral Growth – From selfishness to selflessness

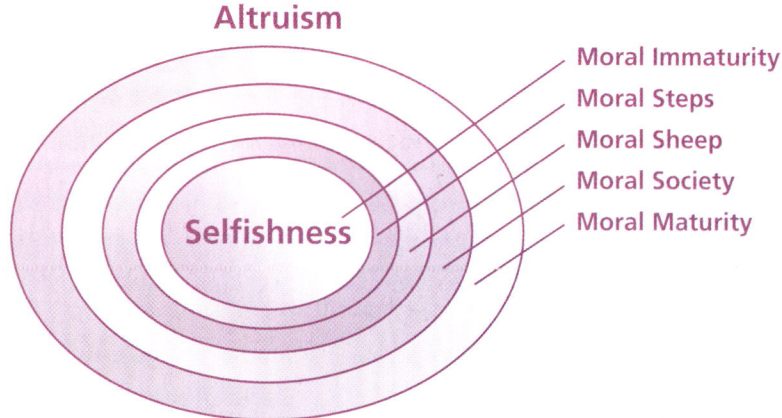

From the five stages of moral growth, we can see that a person's motivation to do the right thing moves from the stage of reward and punishment, through the need to be liked and to have approval, towards the stage where a person behaves out of a personal conviction. In other words, to be fully mature is to move from selfishness to altruism (selflessness). This is what it means to develop a personal morality. Jesus is an example of someone who was fully mature.

5-4-3-2-1

1. Name and explain the **five** titles given to the stages of moral growth.
2. Which **four** stages are not possible to achieve as a toddler? Why?
3. Give examples to explain **three** of the stages of moral growth.
4. What **two** words describe the personal progression from moral immaturity to moral maturity?
5. Identify the **one** stage of moral growth that you think you are at. Give reasons to explain your answer.

KNOW IT ALL
Complete the following sentences in your Religion folder.

1. Moral growth involves changes in our…
2. Sometimes people can get stuck at one stage because…
3. Achieving moral maturity takes effort because…

DIGGING DEEPER
1. If everyone stayed at stage one or two, what kind of world would we live in?
2. If we were only motivated to do good in order to gain the approval of others, what would this mean for our society?
3. What stage of moral maturity do you think you have reached? Give reasons for your answer.

Changing and Growing

Growth and change are human activities. Human beings want to change and grow for the better. All the time, we are making plans for the future. For example, we study specific subjects today in order to be successful in a specific career in the future; we save a specific amount of money this week in order to buy a particular item next week.

The human need to move beyond our present situation includes our need to move through the stages of moral growth. Our religion supports us in our need to move from selfishness to altruism, from moral immaturity to moral maturity.

But why do we need to attain moral maturity? It is because our actions have consequences for ourselves and others, and we have a moral responsibility to ensure that these consequences are good.

Story: The Woodcutter's Bowl

High up in the mountains lived a woodcutter and his father. The boy's mother had died when he was a child and the young boy had learned his trade from his father. One day, while at the market in the valley below, the woodcutter met the love of his life and eventually they were married. She came to live up the mountain with her new husband and his father.

In time, the woodcutter and his wife had a son – their pride and joy. But, as the child grew older, so too did the grandfather. The old man's hand shook a lot and he always made a mess at the table. Now, the wife was a very house-proud woman and she grew more and more irritated with the old man. She nagged at her husband to do something about him, so eventually, for peace sake, the woodcutter acted. He carved out a small wooden bowl. The old man was then moved away from the table at mealtimes and his food was put into the bowl. Now, though the father had become feeble in body, he was not feeble in mind, and this action of his son and daughter-in-law hurt him a lot. But he kept his sorrow to himself and did not complain.

Then one day something terrible happened. The young boy, who was now about seven years old, went missing. The woodcutter and his wife were beside themselves with worry. The woodcutter noticed that his carving shed was lying open and that some of his tools were missing. Eventually, they found the boy in the forest, chopping some wood from a tree. 'Son,' said the mother, 'what are you doing?' 'Don't worry!' said the boy. 'I'm doing a job for you.' 'What job are you doing?' the father asked, amazed. 'I'm cutting some wood to make a bowl, father,' the boy said, 'so that when you're old like Granda, you'll have your own bowl for when we put you in the corner.'

Granda was back at table from that evening onwards.

KNOW WHAT

1. What would you say about the woodcutter's conscience? Was it strong or weak? What stage of moral growth would you say the woodcutter had reached?
2. What about the woodcutter's wife? What stage of moral growth do you think she was at? Give a reason for your answer.
3. What were the consequences of the couple's actions for the old man?
4. How did the actions of the parents influence the child's actions? Explain your answer.
5. Would you say the child acted out of moral maturity or simply in imitation of his parents? What does that say about the power of influence?
6. What were the consequences of the child's action for the situation?

DIGGING DEEPER
Why is it important for people to reach moral maturity?

Moral growth: The process whereby our morality changes, grows and matures over time. A person's moral growth is reflected in their choices.

Moral maturity: Fully developed ability to make good choices.

See pages 497, 498 and 499 for past exam questions on this topic.

KNOW THE WAY

LESSON 123 Conscience and Morality

GROUNDWORK
In this lesson we plan to:
- explore the meaning of conscience and its importance in moral maturity.

DIGGING DEEPER
How does my conscience help me to move towards moral maturity?

 **Key Concept**
Conscience

We reach the stage of moral maturity when we make good choices based on our concern for others and not just for ourselves. What part of us is actually engaged in the process of developing moral maturity? Let's try to find out!

What would you do if…

- you saw someone with a combat knife at school?
- you were offered alcohol at a party?
- you saw someone in your class being pushed around?
- you got the chance to go out with someone else's boyfriend or girlfriend?
- you were offered a lift home from a party by a friend who appeared to have been using drugs or alcohol?
- you were travelling home with a friend and they started to drive over the speed limit?

In small groups, choose *one* of the situations above and discuss the following questions.

1. What would be your immediate response in the situation (in the instant after it happens)?
2. What other people, apart from yourself, would be affected by the situation?
3. What thoughts go through your mind as you decide what you would do in the situation: is it only about following a rule? Is it only about following what you feel at that moment, or would you say there's more to what's involved as you make a decision? If so, what does this 'more' include?
4. What would guide you in the situation and in any choice or decision you would make about it?

Conscience

Our **conscience** helps us to respond to moral situations. But what does the word 'conscience' really mean? Is it a little voice inside our heads? Something we feel when we are making the wrong decision? Here is what some famous people had to say about conscience:

*'**Conscience** is the inner voice which warns us that someone may be looking.'*
(H. L. Mencken)

*'The person that loses their **conscience** has nothing left worth keeping.'* (Izaak Walton)

*'War is so unjust and ugly that all who wage it must try to stifle the voice of **conscience** within themselves.'* (Tolstoy)

*'Good friends, good books and a sleepy **conscience**: this is the ideal life.'* (Mark Twain)

*'Courage without **conscience** is a wild beast.'* (Robert G. Ingersoll)

KNOW WHAT
1. How would you describe your understanding of 'conscience'?
2. Choose the definition that you think is the most effective in explaining the word 'conscience'. Give reasons for your choice.
3. Which statement do you think is the least effective? Why?

A Guidance System

Our conscience is a guidance system working within us. We can think of our conscience as our 'SIM card', without which we would not operate properly. Like our morality, it is part of who we are.

Our **CONSCIENCE** (our SIM!) guides us in three ways:

S It **sees** the difference between right and wrong, good and bad, and lets us know when we have made a choice that is good and when we have made a choice that is bad.

I It gives us an **inner** sense of what is right and wrong, even if we cannot fully explain why this is so. It is inside/within us, even if others put pressure on us to make other choices.

M It makes us want to choose what we think is for the best. It acts like a **magnet** and draws us towards what we feel is right and good.

An Informed Conscience

To make a moral decision, i.e. a decision that involves right or wrong, good or bad, is not always an easy task. Because our conscience is part of who we are as human beings, it can be strong or weak, full of knowledge or lacking in knowledge. So when we are making a moral decision, it is really important to have as much *information* as possible.

This means that we must *inform* our conscience with the necessary information to make good moral decisions. An informed conscience will be up to date with the moral teachings from all the sources of morality, particularly from the faith community to which we belong. The leaders of faith communities continue to address the moral questions of today and provide guidance for their members, e.g. Catholics receive guidance from the Pope and the bishops.

Think of conscience in terms of a computer. When we log on to the internet, we make sure that our computer has all the information it requires in order to protect it from viruses; we make sure our virus protection system is constantly updated against all new virus attacks. In the same way, we need to provide our conscience with constant updates in order to support its work. If we don't keep our conscience informed, we can make a wrong decision due to lack of information.

An Informed Christian Conscience

For a Christian, conscience does not act alone, but works under the guidance of the authority and tradition of the Church. Through the religious leaders and the teachings of the Church, the Christian conscience receives the information that is required to make good moral decisions.

> 'Conscience is not merely somebody whispering in my ear; it is not just a feeling or an instinct. It is my judgement of what is the best thing to do in a particular situation. The judgement is not just about how I feel. Sometimes a person may feel no guilt about a proposed action, but someone else may feel equally strongly that it wrongs them.' (The Irish Catholic Bishops' Conference, 1998)

Catholics believe that their conscience is informed by the Holy Spirit in different ways:

- Through the Bible, where they learn about how God sees the world and how they are called to serve one another.
- Through the Tradition of the Church, which passes on the truth of the faith under the inspiration of the Holy Spirit.
- Through the teaching of the Pope and the bishops.
- Through inspirational people, who show what it means to follow Jesus and to make good moral choices. The saints are a good example.
- Through prayer, which enables believers to become more aware of what God wants and of how God loves all people.

Such information helps people to live good lives and to make good moral decisions.

TAKE FIVE

1. What does the word 'conscience' mean?
2. Why can our conscience be described as our 'SIM card'?
3. How can the letters S I M help us to remember the three ways in which our conscience acts as a guidance system?
4. What is an informed conscience?
5. What informs or guides a Christian conscience?

DIGGING DEEPER

1. Why is it necessary to inform our conscience?
2. Do you feel that your conscience is informed? Why?/Why not?
3. What or who informs your conscience? Give examples to support your answer.
4. How does our faith support us in our moral growth?
5. Do you feel that your faith tradition helps you to progress towards moral maturity? Why?/Why not?

Activating our Conscience

We know that our conscience is part of us, but it is not always activated! This means that we can make some choices without the help of our conscience. See if you can work out which of the following situations require the help of your conscience:

1. You have just noticed your friend stealing from a supermarket.
2. You decide to go into the kitchen to boil the kettle.
3. You must choose to wear trainers or shoes.
4. You are asked to take part in the Concern fast at school.
5. You discover that a student at school is being bullied.
6. You have to go to your guitar lesson at five.
7. Your best friend wants to copy your homework.
8. You have found money in the school toilets.

KNOW WHAT

1. Which situations would cause your conscience to be activated/not to be activated? Explain your choices.
2. Is it possible to ignore your conscience? Give some examples to support your answer.
3. How does our conscience help us to develop moral maturity?

DIGGING DEEPER

1. How does having an informed conscience help relationships in the world?
2. Do you think you could name a person who always acts with an informed conscience? Give reasons for your answer.

 **Conscience: Capacity/ability for judging the best thing to do when free to choose.**

Religious Morality in Action

LESSON 124 Moral Decision-making

GROUNDWORK
In this lesson we plan to:
- explore the process of moral decision-making.

DIGGING DEEPER
What can help me in my moral decision-making?

Key Concept
Decision-making

Introductory Activity: You Decide!

In pairs, decide who is going to ask the question and who is going to answer.

Run through the questions briskly – your answers need to be immediate!

Chalk or cheese?	Guitar or drums?	Text or chat?
Male or female?	Hair long or short?	Chess or monopoly?
Meat or veg?	Hoodie or shirt?	Dog or cat?
Walk or bus?	French or Physics?	Fish or chips?
	Corrie or Eastenders?	Drama or gig?

You did not require a lot of thought or reflection to answer the above questions. Making a moral choice is quite the opposite! It calls for a detailed process of consideration. We will now look at the D.E.C.I.D.E. process of **decision-making**.

D.E.C.I.D.E

D	**Define**	**Define** the facts and find out all the relevant information.
E	**Experience**	Listen to advice from the voice of **experience**, particularly to the traditions of your faith community/church. Your family, friends and community can also be of help.
C	**Consequences**	Think of all the possible **consequences** of your decision. Who will they affect? How will they affect your relationship with others, self and God?
I	**Inner self**	Listen to your conscience and allow your **inner self** to guide you. It is at this point that people of faith turn to their religion for guidance.
D	**Decide**	**Decide** what to do and have the courage of your convictions.
E	**Evaluate**	**Evaluate** your decision and learn from your own experience.

The D.E.C.I.D.E. Process in Action

Let's look at a moral dilemma (problem) and work through the D.E.C.I.D.E. process in order to figure out a moral solution.

Penny and Josh have been asked to collect and take care of all the third-year fundraising money at school. Penny just adores rock bands and she would love to see her favourite band play live in the city on Friday night, but she doesn't have enough money to buy a ticket. The fundraising money is just sitting there and if she were to 'borrow' the price of the ticket from it, she could find a weekend job and then pay it back. Josh suggests that he should take the cash home to his parents' safe for the weekend. What should Penny do? She thinks this is a 'once in a lifetime' chance to see her favourite group.

D – Define the facts

Penny and Josh have been given a position of trust. They have been asked to collect and keep safe the fundraising money.

E – Experience

Whom should Penny talk to? What will she say? Do you think Penny already knows what her family, friends, community and faith tradition would say about the situation? What would they say, and do you think they would all say the same thing?

C – Consequences

What would happen if Penny took the money and was able to pay it back? What would happen if she took it but couldn't pay it back? Who would be affected by Penny's decision to take the money? What relationships would be affected? What would be the impact of Penny's decision if she took the money? What would be the impact of Penny's decision if she did not take the money?

I – Inner self

Penny has to take the time to listen to her inner self, her conscience. Remember, our conscience helps us to decide what is best. Penny and Josh would not have been asked to take care of the money if they had not already shown that they could be trusted. This means that they had already made good moral decisions. At this point, Penny needs to take time out to pray for guidance. If she makes a quick decision, it could have devastating consequences and affect her reputation for a very long time.

D – Decide
Did you ever make a decision and then change your mind about it several times? When you are making a moral decision, it is important to complete each stage in the process and be happy with your decision before acting on it. At this stage, Penny must make a decision and be happy with it. Then she must act on it.

E – Evaluate
Just as we can learn from our mistakes, we can also learn from our successes. Whatever Penny has decided to do, it is important that she evaluate (examine and judge) the outcome and learn from the process that she has engaged in.

KNOW HOW
With the help of the D.E.C.I.D.E. process, see if you can work out what you think is the best decision to take in the following moral dilemmas.

- Cathal's younger brother Gerard is always annoying him. He doesn't know when to get lost and he embarrasses Cathal in front of his friends. One weekend, Cathal is left at home to babysit Gerard. When Gerard goes off to bed, Cathal relaxes in front of the TV. Before long, three of Cathal's friends call round to invite him to a party. Cathal really wants to go and he knows that Gerard is fast asleep. What should he do? Would it be so bad to leave a nine-year-old at home alone?
- Ruby would love to go to College, but she has to study really hard for every grade she gets. Her pals are always on at her to chill out but she reckons it is easier for them: they get the same grades and don't have to spend half the time studying, or so it seems anyway. On Monday morning, Ruby's Junior Cert mocks will begin, so she spends the whole weekend studying. When she reaches her school, she meets two of her friends, who are really excited; one of them found the exam papers and they have until twelve thirty to gather all the answers. Ruby is excited too, but in her heart she is disappointed. What should she do? Should she ignore the papers; after all, she has studied hard? Or perhaps she should tell the teacher concerned?

KNOW WHAT
How did the D.E.C.I.D.E. process help you to reach a moral solution to each dilemma?

DIGGING DEEPER
1. If we take time with a moral decision, how is the end result affected?
2. What would happen if you left out one or more of the stages in the D.E.C.I.D.E. process? Explain your answer.
3. Do you think this process would be helpful to you if you were faced with a moral dilemma in your own life? Why?/Why not?

 **Decision-making:** Process involved in making a choice.

LESSON 125 A Religious Moral Vision

GROUNDWORK
In this lesson we plan to:
- explore how a religious moral vision can influence the moral decisions of believers.

DIGGING DEEPER
How does my faith influence my moral decisions?

Key Concepts
Decision-making/Forgiveness

Meet Saala and Susie…

Saala and Susie are both sixteen. Saala is a Muslim. Islamic religious laws forbid Muslims from drinking alcohol. Susie is a Roman Catholic. Her religion asks her to show respect for herself and others. The laws of the State forbid both of them from drinking alcohol in a public place. They are at a party and have access to alcohol. Before they decide if they will take a drink, what kind of questions do you think go through their minds.

Saala and Susie face the same dilemma.

- Do you think they would both respond in the same way?
- What would be different about the approach of each one to their decision?
- How might their approach affect their decision?
- How could the following influences affect their decision: media, friends, family, school, State, religion?

The Moral Vision of Judaism, Christianity and Islam

To help us to understand how a religion would have an influence on the moral decision-making of believers, let's take a closer look at the moral vision of Judaism, Christianity and Islam.

The Jewish Moral Vision
- Life is sacred because all people are created in the image of God.
- Because God created the world, all of creation should be treated with reverence and should be considered holy.
- Acts of cruelty are a disgrace to God. All people deserve to be treated with compassion.

- The Jewish people believe that God has spoken to them through the events of their history and that God continues to speak to them through the events of the present.
- Jewish people are guided by prayer and sacred scripture, particularly the Torah and the Ten Commandments.
- They are also guided by the Talmud, which is an interpretation of the Torah.
- At the heart of Jewish morality is justice.
- Freedom is another important value. This includes political and religious freedom and the freedom of all people to shape their own lives.

The Golden Rule of Judaism: *'What is harmful to yourself, do not to your fellow men.'* (Talmud)

The Christian Moral Vision
- Life is sacred because all people are created in the image of God.
- Because God created the world, all of creation should be treated with reverence and should be considered holy.
- God offers all people the gift of freedom to choose between good and evil.
- The way of Jesus Christ – as shown by his life, death and resurrection – is at the centre of the Christian moral vision.
- At the heart of Christian morality is love. The Christian community is a community of love. Jesus said: 'Love one another as I have loved you.'
- **Forgiveness** is an important part of that love: Jesus taught that God forgives and that God asks all people to forgive one another.
- Christians are guided by the Bible and especially by the Ten Commandments and the Beatitudes.
- Jesus Christ gave the apostles and those who succeeded them the responsibility to teach the community in his name. So, Christians listen to what the Church teaches as a guide to Christian living.
- Christians are also guided by the experience of others in their faith community (past and present), particularly by the lives of the saints and those who shine out as an example of God's love in the world.
- Scripture, prayer, the teachings of the Church and the example (or witness) of others all help Christians to inform their conscience.

The Golden Rule of Christianity: *'Always treat others as you would like them to treat you.'* (Matthew 7:12)

The Commandment of Jesus: *'Love one another as I have loved you.'* (John 15:12)

The Islamic Moral Vision
- Men and women are religious beings because God has created them. All that God has created is dependent on God.
- Sacred law, called Sharia, teaches Muslims how to behave. This law is based on the Qur'an (the sacred text of Islam), the example of Muhammad and the teachings of Muslim scholars. It covers social, political, economic, educational and spiritual aspects of life.
- The Qur'an is considered the perfect revelation from God and is treated with great respect.
- Islam's code of behaviour is expressed in the Five Pillars of Islam: Shahada ('There is no God but Allah and Muhammad is his messenger'), Salah (prayer), Zakat (giving to the poor), Sawm (fasting during Ramadan) and Hajj (pilgrimage to Mecca).

The Golden Rule of Islam: *'No one of you is a believer until he desires for his brother that which he desires for himself.'* (Sunna)

How does a religious moral vision influence the moral decisions of believers?

KNOW IT ALL

Table Quiz (The marks are given in brackets.)
1. Who has given Christians the freedom to choose between good and evil? (2)
2. What does Judaism say about compassion? (2)
3. What did Jesus Christ give the apostles? (2)
4. What does Islam say about all that God has created? (2)
5. Where do Muslims find their code of behaviour? (2)
6. What does the Bible offer Christians? (2)
7. What does Judaism teach about creation? (2)
8. How does prayer impact upon the moral life of a Christian? (2)
9. What is at the heart of Jewish morality? (2)
10. Where is the Islamic code of moral behaviour expressed? (2)
11. Name four of the Pillars of Islam. (4)
12. How does the experience of others guide the morality of Christians? (2)
13. Name and describe an important value in Judaism? (4)
14. Explain the importance of forgiveness in Christian morality? (4)

Human Life is Sacred

One of the deepest held beliefs of Christians is that human life is sacred.

'Human life is a precious gift to be loved and defended in each of its stages. The Commandment "You shall not kill" always requires respecting and promoting human life from its beginning to its natural end.' (Pope John Paul II)

'The inalienable rights of the person must be recognised and respected by civil society and the political authority. These human rights depend neither on single individuals nor on parents; nor do they represent a concession made by society and the state; they belong to human nature and are inherent in the person by virtue of the creative act from which the person took his origin. Among such fundamental rights one should mention in this regard every human being's right to life and physical integrity from the moment of conception until death.' (Catechism of the Catholic Church, 2273)

Suicide and Abortion

All people experience difficult times in their lives. However, for some it can seem that there is no end to the darkness and no hope in sight. During these times, the Catholic Church encourages all Christians to look to the life and death of the Risen Jesus for comfort, in the hope that those who may be thinking about suicide or abortion might reconsider their situation. Christians are assured that there is life after death and that God is loving and merciful and understands the sufferings of the human heart.

On the issue of suicide, the *Catechism of the Catholic Church* states:

'Everyone is responsible for his life before God who has given it to him. It is God who remains the sovereign Master of life. We are obliged to accept life gratefully and preserve it for his honour and the salvation of our souls. We are stewards, not owners, of the life God has entrusted to us. It is not ours to dispose of.' (CCC, 2280)

On the issue of abortion, the Catechism states:

'Human life must be respected and protected absolutely from the moment of conception. From the first moment of his existence, a human being must be recognised as having the rights of a person – among which is the inviolable right of every innocent being to life.' (CCC, 2270)

We will now take a closer look at the religious moral vision on Euthanasia.

Case Study – Active Voluntary Euthanasia

Active voluntary euthanasia is the phrase used to describe the situation where someone who is ill and dying asks to die (voluntary), and they request the help of someone else to bring this about (active). There are thirty-three 'right to die' groups from all over the world in the pro-euthanasia organisation called ERGO. To date in Ireland, there has been no State law passed that will allow euthanasia.

The Christian Moral Vision on Euthanasia

The Christian moral vision *goes against* active voluntary euthanasia. This is because Christians believe that each person is created by God and that human life is sacred (holy). It is very difficult for a person who is terminally ill to journey through their pain and it is also difficult for family and friends to journey beside them. This difficulty is appreciated by the Christian churches and much thought and effort has gone into the many church documents that express the

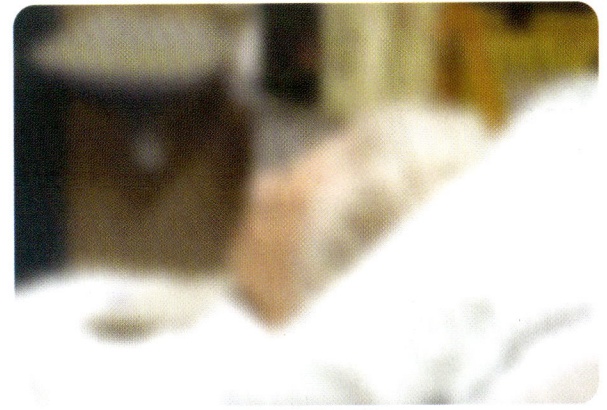

moral teaching on euthanasia. Two such documents from the Catholic Church are:

- *The Declaration on Euthanasia* (Sacred Congregation for the Doctrine of the Faith, 1980)
- *Evangelium Vitae* (Pope John Paul II, 1995)

In the *Declaration on Euthanasia*, the Catholic Church states that:

- human life is sacred and no one has the right to dispose of it;
- human life is a gift from God that must be preserved.

This teaching is repeated in the *Catechism of the Catholic Church* when it states that it is in the hands of God alone to give and take life. It goes on to say that to directly take someone's life, even if they request it, is to break the moral law of respect for life.

In *Evangelium Vitae*, Pope John Paul II teaches that 'euthanasia is a grave violation of the law of God, since it is the deliberate and morally unacceptable killing of a human person' *(EV, 65)*. The Church places its teaching within the context of the care that is available to people who are near death, particularly through the work of the hospice movement.

KNOW IT ALL

Complete the following sentences in your Religion folder.

1. The Christian moral vision is opposed to euthanasia because…
2. Two of the documents that express the Catholic Church's teaching on euthanasia are…
3. The *Declaration on Euthanasia* states that…
4. The *Catechism of the Catholic Church* states that to take someone's life is to break…
5. Pope John Paul II wrote that…
6. The Catholic teaching on euthanasia is placed within the context of…

The Islamic Moral Vision on Euthanasia

The Islamic moral vision *goes against* euthanasia. Islam teaches that men and women are sacred beings because God has created them, and all that God has created is dependent on God. The Qu'ran states: 'To Allah belongs the kingdom of the heavens and the earth. He creates what He pleases' (Sura 42:49) and 'Destroy not yourselves. Surely Allah is ever merciful to you' (Sura 4:29).

The prophet Muhammad, the founder of Islam, was very much opposed to a person taking their own life. The Islamic faith teaches that when people are suffering badly, they should ask Allah for help, as no one has the right to decide when they will die.

KNOW IT ALL

Copy the following exercise into your Religion folder and mark each sentence as true or false.

1. Islamic moral teaching holds that euthanasia goes against God.
2. Muslims believe that all that God has created is not dependent on God.
3. Islamic moral teaching holds that human life is sacred.
4. Muhammad did not give an opinion on moral issues.
5. When Muslims are suffering, they should ask one another for help first.

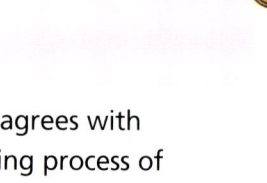

The religious moral vision of both Christianity and Islam fundamentally disagrees with euthanasia. Both religious moral visions would influence the decision-making process of believers if the moral issue of euthanasia arose. Both religions offer much support to their followers in order that they make moral decisions in keeping with the teaching of their faith.

KNOW HOW

In order to be properly informed on a moral issue, such as euthanasia, we seek guidance from the sources of authority and tradition of our religion. This guidance works to inform our conscience and, therefore, influences our decision-making process.

1. In pairs, think of one other moral issue that would call for information and guidance from your religion in order to inform your conscience in relation to it.
2. Try to find out what the moral teaching of your religion is with regard to your chosen moral area.
3. Discuss your information and your viewpoints in class.

 **Forgiveness:** The act of pardoning, excusing or making allowance for an offence.

See page 499 for past exam questions on this topic.

KNOW THE WAY

LESSON 126 Morality in Action

GROUNDWORK
In this lesson we plan to:
- explore the concept of love as an expression of morality in action.

DIGGING DEEPER
What is Christian love?

Key Concepts
Truth/Integrity/Life/Respect

Love is All you Need!

The word 'love' is often over-used. Look at all these phrases – what meaning does love have in each of them?

I'd love to live in Egypt.

The twins argue a lot, but it's obvious that they really love each other.

I love your dress. Where did you get it?

I LOVE MY FAMILY, BUT SOMETIMES THEY DRIVE ME MAD.

Paula loves Bruce.

Bernadette is my brother's girlfriend – I think he's in love.

'I love my cat,' said Niamh.

They never argue - it must be love.

We sometimes use the word 'love' in a general sense to show that we really like some particular thing or experience. However, love is most properly spoken of in the context of relationships. Love is an 'umbrella term' for all the values within a relationship: when you respect someone, you show them love; when you share with someone, you show them love; when you are honest and true with someone, you show them love, and so on.

445

SECTION F THE MORAL CHALLENGE

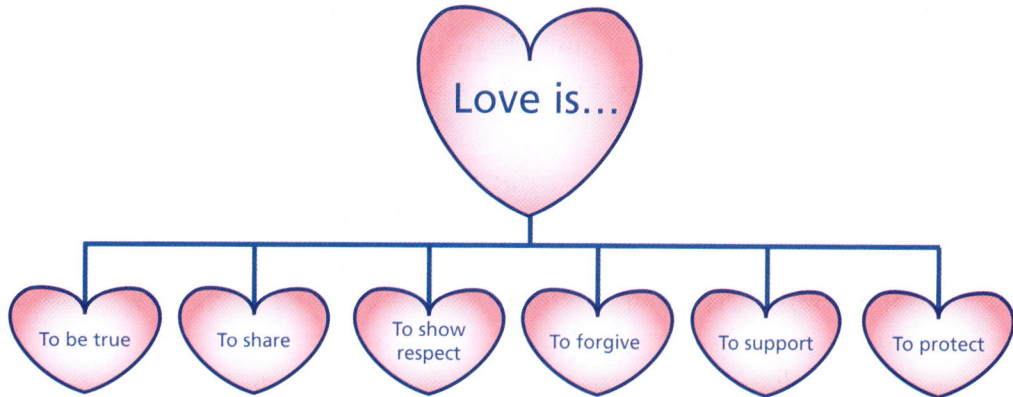

What other values can you add that may be found within a relationship?

There are many different types of love, just as there are many different types of relationship. The first love a baby experiences is the love of family. The bond within a family is a special type of love. This love can inspire great sacrifice in a parent or guardian. Later in life, a person experiences the love of friends, particularly the love of close friends. We say that a person 'falls in love' when they are physically and emotionally attracted to another person. Love is the all-embracing value that surrounds all the other values found within a relationship.

KNOW HOW
Write an acrostic poem based on the word 'Love'.

Truth and Integrity

Truth is a leading value in any right relationship. When we are honest and true in our dealings with others, we show that we have **integrity** and that we make our choices based on a moral vision. When we tell the truth, we are showing our integrity. Of course, it is not always easy to be truthful and honest, but when we succeed, we earn the trust of others and show the depth of our integrity.

Truth is an important Christian value. Jesus equated himself with truth; he said: 'I am the way, and the truth, and the life' (John 14:6). He taught that truth and honesty set people free from the burden of lies and deceit: '…you will know the truth and the truth will make you free' (John 8:32). Love cannot survive without truth.

Respect

The major world religions teach that human **life** is sacred and, therefore, it should be treated with **respect**. To respect means to value, to show consideration and to avoid causing harm to someone or something. Jesus showed a deep respect for all people, regardless of their place in society. He also showed respect for all of creation. We see this respect reflected in the values he singled out in the Beatitudes. Just as love cannot survive without truth, neither can it survive without respect.

Christian Love – Morality in Action

Christian love is most clearly seen in the person and example of Jesus. Jesus said, 'I give you a new commandment, that you love one another. Just as I have loved you, you also should love one another' (John 13:34).

The relationship of love between Jesus and his Father meant that he was prepared, with the help of the Holy Spirit, to sacrifice himself in response to the will of his Father. Christian love is about God's relationship with people and about their relationship with God and with one another.

Christian love does not mean going around hugging and kissing people all of the time! As members of the body of Christ, Christians are called to act together to take care of, support and forgive one another. This is how St Paul explained the Christian definition of love to the early Christian community: 'Love is patient; love is kind; love is not envious or boastful or arrogant or rude. It does not insist on its own way. It is not irritable or resentful; it does not rejoice in wrongdoing, but rejoices in the truth. It bears all things, believes all things, hopes all things, endures all things' (1 Corinthians 13:4-7).

This sense of Christian love grows and develops within each person. Christian love is nourished by God's deep love. The more people accept that they are loved by God, the more they will reflect God's love in the way they care for others and show respect for all life.

Characteristics of the Christian art of loving:
- To see Jesus in others.
- To be the first to love – to take the initiative.
- To love one's enemies.
- To love your neighbour as yourself.

KNOW WHAT
1. Why is love an essential value in relationships?
2. How is truth expressed in relationships?
3. How is respect expressed in relationships?

DIGGING DEEPER
1. What is Christian love?
2. How did St Paul describe Christian love?
3. How are the values of truth and respect linked to the value of Christian love?
4. How does love support and nurture (take care of) all the values in people's relationships?
5. How do right relationships show religious morality in action?

 **Truth:** Facts or beliefs that may be relied on.

Integrity: Not open to bad influences; choices always based on a moral vision.

Life: Found in things or beings that are alive; energy for living.

Respect: To honour; to value; to treat properly.

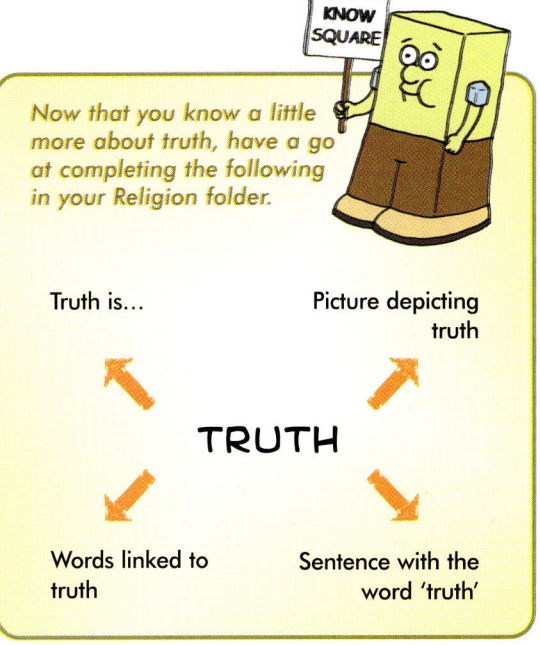

Now that you know a little more about truth, have a go at completing the following in your Religion folder.

Truth is… | Picture depicting truth
TRUTH
Words linked to truth | Sentence with the word 'truth'

LESSON 127 Social Justice

GROUNDWORK
In this lesson we plan to:
- explore the meaning of justice.

DIGGING DEEPER
How does my community of faith work for justice?

Key Concept
Justice

Justice

The first element of justice is to recognise that we are totally dependant on God and must therefore place God before everything else in our lives. As a human being, you have worth and value. You have human dignity, no matter who or what you are, no matter what your religion is, or your gender, or what mix of abilities and disabilities you may have, etc. As a human being, you have human rights. To be denied one's human rights is to be denied **justice**.

Justice is about giving people what is rightfully theirs. A good way to describe justice is to say that it is about *right* relationships with other people, no matter who they are. That includes both close friends and people we don't know, even people we don't particularly like or get along with. Building up right relationships means creating the conditions between ourselves and others that will enable everyone to get along together. When relationships are right, justice is the result. You destroy justice when you destroy right relationships between yourself and other people.

What do we spend more money on?

   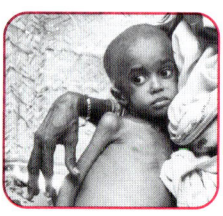

Labels or the fight against child labour?   Women's make-up or women's food?

 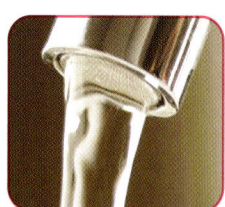  

Fizzy drinks or clean water?   Pets or child poverty?

- What are your initial thoughts about these pictures?
- Does the stark contrast in images help you to focus on the differences in our world? How?
- Of the choices listed, what do we spend more money on? Is this morally right?
- In your opinion, which pair of images is the cause of most concern in the world? Give reasons for your answer.
- How can you personally make a difference?

- From magazines and newspapers, see if you can come up with one other set of contrasting images.

We live in a very unjust world. However, as the following story illustrates, each one of us can make a difference if we start right here, right now.

Story: The Starfish

A young man was walking down a deserted Mexican beach at sunset. As he walked along, he saw an old man in the distance. When he came nearer, he noticed that the old man kept bending down, picking something up and throwing it out into the water. As he moved even closer, he noticed that the old man was picking up starfish that had been washed up on the beach and, one at a time, he was throwing them back into the water.

He was puzzled. He approached the man and asked him what he was doing. 'I'm throwing these starfish back into the ocean,' the old man said. 'You see, it's low tide right now and all of these starfish have been washed up on to the shore. If I don't throw them back into the sea, they'll die up here from lack of oxygen.' 'I understand,' said the younger man, 'but there must be thousands of starfish on this beach. You can't possibly get to all of them. There are simply too many. And don't you realise this is probably happening on hundreds of beaches up and down this coast? Don't you see that you can't possibly make a difference?'

The old man smiled, bent down and picked up yet another starfish. As he threw it back into the sea, he replied, 'Made a difference to that one!'

A World Divided

Our world is divided by enormous wealth on the one hand and great poverty on the other. From the 'wealthy' north to the 'poor' south, we can literally draw a line to show the division.

In 1984, Bob Geldof and Midge Ure brought the Band Aid experience to the world with the release of the song 'Do They Know It's Christmas?', which raised fifteen million euro for famine victims in Ethiopia. This was followed by Live Aid, which in turn raised over one hundred million euro. Similarily, 'Comic Relief' and 'Red Nose Day' raised even more funds.

In 2005, twenty years after Band Aid, Bob Geldof and others organised another major event: Live 8. The injustice caused by poverty and debt remained as fundamental as ever. Live 8 was planned in an effort to urge governments to act. Geldof stressed that the event was about *justice,* not charity. He said:

> 'This is not Live Aid 2. These concerts are the start point for the long walk to justice, the one way we can all make our voices heard in unison. This is without doubt a moment in history where ordinary people can grasp the chance to achieve something truly monumental and demand from the eight world leaders at G8 an end to poverty. The G8 leaders have it within their power to alter history. They will only have the will to do so if tens of thousands of people show them that enough is enough. By doubling aid, fully cancelling debt, and delivering trade justice for Africa, the G8 could change the future for millions of men, women and children. Live 8 has always been about combining political, public and media pressure to make poverty history.'

Note: The G8 is a meeting or summit that brings together the leaders of eight of the world's most powerful countries – the USA, Canada, Great Britain, France, Germany, Italy, Japan and Russia. In 2005, Britain's then prime minister, Tony Blair, hosted the summit. The Live 8 concert was held at the same time so that the leaders would know that the world was watching and waiting for their plan.

Log on to the following websites to find out more about Live 8:

http://www.live8live.com/whatsitabout/

http://www.live8live.com/videos/?clip=ricky1

Many people make an enormous effort to fundraise and create awareness of social injustice in our world. We have all experienced fundraising campaigns in our school, in our locality, in the media, in fact all around us. By taking part in such campaigns, and even organising our own, we can all work together for justice.

KNOW WHAT
1. What does the phrase 'a world divided' mean? How is this situation unjust?
2. How has the work of Bob Geldof contributed to the pursuit of a just world?

DIGGING DEEPER
1. Why is it important to work for justice in our world?
2. Does the issue of justice impact on your moral decision-making? How does it do this?

KNOWING ME KNOWING YOU
Choose one justice project that your school was involved in over the past year. Describe what was done, who was involved and what the outcome was. Then make a poster to summarise your findings.

A religious moral vision can greatly influence a believer's attitude to social justice. Rooted in the beliefs of all religions is the value of justice. The Golden Rule of each of the major world religions speaks about treating others with justice.

The Christian Moral Vision on Justice

Christians believe that it is their religious duty to work for social justice. This means helping to eradicate poverty and the unfair distribution of global wealth. Justice is at the heart of Jesus' message:

> *'You must love God with all your heart, and with all your soul, and with all your mind, and with all your strength; and love your neighbour as yourself.'* (Mark 12:29-31)

In these words, Jesus gives people a way of measuring what is right and what is wrong. When Christians are faced with the moral issue of social justice, they should ask themselves: 'If I do this, will I be showing that I love God? If I do this, will I be showing that I love my neighbour?'

The Catholic Church supports and informs the moral decision-making of its members by its teachings on social justice. These include documents like *Pacem In Terris* (Peace on Earth) from Pope John XXIII. This document works to establish universal peace through promoting truth, justice, charity and liberty. Nearer to home, the Irish Catholic Bishops produced *The Work of Justice*, a document that interprets the Scriptures and their invitation 'to do justice, and to love kindness, and walk humbly with your God' (Micah 6:8).

In Section A, we looked at Trócaire's work for justice and peace in the world. The Christian moral vision inspires and motivates Trocáire's campaign. It has a vision of a world where there is justice for everyone, where people's human dignity is ensured, where human rights are respected and basic human needs met. In a just world, resources would be shared fairly and people would have control over decisions that affect their lives and their future.

KNOWING ME KNOWING YOU

You can find out more about Trócaire and its work for a just world at: *www.trocaire.org*

KNOW WHAT

1. Where does the Christian moral vision come from?
2. See if you can think of two examples of how the Christian moral vision has influenced Christians in their moral decision-making.

The Jewish Moral Vision on Justice

Judaism states that because God created the world, all of creation is holy (sacred) and should be treated with reverence and compassion. Justice is a very powerful theme in the Jewish sacred text. In the Psalms, there is an endless cry for justice for the oppressed, the poor, the powerless.

At the heart of Jewish morality is justice. Jewish people believe that they have a basic responsibility to be fair and act in a just way. They have a passion for what is just and right. They believe in right relationships and this belief expresses itself in charity, compassion and kindness.

> 'Why does the workman ascend the highest scaffolding and risk his life, if you do not pay him his wages as soon as they are due?' (The Talmud)

The moral decision-making of Jewish people is greatly influenced by their religious moral vision. One example of this vision in action is the work of the organisation called the American Jewish World Service (AJWS), an international development organisation dedicated to bringing compassion, dignity and justice to people who are suffering from the oppression of poverty.

KNOWING ME KNOWING YOU

You can find out more about the American Jewish World Service and its work for a just world at: *http://www.ajws.org/index.cfm*

KNOW WHAT

1. Where does the Jewish moral vision come from?
2. Give an example of how the Jewish moral vision has influenced Jewish people to work for justice.

DIGGING DEEPER

1. How can a person's faith help them to work for justice?
2. How is a person's moral vision evident in the way they live their life?
3. Name and describe two ways in which your community of faith works for justice in the world.
4. Write about a time when you were influenced by the moral vision of your religion.

Or

Write about a person you know or have heard about whose moral decision-making was influenced by the moral vision of their religion.

Justice: Fairness and respect, which leads to good relationships.

See page 500 for past exam questions on this topic.

LESSON 128 Moral Failure

GROUNDWORK
In this lesson we plan to:
- come to a greater understanding of moral failure and its consequences.

DIGGING DEEPER
How does a refusal to love lead to the breakdown of relationships?

Key Concepts
Sin/Conscience

The Parable of the Prodigal Son

A farmer had two sons. One day the younger son said to his father, 'Dad, it's time you handed over the farm to the two of us.' The father did as the son asked. He divided up the farm between his two sons. The younger son sold his share of the farm, quickly packed his things and went abroad. There, he wasted his money having a 'good time'. Finally, his pockets were empty. He found himself with no money and no food.

Then he realised what a fool he had been and he decided to return home. 'I have wronged God and I have wronged my father. I'll tell my father that I don't deserve to be his son any more; he can take me on as a hired worker.'

When the younger son was still a long way from home, his father saw him coming and he ran out to meet him. He threw his arms around his neck and kissed him. 'Dad,' the son said, 'I have wronged God and I have wronged you. I don't deserve to be called your son.'

'Quick!' his father called to the servants, 'go and get the best clothes out. Get a ring and sandals and dress my son properly. Then kill the calf we have fattened. We'll have a feast and a grand time tonight. My boy was dead and lost, but here he is alive and back home again!'

Now the older son had been out on the farm. When he heard that his brother had returned and that his father was preparing a feast for him, he was furious. He wouldn't even go inside the house. His father came out and pleaded with him. But the older son answered, 'Look, I have slaved for you all these years. But did I get anything for it? Not even some money to have a good time with my friends. Now, this son of yours throws your money away on the high life, and then comes home again, and you go and kill a calf for him.'

'Look son,' said the father, 'we're always together. The whole farm is yours – you know that. But we have to celebrate tonight. Your brother was dead and lost, but now he is alive and back home again!' (Based on Luke 15:11-32)

KNOW WHAT

1. What do you think was going on in the mind of the younger son when he asked for his share of his inheritance and then went off and wasted it all?
2. What do you think was going on in his mind when he chose to come back?
3. Why do you think the older son was upset?
4. Where are the examples of selfishness in this parable? Explain your answer.

DEEPER DEEPER
1. Where is there a lack of respect shown towards the father in this parable?
2. If someone always gets their own way, does that make them happy? Why?/Why not?
3. Give examples of someone today going their own way rather than going God's way.

The Christian Vision of Moral Failure

The parable of the prodigal son is a good example of how people can be selfish. Selfishness leads to lack of respect for others. People can be selfish in their dealings with other people, in their treatment of the environment and the resources of the world, etc. When we act selfishly, we put our own needs before the needs of others. In this way, we refuse to love others. This kind of behaviour leads to the breakdown of relationships and can be described as moral failure. Another name for moral failure is **sin**.

For Christians, sin refers to anything that goes against God. This includes bad moral decisions, through which people hurt themselves or others or damage the environment. Selfish choices usually lead to sin.

KNOW WHAT
1. When Christians talk about moral failure, what do they mean?
2. How does sin affect the Christian moral vision?

DIGGING DEEPER
1. How do you know if you have sinned? Is it difficult to figure out? Why?/Why not? What part of your inner self helps you to figure it out?
2. Why do you think we can be selfish over and over again, even when we know what happens as a result?

Story: The Storeroom

'Right Mark, everyone else is away; now's our chance,' said Jeff.

'Our chance to what?' enquired Mark.

'It's our chance to raid the computer storeroom. I worked out that today is delivery day.'

'But the storeroom is always locked and the technician left just now with the keys,' said Mark.

'Yes,' said Jeff, 'but not before he opened the storeroom to get me a blank disc. Remember?'

'But you didn't really need a blank disk,' said Mark.

'Clever, eh?' said Jeff, with a smirk on his face. 'And now that he's out of the way, we're wasting valuable time', and he walked purposefully towards the storeroom door.

'You're not going to do what I think you're going to do, are you?' asked Mark in disbelief.

'Yep! You keep watch here until I get the goodies,' said Jeff.

'Ah, you can't be serious! We'll be found out, and even if we're not, it's wrong,' said Mark.

'It feels all right to me! Don't be such a wimp, Mark. Now go and watch at the door,' ordered Jeff firmly, 'or is that "wrong" too?'

Reluctantly, Mark went over to the door to keep watch.

KNOW WHAT

1. Jeff makes a moral decision in the story. Do you think Jeff's decision is wrong? Why?
2. Mark feels pressured into going along with Jeff. What do you think about his final decision?
3. Which character in the story has the stronger conscience? Give reasons for your answer.

DIGGING DEEPER

1. Have you ever found yourself being pressured into making a bad moral decision? What happened?
2. What can help us in a situation where we feel we are about to make a bad moral decision?

Some sins are more serious than others

There are three factors that determine whether something is sinful or not, and how seriously sinful it is.

1. **The action you choose**, i.e. what you do. Choosing to drive while under the influence of drugs or alcohol is more serious than choosing to steal a biscuit from the kitchen.
2. **Your intention in choosing this action,** i.e. why you choose to do it. Young children intend no harm by playing with matches, yet the outcome may be serious. Sometimes, however, people intend to do harm and make bad moral decisions as a result.
3. **The circumstances of your decision,** i.e. how free you are to make this moral decision. If you are put under pressure to make a bad moral decision, then that decision is less sinful for you than if you choose it freely.

There are two main types of sin:

- **mortal sin,** which is the most serious type of sin;
- **venial sin,** which is any other type of less serious sin.

A *mortal sin* results when all three of the above factors are present, when the action is fully understood, there is knowledge, and it is freely chosen. For Christians, mortal sins are so serious that they break a person's relationship with God. Usually, they also cause great harm and damage to others or to the environment. An action has to be very serious before it can be called a mortal sin.

Bad moral decisions may be called *venial sins* when the act, the action and the result are less serious, when the person did not intend the harm or damage caused, or the person was not fully free in making their decision. Venial sins weaken a person's relationship with God; they do not break a relationship with God.

Bad moral decisions may lead to friendships being shattered, trust being broken, fear being aroused and enemies being made. In other words, right relationships break down. This is why such decisions are called sins.

Your **conscience** is your inner ability to know whether a moral decision is good or bad. For people of faith, praying and staying aware of God's love will make their conscience stronger. So, too, will reading the sacred text, knowing the tradition of one's faith and looking at the good example of inspiring people.

KNOW IT ALL
Complete the following sentences in your Religion folder.

1. The three factors that determine the seriousness of a sin are…
2. For Christians, there are two types of sin. They are…
3. Mortal sins are the most serious because…
4. Mortal sin breaks a relationship with God and usually causes…
5. Our conscience helps us to know when something is a sin because…
6. Our conscience can grow stronger with the help of…

The Jewish Vision of Moral Failure

Any situation, experience or event that prevents the Jewish people from being in a full and right relationship with God is a cause of moral failure and is seen as a sin. The Jewish New Year, Rosh Hashanah, begins with ten days of repentance. During this time, a ram's horn, called a *shofar*, is blown. Jews see this as a summons to repent and return to God so that they can begin the New Year in a proper way. The Jewish people look forward with hope to the future and they repent for the past.

KNOW WHAT
When Jews talk about moral failure, what do they mean?

 **Sin:** An offence against God. Turning away from a relationship with God and others.

LESSON 129 Stewardship of the Earth

GROUNDWORK
In this lesson we plan to:
- explore the meaning of stewardship and how a lack of stewardship of the earth is a moral failure on the part of humans;
- explore the Christian moral vision of stewardship.

DIGGING DEEPER
What is the Christian moral vision of stewardship?

Key Concepts
Stewardship/Respect

Stewardship of the Earth

For Christians, Jews and Muslims, the earth is a sacred gift given to human beings by God, to be cared for and respected. Each person has a responsibility to care for the earth. In religious terms, we call this **stewardship** of the earth. To be stewards of the earth is part of our religious moral vision. We have a responsibility to look after the earth and hand it on to each new generation in a good and wholesome condition. Unfortunately, we only have to look around us to see the contrast between what God asks and what people do.

KNOW HOW
In groups of two, name and describe two examples of damage caused to the earth by the people who live on it. Discuss your answers.

KNOW IT ALL
Copy the following exercise into your Religion folder and fill in the blanks using the wordbank given below.

Many religions believe that the earth is a _____ gift from God. We have a _____ to care for the earth. This responsibility is called _____. We look after the earth in order to _____ it on to each new _____. To be stewards of the earth is part of our religious _____ _____.

WORDBANK
Generation • Sacred • Stewardship • Moral Vision • Hand • Responsibility

DIGGING DEEPER
1. Give an example of a time when you showed stewardship of the earth.
2. Give an example of the way your school shows stewardship of the earth.
3. Name one thing you could do to show respect for the earth.

Lack of Stewardship – A Moral Failure

A lack of stewardship of our planet has dreadful consequences and is a moral failure on our part. Let's take a look at some issues that show a lack of stewardship of our planet. The future of humanity depends on our awareness of these issues.

Global Warming

Over the last century, human beings, by their actions, have greatly increased the amount of carbon dioxide in the atmosphere. Every time we drive a car or use electricity from a coal-fired power plant, or heat our home with oil or natural gas, we produce carbon dioxide. High levels of this gas are turning the atmosphere into a heat-trap. Most scientists agree that the earth is becoming warmer.

The Ozone Layer

Without a layer of ozone above us in the atmosphere, human skin would be burnt by the sun even on the dullest days and more skin cancer would occur. The ozone layer blocks the sun's most harmful ultra-violet (UV) rays. Up to recently, CFC (chlorofluorocarbon) gases were used widely in fridges and aerosol cans, and some countries still use them because they are cheaper to produce. These gases damage the ozone layer, which has been getting thinner. Over the Antarctic, it has virtually disappeared, leaving a huge area of the earth unprotected. Recently, a group of scientists stated that the international ban on CFCs is beginning to work. (This ban was put in place after three scientists won the 1995 Nobel Peace Prize for showing how CFC gases can break down the ozone layer). There are signs that the ozone layer is returning.

Acid Rain

Gases from cars and factories go into the atmosphere and dissolve in droplets of rain. In this way, rain can turn to acid. As this acid rain falls, it causes burns in plants, trees and animals. The tropical rainforests of South America are in particular danger – at the very time when they are needed to take carbon dioxide out of the atmosphere.

Fresh Water

A United Nations report for the World Water Forum warned that the amount of fresh water per person is decreasing; it may be 33 per cent less by 2020. This decrease is due to wasteful use, pollution and climate change. Water may become a major cause of conflict in this century (just like oil in the twentieth century). There are already tensions over the supply of water between Israel and Palestine, between India and Bangladesh and between Egypt and countries further up the Nile River.

Statistics show us that:

- 80 per cent of illness in the world's developing countries is water-related;
- more than five million people die in poor countries each year from diseases caused by unsafe drinking water, lack of sanitation and lack of water for hygiene.

Did you know?

- It takes between three and five gallons of water to flush a toilet.
- If you let the water run, you can use up to three gallons of water while brushing your teeth or washing your hands.
- A washing machine can use up to thirty gallons of water in one cycle.
- We use thirty to forty gallons of water when taking a bath.
- A shower uses seven gallons of water per minute.

Air Pollution (Smog)

Gases from cars and factories do not always blow away. When there is no wind, the amount of these gases in the air increases. Then the air becomes dangerous to breathe. This is called air pollution. Air pollution causes many problems for us today. For every fifty people who have heart attacks in London, one is triggered by air pollution. Scientific evidence links cancer to air pollution and suggests that women exposed to pollution are more likely to have babies with heart problems.

Electronic Waste (E-Waste)

E-waste is old computers, mobile phones, computer and television screens and other electronic gadgets. Statistics show that one computer is thrown out for every new one put on the market. Millions of tons of old computers and other e-waste are dumped into landfills in the US every year. On average, computer and TV screens contain between two and four kilogrammes of lead, which gets into the soil. Lead is poisonous to humans and to animals. Mobile phones also contain many toxic metals and other health hazards. Unfortunately, the brilliance and speed of electronic innovation matches the rate of electronic waste and the problem is where to dispose of the mountain of e-waste that is piling up.

See *www.cawrecycles.org/Ewaste/background%20e-waste.html*

KNOW HOW

Divide your class into six groups. Each group must choose and research *one* of the issues outlined above.

Each group then creates a poster for the issue they have chosen, which should provide answers to the following questions:

- What is the problem?
- Where is the evidence?
- How does this impact on the earth today?
- How does this impact on the future of the earth and its inhabitants?
- What solution is possible?
- How are these issues examples of moral failure?

KNOWING ME KNOWING YOU

What can we do to protect the earth and care for our environment? Log on to some of the following websites and find out!

www.bbc.co.uk/nature/environment/conservationnow/global, www.eicni.org, www.enfo.ie
www.environment-agency.gov.uk/fun, www.ulsterwildlifetrust.org, www.kidsagainstwaste.org
www.wakeuptowaste.org, www.rethinkrubbish.com, www.recycle-more.co.uk, www.realnappy.com
www.dogstrust.org.uk

The Christian Vision of Stewardship

Then God said, 'And now we will make human beings; they will be like us and resemble us…' (Genesis 1:26)

In the book of Genesis, which is part of the sacred text of both Christians and Jews, we are told that humans are made in the image and likeness of God. The story of Creation tells us that God created the world and then saw that it was good. By creating human beings in the image of God, God is inviting us to share in the work of caring for creation.

We show that we are made in the image and likeness of God when we:

- **respect** and care for ourselves and one another;
- respect and care for the earth;
- work to make the world a good place for everything that lives in it.

'Christians, in particular, realise that their responsibility within creation and their duty towards nature and the Creator are an essential part of their faith.' (*Peace with God the Creator, Peace with All Creation*, Pope John Paul II, 15)

Jesus grew up in the Jewish tradition of seeing the world as God's creation. He loved and respected the world of nature. Like the people who wrote the psalms in the Bible, Jesus found that the earth and the natural world helped him to know God his Father better. Jesus spoke often about the earth to help others to learn about God and about life. Here are some examples from the Gospel according to Luke:

- Trees show their character in their fruit; people show their character in their actions. (Luke 6:43-45)
- Rock is a good foundation on which to build, just as the teaching of Jesus is a good foundation for life. (Luke 6:46-49)
- Seeds give a harvest despite difficulties; what God wants will happen too despite difficulties. (Luke 8:5-8)
- God cares for the birds of the air and for the flowers of the field; God cares for us. (Luke 12:22-28)
- Gardeners want their plants to grow; God wants us to grow. (Luke 13:6-8)
- The mustard seed grows into a big plant and a little yeast makes a lot of bread; our little efforts can allow God's kingdom to be more present to others. (Luke 13:18-20)

Jesus valued the world of nature for another reason too: when Jesus was alone with nature, it gave him the space to make important decisions about his life and to reflect on what his Father wanted him to do.

- As he started his work: he went into the wilderness and returned with fresh strength. (Luke 4:1-14)
- Before a typical day's work: he went off to a lonely place to renew himself and to give special time to his Father. (Luke 4:42)
- Before a big decision: Jesus spent the whole night on the mountain in prayer to God before he chose the twelve apostles. (Luke 6:12)
- Before going to Jerusalem to face suffering and death: he went up a mountain to pray and was transfigured (changed). (Luke 9:28)
- Before the end: Jesus went to a garden to pray for strength. (Luke 22:39)

KNOW WHAT
1. Jesus showed a great fascination for the riches of the earth. How do we know this?
2. Jesus used many examples from nature in his parables. Name two of them.

DIGGING DEEPER
1. Why do you think Jesus benefited from his natural environment?
2. Do you spend time enjoying the natural environment around you? Why?/Why not?
3. In what way do you benefit from your natural environment? List two examples.

St Francis of Assisi – Patron Saint of Ecology

St Francis, the founder of the Franciscans, is well known for his love of nature. In a famous prayer he called the sun his 'brother' and the moon his 'sister'. Francis is even said to have preached to the animals. Like Jesus, Francis saw everything in the world as God's creation. Like Jesus, Francis grew closer to God through the world of nature. He believed that all created things are connected and that everything in the world is part of one great family. In 1228, just two years after his death, Francis of Assisi was made a saint. Then in 1979 Pope John Paul II named Francis as the patron saint of ecology. He is among the best known and greatest examples of Christian stewardship of the earth.

KNOWING ME KNOWING YOU
Find out more about Francis of Assisi at your local library or on the internet. Share your findings with the class.

DIGGING DEEPER
Name and describe one way in which your class could pay tribute to the beliefs and work of St Francis of Assisi. Choose a time and date to carry out your tribute.

KNOW HOW
The Five 'R's: RESPECT * REDUCE * RECYCLE* REUSE* REFLECT

1. Divide up into pairs and, using each of these five words, write three sentences to explain how people can show their stewardship of the earth.
2. Have a go at designing a poster for each R.
3. Take up the 'R' challenge:
    - Based on the five 'R's, choose one thing that you will do at home over the next week to show that you take your responsibility for the earth seriously.
    - Write a daily blog of your challenge.

Stewardship: The job of caring for something that belongs to another.

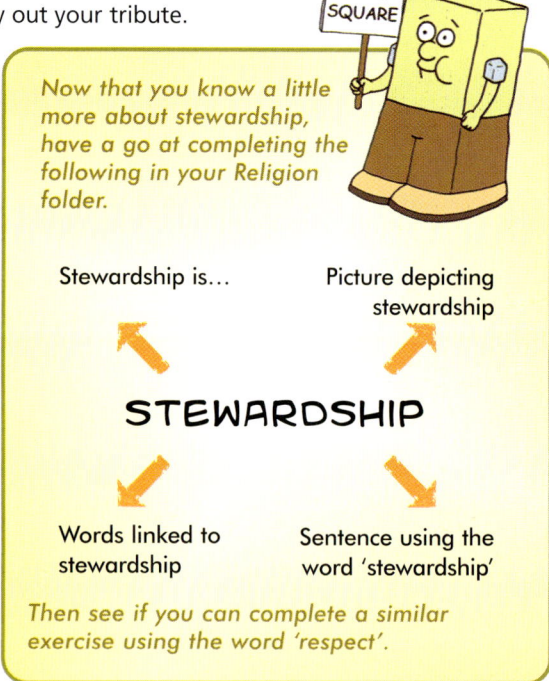

Now that you know a little more about stewardship, have a go at completing the following in your Religion folder.

Stewardship is…   Picture depicting stewardship

STEWARDSHIP

Words linked to stewardship   Sentence using the word 'stewardship'

Then see if you can complete a similar exercise using the word 'respect'.

LESSON 130 Forgiveness and Reconciliation

GROUNDWORK
In this lesson we plan to:
- examine the methods by which religious traditions offer the possibility of restoring relationships.

DIGGING DEEPER
Why is it important to forgive?

Key Concepts
Forgiveness/Reconciliation/Peace/Judgement

Baby Can I Hold You?
Sorry
Is all that you can't say
Years gone by and still
Words don't come easily
Like sorry like sorry

Forgive me
Is all that you can't say
Years gone by and still
Words don't come easily
Like forgive me forgive me

But you can say baby
Baby can I hold you tonight
Maybe if I told you the right words
At the right time you'd be mine

I love you
Is all that you can't say
Years gone by and still
Words don't come easily
Like I love you I love you

TAKE FIVE

1. What is this song about?
2. What are the words that 'don't come easily'?
3. In your opinion, why are words like 'sorry', 'forgive me' and 'I love you' often difficult to say? Do you find these phrases easy to say? Why?/Why not?
4. What does the song tell us about forgiveness?
5. How are forgiveness and love linked to each other?

Forgiveness and Reconciliation

When something is broken, we try to fix it. When we break a relationship (between ourselves and others, ourselves and God, ourselves and our environment), we also try to fix it. In order to set about rebuilding a relationship, we must begin by saying we are sorry. This means we are asking for **forgiveness**. True forgiveness is a very special gift. We can find it difficult to forgive someone who has hurt us in some way. We can also find it difficult to have been the person who has caused the hurt and must ask for forgiveness. Asking for forgiveness is not enough, however; we must work to rebuild the relationship and decide not to cause such hurt again. Only then will the true meaning of forgiveness take full effect in our lives.

When a relationship has broken down, it can cause worry and great sorrow. With forgiveness comes **reconciliation** and **peace**. When we ask for forgiveness, we want to be reconciled (reunited) with those whom we have hurt. Reconciliation is what happens when a broken relationship is healed. For reconciliation to take place, we must first recognise the *need* to rebuild a broken relationship.

The Christian Vision of Forgiveness and Reconciliation

Forgiveness and reconciliation are very important in the Christian faith. Jesus was sent by God the Father to tell all people that they are God's children and to restore a proper relationship between God and the world. Even when a person turns their back on God, God never rejects them. Every time a Christian makes a decision that is against the Christian moral vision, they hurt themselves and damage their relationship with God and with others. Recognising this is the first step. Then there is the need to say sorry, to try to correct the damage done and then to ask for forgiveness. This same principle applies to all other relationships. Christians celebrate this process in the sacrament of Reconciliation.

DIGGING DEEPER

Through the example of his life, Jesus showed the forgiveness of God. Read about the sinful woman who was forgiven in Luke's gospel (Luke 7:36-50).

1. Why did Jesus forgive this woman?
2. Can you explain the response of those who were at table with Jesus?

3. What can we learn about forgiveness from this incident?
4. Name one other story or incident in the New Testament where we can read about God's forgiveness.

The Jewish Vision of Forgiveness and Reconciliation

Forgiveness and reconciliation are also important for Jews. The festival of Rosh Hashanah ends with the day known as Yom Kippur, the Day of Atonement (at-one-ment with God). This is the most holy day of the Jewish year. On this day, the Jewish people fast, pray and ask God's forgiveness for their sins. Some devout people wear a white robe as a symbol of purity. In the evening, Jewish families have a special meal at home and then go to a service at the synagogue. This is a time of reconciliation and peace.

Meet Paula and Robert – which one of them is genuinely looking for forgiveness and reconciliation?

Paula: 'Listen, I am really sorry about not turning up yesterday. I know I said I would meet you in town, but my brother offered to bring me for a drive in his new car and I really wanted to go with him. I realise now I was selfish. I should have let you know I wasn't going to turn up. I would understand it if you never wanted to talk to me again, but please, give me another chance.'

Robert: 'Yeah, yeah, yeah, so you were waiting for me. You didn't have anything better to do, did you? Don't get all steamed up, it's not worth it. Forget about it… let me tell you about my brother's new car.'

TAKE FIVE
1. What is forgiveness? Why do we ask for forgiveness?
2. What is reconciliation and how does it come about?
3. What does the Christian moral vision say about forgiveness and reconciliation?
4. What does the Jewish moral vision say about forgiveness and reconciliation?
5. In the above example, which person was genuinely looking for reconciliation?

DIGGING DEEPER
1. Why do you think reconciliation is an important part of the Christian moral vision?
2. Why do you think reconciliation is an important part of the Jewish moral vision?

The Catholic Sacrament of Reconciliation

The sacrament of Reconciliation offers the possibility of restoring broken relationships. During the sacrament of Reconciliation, the priest, who represents the Risen Jesus, forgives the person for anything wrong they may have done. We must remember that when we sin, we damage our relationship with God and also with other people.

There are four elements in the sacrament of Reconciliation:

Contrition	The person must be sorry that they have sinned.
Confession	The person must confess their sins.
Absolution	The person receives forgiveness.
Satisfaction	The priest gives the person an act of penance.

What happens during the individual celebration of the sacrament of Reconciliation?

- The person comes to celebrate the sacrament with contrition (sorrow for their sins).
- The priest greets the person and they make the sign of the cross together.
- The priest encourages the person and invites them to trust in God's mercy.
- The priest reads a scripture passage to remind the person that the call to live like Jesus is a call to change and grow.
- The person confesses their sins. They tell the priest about the times when they have damaged their relationship with God because of their behaviour and the choices they have made. The priest gives some advice and guidance.
- The priest gives an act of penance. He may ask the person to recite one or more prayers or to reflect on a particular passage of scripture. Doing this will help them to bring about a change in their life.
- Then follows the 'Act of Sorrow'.
- The priest extends his hands and gives absolution — a blessing that brings God's forgiveness and that reconciles the person with God, with the Church community and with themselves.
- The rite ends with praise of God and the sending out of the person to live like Jesus.

Preparation for the Sacrament of Reconciliation

Each person should spend some time in preparation before they celebrate the sacrament of Reconciliation. Some of the questions they might ask themselves are:

- Have I spent time in prayer?
- Have I made Sunday a special day during which I honour God as I ought?
- Have I shown care and respect for my parents, my friends, those in school and the people I meet every day?
- Have I made sure that I treat my body with the respect it deserves?
- Have I shown care and respect for the environment?
- Have I always told the truth?
- Have I been lazy or reluctant to do my work or chores?
- Have I taken the time to listen to those who want to talk to me, and have I spent time with those who need my company?

Can you suggest any other questions that should be asked before the sacrament of Reconciliation?

KNOW IT ALL

Complete the following sentences in your Religion folder.

1. The sacrament of Reconciliation is…
2. The person coming to celebrate this sacrament must feel…
3. This sacrament is especially helpful in developing…
4. Absolution is…
5. At the end of the sacrament, the priest…
6. Preparation for the sacrament of Reconciliation means…

DIGGING DEEPER

Why do you think it is important to spend time in preparation before celebrating the sacrament of Reconciliation?

Judgement – Heaven, Hell and Purgatory

When we do something that leads to the breakdown of a relationship, we need to take time to think about the cause of our error of **judgement**. Why did we behave in a particular way? Why did we make a poor moral choice? Christians believe that at the end of time there will be a Day of Judgement. This means that God will judge people on the way they freely chose to behave during their lifetime. This is what will determine their future after death.

Heaven is where people finally become fully alive. St Paul says, 'No eye has seen nor ear heard, nor the human heart conceived, what God has prepared for those who love him' (1 Corinthians 2:9). 'Heaven is the ultimate end and fulfillment of the deepest human longings, the State of supreme, definitive happiness' (*Catechism of the Catholic Church* (*CCC*), 1024). It is where people find and live their true identity (*CCC*, 1025). It is a state of happiness, of life with God and others for ever in a relationship of knowledge and love.

At the moment of death, few people are fully perfect. They have not reached their full potential to be what God made them to be. There is a gap to be crossed. Purgatory is the name Catholics give to the stage between death and heaven – in which God makes people ready to enter the joy the heaven (*CCC*, 1030). Catholics believe that they can unite themselves with God and with those who have died through prayer – especially at Mass – and through good deeds. In this way, they can continue to help those who have died (*CCC*, 1032). This is what is meant by the Christian belief in the 'communion of saints', which is expressed in the Apostles' Creed.

God never fails to love us, no matter what we do; even if we turn away from God, God is always waiting to welcome us back. Because God made people free to choose, we have to imagine the possibility that people may reject the love of God and of others. They may turn away from God, ignore their conscience and ignore what God and others tell them. As St John says, 'There is sin that is mortal' (1 John 5:16): this includes the attitudes and actions through which people cut themselves off from God. This state of definitive separation from God has often been called *hell*.

DIGGING DEEPER

1. What is the Day of Judgement?
2. What determines where a person's final resting place will be? Give reasons for your answer.
3. Give a brief explanation of each of the following; heaven, hell, purgatory.

Peace: Presence of harmony; absence of disputes.

Reconciliation: Restoring friendship, harmony and good relationships.

Judgement: A decision about someone or something, usually arrived at after careful consideration.

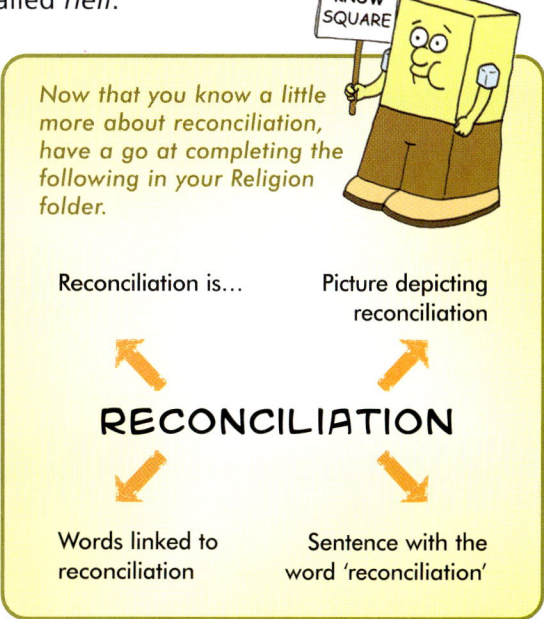

Now that you know a little more about reconciliation, have a go at completing the following in your Religion folder.

(Higher Level Only)

Law and Morality

LESSON 131 The Relationship between Law and Morality

GROUNDWORK
In this lesson we plan to:
- explore the relationship between State law and personal morality.

DIGGING DEEPER
How does the law of the State impact on personal morality?

 **Key Concepts**
Civil law/Constitution

Introductory Exercise: School Rules OK!

Like all schools, yours will have a set of rules, which are probably listed in your School Journal. These rules will include a Code of Behaviour, outlining how you are expected to act while in school. Have a read through your school's rules before completing the following exercise:

Choose six school rules and briefly explain why these rules are for the good of your school community.

DIGGING DEEPER
1. Why do you think we have rules and regulations?
2. How do rules help us to work together as a community?

3. If there were no rules, what do you think life would be like?
4. Can you think of some other situations where people accept certain rules for the good of a group? How do the rules help in these situations?

State Law

We have school rules to ensure that each person within the school community is treated with fairness and respect. In our country, we have State rules (laws) which tell us how we should act so that each person's rights are protected.

State law is prescribed (laid down) by the lawful authority of the State and imposed on society to protect the rights and freedom of individuals and the common good of the members of that society. State law includes 'civil law' and 'criminal law'. **Civil law** applies to ordinary life, as opposed to criminal law, which applies to criminal activity.

The fundamental principles and laws of the Irish State are outlined in the Irish **Constitution**. The Constitution reflects the values we want to promote as a society. The first paragraph of the Constitution of Ireland reads:

> *The Irish nation hereby affirms its inalienable, indefeasible, and sovereign right to choose its own form of Government, to determine its relations with other nations, and to develop its life, political, economic and cultural, in accordance with its own genius and traditions.*

Irish civil laws reflect the values that are promoted in the Constitution. Failure to obey these laws will bring a person into conflict with the State. The following are some of the civil laws that apply to all inhabitants of the Irish State. See if you can add to the list:

- Front- and back-seat passengers must wear seat belts.
- People who own a television must pay a TV licence fee.
- Those who drive cars must do so responsibly.
- It is forbidden to put graffiti on public buildings.
- People of school-going age must attend school.

It is also against the law to:

- assault or murder another person;
- steal;
- travel on public transport without paying the proper fare;
- sell items on the streets without a licence;
- fundraise for charity in a public place without a licence.

TAKE FIVE

1. What is State law?
2. What is the purpose of a Constitution?
3. In your own words, describe what rights are affirmed in the first paragraph of the Irish Constitution.
4. List *three* Irish civil laws and state their purpose.

DIGGING DEEPER

1. Do you agree with the civil laws listed above? Why?/Why not?
2. Is there anything that is not against the law that you think should be illegal? Give reasons for your answer.

Personal Morality v. State Law

Our personal morality is guided by our conscience and our sources of morality. Personal morality and State law cannot be totally separate because it is individuals who shape and enforce the law in the first place. What binds a community together is the sharing of core values. For example, Irish society believes that stealing is wrong, and Irish State law reflects this value. The conviction that it is wrong to steal comes from each person's conscience, so personal morality is also a foundation for State law.

However, not everyone agrees with all of the civil laws or with proposed changes to the law. In a democracy, people have the freedom to protest peacefully against laws and issues that concern them. Consider the following examples of conflict between State law and the personal morality of those who protest:

- In 2002, the Irish Government put a Disability Bill before the Oireachtas, but it was forced to withdraw the bill after strong protests from individuals and groups involved with disability issues, who argued that the rights of people with disabilities were not being adequately catered for. There were many aspects of the bill with which they disagreed; for example, trains would not have to be accessible to people with disabilities until 2015, and the railway platforms would not be accessible until 2020. As Fintan O'Toole, a columnist for *The Irish Times*, put it: 'You wait thirteen years for the train to come and then discover that you can't get into the station for another five.' Pressure was put on the Government, through the public representatives and the media, to influence this issue of State law.
- Another example of such conflict would be where factory owners or managers ignore safety regulations and laws because they are more interested in making profit than in protecting workers from danger. In situations like that, there can be a serious conflict between the personal moral stance of the individuals concerned and the protection offered to them by the laws of the State.
- Greenpeace volunteers work tirelessly to stop climate change, save our seas, eliminate toxic chemicals and end our nuclear age. These are only some of the projects that they are involved in on a worldwide scale in an effort to protect our fragile planet. How often do you think they come into conflict with State law?
- Donald Woods (1933-2001), a native of South Africa, grew up in the days of apartheid, the South African legal code that allowed white people to discriminate against non-whites. As the editor of the *Daily Dispatch* newspaper, Woods was very critical of the South African government. He was also critical of the emerging Black Consciousness Movement under the leadership of Steve Biko. A young black woman accused Woods of writing misleading stories about the movement. She invited him to meet with Biko. After the meeting, the two men became friends, and Woods began to provide political support for Biko. He wrote editorials in his newspaper and controversially hired black journalists.

Greenpeace protesters

In 1976, following riots, Steve Biko was arrested and battered to death by some policemen. The Government claimed that he had died on hunger strike. Woods went to the morgue with Biko's wife to see his friend's body and he managed to get some photographs. When the photographs were published, he and his family had to flee South Africa because their own lives were at risk. From his new home in London, he continued to campaign tirelessly against apartheid.

(You can read the full story at: *http://www.actsascotland.org.uk/woods.html*)

KNOW WHAT

1. How is State law connected to personal morality?
2. What are the benefits of the relationship between State law and personal morality?
3. Give some examples of situations where conflict may arise between State law and personal morality.

DIGGING DEEPER

Conflict can also arise when the State wants the individual to act or behave in a way that the individual rejects.

1. What would you do if your country was involved in a war but you were a pacifist, someone who does not believe in solving conflict through violence? You could be called a traitor!
2. Find out about any situations in Ireland where people have protested and brought about a change in the Government's opinion.
3. The film *Cry Freedom* is based on the story of Steve Biko and Donald Woods. Your teacher might arrange for your class to watch this film. With the help of your teacher, see if you can identify the following:
   a) One example of where Steve Biko's personal morality brought him into conflict with the State.
   b) One example of where Donald Woods' personal morality brought him into conflict with the State.

> **Civil law:** Collection of rules about behaviour, decided upon and enforced by the State authorities.
>
> **Constitution:** Code (statement) of values and guidelines for a group or country.

LESSON 132 State Law and Religious Morality

GROUNDWORK
In this lesson we plan to:
- explore the relationship between State law and religious morality.

DIGGING DEEPER
How could my religious morality bring me into conflict with the State?

Key Concepts
Pluralism/Religious fundamentalism/Libertarianism

State Law and Religious Morality

Different people have different views or theories about the relationship that exists between State law and religious morality. Here are some of those views.

- **Pluralism** reflects the belief that State laws ought not to be based on or determined by any single religious tradition. Each group within the society – whether ethnic, racial, religious or social – has a right to participate in and develop its own culture and interests. A pluralist society is enriched when the views or outlook of different groups are accepted and people are encouraged to be tolerant of others' viewpoints.

- **Religious fundamentalism** takes a literal, rigid and fixed view of religious beliefs. Religious fundamentalists stick rigidly to their sacred text or teachings. Attempts to modernise or update beliefs are strongly resisted, and those who seek to do this are excluded from the group. So, for example, a Christian fundamentalist may take the Creation story from the Bible as the literal truth. Any truths based on scientific discovery that appear to conflict with their religious text or teaching are likely to be dismissed as lies. A religious fundamentalist would like if the laws of their religion were implemented as the laws of the State in which they live.

- **Libertarianism** is the belief that each person has the right to control their own body, actions, speech and property. Libertarians believe that they are free to do what they choose once they do not interfere with the right of another person to do as they choose. Libertarianism rejects laws that restrict the freedom of the individual. It believes that moral issues should be left to the individual's conscience. From a libertarian point of view, the Government's role is only to protect the individual from harm, violence or fraud.

KNOW IT ALL

Copy the following grid into your Religion folder and write three brief points about religious fundamentalism and libertarianism. Pluralism has been filled in as an example.

World view	Point 1	Point 2	Point 3
Pluralism	Laws are not determined by any one religious tradition.	Each group can develop its own culture and interests.	There is a tolerance of different viewpoints.
Religious fundamentalism			
Libertarianism			

'No one should have more of a say than others in how we run our country. Your traditions are as valuable to you as my traditions are to me. Just because my traditions lead me to reject certain things, doesn't mean that I should deny these things to you. I can't limit your life just because of my beliefs. A person's religion is their own private business.' **(Mrs B. Mee)**

'What do I value? Well, of course I value freedom! What else is there to value? Our freedom to be who we are is the most important thing I can think of. Laws are really very oppressive. It's up to me to decide at what age my child will see a particular film or start to drink alcohol. It's up to me to decide whether or not my child will go to school. People shouldn't hurt anyone; what else can laws add to life? Yes, I know you disagree with me. But then you are lucky: I would defend your right to disagree. That's what freedom is all about.' **(Mr A. Freeman)**

'You know, it's all in the Bible. That's all we need. If people did exactly as the Bible teaches, then God would not need to punish the world. The people who were killed in that earthquake were punished because they were not living as God asked. God's patience could only last so long. There is only one way to live. People who vote for candidates who represent any other way have been warned: God will punish them!' **(Miss C. Strict)**

KNOW WHAT

1. Identify the pluralist, the fundamentalist and the libertarian. Give reasons for your choice.
2. Could any of these people's opinions bring them into conflict with the State?
3. Is it possible that the laws of a country could take into account opinions such as those above? Whose opinions might the State find it most difficult to accommodate?

Christianity and State Law

For the sake of the 'common good', everybody must obey State laws. Christianity teaches that being a good person includes being a good citizen. If people live by God's love for all, they will respect the laws that are put in place by the State to protect people's rights.

What happens when a State is found to promote bad laws? For instance, South Africa once had laws that promoted prejudice and discriminated against individuals on the grounds of race and colour. A Christian could not, in such instances, either obey or promote such laws because they go against the moral vision that Jesus taught.

DIGGING DEEPER

The *Catechism of the Catholic Church* holds that: 'The Church respects and encourages the political freedom and responsibility of the citizen. It is part of the Church's mission to "pass moral judgements even in matters related to politics..."' (CCC, 2245-2246)

1. How does the relationship between State law and religious morality impact on the citizens of a country?
2. In recent years, the death penalty has arisen as a moral issue in some countries. The member states of the European Union have removed this form of punishment from their laws. However, other countries around the world have not. What do you think would be the reaction of the following to this issue?
   • A pluralist • A libertarian • A religious fundamentalist

KNOW HOW

Divide your class into groups of four. Each group should gather as many newspapers as possible over the coming week. On a designated day, each group look through their newspapers and try to find articles that show how personal morality can come into conflict with State law or how religious morality can come into conflict with State law. Examine each issue in the following way:

- Outline the issue that has caused the conflict.
- Describe the conflicting viewpoints involved.
- Suggest how this conflict could be resolved.
- Discuss your findings with the other groups.

 **Pluralism:** A state of society where the views of people of all traditions and none are tolerated.

Religious fundamentalism: A literal, rigid style of belief. Relies solely on a literal interpretation of the community's sacred text and teachings. Rejects attempts to update or modernise the way in which community belief is expressed.

Libertarianism: The belief that a person is free to do what they choose once they do not interfere with the right of another person to do as they choose.

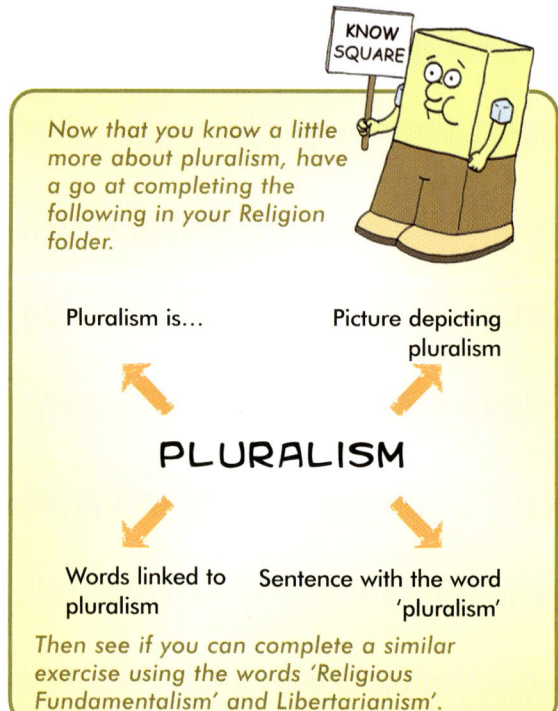

Now that you know a little more about pluralism, have a go at completing the following in your Religion folder.

Pluralism is... / Picture depicting pluralism / **PLURALISM** / Words linked to pluralism / Sentence with the word 'pluralism'

Then see if you can complete a similar exercise using the words 'Religious Fundamentalism' and 'Libertarianism'.

See page 500 for past exam questions on this topic.

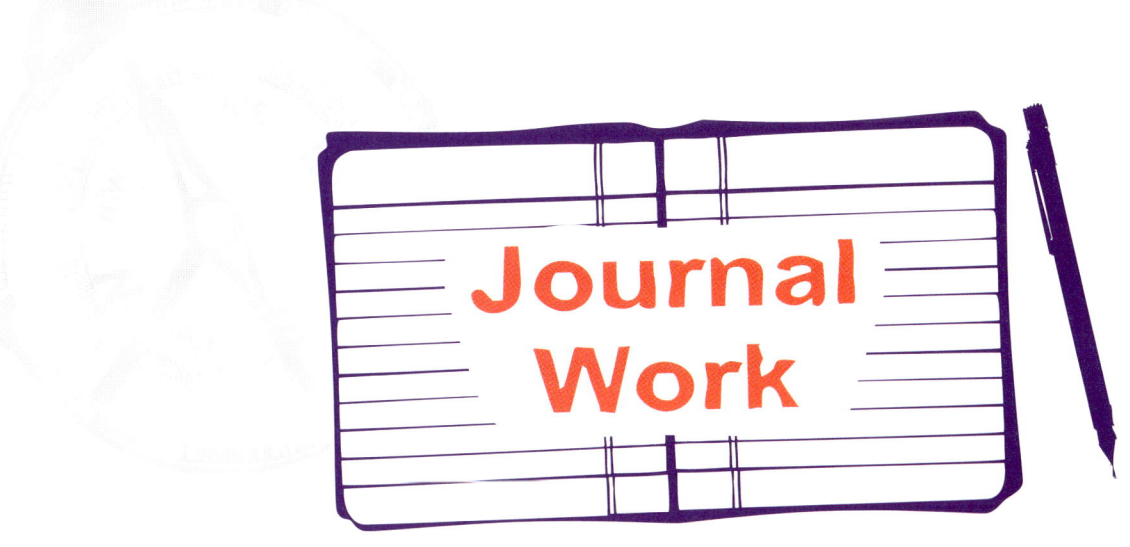

The Junior Certificate Religious Education Examination is made up of two components. The first component is the written exam paper, which makes up 80 per cent (Higher Level) or 75 per cent (Ordinary Level) of the total marks awarded in the final grade. The second component is the written journal, which makes up 20 per cent (Higher Level) or 25 per cent (Ordinary Level) of the marks awarded in the final grade.

We will now take a closer look at the journal and explore the different elements in it.

Aims of Journal Work

Journal work is included in the Junior Certificate Religious Education Examination in order to give you, the student, a chance to experience religion as part of your everyday life. It offers you the chance to work on an area of personal interest or concern to you. As you do this work, you will be building on what you have learned through the Religious Education course and relating it to your own personal experience.

Range of Skills

You will be using many different skills in the process of your journal work. Before you begin, it is important to explore the types of skills involved and to know how each one can be developed.

Type of Skill	This skill can be developed by
Enquiry skills	Asking questions about people, places, organisations and the planet.
Observational skills	Paying particular attention to somebody or something and recording details of what is observed.
Problem-solving skills	Working on a solution to a given problem through various tasks and activities.
Reflective skills	Taking the time to look back and think about past experiences and work that you have been engaged with.
Research skills	Finding out more about someone or something using the library, the internet, local knowledge and so on.
Critical evaluation skills	Learning how to evaluate (examine and judge) one's findings or experiences.
Organisational skills	Learning how to organise time and effort effectively while planning and managing various tasks and activities.

As you engage in the journal work, you should be able to identify which skills you are using at each stage of the process and understand their meaning. In the journal exam booklet, you will be asked to choose *two* of the skills you used and to explain how you put them into practice.

The Journal – A Four-Stage Process

The four stages involved in creating the journal are as follows:

- **P**lanning – Choosing a title and planning the whole project
- **P**articipation – *Doing* the work
- **P**ractice booklet – Writing up a rough draft
- **P**erfected exam booklet – Writing up the final exam version

Stage 1: Planning

This stage is about finding the correct journal title and then planning the work that will be involved. Each year, twelve journal titles are sent to each school, two for each of the six sections of the syllabus. While students may decide to work in groups or individually, for the final exam each student must submit an individual piece of work.

When choosing a title, it is important to look for something that is of special interest to you or that covers a specific section that you really enjoyed learning about. The following questions may be of help:

1. Will I work on *my own*, as part of *a group* or with the *whole class*?
2. Will this topic *maintain my interest* throughout the process?
3. Have I good access to *information* about this topic?
4. What do I hope to *achieve* by working with this topic?

The next stage of planning is where you 'map out' how you are going to research and explore the information necessary to complete a journal on your chosen topic. The following exercises will help you to decide how best to proceed.

Preparatory Exercises

The following is a list of research methods that you might use when carrying out work on your chosen title. Identify with a tick (✓) the ones you think are particularly suitable for the title you have chosen and explain how you might put them into practice.

Research Method	✓	How I might use this method
Conduct an interview		
Organise a survey		
Engage in group-work		
Use the library		
Look up information on the internet		
Observe or take part in an experience of worship		
Invite a guest to speak to the class		
Make a video		
Keep a diary		
Take part in role-play		
Create a questionnaire		
Other		

2. Which of the methods that you have ticked include:
   - (a) Enquiry skills
   - (b) Observational skills
   - (c) Problem-solving skills
   - (d) Research skills
   - (e) Reflective skills
   - (f) Organisational skills
   - (g) Critical evaluation skills

3. Which of these skills do you plan to use?

You might like to list all the possible methods on a chart as follows:

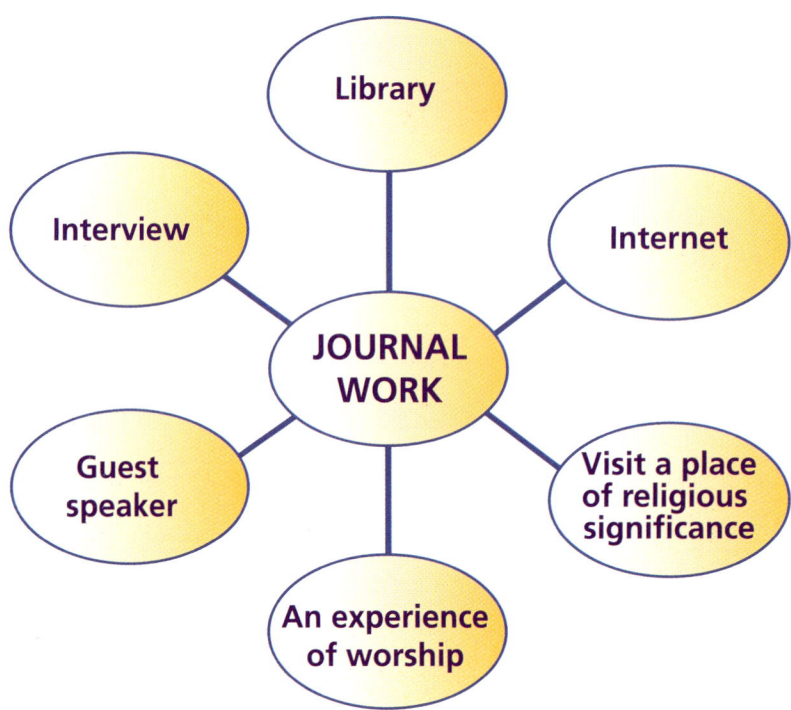

You could draw a more detailed chart when you have made your mind up about your exact plan and how you are going to carry it out. Whether you are working as a group or as an individual, the second planning chart will help you to clarify your thoughts.

For example, if your chosen title was 'Prayer and Young People' (Junior Certificate Exam 2004/Section E), you might find the following types of planning chart helpful. Note that in the first example, the tasks have been divided up between the different students in the group.

For group research:

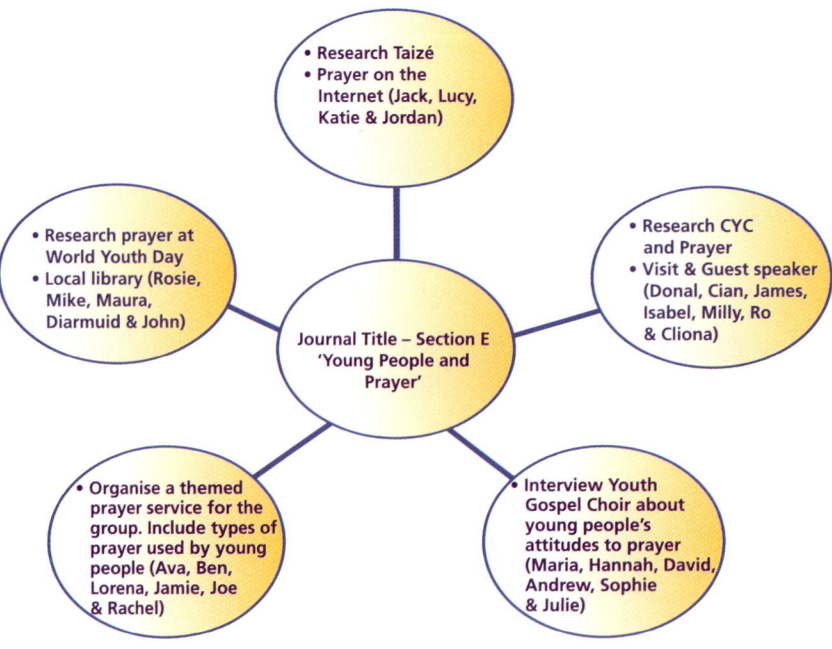

For individual research:

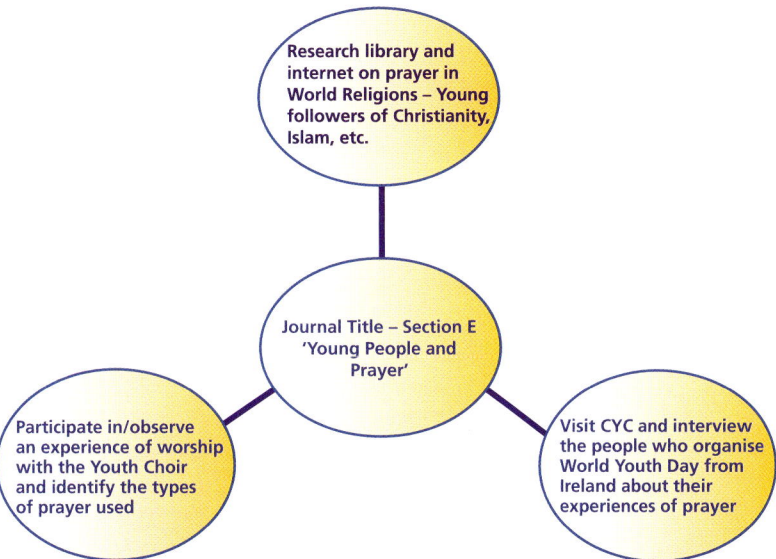

If planning is carried out in a clear and precise manner, then each person knows exactly what they are doing and they can write up and share their information in a clear way.

It is essential that you are focused on the journal title at all stages of the process and that you know which parts of your Religious Education course it relates to and, particularly, which key concepts it relates to. The Department of Education and Science has issued *Guidelines* on the completion of the journal work. With the assistance of your teacher, you should make yourself aware of these guidelines and be clear about them when doing your work. They are a useful checklist for you to tick off as you complete each stage of the journal work. Don't forget that while your teacher and the syllabus can act as very useful *guides* throughout the process, the actual material that you produce must be your own unaided work.

Stage 2: Participation

This is the stage at which most of the 'real' work takes place. It is important to note that the more time, energy and effort you put into this stage, the more information you will have for the next stage, i.e. writing up the practice journal. The participation stage involves the *doing* of the work as opposed to talking about it, i.e. gathering the information, organising trips, making visits, inviting in guest speakers and so on. While many people will have the same job in the project, often students can carry out their job in a different place or take a different angle, and this serves to add to the wealth of information.

It is really important that each student keeps ***a record of the work undertaken*** and that they engage with the project and, therefore, have a valuable, personal experience.

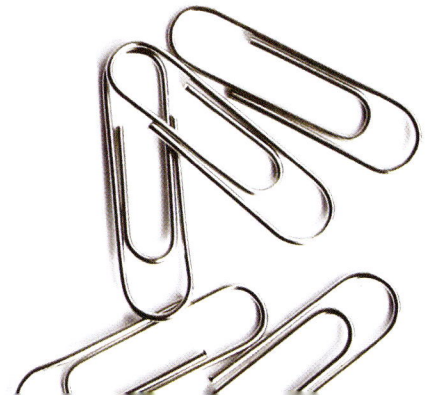

Stage 3: Practice Booklet

You will be submitting your final journal work in a booklet supplied for that purpose. The booklet will be divided into five sections, with clear instructions on what is required for each section. The 'Practice Booklet' involves your first attempt at writing up these five sections, i.e.:

Section One – Introduction
Section Two – Getting Started
Section Three – Work
Section Four – Discoveries
Section Five – Looking back

Each section has a certain number of marks allocated to it. We will now take a closer look at the individual sections.

Section One – Introduction (12 Marks)

In this section, you are asked to identify your chosen title and to explain why you made that choice. You are also asked to indicate whether you did your journal on your own or as part of a group/whole class.

Under the heading 'Title', there are three spaces to fill in:

- *The title I chose for my journal work is …*
  Here you fill in the prescribed title from the Department of Education and Science's list of titles.

- *The personal title of my journal work is …*
  Your chosen title may be the prescribed title or it can be your own personal interpretation of that title. For example, in 2003, Section A 'Communities of Faith' had as one of its prescribed journal titles: 'A profile of a local or a national religious organisation.' (Note: In a *profile* you are expected to outline or trace the development of the organisation you have chosen.) An example of a personal interpretation of this title might be: 'A profile of a Methodist church in my local community.'

- *I chose this title because …*
  You should give one or two reasons why you chose this title. For example: 'There are people of different faiths in my school and we held an ecumenical prayer service this year at Christmas. Because of this, I would like to know more about other religious organisations in my locality.'

Then, you will be asked to explain what you hoped to achieve by working on this title. Perhaps it was something that you wanted to learn more about or maybe you had already covered this section in class and wanted to find out more about this particular area. It would be a good idea to give at least two reasons for your choice.

An example of some reasons for doing journal work on the above title:
To learn more about the Methodist Church and to see how it is the same and how it is different from the Catholic Church. I also hoped to be able to know about and understand the beliefs and practices of Methodists.

Section Two – Getting Started (12 Marks)
In this section, you are asked to describe and explain the *preparatory work* you did in order to write up the journal booklet. This section is about all the work you did at the *planning* stage, described earlier. You may not have completed all that you planned to do, but it is important to include all your original ideas here because they can be relevant when you come to look back and reflect on the whole process of creating your journal.

An example of how to describe your preparatory work:
We planned to divide our class into five different groups. Each group would be given a different task. My group planned to find out about how the Methodist Church was set up. I planned to go to the library and find some books on the Methodist Church. I hoped to compare the information with what we had learned about the Catholic Church in my local area. The others in my group planned to write out a list of the similarities and differences in the organisation of both churches. My grandmother's neighbour is a member of the Methodist Church, so I planned to interview her about the church. I then planned to visit the minister with the rest of my group. We prepared a questionnaire about religious organisations before we went and about the inspiring vision, work and variety of roles in the Methodist Church.

Section Three – Work (24 Marks)
In this section, you are asked to describe *all* the work you did *during* your journal project.

To do my journal work I …
Detail the research, assignments, interviews, trips, etc. that you engaged in. If you worked as a group, describe your role in the group and also the work that was done by the rest of the group. Aim to describe at least three different types of work carried out on your chosen title. For example: I wrote up a chart based on my findings in the library. This chart showed the similarities and the differences in how the Catholic and the Methodist churches are organised. I also worked with my group when we were deciding on the questions for the minister. I had the job of writing the questions out and then another student in the group typed them out. I made the appointment with the minister and went along with two other girls from my class. We asked the minister two questions each and we took turns in writing the answers down. The questions I asked were: 'What is the inspiring vision of the Methodist Church?' and 'What work does the Methodist Church do in this area?' One of my other jobs was to collect money from my group to buy a present for the minister as a way of thanking her for her time. I collected the money and another girl bought a box of chocolates and a card. I was in charge of making the presentation to the minister and she said she was very happy to answer our questions. She also brought us into the Methodist chapel and explained the different roles that people have in the church.

I included this in my journal because ...

Here you explain why you chose the particular methods that you outlined above, such as why you decided to interview a person of faith, make a trip to a place of religious significance or research a website and so on. For example: 'It gave me a great insight into how the Methodist community of faith is organised, how it was founded and about the work it does in my local area. I was never in a Methodist chapel before and I enjoyed learning about the different roles the people have in the church.'

My reaction to doing this work was ...

Here you are asked to:

- describe your own reaction to the work on the chosen title, i.e. how interested or engaged were you? Were you surprised, disappointed, delighted or fascinated by the information you researched, compiled, observed, learned?
- if you worked in a group, describe how the group reacted to the work, i.e. how did the group find the activities and the whole journal project? Was it a good experience?
- describe and explain how your reaction to the journal work was the same or different to that of the other members in your group.

An example of how you might answer these questions:

I was really pleased with the information I received. I learned a lot of new things and I really enjoyed meeting the minister. I like the way women can be ministers in the Methodist Church. One other piece of information that impressed me was how the Methodist and Catholic communities help each other out when fundraising for church projects.

Everyone in my group found the information very interesting. We thought that there would be more statues and artwork in the Methodist chapel, but in this regard it is not at all like a Catholic church building.

The most difficult part of the work was to get all the minister's answers written down. When all the information was eventually down on paper, I realised that I had known very little about the Methodist Church before undertaking the project.

Section Four – Discoveries (42 Marks)

This section is specifically about you and how the journal impacted on you.

You are asked to explain what you have learned from your journal work. (Note: We can learn about something by gathering facts, but we can also learn from our experiences, i.e. from what we do.) You should mention some of the facts that you learned here, but you can also mention what you learned from the experience of doing journal work, i.e. your 'personal' response to the work.

You are also asked to describe how your work on the journal has affected your *attitude*. You should describe two or more ways in which the journal work has changed/impacted on your attitudes/opinions. You should identify clearly what difference engaging in the work has made to your knowledge, understanding or experience.

An example of how you might answer these questions:

I learned…

that the Methodist place of worship, i.e. their chapel, is a lot different from the Catholic one. It is quite small and has a pointed roof. It is not as ornate as the Catholic place of worship. I also learned that Methodists believe that preaching the Word of God is very important. When they worship together on Sundays, they listen to the minister preach a sermon, and they pray and sing hymns together. Singing together is a very important part of worship in the Methodist community of faith. I learned that Methodists have two sacraments, Baptism and Holy Communion (or the Lord's Supper). They usually celebrate the Lord's Supper at the morning service of the first Sunday of every month. The leader of the Methodists in Ireland is called a President. The name of the Methodist President is Reverend Ivan McElhinney.

As a result of what I have learned I will…

appreciate more the faith of the Methodist community. I feel that because of this I am now more respectful of that faith. I have learned that to find out about another faith helps you to understand more about your own faith. I have a deeper respect for my own faith because I am not taking it for granted as much now. I also think it is important for all Christians to know about the different denominations in Christianity and how we can take part in ecumenical celebrations.

Skills: Here you are asked to choose two skills that were specific to your journal and to describe how you used them. For example, in order to *research* your title, you went to the library, became quite efficient at working with your internet search engine, made some trips to places of significance and so on. (When answering this question, it is important to give only those details and information that are relevant to the two skills you have chosen.)

An example of how you might answer this question:

*I used **research** skills when I…*

went to the library and searched the internet to find out lots of new information about the Methodist Church. I also used research skills when I visited my granny's friend and asked her questions about her beliefs and practices.

*I used **organisational** skills when I...*

organised for my group to visit the minister. I also used my organisational skills when I wrote out the questions and got them photocopied for everyone. Finally, I used my organisational skills by recording, ordering and writing up all of my work.

Linking: Here you are asked to explore the links between your journal work and the religious education course. You must describe two areas that your journal is linked to. These can come from within the same section of the course or from two different sections of the course. You must explain how these areas relate to the work you undertook on your chosen title.

For example, if your chosen title was 'A profile of a local or a national religious organisation', your chosen links might be the following:

Section A, Part 2 – Communities at Work:
- 'Variety of roles' – different roles within the religious organisation, i.e. the Methodist Church.

Section A, Part 3 – Communities of Faith:
- 'Inspiring vision' – the story of the founder of the Methodist Church – John Wesley.
- 'Impact of this work' – the work of the Methodist Church in the local area.

An example of how you might answer this question:

My journal work reminded me of studying...

Parts two and three of Section A – Communities of Faith. We studied this section in first year. It reminds me of section A *because* that section was all about communities working together, especially communities of faith. My journal work is linked to this section because it is about the Methodist community of faith and how they work and worship together. It is also linked to the fourth part of Section A because Christians can only take part in ecumenism if they know and understand more about each Christian denomination. Through my journal work, I have learned many new and interesting things about the Methodist Church.

My journal work also reminded me of studying ...

Section E – Celebration of Faith *because* in that section I learned about the places and the times of significance for the Methodist community of faith. The Methodist chapel is a place of significance because that is where Methodists worship and celebrate together. Sunday worship is a time of significance, when the members of the Church gather to pray, sing and listen to the Word of God.

Section Five – Looking Back – (10 Marks)

The final section of the journal asks you to think about the journal work you have completed and to describe what you really enjoyed about it. It also asks you to note any changes you would make if you were to begin again.

Here, you are being asked to reflect (look back) on the entire process (from start to finish, i.e. from the time you chose your title to the writing up of the journal exam booklet) and to evaluate (examine and judge) your planning, participation and practice journal. There are various questions given in the journal booklet to help you to answer this particular section, e.g. 'Imagine someone else in your school is starting out on journal work and has chosen the same title as you. What advice would you give?' In this section, you can write about what went well and also about any part of the plan that did not work out so well. Remember that you are *not* being asked here to recall all the 'facts' that you learned, so try not to repeat here what you have already written in the previous section.

An example of how you might answer this question:

Looking back at my experience of doing journal work on this title …

I think that it all went really well. I enjoyed working with my class on the project and I think that it was a good idea to work as a group instead of choosing different titles and splitting up as individuals. Working in groups allowed us to look more closely, from different angles, at how the Methodist Church is organised nationally and locally. For example, I was really happy with our interview with the minister, as it was interesting to hear her tell us lots of new things about the Methodist Church in my area.

If I were to start again, one thing I would do differently would be to spend a little more time in the library and on the internet. I would look at more internet sites about the Methodist Church in different countries and not just in Ireland. I would pay more attention to things like the story of John Wesley, the founder, and how the roles of people in the Methodist Church are different from those in my church.

I would definitely arrange to meet the minister again, but maybe the next time I would invite her into our school to meet the whole class group. This would have been easier than explaining what she said to the class, and it would also have been better if the whole class had visited the Methodist chapel.

I would recommend to anyone doing a similar journal title to interview a young person from the religious organisation to find out if they have a similar or different role in their church and maybe invite them to take part in an ecumenical service with our class.

Stage 4: Perfected Exam Booklet

This is the booklet that you will be given on which to write up the final version of your journal. This will be handed up with your written examination on the day of the Religious Education Junior Certificate Exam, so it is really important to write it up as best you can.

At this stage, it is important to make sure that you have followed all the guidelines suggested and that you have answered every question to the best of your ability. You can transcribe your work from the practice journal, making any changes that are necessary.

You may not add any extra inserts or pages to your exam journal booklet, as they will not be marked.

Remember that if you do not submit a journal, you will lose 20 per cent (Higher Level) or 25 per cent (Ordinary Level) of your final grade.

Some Important Points to Remember

Before beginning your journal work:
- Become familiar with the key concepts in the syllabus that relate to your chosen title.
- Read the Department of Education and Science's *Guidelines for Completion of the Journal Booklet*, Circular S98/02.

Before writing up your practice journal:
- Think about how working on your chosen title affected your knowledge, understanding, skills and attitudes. Consider any new insights, changes of attitude or positive reactions you have had during the process.
- Reflect on the whole process of creating your journal, from beginning to end.
- Think about what worked well for you, what would be useful to other students, and what you would do differently if you or others were to work on the journal title all over again.

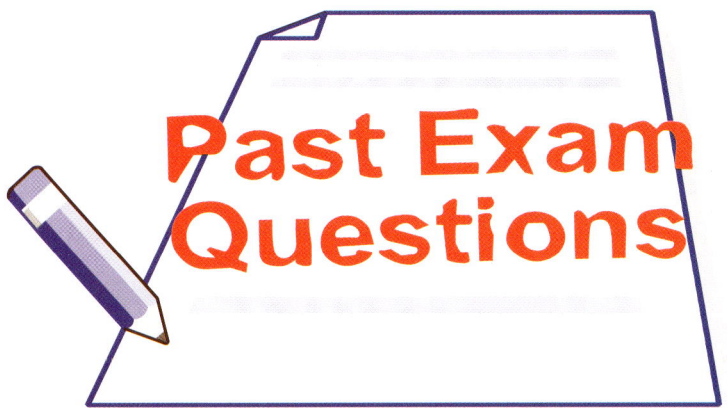

Section A

Lesson 15 2006 Higher Level/Section 4
Question 1. Communities of Faith

A Name a church **or** religious organisation **or** a religious order found in present day Ireland, and outline **two** ways in which its beliefs influence the way of life of its members. *(24 marks)*

B a. Outline **one** challenge that a church **or** a religious organisation **or** a religious order faces in Ireland today. *(10 marks)*

b. Briefly outline how the beliefs of the church **or** the religious organisation **or** the religious order you have named above could help its members to deal with this challenge. *(16 marks)*

Lesson 15 2006 Ordinary Level/Section 4
Question 1. Communities of Faith

Communities of faith work locally and nationally.

A a. Name **one** community of faith that you have studied which works *either* locally *or* nationally. *(3 marks)*

b. Outline the work done by the community of faith you have named above. *(10 marks)*

B Explain **one** way in which the needs of people are being served in the work done by a community of faith. *(12 marks)*

C Explain how any **one** idea of the founder/earliest followers can be seen in the work of a community of faith. *(15 marks)*

Lesson 15 2007 Higher Level/Section 5
Question 6.

Outline the work being done by **one** community of faith to promote justice.

In your answer you should describe the religious moral vision on which the work is based. *(70 marks)*

Lesson 17   2005 Higher Level/Section 4
Question 1. Communities of Faith

A   'Archbishop Eames calls for a "determined effort" to end sectarianism' – *Irish Times*, December 2004

    a. What is sectarianism? *(5 marks)*

    b. Outline **one** example of sectarianism *(10 marks)*

    c. Identify **two** effects that sectarianism can have on a community of faith. *(10 marks)*

B   a. What is ecumenism? *(5 marks)*

    b. Briefly outline **one** example of ecumenism. *(10 marks)*

    c. Give **two** reasons why people work for ecumenism. *(10 marks)*

Lesson 17   2007 Ordinary/Section 4
Question 1. Communities of Faith

A   a. Hatred of another person because of his/her religion is – (Tick the correct box)

☐ Ecumenism   ☐ Humanism   ☐ Sectarianism   *(8 marks)*

    b. Describe **one** example of people being in conflict because of their religion. *(10 marks)*

B   a. Describe **one** example of people working to build respect for the beliefs of others. *(10 marks)*

    b. Give **two** reasons why people work to build respect for the beliefs of others. *(12 marks)*

Lesson 20   2006 Higher Level/Section 5
Question 1.

    a. Outline **one** example of inter-faith dialogue that you have studied

    b. Discuss the reasons why people take part in inter-faith dialogue. *(70 marks)*

Lesson 20   2005 Higher Level/Section 5
Question 1.
Outline **two** styles of leadership found in a community of faith. *(70 marks)*

Lesson 23   2007 Higher Level/Section 4
Question 1. Communities of Faith

A   Giving direction is one way a person can lead a community. Outline what is involved in **two** other ways of leading a community that could be used by a leader. *(20 marks)*

B   Explain how the way in which a community is led can have an effect on its members. *(20 marks)*

C   Being a leader is one role a person can have within a community. Describe another role a person can have within a community. *(10 marks)*

Section B

Lesson 30   2007 Higher Level/Section 5
Question 2.
Outline **two** historical sources of information about the life of Jesus of Nazareth and discuss the ways in which they are similar to what the gospels say about his life and death.   *(70 marks)*

Lesson 32   2004 Higher Level/Section 5
Question 2.
Imagine you have been asked to give a talk at a Bible meeting explaining the stages involved in the development of the Gospels from the oral tradition to the written word. Outline the talk you would give making reference to the importance of the Gospels in the Christian community of faith.   *(70 marks)*

Lesson 37   2005 Higher Level/Section 5
Question 2.
In the parables Jesus tells people what the kingdom of God is like; in the miracles he shows people the kingdom of God among them. – Mark Link

Outline what is revealed about the kingdom of God in **one** parable and **one** miracle you have studied.

(70 marks)

Lesson 37   2005 Ordinary Level/Section 4
Question 2. Christianity

A   Outline **one** miracle Jesus performed.   *(12 marks)*

B   State what Jesus taught about the kingdom of God in the miracle you have chosen above or in one other miracle Jesus performed.   *(14 marks)*

C   Describe **one** way in which Jesus' teaching about the kingdom of God influenced the way of life in the first Christian communities.   *(14 marks)*

Lesson 40   2003 Ordinary Level/Section 4
Question 2. Jesus in Conflict with Authority

A   Jesus was in conflict with members of each of the following groups. Tick **one** and explain why Jesus was in conflict with this group.

   Pharisees ☐   Romans ☐   Sadducees ☐   *(12 marks)*

B

CHIEF PRIESTS CRITICISE JESUS	Leaders say Jesus is a troublemaker	Angry scenes as Jesus overturns tables in Temple
- Capital News	*- Galilee Times*	*- Jerusalem Herald*

These headlines might have appeared when Jesus came into conflict with people in power. Imagine you are a journalist covering the events in the life of Jesus. Write a newspaper report describing **one** of the times Jesus was in conflict with people in power.

a.	What was the event?	(5 marks)
b.	What did Jesus say or do?	(10 marks)
c.	How did the people in power react?	(5 marks)
d.	Why did they react in this way?	(8 marks)

Lesson 40   2007 Ordinary Level/Section 4
Question 2. Foundations of Religion – Christianity

A These headlines might have appeared in Palestine at the time of Jesus.

a. Tick **one** of the following headlines and name **one** event from the life of Jesus which it could describe.

Jesus welcomes sinners	Jesus treats women as equals	Jesus says the poor are blessed	Love your enemies says Jesus
- *The Galilee Gazette*	- *The Bethlehem Bulletin*	- *The Nazareth News*	- *The Jerusalem Journal*
☐	☐	☐	☐

Name of the event from Jesus' life.   (8 marks)

b. Describe what happened in the event from the life of Jesus which you have named above.
(10 marks)

B Explain why people were surprised by what Jesus said about the Kingdom of God.   (12 marks)

C Describe one situation where religious leaders were in conflict with Jesus because of what he said about the kingdom of God.   (10 marks)

Lesson 43   2007 Higher Level/Section 4
Question 2. Foundation of Religion – Christianity

A Describe **one** incident from the life of Jesus that led to his death.   (15 marks)

B Outline **two** reasons why the incident you have described above led to the death of Jesus.
(20 marks)

Lesson 44   2005 Higher Level/Section 4
Question 2. Foundations of Religion – Christianity

A a. Below you will find a list of some of the events leading up to the death of Jesus. Number these events in the order in which they occurred. Number 1 should be the first event and number 5 should be the last event.

Number	Event
	The Crucifixion
	Jesus is brought to Pontius Pilate
	Jesus is brought before the Sanhedrin
	The Last Supper
	Temple guards arrest Jesus

(10 marks)

    b. What was the role of the Sanhedrin in Palestine at the time of Jesus? *(6 marks)*

    c. What position did Pontius Pilate hold in the political life of Palestine at the time of Jesus? *(6 marks)*

B Imagine you were **one** of the disciples who witnessed Jesus' death and was present when Jesus appeared after his resurrection.

    a. Describe the impact that the death of Jesus had on your life. *(12 marks)*

    b. Describe **one** of the appearances of the risen Jesus you witnessed and the effect it had on you. *(16 marks)*

Section C

Lesson 54 and 67   2006 Ordinary Level/Section 4
Question 3. Major World Religions

A Tick **one** of the following world religions you have studied:

    ☐ Buddhism   ☐ Hinduism   ☐ Islam   ☐ Judaism

    a. Name a text that is sacred for members of the world religion you have ticked above. *(8 marks)*

    b. Give **one** reason why this text is sacred for members of the world religion ticked above. *(10 marks)*

B Sacred texts have been passed on by word of mouth and by written word.

    Describe what happened in the development of the sacred text you have named above at *either* the word of mouth stage *or* the written word stage. *(10 marks)*

C • Buddhism   • Hinduism   • Islam   • Judaism

    Describe a religious ritual that shows the importance of a sacred text for members of **one** of the world religions listed above. *(12 marks)*

Lesson 54 and 67 2005 Higher Level/Section 4
Question 3. Major World Religions

A *Every religion has ideas about God, the world, humanity – ideas that shape the beliefs and rituals of that religion.*

   a. State a key belief about God from **one** of the following world religions
   - Buddhism
   - Hinduism
   - Islam
   - Judaism *(8 marks)*

   b. Describe how their belief about God influences the way of life of followers of the world religion today. *(10 marks)*

   c. Outline how the life of an important person in the story of this world religion was influenced by his/her beliefs about God. *(15 marks)*

B a. Name a religious ritual associated with **one** of the following world religions:
   - Buddhism
   - Hinduism
   - Islam
   - Judaism *(5 marks)*

   b. Explain the meaning of this ritual. *(12 marks)*

Lesson 54 and 67 2006 Higher Level/Section 4
Question 3. Stories of Faith

A a. Tick **one** of the following world religions you have studied and name the sacred text associated with it:
   - ☐ Buddhism
   - ☐ Hinduism
   - ☐ Islam
   - ☐ Judaism *(5 marks)*

   b. Briefly explain why this sacred text is a document of faith. *(10 marks)*

B a. Outline **one** religious ceremony in which the sacred text you have named above is used. *(10 marks)*

   b. Describe **two** ways in which this sacred text influences the way of life of a follower of this world religion. *(10 marks)*

C
   - Buddhism
   - Hinduism
   - Islam
   - Judaism

   Briefly describe a time of growth and development in **one** of the above world religions. *(15 marks)*

Lesson 55 and 71 2004 Higher Level/Section 5
Question 3.

A tradition can be described as a long established belief or custom. Describe **one** tradition that is popular in one of the following world religions that you have studied. Explain its origins and its significance for followers today.

   - Buddhism
   - Hinduism
   - Islam
   - Judaism *(70 marks)*

Lesson 56 and 71   2003 Ordinary Level/Section 4
Question 3. World Religions

Imagine you are bringing a group of young people on a tour of a place of worship used by members of **one** of the following world religions:

- Buddhism
- Hinduism
- Islam
- Judaism

A a. Name a place of worship associated with your chosen world religion. *(6 marks)*

b. Briefly describe this place of worship. *(20 marks)*

B The group of young people would like to know about the rites and rituals of this world religion. Briefly describe any **two** rites or rituals that happen in this place of worship.

(14 marks)

Lesson 56   2007 Higher Level/Section 5
Question 5.

Ritual can help people express their faith.

Discuss the importance of ritual for members of **one** of the following world religions:

- Buddhism
- Christianity
- Hinduism
- Islam
- Judaism

(70 marks)

Lesson 59 and 72   2004/Ordinary Level/Section 4
Question 3. People of Faith

A In every world religion there are people whose vision and commitment are a worldwide inspiration to others. Under the following headings briefly outline the story of **one** such person from the world religion you have studied.

Tick the world religion:

☐ Buddhism   ☐ Hinduism   ☐ Islam   ☐ Judaism

a. Name of person: *(4 marks)*

b. His/her religious vision: *(8 marks)*

c. One example of his/her commitment: *(8 marks)*

B In the history of every world religion there are important moments. Tick **one** of the following words which describes such a moment.

☐ Expansion   ☐ Schism

Explain how the word you have ticked describes an important moment in the story of **one** of the following world religions:

- Buddhism
- Hinduism
- Islam
- Judaism   *(12 marks)*

C a. Sometimes people suffer persecution because of their religious commitment. Describe **one** example of persecution in the story of **one** of the following world religions:

- Buddhism
- Hinduism
- Islam
- Judaism   *(4 marks)*

b. Outline **one** effect this persecution could have on a follower of your chosen world religion.

(4 marks)

Lesson 61 and 74   2003 Higher Level/Section 5
Question 3.
You have been asked to write an article about a leader in **one** of the following world religions:

- Buddhism
- Hinduism
- Islam
- Judaism

In your article you should outline the role of the leader in relation to **two** of the following points:

Community structure

Follower/discipleship

Tradition *(70 marks)*

Lesson 61 and 74   2004 Higher Level/Section 5
Question 3.
A tradition can be described as a long established belief or custom. Describe **one** tradition that is popular in one of the following world religions that you have studied. Explain its origins and its significance for followers today.

- Buddhism
- Hinduism
- Islam
- Judaism *(70 marks)*

Lesson 61 and 74   2006 Higher Level/Section 5
Question 3.

- Buddhism
- Hinduism
- Islam
- Judaism

Discuss how the style of leadership in **one** of the above world religions is influenced by the views of its founder/earliest followers. *(70 marks)*

Lesson 73   2005 Ordinary Level/Section 4
Question 3. Major World Religions
Choose **one** of the following world religions you have studied. (Tick **one** box)

☐ Buddhism   ☐ Hinduism   ☐ Islam   ☐ Judaism

A   Name the founder/earliest followers of the world religion you have ticked above. *(8 marks)*

B   a. State a belief about the way people should live which was taught by the founder/earliest followers of the world religion ticked above. *(10 marks)*

   b. Explain why the belief you have stated above attracted people to this religion when it began. *(12 marks)*

C   Outline how **one** belief of the founder/earliest followers of the world religion ticked above influences the way of life of followers today. *(10 marks)*

Section D

Lesson 76   2003 Ordinary Level/Section 4

Question 4. The Development of Faith

A   Read the following:

'I can remember my mum dropping me off to Sunday school, as the rest of the family headed off to "Big Church". I can recall the stories I was told about a kind man who performed miracles. I can also remember proudly displaying a picture I had coloured in of Jesus when my mum came back to collect me.' (*Redemptorist Publications - Adapted*)

   a. In what two ways did this person's mum influence his/her religious beliefs and practices as a child. *(10 marks)*

   b. Apart from the influence of parents, name two other factors which influence the religious beliefs and practices of teenagers and explain how these factors influence those beliefs and practices. *(20 marks)*

Lesson 80   2003 Higher Level/Section 5

Question 4

Imagine you have been asked to talk at a parent's night in a primary school, about the difference between the faith of a child and that of a teenager. Outline the talk you would give, describing **two** things that could influence the way in which a child's faith might develop into a more adult faith.

(70 marks)

Lesson 80   2006 Higher Level/Section 4

Question 4. The Search for Meaning

C   People today express the search for meaning in many ways.

   Give **two** examples of how the search for meaning is expressed in today's world and give a brief account of each example: *(18 marks)*

Lesson 80   2006 Ordinary Level/Section 4

Question 4. The Search for Meaning

A   a. All human beings ask questions. Give two examples of important questions that a person asks in his/her search for meaning in life. *(8 marks)*

   b. The questions young children ask are often different from those asked by teenagers. Explain why this is so. *(10 marks)*

Lesson 82   2006 Higher Level/Section 4

Question 4. The Search for Meaning

A   Briefly explain how religious faith can grow out of the questions that a person asks in his/her search for meaning. *(16 marks)*

Lesson 82   2006 Ordinary Level/Section 4
Question 4. The Search for Meaning

B   Which of the following gives non-religious answers to questions about the meaning of life?

(Tick **one** box only) ☐ Humanism   ☐ Monotheism   *(10 marks)*

Lesson 82   2005 Ordinary Level/Section 4
Question 4. The Question of Faith

A   World religions refer to God by different names. Tick **one** of the names listed below:

☐ Allah   ☐ Brahman   ☐ Jesus   ☐ Yahweh/YHWH

With which world religion is the name you have ticked above associated?   *(8 marks)*

B

- God is someone I trust
- God is an old man with a beard
- God is a spirit
- God is a judge sitting high up in the heavens watching me

a.   Describe the image of God in a world religion you have studied.   *(16 marks)*

b.   Outline a story from the sacred text of a world religion you have studied in which the image of God described can be found.   *(16 marks)*

Lesson 83   2004 Ordinary Level/Section 4
Question 4. The Search for Meaning

B   Read the letter below.

'There was a time when I thought God was an old man sitting in Heaven looking down on us. Now I think God is more like a friend. When I pray I don't see God as a man or a woman, I see God as a spirit. I pray every day, talking to God the way I talk to you.'

a.   State **one** way in which this letter shows personal faith.   *(10 marks)*

b.   State **one** thing that could have influenced the religious belief of the person who wrote the letter.   *(10 marks)*

Lesson 87   2006 Ordinary Level/Section 4
Question 4. The Search for Meaning

C   Tick **one** of the following world religions you have studied:

☐ Buddhism   ☐ Christianity   ☐ Hinduism   ☐ Islam   ☐ Judaism

Describe how religious belief had an affect on the life of an important person in the story of the world religion you have ticked above.   *(12 marks)*

Lesson 88 2006 Higher Level/Section 5
Question 4.

Religion and science have points in common and points of difference in their understanding of creation.

Outline **one** point in common and one point of difference. *(70 marks)*

Lesson 89 2005 Higher Level/Section 4
Question 4. The Question of Faith

B Agnosticism and humanism can be described as non-religious ways of looking at the world.

Briefly explain the way **either** agnosticism **or** humanism has of looking at the world. *(14 marks)*

Section E

Lesson 90 2006 Higher Level/Section 4
Question 5. Prayer

A

Why is prayer important in the life of a person who has religious belief? *(15 marks)*

B ☐ Buddhism ☐ Christianity ☐ Hinduism ☐ Islam ☐ Judaism

Tick **one** world religion you have studied from those listed above and name the place of worship where members of this world religion regularly gather for prayer.

a. Name of place of worship. *(5 marks)*

b. Describe the place of worship you have named above. *(15 marks)*

c. Explain how the place of worship you have described above can help people to pray. *(15 marks)*

Lesson 93 2007 Ordinary Level/Section 4
Question 5 The Celebration of Faith

A World religions have special seasons and days of the year which are of religious importance for their members.

a. Name **one** special season *or* day of the year that has importance for members of a world religion you have studied. *(8 marks)*

b. Give **one** reason why the time you have named above is important for members of the world religion with which it is associated. *(12 marks)*

B   a.   Name **one** religious ceremony which marks the importance of *either* a special season *or* day of the year in a world religion you have studied. *(8 marks)*

b.   Outline what happens in the religious ceremony you have named above. *(12 marks)*

Lesson 96   2005 Higher Level/Section 4
Question 5. The Celebration of Faith

A   a.   In major world religions worship means… *(5 marks)*

b.   Briefly outline **one** act of worship you have observed or participated in. *(12 marks)*

c.   Describe **one** religious symbol that is used during an act of worship. *(6 marks)*

d.   Explain the meaning of this religious symbol. *(12 marks)*

e.   Give **three** reasons why people pray during worship. *(15 marks)*

Lesson 98   2003 Higher Level/Section 4
Question 5. Mystery

A

Statement Number 1	Statement Number 2	Statement Number 3
'Every human person is a mystery, which must be learned slowly, reverently, with care, tenderness and pain, and is never learned completely.' - Anon	'I can see nothing plain; all's mystery. Yet sometimes there is a torch inside my head that makes all clear, but when the light is gone I have but images…' - W.B.Yeats	'A mystery is not a wall against which you run your head, but an ocean into which you plunge. A mystery is not a night; it is the sun, so brilliant that we cannot gaze at it…' - E. Joly

a.   Which of the above statements best describes encountering mystery in life? Explain your choice. *(10 marks)*

b.   People often look back on life and recognise the experience of mystery at certain times and in certain places. Identify **one** life experience and explain how it could hold a sense of mystery for a person. *(15 marks)*

B   a.   Sometimes people give expression to the experience of mystery through worship.

       Describe **one** example in which people express their experience of mystery in life. *(10 marks)*

b.   Explain how this act of worship helps people to express their experience of mystery in life *(15 marks)*

Lesson 98   2005 Higher Level/Section 5
Question 5.

I feel at home in a Hindu temple. I am aware of Presence, not personal … but something larger.

       - Yann Martel

Outline how places of worship help people to respond to the experience of mystery of life. *(70 marks)*

Lesson 103 2005 Ordinary/Section 4
Question 5. The Celebration of Faith

A World religions have different places of worship. Tick **one** of the following places of worship and name the religion associated with it.

☐ Church ☐ Mosque ☐ Shrine ☐ Synagogue ☐ Temple

(8 marks)

B a. Name **one** religious symbol that can be seen in the place of worship you have ticked above. *(8 marks)*

b. Explain the meaning of this religious symbol. *(12 marks)*

C Describe a religious ceremony for which people gather in the place of worship you have ticked above. *(12 marks)*

Lesson 111 2007 Higher Level/Section 4
Question 5. The Celebration of Faith

A a. Give **one** example of a symbol people use when they are praying. *(5 marks)*

b. Explain why people use the symbol you have given above when they are praying. *(9 marks)*

B Suggest **two** reasons why people can sometimes find it difficult to pray. *(12 marks)*

C a. ☐ Meditation ☐ Penitence

Tick **one** of the above types of prayer that you have studied.

Outline what is involved in the type of prayer you have ticked above. *(10 marks)*

b. Outline **two** reasons why prayer is important for members of a world religion that you have studied. *(14 marks)*

Section F

Lesson 122 2006 Higher Level/Section 4
Question 6. Morality

A What is moral maturity? *(14 marks)*

B Family, friends, religion, etc. can influence a person's ideas of what is right and wrong.

Outline how **two** such influences can affect a person's idea of right and wrong. *(16 marks)*

C In making a decision, how would a morally mature person deal with the many influences on his/her idea of right and wrong. *(20 marks)*

Lesson 122 2005 Higher Level/Section 4
Question 6. The Moral Challenge

A *Moral codes express the rights people are entitled to, as well as the responsibilities they have towards others.*

    a. Name **one** moral code you have studied. *(5 marks)*

    b. State **one** right it expresses. *(5 marks)*

    c. State **one** responsibility it expresses. *(5 marks)*

    d. Explain how the moral code you have named above could help a person in making a moral decision. *(10 marks)*

B   a. Outline a situation in which a person has to make a moral decision.

    b. Explain how a person's religion could influence his/her moral decision-making in the situation you have outlined above. *(15 marks)*

Lesson 122 2006 Ordinary Level/Section 4
Question 6. The Moral Challenge

A A person's understanding of right and wrong is influenced by many factors.

    Family ☐   Friends ☐   School ☐   State ☐

Tick **one** of the above and give an example of how it could have an effect on a person's understanding of right and wrong. *(15 marks)*

B Tick **one** of the statements listed below that is associated with a world religion you have studied.

Buddhism	Christianity	Hinduism	Islam	Judaism
Act towards others exactly as you would act towards yourself.	Treat others as you would like them to treat you.	Do nothing to others which, if done to you, could cause you pain.	None of you truly believe, until you wish for others what you wish for yourself.	What is harmful to yourself do not do to others.
☐	☐	☐	☐	☐

Describe how the idea expressed in the statement ticked above can have an effect on the behaviour of members of this world religion today. *(16 marks)*

C Give **one** example of how the idea expressed in the statement ticked above can still be seen in the life of the founder/earliest followers of the world religion with which it is associated. *(14 marks)*

Lesson 122   2005 Ordinary Level/Section 4

Question 6. The Moral Challenge

A a. Moral issues arise in situations where people have to make decisions about the right thing to do.

Tick the box that shows the moral issue arising in each situation below. The first situation has been matched to a moral issue as an example for you.

Situation 1
Two of your friends have a row and are not speaking to each other. You get tickets to a concert and bring them both to it. The row is soon forgotten and they enjoy the concert together.

The moral issue solved in this action is –

(Tick the correct box)

- Truth ☐
- Justice ☐
- Authority ☐
- Reconciliation ☑

Situation 2
You have seen a classmate taking another student's schoolbag without permission. The student whose bag has been taken asks if you know anything about the missing bag. You have to decide what to say.

The moral issue solved in this action is –

(Tick the correct box)

- Truth ☐
- Justice ☐
- Authority ☐
- Reconciliation ☐

Situation 3
You are organising a class outing to the cinema. One of your classmates uses a wheelchair. You discover that the bus with wheelchair access will cost more. You have to decide whether to go ahead without this classmate or do more fundraising so that no one will be left out.

The moral issue solved in this action is –

(Tick the correct box)

- Truth ☐
- Justice ☐
- Authority ☐
- Reconciliation ☐

(8 marks)

  b. Explain how **one** of the moral issues ticked above arises in the situation it is matched with.
  (10 marks)

B Outline how a morally mature person would decide what is right or wrong in any one of the situations described. *(12 marks)*

C Explain how a person's religious beliefs could influence his/her views of right or wrong in any one of the situations described above. *(10 marks)*

Lesson 125   2003 Higher Level/Section 4

Question 6. Morality Decision-making

Imagine you are on a train with a woman and a man sitting opposite you. During the journey the woman leaves her seat without taking her bag. A moment later you see the man getting ready to leave the train with the woman's bag under his coat.

A Describe two different ways of dealing with this situation. *(14 marks)*

B Explain the consequences of **one** of the above ways of dealing with this situation for each of the following:

The Woman;

The Man;

Yourself. *(15 marks)*

C Explain how a person's religious moral vision could influence his/her decision-making in this situation. *(21 marks)*

499

Lesson 127 2004 Ordinary/Section 4
Question 6. Justice and Religious Moral Vision

A   A religious moral vision can inspire people to work for justice.

    a.   Outline **one** religious moral vision you have studied.   *(12 marks)*

    b.   Explain how this religious moral vision could inspire people to work for justice.   *(8 marks)*

B   Explain how this religious moral vision can be seen in the work for justice of a member, or members, of any religious organisation you have studied.   *(20 marks)*

Lesson 132 2004 Higher Level/Section 4
Question 6. Morality and Religion

'PRIEST OBJECTS TO GOVERNMENT LAWS ON CHURCH DESIGN'

A   The headline above refers to a situation where conflict arose between government law and the views of a religious leader.

    Outline another situation where there could be conflict between a country's law and religion.   *(10 marks)*

B   Explain how **two** of the following could influence a person's judgement of right and wrong in the situation you have described above.

    • Family   • Peer group   • Civil law   • Religion   *(20 marks)*

C   Explain how a morally mature person would judge between right and wrong in the situation you have described above.   *(20 marks)*

Glossary of Key Concepts

Section A

Authority: The power that a person in a position of leadership has to make decisions for or about a group or community.

Church: A community of faith. Also used to describe a building in which people worship.

Community breakdown: Occurs when a group stops working/sharing and breaks apart.

Commitment: Pledge/promise to a group or community to carry out a task or role.

Communication: Sharing of experiences, thoughts or feelings.

Co-operation: Working together to achieve a common goal.

Denomination: Community of faith, with its own particular organisation and practices.

Ecumenism: Name given to the movement that works to promote greater unity between the different Christian denominations.

Faith/belief: Something accepted as true by a person or group. Our faith or belief in God is at the heart of our religion.

Founder: A person whose teaching and example leads to the formation of a group or community vision.

Gospel: Means 'good news' and refers to the Good News of God's love that Jesus brought to all people. The first four books of the New Testament are called gospels because they tell of the new life that Jesus offers to all.

Identity: That which makes it possible to know who a group or a person is.

Inter-faith dialogue: When members of different communities of faith (different religions) talk together in order to come to a better understanding of their beliefs.

Lack of co-operation: Not working together.

Leadership: Setting a goal or aim for a person or a community and guiding them towards it. Always involves some degree of authority.

Ministry: Role of service given to a member by a community and/or its leader.

Mission: A specific task given to a person or group.

Religions: Systems of practices and rules to express and respond to the search for and belief in God.

Religious commitment: Pledge/promise to live as God asks; may involve taking on a new task or role.

Religious conflict: Occurs where two or more groups oppose one another because of their differing faiths or religious beliefs.

Roles: Specific tasks or functions within a group, e.g. member, leader, secretary, etc.

Sacred text: Writings relating to a community of faith, which are considered holy and inspired.

Sectarianism: Excluding (even hating) others who do not belong to one's own community of faith.

Service: Work done by a person or group for the good of another person or group.

Sharing: Willing and unselfish giving to others.

Tolerance: Being willing to recognise and respect the beliefs and practices of others, while valuing and studying one's own beliefs and religious practices.

Vision: A powerful image of what the world or a person or a group could be.

Vocation as a calling to serve: God calls people to carry out their roles/tasks in their community of faith for the benefit of others.

Section B

Ancient Judaism: The religion into which Jesus was born, based on the Five Books of Moses (also called the Torah), which are the first five books of the Bible.

Christ/Messiah: 'Christ' and 'Messiah' are English versions of the same word in Greek and Hebrew, meaning 'anointed'. For the first Christians, Jesus was the Messiah promised by God, for whom the Jewish people had waited.

Conflict with authority: An open clash with the person/group that makes the community's or group's decisions. Jesus clashed with the Pharisees and, more particularly, with the Sadducees.

Eucharist: Literally 'to give thanks'. It is the name that Christians give to the sacrament based on the command of Jesus: 'Do this in memory of me.' Also used to refer specifically to the body and blood of Christ, who is truly present in the Eucharist under the appearances of bread and wine.

Evidence: Information that provides a reason for believing in something.

Evidence from oral tradition: Information that is handed on by word of mouth from one group to another.

Evidence from written tradition: Information that is written down, e.g. in the gospels and the letters of the apostles.

Evangelist: The name given to each of the four writers of the gospels: Matthew, Mark, Luke and John.

Gospel: Means 'good news' and refers to the Good News of God's love that Jesus brought to all people. The first four books of the New Testament are called gospels because they tell of the new life that Jesus offers to all.

Kingdom of God: God is always present in the world. The Kingdom of God is brought about when people respond to God's presence in their words and actions and by treating others and the earth as God calls them to. The Kingdom of God, therefore, refers to a way of life rather than a physical place. It means trusting in God and listening to the voice of the Holy Spirit.

- **in parable:** Jesus told short stories called parables to teach his followers what he meant by the Kingdom of God. These stories invited people to respond by changing their behaviour.

- **in miracle:** Jesus performed wonderful actions called miracles to show people that the Kingdom of God is present and at work in the world. These miracles invited a response.

- **in table-fellowship (shared meals):** Jesus loved to share meals, especially with those who were looked down upon or excluded by others. By doing so, he showed that the Kingdom of God includes everyone.

- **in discipleship:** Becoming a follower or disciple of Jesus means working to build the Kingdom of God in the world.

Martyrdom: Suffering or being put to death because of your religious beliefs.

Memorial: An action that recalls the past. The Eucharist is a memorial because it recalls and makes present the actions of Jesus at the Last Supper and it reminds us that the Risen Jesus continues to be with us.

Messianic expectation: The belief of the Jewish people that God would send a great political and religious leader to solve their problems.

Mission: Task given to a member of a community of faith to continue the work of Jesus, i.e. making people aware of God's presence and action in the world and inviting a response.

Missionary: The word used to describe a person or community that continues the work of Jesus, telling others about the Good News of God's kingdom and inviting their response.

New Creation: St Paul described Jesus as God's 'New Creation' to underline how the presence of Jesus was God's new start in the world.

Passover: The name given to the meal and the festival that celebrates God's action in freeing the Hebrew people from slavery in Egypt.

People of God: The term used to describe the Hebrew people whom God freed from slavery in Egypt. In Christian use, it is the name given to the community of those who believe in Jesus. (See Acts 2:44-46 for the first written description.)

Presence: Opposite of absence. Something seen or felt or heard or available.

Pentecost: The day, described in Acts 2, when the followers of Jesus experienced God's gift of the Holy Spirit.

Resurrection: The event in which Jesus was raised to new life after his death on the cross.

Sacrifice: Giving of oneself out of love in order to achieve a goal or purpose.

Son of God: A name for Jesus that helped Greek-speaking Gentiles to understand the unity of Jesus and God.

Son of Man: A title that Jesus gave himself, especially in the gospel according to Mark.

Synoptic: Means sharing a point of view. The gospels of Matthew, Mark and Luke are called synoptic gospels because they share so many of the same stories about Jesus.

The Holy Land: The country where Jesus lived and taught. Called Palestine, prior to the creation of the modern state of Israel.

The Roman Empire: The name used to describe the regions of the world ruled by Rome. Palestine was part of the Roman Empire.

Transformation: A core change in a person or thing, i.e. a change in essential qualities or character or way of life.

Vocation: Calling to a particular kind of work or role. As a religious term, it is a calling from God to serve others as Jesus did, by taking on a role/task in the community of faith for the benefit of others.

Witness: Something that serves as evidence or proof. The gospels give witness to the story of Jesus.

Section C

Calendar/Sacred time: A calendar is a system for dividing the year into definite periods. Sacred time refers to times of special religious importance, e.g. religious festivals.

Ceremony: A formal event to celebrate and to show respect for something, for example, a baptism or a wedding.

Commitment: Pledge/promise to a group or community to carry out a task or role.

Community Structure: Way in which a group of people with a common interest is organised, especially in its roles (leadership, membership, etc).

Creed: A statement of religious beliefs.

Cultural context: The events, facts, stories and customs of a particular culture or society that connect with and influence other events, e.g. the founding of a major world religion.

Development: Growth or change, e.g. the way in which a community of faith grows or matures over time.

Education: The teaching or passing on of knowledge.

Evidence: Information that provides a reason or basis for believing something.

Expansion: Increase in size, area or number. A religious community expands when more people join it and when it spreads to other places.

Festivals: Special celebrations that recall the events, facts, stories and customs of a particular group, nation or religion.

Follower/Discipleship: A person becomes a follower when they take on discipleship. This means that they begin to live by the traditions of a community of faith.

Founder: A person whose teaching and example leads to the formation of a group or community vision.

Inspiration: Something that stirs our imagination and that influences us to new thinking or action.

Leadership: Setting a goal or aim for a person or a community and guiding them towards it. Always involves some degree of authority.

Location: A particular place, e.g. a town, city or country.

Meditation: Focusing attention/thoughts on a story, object or person in order to be more aware of them. Christian meditation focuses on God and the love of God as shown in Jesus Christ.

Oral tradition: Information that is handed on by word of mouth from one person or group to another.

Persecution: Deliberately causing loss, pain or death to a person or a group because of race, religion or way of life.

Pilgrimage: A journey to a sacred place.

Places of Worship: Places set apart for religious rituals.

Prophet: A person who speaks on behalf of God.

Practice: The practice of a faith tradition means the living of that faith according to its central beliefs and teachings.

Prayer: Communication between people and God.

Revelation: The act of revealing or showing something. Used to describe how God and God's message were revealed to the founders of Judaism, Christianity and Islam.

Rite: A set of words or actions used to celebrate or mark an important event. 'Rites of passage' celebrate different stages in a person's life.

Ritual: A series of actions carried out in a set way. Religious rituals are usually repeated regularly by the faith community to express the relationship between God and the community.

Sacred text: Writings relating to a community of faith, which are considered holy and inspired.

Schism: A split, especially in relation to a religious tradition.

Sign: A word, drawing or action that gives information.

Symbol: A type of sign, but with a deeper meaning. A symbol is a visible sign of something invisible.

Tradition: The handing down of information, beliefs and customs from one generation to the next. Religious tradition involves the handing on of religious practices, beliefs, etc.

Vision/dream: A powerful image of what the world or a person or a group could be.

Section D

Agnosticism: World view that neither includes nor excludes God. Belief that there is not enough proof to decide one way or another whether God exists.

Atheism: World view that does not include God and in which the term 'God' does not refer to anything real.

Awe and Wonder: Emotion (combining amazement and reverence) inspired by deep (significant) experience.

Childhood Faith: A child's first stage or expression or personal response to God and what is known about God.

Creation: The coming into existence of the world. In religious terms, God's unique act of causing the whole world to exist.

Experiencing God: Being aware of God's presence in an immediate and personal way.

Faith: The response of a person or a group to God's revelation.

Fundamentalism: A literal, rigid style of belief. Relies solely on a literal interpretation of the community's sacred text and teachings. Rejects attempts to update or modernise the way in which community belief is expressed.

Humanism: Looks to life (not religion) as a source of meaning; to base one's plans or beliefs on factual evidence and scientific ways of enquiry only.

Materialism: World view that includes only physical and measurable things. Since we cannot see or measure God, materialists say that God does not exist.

Mature Faith: A fully developed (worked out) expression of a personal response to God and what is known about God.

Meaning: When people search for meaning in life, they look for relationships or things that make life feel worthwhile, that bring satisfaction and that make sense of life.

Meaninglessness: People experience meaninglessness when they feel life is not worthwhile, when they can find no reason to suffer their present difficulties.

Monotheism: The belief in only one God.

Personal Faith: One's personal response to God and what is known about God. Grows and develops as a person grows.

Prayer: Communication between people and God.

Polytheism: The belief in many gods.

Question: To ask or argue about things that are uncertain or debatable.

Questioner: Person who asks questions.

Reflection: Inner personal thought. Focusing on or searching for something meaningful in a sacred text, in the events of life or in the world of nature.

Religious belief: What we believe to be true about God and our relationship with God.

Religious practice: The system of behaviour and set of activities people use to express their belief in God.

Search: To look for, to seek out, to enquire, to ask – in order to find meaning or answers.

Secularism: Way of making life choices that excludes God.

Stages of Faith: Different ways of expressing the same faith/belief that go with different stages of life (e.g. childhood, adolescence, adulthood).

Trust: To rely on or to put one's confidence in someone or something.

Worship: Response of a group or individual to the sacred, often expressed through ritual.

World view: Way of thinking about the world (its origin, the way it works, etc.) that guides the way we live.

Section E

Actions of significance: Actions through which people respond to what is meaningful in their lives.

Celebration: Special gathering to honour one or more people or to mark a particular event.

Communal prayer: Taking time with the other members of your community of faith to be with God and to communicate with God.

Communicating experience: Being put in touch with a source of meaning – often through symbols.

Communication: Sharing of experiences, thoughts or feelings.

Communication with God: Sharing one's thoughts and feelings with God.

Contemplation: Focusing one's heart/feelings and being at rest with a particular subject or story. Christian contemplation brings Christians closer to God and to Jesus Christ.

Encountering mystery: Being strongly affected by a meaningful experience that we do not fully understand.

Encounter with God: Being strongly aware of the presence of God in a particular moment or place.

Icon: Picture with a religious content and meaning, used in the worship of the Orthodox Church.

Identity: The individual characteristics that define a person or thing, or by which a person or thing can be recognised.

Meditation: Focusing attention/thoughts on a story, object or person in order to be more aware of them. Christian meditation focuses on God and the love of God as shown in Jesus Christ.

Participation: Taking an active part in an action or activity.

Penitence: Being sorry for past sins or failures.

Personal Prayer: Taking time alone to be aware of God and to communicate with God.

Petition: A request/prayer that asks for a particular help or result.

Praise and Thanksgiving: To express approval of a person or thing; to express gratitude for a favour, kindness or mercy.

Places of significance: Places that have a special meaning for people.

Reflection: Inner personal thought. Focusing on or searching for something meaningful in a sacred text, in the events of life or in the world of nature.

Ritual: A series of actions carried out in a set way. Religious rituals are usually repeated regularly by the faith community to express the relationship between God and the community.

Sacrament: A symbol of God's grace or presence, through which believers can communicate with God.

Sacredness: Regarded as holy, set apart, reserved, connected with God.

Sign: A word, drawing or action that gives information.

Symbol: A type of sign, but with a deeper meaning. A symbol is a visible sign of something invisible.

Times of significance: Times when people respond to what is meaningful in their lives.

Worship: Response of a group or individual to the sacred, often expressed through ritual.

Wonder: Feeling of respect and awe resulting from encountering or coming face to face with something amazing or spectacular.

Worship as a response to mystery or an expression of ultimate concern: When we find something or someone to be deeply meaningful, but normal words and thoughts are not enough to express our relationship or response, we turn to worship.

Section F

Action and consequence: A consequence is something that happens as a result of an action/choice.

Authority: Person or group that makes or carries out decisions for a community or State.

Civil law: Collection of rules about behaviour, decided upon and enforced by the State authorities.

Constitution: Code (statement) of values and guidelines for a group or country.

Conscience: Capacity/ability for judging the best thing to do when free to choose.

Choice: Opting for one thing rather than another.

Decision-making: Process involved in making a choice.

Forgiveness: The act of pardoning, excusing or making allowance for an offence.

Freedom: The capacity to do what we want, i.e. to choose to do good or to do bad.

Influence: Something that affects a person's behaviour/decisions.

Integrity: Not open to bad influences; choices always based on a moral vision.

Judgement: A decision about someone or something, usually arrived at after careful consideration.

Justice: Fairness and respect, which leads to good relationships.

Laws: Rules concerning behaviour.

Libertarianism: The belief that a person is free to do what they choose once they do not interfere with the right of another person to do as they choose.

Life: Found in things or beings that are alive; energy for living.

Morality: The basis on which a person makes moral choices, i.e. between good and bad.

Moral growth: The process whereby our morality changes, grows and matures over time. A person's moral growth is reflected in their choices.

Moral maturity: Fully developed ability to make good choices.

Moral vision: Awareness of what is right and wrong, which guides a person's choices.

Peace: Presence of harmony; absence of disputes.

Pluralism: A state of society where the views of people of all traditions and none are tolerated.

Reconciliation: Restoring friendship, harmony and good relationships.

Relationships: Connections between people, through family, community, country, group or choice.

Religious fundamentalism: A literal, rigid style of belief. Relies solely on a literal interpretation of the community's sacred text and teachings. Rejects attempts to update or modernise the way in which community belief is expressed.

Religious moral vision: Awareness of what is right and wrong, as revealed by the sacred texts or founder of a community of faith.

Respect: To honour; to value; to treat properly.

Sin: An offence against God. Turning away from a relationship with God and others.

Society: The connection that exists between people when they share an outlook and way of life.

Stewardship: The job of caring for something that belongs to another.

Tradition: Guidance that is handed on, e.g. a law or custom.

Truth: Facts or beliefs that may be relied on.